The Transgender-Industrial Complex

# THE TRANSGENDER– INDUSTRIAL COMPLEX

Scott Howard

ANTELOPE HILL PUBLISHING

Cover art by Swifty.
Edited by Margaret Bauer.
Layout by Margaret Bauer.
Index by Malta.

The author can be contacted at scott2hotthoward@protonmail.com

Antelope Hill Publishing | www.antelopehillpublishing.com

Hardcover ISBN-13: 978-1-956887-58-7
Paperback ISBN-13: 978-1-956887-57-0
EPUB ISBN-13: 978-1-953730-42-8

*"It's the rush that the cockroaches get at the end of the world."*

– Every Time I Die, "Ebolarama"

# Contents

# Introduction

*"Men who get their periods are men. Men who get pregnant and give birth are men."*

The official American Civil Liberties Union (ACLU) Twitter account
November 19th, 2019

At this point, it is safe to say that we are through the looking glass. The volume at which all things "trans" and LGBTQ-et cetera in general is now trumpeted, complete with the breathless hysteria with which the media shrieks about the rights of non-binary people of color to have sex changes on demand paid for by someone else in a country that isn't theirs, the "concentration camps" that don't exist to "torture" these trans people, the deeply disturbing assertions that young children be forcibly sterilized to align with their "gender identity" on the one hand, while protesting the "forceful sterilization" of trans people in order for them to change the sex on their birth certificates on the other. . . . Well, it all seems rather bewildering.

Did anyone expect, when we were hurtling toward Y2K and the late-Senator Ted Stevens's pneumatic tube-powered Information Super Highway that we would soon be discussing "trans women's periods" about hairy men in wigs in mainstream society with a straight face? That people of indeterminate gender who pose spread-legged with splotches of blood on their pants-crotches and hashtag their "activism" on social media would be heralded as the epitome of "stunning and brave?" That it would be considered a *human right* for sex predators to declare themselves another gender in order to use the little girls' room? It's at once farcical and tragic, as the Soviet general in *The Camp of the Saints* lamented between sips of vodka: "We're caught in the clutches of the great hermaphrodite, Zackaroff. We're all its serfs. And we can't even cut off its balls!" Possibly, truer words have never been spoken.

In the wasteland of deepening darkness overcoming our civilization, the plagues of opioids and anti-depressants, a steady diet of appointments with the local psychoanalyst, hormone blockers for prepubescent children, demon-drag-queen story time and more untold horrors confront us as the forces of disintegration eat the remnants of our civilization from the inside out. The smug and decadent extensions of the ruling class in the media persistently focus not on the blanket censorship and the personal and professional destruction of any dissidents who aren't totally "with the program," of which they (the media) are willing and eager participants, but rather claim that said censorship is instead reflective of a pervasive *climate of fear* surrounding the wholesale *literal* massacre of the LGBTQ "community" by malevolent hate-mongers lurking around every corner. But is it, in fact, a "massacre?"

The homicide mortality rate for transgender persons in the United States is actually significantly *lower* than the average person:

Kentucky State University associate professor Wilfred Reilly found that the 2017 homicide death rate for transgender people was about 1.48 per 100,000, less than a third of the overall murder rate of about 5 per 100,000 and a fraction of the rate for men in general (6.68) or black people (18.8). . . . His conclusions fly in the face of claims by the Human Rights Campaign, which called transgender deaths "a national epidemic" in its 2019 report, as well as the American Medical Association's June warning of an "epidemic of violence" and approved policies to combat "fatal attacks against transgender people." A Sept. 27 headline in *The New York Times* similarly read: "18 Transgender Killings This Year Raise Fears of an 'Epidemic. . . .'" For those who might accuse him of cooking the books, Mr. Reilly pointed out that he based his conclusions on FBI figures; a 2016 study by the UCLA Williams Institute, which found that 0.6% of the population identifies as transgender; and the Human Rights Campaign's database of transgender homicides. . . . Far from rising, the transgender homicide rate has been notable for its stability. There were 21 such deaths in 2015, 23 in 2016, 29 in 2017, 26 in 2018 and 22 in 2019 so far [December 8th, 2019], "and that's with this very active LGBT lobbying group trying to find as many as possible," Mr. Reilly said.[1]

Yet it is treated as an "epidemic," largely on the back of—surprise, surprise—media lies and manipulation and systemic brain-washing. We see here how vital control of information and its dissemination is to the ruling class. This is a full-on indoctrination campaign operating at all levels, which extends to the very formation of the language we use to communicate our ideas.

To evoke George Orwell's *1984* has become a bit of cliché, but for good reason. Not only did he presage control over the construction of language to suit ideological purposes—a "real world" example is the now-widespread acceptance and use of the term "partner" rather than husband, wife, boyfriend, or girlfriend, which not only removes the sex of the so-called "partner" from the equation but also has a connotation of a contractual rather than romantic relationship, such as a business partner— but he also understood that limiting language in such a way as to prevent the expression and even formulation of thoughts that might dispute the anti-reality mantras of the ruling class was essential for controlling and conditioning the population.

The formation of words and the alteration of grammatical and stylistic conventions to suit the prevailing orthodoxy is now rampant: consider the grammatically-incorrect "people of color" versus the grammatically-correct "colored people," or the Associated Press's decision to capitalize the word "Black" when used in the context of race and culture but not to do the same for "white," signaling the latter's delegitimization as a unique racial group with legitimate interests. "It seems like such a minor change, black versus Black," *The New York Times*'s national editor, Marc Lacey, said. "But for many people the capitalization of that one letter is the difference between a color and a culture."

"Not having a capital letter has felt disrespectful," said David Lanham, director of communications for the Brookings Institution's Metropolitan Policy Program. "There is a shared cultural identity with Black Americans and that goes through our shared experiences. That also goes to the lack of geographic history as a result of

---

[1] Richardson, "Transgender homicide rate."

slavery." So *not* having a shared geographic space (aka a homeland, like Europe) is what constitutes a legitimate race, then? I can see where Lanham probably got his talking points.

Now here's where it gets downright genocidal: "White doesn't represent a shared culture and history in the way Black does, and also has long been capitalized by hate groups," *The New York Times* said in explaining its decision to go with the AP's change. "We agree that white people's skin color plays into systemic inequalities and injustices, and we want our journalism to robustly explore these problems," John Daniszewski, the AP's Vice President and Editor-at-Large for Standards, said in a memo to staff. "Capitalizing the term white, as is done by white supremacists, risks subtly conveying legitimacy to such beliefs." CBS News said it would capitalize "white," although not when referring to white supremacists, white nationalists, or white privilege.

One change really does speak volumes. This cannot be viewed as anything but the next step in de-humanizing whites in what will produce the most appalling levels of violence if the rhetoric continues down this path. Similarly, the use of "community" as a legitimate expression is applied liberally in all cases except in those that pertain to positive white or Christian identity, or to heterosexuality. Thus the "diverse" but also somehow monolithic LGBTQ-et cetera "community."

But is this a community? For starters, lesbians and gays generally do not get along: "trans" is supposedly a gender incongruence and/or variance, not a sexuality (or is it?—we'll come back to this); and intersex, as opposed to transgender, is a condition whereby the individual in question has atypical sex traits and/or reproductive anatomy. Nevertheless, whether they like it or not, intersex people have been engulfed in the oppressive rainbow embrace, their identities weaponized for ideological means by the pillar of the neo-liberal Establishment that is the *transgender-industrial complex.*

There are several "intersex advocacy organizations" supposedly representing these people's interests. One such organization is Organisation Intersex International (OII) Europe, which is funded by the Astraea Lesbian Foundation for Justice, Dreilinden, the Sigrid Rausing Trust, and the European Union, and has partnered with Heinrich Böll Stiftung. The intersex organizations are usually used as support for the broader LGBTQ agenda.

In the summer of 2019, the United Nations Office of the High Commissioner for Human Rights (OHCHR) hosted a meeting with NGO and business representatives at Deutsche Bank's PalaisPopulaire[2] for discussion on the working OHCHR publication "Engaging the Private Sector in LGBTI issues: a guide for Human Rights Defenders." OII Europe staff attended the meeting, "representing intersex perspectives." Also in 2019, an international intersex activist meeting was held at the Seta

---

[2] In September 2020 a delightful sculpture titled *Die Doppelgängerin* (2010/20) by the Austrian filmmaker, media, and performance artist Valie Export was put on view in front of the PalaisPopulaire: "Two gigantic scissors are interlocked to form a figure that is both delicate and threatening. The work, which is over four meters high, triggers myriad associations. Traditionally, scissors are associated with sewing, tailoring, and other 'feminine' spheres, but also with the male fear of castration and violence with 'female' connotations . . . Export is one of the pioneers of the feminist avant-garde and conceptual media, performance art, and film art."

office in Helsinki, Finland.[3]

Transgender Europe (TGEU) is Co-Chaired by Tanja von Knorring (who, according to their website, is also "Chairperson of Transgender political committee of Seta – LGBTI Finland, board member in Trasek[4] and [an] array of other LGBTI associations") and Tina Kolos Orbán (Hungary, "active in the LGBT movement since 2005 before the founding of Transvanilla Transgender Association in 2011. . . . Also served on the International Trans Fund's Grant Making Panel for 2 years"). Other persons involved with Transgender Europe include:

- Erika Castellanos, an HIV positive transgender activist from Belize residing in the Netherlands
- Jorge María Londoño, who Has been active in queer and LGBTQ-activism since 2013. Their value-based activism has been shaped by anti-racist, post-colonial, and queer feminist approach to trans/queer activism. They were born in Colombia but are now based in southern Sweden. Jorge María work[s] with youth and child rights and has a background as a Board Member of IGLYO (2017–2019). They are currently chairing Youth Against Racism Sweden.
- Mimi Aum Neko: Active member of Acceptess-T and Strass (Sexworkers' trade union), Mimi began her LGBTQI activism 12 years ago against the military coup d'Etat in Thailand. Threatened by the military regime, she sought asylum in France and started to fight against transphobia, racism, HIV and stigmas, poverty and dictatorship for the rights of trans migrants and sex workers.
- Anwar Ogrm: An activist from France, combining different struggles, such as queer and trans rights, gender equality and anti-racism. Back in Paris, Anwar was engaged in several grassroots organisations addressing racism as well as queerphobia from an intersectional perspective. Advocacy work and empowerment for queer and trans Muslim people is one of his priorities.
- Miles Rutendo: Founder of Queerstion Media, Miles is a journalist and brings 10 years of experience within media & communication, LGBTQ and migration activism. Miles has worked previously for RFSL as coordinator for a Global LGBT Leadership training Rainbow Leaders as well as Editor for Soginews global LGBT news site. Miles wants to amplify the voices of trans asylum seekers and refugees in Europe and intersectional perspectives.

---

[3] "Seta's Gender Diversity & Intersex Centre of Expertise (former Trans Support Center / Transtukipiste) offers services to all trans and intersex persons, people pondering their gender and also to their families and loved ones." Seta's main contributors are the Funding Centre for Social Welfare and Health Organisations (STEA) and the Ministry of Education and Culture; it is a member of ILGA Europe, Transgender Europe, IGLYO, SOSTE, Finnish Youth Cooperation – Alliance, and the Family Federation of Finland.

[4] An NGO which provides a template for any resident in Finland who "want[s] to start the gender reassignment process" to take to a doctor explaining the process so that the doctor may write a referral. Finnish law guarantees the right to a referral in any case, this is just to grease the skids. Core services are provided by the National Public Health System based on two Transgender Health Programs, one at the Helsinki University Hospital and one at the Tampere University Hospital. This is based on a decree by the Ministry of Health and Social Security.

If this seems a bit like everything but the kitchen sink, in many ways it is, but this is not just a bunch of "kooky liberals"—it is systemic and it is by design, as we will see.

For example, the official position of the 150-plus-member-organization Transgender Europe, according to their website, is that "the struggles for racial justice and trans liberation are interconnected" and that "Black trans refugees and asylum seekers also face structural violence in heavily policed and militarised areas such as border controls and migration offices." Transgender Europe, in turn, is supported financially by George Soros's Open Society Foundations, the European Commission, the Council of Europe, and the Government of the Netherlands, and has in the past received support from the German Federal Foreign Office, the US State Department, the Austrian Agency for International Cooperation in Education and Research (Österreichischer Austauschdienst, or OeAD), the Arcus Foundation, and Heinrich Böll Stiftung.

We see the misleading linkage of intersex with "trans" as well as sexuality (although the link between trans and sexuality is a firm one) *and* the perpetual linkage of "youth" (which we will also see recur, particularly as it pertains to "diversity," "refugees," and the like) with the International Lesbian, Gay, Bisexual, Transgender, Queer, and Intersex Youth and Student Organization (IGLYO), which admits that it is little more than a training camp for "activists": "IGLYO is a youth development and leadership organisation building LGBTQI youth activists, ensuring LGBTQI young people are present and heard and making schools safe, inclusive and supportive of LGBTQI learners." Further, directly from their website:

> With 90+ member organisations, situated in 40+ countries, the IGLYO network unites a great variety of individual and group experiences. LGBTQI youth in the Council of Europe region hail from diverse ethnic, racial and religious backgrounds. IGLYO is cognisant of the intertwined realities of racism, LGBTQI-phobia, sexism, classism, ableism and ageism that are part of the lived experiences of LGBTQI-youth of colour. At the 2019 Annual Member's Conference, IGLYO members unanimously voted to constitute an Anti-Racism Task Force.[5] The amended 2020 Work Plan states that the Anti-Racism Task Force will: "Lead and direct IGLYO's intersectional methodology, and anti-racist and decolonial perspective." In the spirit of the AMC's decision, the 2019 IGLYO Board is honoured to facilitate the constitution of IGLYO's first Anti-Racism Task Force. . . . The 2020 IGLYO Board extends a warm invitation to applicants to join the IGLYO Anti-Racism Task Force Member. Applicants must meet the following criteria: Identify as LGBTQI+; Not be older than 30 years; Live in the Council of Europe region; Identify as Black, as a Person of Colour, as Indigenous, as Roma, as a member of racialised groups/indigenous communities/minority faiths/ethnic minorities. . . . The IGLYO Anti-Racism Task Force represents an opportunity to shape the future of LGBTQI Youth activism in Europe and beyond.

---

[5] The Council of Europe itself has a task force in the European Commission against Racism and Intolerance (ECRI).

Notice that European peoples will *never* be referred to as indigenous. These anti-reality and often gaslighting constructs serve a clear ideological purpose and are central to the project.

Outside of Europe, in linking "de-colonialization" and "queerness," many of these "activists" work to conflate European colonialism with an artificial imposition of the notions of gender and sexuality. Elizabeth Kerekere is one such figure in New Zealand who states that pre-colonial Māori were sexually experimental people who openly accepted gender and sexual fluidity. Maybe they were or maybe it's a Margaret Mead-tier ideological position, but then again maybe not: New Zealand's first transgender mayor and Member of Parliament Georgina Beyer—part of the Wellington gay nightclub scene, initially as a singer and drag queen performer, and later as a prostitute—has Māori ancestry.

In any case, for what is germane to the present argument is that "de-colonization" is employed not just in nations constructed through European settler colonization, *but in Europeans' ancestral homelands*. To justify Third World displacement of indigenous Europeans, white Europeans have seen their claims to their own homelands rendered illegitimate. The BBC claims in what is a frankly genocidal assertion that "the Sami are the only indigenous people in the EU," which frames Europeans as colonists in their *own* homelands. Thus, "de-colonization" can *only* mean white eradication and replacement since whites cannot in this ideological construction be indigenous to anywhere and are themselves a constructed race. These are the stakes.

IGLYO, by the way, is funded by the Government of the Netherlands (the Dutch Ministry of Education, Culture, and Science), the Council of Europe European Youth Foundation, and the European Union, and has also received funding from UNESCO, which should communicate to the reader precisely the aims of the ruling class.

A precursor to the IGLYO report "LGBTQI Inclusive Education" was presented at the European Parliament in January 2018, with IGLYO receiving official feedback from the following governments: Andorra, Austria, Belgium, Denmark, Estonia, Germany, Kosovo, Luxembourg, Malta, Montenegro, the Netherlands, Norway, Portugal, Slovenia, Sweden, and the United Kingdom. The Parliamentary Assembly of the Council of Europe called on Member States to "ensure access by LGBTI children to quality education by promoting respect and inclusion of LGBTI persons and the dissemination of objective information concerning sexual orientation and gender identity, and by introducing measures to address homophobic and transphobic bullying." Yeah, I'm sure the information will be objective!

These efforts are, quite literally, state sponsored, although, as we've already seen, support is by no means limited to the state and various supra-governmental apparatuses with the NGOs, corporations, and more. They are all essentially uniform in their support for this particular pre-packaged agenda, sometimes referred to as "globalism," anyway. Due to said uniform nature and shared interests and aims externally—meaning there are internal disagreements about the allocation of power and there is at least one major fault line factionalizing the push for domination—from a practical perspective, i.e. how these disagreements affect the 99% of the planet's population being treated as pawns, these disagreements have little bearing on the overall thrust of the Establishment. Though it sounds ironic for self-styled revolutionaries to be the Establishment, they are in fact part of the same power structure. *I challenge you to identify one single institution that they do not control.* Furthermore, this "revolution" is being carried out against nature, order, and the very fabric of reality, is degrading by every measure, and is fundamentally anti-truth and anti-reality.

Beyond the usage of intersex people as pawns by the Establishment, intersex is used as a cudgel against people who object to the un-coupling of biological sex and "gender" and thus represents a manifestation of this "spectrum." Intersex and transgender are not the same, however, as one is a biological abnormality and the other a psychological one. This is obviously not to imply that there is something inherently "wrong" with intersex people, but rather to simply state that a few biological abnormalities do not undo the entire basis for what we know to be biological sex, nor does this negate the sexual dimorphism of men and women.

Transgender people need psychological interventions, not medical ones: percentages of transgender suicidality vary dramatically, from 18–45%, but even on the low end, that is astronomical. Most estimates are north of 30%. A litany of studies agree on one thing, however: "Such high prevalence rates of suicide ideation and attempts among transgender individuals seem closely tied to their gendered experience."[6] Furthermore, "This gender disorder does not seem to be associated with any molecular mutations of some of the main genes involved in sexual differentiation."[7] In other words, there is no biological evidence that the "body is wrong" for transgenders, but rather, that it is a psychological condition which surgery does not only *not* fix, but the evidence indicates that it *exacerbates* the tendencies to self-harm. The people pushing this idea that transgenders are "born in the wrong body" are lying for self-serving and deeply harmful reasons.

In many places, what I've already stated, despite its obvious factuality, is considered "hate speech" and is punishable by law because we all know the more self-evidently true something is, the more it needs to be accompanied by draconian punishments for anyone who questions it. When the law isn't called upon to suppress contradictory evidence, an army of professional "activists," grievance-mongering NGOs, corporations, academics, and media functionaries lie in wait for any excuse to swarm Wrongthinkers.

*eNeuro* published a paper in December 2019 by University of Michigan neuroscientist Stephen Gliske challenging the prevailing orthodoxy of transgenderism. Among his conclusions were that:

> The experience of incongruence between one's body and desired gender could be due to changes in an individual's sense of gender, rather than an individual having the brain sex of the desired gender . . . this paradigm shift—from fixed anatomical sizes to dynamic activity in brain networks—means that there may be many more options to decrease the distress experienced with gender dysphoria than we have ever realized.

But that would grind the sex change assembly line to halt, and that cannot happen.

In response to the publication of Gliske's paper, Troy Roepke of Rutgers University immediately started a petition on Change.org to have the paper retracted, alleging (as these types of whipped-up screeds always do) that there were "numerous scientific and theoretical short-comings" without identifying what, exactly, those

---

[6] Wolford-Clevenger, et al., "Suicide Risk Among Transgender People."
[7] Lombardo, et al., "Hormone and genetic study."

were, and that "this is not merely an example of difference in scientific opinion, but a direct attack on a vulnerable community." How? It seems Gliske is the one being attacked. What it *is* is an attack on the lucrative industries profiting from transgenderism and a gaslighting operation driving the population mad with its contradictions and ever-accelerating nature.

Of particular issue, echoing Queen Gertrude from *Hamlet* ("The lady doth protest too much, methinks"), is Roepke's contention that (and pay close attention to the order the "awarenesses" are listed):

> None of the three reviewers were sufficiently socially-, politically-, or scientifically-aware of the true intent and meaning of the clinical implications paragraph that was not only disregarding decades of research on the effectiveness of transitioning but actively promoting "chemical conversion therapy."

What is the whole process of "transitioning" *but* chemical conversion therapy?

Naturally *eNeuro* caved and retracted the paper on the back of these accusations and over 900 signatures of Roepke's petition. Rather ironic when you consider that in 2018, the European Parliament adopted a resolution where it condemned vis-à-vis Hungary "the attacks on free teaching and research, in particular on gender studies." It is as James Mason wrote:

> It's who you are and what you stand for, not what you do or how you do it. Mass graves are perfectly all-right as long as they are filled with dead Europeans killed while defending their homeland. Horrible killing is okay as long as it is state sanctioned. Vile and perverse videotapes are readily available and completely legal. But put 'em all together–private enterprise style–and watch out!

Indeed, for Savitri Devi, "It is not violence, but honesty about violence, which rapidly decreases at the end of the Dark Age."

There are real concerns here, and "hate" has nothing to do with it, unless of course we're talking about the "hate speech" legislation being used to wipe out dissent or hating what's being done to psychologically vulnerable people and children. It should go without saying that children are off-limits, but this perverse and disgusting agenda is zeroing-in on them as guinea pigs for hormonal and surgical experimentation, and for ideological reasons. While the media insists that detaining any random person who shows up in the West demanding entry (if the government even bothers to stop them anymore) is "torture," children who have just learned to talk are apparently able to determine their "gender identity" and to consent to the introduction of puberty blockers which stunt growth and cause infertility, bone and other health complications, and even death. As Corey Lynn reports:

> There are over 25,000 adverse reports including 1,500 deaths on Lupron products for puberty blockers, endometriosis, and prostate cancer. Manufactured by AbbVie, Lupron Depot-Ped is the number one prescribed puberty blocker, which is being used on children for early stages of gender

transitioning, despite never having been approved by the FDA for that purpose.

If a female child "identifies" as a boy, she may be given so-called "puberty-blockers" to prevent her from going through the natural human process of development. In some cases, she would then be given testosterone in an attempt to make her "become" a male. Endocrinologist Michael Laidlaw states that:

> An endocrinologist may be giving high levels of testosterone to a female to "transition" her. In this case, it's being induced by the medication. . . . When you look at the dosing that they're doing for females, for example, they give them a dose such that their testosterone levels would be in the normal range for a male, but for a female it's 10 to 40 times higher than normal. The rates for estrogen given to males are similarly high and unhealthy. When people are given far more of the opposite sex hormone than their bodies can handle, they are at increased risk for cardiovascular disease, cardiovascular death, deep vein thrombosis. They've looked at adults taking these hormones and have seen already these cardiovascular risks. When these drugs are administered to children, one would presume it's the same or even worse, in the long run.[8]

Laidlaw warns of similar effects from "so-called puberty-blocking medication like Lupron . . . [which] may be used for prostate cancer or have a use in females for endometriosis. They stop the pituitary gland from functioning correctly." The pituitary gland is sometimes called the "master gland" due to its central importance in the secretion of a host of essential hormones. Why do you think endocrinologists are so interested in studying "trans people," especially children? They're being used a guinea pigs!

By interfering with the natural processes of the pituitary gland in developing children, Lupron "blocks development of their organs, and their growth is stunted. If it's started in early puberty, these kids will not develop mature sperm or eggs, they will be infertile. If they have gonads removed, they will be sterilized." Laidlaw also states that:

> Under the Dutch protocol, as of Dutch law, these kids couldn't take cross-sex hormones until they were 16. In the U.S., the age was lowered to 12. I filed a Freedom of Information Act request and found that in [one] NIH study they actually recommended kids as young as 8 years old getting on to these opposite-sex hormones. They're going to end up with lower bone density, perhaps stunted brain development. A lot of the brain impact is unknown. There seems to be some brain development that is sex hormone-dependent.

There is actually quite a bit of evidence that is the case. First off, new research published in *Biological Psychiatry* indicates that these hormonal treatments also alter brain chemistry, which is anecdotally supported by anyone who's ever taken exogenous hormones—or, indeed, can attest to endogenous fluctuations. Researchers at

---

[8] O'Neil, "Medical Expert."

the Medical University of Vienna, led by senior authors Dr. Siegfried Kasper and Dr. Rupert Lanzenberger, show that administration of the male hormone testosterone in female-to-male transgenders raises brain levels of SERT, the serotonin transporter. On the flip side, male-to-female transsexuals who received a testosterone blocker and the female hormone estrogen showed *decreased* levels of this protein. SERT plays an important role in regulating mood, and in the treatment of mood and anxiety disorders, many common antidepressants called selective serotonin reuptake inhibitors (SSRIs) bind directly to the serotonin transporter protein and inhibit recycling of the neurotransmitter. "This study is the first to show changes in brain chemistry associated with the hormonal treatments administered in the sex change process," says Dr. John Krystal, editor of *Biological Psychiatry*:

> It provides new insight into the ways that the hormonal differences between men and women influence mood and the risk for mood disorders. What we see is a real quantitative difference in brain structure after prolonged exposure to testosterone. . . . In more general terms, these findings may suggest that the genuine difference between the brains of women and men is substantially attributable to the effects of circulating sex hormones. Moreover, the hormonal influence on human brain structure goes beyond early developmental phases and is still present in adulthood.[9]

We would imagine, then, that altering hormonal levels in developing children and adolescents could have profound and decidedly negative ramifications—or, instead of imagining, we can look at concrete proof.

Published in the journal *Frontiers in Human Neuroscience*, a 2017 study looked at an eleven-year-old boy both before and after he was administered hormone suppressors to "transition," the purpose being "to review the effects of puberty suppression on the brain white matter during adolescence." Upon being given anti-puberty pharmaceuticals, the young boy's intellectual performance began to decrease. The scientists who evaluated the child reported that they observed "immaturity in [his] cognitive development" as a result of taking the drugs. After twenty-eight months, the child's white matter was observed to be "unchanged," which the research team concluded "may be related to reduced serum testosterone levels." Additionally, the boy's global IQ, or GIQ, was found to be:

> [F]urther slightly reduced during the follow-up with [hormone disruptor] treatment. In fact, the low average GIQ together with impairment in the perceptual organization of intelligence and processing speed index presented even before treatment suggest that any neurodevelopmental immaturity may have been potentiated by pubertal suppression. . . . Some questions emerge from these findings, especially regarding the influence of sex steroids on cognition during puberty. It is likely that the structural and microstructural changes in the brain during adolescence . . . may interfere on the achievement of complete cognitive potential.

As Peter Hayes comments:

---

[9] "Sex change hormonal treatments."

Gonadotropin releasing hormone agonists (GnRHas) have been found to impair memory in adults, so the study by Wojniusz et al. (2016) on the possible cognitive effects of these drugs on children treated for idiopathic central precocious puberty (CPP) represents an important contribution to research in this area. Recent findings that GnRHas increase depression symptoms (Macoveanu et al., 2016) and slow reaction time (Stenbæk et al., 2016) in healthy women, and reduce long-term spatial memory in sheep (Hough et al., 2017) underline the importance of the research that Wojniusz et al. (2016) have undertaken. However, their reassuring statement in the abstract that girls undergoing GnRHa treatment for CPP and controls "showed very similar scores with regard to cognitive performance" and their conclusion that "GnRHa treated girls do not differ in their cognitive functioning . . . from the same age peers" (Wojniusz et al., 2016) may be overly optimistic. . . . Girls treated for CPP with triptorelin acetate were tested with the short form Wechsler Intelligence Scale for Children III. It was found that the girls had a mean IQ of 94, as against a mean IQ of 102 for the matched control group (Wojniusz et al., 2016). These IQ estimations are presented as standardized IQ scores, which places a girl scoring 102 at the $55^{th}$ percentile, and a girl scoring of 94 at the $34^{th}$ percentile. It is questionable whether scores that indicate a percentile gap of this size can be described as "very similar". . . . . The contention that a decline only becomes clinically interesting if it is of at least 1 standard deviation is unconvincing. Any findings which indicate that GnRHas cause a decline, even a modest decline, in IQ are likely to be of considerable interest to patients and their parents. It is a factor that they may well want to consider in deciding whether or not to take the drug. They may, for example, wish to consider the possible effect of GnRHas on a child's school and exam performance. In this respect it can be noted that 2 of the treated girls had been held back a year at school.

A 2001 study in which 25 children treated for early puberty with triptorelin acetate were tested with the short form Wechsler Intelligence Scale for Children (Mul et al., 2001). In this study, children took the IQ test before treatment and again after two years of treatment. It was found that their IQ dropped 7 points from 100 to 93. With 25 treated participants, this 7-point drop was significant.

Staphorsius et al. (2015) conducted a study in a gender dysphoric (GD) adolescent group under hormonal suppression to investigate the impact of pubertal suppression on executive function (EF); they compared GD adolescents under GnRHa treatment to GD adolescents undergoing physiological puberty and compared them to male and female control groups using the Tower of London test. What they found was a negative impact of pubertal suppression on EF.

Additionally, a global IQ decrease was reported in a longitudinal follow-up of girls with central precocious puberty treated with GnRHa in Schuerger and Witt (1989). In an animal study with pre-pubertal castrated sheep (Hough et al., 2016, 2017), researchers reported an impairment in long-term spatial memory that was *not* reversed by subsequent hormone replacement treatment. Finally, another study correlated verbal skill impairment to pubertal suppression in a GD group (Costa et al., 2015).

To call this child abuse is the understatement of the century. There is nothing stunning and brave about this; it's sick, and people are profiting from it. Michael Laidlaw states that the puberty blocker Lupron costs $775 a month alone; consider that "that's a $27,000 'pause button' at 5 years [of age]. . . . Multiply this together with the huge rise in cases documented or observed in Western nations and a major windfall is to be had." Now we're starting to get to the heart of one of the major motivations: profit. And, by the way, as we've just seen, Lupron is *not* a "pause" on puberty, but a significant harm-inducer on otherwise healthy children.

Back in 2004, *The Guardian* (of all places) reported that a review of more than one hundred international medical studies of post-operative transsexuals by the University of Birmingham's aggressive research intelligence facility (ARIF) found no evidence that gender reassignment surgery is clinically effective, but that has been memory-holed:

> [The Aggressive Research Intelligence Facility], which conducts reviews of health care treatments for the [National Health Service], concludes that none of the studies provides conclusive evidence that gender reassignment is beneficial for patients. It found that most research was poorly designed, which skewed the results in favor of physically changing sex.

Not only that, but *The Guardian* also noted, "the results of many gender reassignment studies are unsound because researchers lost track of more than half of the participants."

The exact rate of desistance (children "growing out" of their transgender feelings) varies by study, but on average about 80% of so-called "trans kids" eventually identified as their "sex at birth." As opposed to being "born in the wrong body," cross-sex stereotypical behavior is often predictive of later same-sex attraction. In other words, most transgenders are simply homosexual.

Additionally, for many people classed as transgender, there is the uncomfortable fact that this is, in fact, a kink for some adults, albeit an extreme one. These are called "autogynephiliacs," men who are sexually aroused at the thought of transforming into a more feminine form. This can range from transvestitism to full-on "gender reassignment." In addition to the multiple "genders" posited by Magnus Hirschfeld, he also believed that there were five kinds of sexuality: homosexual, bisexual, heterosexual, asexual, and automonosexual. For Hirschfeld, automonosexuals were men who derived excitement at the thought or image of themselves as women; they "feel attracted not by the women outside them, but by the woman inside them." Indeed, there is an entire subset of modern pornography under the umbrella "femdom" (female domination) that caters to these kinds of transformation or feminization fantasies. Kink.com was one of the partners for the Transgender Law Center's 10th anniversary celebration in 2012. One of the major projects of modern psychology has been to "de-pathologize" pedophilia alongside gender identity disorder/gender dysphoria. The consistent and inescapable overlap of sexuality and "trans" has seriously disturbing ramifications. Once again, I must state that this is no territory for children. Unfortunately, the ruling class does not see it that way.

Instead, the mainstream view is that of Elizabeth Warren, who made the insane pledge in her 2020 presidential bid that if elected she would allow a "transgender child" to pick her Secretary of Education ("I'm going to have a Secretary of Education that this young trans person interviews on my behalf") or that of transgender "activist" and tenured College of Charleston professor Veronica Ivy/Rachel McKinnon,[10] who stated in a YouTube video released on Mother's Day 2017 that if children's parents won't support their "gender identity"—calling it "abuse"—that "it's okay to walk away . . . and I want to give you hope that you can find what we call your glitter family. Your queer family."

The mainstream view is that of *National Geographic* magazine, which ran the single-issue "Gender Revolution" in January 2017 in conjunction with a documentary film of the same name and produced a discussion guide for teachers and parents, which uses the World Health Organization's definition of and support for transgenderism. The discussion guide refers to Jewish feminist Gloria Steinem and Jewish COO of Facebook Sheryl Sandberg and asks: "How have Gloria Steinem and Sheryl Sandberg contributed to our understanding of gender by the lives they have lived and the positions they have taken?" I will be answering this question regarding Steinem later, but for addressing Sandberg, her donations to the Anti-Defamation League, and her position as founder of LeanIn.org, which is dedicated "to offering women the ongoing inspiration and support to help them achieve their goals," and its partnering with Salesforce, well . . . read on for that as well.

From the magazine's Jewish editor-in-chief Susan Goldberg, this "gender revolution" is very positive. In her piece "We are in the Midst of a Gender Revolution," she writes:

> The popular dating app Tinder announced it was expanding its options for gender identification to nearly 40 choices, following in the footsteps of Facebook, which now has more than 50 gender options to choose among. Pew Research reports five federal agencies are collecting data about gender identity. . . . Now that we know XX and XY, and blue and pink, don't tell the full story, it is time to write a new chapter to ensure that we all can thrive in this world no matter what our gender—or decision to not identify a gender. . . . This is why we're devoting the January issue of *National Geographic* magazine entirely to an exploration of gender issues—in science, social systems, and civilizations—and why we decided to feature a transgender person for the first time on the cover of our magazine: nine-year-old Avery Jackson.

The discussion guide, with no evidence, confidently states that, "Gender is a social construct, and Western culture starts to impose its values before we are born, even in the way we decorate nurseries for babies."

The mainstream view is that of the Netflix show *AJ and the Queen* where a ten-year-old accompanies RuPaul to various "performances" across the country (the child is apparently "trans" as a response to, in a rare moment of truth-telling, significant childhood trauma). Netflix also heavily-promoted the French film *Cuties*, which "explores the challenges faced by a group of young and diverse girls in their quest for authenticity and belonging when their inherited cultures, faith, and traditions clash with secular liberal French society." The trailer opens with a clearly pre-pubescent black girl in a headscarf watching another pre-pubescent brown girl grinding her pleather-clad rear end in the air while doing laundry and ironing her hair,

---

[10] The biologically male McKinnon/Ivy has been winning championships and setting world records competing as a women's cyclist. Ivy states that this ability to compete against women is a "human right."

which inspires her to want to join the posse of the cool girls and their dancing troupe.

Forbes writer Scott Mendelson ("Even as a secular Jew, I always enjoyed that cartoon [Veggie Tales] as it really stressed the 'Don't be a jerk' component of spirituality and Christianity") states that your outrage is "totally ridiculous" and the result of a "false flag controversy": "Maybe, just maybe, Doucouré's (a Black woman, by the way, making her presumably immune from criticism) feature is intended for young girls who themselves are coming to terms with their sexuality and/or their potentially discomforted parents. Once again, it's up to girls to protect boys and men from their own uncontrollable libidos." Is that right, Scott?

The film is supposed to be a critique of both the hyper-sexualization of young girls in decadent Western societies, terraformed by the "elite" and spread, cultivated, and incentivized by social media and that of the more repressive elements of Islamic culture. I'm a bit ambivalent about the film given some of the explicit situations but my read is that it was designed to make the viewer uncomfortable and to elicit disgust. The marketing of the film as essentially soft-core pedophilic porn is really the issue past the fact that a "multi-cultural" France is an obvious non-starter that must be categorically rejected, "happy medium" of the film's ending or no. Given that one of the co-founders of Netflix is a descendent of Sigmund Freud and Edward Bernays, though, marketing the film in this fashion—and Mendelson's defense of it—and running shows like *AJ and the Queen* and many of Netflix's other "woke" programs is to be expected.

The mainstream view is that of Cathy Maser of the Lawrence S. Bloomberg Faculty of Nursing at the University of Toronto and the Transgender Youth Clinic at SickKids who believes "the earlier transgender and non-binary youth access resources to help discover who they are, the better." Planned Parenthood Toronto has awarded Maser for her work. As a lecturer at the University of Toronto:

> Maser challenges students to develop an understanding of the relationship between a youth's health and his or her socioeconomic context. She helps them explore how social class, gender, migration, race/ethnicity, ability/disability and sexual orientation come together to affect the ability of an adolescent to access adequate health care.

The mainstream view is that of the ACLU, ACLU-Idaho, Cooley LLP, and Legal Voice, co-filers of a federal lawsuit challenging Idaho Governor Brad Little signing into law prohibitions on transgender "girls" and "women" from competing in sports as female. Legal Voice describes itself as a:

> Progressive feminist organization using the power of the law to make change in the Northwest. We use that power structure to dismantle sexism and oppression, specifically advocating for our region's most marginalized communities: women of color, lesbians, transgender and gender-nonconforming people, immigrants, people with disabilities, low-income women, and others affected by gender oppression and injustice.

According to the lawsuit, "H.B. 500 requires women and girls, upon a 'dispute regarding' their sex, to submit to invasive physical examinations and genetic testing in order to 'verify' a vague and indeterminate notion of 'biological sex.'" What is vague and indeterminate about determining whether someone's chromosomes are XX or XY, or even more simply using the rubric from *Kindergarten Cop*?

The mainstream view is that of *Huffington Post* "trans advocate" Brynn Tannehill, who writes, "The desistance myth was promoted by reparative therapists, concern trolls, and charlatans. It's time for the 80 percent desistance figure to be relegated to the same junk science bin as the utterly discredited link between vaccines and autism." Any hard evidence to support that claim, Brynn? Of course not. Buyer's remorse is common for men, women, boys, and girls who are often railroaded or pressured into what's proven to be a financial windfall for the pharmaceutical, biotech, plastic surgery, and, yes, retail industries. Gender is, after all, a consumer choice the market is more than happy to cater to, and even more so, it is an ideological construct designed to further meld humanity into one indeterminate mass of easily-controlled serfs and consumers. What will be indeterminate is any unique or differentiating characteristics among these Eloi.

Like race, gender is framed by the ruling class as essentially only skin-deep (although this framing is fraught with contradiction at basically every turn), when the reality is that sex and race reflect something much deeper and more profound. For an indoctrinated and dumbed-down population raised on sloganeering and devoid of critical thinking faculties, this does not matter. It's plug-and-play.

Transgenderism is a vehicle for social engineering by the Establishment, and its methods of recruitment and mental re-configuring map very closely with those of notorious cults like Synanon—and with very good reason, as we shall see later. It preys on the mentally ill and vulnerable, breaking them down and re-forming their identities in the desired image of the cult leader or leaders. Extensive research shows that between 52% and 82% of self-identified transgender persons have *at least* one or more DSM-listed psychiatric conditions or personality disorders *beyond* their gender dysphoria. Happy, well-adjusted people do not join cults, and, as Margaret Singer noted, "If the social structure has not broken down, very few people will follow."

So the intent is clear: to serve as a potent means of propaganda and mind control; to demoralize, weaken, and dumb down the population to make them more compliant; to create a new "victim class" for political exploitation and to further splinter the family and atomize the native population; and to produce new "markets" for increased profit. Some of the worst excesses are very obviously done for sport or out of malice, showing that beyond the horizontal view, it is a rejection of natural law, representative of the advanced decay of a civilization being eaten alive from the inside-out, spreading its diseased anti-morality across the globe. It is, in no uncertain terms, *pure evil*, and the people and organizations so far introduced are just the tip of the iceberg.

## 1

## All My Friends Are Going Trans

*"[Jesse] Singal is attempting to provide hope to parents that their child who says they're trans might not be. He leaves enough doubt for you to consider gatekeeping your child's identity. This is irresponsible. Singal goes on to express how investigating that identity could cause harm, if adolescents begin physical transitions: 'Some of these interventions are irreversible. People respond differently to cross-sex hormones, but changes in vocal pitch, body hair, and other physical characteristics, such as the development of breast tissue, can become permanent.' Here, it sounds like Singal is essentially trying to scare readers into not letting young trans people be themselves.*

– Robyn Kanner[11]
"I Detransitioned. But Not Because I Wasn't Trans,"
*The Atlantic*, June 22nd, 2018

For Richard Dawkins, the meme ("a unit of cultural transmission") is a viral phenomenon that exhibits evolutionary behavior and responds to selective pressures at the inter-generational level of a group or society (think ideas, traditions, symbols, et cetera—anything that can be imitated and mentally internalized). The meme is also capable of spreading even while simultaneously harming the host (for Aaron Lynch, the meme can double as a "thought contagion"). Thus, what is appealing and has enough resonance with enough people can spread even if the content of the meme is harmful or, in some cases, lethal. The digitization of the world allows for the speed with which a meme can spread like a virus (hence the phrase "going viral"). Oftentimes these destructive memes are packaged in Trojan Horse fashion, thus ushering dangerous concepts such as multi-culturalism right past the usual defenses as they are attached to and cloaked by seemingly-benign or generally "agreeable" sentiments. We will later explore the effectiveness the meme "love is love" had in the

---

[11] Robyn Kanner is the Senior Creative Advisor of Biden for President and formerly of Jigsaw, a "Minority Report"-esque unit managed by Google that "forecasts and confronts emerging threats" online; its CEO, the Jewish Jared Cohen, is alleged to have used his position in Jigsaw's precursor Google Ideas to foment unrest targeted at regimes dis-favored by the US in the Middle East in the years preceding the so-called Arab Spring; Stratfor's vice-president of counter-terrorism Fred Burton writes that "GOOGLE is getting WH [White House] and State Dept. support and air cover. In reality, they are doing things the CIA cannot do." Cohen was an intern at the US State Department and served as a member of the Secretary of State's Policy Planning Staff from 2006 to 2010. He headed Google Ideas and now Jigsaw, was named a World Economic Forum Young Global Leader, and is an adjunct senior fellow with the Council on Foreign Relations focusing on "counter-radicalization."

institutionalization of gay marriage. The disingenuous argument of letting so-called trans kids "be themselves" is along these same lines.

One of the primary causes of the explosion of "trans youth" in recent years can be explained by the social contagion effect. A study published in 2018 by Dr. Lisa Littman compellingly argues that social contagion may well be a significant factor in the increase of trans-identifying young people, who are obviously much more impressionable than adults—which is why the ruling class pushes "trans" and the other colors of the rainbow so heavily in schools, libraries, and in children's programming.

In 2009, the American Psychological Association (APA) in its "Report of the APA Task Force on Gender Identity and Gender Variance" estimated the number of transgender individuals in the United States at 115,000 to 450,000, or 38 to 147 per 100,000 by using US Census data for that year's total population size—meaning at the low end we're looking at .04% and at the high end .15% of the population. Seven years later, a 2016 study from the Williams Institute at UCLA estimated that transgenders represented about 0.6% of the adult population. The Williams Institute had five years earlier placed the percentage of adult transgenders in the US at 0.3%, which may mean that given the Census figures versus the Williams Institute's, the Institute may well have inflated their numbers or have used a much more flexible definition of trans, although it is also possible people previously felt less comfortable self-identifying as trans whereas increasingly they're actually receiving benefits from doing so.

The APA and the Census aside, if we consider the 2011 versus 2016 Williams Institute percentages, a doubling of self-identifying trans people seems to suggest that the spike can be largely attributed to massive social-reprogramming efforts and incentives for becoming or identifying as transgendered. That number has continued to explode, with the number of transgender-identifying high school students now estimated to be at around 2%. A self-serving report published by GLAAD in 2017, tellingly called the Accelerating Acceptance report, surveyed over 2,000 American adults ages 18 and over in November 2016 in partnership with Harris Poll. The report revealed a whopping 20% of the youngest respondents (18–34) identified as LGBTQ, compared with 12% of Generation X (ages 35–53) and 7% of Baby Boomers (52–71). It is entirely possible—probable, even—that the numbers are exploding due to social contagion and incentivizing efforts as well as being dramatically inflated, which in turn accelerates self-identification.

In case you were wondering if GLAAD is some fringe organization, presenting partners of the GLAAD Media Awards are Gilead Sciences, Wells Fargo, Ketel One Vodka, and Delta Airlines; additional corporate and foundation partners include Google, Target, Facebook, Hilton, Netflix, ViacomCBS, Comcast/NBCUniversal, the National Basketball Association, AT&T, Morgan Stanley, Coca-Cola, Walt Disney Television, the Tides Foundation, the TAWANI Foundation, Tinder, and Grindr, the last two being "hook-up" apps—Grindr, founded by the Jewish Joel Simkhai, specifically for homosexuals.

The spread among the youth has happened in various other ways as well. Some parents are incentivized to claim their children are transgender for reasons related to social attention and/or approval and to foster a sense of belonging. Of these, a percentage are likely suffering from Munchausen by proxy syndrome, where typically the mother harms their child or children for sympathy and affection. Dr. Michelle Cretella states that, "Munchausen by proxy is a disorder in which an adult feigns either physical or psychological condition in a child for their own subconscious reasons. Most often the perpetrator is the biological mother and she often has a background in health or medicine."[12]

A prime example is the saga of a Dallas, Texas family court case begun in late 2019 involving a non-biological mother's attempts at forcing a sex change on her now-eight-year-old son. The non-biological mother in question is pediatrician Anne Georgulas, who gave birth via IVF using an egg donor, and claims the boy James should be called "Luna" and transitioned into a girl because he once asked for a girl's toy at McDonald's and imitated female characters from *Frozen* after viewing the movie. He allegedly asked to wear dresses, which the father initially acquiesced to until he found the girls' clothing in his trash one morning (thrown out by James himself).

The jury believed that her ex-husband, the biological father, should not have a say in the matter, but Judge Kim Cooks ultimately overruled the jury's decision and awarded joint custody provided the father attend counseling with James, his twin brother, and Georgulas. Cooks stated that Georgulas must receive permission from the boy's biological father before allowing the boy to undergo any "transitioning" measures; if the parents could not agree, a court-appointed parenting coordinator would be the tie-breaker. Cooks found that Georgulas was "overly affirming in instances when James supposedly showed a desire to be a girl," including taking him to Pride parades, buying him dresses and fake hair, and enrolling him in kindergarten as a girl under the name Luna.

Georgulas's attorneys filed a motion to have Cooks replaced in November 2019, and in January 2020 Judge Mary Brown was appointed to the case. After initially upholding joint custody, Brown reversed course in August 2020 after an appeal by the Georgulas camp, and granted her request to force the father to pay for and attend counseling without a proper hearing; Georgulas was also given sole custody and decision-making power over the future of the child, which will presumably begin with the administration of puberty blockers and the full "transition" of James into Luna. This is legal but no less criminal. As Cretella explains:

> In the case of imposing gender dysphoria on a son, there are cases in the scientific literature of severe maternal depression triggered in a mother longing for a daughter. The mother's depression lifts when the boy dresses and acts as a girl. This has been termed "gender mourning."

When with his father, James is happy behaving like a normal boy. Whenever James is with his mother, however, she only addresses him by the name Luna and will only allow him to dress in girl's clothing; the mother also specifically chose a therapist who specializes in gender transitioning.

For her part, Cretella, Executive Director of the American College of Pediatricians, has been targeted as a kind of heretic, in her description, which is not all that far from the truth given the religious fervor with which pro-trans groups push this insanity on children. She and the American College of Pediatricians have come under fire from the American Academy of Pediatricians and were actually labeled a

---

[12] O'Neil, "Mothing Forcing Transgenderism."

"hate group" by the Southern Poverty Law Center (SPLC). Why is the SPLC weighing in on a struggle between two pediatric associations? Because it's an ideological orthodoxy enforcer and wants to push the delusions of transgenderism on the population and silence anyone who gets in their way. If anything, Cretella is motivated by concern for vulnerable children at the mercy of their parents, weaponized bureaucratic, educational, and judicial systems, and a society that is rapidly disintegrating around them, not "hate." This is infantile, but for a sentimentalized and dumbed-down population, evidently it is a sufficient explanation.

The social contagion's spread is hastened by the internet and social media use in particular, as Littman's study, "Parent reports of adolescents and young adults perceived to show signs of a rapid onset of gender dysphoria," found:

> Adolescent and young adult (AYA) children, who have had no histories of childhood gender identity issues, experienced a perceived sudden or rapid onset of gender dysphoria. Parents have described clusters of gender dysphoria in pre-existing friend groups with multiple or even all members of a friend group becoming gender dysphoric and transgender-identified in a pattern that seems statistically unlikely based on previous research. Parents describe a process of immersion in social media, such as "binge-watching" YouTube transition videos and excessive use of Tumblr, immediately preceding their child becoming gender dysphoric.

As we put the pieces of the puzzle together—viral memes and thought contagions, the ubiquity of support and increasingly incentivizing of "trans" by every significant and many insignificant institutions, the role of technology and social media in isolation and recruitment/grooming, various social pressures, the break-down of the family and other institutions that provide stability and meaning, the "halo effect" of abnormal sexualities, and more—we see once again a deeply-enmeshed set of conditions that work synergistically in spreading and amplifying harmful beliefs.

The grooming factor is very real. A Queens University (Canada) professor found that the percentage of pedophiles who were homosexuals was four times that of the general population. 59% of male child sex offenders had been a "victim of contact sexual abuse as a child." As Lynda S. Doll reported in her study, "Self-Reported Childhood and Adolescent Sexual Abuse among Adult Homosexual and Bisexual Men" (1992), "This study of 1,001 adult homosexual and bisexual men found that 37% reported they had been encouraged or forced to have sexual contact with an older or more powerful partner before age 19. Median age at first contact was 10." So the young *are* being groomed by powerful predators, and it is becoming legalized.

In the United States, lesbian Assemblywoman Susan Talamantes Eggman and Jewish homosexual State Senator Scott Wiener's proposed legislation (Bill SB 145) "to end blatant discrimination against LGBT young people regarding California's sex offender registry" echo an extremely disturbing mindset within this "community," as do these comments from Jewish homosexual Milo Yiannopoulos said during a live-stream:

> We get hung up on this child abuse stuff. . . . This is one of the reasons why I hate the left, the one size fits all policing of culture, this arbitrary and oppressive idea of consent. . . . Pedophilia is not a sexual attraction to somebody

who is 13 years old and sexually mature. . . . In the gay world, some of the most important, enriching, and incredibly life-affirming, important, shaping relationships are between younger boys and older men. They can be hugely positive experiences very often for those young boys.

Jewish California State Assemblywoman Laura Friedman calls the SB 145 bill "purely an equity issue," as Sen. Wiener explains:

> Currently, for consensual yet illegal sexual relations between a teenager age 15 and over and a partner within 10 years of age, 'sexual intercourse' (i.e., vaginal intercourse) does not require the offender to go onto the sex offender registry; rather, the judge decides based on the facts of the case whether sex offender registration is warranted or unwarranted. By contrast, for other forms of intercourse—specifically, oral and anal intercourse—sex offender registration is mandated under all situations, with no judicial discretion.

Something else to consider: a *Computers in Human Behavior* survey from a general population of Internet pornography users found that users of pornography depicting sexual abuse of children also consume both hardcore pornography (featuring ostensibly adult performers), as well as animal pornography. There were no consumers of child sexual abuse images who only collected child sexual abuse images.

A separate study from *BMC Psychiatry* examining 231 Swiss men charged in a 2002 case for possession of child pornography found that 60% percent also had pornography that depicted sexual acts with animals, excrement, or brutality; 33% consumed at least three or more types of deviant pornography. Researchers also found that those convicted for possessing child sexual abuse images were more likely to subscribe to commercial websites containing legal pornographic material.

The increasing need for more hardcore pornography leads individuals to pursue very perverse prurient interests which include, but are not limited to, transgender pornography: using functional MRI, a 2014 study from by Valerie Voon found that compulsive sexual behavior is characterized by novelty-seeking, conditioning, and habituation to sexual stimuli in males—meaning users need more extreme content over time in order achieve the same level of arousal. By its own admission, porn outlet xHamster concluded that the more porn you watch, the more likely you are to identify as bisexual.

If porn also makes people more sexually unsure, and we add all of the de-stabilizing and alienating factors of (post-)modernity previously discussed into the equation, not least of which is the social contagion effect outlined by Lisa Littman and the active recruitment/grooming of the mentally ill and/or vulnerable by homosexuals and/or transgenders, then the explosion of self-identifying transgender persons, *particularly among the youth*, makes sense. How many of these groomers/recruiters are in positions of power? As we will see, a great many.

Critics blame the lack of research on the increasingly-common phenomenon of "de-transitioning," which is basically an attempt to revert back to the original sex with varying degrees of success given some of the changes, as evidence that surgery and hormonal therapy work and that "correcting" the mistake of "being born in the wrong body" then sends the person in question out into the rainbow yonder of cupcakes and Gender Unicorns. More likely it's something closer to what James Caspian encountered when his proposal to study gender reassignment reversal was turned down by Bath Spa University in the UK, because it was "potentially politically incorrect" and that "the posting of unpleasant material on blogs or social media may be detrimental to the reputation of the university."

Beyond the cowardice, it certainly can't have anything to do with the fact that a male-to-female genital surgery ranges up to $12,000 for a "penile inversion" and up to $28,000 for a "rectosigmoid transfer" procedure, where surgeons use *rectal tissue* to "construct a vagina." Yes, rectal tissue. For female-to-male surgeries, the range can be anywhere from $6,000 for a mastectomy to $80,000 for the "construction of a penis capable of achieving erection and permitting a person to urinate while standing,"[13] and these are just the baseline surgeries, not the hormones, the other procedures like plastic surgery, the new outfits, the puberty blockers depending on the age, et cetera. You can actually compare prices online to find the cheapest vaginoplasties!

In any case, the Jewish transgender "activist" Riki Wilchins ("I had been raised in the tightly-knit Jewish community in Cincinnati, Ohio. My grandfather had studied to be a rabbi at Hebrew Union College") counters that Caspian's research would be a waste of time anyway since only a "very small fraction of people de-transition." And besides, Wilchins says, the bigoted "strong political undercurrent in previous studies" had been used to "restrict transgender people's access to surgery."

The transgender phenomenon is fully backed by the state and supported with "evidence" by "experts" like Sheree Bekker and Cara Tannenbaum, who claims gender is fluid and when asked to weigh in on hormonal advantages in women's athletics, claims that there is "a lack of evidence about testosterone's effects." Congresswoman Ilhan Omar also saw fit to send a letter to USA Powerlifting demanding that they allow biological males who identify as women to compete in women's events, because biological differences between the sexes are a "myth" unsupported by "medical science." In 2015, the Court of Arbitration for Sport found that the way the International Association of Athletics Federations (IAAF) regulated intersex athletes (through testosterone levels) was scientifically unsound. None of this could be further from the truth, but this is central to the anti-reality agenda of the ruling class. As Mark Regnerus writes for *First Things*:

> This is the queering of science. Its academic roots have been around for decades, but it is now swelling in practice. A pair of colleagues at the University of Texas outline it in considerable detail in "Queering Methodologies to Understand Queer Families," a federally funded review that appeared recently in Family Relations. Long-standard (or dominant) research methods, they hold, stand in need of adaptation: "Queering questions that which is normative." They openly counsel tying science to politics, imploring scholars to put their research to work "in ways that best represent and strengthen (queer) families."

This is one hundred percent an extension of the "culture of critique" that's been metastasizing in academia for generations.

There's serious money behind this endeavor, and it has full institutional support.

---

[13] Levy, "Two transsexuals reflect."

Parents can even be overruled by the courts. As CNN reported in February 2018:

> A Hamilton County, Ohio, judge . . . gave custody of a transgender teen to his grandparents rather than his parents, allowing them to make medical decisions regarding his transition. The parents didn't want the teen, a 17-year-old who identifies as male, to undergo hormone treatment and refused to call him by his chosen name, triggering suicidal feelings, according to court testimony. The parents wanted custody in order to make medical decisions for the teen and prohibit the treatment that his medical team had recommended.
> . . . A team at Cincinnati Children's Hospital Medical Center, where the teen has been treated since 2016, advised the court that he should start treatment as soon as possible to decrease his suicide risk.

The hospital's Transgender Health Program "offers medical care for transgender and gender-nonconforming youth from age 4 to their 25th birthday." Lee Ann Conrad, pictured right, is its Director and founder.

In April 2019, the Arizona Supreme Court made the decision that judges can overrule parents on so-called "treatment" for transgender children, requiring them to seek "expert help" for children who "may be transgender," according to *AZ Central.*

"In a lot of these cases, children are stating, 'I don't want to live,' or they're getting admitted to Phoenix Children's because they're slamming their heads against floors," says Cammy Bellis, founder of Mothers in Transition. The nonprofit group "connects moms of gender non-conforming children with legal resources." Bellis continues, "Parents feel that it's their right to be able to make legal and medical decisions about their child, but when your child's making death statements and having suicidal ideations, when do the courts plan to step in?"

Early and often, I can imagine; the American Psychiatric Association (APA) claims that "cross-gender behaviors" can manifest themselves from *age two.* Frankly, though the APA is treated as an "authority," they lost their credibility long ago. They've been weaponized as an activist institution since at least the 1970s.

The Jewish "activist" Frank Kameny (co-founder of the Washington, DC branch of the Mattachine Society) was at the forefront of pressuring the APA to reconsider its position on same-sex attraction, along with Barbara Gittings (in 1971, Gittings became the second head of the American Library Association's Task Force on Gay Liberation), though how much pressure the APA really needed is debatable. In 1973, the APA declared that "by itself, homosexuality does not meet the criteria for being a psychiatric disorder" and removed it from the second edition of its Diagnostic and Statistical Manual of Mental Disorders (DSM-II). Eventual DSM-III committee Chair the Jewish Robert L. Spitzer (Columbia University) was generally credited with spearheading the decision. Removing homosexuality from the DSM is not, in and of itself, necessarily a problem, per se, but it is indicative of a larger pattern of behavior as regards the politicizing of institutions such as the APA, the weaponization of psychoanalysis and mental health more broadly (and insidiously), the re-definition of terms and behaviors to suit their agenda and fit their narrative, and the jointly subversive and collusive means of forcing policy changes on an unwilling or unaware public. It also removes the clear link between homosexuality and pathology.

Another insidious example of re-defining is the constant linking of everything and anything deemed unfavorable by the in-group to the Holocaust and anti-Semitism, with Kameny writing in June 1965: "There is but a short step from prison sentences for homosexuals to gas ovens for Jews, and amazingly little difference between [Sir Cyril] Osborne and Hitler." Kameny wrote to CBS in November 1966: "I am sure that you see the similarity between the charges of a 'homosexual mafia' and the charges of a 'Jewish conspiracy,' which one hears endlessly from anti-Semitic sources. Both charges are a discredit only to those making them and to those believing them." For added significance, Jewish publication *The Forward* refers to Kameny as "the Moses of the LGBT movement."

The debatable removal of homosexuality from the DSM is reflective of this pattern of "activism" and behind-the-scenes machinations that would take place elsewhere with the homosexual agenda as a precursor to "trans" and the like, and with the APA itself as a harbinger of the transformation of society more widely. Gender identity disorder was dropped from the DSM-V, which was published in 2013, to "remove the stigma associated with the term disorder," and the new term "gender dysphoria" was added as per the APA, "The presence of gender variance is not the pathology but dysphoria is from the distress caused by the body and mind not aligning and/or societal marginalization of gender-variant people." There are still plenty of other disorders in the DSM, though. Gender dysphoria will probably be removed from the next volume altogether.

The APA has no problem calling the very nature of masculinity itself toxic, however, as to quote Erielle Davidson of *The Federalist*:

> For the first time in its history, the American Psychological Association released a report to assist psychologists working with men and boys. One of the biggest "takeaways" of the report alludes to a crisis of masculinity: "traditional masculinity—marked by stoicism, competitiveness, dominance and aggression—is, on the whole, harmful. . . ." The APA report evinces a growing and unfortunate trend within our "woke" society of using traditional masculinity as a convenient scapegoat for a host of societal ills. Instead of considering the complexity of the human condition, we seem compelled to reduce issues of male mental health to question of men merely being too "manly." The subtext of the report is that, in order to address male mental health, we must restructure society to reject masculine norms and simultaneously reprogram men to reject their biological inclinations.

No agenda, right? In the article "The New Voices of Masculinity" by the Jewish Nora Caplan-Bricker, part of *GQ*'s New Masculinity issue, "an exploration of the ways that traditional notions of masculinity are being challenged, overturned, and evolved," we are treated to soy-addled and Cult-Marx-informed and -distorted takes on how men should no longer be men from a variety of Caplan-Bricker's interviewees, most of whom are not male, nor, as we might expect, White. Let's investigate what the New Masculinity looks like filtered through this particular lens.

Caplan-Bricker leads with a mixed-race *Daily Show* writer who laments the fact that homosexuality is not considered masculine and follows that up with a transgender boxer who "confronts his (said in context) privilege in a weaponized, white male body." Next is Asia Kate Dillon, known for playing Hollywood's first gender-nonbinary characters. Off-screen, Dillon, "who uses the singular 'they' pronoun," has become "a powerful advocate for greater inclusivity in popular culture." Some of Dillon's insights include:

> For one person, masculinity might mean a dress and a face of makeup, because that's how they see themselves. . . . I think that the "actress" category should be removed from awards shows. . . . As someone who was assigned female at birth, I was already a marginalized person, and then on top of that I'm queer and nonbinary and trans. So I have several marginalized identities. And I also carry white-bodied privilege. That doesn't negate my talent, my innate gift. It just means that even though I carry these marginalized identities, I still hold power in rooms where there are queer people of color, for example.

Jewish dog-sled racer Blair Braverman "puts a feminist spin on adventure-writing" and talks about the need for women in male spaces, generally-imagined sexism, and a de-constructing of the white male American mythos. Braverman says:

> From the time settlers came to what would become the United States, the American narrative has been one of (white) men risking everything to tame the wilderness and shape it for their own purposes, whether they're pioneers or cowboys or prospectors. For a woman to participate in adventure sports or expeditions, on her own terms, complicates the narrative: What if it's not man versus nature anymore? What if we're not—gasp—conquering the wilderness at all? What if a woman's skills can surpass a man's in a realm that's been safely cordoned off as male—which is to say, a realm that's been safe from the possibility of a woman coming in, succeeding, and thereby threatening the supremacy of masculinity itself? If any part of that man-versus-nature narrative is fallible, it calls into question some very deep-seated stories and values that our country is based on.

We are also treated to such gems as Liz Plank (a self-proclaimed feminist), Tarana Burke (the founder of the #MeToo movement), Aymann Ismail (complains about Islamic stereotypes), Hannah Gadsby (a misandrous quote-un-quote comic), and Al Freeman (a quote-un-quote artist who specializes in under-stuffed pillows of things like genitalia and beer cans, which she describes as "soft sculpture"). Freeman states:

> I've never tried to make funny work. But I guess it's castrating humor, to some degree. It robs the masculinity of its power and its potency. There's also the idea of all of these kinds of macho objects being cuddly pillows. The idea of a frat boy seeking comfort in a pillow version of his Jägermeister bottle, as if the pillows are teddy bears that would comfort some terrible man.

Also present among the grab-bag is Katrina Karkazis, author of the book *Testosterone: An Un-Authorized Biography*, where she makes the demonstrably false argument that, "High T is thought to be the substance in the body that produces masculinity—physically, through muscles and hair, but also behaviorally. But it doesn't actually map on very well to what we understand as masculinity." Phil Daoust agrees, stating in a *Guardian* piece from 2017 that testosterone is "trouble" and leads to "impaired decision-making." He then follows that up with the erroneous and harmful claim that "testosterone makes you stupid." Clearly not, since Daoust has a room-temperature IQ at best. Far from making you stupid, University of Alberta researcher Marty Mrazik published a paper in *Roeper Review* linking giftedness (having an IQ score of 130 or higher) to prenatal exposure to higher levels of testosterone.

One thing is clear, however: testosterone in men is, for the ruling class, a problem. Trying to create a self-fulfilling prophecy, *The New York Times* has declared our current era, "The Age of the Twink" (emphasis added):

> Female body types have always cycled in and out of style; yet with men, alternatives to the ideal of imposing physicality have usually been ignored or lampooned. But as women continue to use their voices to undo that legacy of toxic masculinity, a different kind of change is taking place from within the culture: These twinks, after all, aren't just enviably lean boys or the latest unrealistic gay fantasy, *but a new answer to the problem of what makes a man.*

So men are a "problem" that need to be solved.

The Jewish Leah Berkenwald's[14] "Androgyny: Progressive or Exclusionary?" also from *The New York Times* first favorably quotes the Jewish developmental and clinical psychologist Diane Ehrensaft (who we will return to later) before delighting in the fact that androgynous fashion has the potential to "explode gender norms," using Jewish women Barbara Streisand and Molly Picon as models "who can look convincing as an adolescent boy." So much of the gender non-conforming/transgender agenda involves children or the invocation of children, and it is becoming increasingly obvious that the "slippery slope" is not always a logical fallacy, and certainly not in this case. Disturbingly, there is a very clear reason why "gay rights" has quickly birthed the non-binary/queer/trans hysteria: they are all of a piece, telegraphed by their ever-expanding acronym, LGBTQ+(*ad infinitum*). Feminism, like it or not, has done the same.

As regards the persistent link to sexual perversity, let us consider the "saga" of ILGA: ILGA started out as the International Gay Association at a conference in Coventry, England, in August 1978 when members of small organizations from Australia, the UK, the Netherlands, Ireland, the United States, Denmark, France, and Italy pledged to create an international organization to pool their resources, in order to "combat homophobia" and campaign for "gay rights" on the global stage. It became the International Lesbian and Gay Association in 1986, and though it still uses the ILGA acronym, the official name of ILGA is now the International Lesbian, Gay, Bisexual, Trans, and Intersex Association. Today, ILGA has six continental/regional affiliates, such as ILGA-Europe and ILGA Latin America and Caribbean, and over 1,600 member organizations. ILGA World's primary donors in 2018 were Tides, the Open Society Foundations, the Arcus Foundation, the Swedish International Development Cooperation Agency (SIDA), the Ministry for Foreign Affairs of Finland,

---

[14] Berkenwald also favorably quotes the Jewish anarchist Emma Goldman in her 2012 blog for the Jewish Women's Archive "Enthusiastic Agitators: Jewish women on birth control," and closes with: "Whenever you're feeling stuck, just ask yourself: WWEGD? (What would Emma Goldman do?)."

the Astraea Lesbian Foundation for Justice, the Australian Government Department of Foreign Affairs and Trade, Burberry, Wattpad, Humble Bundle, ProtectDefenders.eu (which is funded by the European Union), and the Yogscast. Past funding has also come from the Ford Foundation, the City of Geneva, RIWI (a global trend-tracking and prediction technology firm), the UNDP, BT, UN Women, Google, Hivos, the Norwegian Ministry of Foreign Affairs, Thomson Reuters, and the Foundation Against Cancer. Why is a *cancer* foundation funding an LGBTQ organization?

Pamela Valenti is a prime example of the inter-connectedness of the people involved in promoting this agenda; she is a senior advocacy specialist at the Open Society European Policy Institute in Brussels, where she works on EU digital policies and foreign affairs. She joined the Open Society European Policy Institute in 2015, having previously worked as an EU advocacy consultant for the Open Society Eurasia Program on "human rights and democracy" in the Eastern Partnership countries and Central Asia, as a grant-making assistant for the European Endowment for Democracy, as a researcher for the European Parliament, and as a trainee for ILGA-Europe.

Heather Grabbe, Director of the Open Society European Policy Institute, is another. The Open Society European Policy Institute "works to ensure that open society values are at the heart of EU policies and actions, both inside and outside its borders." Grabbe is an "advocate for democratic pluralism and open societies." She was ranked highly among "the women who shape Brussels" by Politico, gave a TED talk on the "importance of critical thinking and mindful engagement with post-truth politics," and has written recently on "how climate change and technology are affecting the quality of democracy and economic and social justice." From 2004 to 2009 she was senior advisor to then-European Commissioner for Enlargement Olli Rehn, responsible for EU policy on the Balkans and Turkey. Previously, she was deputy director of the Center for European Reform, where she wrote extensively on EU external policies and enlargement. She also conducted academic research at the European University Institute (Fiesole, outside Florence), Chatham House (London), Oxford and Birmingham Universities, and taught at the London School of Economics.

With all of that in mind, the institutional support for the following is all the more abhorrent. The North American Man/Boy Love Association (NAMBLA) was a member of ILGA, and only after substantial external pressure and after the United Nations Economic and Social Council (ECOSOC) suspended ILGA's consultative status did they vote to expel NAMBLA in 1994. ILGA's application to be reinstated was rejected in 2002 "based on concerns raised about its member organizations or subsidiaries that promoted or condoned paedophilia." Subsequent applications in 2003 and 2006 were also rejected; ILGA blamed the Organization of Islamic Cooperation (you know, the same countries that organizations like ILGA want to import wholesale into the West). Late in 2006 ILGA-Europe was granted ECOSOC consultative status, and in 2011 the central ILGA organization was finally successful. Their pedophilic affiliations have not stopped their return to "legitimacy" nor their growth into one of the largest and most well-funded LGBTQ networks in the world.

For NAMBLA member Bill Andriette, "It's kind of a mythical concept—consent. . . . People who don't like pornography or people who don't like sadomasochism might say, 'Well those things are so degrading that people who engage in them cannot really be consenting, no matter what they tell you.'" Jewish journalist Donna Minkowitz, self-described as a "dyke leather and S/M activist," respects NAM-BLA's right to exist and states that "discrimination arising from age-of-consent laws can be 'problematic,'" that favorite word, along with "complicated," used by the ruling class for anything they don't disagree with but don't want to appear to support.

Minkowitz, it should be noted, went undercover to "out" American Renaissance conference attendees on behalf of Political Research Associates, founded by North-western alum and "lesbian feminist activist" Jean Hardisty. They are committed to "researching" such concerns as "anti-Semitism" and "racial and immigrant justice." From 2011–2015, Political Research Associates received grants totaling $900,000 from the Ford Foundation. In Minkowitz's interview with *Lilith* ("Independent, Jew-ish & Frankly Feminist"—entitled their Fall 2009 issue "boys* are the new girls," which features articles such as "Bottoming for God") she whined about American Renaissance's supposed "anti-Semitism" and highlighted Sam Dickson's proposal to get White women to have more babies as an issue. She stated that groups like American Renaissance "pose a tremendous danger to the rest of us." Who is "us"? Can we guess? And what "danger" does it, in fact, pose?

# The Gaslight Anthem

*"Power is in tearing human minds to pieces and putting them together again in new shapes of your own choosing."*
— George Orwell, *1984*

One of the most powerful weapons in the ruling class's arsenal is gaslighting, and with their stranglehold not just on the media apparatus and academia, but also on all of society's institutions, their job is made that much easier. According to *Random Lengths News*, gaslighting is defined as:

A form of psychological manipulation in which a person seeks to sow seeds of doubt in a targeted individual or in members of a targeted group, making them question their own memory, perception, and sanity. Using denial, misdirection, contradiction, and lying, gaslighting involves attempts to destabilize the victim and delegitimize the victim's beliefs.

This is occurring in our society on a massive scale, and the virtual omnipresence of media—and the media monopoly by the Establishment—is profoundly effective for not just social control, but social engineering. Gaslighting is abuse, and deeply harmful, but its coercive power lies in its apparently "soft" nature. Such coercion is generally much more effective, for the victim is not aware that they are being manipulated and may even come to question their own sanity. Patricia Evans describes the mechanisms typically employed by the abuser:

- Withholding of information
- Countering information selectively to fit the abuser's perspective
- Discounting information
- Indirect verbal abuse, often in the form of humor
- Blocking and diverting the victim's attention from outside sources
- Trivializing the victim's perspective or even worth
- Undermining the victim by gradual erosion

There is a reason why the media mouthpieces refer to everything that runs counter to the narrative a "conspiracy theory," or why the truth is always the exact opposite of what's being stated by the commentariat and the critical theoretical priestly class in academia. That's why everything is a "phobia" or framed in negative.

In a great irony, the article I sourced the aforementioned definition of gaslighting from uses it to insist that it is Donald Trump who is gaslighting "us" into insanity. On the contrary, it was whenever he said something that cut to the heart of the matter, or proposed something to upset the apple cart, that the media went most apoplectic. Trump exaggerating how many people attended his inauguration or the size of his hands is far more useful as "proof" of his apparent "existential threat" than when he wonders aloud about the usefulness of NATO. Remember, the same people who support chemically castrating children are the ones screeching "Think of the children!" the loudest *in favor* of letting in a seemingly infinite stream of adult male migrants from the most violent, dysfunctional countries on earth—and moving them into *your* neighborhood.

Transgenderism is the ultimate form of gaslighting. If you can get a population to accept multitudinous genders when in reality human beings are sexually dimorphic, you can get them to accept anything, even eating maggot sausages to delay the carbon-induced apocalypse. It serves other purposes, too, such as the humiliation and degradation of an occupied state's population, the literal mental retardation of the affected population, and the added consumer economy windfall produced by people "switching genders" and "identifying" with consumer goods that have been linked to this political/lifestyle/identity choice. It is materialistic, hyper-individualistic, and also totally at odds with reality. The prostate of a "trans woman" doesn't magically become something else; surgical modifications and hormones and lies do not undo nature. If you accept that sex and gender are independent of each other, then it is axiomatic that a transgendered individual may believe themselves to be "born into the wrong body" despite not having the corresponding chromosomes, whereby they may endeavor to undergo hormone treatments, surgical modifications, and a wardrobe change.

The concept of transgenderism relies on the fundamental premise that biology and expressed "gender identity" need not correspond. Therefore, the intellectually honest person must also conclude that trans-racialism is a legitimate phenomenon, "skin color" is not phenotypical at all for it must be totally divorced from any biological considerations, and thus, skin color is *not* a reflection of genetics but an arbitrary marker of "race" in the same way genitalia are arbitrary markers of "sex." You cannot hold one belief and not the other and claim to stand on principles or to have a logically coherent worldview. The discussion then shifts to articles of faith, which is squarely in the realm of the theological—a great irony for a largely atheistic and materialistic ideology based on "science" and "progress." Contradictorily, race is somehow a construct, yet also totally fixed, except that its fixity only applies when it is useful, likewise its "constructed" nature.

Sex is even more clear-cut than race, though. There are mixed-race people, but nobody is mixed-sex. You are either male or female. While some may argue that people with intersex conditions create some sort of third category, this is really a misnomer, as people with various intersex conditions simply have a disorder that affects sexual development and reproductive function. These people are still male or female, even if they appear ambiguous or are infertile. No human is both sexes biologically, and no one is neither. Though intersex conditions certainly are medically interesting, they are extremely rare and should not be cited as a justification for pushing gender fluidity or gender choice, especially on children.

Princeton University researcher and psychologist Kristina Olson (PhD from Harvard), who since 2013 has been studying "gender-nonconforming kids, who consistently defy gender stereotypes but have not socially transitioned," mostly when she was with the University of Washington, says, "My findings are often 'duh' findings." Oh wait, she's talking about a three-year-old being situated to "transition" because they "*already* have a strong sense of their identity." At *three*. I would hardly call that a "duh" finding.

Olson and many members of the TransYouth and Gender Development Project through the Social Cognitive Development Lab at the University of Washington moved to Princeton in September 2020 to continue their research there. Notable figures include postdoc Dominic Gibson, who received his PhD in Developmental Psychology from the University of Chicago where he worked with Susan Levine and Susan Goldin-Meadow, and alumni now situated in positions at the University of Lisbon (Portugal), Procter & Gamble, the University of Zurich (Switzerland), the University of Chicago, Google, and Victoria University of Wellington (New Zealand).

Charlotte Tate, a psychologist from San Francisco State University, agrees with Olson and her acolytes, saying that from interviews with trans people, "one of the most consistent themes is that at some early point, sometimes as early as age 3 to 5, there's this feeling that the individual is part of another gender group," as reported by Ed Young for *The Atlantic*. Aaron Devor, the University of Victoria in British Columbia, Canada's Chair of Transgender Studies—who is transgender—says that Olson's work is very reminiscent of that of Evelyn Hooker, and "will have an Evelyn Hooker effect" in dispelling the notion that transgender people are mentally ill.

Devor may be on to something: despite the contradicting evidence I am about to present, LGBTQ ideologues maintain that there are no negative disparities in psychological health in the homosexual brain relative to the heterosexual brain, with Evelyn Hooker's 1957 study, "The Adjustment of the Overt Male Homosexual" as the be-all end-all study, functioning much the same as Alfred Kinsey's 10% male homosexual figure.

A psychologist based out of UCLA, where one of the first official gender clinics in the US was founded in 1962 and where some of the country's first "sex changes" were being performed by urologist Elmer Belt, Hooker's "research" was unscientifically designed to prove the point that homosexual men did not differ from heterosexual men in psychopathology. Hooker only used thirty subjects from each group, eliminated any subjects who were currently in psychiatric therapy, administered three diagnostic tests with no oversight and discarded the results of two of them because she didn't like the results, and in the one remaining test decided to create her own personal criteria to interpret the results. This sounds eerily reminiscent of the self-serving methodology "proving" anti-Semitism-as-psychosis from *The Authoritarian Personality* crowd. It is also worth noting Hooker's priors: in 1937, Hooker received a fellowship to the Berlin Institute of Psychotherapy and lived with a Jewish family while studying there. Before returning to the United States, Hooker was part of a group tour of the USSR, notorious for weaponizing psychology against the population, going so far as to "commit" dissidents.

So about that homosexual psychopathology: a government-sponsored study of 5,998 Dutch adults ages 18 to 64 featured in the January 2001 issue of the *Journal of the American Medical Association* found that compared to heterosexual women, females who engage in homosexual behavior are 405% more likely to have suffered a substance use disorder, 241% more likely to have suffered mood disorders during their lifetimes, and 209% more likely to have suffered two or more mental disorders during their lifetimes. In the Netherlands, male homosexual relationships last an average of 18 months and gay men have an average of eight partners a year outside of these relationships. Those with borderline personality disorder are more likely to exhibit greater sexual preoccupation, have earlier sexual exposure, engage in casual sexual relationships, report a greater number of different sexual partners as well as increased promiscuity, and engage in homosexual experiences. Those, for the most part, are also side effects of early and/or consistent exposure to pornography.

Patients with borderline personality disorder appear to be characterized by a greater number of high-risk sexual behaviors and a higher likelihood of having been coerced to have sex, experiencing date rape, or being raped by a stranger.[15] Recall here the strong association between abuse and trauma causing illness and/or homosexuality and/or transgender identification. Yet these behaviors, which are clearly self-destructive and often beget more abuse, are condoned and even encouraged by the media, academia, and every institution of any significance and then some.

The same 2001 Dutch study in the *Journal of the American Medical Association* found that compared to heterosexual men, males who engage in homosexual behavior are: 727% more likely to suffer from bipolar disorders and 502% more likely to have suffered symptoms in the last twelve months; 620% more likely to suffer from obsessive-compulsive disorder and 718% more likely to have suffered symptoms in the last twelve months; 454% more likely to suffer from agoraphobia (fear of leaving home or being in public) and 632% more likely to have suffered symptoms in the last twelve months; 421% more likely to suffer from a panic disorder; 229% more likely to have suffered social phobia at some point in their lives; 375% more likely to have suffered simple phobia in the last twelve months and 361% more likely at some point in their lives; 311% more likely to suffer from mood disorders and 293% more likely to have suffered from symptoms in the last twelve months; 261% more likely to have suffered from symptoms associated with anxiety disorders in the last twelve months and 267% more likely over the course of their lifetimes; 270% more likely to have suffered two or more psychiatric disorders during their lifetime; and 235% more likely to have suffered major depression at some point in their lives.

These findings are echoed by King et al. (2008), "LGB people are at higher risk of mental disorder, suicidal ideation, substance misuse, and deliberate self harm than heterosexual people," Semlyen et al. (2016), "In the UK, LGB adults have higher prevalence of poor mental health and low wellbeing when compared to heterosexuals," and more. Additionally, the 2002 National Survey of Family Growth found that nearly 75% of all lesbians were overweight or obese.

Another main tactic employed by transgender "activists" is to obsess over conversion therapy, which to the average person has marginal credibility at best, if they've even heard of it. Yet it was turned into a major talking point by the media in conjunction/coordination with these organizations and "activists," used to paint Mike Pence as a bogeyman to rally support against, as well as to poison the well against anti-foreign interventionist Tulsi Gabbard's 2020 presidential campaign. The real purpose was not to protest conversion therapy, but to politically assassinate an

---

[15] Sansone and Sansone, "Sexual Behavior in Borderline Personality."

Establishment outsider in the latter case and to create a Trump-adjacent "monster" to serve as a villainous focal point as well as a rallying cry for "activism" akin to the absurd and egregious lies spread about border detention facilities operating as concentration camps in the former case. If anything, "transitioning" someone to "cure" them seems more like conversion therapy—a very lucrative conversion therapy—than anything, and what's more, after promising these mentally ill people the world, the evidence suggests that suicidality *increases* after surgical "intervention" because nothing psychological has been resolved.

One comprehensive thirty-year study in Sweden by Dhejne, et al. in 2011 that captured almost the entire population of surgically-reassigned transgender individuals in the country from 1973–2003 showed that post-operative transgender individuals were at *over nineteen times* greater risk for dying by suicide than the general population, and overall the study found:

> Substantially higher rates of overall mortality, death from cardiovascular disease and suicide, suicide attempts, and psychiatric hospitalisations in sex-reassigned transsexual individuals compared to a healthy control population. This highlights that post surgical transsexuals are a risk group that need long-term psychiatric and somatic follow-up. . . . [Additionally,] Immigrant status was twice as common among transsexual individuals compared to controls, living in an urban area somewhat more common, and higher education about equally prevalent. Transsexual individuals had been hospitalized for psychiatric morbidity other than gender identity disorder prior to sex reassignment about four times more often than controls.

Furthermore, the conversion therapy hysteria serves a rhetorically dis-arming purpose, as the World Professional Association of Transgender Health (WPATH)'s Standards of Care states that "treatment aimed at trying to change a person's gender identity and expression to become more congruent with sex assigned at birth" is "no longer considered ethical." What's more unethical, though: chemically castrating or sterilizing a child, mentally and developmentally retarding them, or waiting a few years to see if they'll grow out of this supposed "transgender" identity? Pursuing legitimate psychological treatment methods or embracing this "identity"? Most of the supposed "trans kids" have their trans-need projected upon them by parents and/or the Establishment, and, most eventually identify as "just" homosexual. This is before considering whether children even understand these concepts of "gender," and beyond that, if we're talking about sexuality and children, then we are nowhere near ethical in any universe but the depraved one of the people pushing this agenda. Is this in some manner a gateway to pedophilia? In many ways, it really looks like it.

The simple and tragic fact is that the ideology of transgenderism has become institutionalized. Schools themselves encourage gender confusion from the moment children are put into them. This is a page quite literally right out of the Soviet Union playbook. In 2017, the University of Minnesota published a study claiming that 2.7% of children in the state "identify as transgender or gender nonconforming." Many North American primary schools have adopted the notorious Gender Unicorn, which encompasses not only "gender identity" but *sexual attraction.*

The Gender Unicorn was created by Trans Student Educational Resources

(TSER), co-founded by the Jewish Eli Erlick and Alex Sennello ("two 16-year-old transgender women"), which changed its name in 2014 from Trans Student Equality Resources stating that "equality is not enough" for the "transgender community." Erlick was called a "New Face of Feminism" as a "young feminist changing the game" by *Teen Vogue* in 2016; Erlick was instrumental in lobbying for the passing of the School Success and Opportunity Act in California which "extends gender identity and gender expression discrimination to transgender and gender-noncon-forming K-12 students in public schools." Their Program Director is Harper Rubin, "the first trans athlete at Bard College." TSER states that, "As with all our jobs, we prioritize trans youth of color (particularly Black and Indigenous trans youth) in our selections." I'm not a lawyer, but I'm pretty sure that violates basically every anti-discrimination law on the books. Or it would, if the ruling class gave a shit. So much for fighting discrimination . . . or is it?

In 2016, the Jewish George Soros's Open Society Foundations published the last of its subsequent issue-specific briefs in the "License to be Yourself" series, entitled "License to be Yourself: Responding to National Security and Identity Fraud Arguments" where we see "trans issues" used as a way to neuter countries' border control and enforcement capabilities under the guise of "human rights":

> The disproportionate impact of counter-terrorism measures on trans people has been documented by Martin Scheinin ["Although Scheinin received a Lutheran upbringing, his father's Jewish ancestry made him read books on the Holocaust and thus he became interested in human rights"], the United Nations Special Rapporteur on the Promotion and Protection of Human Rights and Fundamental Freedoms while Countering Terrorism. In 2009, he specifically mentioned two threats to trans people's right to recognition before the law:
>
> - Greater suspicion and harassment of trans people can occur when immigration controls focus on detecting male bombers who may be dressed as females.
> - Stricter procedures for issuing, changing and verifying identity documents risk unduly penalizing transgender persons whose personal appearance and data are subject to change.
>
> The Special Rapporteur recommended repealing "restrictive immigration controls and asylum procedures that violate the human rights, including the right to freedom of movement, of transgendered persons. . . ." In June 2014, the UN General Assembly adopted a resolution reaffirming and updating the UN's 2006 global counter-terrorism strategy stating that, "Any measures taken to counter terrorism should not be based on profiling."

National security out, social justice in. As if it couldn't get any more preposterous (and dangerous), the brief continues:

> Body scanning and pat-down searches are often very stressful situations for trans and intersex people. This can be due to concerns about how their body

diversity will be perceived by others, and whether prosthetics (to create the shape of breasts or a penis, for example) will be identified as anomalies by a scanning device. Such stress can be interpreted as suspicious by airport security and border control agencies. Other people may not have any identity documents, including many refugees and asylum seekers. Refugees by definition are unable, or unwilling for reasons of fear, to avail themselves of the protection of their country of nationality. This is likely to mean they are no longer able to access official records of their identity once they are accepted as refugees in another country. Many refugees flee without necessary identity documents. Trans refugees (and those intersex refugees who have transitioned) face the additional barrier of having to establish a link between their previous sex and their current sex and/or gender identity. As refugees, they are unable to return to their country of origin in order to verify their identity and typically cannot obtain documents issued under their previous name, sex or gender identity. This can have ongoing implications when they are required to verify details such as an employment history or qualifications. The particular difficulties faced by trans refugees can have serious consequences at the point of entry. In many countries, refugees and undocumented individuals are held in detention centers while (a) their claim for asylum is processed and (b), if their claim is rejected, pending their removal from the country. If a trans person does not have accurate documentation, this can mean that they are placed in incorrect detention centers. For example, in the United States, there have been numerous stories of trans women (often trans women of color) being subjected to significant violence and abuse because they have been placed in a male detention center.

Don't worry, though: Transgender Europe has produced its "Welcome to Stay: Building Trans Communities Inclusive of Trans Asylum Seekers and Refugees in Europe," which was produced with financial support from the Rights, Equality and Citizenship Program of the European Union. In it, the Somali Farah Abdi complains that:

> LGBTQI refugees need safe accommodation. It doesn't make sense for LGBTQI refugees who have run away from homophobia and transphobia to come to a safe country and be grouped together with other asylum seekers who are very homophobic and transphobic.

So why would these other people be invited to stay in these countries, particularly as they continue to arrive *en masse* and transform their environs?

It seems the Steve Sailer Magic Dirt is at work here: meaning that simply because someone stands on German soil, they are immediately as, if not more, German than those whose ancestors are, well, Germanic, and that their tolerance exceeds anything imagined by an overweight feminist working in HR for some corporation. Logically, it makes no sense, but we are *way* past that now. Every two years TGEU holds the European Transgender Council—the largest gathering of political transgender activists in Europe: "With 200 delegates, first class key note speakers and panelists, ample workshops and diverse cultural program the TGEU Councils are both—a forum setting the agenda for transgender politics in Europe."

If you organize any events, Transgender Europe says to "make sure that events do not require people to show their ID cards, which may out trans people." Mimi Aum Niko from Thailand states that, "In France, asylum seekers are able to apply for state social insurance, which includes access to hormones. But first they need to know someone who can speak French and can guide them to go see the right doctor. This is a big problem." Indeed. But *mon Dieu!* the authors cry: "They may experience physical and mental health crises, including depression and suicidal thoughts. Some even consider returning to their home country solely to access hormones." But if it's safe enough to go get a testosterone injection, surely it's safe enough to stay?

The lies just keep coming: in 2011, then-United Nations High Commissioner for Human Rights Navi Pillay condemned the "growing tide of violence against LGBT people around the world." It seems this tide, like that of anti-Semitism, is perpetually swelling. Pillay made sure to emphasize that "transphobia" and "homophobia" are no different from sexism, racism, or prejudice against immigrants:

> Violence against trans people, like violence against women or racial minorities, feeds into a cycle of inequality in which established social and economic structures determining the distribution of power and resources ensure that those who have more advantages continue to profit.

Gaslighting at its finest.

Those profiting most handsomely from not just the transgender-industrial complex but also the LGBTQ agenda more generally are the exact same beneficiaries of the entire neo-liberal globalist Establishment, and it serves their purposes to "link" all of these "social justice" causes together as inextricably as their system itself is inextricably intertwined. One cannot break from the Establishment orthodoxy on a single issue or they will have transgressed and will be destroyed. The maintenance of this orthodoxy is absolutely vital from a conditioning perspective, and contradictory beliefs or especially evidence must be suppressed at all costs. It helps to have a ready-made phalanx of professional "activists" to out-source the work to.

*PLOS One*, which published Lisa Littman's study discussed in Chapter One in 2018, was almost immediately inundated by "activist" complaints, and felt compelled to issue a statement that it would seek "further expert assessment on the study's methodology and analyses," citing reader concerns, followed by an official apology. The Dean of Brown University, home of researcher Lisa Littman, was deeply unhappy with Littman's findings, claiming that they could be used to "invalidate the perspectives of members of the transgender community." Brown removed a press release highlighting Littman's findings, and a "trans graduate student" at Brown's School of Public Health named Arjee Javellana Restar published what *BuzzFeed* calls "the most thorough and damning description of the research to date" in the *Archives of Sexual Behavior*. Among the conclusions *BuzzFeed* finds "damning" are that there were "survey responses from parents who had visited sites promoting anti-trans views" and that Littman's approach "pathologizes trans people." Trust me, it is not Littman's approach that's pathologizing anyone.

This kind of wording (and obvious lack of any concrete evidence) by ideologues like Restar is par for the course. Consider the following from George Soros's Open Society Foundations' May 2014 "License to be Yourself" Report: "The pathologization of gender identity means governments typically privilege the views of medical experts over those of trans people themselves." Subjectivity over objectivity. Classic Frankfurt School critical theory. But the so-called experts themselves seem to be really into the junk science, concern trolling, and charlatanry Brynn Tannehill seems to think is reserved for anyone who criticizes the agenda or highlights its significant issues, from self-serving methodology to legitimate harm.

Lisa Littman found that 62.5% of the adolescents and young adults (AYAs) had reportedly been diagnosed with at least one mental health disorder or neurodevelopmental disability *prior* to the onset of their gender dysphoria and nearly half had reportedly experienced some kind of trauma prior to their "rapid onset gender dysphoria." Littman continues:

> Concern has been raised that adolescents may come to believe that transition is the only solution to their individual situations, that exposure to internet content that is uncritically positive about transition may intensify these beliefs. . . . The presentation of gender dysphoria can occur in the context of severe psychiatric disorders, developmental difficulties, or as part of large-scale identity issues. . . . Adolescents with gender dysphoria 'should be screened carefully to detect the emergence of the desire for sex reassignment in the context of trauma as well as for any disorder (such as schizophrenia, mania, psychotic depression) that may produce gender confusion. . . .' Parents reported subjective declines in their AYAs' mental health (47.2%) and in parent-child relationships (57.3%) since the AYA "came out" and that AYAs expressed a range of behaviors that included: expressing distrust of non-transgender people (22.7%); stopping spending time with non-transgender friends (25.0%); trying to isolate themselves from their families (49.4%), and only trusting information about gender dysphoria from transgender sources (46.6%). Most (86.7%) of the parents reported that, along with the sudden or rapid onset of gender dysphoria, their child either had an increase in their social media/internet use, belonged to a friend group in which one or multiple friends became transgender-identified during a similar timeframe, or both.

In this case, the trans recruitment process and subsequent mental re-configuring is uncomfortably similar to Synanon, for as Jenn Smith outlines:

> Whereas Synanon would break down the recruit and then "build up a new personality not drug oriented," trans activists break down potential recruits and then "build up a new personality not traditionally gender (or what they call 'cis gender') oriented. . . ." While Synanon utilized a brainwashing technique called the "Think Table" in which daily messages and support would be broadcast each morning to the breakfast table (People's Temple founder Jim Jones used a similar system), social media sites now serve as a kind of "Think Table" for trans activism, broadcasting daily brainwashing messages. . . . Total self surrender necessarily involves pulling away from anybody that would pull you back to former ways of thinking and behaving. Friends and family have always been the biggest threat to cult agendas. Synanon thus encouraged recruits to destroy their former selves and come join "the Synanon family."

Unsurprisingly *Medium* banned Smith's article for some obscure rules violation. I think we all know what rules Smith really broke.

Remember Veronica Ivy/Rachel McKinnon's video to "walk away . . . and find what we call your glitter family. Your queer family"? Consider here as well Littman's findings that the "newly-transgendered" stopped spending time with non-transgenders, mis-trusted non-trans people, tried to isolate themselves from their families, and only trusted "trans news" from trans sources, among other behaviors. Breaking people down further is so much easier when they are *already* broken down, isolated, gaslit, propagandized, and stripped of any meaningful sources of identity; as Smith continues:

> Transgender leaders and activists can thus just parachute into the lives of these troubled, wounded minds and start rebuilding them with their new "trans identity," and they tend to become as dedicated to the trans cult as any Synanon member ever was. Although it should be noted that with all of the non-stop propaganda and pro-trans coverage in the media and Holly-wood, "parachuting in" is not even required, because brainwashing and suggestion are constantly being broadcast on almost every TV channel. The rebuilding of the personality thus can be done by a form of electronic correspondence, without ever coming into physical contact with an actual recruiter. The use of incredibly slick multi-media presentations, the likes of which Dederich et al. could only dream of, makes this kind of programming even more effective.

The Dederich in question would be Charles E. Dederich, an alcoholic test subject administered LSD during a series of tests in the 1950s at UCLA which also included Alcoholics Anonymous (AA) founder Bill Wilson. The hypothesis was that psychoactive substances could modify addictive behavior. Dederich believed that his "full surrender" and the destruction of his ego during the experience had cured him, and actually given him powers of omnipotence. Wilson came to a similar conclusion—as did the CIA—that the person needed to be broken down completely in order to be built anew. Dederich joined AA and became an acolyte of Wilson's while the CIA was running its own LSD-based experiments, via Smith:

> The Central Intelligence Agency (CIA) focused many of its MK Ultra LSD experiments on the drug's ability to clear the mind, and thus allow for the programming or brainwashing of a subject. Most of the MK Ultra documents were deliberately destroyed in 1973 under orders of CIA Director Richard Helms to avoid public scrutiny, but it appears from the documents that survived as if one of the goals was the creation of so-called "Robot Agents", or sleeper agents brainwashed by the agency to serve its goals.

Dederich apparently strove to accomplish something similar, and left AA in 1958 to found Synanon, however Dederich believed LSD to be too unpredictable and would instead rely on the "ego-crushing [power of] peer pressure." This became The Game, an exercise in ego-destroying abuse and humiliation designed to make someone feel so worthless that they totally capitulate. Sounds like what every organ of the Establishment is doing to white people every day—a relentless assault on "whiteness," "privilege," *ad infinitum* designed to break our will so we surrender. Then we can be re-born into good soldiers for diversity and dis-avow our privilege, just as "a 'Synan-ist' . . . would lead an all-out group assault on the person. The technique, which could last for days or weeks, eventually led to an emotional breakdown and complete psy-chological exhaustion in which the person disavowed their former selves and ways completely." Continuing with Smith:

> This kind of intense and prolonged assault had much in common with some of the "psychic driving" techniques employed by Doctor Ewen Cameron in his ghoulish MK Ultra experiments conducted in Canada.[16] "The Game" was recognized by Dederich and others as a form of highly effective brain-washing. Its ability to break down drug addicts and reshape them garnered Synanon the attention and financial support of Fortune 500 companies, Hol-lywood stars, and an endorsement from LSD guru Tim Leary. Synanon's success resulted in countless cult-like copycat rehab organizations that used the same "game" tactics, including another well-known group named Straight Inc. The Straight operators discovered that age-specific peer pres-sure was more effective than just the general group pressure Synanon used. . . . The goal was to change behavior in such a way that addictive personalities would become addicted to people (the group) instead of drugs. The average age of Straight recruits was 17, with members as young as 12 and 13.

This kind of preying on the youth is, as previously stated, a grooming process, and whether it be a physical preying or a psychological preying—often both—the goal of the Establishment is to get them young. The implications are well past disturbing, well past even criminal, particularly when we consider the cascade effect of self-destructive behaviors, psychopathologies and mental illnesses, and lives led to ruin. Furthermore, the introduction of sex hormones in the name of "transitioning" is harmful enough in adults, but with children the results are downright catastrophic. As we can see, however, the full extent of the damage is being actively suppressed by the Establishment and its lackeys.

---

[16] Initial seed money for the Allen Memorial Institute in Montreal, where Cameron became the first Di-rector, was supplied in part by the Rockefeller Foundation.

### Sex (Education) as a Weapon

*"From children's books to TV shows and movies, media geared towards young people is more LGBTQ-inclusive than ever. Broadway and TV star Billy Porter recently guested on an episode of Sesame Street . . . donning the fabulous black dress that blasted away boundaries at last year's Academy Awards ceremony. Netflix just released a new show,* Chip & Potato, *geared towards toddlers that features a two-dad family in the neighborhood and gender-neutral bathrooms. Drag queen story hours are sashaying into public libraries across the U.S."*

– Allison Hope,
"The Right's New Target: LGBTQ Children," *Slate*, March 23rd, 2020

Once again we see the absolutely egregious falsehood that somehow the *right* is "a highly coordinated, well-resourced political movement that is targeting the most vulnerable among us: our children," according to Allison Hope. This is demonstrably false, but for these ideologues, facts do not matter. Hope is right about one thing, though: "Children are often the innocent casualties for much of what ails society."

Thousands of schools across the United States have chapters of the GSA Network; formerly the Gay-Straight Alliance, in 2016 they officially changed their name to the Gender and Sexualities Alliance Network, "after hearing from countless youth leaders who understand their genders and sexualities to be uniquely theirs and have moved beyond the labels of gay and straight, and the limits of a binary gender system."

The GSA Network has produced "educational materials" for the University of North Carolina and has chapters across the country, operating as propaganda nodes and training grounds. Also embodying the intersectional approach we've come to expect, their website proclaims that:

GSA clubs build power for a growing movement of LGBTQ+ youth of color and we actively support youth through training in leadership, organizing, and advocacy for racial and gender justice. We empower trans and queer youth to educate your schools and communities [and] organize in coalition with other youth across identity lines.

*Your schools.* Hmm. . . .

There are at least 4,000 GSA clubs across the US. Where does the GSA Network derive its funding? I'm glad you asked: the Open Society Foundations, the Ford

Foundation, the Horizons Foundation, the Silicon Valley Community Foundation, the Arcus Foundation, the Weingart Foundation, the Foundation for a Just Society, the California Endowment, the William and Flora Hewlett Foundation, the LGBTQ Racial Justice Fund administered by the Astraea Lesbian Foundation for Justice, the Tides Foundation, Vans, the Liberty Hill Foundation, the Communities for Just Schools Fund, and the Tikkun Olam Foundation,[17] among others.

In turn, the Communities for Just Schools Fund donor organizations include the Open Society Foundations, the NEA Foundation, the WK Kellogg Foundation, Casey Family Programs, the Wellspring Philanthropic Fund, the NoVo Foundation, the Arcus Foundation, the Ford Foundation, and the Einhorn Family Charitable Trust, also known as the Einhorn Collaborative. Its founder, the Jewish David Einhorn, net worth approximately $700 million, is a hedge fund manager and graduate of Cornell University. Jon Gruber, Strategy Lead-Building, was formerly the Director of Education at the Jewish Foundation for the Righteous ("We would like to thank the Conference on Jewish Material Claims Against Germany for their support of our rescuer support and education programs"). Executive Director Jennifer Hoos Rothberg was previously the Director of Development for Cornell Hillel.

According to their website, in 2015, the GSA Network:

> Transitioned its leadership to a Co-Executive Director model and made it an organizational priority to have LGBTQ+ people of color in the top echelons of management and governance to ensure that the organizational identity reflect[s] the identity of the LGBTQ+ youth that participate in our programs.

One thing that is very striking is the paucity of whites and especially white men involved with most of these organizations. This observation is supported by the Evelyn and Walter Haas, Jr. Fund-funded Funders for LGBTQ Issues' 2018 "Diversity Among Philanthropic Professionals" report, which found that:

- People of color made up 45.6 percent of the staff and board at foundations with a social justice focus
- Women accounted for nearly 70 percent of the staff and board at all participating foundations
- Nearly half of women at foundations with a social justice focus were women of color
- Among lesbian, gay, and bisexual people in philanthropy, 43.1 percent of those at foundations with a social justice focus were people of color
- Among transgender people, 57.1 percent of transgender people at foundations with a social justice focus were people of color

---

[17] An explicitly-Jewish NGO focused on "social justice," probably their most substantial project is partnering with the Nigerian government on the implementation of a "strengthened health system." This sounds noble, and I'm sure there will be some benefit to the Nigerian people, but given what we're investigating in this book, I have to think the implications are more ominous than anything. You have to read between the lines, but look at this statement from their website: "To achieve development in a sustainable manner, TOF promotes gender equity and empowerment of women. In line with the millennium development goals, TOF creates awareness and sensitize[s] communities against harmful practices and customs that limit women and children from becoming useful citizens and major contributors to their society."

By their own admission, non-Whites, especially Blacks, appear to have higher incidence rates of homosexuality; as reported by the Arcus Foundation-funded Applied Research Center in 2010, "Don't Ask, Don't Tell affects African-American women disproportionately," and another black-focused "activist" organization reported in 2019 that, "According to the most recent data from the Gallup Daily Tracking Poll, 5 percent of Black people identify as LGBT compared to 4 percent of white people. Latinx and Asian adults are also more likely than their white counterparts to identify as LGBT." A Gallup survey of over 121,000 Americans in 2012 found basically the same predispositions, although the percentages for each respective group who identified as homosexual were slightly lower: 4.6% Black, 4.3% Asian, 4% Hispanic, 3.2% White. The same is true of transgenders: "Among adults who identify as transgender, 55 percent identify as White, 16 percent identify as African-American or Black, 21 percent identify as Latino or Hispanic, and 8 percent identify as another race or ethnicity." Other than Whites, all of those percentages are higher than the respective races' population share.

The proportion of Whites is probably even lower given that Jews are classed as White. Five percent of representatives of households responding to the question "Do you consider yourself (or does anyone in the household consider themselves) to be gay, lesbian, bisexual, or transgender?" from the Jewish Community Study of New York, 2011, covering the Five Boroughs of New York City plus Nassau, Suffolk, and Westchester Counties responded "yes." In the 2007 Annual Survey of American Jewish Opinion administered by Synovate, Inc. for the American Jewish Committee, the proportion of LGBT individuals among American Jews was at least 7%.

This reality helps explain why LGBTQ is pushed so hard on whites, and it also explains in part the conscious undertaking by the LGBTQ Establishment to cater to these groups in order to weaponize them as another intersectional grievance vector, as exemplified by organizations such as Soros's Open Society Foundations and Funders for LGBTQ Issues; regarding the latter:

> In 2007, [Funders for LGBTQ Issues] announced its new mission: to mobilize philanthropic resources that enhance the well-being of lesbian, gay, bisexual, transgender and queer communities, promote equity, and advance racial, economic and gender justice. It also launched a new program: the LGBTQ Racial Equity Campaign. The LGBTQ Racial Equity Campaign is a multi-year initiative to increase philanthropic support for LGBTQ communities of color, their leadership and organizations, and to support grant-making institutions that embody fairness and inclusiveness. Through the campaign, Funders conducts research, maintains an online racial equity toolkit, and makes the case nationally for increases in funding for LGBTQ people of color organizations and projects. The Racial Equity Regranting Initiative, another of the campaign's elements, supported the capacity of local LGBTQ communities of color through grants to LGBTQ public and community foundations.

On the level of governance, Renew Europe, a successor to the Alliance of Liberals and Democrats for Europe (ALDE) in the European Parliament comprised of 98 Parliamentarians (MEPs), wants even more bureaucratic and political heft behind "the fight against racism and discrimination," particularly at the highest levels. It is vital here to note that the leader of the ALDE, Guy Verhofstadt, stated on March 1st, 2019: "Let's create a single Euro-African economic area. It would have an enormous potential that remains untapped: 1.5 billion consumers, 20 trillion in value, able to rival with China." This would be the end of Europe as we know it, and he knows it.

Focusing specifically on education/indoctrination, UNESCO received financial support from the Dutch Ministry of Education, Culture, and Science, and the Norwegian Agency for Development Cooperation for its work on "preventing and addressing homophobic and transphobic violence in educational settings, including the global review on the extent of the problem and education sector responses." UNESCO's 2016 report "Out in the Open: Education sector responses to violence based on sexual orientation and gender identity/expression" was followed in November 2018 by the Council of Europe's report "Safe at school: Education sector responses to violence based on sexual orientation, gender identity/expression or sex characteristics in Europe," in partnership with UNESCO.

The "epidemic of violence" myth has already been dispelled in this book, but we can see here the standard tactics employed to play on people's emotions and artificially manipulate them into supporting the various aspects of the One World globalist project. The "recommendations" in this report are actually mandates, as "Member States' education sectors *must* (emphasis added)":

- Provide information to educational communities on equality and non-discrimination for all, including on grounds of gender, sexual orientation, gender identity/expression and sex characteristics. Information campaigns are a good way to disseminate this information.
- Review [educators'] curricula to ensure they include factual and non-judgmental information about sexual and gender diversity. At minimum, curricula must refer to equality and non-discrimination on all grounds. Ideally, curricula must explicitly mention the grounds of sexual orientation and gender identity/expression or sex characteristics. At best, curricula must explore specific issues related to sexual and gender diversity across several topics.
- Partner with civil society to benefit from their expertise in preventing and addressing [sexual orientation, gender identity and expression, and sex characteristics] SOGIESC-based violence. As education sectors acquire experience with the topic, their partnerships with civil society organisations should evolve to continue complementing official responses to violence.

All of this of course simply frames as anti-discrimination what is actually indoctrination and the stamping-out of any dissent through crushing uniformity. The report also references "binding international law" to mandate compliance with the UN's Sustainable Development Goals, again using "anti-discrimination" as an interpretative leap to pushing the LGBTQ propaganda. Preventing violence based on sexual orientation is a far cry from mandating transgender propaganda in teachers' curricula. It's like a version of the perversion of the American Constitution's 14th Amendment on a global scale. According to the "Safe at school" report:

In 2015, the United Nations General Assembly formally adopted a set of 17

Sustainable Development Goals (SDGs) to achieve the 2030 Agenda for Sustainable Development agreed by all UN Member States. Several goals require States to prevent violence against LGBT students in education:

- Goal 3: Ensure healthy lives and promote wellbeing for all at all ages
- Goal 4: Ensure inclusive and quality education for all
- Goal 5: Achieve gender equality and empower all women and girls
- Goal 10: Reduce inequality within and among countries
- Goal 16: Promote peaceful and inclusive societies for sustainable development

These goals cannot be achieved unless States take positive action to prevent and address violence in the education sector, including SOGIE-based violence.

The report, authored by Jasna Magić and Bruno Selun with additional input by Sophie Aujean (ILGA-Europe); Rubén Ávila and Euan Platt (IGLYO); Michael Barron (EQUATE Ireland); A. Chaber (Campaign Against Homophobia, Poland); Christophe Cornu and Yongfeng Liu (UNESCO); Eunice Den Hoedt (formerly seconded to UNESCO from the Dutch Ministry of Education, Culture and Science); Joe Kosciw (GLSEN, USA); and Oren Pizmony-Levy (Teachers College, Columbia University, USA), also states that in Ireland:

The Professional Development Service for Teachers (PDST, the largest provider of in-service teacher training) trains teachers to deal with issues linked to sexual orientation or gender identity/expression, including on best practices when implementing the national anti-bullying procedures.

And in Belgium:

Regional pedagogical guidance services commission NGOs and businesses to deliver both pre- and in-service training for staff. Regional education ministries also support a federal centre for expertise in sexual health, which provides LGBT-inclusive teacher training.

Flanders's regional Ministry of Education has been allowing LGBTQ NGOs to "raise awareness in schools" since 1999; apparently, "for the ministry, this tailored support to schools is essential to address SOGIE-based violence, but also the gender roles and stereotypes at the root of this violence." Per the report, in France:

The Ministry of Education set up a national network of experts on SOGIE-based violence, each based in the ministry's regional branch in one of France's 26 academic regions. In addition to their expertise on LGBT issues, these staff members also variously specialise in gender-based violence, gender equality, or discrimination. They relay resources and training from the ministry to teachers in their region, and act as a link on SOGIE-based violence between the regional and national levels. These specialised support staff receive continuous training, including on racist, sexist, and SOGIE-based violence and their discriminatory aspects. They follow and organise seminars on preventing and addressing violence, and share resources with colleagues in their region.

The Council of Europe has increasingly begun pressuring member states to adopt the instantly-recognizable uniform policy regarding "gender identity" and sexual orientation; in 2010, the Recommendation CM/Rec(2010)5 from the Committee of Ministers to member states in the realm of education specifically stated that the nations of the Council are urged to "take appropriate legislative and other measures, addressed to educational staff and pupils, to ensure that the right to education can be effectively enjoyed without discrimination on grounds of sexual orientation or gender identity." All well and good in essence, but by 2016, Resolution 2097 of the Parliamentary Assembly of the Council of Europe on "Access to school and education for all children" called on members to:

> Ensure access by LGBTI children to quality education by promoting respect and inclusion of LGBTI persons and the dissemination of objective information about issues concerning sexual orientation and gender identity, and by introducing measures to address homophobic and transphobic bullying.

We have seen what "objective information" looks like in this context, as well as the kinds of "measures" instituted to force compliance and stifle objection or even debate. In short, bullying.

As with all of these Trojan horse causes, the goalposts continue to move and the terminology is subject to constant revision. In its advanced stages—as in now—the statements of truth are diametrically opposed to the *actual* truth. This is part of the global gaslighting operation conducted by the Establishment and why control of the media apparatus and of education are so vital. As Catherine J. Nash and Kath Browne write in "Resisting the mainstreaming of LGBT equalities in Canadian and British Schools: Sex education and trans school friends":

> Once-invisible heternormativities are now being challenged through LGBT curricula and support for trans students. This creates classrooms as pivotal, geographical, social and political spaces that operate at the juncture of the public/private spaces of the home, public spaces of the neighbourhood and the imagined space of the nation and nation-building citizenship. Oppositional ideologies can no longer be understood through the labels of 'anti-gay', 'homophobic' or 'transphobic', and these oppositions go beyond 'anti-gender', such that the term heteroactivism names the activisms and ideologies that seeks to reassert the superiority of monogamous, binary cis-gendered, coupled marriages as best for children and for society.

In other words, the "assumption" that nuclear families of loving, committed couples raising healthy children together is best for those children and for society is "problematic," and it *must* be challenged, nay *dismantled*—just like the "patriarchy" and "white supremacy," et cetera.

The Manitoba Teachers' Society acted as a partner organization for a project led by Catherine Taylor (the University of Winnipeg), primarily funded by the Social

Sciences and Humanities Research Council of Canada with additional funds provided by The Manitoba Teachers' Society, Egale Canada Human Rights Trust, the Legal Research Institute at the University of Manitoba, and the University of Winnipeg, with additional authorial support for Taylor from other academicians from the Universities of Winnipeg and Manitoba and Elizabeth Meyer (University of Colorado; co-editor of *Gender and Sexuality in Education* and *Supporting Transgender and Gender-Creative Youth: Schools, Families, and Communities in Action*); this research became the "Every Teacher Project on LGBTQ-Inclusive Education in Canada's K-12 Schools." In it, the authors provide recommendations sure to become mandates such as:

- Develop appropriate curricular content at all grade levels and provide teachers with support to implement it. Make LGBTQ-inclusive content mandatory.
- Develop legislation/school board policy to require all publicly funded schools to provide a Gay-Straight Alliance.
- Actively work with Ministries of Education to create and implement effective legislation supporting LGBTQ-inclusive education.
- Ensure that student coursework has LGBTQ content integrated throughout Bachelor of Education programs.

The New Zealand Ministry of Education provides suggestions for schools and teachers in their role of "supporting LGBTIQA+ students," recommending: developing inclusive classrooms; using language to affirm diversity; making LGBTIQA+ content and themes visible across the curriculum; using targeted programs to facilitate opportunities for healthy discussion about sexuality, gender identity, and diversity; planning and delivering sexuality and gender education within the New Zealand Curriculum, years 1 to 6; and planning and delivering sexuality and gender education within the New Zealand Curriculum, years 7 to 13. As Howie Bruce and Jenny Horsley write, "Further delving into this material reveals resources that link to other groups supportive of education around diversity, including The Rainbow Trust and the Safe School Coalition in Australia." The Safe Schools Coalition Australia (SSCA) was a national network of organizations "working with school communities to create safer and more inclusive environments for same sex attracted, intersex and gender diverse students, staff and families" that began in Victoria in 2010 and went nationwide in 2013; it ceased to be a national organization several years later, however, with the cessation of federal funding.

In the UK, the Government Equalities Office and Department of Education in England and Wales started providing specific funding to 1,000 primary and secondary schools "with no or ineffective measures against SOGIE-based violence," which includes teacher and staff training. In England, as Neal Baker reported in February 2019 for *The Sun*, "Primary school children from the age of five are reportedly set to receive compulsory lessons about gay and trans relationships. New guidance . . . will also *ban parents from opting their kids out* of sex education in secondary school (emphasis added)." The preposterously-named Paul Twocock believes that the new regulations are "a great step forward for society."

In October 2019, the Northern Ireland Education Authority published its "guidance for schools on supporting trans children." The Scottish Government's LGBT

Inclusive Education Implementation Group has created a national framework including curriculum content, teaching materials, teacher training, and assessment criteria to "ensure LGBT inclusion in Scottish schools." Per IGLYO's 2018 LGBTQI Inclusive Education report:

> In 2014 the government allocated £2 million to a programme in England to help build schools' capacity to tackle homophobic, biphobic and transphobic bullying (the Anti-Homophobic, Biphobic and Transphobic (HBT) Bullying programme), in cooperation with relevant NGOs. In July 2016, the government provided a further £2.8 million to extend the programme from September 2016 to March 2019. . . . Public Sector Equality Duty requires that activities should be inclusive of sexual orientation and gender identity. Statutory Relationships and Sex Education (from 2019) will have to be inclusive of LGBTQI issues. . . . [In 2015] the National Children's Bureau (NBC) was awarded funding from the Department of Education and Government Equalities Office to deliver training for 1,500 primary and secondary teachers in seven local authority areas. The training is said to build teachers' ability to deliver a curriculum of sex and relationships education, within personal, social, health and economic (PSHE) education, which is inclusive of lesbian, gay, bisexual and transgender (LGBT) issues. . . . Furthermore, some universities or schools provide this training, often in collaboration with civil society organisations. In England, Stonewall offers training to universities. LGBT Youth Scotland works with six of the eight teacher training universities in Scotland. Through lectures, workshops and seminars, trainee teachers are signposted to LGBTI inclusion resources and are given a basic overview of LGBTI inclusion. . . . In England, the Proud Trust provides support and training to LGBTQI learners to make a positive change for themselves and their communities through youth groups, peer support, delivering of training and events, campaigns, undertaking research and creating resources. . . . The Scottish Government and LGBT Youth Scotland have developed a Toolkit for Teachers: Dealing with Homophobia and Homophobic Bullying with information, guidance and specific lesson plans for teachers to include LGBT topics across all subjects. More recently, LGBT Youth Scotland, funded by the government's Equalities Unit, has also developed a Guidance for Supporting Transgender Young People aimed to help primary and secondary education staff in Scotland support trans and non-binary learners.

In May 2019, the parents of a kindergartener in Andorra claimed that not only was their child transgender, but that the teachers in the facility needed to be educated about gender identity in childhood; the Catalan Association of Parents with Trans Children, Chrysallis, delivered the seminar. Andorra's health insurance system already covers hormone therapy, but in 2019 it was decided that "trans-specific" healthcare at a facility in Barcelona would also be covered. Also in 2019, the Department of Equality produced a short film entitled "#lovingdiversity," and handed out rainbow stickers and promoted online information on "sexual and gender diversity" in conjunction with this project; that same year the law on the rights of children and adolescents was amended to reflect "the right to identity," and establishing that "trans children must be respected in their gender identity." DiversAnd is the most prominent LGBTQ NGO currently active in Andorra: "The idea we have is to visualize the diversity that exists and put pressure on the administration to be sensitive to the group," said the president of the association. In 2016, Andorra's Ministry of Education teamed up with LGBTQ NGO Som Com Som to provide "a training session for teachers on LGBTQI issues."

In 2015, Estonia's Ministry of Education and Research tasked Tallinn University with delivering an in-service training course for teachers on LGBTQ "issues." Also in Estonia, at Tartu University LGBTQ topics are included in Diversity in Education, which is compulsory for teachers who study "Teaching Humanities and Social Subjects in Basic School" and voluntary for teachers who study "Teaching Natural and Exact Sciences at Lower Secondary School."

The Eötvös Loránd University in Budapest, Hungary has offered two courses on diversity which are part of the teacher training curriculum. In the course "Pedagogical experiences and approaches, representations of children, and individual specificities" diversity and inclusion are mentioned, with "LGBT youth" typically included; "Everybody's society—everybody's school" may also include "LGBT youth issues," but it is dependent on the professor.

In Spain, the Institute of Women and for Equal Opportunities and Complutense University of Madrid started in-service training to "prevent SOGIE-based [sexual orientation or gender identity/expression] violence" in 2016; Complutense University of Madrid also has an MA program in LGBTIQ+ Studies and set up a specific LGBT support office in 2017, which supports transgender students seeking to change their name and gender in the register. Spanish primary and secondary schools in Sevilla, Madrid, and Tenerife work with local LGBTQ organizations to incorporate "sexual, gender and family diversity" in both class content and extra-curricular activities, whatever those may entail. The Action Protocol on Gender Identity in Andalusia's Education System "address[es] trans realities in schools in a detailed, comprehensive and depathologising manner." IGLYO reports that:

> The government of Catalonia stated in 2014 (Law to grant the rights of LGBTI people and to eradicate homophobia, biphobia and transphobia) that there must be regulations for trans and intersex people to be treated according to their own gender even if they are minors, especially in educational institutions.

In March 2019, the Portuguese Secretary of State of Education, João Costa, published a statement on the importance of educating students about "gender equality" and condemned attempts to label the ongoing work in schools as spreading "gender ideology," even though it obviously is. Costa writes:

> In the week that we celebrate Women's Day, it is worth remembering why the theme *Gender Equality* was introduced in the area of Citizenship and Development for all students. . . . I receive letters and some petitions against the inclusion of the theme of Gender Equality in the curriculum. Interestingly, they do not speak of Equality, but of Gender Ideology. With bizarre arguments, such as the alleged imposition of a culture of death, the annulment of biology or the destruction of the family.

I promise I didn't write to him! He continues:

> Human Rights are not negotiated, are not postponed and are not optional, Citizenship in schools is not optional. The word ideology was transformed, by some, into an insult, in the famous imprecation "that is ideology". The Universal Declaration of Human Rights, whose 70th anniversary we are celebrating, is an ideological project. I'm glad. It is a good thing that we continue to strive for compliance.

In 2012, ILGA Portugal launched a call for an illustrated LGBTQ children's book with the winner being a story about a five-year-old girl with two fathers ("Primeiro Cresci no Coração" - First I grew up in their hearts"). The book has been provided for free to primary schools and public libraries, with sponsored readings.

In Serbia, NGO Labris has been organizing LGBTQ-centric training seminars for college professors, high school teachers, and school psychologists since 2011. From ILGA-Europe's 2020 Annual Review:

> Labris convened two national conferences for LGBTI liaison officers in July [2019], in Belgrade and Borkovac, to build their capacity in handling anti-LGBT hate crimes. Labris also held three meetings, bringing together liaison officers and the LGBTI community in Belgrade in April, and in Novi Sad and Niš in July. The meetings helped build trust in the community, and increase the knowledge of liaison officers about the needs of LGBT people.

Labris conducted a textbook analysis in 2014 and found—by what metric we do not know, surely not a scientific one—that school textbooks in the areas of biology, medicine, and psychology contained "discriminatory content."

Per ILGA-Europe's 2020 Annual Review, in 2019:

> The Flemish parliament introduced mandatory education on gender and sexual identity for first grade students in high schools, the fulfilment of which will be monitored by school inspections. Two universities, ULB and VUB, co-organised a workshop with four other European universities, on good practices on LGBTI inclusion.

Çavaria vzw provides materials to kindergarten teachers, and states that kindergarten is a better place to start indoctrinating children because "giving pre-schoolers a positive view of the evident diversity in our society is an exciting, but not always easy task for any pre-school teacher." They do, however, provide information about "Talking to preschoolers about diversity": "In a broader sense than what you say, ask yourself what the added value is of certain divisions in boys and girls that you make. Each time you divide them up like that, you reinforce the image that boys and girls are fundamentally different."

The Netherlands's Ministry of Education, Culture, and Science developed a guide in 2017 to help schools "attain educational goals linked to sexual and gender diversity." Peggy Cohen-Kettenis was Chair of Gender Development and Psychopathology at the University Medical Center Utrecht before becoming Professor of Medical Psychology at the Free University (VU) Medical Center in Amsterdam and the head of a gender clinic for children, adolescents, and adults. For the fifth revision of the DSM, Cohen-Kettenis was the Chair of the Gender Identity Disorders sub-committee under the Sexual and Gender Identity Disorders Work Group, Chaired by Kenneth Zucker. A trio of studies conducted by Peggy T. Cohen-Kettenis in conjunction with other researchers are often used as proof that surgical and hormonal intervention is only ever a good, and the younger the better.

In Sweden, the National Agency for Education uses a "norm-critical approach to familiarise educational staff with LGBT issues."[18] The Swedish government monitors "homophobic, biphobic, transphobic and interphobic bullying" through the Swedish Schools Inspectorate. The Service Santé de l'Enfance et de la Jeunesse is responsible for sex education in Geneva, Switzerland's schools and includes "LGBTQI issues" in the curriculum.

The Finnish Ministry of Education and Culture promotes a teacher guide developed by a national LGBTQ NGO, which includes "pedagogical materials to discuss sexual and gender diversity in class"; also in Finland, the National Agency for Education published an official guide in 2015 for basic schools to develop their "equality planning." Between 2014 and 2016, Finland updated the core curricula for pre-primary, primary, and general upper secondary education to "explicitly acknowledge that students' conception of their own gender identity and sexuality would evolve during these years," as the "Safe at school" report puts it.

In Ireland, per IGLYO:

> LGBT SASS was developed in 2016 by BeLonG To and Health Promotion within Ireland's national Health Services Executive. It is a comprehensive whole-school-community model for school change in order to become safe, supportive and inclusive of LGBT+ students. It was piloted in the NW of Ireland, in Donegal. Funding is now being sought to roll-out SASS nationally. . . . BeLonG To's Stand Up LGBT+ Awareness Week is a national event in November in secondary level schools across Ireland. . . . BeLonG To sends Stand Up packs (with posters and teachers' booklets) to all secondary level schools in Ireland. Stand Up Week address[es] sexual orientation and gender identity/expression.

Montenegro's Ministry of Education offered a training course for teachers and school psychologists and counselors in 2013, in collaboration with another of these LGBTQ NGOs; Montenegro has incorporated "sexual and gender diversity" in its national curriculum. One NGO delivered a training seminar on "the human rights of LGBT people" to pre-primary education professionals in 2017. In no universe but this one is this apparently acceptable, and accept and promote it major Montenegrin NGO Juventas and its donors (the Open Society Foundations, USAID, UNDP, the

---

[18] "In Sweden, future teachers must follow compulsory university training to prevent discrimination and violence. The National Agency for Education also provides in-service training; it uses a norm-critical approach to discuss the inclusion and representations of LGBT young people and the issues they face. A norm-critical approach implies discussing and evaluating prevailing social norms, rather than individuals who fall outside them. In 2014, the Living History Forum (a public authority) also launched new training materials for teachers and pupils in primary and secondary education titled 'LGBTQ [issues], norms and power,' outlining how prevailing rights and norms have developed through history."

Global Fund, the Rockefeller Brothers Fund, the European Commission, the Westminster Foundation for Democracy, the US and British Embassies in Podgorica, and the Delegation of the European Union to Podgorica, among others) do.

In Greece, the educational section of the Educational Radio-Television broadcasts from the Hellenic Parliament TV Channel, which includes student productions that were distinguished within the framework of educational activities of the Educational Radio TV. The episodes' themes are in accordance with the educational priorities of the Ministry of Education and Religious Affairs, such as: respect for diversity, the refugee crisis, sustainability, and gender equality. The Department of Early Childhood Education at National and Kapodistrian University of Athens offers the following:

- "Gender Theories": This lesson focuses on the way social sciences analyse the aspect of gender in sociability. It focuses on gender, as the principle that organises social life, and the ways it interacts with other analytical categories, such as sexuality, race, etc.
- Thematic week "Gender, body, otherness": This thematic week covers issues related to norms about gender, bodies and sexual orientation. It features movies, lectures and presentations from experts of different fields. Colour Youth (along with other LGBTQ organisations) has participated in this week with presentations.

Colour Youth is a grantee of the Open Society Foundations, which states that "Greece is susceptible to outside pressure." The European Court of Human Rights has in the past fined Greece for excluding same-sex couples from the civil union law.

Armenia decided funding a film on transgender weightlifting champion Mel Daluzyan was a good use of funds, and the Civil Status Acts Registration Agency of the Ministry of Justice decided that a psychiatric opinion from a licensed professional was not necessary for a trans person to change their name. That said, IGLYO whines that, "an analysis of elementary school textbooks revealed a disproportionate representation of gender roles with clear domination of the male roles depicted . . . [and] the State Yerevan University . . . consider[s] gender as a binary topic." According to the European Commission against Racism and Intolerance, "topics related to sexual orientation and gender identity and expression, or the issues of homophobia, biphobia, transphobia or interphobia are not properly covered in sex education classes in schools."

In Austria, the University of Applied Arts Vienna offers a course on the topic of diversity and (trans)gender in the context of didactics. The University of Vienna offers courses on gender diversity where "queer pedagogy" is taught. Verein Ausgesprochen is an association for LGBTQI teachers in Austria that provides specific workshops and guidelines for teachers. "Rainbow families" NGO FAmOs receives funding from the Austrian Ministry of Labor, Family, and Youth.

In Germany, the State of Berlin adopted an action plan against homo- and transphobia back in 2010 that lists measures for the education sector to "prevent and address LGBT discrimination." Berlin now organizes regular teacher training seminars pertaining to SOGIE-related "issues" in partnership with NGOs; Berlin's regional action plan "against homophobia" mandates every school to have "a contact person with specific knowledge of LGBT issues." Berlin's State Office for Equal Treatment and against Discrimination and two other regional agencies support LGBTQ NGOs to carry out actions mandated by the 2013 Berlin LGBT Action Plan, which includes regularly offering training courses on LGBTQ topics for school staff, including child and youth welfare workers, as well as organizing the annual Queer History Month and other campaigns to "address LGBT issues in schools." Immediately upon the fall of the Berlin Wall the LGBTQ agenda was being implemented in Berlin with the establishment of the Unit for Same-Sex Lifestyles in 1989. Originally part of the Department for Education and Youth Affairs, it was subsequently relocated to the Department for Labor Integration and Women, which speaks volumes.

Albania's Ministry of Education, Sport, and Youth and the Institute of Educational Development developed a module "Competencies for life and sexual education," alongside a module on "LGBT issues and heterosexism" in 2015; that same year, the Ministry of Social Welfare and Youth of Albania held a consultative meeting on LGBTI rights, with the participation of educational experts and LGBTQ and "human rights organizations" along with relevant government ministries. As a result of this meeting, a national action plan on "LGBTI issues" was presented: the National Action Plan on LGBTI People 2016–2020 defines the:

> Inclusion of LGBTI issues in the field of legislation and policy development, safety and protection of rights and access to service. . . . The Ministry of Education [and of Sport and Youth] is obliged to reduce discrimination of LGBTI people in education by reviewing the curricula at all educational levels and training educational employees (objective 3.2) and to prepare the training curriculum for pre-university education teachers (objective 3.2.4).

PINK Embassy is an NGO tasked with implementing many of these objectives in the school system and providing training to teachers and students; according to IG-LYO:

> PINK Embassy signed a cooperation agreement with the Ministry of Education and Sports to raise awareness of teachers and youth in Albanian schools in relation to bullying and discrimination [and] present tools on how to tackle it, and to assist the government in its efforts to review school curricula and education programs.

The first PINK Embassy program came courtesy of support from the Ministry of Foreign Affairs of the Kingdom of the Netherlands in collaboration with COC Nederland/Netherlands; their first major event was on May 17th, 2012, called the "Festival of Diversity." Other significant supporters and/or partners with Albania's PINK Embassy include the Canada Fund for Local Initiatives, ILGA-Europe, the US Embassy in Tirana, and the Delegation of the European Union to Albania.

The Institute of Educational Development has collaborated with UNESCO in the past. In UNESCO's August 2017 "Albania Education Policy Review: Issues and Recommendations" extended report we learn:

The Republic of Albania is undergoing significant education reforms, including the implementation of the Pre-University Education Development Strategy 2014–2020. These reforms reflect the high priority given to education in Albania, in the perspective of European Union integration and the country's international commitments. Looking beyond the year 2020, these and other reforms are expected to help align the education sector with Sustainable Development Goal 4 (SDG4) of the international 2030 Agenda for Sustainable Development. SDG4 is to 'ensure inclusive and equitable quality education and promote lifelong learning opportunities for all.' This means building upon the range of actions taken by the government and other stakeholders to achieve inclusion, equity and quality in education. . . . It is our hope that through this EPR, UNESCO contributed to policy analysis and dialogue to guide the implementation of the Pre-University Education Development Strategy 2014–2020 and to eventually align the national reform agenda with SDG4-Education 2030.

In 2018, the United Nations' Free & Equal initiative began a major online campaign in Albania called "I Am Your Child," which "seeks to change the narratives around family values through videos and other social media content carrying a simple message; supporting your kids – no matter who they are or whom they love – is what family is all about." Additionally, as the UN reports:

In 2019, the roll out of the social media campaign was amplified by well-known and respected psychologists, teachers and sociologists, as well as the Anti-Discrimination Commissioner, the Albania People's Advocate and the UN Resident Coordinator, who used their reputation, platform and strong arguments to help spread the message of the campaign. . . . The Free & Equal team moreover worked directly with parents of LGBTI individuals, setting up a support group for parents in rural areas together with the NGO Open Mind Spectrum Albania. . . . Presentations by UN staff and community members helped increase the group's understanding of the issues their children face and the importance of family support. . . . Over the past few years, Free & Equal Albania has also been working with journalists to eliminate use of stigmatizing language and negative stereotypes about minorities in traditional media. . . . In 2019, the team hosted 40 journalists from traditional and conservative regions of Albania in a training workshop on fair and ethical reporting, resulting in five media stories in the local press. . . . Plans for 2020 include continuing the "I am Your Child" campaign both online and with in-real-life parents' groups. The team will also, in collaboration with Free & Equal Serbia, focus on outreach to the business community using the Standards of Conduct for Business that were recently translated into Albanian.

In January 2016 in Iceland, an elementary school in Reykjanesbær removed sex-specific bathroom signs as well as stipulations for specific swim attire, with the school's principal stating that "since there are currently children attending the school who are gender-fluid or trans, it's not up to us, the school, to force them or anybody else into a pre-designed form." The Ministry of Welfare supports the national

LGBTQ organization Samtökin 78; Samtökin also has a contract with the Municipality of Reykjavík to provide "LGBTQIA education" in schools. The Hafnarfjörður municipality commissioned Samtökin 78 to train teachers and staff in its schools and "to make the curriculum more inclusive in compulsory education (ages 6–16)." When locals protested the inclusion of these materials in the Hafnarfjörður compulsory schools, ten individuals were charged with hate speech.

In August 2020, the US Embassy in Prague published a Declaration on the Occasion of Prague Pride, which the US Embassy both participated in and supported:

> Inclusivity and diversity make our communities more peaceful and prosperous, whereas employing rancor for political gain has tangible social costs. Sexual orientation and gender identity are the lived experience of each individual – they are not a political ideology. . . . The celebration of diversity is an important way to promote respect for human rights. We support the work of those who promote equal treatment for all LGBTI+ people, and who contribute to the creation of a more just and inclusive society.

This is pure projection; it's difficult to read these words and not become infuriated while realizing the horrors carried out under this banner of inclusion and tolerance. It's really quite sickening. As I quoted Savitri Devi in the Introduction and is worth repeating: "It is not violence, but honesty about violence, which rapidly decreases at the end of the Dark Age."

In the Czech Republic, according to IGLYO:

> Several books and guidelines have been published on the topic of sexual orientation: 'Homophobia in School Environment' (authors Smetáčková, Braun) by the Government Office; PROUD's handbook for teachers available during PROUD's trainings of teachers and online; 'Adolescence, Parenting and (Homo)Sexuality' (Zdenek Sloboda, 2016, Pasparta Publishing) includes [a] chapter on coming out and school environment where GALE's Toolkit for Schools is reviewed.

GALE is the Global Alliance for LGBT Education. Toolkit 1.0 was made possible through funding from Hivos, the Tides Foundation, EduDivers, and the American Jewish World Service. EduDivers clients include several major municipalities in the Netherlands and the European Union. GALE's mission in producing educational materials is to indoctrinate and enforce orthodoxy: "Education to combat discrimination should not only focus on emancipating people who label themselves as a minority. It should deconstruct the limiting norms that create discredited identities and imagined minorities (the norm of heterosexuality)." GALE applied for and got consultative status with UNESCO in 2008; their Strategic Plan 2018–2022 informs that:

> The Dutch government decided that GALE could be a partner in the Dutch strategy to help shape an international 'equality' coalition of States, cities and NGO's. In 2011, the Dutch government funded GALE with an annual budget of €50.000 for stimulation and cooperation. This was focused at supporting UNESCO with the anti-homophobic bullying research project (2011–2016). Accepting this grant implied that GALE had to set priorities. This project

focused on schools only. . . . At the same time, there was an international discussion about the end of the old Millennium Goals and the new SDGs. . . . UNESCO's new strategy blends comprehensive sexual education and combating violence into a strategy on "gender-based violence."

Cyprus's Ministry of Education and Culture sponsored a multi-year training program called "HOMBAT-Combating HOMophoBic And Transphobic bullying at schools" for hundreds of teachers and college professors; the program ran from 2017–2019 and also involved schools in Greece and Lithuania. It was run by GALE. In 2019, the UN "recommended" Cyprus institute measures to "combat discrimination" and change its gender identity laws, which it accepted.

The aforementioned Czech NGO PROUD co-organized with government ministries and officials a conference on homophobia in schools in 2014; PROUD offered over 100 school seminars (attended by more than 3,000 pupils) during 2013–2016 on "LGBT awareness." PROUD has received funding from the PlanetRomeo Foundation (which funded school seminars on "LGBT issues"), the US Embassy in Prague, ILGA-Europe, Lush Cosmetics, and the Open Society Foundations. EEA Grants (a joint funding initiative of the governments of Iceland, Liechtenstein, and Norway) funded the "Invisible Minorities" project in the Czech Republic:

During the project, the following activities took place: educational activities for the pupils of elementary schools, secondary schools, vocational schools and secondary grammar schools; seminar for future specialists; four seminars for social worker experts; two seminars for pedagogical workers and two seminars for workers from services for seniors. . . . The first workshop took place in Prague in August 2015 with participation of representatives of [what is now FRI] . . . . Special attention was paid to the area of migrants in the context of the LGBT community, the system of education on LGBT issues in Norway, and LGBT elder adults. . . . The second workshop took place in Bergen. It was attended by representatives of PROUD, Zdeněk Sloboda, Jolana Novotná and Petr Pávek.

The "rainbow city" of Bergen provides funding to the Norwegian FRI, Foreningen for kjønns- og seksualitetsmangfold (The Norwegian Organization for Sexual and Gender Diversity); Erlend Horn, city councilor for social matters, housing, and inclusion, informs that, "We cooperate with FRI in order to raise awareness among pupils, and we inform newly arrived immigrants in Bergen about the legal status of the LGBT population." In June 2016, the Norwegian Government launched a new cross-ministerial LGBTQ action plan entitled "Safety, diversity, openness – The Norwegian Government's action plan against discrimination based on sexual orientation, gender identity and gender expression (2017–2020)." Five years earlier, Norway's Directorate for Education and Training had published a guide on relationships and sexuality for primary school teachers. Regarding Bergen specifically, as Horn relates in "The Rainbow City of Bergen, Plan for gender and sexual diversity 2017–2021":

Unfortunately, it is quite common to hear homophobic language in public spaces. Hilde Slåtten at the University of Bergen presented her doctoral thesis last June, regarding derogatory words for homosexuals among pupils in the ninth grade in a selected number of Norwegian schools. In her thesis it appears that almost half of the pupils had called someone "homo" the past week. This is unacceptable, and we will step up our efforts to communicate this message to our children and youngsters. Our goal is that representatives from FRI shall visit all pupils in lower and upper secondary schools, that representatives from pupil's councils join courses in connection with the annual Rainbow days and that teachers in the Bergen schools increase their competence about group-based prejudices. A friendly wind is blowing in the city's rainbow flag. In our plan we propose a number of measures to make the city more including. Many of these measures do not cost much for the majority, but may mean a lot to the minorities in question: for instance avoiding the usual gender segregation at public toilets and in forms to fill out. We wish Bergen to host Europride in order to show Bergen as an open and welcoming city, but also to increase our international dedication in this area. A safe haven for people who fled their countries; LGTB-refugees are in a particular vulnerable situation, and in the years to come Bergen will give residence to an increasing number of refugees, which appears in this plan.

In order to stamp out Wrongthink, Bergen will send representatives of FRI into the lower secondary schools, as per "The Rainbow City of Bergen, Plan for gender and sexual diversity 2017–2021":

It is important to make children understand and get knowledge of different kinds of families to prevent prejudices, bullying, harassment and hate crime. It is also essential that the staff in kindergartens and schools are aware that children can deviate from gender norms and may have a different gender identity than the one they were registered under when born. . . . All pupils in Norwegian schools must learn about homosexuality. One competence aim for 1st to 4th grade is to enable pupils to discuss various types of family, including same-sex parents. Pupils from 5th to 7th grade shall be able to "discuss various sexual orientations in relationships, couples and families". Furthermore they should be able to "describe roles in their own everyday life and find out which expectations are connected to these roles. . . ." Bergen municipality also carries out yearly following-up training at the primary and lower secondary schools in Bergen. . . . We know that many asylum seekers in reception centers in our region have an identity that break with the traditional view on gender and sexual identity, and many of them are in a particularly vulnerable situation. In Nuremberg (30 places) and Berlin (122 places) in Germany they have established proper reception centers to attend to this group. . . . Bergen municipality has had a good cooperation for several years with FRI, previously LLH. It is important for the municipality to continue and strengthen this cooperation. In order to give information to schools, newly arrived immigrants and others, the municipality depends on this cooperation to obtain the objectives in this plan. In addition to this information campaign FRI and other organizations, such as Skeiv Verden, Skeive studenter, Skeiv ungdom and HomoHib, organize cultural events and other important meeting points for lgbti-persons in Bergen, thus the above mentioned organizations contribute to make Bergen a diverse city to live in.

FRI works for "equality and against discrimination of people who break the norms of gender and sexuality in Norway and in the rest of the world" and has a mission statement that, "The queer movement must be anti-racist." FRI's youth organization is Skeiv Ungdom; it features the following extremely bizarre and disconcerting statement on its website:

Skeiv Ungdom has several selections. One of these is Young BDSM. We believe that BDSM and fetishism have a natural place in Skeiv Ungdom's struggle against norms that limit people's ability to live free and secure lives on their own terms. Skeiv Ungdom's UngBDSM selection works in two parts. The first part of this work is information-based. Sexuality education is an important topic that Gay Youth works with. . . . UngBDSM provides input on what is important to include in sex education for young people. Among other things, Skeiv Ungdom works to ensure that knowledge about BDSM and fetishism becomes part of the teaching of sexuality. . . . In the long run, this can help increase the level of knowledge about BDSM and fetishism. . . . Skeiv Ungdom also works to ensure that BDSMers and fetishists have special legal protection on an equal footing with other queer identities.

For IGLYO:

The project Rosa kompetanse (Pink competency) is run by the Norwegian organisation for gender and sexual diversity (FRI) and financed by the Department of Education and the Department of Health. The project has given courses to teachers (and pre-service teachers) since 2011. It offers knowledge-based courses relevant to the school setting, given by people with a school background. It talks about gender identity, norms, sexual orientation and varied types of families, in accordance with the curriculum. The project also cooperates with Skeiv Ungdom, so that at some schools, Pink competency gives courses to teachers while Skeiv Ungdom educates the students.

Are they teaching them about BDSM and other fetishes needing "special legal protection on an equal footing with other queer identities"?

The project Restart, supported by the Directorate for Education and Training and the Directorate for Children, Youth, and Family Affairs, sponsors "activists" from Skeiv Ungdom to go into schools and discuss sexual orientation, gender identity, and gender expression with students as well.

# Drag Me to Hell

*"The effect of the drag system is to wrench the sex roles loose from that which supposedly determines them, genital sex."*

– Esther Newton

One of the most insidious targeted propaganda and recruitment vehicles of this agenda is the much-publicized Drag Queen Story Hour, which is typically hosted at public libraries. The Drag Queen Story Hour (DQSH) was first launched in San Francisco in 2015 by lesbian Michelle Tea and "queer literary arts organization" RADAR Productions under the leadership of Virgie "lose hate not weight" Tovar and Juli Delgado Lopera; there are now dozens of branches in the United States and abroad as far afield as Berlin and Tokyo. These "events" feature provocative dancing and BDSM accoutrements such as dog collars; one event featured a drag queen spreading his legs to a group of children revealing his naked genitalia under a short skirt, and another in Texas was run by a pair of convicted sex offenders named William Travis Dees and Albert Garza. Said one drag queen, "We are trying to groom the next generation." Indeed.

While the mainstream focuses on the drag queens themselves – usually in a way that glorifies them and advertises this depravity to children ("drag kids" is now a thing), I'd instead like to focus on this important question: who is actually bankrolling these perverse pedophilic grooming gangs? You can donate to Drag Queen Story Hour through Amazon Smile, and they receive funding from the Hachette Book Group, Chronicle Books, and HarperCollins Children's Books. RADAR receives funding from the San Francisco Foundation and Poets & Writers as well as, as Kay Elle Lothbrook reports:

The California Arts Council, The San Francisco Public Libraries, The Horizons Foundation, and notably The Walter and Elise Haas Fund and The Zellerbach Foundation. The Walter and Elise Haas Fund is a Bay Area "philanthropy" founded by Walter Haas. Walter Haas is the son of Jewish Bavarian immigrants, who married Elise Stern, daughter and niece of the founders of Levi Strauss Jeans. Haas is best known for being the President of Levi Strauss from 1928–1955, he is credited with saving and growing the brand. The Walter and Elise Haas Fund focuses their energy and capital on 5 areas, according to their website: The Arts, Economic Security, Education, Jewish Life, and Net Safety. The site prominently features articles like "How the World

Should Be: Jews, Social Justice and GLIDE" by Rabbi Michael Lezak. . . . The Zellerbachs are a wealthy family of Jewish immigrants known for owning a huge paper and paper pulp conglomerate and enormous timber and land holdings in the Pacific Northwest. . . . They were the subject of a 1958 antitrust investigation by the U.S. Justice Dept. . . . A huge portion of The Zellerbach Family Foundation's operating budget is also devoted to encouraging mass immigration and refugee resettlement. . . . The Zellerbach Foundation has donated over $46 million dollars to date, and is devoted to "building vibrant communities" by supporting refugee and resettlement NGO's like The Tahirih Justice Center who have "served over 25,000 courageous individuals fleeing violence since 1997." Tahirih Justice Center Executive Director, Morgan Weibel states, "without the critical support of the Zellerbach Family Foundation, Tahirih would be unable to continue its necessary work to support immigrants."

The Walter and Elise Haas Fund and the Evelyn and Walter Haas, Jr. Fund are the two primary funds through which the Haas family disburses donations. The Walter and Elise Haas fund has over $216 million in assets, and it has donated to the ACLU, Bend the Arc: A Jewish Partnership for Justice, the J Street Education Fund, the Tides Center, the New Israel Fund, the Horizons Foundation, the Center for Popular Democracy, the National LGBTQ Task Force, the National Committee for Responsive Philanthropy, Grantmakers Concerned with Immigrants and Refugees (GCIR), Mujeres Unidas y Activas (MUA), the SPLC, and the ADL, which, by the way, produces guidelines for "Toys and Gender" aimed at kindergarteners:

Learning Objectives:

- Students will reflect on how toys are categorized as "girl toys," "boy toys" or both
- Students will develop an understanding of gender stereotyping
- Students will explore the concept of gender-neutral toys
- Students will re-create packaging for their favorite toys to make them gender-neutral

Be sure to use terminology such as firefighter instead of fireman, police officer instead of policeman, trash collector instead of garbage man, flight attendant, humankind, etc. When singing nursery rhymes, change the lyrics to make verses gender neutral (i.e. For "Wheels on the Bus," use "parents" instead of "mommies"). . . . [Pre-K adaptation: Instead of the handout, use real toys from the classroom or toys you bring from home or borrow. Find some toys that are gender-specific like dolls or princesses (with lots of pink) and superheroes as well as toys that are more gender-neutral like a teddy bear.]

The SPLC claims that objections to the Drag Queen Story Hour are evidence of "escalating white nationalist threats against transgender people."

The Evelyn and Walter Haas, Jr. Fund is the other major Haas family foundation and has almost $464 million in assets to date. It donates to many pro-open borders groups like La Raza in addition to the Tides Foundation, the Tides Center, the

Transgender Law Center, the National LGBTQ Task Force, the ACLU, the Civil Marriage Collaborative, the Astraea Lesbian Foundation for Justice, the Haas Institute for a Fair and Inclusive Society, the Proteus Fund, National Committee for Responsive Philanthropy, and the East Bay Alliance for a Sustainable Economy, which also receives funding from the Zellerbach Family Foundation. Levi Strauss has its own foundation, the Levi Strauss Foundation, which donates millions to LGBTQ "causes."

A full funding list for the Tides Foundation from 2005,[19] sourced from their IRS 990 form, though it is a bit dated, provides insight into the kinds of projects they support; as an illustrative and far from exhaustive sample:

| | |
|---|---:|
| ALSO for Gay Youth | $5,000 |
| AIDS Foundation of Chicago | $100,000 |
| AIDS Action Committee of Massachusetts | $100,000 |
| ACLU | $189,950 |
| Alabama Coalition on Black Civic Participation | $54,375 |
| American Foundation for AIDS Research | $100,000 |
| American Jewish World Service | $20,200 |
| American Jewish Committee | $5,000 |
| American Friends of the Israel Democracy Institute | $5,000 |
| Asian Pacific Network of People Living with HIV/AIDS | $29,500 |
| Astraea Lesbian Foundation for Justice | $25,000 |
| Astraea Media, Inc. | $10,000 |
| Aswat (Palestinian Gay Women) | $3,600 |
| Bat Shalom, The Jerusalem Women's Action Center | $5,000 |
| Bay Area Coalition for Equitable Schools | $33,333 |
| Brothers Against Guns | $50,000 |
| Canadian HIV/AIDS Legal Network (which received $225,000 from the Open Society Foundations in 2012) | $49,706.50 |
| Center for American Progress | $530,000 |
| Columbia University | $122,750 |
| Congregation B'nai Jeshurun | $26,008 |
| Congregation Emek Beracha | $50,000 |
| Demos (a dynamic "think-and-do" tank that powers the movement for a just, inclusive, multiracial democracy) | $282,245 |
| Estonian Network of HIV-Positive People | $9,992 |
| Gay and Lesbian Advocates and Defenders | $12,000 |
| Gay and Lesbian Leadership Institute | $10,000 |
| GLSEN | $12,000 |
| Golos AntiAIDS (Russia) | $10,000 |
| Health, Hope, and HIV Network (Antigua and Barbuda) | $13,000 |

---

[19] The Jewish Joanie Bronfman of the Bronfman Seagram's fortune was a long-time Tides Board member, and the Jewish Suzanne Nossel, who we will re-visit later, is another. Interim CEO Tuti B. Scott's biographical description on the Tides' website includes that "Tuti has been a featured speaker and workshop producer for the Women's Funding Network, the Jewish Women's Funding Network, and several of the member funds of these networks. . . . Tuti currently serves as Chair of the Board of Directors of Tides and a founding Board member of the Women Win Foundation, and is proud to call herself an intersectional feminist."

| | |
|---|---:|
| Horizons Foundation | $2,500 |
| Human Rights Watch | $300,061.30 |
| Hyacinth AIDS Foundation | $100,000 |
| Indian Network for People Living with HIV/AIDS | $40,039.66 |
| International Community of Women Living with HIV/AIDS (UK) | $203,533 |
| International Gay and Lesbian Human Rights Commission | $27,464 |
| International HIV/AIDS Alliance | $68,615 |
| International Sephardic Education Foundation | $20,000 |
| Israel Policy Forum | $27,000 |
| Jacksonville Area Sexual Minority Youth Network | $38,000 |
| Jews for Racial and Economic Justice | $2,500 |
| Jewish Community Center in Manhattan | $78,900 |
| Kolot: The Center for Jewish Women's and Gender Studies | $10,000 |
| Lambda Legal | $73,220 |
| Mama Cash | $20,000 |
| Media Matters for America | $1,074,453.76 |
| Mount Sinai School of Medicine | $36,000 |
| Multi-Ethnic Immigrant Organizing Network | $35,000 |
| National Center for Lesbian Rights | $50,500 |
| National Coalition on Black Civic Participation | $97,500 |
| National Gay and Lesbian Task Force (now the National LGBTQ Task Force) | $7,000 |
| Network of African People Living with HIV/AIDS | $112,768 |
| New Israel Fund | $16,800 |
| Northwestern University | $5,000 |
| Positive Muslims (South Africa) | $9,953 |
| Sierra Club and the Sierra Club Foundation (combined) | $152,383 |
| Sylvia Rivera Law Project | $2,500 |
| Tides Canada Foundation | $140,400 |
| Tides Center | $1,500,000 |
| Tides, Inc. | $157,760.03 |
| Topeka AIDS Project | $53,148 |
| TransFair USA | $1,000 |
| Transgender Law Center | $5,000 |
| UCLA School of Medicine | $296,928 |
| Udmurtia-AntiAIDS (Russia) | $10,000 |
| Upwardly Global | $25,000 |
| Yale University | $318,574.80 |

Tides also disbursed funds to over *seventy* regional Planned Parenthoods.

Also mentioned as a primary funder of RADAR Productions is the Horizons Foundation. The Horizons Foundation was founded in 1980 by San Franciscans seeking to create "a gay United Way." Today, Horizons receives funding from major companies like Facebook and PricewaterhouseCoopers, financial institutions like BNY Mellon Wealth Management and Morgan Stanley Wealth Management, and absurdities like the San Francisco Police Officers Pride Alliance; as of mid-2019, Horizons had total assets in excess of $36 million. They've come a long way. They also receive funding from the Gill Foundation, the Arcus Foundation, the Evelyn and

Walter Haas, Jr. Fund, the Levi Strauss Foundation, the William and Flora Hewlett Foundation, the Wellspring Philanthropic Fund, and the Laughing Gull Foundation. The Queer Cultural Center is another LGBTQ incubator, funded by organizations such as the William and Flora Hewlett Foundation, the Zellerbach Foundation, the Horizons Foundation, the California Arts Council, and the National Endowment for the Arts; the Queer Cultural Center also supports RADAR Productions.

The Horizons Foundation's grantees for 2018–19 include, via the grant directory on their website (and this is not even close to a comprehensive list, but is simply a representative list of the kinds of projects and organizations they're funding, and to give the reader an idea of the resources at their disposal as well as the ways in which they are advancing their agenda):

| | |
|---|---:|
| The LGBT Asylum Project - Center for Immigrant Protection | $10,000 |
| Jewish Family & Community Services East Bay | $3,290 |
| Auburn Theological Seminary | $10,000 |
| Planned Parenthood Federation of America, Inc. | $60,000 |
| Sexual Minorities Uganda - USA dba Smug International | $60,000 |
| St. James Infirmary | $1,000 |
| Queer and Asian Conference, 2019 at UC Berkeley, 2 Grants | $1,500 |
| National Center for Lesbian Rights | $10,000 |
| Topsy Turvy Queer Circus | $10,000 |
| San Francisco Trans March | $10,000 |
| Genders & Sexualities Alliance Network | $8,000 |
| Transgender Law Center | $40,000 |
| University of California Berkeley Foundation | $6,480 |
| Miami-Dade Gay & Lesbian Chamber of Commerce | $7,000 |
| Instituto Familiar de la Raza | $1,000 |
| New Venture Fund | $10,000 |
| Media Matters for America | $60,000 |

The Horizons Foundation also grants a host of scholarships, mostly to universities central to the incubation and advancement of the transgender-industrial complex:

**Markowski-Leach Scholarship Fund Grants**

| | |
|---|---:|
| San Francisco State University, 2 Grants | $4,000 |
| Stanford University, 2 Grants | $14,000 |
| University of California, Berkeley, 3 Grants | $11,000 |
| University of California, San Francisco, 2 Grants | $3,000 |

**eQuality Scholarship Fund Grants**

| | |
|---|---:|
| Boston University | $6,000 |
| Brown University, 3 Grants | $9,000 |
| David Geffen School of Medicine at UCLA | $6,000 |
| Golden Gate University | $3,000 |
| Lewis & Clark College | $6,000 |
| Reed College | $6,000 |
| SIU School of Medicine | $6,000 |
| Stanford University, 2 Grants | $6,000 |

| | |
|---|---|
| Stanford University School of Medicine | $6,000 |
| UC Hastings College of the Law | $6,000 |
| University of California, Davis - School of Medicine | $6,000 |
| University of California, Los Angeles, 4 Grants | $14,500 |
| University of California, Berkeley, 3 Grants | $14,000 |
| University of California, San Francisco, 2 Grants | $12,000 |
| Yale University, 2 Grants | $4,000 |

The connection with higher education is essential, not just for its infrastructure and role in legitimizing all things "trans," but for its uses as an indoctrination center. Facilitating as many pliable minds' entry into these indoctrination factories as possible is essential. Consider the Point Foundation, the largest LGBTQ scholarship-granting organization in the country, including the earlier-mentioned Harper Rubin. The following have scholarships sponsored through Point: ViiV Healthcare, Toyota, NBCUniversal, Wells Fargo, Novo Nordisk, FedEx, HBO, HSBC, the Barbara Epstein Foundation, and more. Involved with recent Point Honors events are included: the Jewish fashion designer Rachel Antonoff, Cadillac, Merrill Lynch, Hilton, Wells Fargo, American Airlines, Warner Media, Verizon, J. Crew, and BNY Mellon Wealth Management.

It's not just higher education, either; as I mentioned, for the Establishment, getting children as young as possible is ideal. Karen Zelermyer outlines the specific strategy targeting the youth undertaken by these LGBTQ "philanthropies":

Many funders, including the Adam R. Rose Foundation, the Arcus Foundation, the California Endowment and the Johnson Family Foundation have continuously carved out funding for queer youth through leadership development, direct service, scholarship and safe schools programs. As past annual tracking reports and this research show, children and youth have received the most funding of any LGBTQ population sub-group throughout the movement's history. . . . During this era, funders invested millions of dollars towards creating safer educational environments for LGBTQ and allied youth, with the Gay, Lesbian and Straight Education Network (GLSEN) receiving the second highest amount of foundation funding among all LGBTQ organizations. Local funders have been able to direct grants towards area high schools and colleges for curriculum development and to support gay-straight alliances. Organizations that work directly with LGBTQ youth outside school environments have also benefited during this period, due in no small part to funding from the Queer Youth Fund at Liberty Hill Foundation (a progressive foundation primarily serving Southern California). Founded in 2002 by Ralph Alpert, Jim Johnson, and Weston Milliken, the Queer Youth Fund provides large, multi-year grants to innovative and effective leadership development and organizing projects nationwide that empower LGBTQ youth. The Fund has received foundation support from the Johnson Family, Threshold, Tides, Liberty Hill and Gill foundations and The Palette Fund, and has awarded more than $3 million to organizations working in 21 states and Canada. . . . The State Equality Fund, a partnership of five major foundations in conjunction with the Tides Foundation, has awarded more than $7.5 million since 2007 for organizations working to pass sexual orientation and gender-identity nondiscrimination statutes; implement safe-school policies for LGBTQ and LGBTQ-perceived students; and secure adoption and foster care rights for LGBTQ parents. The Fund, for example, awarded the Illinois Safe Schools Alliance, a network of organizers, $80,000 in 2008 to pass local safe schools ordinances, and, eventually in 2010, the Illinois legislature passed a statewide safe-schools law. The Fund also gave Love Makes a Family Connecticut $10,000 in 2008 for its efforts to extend statewide non-discrimination protections to transgender people, which was later passed in July 2011.

The Johnson Family Foundation has also donated extensively to the Williams Institute at UCLA, as well as the Transgender Foundation of America, the Tree of Life Synagogue, the SPLC, Planned Parenthood, the New York City LGBT Community Center, the New Venture Fund, MAP, the National LGBTQ Task Force, the Hebrew Immigrant Aid Society (HIAS), GLSEN, Funders for LGBTQ Issues, the LGBTQ Victory Institute, the ACLU, the American LGBTQ+ Museum, the Center for American Progress (CAP), the Environmental Defense Fund, Lambda Legal, the UCSF Program on Reproductive Health and the Environment, the National Center for Lesbian Rights (NCLR), and Outright Vermont.

The UCSF Program on Reproductive Health and the Environment's partnerships include the Pan-American Health Organization (PAHO), the Endocrine Society, the NIH, the CDC, the EPA, the World Health Organization (WHO), and the Natural Resources Defense Council, which itself has received ample funding from the MacArthur Foundation. Laurence Rockefeller is on its Board of Trustees and Joan Davidson, President Emerita of the JM Kaplan Fund (a former CIA front named after Jewish financier Jacob Merrill Kaplan), is an Honorary Trustee.

Vermont is a rural state with a small population. Yet, even with its small population, the 501(c)(3) NGO Outright Vermont, which has also received funding from the Tides Foundation, "serves over 2,100 LGBTQ youth and their families, and nearly 5,000 educators and service providers in every county in Vermont." Outright Vermont runs summer camps and provides "gender-identity programs" to Vermont public schools. They have more than sixty volunteers who go into schools across the state. They run summits, an annual Gender and Sexuality Alliance Conference "which connects students and advisors" (both middle school and high school students), and they have a "drop-in space" in Burlington.

Outright Vermont states that no age is too young for transitioning. Dr. Rachel Inker of Community Health Center of Burlington states that, "The choice to have surgery is a personal one that should be explored in every age group." According to Iris Lewis:

> Both Outright Vermont and the Community Health Centers of Burlington— the organizations that Kaplan and Inker are a part of, respectively—participated in drafting and providing feedback on the rule. According to Inker, the process began last fall, and several additional groups took part.

Kaplan would be Dana Kaplan, the Executive Director of Outright Vermont. Kaplan identifies as "queer, trans masculine, and Jewish." According to Kaplan, eliminating an age minimum for the introduction of sex hormones and so-called "social transitioning" is a means of suicide prevention, which we have already established to be absolutely false. The suicidality lies are akin to the insistence on the "targeting of trans people." They are pages from a familiar playbook. The opposite of compassionate, these projects are of the vilest nature, encouraging the unconscionable grooming and mutilation of children and the most vulnerable among us.

Also complicit in the Drag Queen Story Hour's grooming efforts is the American Library Association (ALA) which, like the American Psychological Association (APA), has used its patina of respectability to push this radical agenda. In the 1960s, the ALA began constructing various "task forces" along ideological lines, predominantly those of feminism and "civil rights." The Jewish Israel David Fishman (Columbia University, Head of Technical Services at the Jewish Theological Seminary library, son of a rabbi), was the driving force behind using the ALA as a vehicle of "gay liberation" starting in 1970 when he founded and became the inaugural head of its Task Force on Gay Liberation. The ALA and these other foundations and institutions are aided in their endeavors by familiar faces in the ADL, the ACLU, Planned Parenthood, and complicit teachers' unions such as the California Teachers Association, which promotes sexuality and transgenderism to children in single-digit ages.

The Jewish lesbian head of the American Federation of Teachers Randi Weingarten has been at the forefront of pushing the transgender agenda in schools nationally. Weingarten achieved prominence as the head of New York's United Federation of Teachers in 1998 despite one semester of teaching experience. Her rise is reminiscent of fellow New Yorker Joel I. Klein, husband of Nicole Seligman. Additionally, as *The Times of Israel* reported in August 2018:

> Rather than join BDS, the Jewish president of the American Federation of Teachers hopes her group's progressive Zionist message will 'help bring Israel to its better angels. . . .' AFT is not the only union to have a history of supporting Israel. American labor unions had heavy Jewish representation at the time of Israel's birth. . . . Labor unions have also given millions of dollars to the Yitzhak Rabin Center. . . . Weingarten in particular has leaned into AFT supporting Israel's progressive camp. In 2016, Stav Shaffir, a young liberal Israeli lawmaker from the Labor Party, spoke at the AFT convention. . . . Supporting Israel is also a personal cause for Weingarten. She grew up in an involved Jewish home and attended Camp Ramah in New England. She is a member of Congregation Beit Simchat Torah in New York City and is newly married to its senior rabbi, Sharon Kleinbaum. And she is the latest Jewish AFT president, following predecessors like Sandra Feldman and Albert Shanker.

The National Education Association (NEA) teamed up with Gender Spectrum, the Human Rights Campaign (HRC) Foundation, the ACLU, and the National Center for Lesbian Rights (NCLR) to produce the 2015 guideline paper "Schools in Transition: A Guide for Supporting Transgender Students in K-12 Schools," with Jews Joel Baum and Asaf Orr as lead authors. A sample:

> Depending on the youth's particular circumstances, they may begin taking medications that delay the physical changes associated with puberty. Those medications act as a pause button and give the youth an opportunity to explore their gender identity without the distress of developing the permanent, unwanted physical characteristics of their assigned sex at birth. During this

time, the youth will work with their family and healthcare providers to develop a treatment plan, which may eventually include taking cross-sex hormones to induce a puberty that is consistent with their gender identity.

In California, the California Healthy Youth Act became law in 2015 and mandates sex education for grades 7–12 that will "teach pupils about gender, gender expression, gender identity, and explore the harm of negative gender stereotypes." There are now four US states that have passed laws effectively mandating the teaching of "LGBTQ history," with Illinois passing a law that took effect in July 2020 and had the state join the ranks of California, New Jersey, and Colorado. The Jewish billionaire governor of Illinois, J.B. Pritzker, signed into law the requirement that textbooks purchased with state grant funds must "include the roles and contributions of all people protected under the Illinois Human Rights Act" and that "the teaching of history in the United States shall include a study of the roles and contributions of lesbian, gay, bisexual, and transgender people in the history of this country." Well, why don't we go ahead and look at some of this history both in the United States and abroad, then.

# The She-Male Gaze

*"Nosebleeds and psycho-babble, I know it all too well.*
*The penis was from heaven and it went to hell.*
*I'm not a democrat, I'm a conversationalist.*
*If your aunt had balls, she'd be your uncle,*
*And you just can't seem to get that off your brain.*
*Give a straight answer? Not today and not tomorrow.*
*But why don't you come sit down. Tell the boss what's on your mind."*

– The Red Chord, "Black Santa"

It is difficult to pin-point precisely where the concept of "trans" originates, and though we do have some trace evidence from the ancient world, for our purposes in looking at the Western world we can probably look to Provence and a 1322 poem by the Jewish Kalonymus ben Kalonymus cursing having been born male and wishing to have been born a woman, with his penis referred to as "a lasting deformity." Professor Ruth Mazo Karras, whose "current research concerns masculinity in medieval Western Europe in both Christian and Jewish society," argues that a late-fourteenth-century London transvestite prostitute going by the name Eleanor Rykener was trans. The very first Jew to arrive in Canada was the disguised Esther Brandeau in 1738; prior to leaving France, she had "reinvented herself" as a male sailor under the name Jacques La Fargue. A novelization of Brandeau's story is presented by the Jewish Susan Glickman in *The Tale-Teller* (2012).

In Germany in late 1906, the Jewish Martha Baer, affiliated with B'nai B'rith, underwent one of the first "sex changes" that we know about, "transitioning" into a male as Karl M. Baer, and together with the Jewish Magnus Hirschfeld developed these notes into the semi-fictionalized, semi-autobiographical *Aus eines Mannes Mädchenjahren* (*Memoirs of a Man's Maiden Years*), published in 1907 under a pseudonym. In 1919, the Jewish Karl Grune adapted Baer's book into a script for a silent film.

1919 also marked the founding of the Institut für Sexualwissenschaft, or the Institute of Sex Research, in Berlin by the Jewish, homosexual "sexologist" Magnus Hirschfeld and his associate, the Jewish Arthur Kronfeld. For over twenty years prior, Hirschfeld's Scientific Humanitarian Committee had operated as a proto-LGBTQ "activist" organization. Starting the year before the Scientific Humanitarian Committee in 1896, Adolf Brand's periodical *Der Eigene* aimed to popularize the homosexual lifestyle and pederasty in particular. Brand joined up with Hirschfeld, Kronfeld, and their organization before splitting off on his own in 1903 to start a similar group called the Community of the Special with the Jewish anarchist "sexologist" Benedict Friedlaender, who had helped bankroll Hirschfeld's group. The Community of the Special folded five years later when Friedlaender committed suicide.

Hirschfeld and Kronfeld's Institute offered marriage and sex counseling, had a massive library of homosexual erotica and displays of all kinds of sex machines and contraptions, and provided "sexual education" as well as treatments for a new class of people considered to be "transvestites," as Hirschfeld coined them, or "transsexuals" later coined by David Oliver Cauldwell before the currently-accepted "transgenders" or simply "trans." Hirschfeld is widely credited as the originator of what is now known as transgenderism through the creation of the term "transvestite" as a precursor of sorts. Hirschfeld theorized that there were over fifty male variants on "gender" and is also incidentally credited by Sam Francis as being the inventor of the word "racist." Kronfeld was very interested in Freudian psychoanalysis.

Hirschfeld's group worked hard to diminish the ideas of Jewish, homosexual Marc-André Raffalovich, who had come to embrace Catholicism and understood with great clarity that the work of Hirschfeld and company would result in "moral chaos." Raffalovich accused them of being "propagandists for moral dissolution." For Raffalovich, the homosexual did not have to function as a force of subversion, but could—*should*—be duty-bound to grow personally and enhance society through artistic and spiritual pursuits, rather than being governed by base carnality. Though they may not have the same biological destiny as the heterosexual couple creating the next generation, in this way they might positively shape culture through other contributions. As this takes discipline and restraint, it was at odds with the "work" of the Scientific Humanitarian Committee.

A number of transvestites and transsexuals were "given care" at the Institute, most well-known being Rudolph/Dörchen ("Dora") Richter who worked for the Institute as a housemaid; in 1922, Richter elected to have Hirschfeld's team complete a bilateral orchiectomy (removal of the testicles). Richter's procedure was later documented as a resounding success by the Institute's Head of the Sexual Forensic Department, the Jewish Felix Abraham, whose research "interests" included exhibitionism, BDSM, and "age play," where a person role-plays as a child in a sexual situation.

Within a few years the Institute was drawing significant interest from the Soviet Union. In 1923, Soviet Health Commissar Nikolai Semashko visited the Institute, opening channels between the Institute and Moscow, with a parade of Soviet "researchers" visiting in the years following. In 1926, Hirschfeld's team made a reciprocal visit; Kronfeld would later flee to the USSR.

In 1921, Hirschfeld organized the First Congress for Sexual Reform, which led to the formation of the World League for Sexual Reform, and in 1929, Hirschfeld led the third congress in London, organized by the Jewish "sexologist" Norman Haire (who had changed his last name from Zions) and Dora Russell (Bertrand's second wife). Notable attendees included Sigmund Freud and Margaret Sanger, as well as a number of British feminists and birth control advocates. The last congress was held in 1932 in what is now the Czech Republic, hosted and organized by the

Jewish Hugo Iltis.[20]

The year prior, Jewish Institute physician Ludwig Levy-Lenz performed a penectomy (the removal of the penis) on Richter which was followed a few months later by a vaginoplasty conducted by Erwin Gohrbandt, marking a successful "gender reassignment surgery." Under the supervision of Hirschfeld, Levy-Lenz performed the initial "reassignment" operation on the Danish painter Einar Magnus Andreas Wegener in 1930 with the surgical removal of his testicles as he "transitioned" into Lili Elbe; a few weeks after Richter's vaginoplasty, Elbe's was attempted by Kurt Warnekros, along with a uterus transplant. Unsurprisingly, the uterus transplant was unsuccessful, and post-operative complications resulted in Elbe's untimely death.

Minus the obscure late-nineteenth-century New York City proto-LGBTQ advocacy group Cercle Hermaphroditos of which we know little, the first such significant organization in the United States was the Society for Human Rights in Chicago, founded in 1924 by Henry Gerber, who had been inspired by the work of Magnus Hirschfeld and the culture of decadence in Weimar Berlin while stationed with the US Army in Germany. It had a very short duration, but its influence was vital: in 1929, while cruising for gay sex, Harry Hay met one of the Society's members who inspired him to eventually help found the Mattachine Society, co-founded in 1950 by the major Communist Party figure Harry Hay and the Jewish fashion designer Rudi Gernreich, among others. Most of the original members were also avowed communists.

Hay was very intrigued by the work of Magnus Hirschfeld, Adolf Brand, and the Jewish director Leontine Sagan, whose films contained "lesbian themes." Gernreich is described as a pioneer of "unisex fashion" and stated that fashion and the avant-garde should be used to make political statements. Gernreich was romantically involved with the head of the UCLA French Department Oreste Pucciani, commonly credited with bringing the work of Jean-Paul Sartre into the American academy. Upon Gernreich's death, the ACLU established the Rudi Gernreich-Oreste Pucciani Endowment Fund to "fight for LGBT rights." The Jewish Pearl M. Hart, who fought the federal government's efforts to deport naturalized immigrants accused of subversive activities, was co-founder of Mattachine Midwest in 1965.

Earlier in his life, Hay had married Jewish Marxist Anna Platky at the behest of other Communist Party members who told Hay that homosexuality was the mark of bourgeois decadence. Hay was an outspoken supporter of the North American Man/Boy Love Association (NAMBLA) and wore a sign during the 1986 Los Angeles Pride parade protesting the exclusion of NAMBLA. Hay was a frequent participant in NAMBLA meetings and panels, and in 1994 NAMBLA was invited to join in the Spirit of Stonewall march with Hay's Radical Faeries, ACT UP, and others. For Hay: "If the parents and friends of gays are truly friends of gays, they would know from their gay kids that the relationship with an older man is precisely what thirteen-, fourteen-, and fifteen-year-old kids need more than anything else in the world."

ONE, Inc. was born out of the original Mattachine Society and in January 1953 began publishing its *One* magazine, which the US Postal Service eventually refused to deliver due to its obscene nature. On the basis of the Jewish pornographic publisher Samuel Roth's victory in 1957 (the same year Evelyn Hooker's "seminal"

---

[20] In 1938, Franz Boas and Albert Einstein secured a US visa for Iltis.

study was published) with the Supreme Court ruling in *Roth v. United States*, which redefined the Constitutional test for determining what constitutes obscenity under the First Amendment, ONE, Inc. emerged victorious the year following when the Supreme Court reversed a lower court ruling that the magazine violated obscenity laws. Roth, who attended Columbia University for one year, founded a bookstore and was also a writer. His *Now and Forever* is an imaginary conversation between Roth and Mr. Melting Pot Israel Zangwill. He also wrote *Jews Must Live* and consistently ran afoul of the law for the distribution of erotica.

Three years before the founding of the Mattachine Society, Alfred Kinsey, who received his PhD in biology from Harvard University, founded the Institute for Sex Research at Indiana University, still in operation today as the Kinsey Institute. In 1948, he published his team's first volume of "research," *Sexual Behavior in the Human Male*, and in 1953 its sequel *Sexual Behavior in the Human Female* was published. Kinsey is regarded as the progenitor of the 10% of the male population as homosexual statistic,[21] when numerous subsequent studies have put that percentage at less than half that, for example the Williams Institute at UCLA's 2011 findings that 3.5% of adults in the United States identified as LGB and 0.3% identified as transgender. Additionally, the report's author Gary J. Gates notes that, "In general, the non-US surveys . . . vary from 1.2% to 2.1%, estimat[ing] lower percentages of LGB-identified individuals." The 2004 film *Kinsey* with Liam Neeson gave the familiar Hollywood treatment to this "icon," and in 2014 the United Nations granted the Kinsey Institute "special consultative status." In 2019, the Kinsey Institute was favorably cited by many major media outlets, such as *The New York Times*, the *Huffington Post*, *Vice*, and *Newsweek*, and on December 31st, 2019, Kinsey Institute Research Fellow Justin Lehmiller appeared on an episode of *Dr. Phil*. Their fall 2019 lecture series featured transgender "activist" Jessica Lynn.

Their certification with the American Psychological Association and their Scholarly Concentration in Human Sexuality and Health in partnership with the Indiana University School of Medicine focusing on "competency in practice with LGBTQ+ patients and current best practices" looks an awful lot like the Institute of Sex Research from the outside, although I must state that this is speculative. Lastly, in addition to the in-house members of their Director's Advisory Council, there are also representatives from Northwestern University's Feinberg School of Medicine, the David Geffen Foundation, K&L Gates LLP, the American Institute of Bisexuality, the *Journal of Sex Research*, and the University of Southampton (UK) in the person of Cynthia A. Graham.

Around the time Alfred Kinsey was becoming a rock star, the media also began promoting Christine Jorgensen, about whom Louis Farrakhan recorded the song, "Is She Is or Is She Ain't?" Jorgensen was a patient of the part-Jewish Harry Benjamin, a German émigré who had been an associate of Magnus Hirschfeld's and who was in close contact with surgeons in Denmark, where Jorgensen received hormones, an orchiectomy, and a penectomy. Upon returning to the United States in 1953, Jorgensen became an overnight celebrity, and with Benjamin launched a career as what we might today regard as a "transgender advocate." Benjamin was also the "medical advisor" to Jorgensen's eventual vaginoplasty and wrote of Jorgensen, "Indeed Christine, without you, probably none of this would have happened; the grant, my

---

[21] Kinsey also claimed 37% of men had homosexual physical contact to the point of orgasm at least once.

publications, lectures, etc."

Jorgensen was not Benjamin's first patient; that "honor" goes to a patient simply known as "Van," referred to Benjamin by Alfred Kinsey in 1948. Benjamin set up the appointments for the surgeries in Germany where Van became Susan, at which point Susan apparently moves to Canada and disappears from the historical record. Before sending Van off to become Susan, however, Benjamin had begun to inject his referral with estrogen and to document the effects. Jorgensen would also be prescribed estrogen, the hormonal element previously missing from the "reassignment" equation. Despite the very clear sex-change effects hormones have on the body, however, the idea of the sex change versus the gender reassignment somehow still boils down to a social constructivist element, a collision of contradictions no LGBTQ advocate or theorist has ever been able to square, because they can't.

Benjamin was not finished. In 1963 he oversaw the "successful" female-to-male "transition" of Reed Erickson, and the following year, Benjamin set up a foundation dedicated to homosexual and transgender "rights." As we can see, transgenderism and homosexuality have consistently been framed by even the activists and researchers themselves as inextricable, an acknowledgement also reflected in the LGBTQ-et cetera acronym. Despite the constant talk of "gender identity," there remains this persistent connection to sexuality.

In 1965, John Money and Claude Migeon opened the Johns Hopkins Gender Identity Clinic and commenced surgical "reassignment" procedures the following year. Money had a working relationship with Harry Benjamin, and incidentally, Benjamin's "seminal" work *The Transsexual Phenomenon* was published that same year, 1966. Money received the Magnus Hirschfeld Medal in 2002 from the German Society for Social Science Sexuality Research; other winners include: the Jewish Jonathan Ned Katz, author of *The Invention of Heterosexuality*; the Jewish Ruth Westheimer, who readers will likely know as sex therapist "Dr. Ruth";[22] and the Jewish Richard Green, colleague of Harry Benjamin's and collaborator with John Money on *Transsexualism and Sex Reassignment* (1969) published by Johns Hopkins Press and in coordination with the Harry Benjamin Foundation.

Richard Green was a founding member of the Harry Benjamin International Gender Dysphoria Association (HBIGDA) in 1979, named in honor of Benjamin, which is distinct from Benjamin's own Harry Benjamin Foundation. Green was HBIGDA's President in the late 1990s, taught at UCLA, was on the APA DSM-4's Subcommittee on Gender Identity Disorders, and was co-counsel with the ACLU in a 1998 case challenging the Boy Scouts for refusing to allow a gay man to become an assistant Scoutmaster. Green was the founder of the International Academy of Sex Research and also held several prominent posts in the UK such as research director and consultant psychiatrist at the Gender Identity Clinic (founded in 1966) near Charing Cross Hospital and Professor of Psychological Medicine, Imperial College, London.

One of Benjamin's former patients, Reed Erickson, had established the Erickson Educational Foundation and infused the Johns Hopkins clinic with large sums of

---

[22] "[Dr. Ruth] continues to provide sex advice to young and old alike. This superwoman is also a wine maker: her low alcohol wine supposedly helps men, erm, euphemistically 'stay active' for sexual relations after drinking wine, as the low percentage of alcohol won't inhibit what's going on down there." From Miller, "Six Jews."

money to finance its operations; the Harry Benjamin Foundation also received funding from Erickson during this time period. As with Magnus Hirschfeld's Institute of Sex Research, soon interested parties began visiting Johns Hopkins as a sex change Mecca to learn about their procedures. The Harry Benjamin Foundation and the Johns Hopkins clinic advised figures such as Don Laub on establishing their own gender identity clinics. One of Laub's earlier patients, the Jewish Sandy Stone, is regarded as one of the pioneers of transgender studies as an articulated and distinct discipline. Similar clinics were also opened at the University of Minnesota and Northwestern University.

The influence of Benjamin and his small cohort simply cannot be understated, and they serve as the extension of Hirschfeld's "pioneering" practices; Benjamin's letters are actually archived at the Magnus Hirschfeld Archive for Sexology, Humboldt University in Berlin. Benjamin's colleague, office-mate, and another HBIGDA founding member the Jewish Leo Wollman claimed to have seen more patients than Benjamin himself.

Other affiliates of Benjamin's and his circle included the author of "Psychological Testing of Transsexuals," Ruth Rae Doorbar, who ultimately moved to Jamaica with her boyfriend and began "pioneering" work there, and Columbia University alumnus Wardell Pomeroy, part of Kinsey's research team on *Sexual Behavior in the Human Male* and *Sexual Behavior in the Human Female* and author of several adolescent sexuality books. One of Britain's most famous transgenders, Jan Morris, formerly James Morris, became convinced he had been "born in the wrong body" after meeting with Harry Benjamin. Morris's 1974 book *Conundrum* documents the whole process of "sex change" including the surgical procedures conducted by the French surgeon Georges Burou in Casablanca, Morocco at his Clinique du Parc.

Burou's clinic was a veritable trans factory; one of his most famous patients, Jacques Charles Dufresnoy (Jacqueline Charlotte), had been performing for several years as a showgirl under the name Coccinelle when Burou successfully completed his vaginoplasty in 1958. Dufresnoy founded the organization "Devenir Femme" (To Become Woman) and was a regular performer at the Le Carrousel de Paris nightclub, which also featured regular acts by English "trans woman" April Ashley (also a visitor to Burou's clinic for surgery in 1960) and Marie-Pierre Pruvot, or "Bambi," subject of Jewish homosexual Sébastien Lifshitz's 2013 documentary *Bambi*.

As the tail-end of the so-called "Sexual Revolution" approached, pornography was becoming mainstream, and a new wave of feminism was cresting. "Gay rights" were becoming the next "social justice" frontier in America; the Stonewall Inn riots of 1969 serve as a convenient starting point for many "gay rights historians," and in some ways that's fair, but in others it's simply reflective of the mythologizing of a fringe incident. More consequential from an institutional standpoint is the decision of "activist"-supporting foundation RESIST to begin funding the Gay Liberation Front (GLF) in 1970. Soon the GLF had chapters in at least half-a-dozen major American cities. Though the funding was sporadic and the amounts relatively low, connections such as the New York Foundation's[23] disbursal of $5,000 to Lambda

---

[23] "The New York Foundation was established in 1909 when Louis A. Heinsheimer, a partner in banking firm Kuhn, Loeb & Co., died. In his will Heinsheimer bequeathed $1 million to 'the Jewish charities of New York' under the condition that they choose to federate within a year of his death. One year later when the conditions stipulated in Heinsheimer's will had not been met (the Federation of Jewish Philanthropies would not be founded until 1917) the $1 million bequest reverted into the hands of his brother,

Legal in 1976 established a nascent framework to build upon in later years.

As the 1970s progressed, more clinics were established and advocacy groups formed, such as the Gender Dysphoria Clinic at Queen Victoria Hospital in Melbourne, Australia in 1975, the Astraea Lesbian Foundation for Justice in 1977, what is now ILGA in 1978, and the Harry Benjamin International Gender Dysphoria Association (HBIGDA) in 1979.

The idea for the Gender Dysphoria Clinic was introduced to Queen Victoria Hospital by Trudy Kennedy and Herbert Bower. Kennedy was ultimately investigated by the state's medical board and the clinic forced to shut down temporarily amidst allegations that, as Jill Stark writes for *The Sydney Morning Herald*:

> Patients with psychiatric problems have been wrongly diagnosed as transsexuals and encouraged to have radical gender reassignment surgery. *The Sunday Age* has been told at least eight former patients of the Gender Dysphoria Clinic at Melbourne's Monash Medical Centre believe they may have been misdiagnosed. Some have tried to commit suicide while struggling to live as the opposite sex after the irreversible operations. But as the clinic has limited patient follow-up, it is difficult to determine how many patients may have been adversely affected by the surgery.... One former patient, "Andrew", who was 21 when he had his penis and testicles replaced with a false vagina, was awarded damages after claiming Dr Kennedy misdiagnosed him as a transsexual in the late 1980s.... Since the surgery, he has twice tried to take his own life and has undergone operations to reconstruct a penis and remove breast implants. He says he will never be able to have children, is unable to work and feels like a "mutilated freak".... Countless patients were given sex changes without proper mental health checks before or after surgery.... Dr Kennedy claims the same "political forces" that tried to shut down abortion clinics are trying to close the gender dysphoria facility, which has performed sexual reassignment surgery on more than 600 people—a third of all referrals—since it was founded in 1975 by Dr Kennedy and Austrian-born Dr Herbert Bower.

Bower, "the only child of Austrian Jewish parents ... grew up in the Vienna of Freud," and had been "treating" patients since 1950.

HBIGDA eventually became the World Professional Association of Transgender Health (WPATH) in 2007; several of their presidents trained at Johns Hopkins, and all have been consequential in the spread of transgenderism. Their second president and a founding member, Don Laub, mentioned earlier, was the chief of Plastic Surgery at the Stanford University School of Medicine and as WPATH's "History of the Association" written by Aaron Devor[24] details:

---

Alfred M. Heinsheimer, who, in turn, donated the money to the New York Foundation. The New York Foundation was created by Edward Henderson, Jacob H. Schiff, Isaac Seligman, and Paul Warburg in order that they might 'distribute ... resources for altruistic purposes, charitable, benevolent, educational, or otherwise, within the United States of America.'" From the "New York Foundation" Wikipedia entry.

[24] According to Devor's biography at the LGBTQ Religious Archives Network: "Devor was president of the Jewish Federation of Victoria and Vancouver Island in British Columbia, Canada from 2013-2016 and on the Board since 2011. He has been the Past-President since 2016. He served as a Board member

He managed about 2,000 patients, himself evaluating and treating, along with other members of the Gender Dysphoria Program Committee. Many were accepted into the program which was run both by Stanford University and the Palo Alto Gender Dysphoria Program, of which he was the President. The committee consisted of faculty members, behavioral scientists, social workers and plastic surgeons. This committee drew heavily from multidisciplinary expertise in urology, gynecology, endocrinology, general surgery, and consultations on most patients. In the course of surgery, he invented and popularized three operations: rectosigmoidvaginoplasty (the "Rolls Royce Vagina"), metoidioplasty (using female tissues with hormones to form male structures), post-modern phalloplasty (fasciocutaneus fat and skin, from the abdomen tubularized to form the shaft of the penis). It was made sensitive using a microsurgical nerve transfer from the erotic nerve in the lower abdomen. The placement of a removable silicone urinary assist device (UAD) and also an implanted erectile device, completed the final two functions of urination and sexual intercourse. . . . He organized two international gender conferences at Stanford University and two others in Bordeaux, France, and New York City, New York.

HBIGDA/WPATH's fourth president, the Jewish Ira B. Pauly, worked closely with Harry Benjamin and is credited for undertaking the first global review of the published outcome data on transsexualism in 1965. Their seventh president (1991–1995), Leah Schaefer was:

A pioneer in the field of gender and sexuality. She served two terms as The Association's president and co-authored the first five versions of the Standards of Care. She received an EdD from Columbia University Teacher's College, where she wrote her ground-breaking dissertation later published in 1973 as *Women and Sex: Sexual Experiences and Reactions of a Group of Thirty Women as Told to a Female Psychotherapist.* Leah maintained a large private practice in New York City, and safeguarded the Harry Benjamin archives for many years. In 2007 she, along with executor to the Harry Benjamin estate Dr. Charles Ihlenfeld, donated a substantial portion of these archives to the Kinsey Institute.

---

of Hillel British Columbia 2007-2018. He was the Jewish member on the Greater Victoria Police Diversity Advisory Committee 2005-2010. Devor thinks that he may have been the first out trans man elected to any of these positions. Devor served as a President, Past-President, Vice-President, and board member of Victoria's Conservative Congregation Emanuel 1999-2003. During his time as President and Vice-President Devor was living as a lesbian and may have been the first out lesbian to be elected as a vice-president or president of a Conservative synagogue." Per the *Jewish Independent*, the following were from Devor's remarks read at a July 27th, 2018 Jewish Pride, "organized by the Jewish Pride planning committee and made possible by the support of a record 31 Jewish participating organizations, led by the Centre for Israel and Jewish Affairs, Pacific Region, and the work of numerous volunteers and community members. Funds raised at the Shabbat dinner will go towards supporting future Jewish LGBTQ+ events over the coming year.": "I want to remind you that many of the people who took the risks to fight back against shame and oppression in those early days – and in all the days since – were gender diverse people: trans people, non-binary people, two-spirit people, genderqueer people, transsexuals, transvestites, drag queens and drag kings, and queers, many of whom were also Jews . . . The fact that all of you are here tonight is a beautiful testament to the progressive thread that runs through much of Jewish life and culture."

Ihlenfeld was another associate of Benjamin's; his most famous patient was Renée Richards, born Richard Raskind, "a nice Jewish boy" from Queens. Richards had been receiving hormone injections from Ihlenfeld and had actually planned to travel to Casablanca to see Georges Burou before backing out. Richards was eventually referred to surgeon Roberto C. Granato, Sr. by Harry Benjamin and ended up being successful in forcing the United States Tennis Association to allow "her" to compete as a female professional following a judge's ruling in 1977.

Former WPATH President Eli Coleman is the Chair in Sexual Health at the Program in Human Sexuality (PHS) at the University of Minnesota and has been a frequent "technical consultant" on sexual health issues to the World Health Organization (WHO) and the Pan American Health Organization (PAHO); Coleman is the founding editor of the *International Journal of Transgenderism*.

The University of Minnesota's Program in Human Sexuality is at the forefront of the transgender agenda today. Affiliated researchers and consultants include individuals with WPATH, the University of Toronto, Columbia University, the Mayo Clinic, Yale University, the University of London, the University of Birmingham, University of Tromsø (Norway), KU Leuven (Belgium), John Hopkins, Karolinska Institute (Sweden), the University of Dar es Salaam (Tanzania), the Minnesota Transgender Health Coalition ("We are working for racial, social, and economic justice, and recognize that we are part of a multi-issue movement that includes gender liberation, as well as differences around race, class, age, sexuality, ability, immigrant status, and much more"), and many more.

The Nation Center for Gender Spectrum Health of the Program in Human Sexuality is given financial support by the Jewish transgender billionaire Jennifer Pritzker's TAWANI Foundation and Jennifer Pritzker directly, the General Mills Foundation, Joshua Safer (Executive Director of the Mount Sinai Center for Transgender Medicine and Surgery, Professor of Medicine at the Icahn School of Medicine at Mount Sinai, inaugural president of the United States Professional Association for Transgender Health-USPATH, serves on the Global Education Initiative committee and on the Standards of Care revision committee for WPATH, co-author of the Endocrine Society guidelines for the medical care of transgender patients), and former WPATH Presidents Eli Coleman, Stan Monstrey, and Walter Bockting. Another donor is Lana Wachowski—one of the former Wachowski Brothers (directors of *The Matrix*), both of whom are now apparently the Wachowski Sisters—as is the Jewish Loren Schechter, a "trans advocate" and plastic surgeon specializing in "gender confirmation surgery." Schechter received his medical degree from the University of Chicago Pritzker School of Medicine and is on the Board of Directors of the World Professional Association of Transgender Health (WPATH).

Jane Fonda is a donor to the Pepper Schwartz Professorship in Sexuality and Aging, and the Chair in Sexual Health has received funding from Walter Bockting, Fritz Klein, Jennifer Pritzker, and John Money.

The Bean Robinson Chair in Clinical Sexual Health has received funding from Coleman, the TAWANI Foundation, Gilead Sciences, the American Institute of Bisexuality (founded by the Jewish Fritz Klein), WPATH, the Kinsey Institute, the American Sexual Health Association (John D. Rockefeller, Jr. was an initial financial contributor), the Society for the Scientific Study of Sexuality (Harry Benjamin was a charter member and Richard Green, Leah Schaefer, Eli Coleman, John Money,

Walter Bockting, and Wardell Pomeroy—Columbia University alumnus and co-author with Alfred Kinsey on *Sexual Behavior in the Human Male* and *Sexual Behavior in the Human Female*—are all among its past presidents), and Susan Stiritz. The Jewish Stiritz is the chair of Sexual Health and Education at Washington University in St. Louis, Missouri.[25]

The Joycelyn Elders Chair in Sexual Health Education has received funding from Jennifer Pritzker, the TAWANI Foundation, Eli Coleman, the Planned Parenthood Federation of America, Apothecus Pharmaceutical Corp., the American Sexually Transmitted Diseases Association, and the Guttmacher Institute.

Other University of Minnesota Program in Human Sexuality donors include Agouron Pharmaceuticals (a subsidiary of Pfizer), Bristol-Myers Squibb, California Exotic Novelties LLC, Forest Pharmaceuticals, Roche Laboratories, and Procter & Gamble.

The transgender Marci Bowers is listed as a donor to the Program in Human Sexuality's National Center for Gender Spectrum Health as well as the Chair in Sexual Health and the Joycelyn Elders Chair in Sexual Health Education. Bowers is the protégé of the Jewish Dr. Stanley Biber, the surgeon whose work made "going to Trinidad" a euphemism for "sex change" operations; Biber performed thousands over the course of his lifetime, conducting his first operation in 1969 after studying diagrams from Johns Hopkins, which had been conducting these procedures for a few years by then, and is credited as being an early "pioneer" in transgender surgeries. Bowers took over Biber's clinic in Colorado after his retirement in 2003.

Bowers helped initiate transgender surgical education programs at Sheba Medical Center in Tel Aviv in 2014, the Icahn School of Medicine at Mount Sinai in New York in 2016,[26] Denver Health in Colorado in 2018, and the University of Toronto in 2019. The transgender surgical fellowship at Mount Sinai, the second Jewish hospital to be established in the United States, is considered to be first of its kind in the US; the Mount Sinai Center for Transgender Medicine and Surgery's (CTMS) website states that:

---

[25] Washington University houses one of the "preeminent" "transgender centers" in the United States, where they: "Administer gender-affirming hormones that make a person's physical body match their gender identity . . . [Provide] referrals to surgeons with expertise in gender-affirming surgery . . . pre-exposure prophylaxis (PrEP) and comprehensive HIV and screening for sexually transmitted diseases . . . pelvic care for transmen provided within the transgender clinic . . . [and house an] interdisciplinary group that includes breast and plastic surgeons, urological surgery, speech therapy, reproductive health, dermatology, trans-affirmative gynecologic care and mental health."

[26] The Mount Sinai School of Medicine was re-named the Icahn School of Medicine at Mount Sinai "honoring" the Jewish Carl Icahn, who has been dogged by accusations of financial improprieties all the way back to at least 1982 when Dan River Mills filed a complaint in the Federal District Court for the Western District of Virginia charging that Icahn had acquired its stock with "'proceeds derived through prior acts of extortion, mail fraud and securities fraud." Icahn was the subject of a federal investigation into insider stock-trading abuses in 1987 and Icahn came under federal investigation for insider trading yet again in 2014. Icahn is known to have collaborated with Jewish securities fraudster Ivan "Greed is Good" Boesky on attempted takeovers of Phillips Petroleum Co. and Gulf & Western Industries Inc. in the mid-1980s. Icahn also has ties to another Jewish financial criminal, Dennis Levine. Icahn's name has come up in possible corrupt political dealings of late but nothing concrete has been proven; in 2017, eight senators wrote multiple federal agencies asking them to investigate whether energy companies owned by Carl Icahn financially benefitted from his position as a special adviser to President Trump. In 2018, Icahn faced more allegations of possible insider trading after a federal filing revealed he started selling off millions of dollars in stock for a company that significantly depends on steel just a few days before the Trump administration started publicly considering a steel tariff.

CTMS developed the first full-year fellowship to train doctors in gender-affirming surgery and gender-affirming psychiatric care. Additionally, medical students and residents can sign up for an elective experience to gain exposure to all areas of transgender health. These programs will train the next generation of providers caring for transgender patients.

In 2018 and 2019, Bowers performed the first live surgical vaginoplasties in WPATH-sponsored surgical educational programs at Mount Sinai; Bowers is on the Board of WPATH and has served on the Board for both GLAAD and the Transgender Law Center. A number of the researchers at the Center for Transgender Medicine and Surgery include Joshua D. Safer, Tamar Reisman (who completed her Endocrinology, Diabetes and Metabolism fellowship at UCLA's David Geffen School of Medicine), Zil Goldstein, and Max Lichtenstein.

WPATH Board member Asa Radix is a clinician, educator, and researcher whose main area of expertise is in transgender health and HIV. Radix is the Senior Director of Research and Education at Callen-Lorde Community Health Center and Associate Clinical Professor of Medicine at New York University. Radix is a Columbia University alumnus.

Several of the more recent presidents of WPATH have been from Europe, such as Stan Monstrey, Professor in Plastic Surgery and a leading member of Ghent University Hospital's Center for Sexology and Gender "where both FTM and MTF surgeries are performed weekly" and where Monstrey apparently has a five-year waiting list, and the Dutch Walter Bockting, who completed his post-doctoral fellowship at the University of Minnesota Medical School, and was employed there until 2012, eventually becoming Director of Research for the Program in Human Sexuality, before accepting a leadership position with Columbia University's Gender Identity Program. He is a member of the APA.

Stephen Whittle, "who transitioned from female to male in 1975" and has been teaching at Manchester Metropolitan University since 1993, in 2007 became "the first trans person and non-medic to become President of WPATH." In 1979 Whittle joined Self Help Association for Transsexuals (SHAFT—no pun needed), in 1989 started the UK's FTM Network, in 1992 co-founded and became Vice President of Press for Change (PFC), a UK transgender lobbying group, and from its founding in 2005 until 2011 was with Transgender Europe, eventually serving as President. According to Devor's summary on the WPATH website:

> He has advised the UK government on implementing gender recognition legislation and full protection in all aspects of life in the Equality Act 2010. Stephen has since advised on transgender law to the UK, Irish, Italian, Japanese and South African governments & the European Union, the Council of Europe & the European Commission.

Whittle has also been part of the NHS Gender Identity Services Clinical Reference Group and collaborated with Susan Stryker on *The Transgender Studies Reader* in 2006. Whittle's protégé Jamison Green was on the WPATH Board of Directors during Whittle's two years in charge and eventually served as President. Green is the founder of Jamison Green & Associates, which provides "education and policy consulting on transgender and transsexual issues" to major clients such as the US Securities and Exchange Commission, Macy's, Kaiser Permanente, Genentech, Capital One, IBM, BP, and Booz Allen Hamilton, and helped establish the Human Rights Campaign Foundation's Corporate Equality Index in 2002. The researcher Peggy Cohen-Kettenis, whose work is regarded as "foundational" for "gender reassignment" is a WPATH Board of Directors alumnus.

WPATH's *Standards of Care* revision process was made possible through a grant from Jennifer Pritzker's TAWANI Foundation and an anonymous donor. Pritzker and TAWANI received a Philanthropy Award from WPATH for their "longstanding support." It should come as no surprise, then, to learn that in 2016 the Jewish transgender billionaire Jennifer (né James) Pritzker gave $2 million through the TAWANI Foundation to the University of Victoria in British Columbia, Canada to establish a chair of transgender studies to go along with its Transgender Archives. Jewish "trans man" Aaron Devor, founder of the archives, was named the inaugural Research Chair in Transgender Studies. Pritzker described the donation as a "good investment," and make no mistake, it is an investment.

WPATH's goal is to "promote evidence based care, education, research, advocacy, public policy, and respect in transgender health." It has regional arms in the US with USPATH and in Europe with EPATH. Starbucks was the first company in the world to ask WPATH to help translate their recommended standards of care into a company medical benefits policy.

WPATH member and Brandeis University alumnus Sari L. Reisner's resumé includes current or former positions of: Assistant Professor in the Department of Medicine at Harvard Medical School; Assistant Professor in the Department of Epidemiology at Harvard T.H. Chan School of Public Health; Director of Transgender Health Research at The Fenway Institute;[27] Lead Investigator and Director of Transgender Research at Brigham and Women's Hospital (which is tellingly in the Section of Men's Health, Aging and Metabolism, in the Division of Endocrinology, Diabetes, and Hypertension); and Associate Scientific Researcher in the Division of General Pediatrics at Boston Children's Hospital. Reisner states that "Gender diversity exists in every culture and geographic context. It is to be celebrated, not pathologized." Reisner is the lead author of a paper in *The Lancet*'s first series on transgender health; *The Lancet* in its biographical blurb on Reisner states that "Reisner's work is helping to advance this agenda." Sean Cahill, Director of Health Policy Research at The Fenway Institute, claimed in testimony before the Boston City Council in 2018 that a ridiculous 15% of Massachusetts high school students are LGBT.

Harvard is a major incubator of the LGBTQ agenda; we will get to many more instances later, but one major example is that of Jewish homosexual Instructor in

---

[27] "The Fenway Institute is an interdisciplinary center for research, education, training and policy development with a pioneering history of community and academic collaborations. Our integration with clinical services has enabled technology and health information innovation as well as real-time clinical interventions with key populations. . . . Our strategic priority areas include epidemiology of SGM health, sexual and reproductive health, with a concentration on HIV/AIDS; transgender health; behavioral health interventions; health information technology; health policy research; education, training and technical assistance for health systems and social services; and mentoring early career scholars. We also occasionally engage in targeted research projects, such as COVID-19 vaccine trials, in response to significant public health events and other circumstances."

Medicine at Harvard Medical School and Medical Director of Massachusetts General Hospital's Transgender Health Program Robbie Goldstein. The latter program was established primarily through Goldstein's efforts. In January 2020, Massachusetts General Hospital sponsored the Evening Lecture Series talk by Goldstein, "Trans Rights are Human Rights: The Importance of Gender-Affirming Care."

Harvard Medical School runs the Sexual and Gender Minority Health Equity Initiative, which is according to their website:

> A three-year plan to amend the MD curriculum so that all students and faculty clinicians become well equipped to provide high-quality, holistic health care for sexual and gender minority patients of all ages. Our goals include:
> - increasing visibility of lesbian, gay, bisexual, transgender, nonbinary, and queer (LGBTQ) students, faculty, and staff;
> - discussing issues particular to being an LGBTQ doctor, trainee, and dentist;
> - fostering awareness of the needs and concerns of LGBTQ patients;
> - ensuring understanding in the curriculum and inclusion of LGBTQ health topics;
> - developing a supportive community among students, faculty, and staff.

The Fenway Institute and Harvard Medical School Continuing Education co-hosted the 2020 Advancing Excellence in Transgender Health Conference. Kenneth Mayer is the Medical Research Director and Co-Chair of The Fenway Institute; Professor of Medicine at Harvard Medical School; Professor in the Department of Global Health and Population at Harvard School of Public Health; Director of HIV Prevention Research and Attending Physician at Beth Israel Lahey Health; and Adjunct Professor of Medicine and Community Health at Brown University. He is glad that HIV-positive people can move freely into the country along with the rest of Emma Lazarus's "wretched refuse" because true to form he believes "we are now a global gene pool because of international travel, so the need is to deal with these problems on a global level. One cannot think of them as geographically isolated, or hermetically sealed." This is the kind of sentiment rapidly becoming ironclad law of the Last Men to drag humanity down into the cesspool of the lowest-common-denominators and then go lower still until it's nothing but a debased and sickly horror show being ruled from the top by the Inverted Persons of Dark Age depravity. Feeling disgusted by these people and their agenda is perfectly natural and healthy.

Sabra L. Katz-Wise is an Assistant Professor in Adolescent/Young Adult Medicine at Boston Children's Hospital (BCH), in Pediatrics at Harvard Medical School (HMS), and in Social and Behavioral Sciences at the Harvard T. H. Chan School of Public Health. Katz-Wise's research "investigates sexual orientation and gender identity development, sexual fluidity, health inequities related to sexual orientation and gender identity in adolescents and young adults, and psychosocial functioning in families with transgender youth." Katz-Wise is involved with "advocacy efforts at BCH to improve the workplace climate and patient care for LGBTQ individuals, including her role as co-chair for the BCH Rainbow Consortium on Sexual and Gender Diversity. She also serves on the HMS LGBT Advisory Committee and is a HMS Sexual and Gender Minority Curriculum Development Fellow." According to Katz-Wise's biography, "Dr. Katz-Wise is queer-identified and a strong ally to transgender communities. When she's not learning about LGBTQ health, she likes to practice yoga, travel, and spend time with her wife, toddler, and cat."

Katz-Wise is on the research team of The Trans Teen and Family Narratives Project, a "community-based research study funded by the National Institutes of Health (NIH)," along with individuals such as L.B. Moore who is described thusly:

> LB is a white, non-binary Jew with disabilities who is passionate about racial justice, meaningful relationships with other creatures, and getting enough sleep.... You can find LB at conferences and elsewhere talking about intersectional justice, liberation and anti-oppression, behavioral health, HIV, LGBTQ+ topics, and—of course!—trans and nonbinary youth.

The Advisory Board includes Diane Ehrensaft ("I grew up in a very left-liberal Jewish household in Chicago. We understood what it was to be part of a minority, and we were very focused on social justice. I was part of very progressive Jewish youth groups, and I went to a progressive Jewish camp.") and Roberta Goldman (adjunct professor at Harvard and Clinical Professor of Family Medicine, Warren Alpert Medical School of Brown University).

Among the co-signing individuals and organizations supporting The Fenway Institute's 2014 letter to the Office of the National Coordinator for Health Information Technology, Department of Health and Human Services regarding "new code sets for data collection [for] . . . Sexual orientation: asexual; bisexual; gay; heterosexual; lesbian; questioning (a person who is questioning his/her sexual orientation); decline to answer; and not applicable (ages 0–17); Gender identity: Gender variant; man; intersex; questioning (a person who is questioning his or her sexual orientation); transgender; woman; decline to answer; and not applicable (ages 0–17)" were included: the Williams Institute (UCLA); the University of California-San Francisco (UCSF) LGBT Resource Center; UCSF Center of Excellence for Transgender Health; National Council of Jewish Women; David Moskowitz, New York Medical College; Arthur Lipkin, Mass Commission on LGBTQ Youth; Douglas Krakower, Beth Israel Deaconess Medical Center; Harriet Cohen, Texas Christian University; the Mayo Clinic; the Mazzoni Center; Lambda Legal; William Cohen, Harrington Park Press; Jesse Ehrenfeld, Vanderbilt University School of Medicine; Harvard Law School Center for Health Law & Policy Innovation; the Center for American Progress; and amfAR, The Foundation for AIDS Research.

amfAR was launched in September 1985 with a $250,000 donation from the actor Rock Hudson and the merger of two organizations: the Los Angeles-based National AIDS Research Foundation, spearheaded by Elizabeth Taylor and the Jewish Michael S. Gottlieb, then-assistant professor at UCLA Medical Center; and the New York-based AIDS Medical Foundation, formed by the Jewish Joseph Sonnabend and Mathilde Krim, who had converted to Judaism in 1948 before marrying David Danon. While living in Switzerland, Krim was very active in helping the Zionist-terrorist organization Irgun (responsible for the King David Hotel bombing in 1946, resulting in 91 fatalities) procure arms, and upon moving to the US, was a very active fundraiser for Israeli causes. Krim later re-married, this time to Arthur Krim, lawyer, advisor to Lyndon B. Johnson and other presidents, movie studio mogul, and former head of the Democratic Party Financing Committee. Mathilde Krim was also a major supporter of "gay rights." Harvey Weinstein was central to a very public and very suspect "donation" deal with amfAR in 2015.

Returning to WPATH, another of its most influential members is Dr. Miroslav L. Djordjevic, the leader of the Belgrade Center for Genital Reconstructive Surgery in Serbia. Djordjevic is also a member of the American Academy of Pediatrics, which attacked Dr. Cretella and her organization. He is also a member of EPATH, and has spent time in Boston in affiliation with Harvard University and the Boston Children's Hospital. Djordjevic trained under Dr. Sava Perović, described as "narcissistic" and suffering from a "Freudian God complex" via Aleks Eror for *Vice*:

> Sava Perović started doing these operations in the 80s, and during the 90s a team formed around him that operated in completely criminal circumstances. . . . They earned huge money off of trans individuals, charging them up to five, six, seven thousand Deutsche marks [roughly $8,200–$11,500 in 1993], except that Sava would always change that figure—one day he'd tell you one price, a different day another. He was known to pull patients off the operating table mid-operation, because these were private procedures done in state clinics outside of working hours, and they couldn't let their colleagues see what they were doing. It was all done under the counter and the state tolerated it.

This is because the state will not tolerate intolerance of course. Facing prospective European Union membership, Serbia has diligently held gay pride parades which "have only gone peacefully thanks to a combination of EU pressure and military-scale police operations." Tells you something about "liberal democracy," does it not?

While killing hundreds of Serbian civilians during NATO's "peacekeeping" bombing operations in Yugoslavia, NATO's Supreme Allied Commander Europe (SACEUR) Wesley Clark, whose father was Jewish, said that, "There is no place in modern Europe for ethnically pure states. That's a 19th-century idea and we are trying to transition it into the 21st century, and we are going to do it with multi-ethnic states." Following NATO's bombing campaign, international pressure, and the charging of Slobodan Milošević with a manufactured genocide, the neo-liberal Establishment finally secured the beleaguered president's ouster in October 2000, and one of the first acts of the not-at-all-astroturfed "resistance" in what *Vice* calls an "irrepressible hunger for democracy" was to announce—what else?—a Pride parade in Belgrade scheduled for the following year. Held two days after Milošević was sent to The Hague to stand trial for bogus "war crimes," the parade was disrupted by furious Serbs.[28] Billed by the media as "homophobic," more likely it was a venting of frustration against an obvious expression of occupation with the marchers as an extension of the globalist Establishment. Perhaps there was some "homophobia" there, too, but what is construed as homophobia is more likely a healthy objection to an understanding of what would morph into the horror show parading around today. Five years later, Milošević suffered a "mysterious" heart attack in his cell.

*This* is what "liberal democracy" looks like. By now you should see that this tome

---

[28] Following his arrest, the government was told to extradite Milošević to the International Criminal Tribunal for the Former Yugoslavia (ICTY) or risk losing financial aid from the IMF and World Bank. The US and NATO had backed the "Kosovo Liberation Army," which was literally comprised of various criminals, Muslim terrorists, and drug traffickers.

is not simply a dissection of all things trans, but a dive into all the atrocities wrought by the age of Jewish consumerism. This entire LGBT "movement" (along with all the intersectional pursuits of anti-racism, etc.) masquerades as an organic progression of morality toward the heights of tolerance and goodness, while simultaneously destroying any concept of real love or virtue, as we will further explore.

6

# What's Love Got to Do With It?

In 1979, the American Civil Liberties Union (ACLU) founded the National Gay Rights Project, a program designed to win "lesbian and gay legislative and judicial achievements at the state level." Not long after the ACLU founded the National Gay Rights Project, as Karen Zelermyer writes:

> In 1981, the first private foundations supporting the lesbian and gay communities were established by wealthy gay men and lesbians, including the Howard Gilman Foundation, Newpol Foundation, and the Chicago Resource Center (which went on to become a major funder in the 1980s and 90s). Howard Gilman was the heir of a major paper manufacturer, the Gilman Paper Company. He created the Foundation in 1981 in order to support the arts, animal conservation efforts and medical research.

Gilman has been deceased for some time, and the foundation greatly diminished, but he was a major player in his day. The genesis of the Gilman family and its fortune is a familiar one, as recounted in *Forbes* in 2003's "The Fall of the House of Gilman":

> Shirtsleeves to shirtsleeves in three generations, says the adage about family fortunes. The rise and fall of the Gilmans fits that pattern. Like many American success stories, this one begins on Manhattan's Lower East Side, the first stop for Jews fleeing eastern Europe. Isaac Gilman arrived in the 1880s and peddled trinkets on the crowded streets. By 1907 he had enough money to take over a distressed New England paper company in the village of Fitzdale, Vt., making newsprint and wrapping paper.

Returning to Zelermyer:

> Lesbian and gay issues have also been prevalent in the foundation's grant-making, with nearly $300,000 awarded since 1983 for mostly HIV-related causes. The Newpol Foundation was launched by Marlow Cole. Its most significant grantees have included the National Gay and Lesbian Task Force [now the National LGBTQ Task Force], Services & Advocacy for GLBT Elders (SAGE), the nation's largest advocate of lesbian and gay seniors, and In the Life, a public television series that reports on LGBTQ issues and culture.

In addition to foundations created and funded by lesbians and gay men, progressive and women's foundations have also played an important role in the LGBTQ movement, particularly in supporting local grassroots organizations.

Most of these "grassroots" organizations are completely astroturfed. For example, the Trans Justice Funding Project funds dozens of "grassroots" transgender organizations and "activist" groups across the United States, and presents itself as a grassroots organization in its own right, but it is not. The North Star Fund allows the Trans Justice Funding Project to use their space for its "community grantmaking meeting," and the Trans Justice Funding Project's special "facilitators" include people or organizations such as Rebecca Fox, Laverne Cox, the Amy Mandel and Katina Rodis Fund, Funders for LGBTQ Issues, the Transgender Law Center, the Tides Foundation, Unilever, and Tourmaline. They are funded by the Laughing Gull Foundation, the Arcus Foundation, the Amy Mandel and Katina Rodis Fund, the Liberty Hill Foundation, and the H. van Ameringen Foundation, among others. The Tides Foundation is its "fiscal agent." Totally grassroots.

The Laughing Gull Foundation does not just dispense funds to LGBTQ "causes," most of which are primarily focused on the North Carolina-Virginia region of the US, but they also make "philanthropic impact investments," such as with Coastal Enterprises, Inc. (CEI). I must reiterate: the system is inextricably intertwined, and all of these organizations are enmeshed within it to one degree or another; as another example, the Wild Geese Foundation has donated extensively to Equality Maine, mentioned, like CEI, in John Q. Publius's immigration exposé *The Way Life Should Be?* Equality Maine received $60,000 in 2009, $50,000 in 2012, and $10,000 in 2019 from the Wild Geese Foundation, which also threw $5,000 to the Maine Transgender Network in 2018.

The Amy Mandel and Katina Rodis Fund (AMKRF) "supports social justice work that advances LGBTQ rights, forwards racial justice, and combats anti-Semitism on a global, national, and local scale." In 2012, the AMKRF founded the Tzedek Social Justice Fellowship. Tzedek means "justice" in Hebrew. The AMKRF funds a veritable who's who of "social justice" and LGBTQ-focused organizations, especially if, in their words, they "prioritize combatting anti-Semitism." Among the recipients listed we find: Keshet, the SPLC, Transgender Legal Defense and Education Fund (TLDEF), the Southern Jewish Resource Network for Gender & Sexual Diversity (SOJOURN), the National LGBTQ Task Force, the American Jewish World Service, Bend the Arc, the Astraea Lesbian Foundation for Justice, Carolina Jews for Justice, the Asheville Jewish Community Center, the LGBTQ Poverty Agenda— a project of the Williams Institute at UCLA, GLBTQ Legal Advocates and Defenders (GLAD), the Jerusalem Open House for Pride and Tolerance, and the National Council of Jewish Women (NCJW), which hysterically trumpeted the following before linking to their "Gender Diversity and Judaism NCJW Guide" and its favorable use of the Gender Unicorn on its first page:

The Trump administration is planning to define sex as either male or female, unchangeable, and determined by the genitals that a person is born with. This definition leaves transgender, intersex, genderqueer, and others erased by their own government. This definition not only defies science but is morally repugnant. As Jews, we know that gender is a spectrum, a concept rooted in traditional Jewish texts.

Thank you for that. Then we have their Additional Resources provided:

- A Wider Bridge: Organization devoted to building LGBTQ connections with Israel that offers resources and upcoming programs and trips to Israel. NCJW has funded A Wider Bridge through its Israel Granting Program.
- Eshel: Organization committed to creating inclusive communities for Orthodox LGBTQ Jews and their families whose site offers resources and programming.
- Institute for Judaism and Sexual Orientation: Institute at Hebrew Union College that offers inclusion resources, policy information, and ways to get involved.
- Jewish Transitions: Organization built around celebrating the sacred within every gender and educating Jewish communities.
- Keshet: Organization committed to the inclusion of the LGBTQ community in Jewish life. Their website contains a comprehensive bank of programs and resources.
- National Center for Transgender Equality: Leading advocacy organization working for the rights of transgender individuals.
- Outspirit: Interfaith bank of mind, body, and spirit resources for the LGBTQ community.
- RitualWell: Ritual bank for various points of Jewish life with a large selection of LGBTQ rituals.
- SOJOURN: Organization providing training to advance LGBTQ affirmation and empowerment across the southern United States.
- Svara: Yeshiva centered on reading Jewish texts from an LGBTQ perspective.
- Trans Student Educational Resources [Eli Erlick's Gender Unicorn group]: Youth-led organization offering resources and educational materials.
- Trans Torah: Resource of text and traditions to make Jewish tradition accessible to individuals of all genders.

Bend the Arc is yet another Jewish organization that vociferously pushed for gay marriage and supports other "progressive" causes, as reported in *Tikkun* in 2014:

Jewish activists today seem to reserve their militancy for other liberal causes like immigration reform and marriage equality. . . . In fact, Jews can claim a fair share of the credit for bringing Americans to a tipping point of accepting marriage equality. . . . Jewish activists and leaders at both the national and local/regional levels spearheaded the recent wave of victories for marriage equality (such as state-by-state legalizing of same-sex marriage and the defeat of the Defense of Marriage Act). "We did it in a variety of smaller ways," says [Hadar] Susskind. "[We had to] get rabbis signed on, get other community leaders signed on, do calling drives, get people engaged with their state legislators." Susskind cites the work of regional Jewish groups as key to winning in several states; these include Jewish Community Action (JCA) in Minnesota, Jews United for Justice in Maryland, and Bend the Arc's regional offices in Los Angeles and the Bay Area in California. State Senator Scott Dibble of Minnesota said the work of JCA was "very important" in two major recent fights there: defeating a 2012 amendment to the state's constitution that would have banned same-sex marriage, and the subsequent passage of a state law that legalized it. . . . In California, the Progressive Jewish Alliance (PJA), which is now part of Bend the Arc, joined a local coalition of progressive Jewish faith groups. Called Kol Tzedek, the coalition came together in 2008 to support San Francisco's then-mayor Gavin Newsom's decision to start marrying gay and lesbian couples in open defiance of supporters of Proposition 8, the ballot measure that later passed outlawing same-sex marriage.

More liberal democracy in action!

Alexander Soros is the founding Chair of Bend the Arc: Jewish Action; as *The Forward* reported in April 2012, "Though his father has also given to the group, Bend the Arc has so far played a central role in Alexander Soros's philanthropic profile." We will explore the Soros-Bend the Arc relationship more fully later. Alexander Soros is the Deputy Chair of the Global Board for the Open Society Foundations, and Andrea Soros Colombel is also a Global Board Member of the Open Society Foundations. As reported by *Tablet* in 2020, Bend the Arc continues to:

Function as the "Jewish" umbrella group within a larger progressive political coalition, bringing top-down messaging to synagogues and organizations and providing the validation of Jewish support upstream. . . . Rabbi Aryeh Cohen, Bend the Arc's rabbi in residence explained to reporters that "caging children [and] forcing adults to sleep on cold floors in camps" [at immigration detention centers] meant that the sites could "only be described as concentration camps. . . ." A Bend the Arc-led campaign [supported] President Obama's executive order to enact gender-identity discrimination protections to federal contract employees. . . . Their financial backing comes from a small cohort of foundations and wealthy patrons. . . . From 2005 to 2013, Bend the Arc received annual donations totaling $1.5 million from the Rockefeller Brothers Fund. . . . Toward the end of the Rockefeller fund's support of Bend the Arc, according to public documents, funding began streaming in from another billionaire family via the NoVo Foundation, the philanthropic project of Peter Buffett, son of Warren Buffett, the co-founder of Berkshire Hathaway. With an average annual donation of $2.8 million and a total of $14.2 million in donations between 2012 and 2016, NoVo became one of Bend the Arc's most generous financial supporters.

According to their page on Influence Watch, Peter Buffett's NoVo Foundation:

Provided $350,000 to Borealis Philanthropy for its Fund for Trans Generations. The fund is used to support transgender activists and organizations. In 2019, the fund provided financial support to over 50 transgender-interests projects. The National LGBTQ Task Force received $100,000 from

NoVo. . . . NoVo founded the Create, Connect, Transform project with Allied Media Projects (AMP). Over four years, NoVo will give AMP $3,000,000 for local organizing in Detroit to "fuel social justice, media, art, and technology innovations." AMP, along with the Astraea Lesbian Foundation for Justice, gave funding to Detroit REPRESENT! a group that discusses injustices facing LGBTQ youth of color and make media projects to address it. NoVo gave $300,000 to the Black LGBTQIA+ Migrant Project (BLMP) founded by the Transgender Law Center. The project seeks to highlight how law enforcement and the immigration system targets Black LGBT migrants. The project was started with the support of the Open Society Foundations Soros Justice Fellowship.

The Black LGBTQ+ Migrant Project, which has also received support from Borealis Philanthropy, was, in their words:

Formed in response to increasing harms facing Black LGBTQIA migrants, and gaps in the LGBTQ, immigrant rights, and racial justice movements, the Black LGBTQ+ Migrant Project (BLMP) works to build leadership, reduce isolation, and protect and defend Black LGBTQIA migrants from state and interpersonal attacks. Radical Hope support will be used to build annual leadership cohorts of 100–150 organizers, centering women, femmes, trans and gender nonconforming people; educate the public and shift narratives by publishing original survey research on the experiences and needs of Black LGBTQIA migrants; strengthen local organizing by building Black LGBTQIA immigrant organizing networks and working in coalition with the broader immigrant, racial, and economic justice movements. BLMP envisions a world where all Black LGBTQIA migrants and their loved ones have housing, bodily autonomy, health, and the ability to travel freely and with dignity, free from racism, misogyny, transphobia, and homophobia.

All of this is in line with the UN's Sustainable Development Goals which are the general operating framework of the "elites" for establishing the next mutation of the globalist system. We will continue to see these linked causes and demands, which are anything but organic.

Other NoVo Foundation-funded projects include $2 million to the Florida Immigrant Coalition for "a new initiative, Radical Hope Florida, [that] will sharpen the feminist lens of existing racial, economic, and gender justice organizations, transforming the values and politics of Florida" and $4 million to Grassroots International with Grassroots Global Justice Alliance, Indigenous Environmental Network, and the World March of Women to:

Foster unity and strengthen grassroots feminist movements in six countries where backlashes against women, gender oppressed peoples and communities of color are significantly acute, as a result of right-wing takeovers: Brazil,

Guatemala, Honduras, Palestine, Puerto Rico,[29] and the United States. . . . Centered in the leadership of Indigenous Peoples, peasants, Afro-descendant communities, and other communities of color, this collaboration will contribute to a vision for a global diversity of feminisms (also known as the fourth wave of feminism) that is able to respond to new conditions, including overlapping forces that constrain women's lives, such as systems of oppression based on race, class, sexuality, and gender identity.

Continuing with Bend the Arc, Sean Cooper writes for *Tablet*, "Late in 2014, Rabbi David Saperstein, a Bend the Arc board member, was appointed by Obama to join the State Department as ambassador at large for international religious freedom." According to a 2013 interview with E. Michael Jones, Saperstein, by the way, is:

The man who is responsible for gay marriage in New York City. . . . His wife, Ellen Weiss, was formerly the head of the NPR newsroom, National Public Radio. This is a powerful force and he basically claimed responsibility. He said if it weren't for our group of rabbis, this would have never passed. So what you see is this constant tension for Jewish revolutionary subversive activity.

The CEO of Bend the Arc is Stosh Cotler, described thusly in *Tablet* in 2020:

Cotler's interest in how Jewish activism could potentially alter the American political landscape manifested as early as 2002, on the streets of Portland, Oregon. . . . Leaving Olympia, [Washington,] Cotler found something like a family alternative in Portland, falling in with the city's thriving subculture of self-described "queer-core" musicians, artists, and activists who sought to combat a predatory, male-dominated corporate society hostile and abusive toward women.

Of course, a predatory corporate society that is abusive toward women *and* men, to say nothing of children, is exactly what Bend the Arc supports.

Now here's something *really* telling again from *Tablet* (if the reader is not aware, "goyim" is generally used as a derogatory term for non-Jews):

In an essay published in a zine in 2003 . . . Cotler wrote, "I had danced for D before: a leather butch who came into my club with her old school, high femme wife and their entourage." After Cotler performed her table dance, she was surprised to hear the group discuss their plans for an upcoming Seder. It was a shock to Cotler, "not only of randomly running into other Jews in a goyim-dominated city like Portland, but of meeting freaky Jews at a sex club." When invited to join their Seder, Cotler was unsure about participating in a Jewish ritual after so many years removed from organized religion. The decision to attend was ultimately a profound one for Cotler. "I truly felt like

---

[29] Author's note: Puerto Rico is not a country. I'm not sure where the "right wing takeover" is there unless they mean the Jewish pre-Trump Era GOP-mega-donor Seth Klarman pillaging Puerto Rico? Palestine is an illegally-occupied country, so maybe that's it.

I had found my 'home' in those short hours at the Seder, and after being gone so long I felt scared and lost. . . . When something so deep happens, there is no going back. That Seder marked my return to Judaism and the beginning of my conscious and proud identity as a Jew. . . ." Realizing "that being Jewish was a revolutionary spiritual and political path . . ." Cotler immersed herself in temple life.

Continuing in this same vein, the earlier-mentioned Transgender Legal Defense and Education Fund (TLDEF) was founded in 2003 by Michael D. Silverman, described by *BuzzFeed* as "a cisgender gay man with a long record of LGBT advocacy." As a cooperating attorney with Lambda Legal, Silverman worked on a number of cases, including *Baehr v. Miike* and *Boy Scouts of America v. Dale*. While on a Georgetown University Law Center Women's Law and Public Policy Fellowship, Silverman worked in the legal department at NARAL Pro-Choice America.

Silverman was succeeded by the transgender Jillian Weiss, Board member of the Congregation Beit Simchat Torah and featured speaker at their 2017 Trans Pride Shabbat. Weiss is described by Meredith Talusan of *BuzzFeed* as "a professor and employment attorney who successfully sued companies like Saks & Co. and Deluxe Financial Services on behalf of trans people." Talusan notes that for the TLDEF, "Some of their past highest-profile cases include fighting to allow a transgender then-6-year-old Coy Mathis to use the girls' bathroom in her Colorado school, which paved the way for similar cases in other states."

The TLDEF is currently helmed by Andy Marra, formerly of the Arcus Foundation. Marra previously managed public relations at GLSEN, ("a national organization focused on LGBTQ issues in K-12 education"), was co-director at Nodutdol for Korean Community Development, served as a senior media strategist at GLAAD, and was on the Boards or Advisory Councils of Chinese for Affirmative Action, the Funding Exchange, the Human Rights Campaign, and the National Center for Transgender Equality. Board member Anne Tompkins was detailed to the Regime Crimes Liaison Office in Baghdad, Iraq, where she "assisted the Iraqi Special Tribunal investigation into international humanitarian crimes committed by members of the regime of Saddam Hussein." Board Co-Chair Alaina Kupec, "active fighting the proposed ban on transgender military service," is a Senior Director at Gilead Sciences and was previously with Pfizer for two decades.

The Jewish Council for Public Affairs (JCPA) also opposed the "trans ban" and informed us in 2018 that "Trans Rights is a Jewish Issue; Why Antisemitism is a Trans Issue" courtesy of Barbara Weinstein of the hosting organization and Mara Keisling of the National Center for Transgender Equality. Keisling's writings appeared alongside those of Ilhan Omar, the Jewish Bernie Sanders, Elizabeth Warren, the Jewish Gloria Steinem, Rabbi Sharon Kleinbaum of Congregation Beit Simchat Torah, the Jewish George Lakoff, Linda Sarsour, the Jewish Ilyse Hogue (former President of NARAL, former Board member of Bend the Arc: A Jewish Partnership for Justice, and formerly of the Friends of Democracy PAC founded by Jonathan Soros), the Jewish Allan Lichtman, the Jewish Robert Reich, the Jewish M. Dove Kent (Senior Strategy Officer at Bend the Arc: Jewish Action, formerly Executive Director of Jews for Racial and Economic Justice and author of *Understanding Antisemitism: An Offering to Our Movement*), and the Jewish Paul Krugman, who possessed child pornography on his computer, in the book *What We Do Now: Standing*

*Up For Your Values in Trump's America.* We know what *their* values are.

The lynch-pin for advancing the transgender agenda comes down to the colossal victory of gay marriage, which opened the floodgates with one brilliant stroke of marketing, the phrase "Love is love." Susan Wolf Ditkoff and Abe Grindle focus here on catalysts Tim Gill and his Gill Foundation, and the Jewish attorney Evan Wolfson:

> Tim Gill and other philanthropists who support LGBTQ rights [such as the Evelyn & Walter Haas, Jr. Fund] demonstrated the importance of setting milestones. In the early 2000s, at the urging of movement leaders including attorney Evan Wolfson, they began devoting considerable resources to the very specific objective of legalizing same-sex marriage nationwide.[30] For decades the movement had focused on the broad goal of "advancing LGBTQ rights," and although that work continued, leaders hoped that a significant push on a concrete winnable milestone would more powerfully advance the larger cause. They further concentrated efforts on a targeted set of states in order to build momentum and lay the public and legal foundations for a national victory. . . . The marriage equality movement struggled to connect with the general public as recently as 2008, even losing a well-funded ballot initiative in left-leaning California. In the aftermath of that and other setbacks, supportive philanthropists financed polling and focus groups to help movement leaders understand how to reframe the core message. The research revealed that many voters perceived the movement as driven primarily by same-sex couples' desire for the government benefits and rights conferred by marriage—and they did not find that a gripping rationale. This insight was pivotal: The movement refocused its communications strategy on equality of love and commitment, arguing that "love is love"—a message that struck a chord. Victories piled up, culminating in the 2015 Supreme Court ruling that legalized same-sex marriage throughout the United States.

In 1992, Tim Gill's adopted home state of Colorado passed Amendment 2, a referendum outlawing state and local ordinances, statutes, and regulations that included sexual orientation in their anti-discrimination protections. From Karen Zelermyer, Perhaps sensing an opportunity:

> Tim Gill, the openly gay founder of the Denver-based Quark software company, was a major supporter of the effort to defeat the measure. Its passage prompted him to get more involved in strategic philanthropy, and in 1994 he launched the Gill Foundation. The foundation has gone on to be one of the most significant lesbian and gay funders in the country and through its Out-Giving program has spurred other LGBTQ people to increase their philanthropic giving. Gill is but one example of many donors who created their own philanthropic entities to support LGBTQ issues during the mid- to late 1990s. The largest number of new private foundations established by lesbian and gay donors occurred during this time. . . . To promote philanthropy in the lesbian

---

[30] In the year 2000, the Evelyn and Walter Haas, Jr. Fund gave Evan Wolfson a seed grant that eventually became Freedom to Marry.

and gay community at the local level, a small group of national foundations partnered with Funders for LGBTQ Issues (then the Working Group) in 1993 to launch the National Lesbian and Gay Community Funding Partnership. Local mainstream community foundations were challenged to establish field-of-interest funds specifically for LGBTQ issues, and the Partnership would make the first investments with matching grants of up to $100,000. Thirty-six local community foundations applied and successfully matched an initial grant from the Partnership, itself funded by the Mertz Gilmore, Ford, Gill, Paul Rapoport, Ms. and Levi Strauss foundations, among others. On the local level, funders such as the Jay & Rose Phillips Family Foundation and the Aaron Diamond Foundation helped provide matching grants. Between 1994 (the first year of grantmaking) and 2005 (the last year new sites were added), more than $9 million was invested in LGBTQ work at the local level through the Partnership. Some of the participating community foundations included the Greater Milwaukee Foundation, the Tulsa Community Foundation, the Community Foundation for Middle Tennessee, New York Community Trust and the Rhode Island Foundation.

The Gill Foundation today has in excess of $206 million in assets and it has received donations from organizations such as the Evelyn & Walter Haas Jr. Fund, the Ford Foundation, the David Geffen Foundation, and the Tides Foundation.

Some of the Gill Foundation's grant recipients include the Tides Foundation, the SPLC, the J Street Education Fund, the Clinton Foundation, New Venture Fund, the Los Angeles LGBT Center, Media Matters, the National Center for Transgender Equality, the National LGBTQ Task Force, Trustees of Columbia University, University of North Florida Foundation, Regents of the University of California Los Angeles (UCLA), Texas Association of Business & Chambers of Commerce Foundation, the ADL, Rocky Mountain PBS, Rocky Mountain Community Radio, Colorado Public Radio, Colorado Education Initiative, Interfaith Alliance of Colorado, the Center for Popular Democracy, GLBTQ Legal Advocates & Defenders Inc. of Boston, LULAC, the Barack Obama Foundation, the Indianapolis Chamber of Commerce Foundation, Freedom to Marry, the Palm Center, National Center for Lesbian Rights, NEO Philanthropy, the Pride Foundation, Gender Justice Nevada, and the Jacksonville Area Sexual Minority Youth Network.

Additionally via Influence Watch, we see the intersection with and role of vulture capitalists, specifically in this case the Jewish Paul Singer and the Jewish Dan Loeb:

> The Gill Foundation is a major supporter of Freedom for All Americans (FFAA), which is a campaign run by the American Unity Fund, a Super PAC created by Tim Gill and hedge fund executive Paul Singer. FFAA seeks to enact a federal anti-discrimination law that would prohibit different treatment based on sexuality and gender identity. The group has focused its attention particularly in the South, fighting religious freedom protection efforts in Georgia and North Carolina. Other major donors associated with the group include hedge fund manager Dan Loeb.

As the Associated Press reported in late 2013 about the Employment Non-Discrimination Act:

"I think society continues to evolve on the issue of gay rights," said Sen. Susan Collins, R-Maine, a co-sponsor of the measure. . . . In a sign of the times, the anti-bias legislation has traditional proponents such as the Human Rights Campaign, the largest gay and lesbian advocacy group, plus the backing of a relatively new group, the American Unity Fund. That organization has the financial support of big-name Republican donors—hedge fund billionaires Paul Singer, Cliff Asness, Dan Loeb and Seth Klarman [all Jewish]—and former GOP lawmakers Norm Coleman of Minnesota and Tom Reynolds of New York. . . . "I think that this issue is not so much a Democrat-Republican issue, although more Democrats are for it of course, as it is an age issue," said [Jewish] Sen. Chuck Schumer, D-N.Y.

That or the product of a few wealthy and powerful people, mostly of one ethno-religious group and/or sexual proclivity or proclivities *forcing* the issue. In Gill's case, you'll find his influence everywhere from his more local activities in the early-to-mid-1990s to the 2003 *Goodridge v. Department of Public Health* decision in which Massachusetts became the first US state to allow gay marriage to the Gill Action Fund's political activism such as in 2006 when they targeted 70 "anti-LGBT candidates" to be drummed out of office to the exclamation point of *Obergefell v. Hodges* in 2015 legalizing gay marriage throughout the United States:[31]

After Massachusetts became the first state to legalize same-sex marriage in 2003, the following year 11 states enacted amendments banning same-sex marriage, often by sweeping vote margins. Eager to put substantial funds behind the fight for marriage equality, major funders led by the Gill Foundation and the Evelyn & Walter Haas, Jr. Fund brought together more than two dozen LGBTQ leaders in 2005 to devise a common strategy. What emerged from this gathering became known as the "road map to victory," which would create an electoral and public opinion infrastructure capable of winning and maintaining support for same-sex marriage, one state at a time. It identified 100 tangible battlefields that could then be pursued in sequence as part of a coordinated field operation. . . . Funders came together as the Civil Marriage Collaborative to support the road map. The Haas, Jr. Fund itself contributed $39 million. Marriage equality was a classic example of using a big bet to wage an advocacy campaign. Here, the role of philanthropy is to take a risk that no one else will take. Such a big bet can provide the critical infrastructure required for movements: materials, people, transportation, legal services, research, and more. It can also represent a vote of confidence, especially when the odds against progress are high. When the Haas, Jr. Fund made its first contributions in support of marriage equality, momentum seemed to be going

---

[31] And beyond: in 2016, Gill directed funds from his foundation to the National Park Service to identify "historically significant places related to LGBT history" to be designated National Monuments or included in the National Register of Historic Places. That same year his Gill Action Fund figured prominently in getting Roy Cooper elected Governor of North Carolina as payback against incumbent Pat McCrory for passing the notorious "HB2 bathroom bill," which "forced" transgender people to use the public restroom corresponding with their sex rather than their "preferred gender identity." If you'll recall, the full force of the Establishment came down on North Carolina for daring to be on "the wrong side of history."

in the opposite direction, with more and more states amending their constitutions to ban same-sex marriage. Big investments in advocacy offer leaders the time they need to weather defeats and press forward to create change.[32]

The authors then go on to state that this model is currently being applied to "gun control," the "philanthropic endeavor" currently being spearheaded by the Jewish Michael Bloomberg and his Everytown for Gun Safety. Once again illustrating the "intersectional" nature of the ruling class's agenda—and its incestuousness—while Mayor of New York in 2011, Bloomberg officiated the gay marriage of two Jewish members of his staff, Jonathan Mintz and John Feinblatt. Feinblatt helms the pro-mass migration/H-1B orgy the Partnership for a New American Economy (NAE) founded by Bloomberg, and is also the President of Bloomberg's "gun control" (confiscation) organization Everytown for Gun Safety.

Gay marriage was a sustained, coordinated, and well-funded campaign to manufacture an issue, wear the traditional institutions down, and ultimately impose an agenda through a combination of dubious legislation, judicial activism, bureaucratic machinations, executive fiat, media manipulation, academic indoctrination, mass marketing, and social pressure. These "philanthropic" organizations often serve as a hub for funding and coordination, and their NGO status gives them much more latitude with the implementation of their agenda. It should be clear that (to answer the question posed by this chapter title) *love has nothing to do with it*: it's a calculated agenda designed to bend people to the will of the Establishment.

According to Daniel Siegel, the Rabbinic Director of ALEPH: Alliance for Jewish Renewal, "holiness should not be limited only to certain people and certain relationships." Jewish Supreme Court Justices Kagan, Breyer, and Ginsburg along with Anthony Kennedy and the "lived experience" of feisty Latina Sonia Sotomayor (Princeton then Yale Law) agreed in both *Obergefell v. Hodges* in 2015 and in *United States v. Windsor* in 2013. *United States v. Windsor* was the culmination of the Jewish Edie Windsor suing the US government for recognition of her Canadian marriage to the Jewish Thea Spyer performed in 2007 and officiated by Canada's first openly gay judge the Jewish Harvey Brownstone because she did not want to pay any federal estate taxes after Spyer's death in 2009. Windsor was represented by the Jewish lesbian Roberta Kaplan[33] (Harvard then Columbia Law) who attended the same LGBTQ synagogue in New York City, Congregation Beit Simchat Torah. Kaplan's firm Paul Weiss Rifkind Wharton & Garrison LLP[34] in conjunction with the ACLU filed the case in the US District Court for the Southern District of New York on behalf of Windsor as executor of Spyer's estate on November 9th, 2010, challenging the Defense of Marriage Act (DOMA) Section 3.

---

[32] Foster, et al., "Becoming Big Bettable."

[33] She was good friends with and the prom date of "LGBTQ activist" and UC Berkeley alum Aaron Belkin, now Professor of Political Science at San Francisco State University and Director of the Palm Center, a think tank which focuses on "gender, sexuality, and the military." He blogs for the *Huffington Post* and is a big supporter of transgender people in the military.

[34] Chairman Brad S. Karp is a Harvard Law School graduate, served his clerkship under the Jewish Judge Irving R. Kaufman, and represents or has represented primarily financial institutions such as Bear Sterns, ING, Merrill Lynch, and JP Morgan Chase. I could not independently verify that Karp is Jewish, but the surrounding evidence, including being honored by the Jewish Theological Seminary and receiving his BA from Union College in New York which has traditionally had a very high percentage of Jews in its study body and professorship ranks, seems to suggest that he is.

On July 26th, 2011, Jewish New York Attorney General and Harvard Law School alumnus Eric Schneiderman[35] filed a brief in support of Windsor's claim. Eventually the case wound its way up to the Supreme Court and on December 11th, 2012 the Supreme Court appointed Vicki C. Jackson, a former clerk to Thurgood Marshall (who had been assisted by Kagan's firm when it was just Paul, Weiss in overturning "separate but equal" with *Brown v. Board of Education* in 1954) and a professor of constitutional law at Harvard Law School as an *amicus curiae* to argue two more questions in addition to that posed by Eric Holder's Department of Justice, which had filed its own petition in addition to Windsor's for certiorari before judgment with the Supreme Court on September 11th, 2012 as to "Whether Section 3 of DOMA violates the Fifth Amendment's guarantee of equal protection" for same sex partners. On June 26th, 2013, the Supreme Court declared Section 3 of DOMA unconstitutional and stated that the Constitution does not allow the federal government to treat state-sanctioned heterosexual marriages differently from state-sanctioned same-sex marriages.

*Obergefell v. Hodges* was actually the consolidation of six lower-court cases. One such case took on the character it did following the recommendation of Jewish Judge Bernard A. Friedman to the plaintiffs in a case over which he presided in 2012 that challenged Michigan state adoption law to instead amend their complaint to challenge the state's ban on same-sex marriage. After they agreed, Friedman re-scheduled their hearing for after *United States v. Windsor* "hoping for guidance." Friedman eventually struck down Michigan's constitutional and statutory bans on same-sex marriage; however, and showing the blatant hypocrisy of these people, in November 2018 he ruled that the federal law *against* female genital mutilation (FGM) is unconstitutional, dismissing the charges against several doctors in the first American court case of its kind.[36] This is what we've come to.

The Jewish Elena Kagan of the Supreme Court is known for "queerifying Harvard" as Dean of the Law School from 2003–2009, where Kagan gave over half of her faculty appointments to fellow Jews, by introducing "transgender law courses," inciting student "activists" to help kick military recruiters off campus, and more (and you'll notice a preponderance of Jews represented here), via *Mass Resistance*:

> Kagan encouraged Harvard students to get involved in homosexual activist legal work. . . . To engage in "public interest law" and to get "clinical" legal experience, the Harvard Law School established the LGBT Law Clinic. . . . Kagan recruited former ACLU lawyer (and former ACT-UP activist) William Rubenstein, an expert on "queer" legal issues. Few Americans can comprehend the radical nature of "queer" academics. Rubenstein described one of his courses as taking up "newer identities (bisexuality, trans, genderfuck)" as well as "polygamy, S&M, the sexuality of minors. . . ." Kagan promoted and facilitated the "transgender" legal agenda during her tenure at Harvard. In 2007, HLS offered a Transgender Law course by "out lesbian" Professor Janet Halley and Dean Spade, a transsexual activist attorney. . . . Kagan also brought in Cass Sunstein (Obama's regulatory czar, 2009–2012) who has written in support of free-for-all marriage relationships. . . . There was even

---

[35] Eventually forced to resign his post after four different women accused him of physical abuse.

[36] Snell, "Genital mutilation ban ruled unconstitutional."

a campaign (during her tenure) to make the campus "trans inclusive"—using Harvard's "gender identity" non-discrimination policy (in place since 2006). This included discussions between GLBT student activists and the law school administration (i.e., Kagan) "to make our restrooms safe and accessible for people regardless of their gender identity or expression. . . ." Harvard has become so committed to radical transsexual activism that its health insurance policy now [2010] partially covers "sex-change" breast "treatments" for transsexuals. . . . She moderated a panel on GLBT law at the Harvard Gay and Lesbian Caucus's 25th anniversary celebration in 2008. . . . Elena Kagan was a member of the Diversity Task Force of the ultra-leftist Boston Bar Association during the time of its activism in support of "gay marriage" and advocacy for "transgender rights."

The reader will here recall that Kagan and the other two Jewish Supreme Court justices—Ginsburg and Breyer—voted in favor of legalizing gay marriage in 2015. It would've been four total Jewish justices had Merrick Garland been on the Court (keep in mind Jews are only 1.5% of the American population—quite the overrepresentation), and the same holds true for *United States v. Windsor* two years prior.

The transgenderism floodgates really opened once the one-two punch of *United States v. Windsor* (2013) and *Obergefell v. Hodges* (2015) were successful. These two cases fit into a larger strategic vision by the Establishment which is proceeding exactly along the lines they pre-determined. If this all sounds a bit "conspiratorial," don't take it from me. Take it straight from the horse's mouth. Authors of the "At the Crossroads: The Future of the LGBT Movement," Frances Kunreuther,[37] Barbara Masters, Gigi Barsoum, and Rebecca Fox outlined the 2013 catalyzing strategy that has marked the seeming ubiquity of all things rainbow (this is a bit long, but it's worth excerpting at length):

The LGBT movement maintains significant assets which it has been able to leverage for real progress, including engaged donors and funders; strong national organizations; and political savvy, visible, and influential leaders across a variety of sectors, particularly the entertainment, media, and, increasingly, political arenas. Strategically, these assets have been deployed with a laser-like focus to address specific policy and legislative wins either nationally or in certain parts of the country. . . . Successful public policy change is generally the result of long-term efforts to build a strong advocacy infrastructure and capacity. Advocacy capacity includes various skills, talents, and expertise such as policy analysis, lobbying, and communications. . . . Strategically designed convenings can also lift up new policy priorities, catalyze new relationships and collaborations, promote learning and strategy development, and foster a greater sense of cohesion across the movement. Other movements at similar crossroads are engaging in systematic visioning pro-

[37] Frances Kunreuther, founder and Co-Director of the Building Movement Project, "which works to strengthen U.S. nonprofits as sites of social change" and senior fellow at the Research Center for Leadership and Action at NYU, was also at the Hauser Center for Nonprofit Organizations at Harvard University for five years after heading the Hetrick-Martin Institute for LBGT youth.

cesses. . . . Campaigns for policy change are critical to advancing and codifying social change, but they must align with and move toward the broader vision of the movement. . . . The LGBT movement can build and expand on policy efforts and victories while also building and expanding the movement and its power.

Although the fight against a constitutional amendment banning marriage equality lost in North Carolina in 2012, the campaign engaged a wide range of organizations. Groups ranging from the NAACP and those working on immigrant rights joined the campaign to take a stand against discrimination of any kind. Alliances were built across economic justice and racial justice organizations, and, in the words of one activist, "it has changed the way North Carolina will forever work in terms of coalitions and alliances." Similarly, in Mississippi, a national LGBT advocate reported that they worked with the reproductive justice movement to defeat the so-called Personhood Amendment, which sought to ban all abortions and many forms of contraception. "We saw it as critical to our work around HIV, but more broadly to change views to meet the needs of young people. We may have different angles but we recognize that it's about all people having control over their bodies."

II. STRENGTHEN THE INFRASTRUCTURE Build Organizational Capacity with an Emphasis on the "Fly Over" States

Targeted capacity building support is needed in the Southern and Midwestern parts of the country. As momentum for equality grows, LGBT organizations in those and other overlooked regions will need more support to build the infrastructure for future success and sustainability of the movement. Efforts to strengthen and build the capacity of the "fly over" states should consider the operating needs of these organizations such as board development, leadership and management training, and development support. Efforts should also focus on building advocacy capacity, which can include a range of activities from linking them with peers in other states who can act as coaches, to targeted trainings and convenings, to more systematic efforts to strengthen capacity on a regional level.

Increasing the focus on and investment in LGBT communities of color can give voice to these communities and increase their ability to shape the movement's agenda. This can be done by supporting the non-profit and organizing infrastructure in these communities, building alliances with other non-LGBT organizations serving communities of color, and developing individuals of color as leaders at all levels of the movement.

III. CONNECT WITHIN THE LGBT MOVEMENT AND WITH ALLIES Foster Grassroots – Treetops Connections Within the Movement

The LGBT movement needs a concerted effort to both grow and connect the grassroots through base building and community organizing. Local grassroots groups are typically small and fragile and need operating support to enable them to stabilize and engage in base building over the long term. Ideally, these efforts would lead to the development of alliances with other social justice efforts on the ground. In addition, existing direct service groups, including LGBT community and health centers, are well positioned to play an important role in base building. The second step in supporting grassroots efforts is to link them to state and national policy advocates. Relationships between these groups should be reciprocal and mutually informing.

The LGBT movement can be made stronger if it continues to build alliances with other social change movements. One approach is the establishment of the Strategic Opportunities States within the State Equality Fund, a collaborative supported by the Gill Foundation, Evelyn and Walter Haas Jr. Fund, an anonymous donor, and Ford Foundation, in conjunction with Tides Foundation. Among other things, the investment provides two states with additional resources to create alliances with other powerful forces in that state, such as the African American and Latino communities, and labor unions. Following the passage of several anti-gay ballot measure campaigns and similar attacks on immigrants and communities of color, Basic Rights Oregon (BRO) embarked on a long-term effort to build solidarity among allied communities. One of BRO's three main programs is the Racial Justice and Alliance Building program, which is structured around two activities: lifting up LGBT leadership who are people of color and engaging more white LGBT Oregonians on issues of concern to people of color. That commitment has led BRO to support policy accountability work led by the African American community and participate in immigrant rights campaigns. BRO was able to access training through the Western States Center that emphasized the skills needed to partner with organizations of color. Subsequently, the Basic Rights Education Fund developed an anti-racist toolkit for LGBT Equality groups, entitled, "Standing Together: Coming Out for Racial Justice."

Jewish co-author Rebecca Fox is a Senior Program Officer in the Sexual Orientation and Gender Identity (SOGI) department at the Wellspring Philanthropic Fund, which was founded as the Matan B'Seter Foundation by TGS Management hedge fund partners Andrew Shechtel, David Gelbaum, and C. Frederick Taylor, who have billions of dollars in their "byzantine network." From Influence Watch, we learn:

"Matan B'Seter" is a Hebrew phrase meaning "anonymous gift," according to the *Algemeiner*, a journal serving the Jewish community. The *Algemeiner* noted at least two of the three billionaires are Jewish (*"The Algemeiner* was unable to independently verify Taylor's religion but Gelbaum and Shechtel are Jewish"), and that other subsidiaries within their network (such as one named "Shekel Funding") bore "Hebrew or Israeli-related names. . . ." Andrew Shechtel is an alumnus of Johns Hopkins University and graduated with a degree in math and political economy at the age of 19. Shechtel attended Harvard Business School and reportedly "worked on Wall Street" and joined Princeton-Newport Partners in the 1980s. He was an employee of the firm when it was raided by federal officials. . . . Frederick Taylor reportedly worked at Princeton-Newport Partners, an early investment management company until it was liquidated following an investigation under the Racketeer Influenced and Corrupt Organizations (RICO) Act in the 1990s. It's unclear when Taylor worked for the company.... Wellspring's articles of incorporation from 1999 list three trustees: Allen B. Levithan, George J. Mazin, and Kenneth J. Slutsky. Levithan, the incorporator, is faculty with Rutgers Law School in New Jersey. He is also listed as Of Counsel for the law firm Lowenstein Sandler. Mazin is a retired partner with Dechert LLP, an investment management firm. Slutsky is a New Jersey-based partner with Lowenstein Sandler, a law firm that filed Wellspring's initial articles of incorporation. Wellspring's ... IRS filing covering 2017 lists Slutsky and Levithan as trustees, as well as John L. Berger. Berger is a New Jersey-based partner at Lowenstein Sandler.... Joyce Malombe is a senior program officer for Wellspring's International Children's Education program, a position she's held since 2012. Prior to that, she was an independent nonprofit development consultant. She also worked for the Ford Foundation, the ELMA Foundation, and World Bank. Malombe is a member of the advisory board for the Education Support program of George Soros' Open Society Foundations.

For 2017, we see major donations from Wellspring to the Tides Center, the Tides Foundation, the Center for American Progress, Demos, Borealis Philanthropy, NEO Philanthropy, the National Women's Law Center, the New Venture Fund, Planned Parenthood, the Proteus Fund, the LGBTQ Victory Institute, and the Astraea Lesbian Foundation for Justice. According to Shiryn Ghermezian of *The Algemeiner*:

From 1999 to 2005, the law firm Lowenstein Sandler established more than a dozen anonymous private foundations funded and controlled by limited liability companies. *Businessweek* noted that according to IRS filings, almost all of these companies have links to either Shechtel, Gelbaum or Taylor. The generous donors used these anonymous vehicles, as well as various trusts, to direct more than $13 billion to causes relating to human rights, the environment, and medical research, among others. Using a web of subsidiaries to hide their contributions, the bulk [of contributions to explicitly Jewish organizations] was distributed through the donor advised Jewish Communal Fund ($70 million). Outreach group Aish Ha'Torah also received aid ($17 million), as well as the Israel Project ($2 million), United Jewish Communities ($4 million), American Jewish Congress ($240,000), American Israel Education Foundation ($350,000) and Tarbut V'Torah ($23 million), among others. Other Jewish charities that benefited from their generosity between 2001 and 2012 include: PEF Israel Endowment Funds, American Friends of Tel Aviv Soursasky Medical Center, UJA Federation of New York, Jewish Funders Network, Yeshiva University, Morasha School, Hineni Heritage Foundation, Orange County Jewish Campus, AIPAC Trenton, National Jewish Outreach Program, West Side Hatzolah, American Israel Education Foundation, Jewish Television Network, Hebrew Union College, Orthodox Union Institute, Conference of Presidents, American Friends of Tel Aviv, Mount Sinai Hospital, Auerbach Central Agency for Jewish Education, Israel 21C and the American Jewish Congress.... When *Businessweek*'s reporter introduced himself to Shechtel at a Jewish conference on philanthropy, where his wife gave a presentation, the TGS co-founder declined to talk, dismissed the journalist with a few words and turned away.

This is the way the American system functions, from so-called philanthropy that launders millions of dollars to infuse Jewish organizations with cash to behind-the-scenes machinations to buy elections. As things become increasingly globalized, we will continue to see this pattern replicated on a larger scale.

The Jewish Community Federation and Endowment Fund of San Francisco, the Peninsula, Marin and Sonoma Counties donates extensively to Jewish causes obviously, but beyond that they also dispense funds to a number of "social justice," "diversity," and LGBTQ "causes" and organizations, many of which over-lap: the American Jewish World Service; Bend the Arc; the National Council of Jewish Women; the New Israel Fund; the ADL; Mike Bloomberg's Everytown for Gun Safety; Catholic Charities; the Sandler Foundation; T'ruah; the United Way; Combined Jewish Philanthropies of Greater Boston; the ACLU; GLSEN; the LGBT Alliance; the Center for American Progress; the Council on Foreign Relations; the Foundation for AIDS Research, amfAR; the Gay, Lesbian, Bisexual, Transgender Historical Society (GLBT Historical); the Heartland Alliance for Human Needs and Human Rights; the Horizons Foundation; the Human Rights Campaign; Human Rights Watch; Keshet; Lambda Legal; the Lucile Packard Foundation for Children's Health at Stanford University; MAP; the New Venture Fund; PEN America; PFLAG; the Pride Law Fund; the Tides Network; the Tides Center; the Tides Foundation; Tulane University; the UC Davis Foundation; and the Tzedakah Fund.

The reader may also be interested to know that the Jewish Community Federation and Endowment Fund of San Francisco, the Peninsula, Marin and Sonoma Counties has donated over $200,000 to the "conservative" Prager University Foundation of the Jewish Dennis Prager; Prager University produced a 2018 video featuring Guy Benson who states: "I'm a Christian, a patriotic American, and a free market, shrink-the-government conservative—who also happens to be gay." Jennifer Pritzker has also written an "impassioned plea" to "fellow Republicans" to stop "targeting trans people," and Jewish billionaires and mega-donors like Seth Klarman and Michael Bloomberg switch political allegiances whenever it suits them, thus underscoring the false dichotomy of American politics. In 2020, as Donald Shaw reports:

> A new super PAC that says it will spend $75 million to support Democrats in 2020 is funded in large part by billionaires who run hedge funds, including some with a history of supporting Republicans. . . . The group's top donor is Seth Klarman, the billionaire and former GOP megadonor who is CEO of Baupost Group, a Boston-based hedge fund whose investments include liquid natural gas companies Cheniere Energy and Antero Resources. Klarman gave Pacronym $1.5 million on Dec. 27, 2019, according to the group's year-end FEC filing. . . . Another hedge-fund billionaire backing Pacronym is Donald Sussman, the founder and chief investment officer of hedge fund Paloma Partners.

The Jewish Sussman figures prominently in John Q. Publius's *The Way Life Should Be?* as a figure working to transform the state politically and demographically, and is deeply enmeshed in the shadow architecture of the system, much of it very questionable. Shaw continues:

Other Pacronym donors the group disclosed yesterday include Michael Moritz, partner at venture investment fund Sequoia Capital ($1 million); Kenneth Duda, founder and chief technology office at software company Arista ($1 million); Mimi Haas, director of Levi Strauss & Co. ($600,000); filmmaker Steven Spielberg ($500,000); and Jim Swartz, co-founder of venture firm Accel Partners ($400,000).

Lambda Legal, recipient of major financial support from the Jewish Community Federation and Endowment Fund of San Francisco, the Peninsula, Marin and Sonoma Counties, is an LGBTQ "legal defense" organization, also funded by the homosexual Fred Eychaner and with an extensive network of disproportionately Jewish individual donors and Jewish-helmed or -connected law firms such as: Ropes & Gray; Wachtell Lipton Rosen & Katz; WilmerHale LLP; and Akin Gump Strauss Hauer & Feld LLP. A number of its Board members are Jewish.

Lambda Legal also receives substantial support from a number of prominent "philanthropies" and private-sector donors, not to mention AARP and the National Collegiate Athletic Association (NCAA). Some of these "philanthropies" include: the Klarman Family Foundation (the foundation of Jewish vulture capitalist Seth Klarman); the Open Society Foundations; the Evelyn and Walter Haas, Jr. Fund; the Elton John AIDS Foundation; the Adelson Family Foundation (the foundation of Jewish casino magnate and major GOP donor Sheldon Adelson); and the Shack Sackler Foundation. Private sector donors include: ViiV Healthcare, Bloomberg LP, Google, Facebook, ViacomCBS, JP Morgan Chase, Gilead Sciences, Genentech, PNC Wealth Management, Mastercard, Merrill Lynch, and Wells Fargo.

Keshet is another recipient of major financial support from the Jewish Community Federation and Endowment Fund of San Francisco, the Peninsula, Marin and Sonoma Counties. They are an explicitly-Jewish LGBTQ advocacy organization. Their Chairman of the Board Seth Marnin was on the World Professional Association for Transgender Health (WPATH) Legal Committee; co-authored friend-of-the-court briefs in same-sex Supreme Court cases *Obergefell* and *Windsor*; is the Director of Training and Education for the Office of Equal Opportunity and Affirmative Action at Columbia University; and served as the Vice President for Civil Rights at the Anti-Defamation League (ADL). Secretary Tamar Prager is another Columbia University alumnus. President and CEO Idit Klein, by Keshet's description:

> Spearheaded the creation of leadership development programs for queer Jewish teens and mobilized Jewish communities to help defeat a proposed constitutional amendment to ban same-sex marriage and pass two transgender rights bills in Massachusetts.

Board member Amy Born has degrees from transgender agenda incubators Washington University in St. Louis and Columbia University. Also on the Board, among others are: Gali Cooks (former speechwriter at the Embassy of Israel and former Legislative Assistant at AIPAC); Bennett Decker (a student at the Joint Program between the Jewish Theological Seminary and Columbia University); Liana Krupp (on Planned Parenthood Federation of America's Leadership Council); Joy Ladin (author of *The Soul of the Stranger: Reading God and Torah from a Transgender Perspective*); and Dara Papo (UC Berkeley alum and member of the first cohort of the Pathways LGBT Leadership program—a partnership between Keshet and the Jewish Community Federation of San Francisco—and currently serves as Co-Chair of the Federation's LGBT Alliance).

Keshet's Youth Programs Manager Amram Altzman has a degree in Jewish history and sociology from Columbia University's joint undergraduate program with the Jewish Theological Seminary. Director of Education and Training Rabbi Micah Buck-Yael is a Washington University alumnus, Executive Assistant and Advocacy Assistant Kaden Mohamed is the Young Leaders Council at Fenway Health, Director of Strategic Communications Eugene Patron launched an LGBTQ-specific website for Cox Communications, Associate Director of Education and Training Emily Saltzman was previously employed by Planned Parenthood of NYC, Grants Manager Emily Solomon serves on the alumni committee for Cornell where she interviews prospective students, and Families with Young Children Coordinator Jaime Brody is on the steering committee for Out MetroWest, helping to form one of the first middle school LGBTQ groups in the Boston area.

Other significant recent donations have come from UJA-Federation of New York, the Amy Mandel and Katrina Rodis Fund, the Walter and Elise Haas Fund, the Morningstar Foundation, the Jewish Federation of Metropolitan Chicago, Combined Jewish Philanthropies of Greater Boston, the Klarman Family Foundation, and the Paul E. Singer Foundation (the Jewish vulture capitalist Paul Singer's foundation). It's worth considering at what cost these Jewish vulture capitalists like Paul Singer and Seth Klarman are able to finance their "generous" donations to the LGBTQ "community" and to their fellow Jews. As Andrew Joyce writes:

> Boston-based Seth Klarman (net worth $1.5 billion), who like Paul Singer has declared "free enterprise has been good for me," is a rapacious debt exploiter who was integral to the financial collapse of Puerto Rico, where he hid much of activities behind a series of shell companies. Investigative journalists eventually discovered that Klarman's Baupost group was behind much of the aggressive legal action intended to squeeze the decimated island for bond payments.

Well that's not very philanthropic, now is it? Is this the much-vaunted mitzvah or the tikkun olam we hear so much about? Joyce continues:

> One of the reasons for such secrecy is the intensive Jewish philanthropy engaged in by Klarman under his Klarman Family Foundation. While Puerto Rican schools are being closed, and pensions and health provisions slashed, Klarman is regurgitating the proceeds of massive debt speculation to his "areas of focus" which prominently includes "Supporting the global Jewish community and Israel." While plundering the treasuries of the crippled nations of the goyim, Klarman and his co-ethnic associates have committed themselves to "improving the quality of life and access to opportunities for all Israeli citizens so that they may benefit from the country's prosperity." Among those in Klarman's nest, their beaks agape for Puerto Rican debt interest, are the American Jewish Committee, Boston's Combined Jewish Philanthropies, the Holocaust Memorial Museum, the Honeymoon Israel Foundation, Israel-America Academic Exchange, and the Israel Project.

Klarman, like Singer, has also been an enthusiastic proponent of liberalising attitudes to homosexuality, donating $1 million to a Republican super PAC aimed at supporting pro-gay marriage GOP candidates in 2014 (Singer donated $1.75 million). Klarman, who also contributes to candidates who support immigration reform, including a path to citizenship for undocumented immigrants, has said "The right to gay marriage is the largest remaining civil rights issue of our time. I work one-on-one with individual Republicans to try to get them to realize they are being Neanderthals on this issue."

Though Klarman has now taken his toys to the Democrat sandbox, the insistence on Jewish preeminence, mass immigration, and homosexuality have not wavered—indeed, they've actually found a more receptive audience on all issues save perhaps Israel, and even then, it's mostly window dressing. New kids on the block like homosexual 2020 presidential candidate Pete Buttigieg have not come out of the disaster profiteering in Puerto Rico smelling exactly rosy, either, via Alexander Sammon:

The sincerity of Buttigieg's pledges to Puerto Rico, in particular, has raised eyebrows. Just two days after his Latino outreach plan was unveiled, it was revealed that Team Buttigieg had omitted more than 20 high-powered fundraisers from its official list of bundlers. . . . Buttigieg has already returned funding raised by H. Rodgin Cohen, another bundler his campaign omitted from its initial fundraisers list. Cohen, a Wall Street legend, represented a smattering of banks during the financial crisis, helping to broker more than a dozen deals with financial institutions during the bailout. . . . [Also] among those left out was William Rahm, a senior managing director at the private equity firm Centerbridge Partners. And while it's hardly a surprise that high-ranking private equity titans are allies of the Buttigieg campaign, Centerbridge Partners has a uniquely infamous reputation for its work buying up distressed debt in Puerto Rico. . . . Centerbridge was one of several firms that long concealed its Puerto Rican debt holdings through shell companies. It sat on the steering committee of a coalition of bondholders known as the Ad Hoc group, which fought relentlessly in court for full repayment on $4.5 billion in constitutionally guaranteed general obligation bonds. Centerbridge also at one point carried $390 million in Puerto Rican public-employee retirement system bonds. Hedge funds like Centerbridge have been instrumental in inaugurating a wave of austerity: vast cuts to education, health care, and social services to help facilitate payment of debt scooped up on the cheap. That parasitic work has effectively thwarted recovery from economic depression on the island before Hurricane Maria and reconstruction since, causing Puerto Ricans to flee the island in droves while hedge funds salt away huge profits. . . . Even before the revelation of Buttigieg's ties to Centerbridge, he was dogged by associations to another group known for its work in Puerto Rico: McKinsey. The consultancy firm that Buttigieg worked at between 2007 and 2010 has itself been intimately involved in Puerto Rican politics in recent years. In fact, McKinsey was paid millions in fees for its work on the Promesa board, an unelected financial oversight panel created by the Obama administration to adjudicate the aforementioned austerity measures that have devastated the island. It's known inside Puerto Rico as "la junta." McKinsey worked doing "development, recommendations and writing the Territory's fiscal plan or the amendment to the fiscal plan submitted for approval by the governor of Puerto Rico." In plain English, McKinsey's role was advising how best to slash the budget to provide headroom to pay the vultures. McKinsey also had a self-interest here beyond the $50 million-plus in consulting fees: Affiliates of the company owned Puerto Rican debt, which would be paid back if the consultants managed to devastate public spending enough to find the money. . . . Given the number of McKinsey executives who have already conferred max-level donations upon the Buttigieg campaign, the connection is not insignificant.

In other words, all of the concern for the poor, downtrodden brown people of the world is a sick joke, and with a ruined island, many more brown people are flooding into the US mainland, fleeing the carnage, which is surely by design. Through the "generous" donations of Klarman and others like him to Boston's Combined Jewish Philanthropies, as but one example, that organization is then able to partner with and help fund Catholic Charities to funnel increasing numbers of Third World migrants into the United States, made all the easier in the case of Puerto Rico as it is an American territory. Isn't neo-liberalism wonderful?

## Climate of Queer

*"If you want to take your mind off the fact that you have thousands of dollars of student loan debt but can't get a job, go to the gay disco! Take a walk along the banks of the St. Joseph River under the garish but strangely soothing glow of South Bend's $700,000 gay disco lights as they flash out the rainbow hues that signify that you are now a conquered nation that is ruled by gay commissars like Mayor Pete [Buttigieg]."*

– E. Michael Jones

The mid-1980s marks the time when private foundations' support for the LGBTQ agenda shifted from first gear to second; as Karen Zelermyer writes:

> The Mertz Gilmore Foundation played a critical role in the development of Funders for LGBTQ Issues and encouraged other progressive foundations to support lesbian and gay equality. In 1985 it made its first grant supporting lesbians and gay men to Lambda Legal for its work in providing legal protection for people with AIDS. . . . The Mertz Gilmore Foundation awarded the ACLU of Northern California $10,000 in 1989 for its Domestic Partners Project which sought to "establish legal protection for lesbian and gay male relationships. . . ." A $12,500 grant from the J. Roderick MacArthur Foundation in 1987 to Alternatives to Militarism, a small national peace and justice organization, was the first to address sexual orientation discrimination in the military, specifically military regulations directing the dismissal of a female member of the Air National Guard in New York. . . . .It was in 1987 that total annual funding for lesbian and gay issues first surpassed the $1 million mark. Five years later, the Los Angeles-based David Geffen Foundation awarded two $1 million grants for HIV/AIDS programs: one to AIDS Project Los Angeles ($1,026,500.00), and one to Gay Men's Health Crisis ($1,003,500.00). These were the first million-dollar grants made to lesbian and gay-related endeavors.

The Paul Rapoport Foundation was founded by the estate of the deceased Paul Israel Rapoport who along with Larry Kramer, Nathan Fain, and others founded the Gay Men's Health Crisis (GMHC), which originally operated out of a property owned by Mel Cheren, "The Godfather of Disco." As John-Manuel Andriote writes:

Shortly after the first reports of AIDS hit the press in 1981, Larry Mass asked Donald Krintzman in a *New York Native* interview about being a "cancer patient." Before AIDS had a name, someone with Kaposi's sarcoma was simply called a cancer patient. How, asked Mass, did this new identity fit with his other identities—including gay, male, American, Jewish, and New Yorker. Krintzman [was] the former lover of GMHC cofounder Paul Rapoport (who himself died of AIDS) and the first person with AIDS ever interviewed in the press.[38]

The David Geffen Foundation, founded by its namesake the Jewish homosexual record company magnate, has donated to a number of LGBTQ causes such as the Movement Advancement Project (MAP), "an independent think tank that provides rigorous research, insight, and analysis that help speed equality for LGBT people," which has also been highlighted by Democracy Alliance as part of its "Progressive Infrastructure Map." Based in Chicago, Naomi Goldberg leads MAP's in-depth policy analyses. Prior to joining MAP, Goldberg was a public policy fellow at the Williams Institute at UCLA, where her research focused on "adoption and foster care, domestic partner benefits, and the issues affecting older LGBT Americans."

MAP has worked with SAGE and Columbia Law School, and in late 2017 held a panel discussion on the joint project, "Dignity Denied: Religious Exemptions and LGBT Elder Services" featuring additional speakers from the ACLU and the New Jewish Home. Other principal sources of funding for MAP include: the David Bohnett Foundation, the Laughing Gull Foundation, the H. van Ameringen Foundation, the Wild Geese Foundation, David Dechman (previously a partner at Goldman Sachs and co-founder and current CEO of Summit Rock Advisors) and his partner Michel Mercure, the Gill Foundation, the Evelyn and Walter Haas, Jr. Fund, the Johnson Family Foundation, the Amy Mandel and Katina Rodis Fund, the Palette Fund, and the Ford Foundation, among others.

The Palette Fund was launched in 2008 in the memory of Rand Harlan Scolnick, "a philanthropist who volunteered time, money and corporate commitments to several AIDS organizations in the US and abroad, as well as to Jewish nonprofits and other community groups," by his partner Peter Benassi, a major donor to the Human Rights Campaign, and Terrence Meck. Meck is its President and also sits on the Board of the MAP and is President of Intrinsic Capital, an investment firm "dedicated to providing seed-stage funding to socially progressive startups." MAP's Board also includes a representative of the Ford Foundation.

Palette Board member Blaire Meck is a Soros Fund Management hedge fund alum; Treasurer and Secretary Kristin Resnansky is another of these Stanford MBA/venture capital types like a Tom Steyer; and Board member Todd Sears was a financial advisor with Merrill Lynch where in his description, "he created the first team of financial advisors on Wall Street to focus on the LGBT community and brought $1.5 billion in new assets to the firm." He then moved into "equality leadership" both at Merrill Lynch and Credit Suisse. He is on the Boards of the Williams Institute at UCLA, Lambda Legal, and the US State Department's Global Equality Fund. The Palette Fund focuses on providing financial support to "organizations across the United States that are actively breaking down barriers for the LGBTQ

---

[38] Andriote, *Victory Deferred*, 173.

community." One of their primary focus areas is on "advocacy and services bene-fitting LGBTQ sex workers." Some of their grantees include: Q Clinic (a free clinic serving homeless LGBTQI youths in New York City staffed by students at the Co-lumbia University College of Physicians and Surgeons), The Point Foundation, MAP, GLSEN, GLAD, GLAAD, Funders for LGBTQ Issues, Center for American Progress, True Colors Fund, Association of Transgender Professionals, The Family Acceptance Project at UCLA, Columbia LGBT Health Fellowship, Immigration Equality, The Hetrick-Martin Institute, United Way, Stonewall Community Founda-tion, Liberty Hill Foundation, Callen-Lorde Community Health Center, The Maz-zoni Center, Posse Foundation, Queer Kids, Provincetown TEDx, Human Rights Campaign, Lambda Legal, Children's Radio Foundation, Clinton Global Initiative, MAC AIDS Fund, Princeton Philanthropy in the Classroom, Transgender Law Cen-ter, Queer Consciousness Fund (North Star Fund), Elton John AIDS Foundation, Mount Sinai Hospital, Media Matters for America, Columbia Law School's Center for Gender and Sexuality Law, The Williams Institute at UCLA, and Fenway Health.

The two Co-Directors of Columbia Law School's Center for Gender and Sexual-ity Law are Suzanne B. Goldberg and Katherine Franke (on the steering committee of the Academic Advisory Council of the Jewish Voice for Peace).

The MAC AIDS Fund (now re-named the MAC VIVA Glam Fund) derives much of its funding from the sale of its VIVA Glam products. The first MAC Cosmetics' VIVA Glam brand ambassador/spokesperson was drag queen RuPaul, and other spokespeople include some of the most famous celebrities on the planet such as Nicki Minaj, Ariana Grande, Lady Gaga, and Miley Cyrus. MAC Cosmetics is owned by the Estée Lauder Companies. The Lauder family is Jewish.

Prominent figures of the Williams Institute's Founders Council include: Rabbi Barbara Zacky; Todd Sears; Michaela Ivri Mendelsohn (profiled in 2016 *Jerusalem Post* article: "From Michael to Michaela: A Jewish transition story"); Laurie F. Has-encamp (USC Law School graduate, former President of the Board of Kehillat Israel, former assistant operations officer at Lloyds Bank California, and member of the National Leadership Council of GLSEN); Mike Gleason (Senior Financial Advisor-Wealth Management at Wells Fargo Advisors); Jeffrey S. Haber (lead land use and real estate counsel for Cedars-Sinai Medical Center, The J. Paul Getty Trust, Dream-Works Animation, IAC, and Regent Properties); Tom Morgan (Harvard Business School Executive Education Program graduate, former Home Lending Chief Infor-mation Officer at both Bank of America and JP Morgan Chase and served on the Mortgage Bankers Association's Residential Technology Steering Committee, and former member of Bank of America's Global Diversity Council); Sandra L. Richards (leads the Business Development efforts focused on the Diverse and Multicultural Markets for Morgan Stanley Wealth Management); and Eric Berger (former internal strategy associate for Ethicon, a Johnson & Johnson company, and in 2013 he spear-headed the Credit Suisse LGBT Impact Investing Initiative, which led to the creation of the first-ever LGBT equality index and portfolio).

The Hetrick-Martin Institute is explicitly geared toward "LGBTQ+ youth" ages 13–24. Youth members are provided free clinical services at locations such as the Callen-Lorde Community Health Center and Mount Sinai, as well as the CK Life Trans Clinic at Bronx Lebanon Hospital, Woodhull Hospital (where they can obtain HIV medications and "other comprehensive medical services"), the Q Clinic, and

Planned Parenthood. Both of Hetrick-Martin's Co-Chairs of the Board, Laura Levenstein and Brad Silver of WarnerMedia, are Jewish, as are a number of staff and Board members past and present. Who are their major donors? Bloomberg LP, Bonnie E. Rabin and Suzanne Leibowitz, Facebook, the MAC AIDS Fund, Macy's (where Vice Chair Josh Saterman is something called the Head of Diversity and Inclusion Engagement), New York Life Foundation, HBO, the H. van Ameringen Foundation, the David Geffen Foundation, WarnerMedia, Wells Fargo, ViiV, Calvin Klein, GlaxoSmithKline, Lambda Legal, BlackRock, and the New York Community Trust.[39] They are also partnered with the CDC and a number of New York City- and State-based governmental agencies, as well as the New Jersey Department of Children and Families. They also have a number of "celebrity ambassadors" such as Kimora Lee Simmons, Zachary Quinto, B.D. Wong, and Alan Cumming.

The Transgender Law Center (TLC) collaborated with Harvard Law School on the Transgender Healthcare Advocacy Webinar in early 2020; the Jewish Community Federation and Endowment Fund of San Francisco, the Peninsula, Marin and Sonoma Counties is a major donor. Tessa Lauren, Development Assistant for the Transgender Law Center, is a "Jewish queer trans femme with a background in queer and trans activism throughout the state of California, beginning with her role in the creation of the first trans and non-binary-specific student group at her university back in 2009." Lauren is "a passionate advocate for the intersectional potential of queer/trans and sex worker activism." "Queer Jewish activist" Carrie Kaufman is on their Advisory Board.

Along with eighty-one other organizations, the TLC co-signed support for the 2013 Student Non-Discrimination Act ("SNDA") which would establish "a comprehensive federal prohibition against discrimination and harassment in public elementary and secondary schools across the country based on a student's actual or perceived sexual orientation or gender identity." The Student Non-Discrimination Act was sponsored by Senator Al Franken and Representatives Jared Polis and Ileana Ros-Lehtinen. Franken and Polis are both Jewish; Polis is also homosexual. Ros-Lehtinen is Cuban and was the first Latina elected to Congress. Among the co-signers supporting the bill were the ACLU, the SPLC, the NAACP, the American Psychological Association (APA), the Sargent Shriver National Center on Poverty Law, Amnesty International, La Raza, Union for Reform Judaism, Asian American Legal Defense and Education Fund (AALDEF), the Human Rights Campaign, the Association of Flight Attendants – CWA, the Center for American Progress Action Fund, Lambda Legal, the National Association of School Psychologists, the National Association of Secondary School Principals, the National Black Justice Coalition, the National Council of Jewish Women, and the Log Cabin Republicans! Log Cabin Republicans is "the nation's largest Republican organization dedicated to representing LGBT conservatives and allies."

Speaking of gay neo-cons, Human Rights First, which pledges resources to the LGBTQ agenda, is also very preoccupied with combatting anti-Semitism in addition to "protecting the human rights of LGBT people." Along with the ubiquitous World War II reference, this had my antennae up, and as we should by now expect, we see a massive Jewish overrepresentation in positions of leadership (and they are very well-compensated). COO Zachary Silverstein is a Yale and Northwestern alumnus.

---

[39] Net assets at the end of 2018 were over $2.5 billion.

Senior Advisor for Combatting Antisemitism Ira Forman is a Harvard alum and a Stanford MBA. He was appointed the US State Department's Special Envoy to Monitor and Combat Anti-Semitism (SEAS) in May 2013, serving until January 2017, and from 2011–2012 he was the Jewish Outreach Director for the Obama for America campaign. He also served for nearly fifteen years as the Executive Director of the National Jewish Democratic Council (NJDC). Forman is also a visiting professor and senior fellow at Georgetown University's Center for Jewish Civilization, where he teaches courses "on confronting contemporary antisemitism." Human Rights First is very anti-Russia, and uses "LGBT discrimination" and a "clampdown on dissent"—as well as linking Bashar al-Assad—through what looks like a Log Cabin Republicans-style neo-conservative astroturf job.

Returning to the Transgender Law Center, Marci Bowers helped sponsor its 10th anniversary celebration in 2012, and partnering organizations included: Kink.com, Google, BALIF: An LGBTQI Bar Association,[40] Macy's, the Evelyn and Walter Haas, Jr. Fund, the ACLU, the Jewish Vocational Service, the GSA Network, and Gender Spectrum.[41] The Transgender Law Center (TLC)'s description of activities and funding from their 2018 IRS 990 Form:

> Our representation of trans immigrants . . . expands the ability for people with serious criminal convictions related to being trafficked to obtain asylum. . . . In December 2018, TLC announced litigation against ICE for the wrongful death of Roxsana Hernandez, an HIV+ transgender woman, in immigration detention in New Mexico. . . . Also in December 2018, TLC learned that three trans women living with HIV in the most recent caravan at the border were very ill. Due to our past experiences working with immigrants in the two previous caravans, we decided that it was essential to go to the border and help them enter the United States. . . . We then reached out to contacts in the government and arranged for the women to enter through a port of entry.
>
> [We are] working on an advocacy letter in support of a transgender woman who experienced discrimination while in a coma due to complications in dialysis treatment in a hospital. . . .[42] Besides our general programs, communications and policy advocacy work, we want to highlight the following: Black Trans Circles (BTC) is [a] new program created by Raquel Willis, funded by a Soros Equality Fellowship and hosted by Transgender Law Center . . . TLC's legal challenge to the Veterans Health Administration's sexual reassignment surgery exclusion resulted in a VA call for public comments on

---

[40] Sponsors include Google, Stanford Health Care, AT&T, Uber, and Pritzker Levine LLP.

[41] Featured speakers at their 2016 Gender Spectrum Professionals' Symposium included Jessie Rose Cohen—"Gender Specialist in Private Practice in Oakland, California"; Rey Byrne, self-described as "a white, non-binary, transgender, fat, Jewish, and not-quite-abled therapist"; and Chav Doherty—"MS in Counseling with a concentration in Marriage, Family and Child Counseling from SF State University. He holds a prior MA in Jewish Studies from the Graduate Theological Union in Berkeley, where he studied Feminist Judaism and Jewish Mysticism. Chav has been involved in trans* community in the SF Bay Area for over 2 decades. Chav has written articles on FTM identity and trans* healthcare for publication. An autobiographical essay, 'The Trayf Jew,' was published in the Lambda Literary Award-winning anthology, *Balancing on the Mechizta: Transgender in Jewish Community*. Chav recently retired from UCSF after 29 years of service. He currently works full-time as a licensed therapist at Spectrum Practice of Berkeley—primarily with adolescents and young adults on issues of gender and neurodiversity."

[42] Easily one of the most ludicrous accusations of "discrimination" I've seen.

making SRS available to veterans . . . We co-planned and co-led the national #AbolishICE convening Albuquerque which brought 100 LGBTQ+ migrants, mostly people of color, together for 3 days of community building. On the 3rd day we shut down a major intersection for 3 hours to draw attention to the death of Roxsana in ICE custody as well as the continued detainment of Udoka Nweke and other LGBTQ+ migrants. . . . We are thrilled to report that Udoka Nweke, a Black gay migrant whom we'd been fighting to get out of detention for much of the past year was released on parole. We have begun the process of getting him settled in [a] new location and raising funds he can live on while awaiting his work permit. We have also been assisting a 52-year-old Jamaican trans woman detained at Cibola Detention Center in New Mexico, connecting her with an attorney and raising funds to cover key costs for her.

We took part in the Movement for Black Lives policy retreat and co-authored the Migrant Justice policy paper that will serve as the policy backbone for M4BL's work. We were invited and attended CINEBEH, the largest LGBT conference in Brazil and keynoted the conference where we spoke about the realities for Black LGBTQ+ migrants in the US.

Next up: the Indigenous Two-Spirit Everything-but-the-Kitchen-Sink Foundation's Infinity Migrants Project! These projects are beyond asinine, but the inherent ridiculousness paradoxically seems to strengthen the agenda. What is abundantly clear is that these organizations are being situated as the antithesis of not just Whites and their cultures, and not even of general normality and decency, but of any kind of morality save the Establishment's depraved anti-morality. This kind of degenerate trash is only possible when one drinks the Kool-Aid that we are all "equal," and that equality somehow entitles wide-spread parasitic entitlement at the expense of others. Now that the bottom's dropped out of our civilization, or perhaps more appropriately the drainage system has been sufficiently backed-up, we are drowning in tons of raw sewage while the ruling class looks on and laughs.

In another context, the widely-circulated Google Doc "LIST OF TRANS FUNDS AND RESOURCES" would be tragicomic. In some ways what is obviously a pathetic cash-grab masquerading as activism still is; the list of cash app and Go Fund Me links to HELP INDIVIDUAL TRANS FOLX DIRECTLY belies a roll call of "folx" in various stages of desperation and in need of real help plus an assortment of parasitic freaks (all said in context, and no, I am not making any of this up):

- Demi needs help "black trans and moving to Iowa"
- Help salem get home "help a black nonbinary lesbian move back home"
- Taj Pollard "black trans artist getting top surgery"
- NYC BLACK WOMXN & FEMMES MUTUAL AID LIST
- Help Zaire with therapy housing and medical costs "$theunicornprincess"
- PAY BLACK TRANS WOMEN
- SECURE LONG TERM HOUSING FOR BLACK TRANS PEOPLE BEING RELEASED FROM RIKERS ISLAND
- BLACK EXCELLENCE COLLECTIVE TRANSPORT FOR LGBTQ+ PROTESTORS NYC
- LGBT BOOKS TO PRISONERS

- BLACK TRANS PROTESTERS FUND
- BLACK QT FUND
- BLACK TRANS TRAVEL FUND
- FUND BLACK TRANS WOMEN AND NB PEOPLE IN MN

And on it goes. This horror show continues to spread globally courtesy of friends in high places like the Ford Foundation, a major pillar of the LGBTQ agenda, which, again from Zelermyer:

> In 1990. . . . made the first known international grant to support lesbian and gay people. It went to Atoba, the Homosexual Emancipation Movement, based in Brazil. Atoba, an advocacy organization, was founded in 1985 in response to the murder of a friend of the founders, and became one of the first organizations in South America to engage in AIDS-related work. Ford has gone on to become one of the leading international funders of LGBTI issues, having awarded more than $9 million since that first grant [to the end of 2011], to support NGOs working outside the United States. It has made significant grants to groups in Vietnam, Argentina, Kenya and Nepal and to leading organizations in the United States working internationally, such as the International Gay and Lesbian Human Rights Commission.

On November 28th, 2012, the Ford Foundation brought together LGBTQ leaders and allies, artists, journalists, technologists, policymakers, and funders in a catalyzing event to explore how to best progress the LGBTQ agenda, and how, in their words, "social justice can be inclusive of sexual orientation and gender identity, and how to engage broad communities in securing rights for LGBT people." Featured panel members speak volumes (with accompanying position at the time of the event): Luis Ubiñas, President of the Ford Foundation; Jorge Gutierrez, Project Coordinator of the Queer Undocumented Immigrant Project; Chai Feldblum, Commissioner of the US Equal Employment Opportunity Commission; and Neera Tanden, President of the Center for American Progress, a think tank founded by John Podesta. Podesta served as counselor to President Barack Obama, where he was responsible for coordinating the administration's climate policy and initiatives, and was a member of the UN Secretary General's High-Level Panel of Eminent Persons on the Post-2015 Development Agenda, a panel that also included David Cameron, Horst Kohler (IMF), Jean-Michel Severino (World Bank), Paul Polman (Unilever, Nestlé, World Economic Forum), Abhijit Banerjee (Ford Foundation International Professor of Economics at MIT), and Gunilla Carlsson (UNAIDS, former Swedish Minister for International Development Cooperation, World Bank Group's High Level Advisory Council on Women's Economic Empowerment, European Council on Foreign Relations, GAVI, the Global Fund, Annexin Pharmaceuticals).

   Chai Feldblum is an "openly lesbian" Harvard Law graduate who "once aspired to be a Talmudic scholar. . . . coming from a long line of Orthodox rabbis." Feldblum was an Obama appointee to the Equal Employment Opportunity Commission and was the lead drafter of the Employment Non-Discrimination Act ("legislation proposed in the United States Congress that would prohibit discrimination in hiring and employment on the basis of sexual orientation or, depending on the version of the bill, gender identity by employers with at least 15 employees"); Feldblum cast the deciding vote when the EEOC termed it "unlawful sex discrimination" to limit locker room and shower facilities to those of a single biological sex.

The Jewish Suzanne Nossel is a member of the Council on Foreign Relations (CFR) and was also a senior fellow for the Century Foundation and the Center for American Progress (CAP). She was the architect of the first UN resolution on the rights of lesbian, gay, bisexual and transgender persons, and was the Executive Director of PEN America. As just one example of the kind of work PEN America is doing, PEN America-Los Angeles ran a book drive for migrant children in September 2019 in partnership with the Jewish Family Service Migrant Family Shelter.

According to the Center for American Progress's 2017 issue paper "Advancing LGBTQ Equality Through Local Executive Action" authored by among others Sharita Gruberg, the senior director for the LGBTQ Research and Communications Project at CAP, former law clerk for the American Bar Association Commission on Immigration where she provided support to immigration detainees in removal proceedings including LGBT asylum seekers and filed complaints on detention conditions with the Department of Homeland Security, and formerly held a fellowship with the UN High Commissioner for Refugees where she wrote and submitted refugee resettlement requests and liaised with congressional offices on refugee resettlement cases: "County and city leaders should issue executive orders or mayoral directives that explicitly prohibit discrimination based on sexual orientation, gender identity, or gender expression in government employment."

CAP celebrates four decisions: in 2011, Dwight C. Jones, the mayor of Richmond, Virginia, issued an executive directive prohibiting discrimination against city government employees on the basis of sexual orientation or gender identity; in 2012, Daniel McCoy, the county executive of Albany, New York, issued an executive order adding gender identity and gender expression to the list of classes protected from workplace discrimination in the county government; in 2016, James Ritsema, the city manager of Kalamazoo, Michigan, issued an equal employment opportunity policy for city employment to "increase opportunities based on classifications including race, sex, gender identity, and sexual orientation"; and in 2015, Allan Kauffman, mayor of Goshen, Indiana, signed an executive order expanding the discrimination and harassment policy for city government employees and applicants. The policy already prohibited discrimination on the basis of sexual orientation, but Kauffman's executive order expanded it to include a prohibition on gender identity discrimination and harassment. With this executive order in place, all residents in Goshen could file complaints of discrimination on the basis gender identity, along with sexual orientation and other protected classes.

Similar measures praised by CAP include those of Jersey City, New Jersey, which "actively recruits LGBT individuals to serve within municipal agencies such as the [Jersey City] police and fire departments" and the NYPD:

> Since before 2000, the New York City Police Department, or NYPD, has actively recruited officers from the LGBTQ community. Today, the NYPD's Community Affairs Bureau LGBT Outreach Unit assists in recruiting potential officers from the LGBTQ community.

CAP also celebrates the proliferation of "offices of diversity and inclusion" in cities like San Antonio, Texas and Jersey City. Naturally the authors of this document try to shoe-horn the bogeyman of "conversion therapy" in there despite the fact that their project centers on conversion therapy of its own kind and cult-like mind-re-molding techniques. If the regime can get them young enough so they don't even have to be broken down and re-built into the gender-queer sloganeering automatons of the future, so much the better.

As the 1990s unfolded, politically the onset of the Clinton administration marked a major shift, and 1993 witnessed both the passing of "Don't Ask, Don't Tell" and the appointment and confirmation of Roberta Achtenberg to Assistant Secretary for the Office of Fair Housing and Equal Opportunity, in the process becoming the first open homosexual appointed and confirmed to a federal position by the Senate. The Jewish Dianne Feinstein spoke out strongly on her behalf. In the lead-up to the 1992 presidential election, the UC Berkeley alum and Stanford University teaching fellow Achtenberg had worked on the Clinton campaign, helping to organize fund-raisers and other events. Achtenberg was a member of the committee drafting the Democratic Party's platform, and, as Linda Rapp writes on glbtq, Inc., "she addressed the national convention in defense of the document. In introducing herself to the delegates, she proudly identified herself as a lesbian, a mother, and a Jew."

Though the Boy Scouts ultimately succumbed and then some, back then Achtenberg was one of over fifty members of the United Way Bay Area Board of Directors who voted unanimously to not give funds to the Boy Scouts because of their "discriminatory policy against gay and bisexual boys." Achtenberg states that among her proudest achievements was the forced integration of previously all-white Vidor, Texas, which the libertarians and their freedom of association don't seem to have complained about. Achtenberg helped develop a "public housing project" for Vidor, and "worked with community leaders to ensure successful and peaceful integration." Achtenberg was in charge of the Housing and Urban Development Department's Agency Review Team that helped the Obama administration as it transitioned into office, and in 2011, she was named to the US Commission on Civil Rights.

The Jewish transgender "activist" Riki Wilchins founded LGBTQ political action committee GenderPAC in 1995, which within a year had secured public pledges from predominantly Jewish members of Congress such as Jerrold Nadler and Jan Schakowsky that their offices "would not discriminate against employees because of their gender identity or expression." Sheila Jeffreys contended, rightly, that its aims ignored women in favor of "transgenders, most of whom are men, and homosexuality." GenderPAC ceased operations in 2009. Wilchins co-edited *Gender-Queer: Voices from Beyond the Binary* in 2002 with Clare Howell and Joan Nestle, who sees her work as critical to her identity as a woman, as a lesbian, and as a Jew: "As a woman, as a lesbian, as a Jew, I know that much of what I call history others will not. But answering that challenge of exclusion is the work of a lifetime."

Jewish "LGBT historian" Lillian Faderman (also formerly a visiting professor at UCLA among other things) calls Nestle "the midwife to a revised view of butch and femme." As GenderPAC's Executive Director, Wilchins advised IBM, JP Morgan Chase, and Citigroup among others on their "gender identity and gender expression non-discrimination policies." Her writings have appeared in many places, including anthologies like *The Meaning of Difference: American Constructions of Race, Sex and Gender, Social Class, Sexual Orientation, and Disability: a Text/Reader*, co-edited by Karen E. Rosenblum, and *PoMoSexuals: Challenging Assumptions About Gender and Sexuality* co-edited by the Jewish Lawrence Schimel.

Lawrence Schimel, founding member of the Publishing Triangle, writes and edits works that deal with homosexual and Jewish themes; Publishing Triangle is an association of homosexuals in the publishing world, which also issues annual literary awards in the various subgenres of both literature and sexuality/gender identity. One example is the Publishing Triangle Award for Trans and Gender-Variant Literature; most of the previous winners are college professors such as the transgender Vivek Shraya, Assistant Professor of Creative Writing at the University of Calgary and Board member of The Tegan and Sara Foundation, "which fights for health, economic justice and representation for LGBTQ women." Shraya's 2010 debut is "an illustrated collection of twenty-one linked short stories about a brown, genderqueer child growing up in an immigrant family in Alberta," and 2016 saw the release of the poetry collection *even this page is white*, "an incisive exploration of the effects of everyday racism and colonialism in Canada," longlisted for the Canadian Broadcasting Corporation's *Canada Reads* competition, because institutional racism, sexism, transphobia, and the like precludes a genderqueer person of color from getting any recognition or institutional support such as professorships without the usually-requisite academic qualifications, right? Right.

2018 Publishing Triangle Award for Trans and Gender-Variant Literature winner Tourmaline, "a transgender woman who identifies as queer," has a BA in Comparative Ethnic Studies from Columbia University, where "she" served on the President's Council on Student Affairs, a group which sought to advise the president on professors intimidating Jewish and pro-Israel students amidst the MEALAC Scandal. Tourmaline collaborated with Dean Spade on a series of "prison abolition" videos and has previously worked for the Sylvia Rivera Law Project. Tourmaline co-produced *STAR People Are Beautiful People* (2009) with the Jewish Sasha Wortzel[43] and was featured in *Brave Spaces: Perspectives on Faith and LGBT Justice* (2015), produced by the Jewish Marc Smolowitz and screened at a Human Rights Campaign event.

Tourmaline co-wrote, -produced, and -directed Stonewall-focused short film *Happy Birthday, Marsha!* with Wortzel, and they were awarded a fellowship with Jewish homosexual Ira Sachs's Queer/Art/Mentorship program for 2012–2013. Tourmaline has also been the recipient of a Soros Justice Fellowship (as birthname Reginald Gossett) and was the 2016–2018 Activist-in-Residence (alongside Dean Spade and others) at the Barnard Center for Research on Women's Social Justice Institute, which "marks the next chapter of BCRW's commitment to scholar-feminist praxis and accountable exchange with activists and organizations in New York City and beyond." The Center is "a nexus of feminist thought, activism, and collaboration for scholars and activists" housed at Barnard College, founded by the Jewish Annie Nathan Meyer and affiliated with Columbia University.

The Jewish Dean Spade is an Associate Professor at the Seattle University School of Law. In 2002, as an Open Society Institute and Berkeley Law Foundation Fellow, Spade founded the Sylvia Rivera Law Project, which "works to guarantee that all people are free to self-determine gender identity and expression," and is funded by the Tikkun Olam Foundation, the Tides Foundation, the Elton John AIDS Foundation, the Groundswell Fund, the ARIA Foundation, the New York Community Trust,

---

[43] Wortzel's *42 Butter Lane* was included in the 2014 exhibition *Roaming House* curated by Jewish feminist Mira Schor.

the New York Foundation, the Keith Haring Foundation,[44] Borealis Philanthropy, the Arcus Foundation, and the Rockefeller Foundation, among others.

Spade has also been the Williams Institute Law Teaching Fellow at UCLA Law School, was selected to give the 2009–2010 James A. Thomas Lecture at Yale Law School, and has also taught classes on sexual orientation, gender identity, poverty, and law at Columbia University and Harvard. In 2010, the *Harvard Journal of Law and Gender* published a series of letters between Adrienne Davis and Bob Chang entitled, "Making Up Is Hard to Do: Race/Gender/Sexual Orientation in the Law School Classroom," along with three response pieces by Adele Morrison, Darren Rosenblum, and Spade. Among Spade's other various manifestos and writings on transgenderism, privilege, and the like, "he" edited two issues of *Sexuality Research and Social Policy* with Paisley Currah, who is along with Susan Stryker the founding editor of *Transgender Studies Quarterly* through Duke University Press. The debut issue featured Chelsea né Bradley Manning on the cover, which, for Currah and Stryker, "could be [a] no better illustration of the timeliness or significance of paying careful attention to transgender issues."

Currah, MA and PhD from Cornell University, was a founding Board member of the Transgender Law and Policy Institute, serves on the Board of Directors for Global Action for Trans Equality (GATE), has served on the advisory board of the Human Rights Watch Lesbian, Gay, Bisexual, and Transgender Rights Program, and from January 2005–December 2006 sat on the External Advisory Committee to the New York City Department of Health and Mental Hygiene for the Amendment of Birth Certificates for Transgender Persons. From November 2004 to December 2005, Currah served on the Citizen's Advisory Committee Transgender Subcommittee, New York City Human Resources Administration and co-authored "Recommended Best Practices for Working with and Serving Transgender and Gender Non-Conforming Employees and Clients."

Currah was also a co-founder of the New York Association for Gender Rights Advocacy, and helped draft the legislation to amend the New York City Human Rights Law to include discrimination based on "gender identity and gender expression." Currah has been an advisor to the LGBT Social Science and Public Policy Center at Hunter College, Sexuality and the Law Social Science Research Network, the International Resource Network (a project hosted at the Center for Lesbian and Gay Studies at the City University of New York and funded by the Ford Foundation), and the University Consortium on Sexuality Research and Training. Currah co-edited with Shannon Minter and Richard Juang *Transgender Rights*, published by Minnesota University Press in 2006. Minter, like Currah, is transgender and is also an alumnus of Cornell University (Cornell Law School). Minter has taught at Stanford University and is the legal director for the National Center for Lesbian Rights (NCLR).

The National Center for Lesbian Rights (NCLR), based out of San Francisco naturally, has been active since the 1970s "advancing the civil and human rights of LGBTQ people and their families through impact litigation, public policy, and public education." They were at the forefront of creating what they believe to be the first LGBTQ Immigration Project and they continue to "fight for the rights of LGBTQ

---

[44] The foundation's namesake apparently had a friendship with and collaborated on at least one project with Timothy Leary.

DREAMers, asylum seekers, and immigrants." To that end, they filed an amicus brief with the notorious 9th Circuit US Court of Appeals in *City and County of San Francisco v. Trump* claiming that withholding federal funding from sanctuary cities for violating federal law is unconstitutional. I know, I know.

The NCLR also wrote legislation signed into law by "Moonbeam" Jerry Brown "that guarantees the right of California's foster youth to access gender-affirming healthcare services." According to the NCLR, withholding treatment—which presumably includes hormones and surgery—"worsens dysphoria" and "can increase risk of abuse and stigmatization." No evidence is provided, unsurprisingly, and we know the opposite is in fact true. Google, Gilead Sciences, Genentech, Accenture, Marriott, the Rosenberg Foundation, Ropes & Gray LLP, and the Horizons Foundation helped sponsor their 2018 anniversary celebration. Other donors to the NCLR include: the Evelyn and Walter Haas, Jr. Fund; the Ford Foundation; the Goldman Sachs Philanthropy Fund; the Betsy and Alan Cohn Foundation; the Levi Strauss Foundation; the Jewish Community Federation and Endowment Fund of San Francisco, the Peninsula, Marin and Sonoma Counties; the Liberty Hill Foundation; the Rabbi Barbara Zacky Fund; Morgan Stanley Global Impact Funding Trust; the Tides Foundation; the H. van Ameringen Foundation; the Arcus Foundation; the Gill Foundation; and a huge number of individual Jewish donors.

The general default of Jews toward liberalism (until power is attained, and abroad, not in Israel) is not reflective of some in-born altruism but rather, for Charles E. Silberman:

> American Jews are committed to cultural tolerance because of their belief—
> one firmly rooted in history—that Jews are safe only in a society acceptant
> to a wide range of attitudes and behaviors, as well as a diversity of religious
> and ethnic groups. It is this belief, for example, not approval of homosexual-
> ity, that leads to an overwhelming majority of American Jews to endorse "gay
> rights" and to take a liberal stance on most other so-called "social" issues.

In other words, the more "open" the society, the better from a Jewish perspective. With the unique conditions of modernity, however, Jews have been able to not just attain positions of power in wild disproportion, but to achieve an unprecedented degree of global influence and, it may be said, control. With this power, darker impulses that might otherwise go unacted-upon may find form in the humiliation rituals and daily indignities suffered by the occupied people. While such an idea may discomfort the reader—as it well should—this does not change the psychological and behavioral disposition of a ruling class that feels no *noblesse oblige* to a people who do not belong to their tribe. Even the collaborators, useful as they are and benefitting nicely from the current system, can be burned whenever it is necessary.

Though I am endeavoring to outline the precise architecture of this agenda and its aims in the political and material sense in order to provide incontrovertible proof of its existence and its danger, the most essential component of this project is that it has kept the majority of people from looking beyond their immediate or "terrestrial" surroundings if you like. The more intense the individualism, the less likely one is to understand themselves in relation to their surroundings and, even more crucially, in the flow of time. This also precludes considerations cosmic or religious, depending on how you want to consider it. But the metaphysical plane is where the real war is being waged, and we are being slaughtered.

Whether or not the reader is a Christian, the following is telling and highly significant; the New Jewish Agenda, active from 1980–1992; per their Wikipedia entry, saw:

> Over 1,200 people attended NJA's founding conference on December 25, 1980. . . . The date was purposely chosen to coincide with Christmas. . . .[45] New Jewish Agenda chapters around the country were active in coalitions to combat racism, anti-Semitism and apartheid. . . . A conference on Anti-Semitism and Racism called "Carrying It On: Organizing Against Anti-Semitism and Racism for Jewish Activist and College Students" was held in Philadelphia in November 1991. Over 500 Jewish activists and allies from other communities gathered for workshops aiming to learn about and mobilize against institutionalized racism in the U.S. and to analyze the relationship between anti-Semitism and racism. . . . Jewish Feminist leadership was part of NJA's culture from its earliest days, and the 1985 Conference passed a resolution to begin a Feminist Taskforce (FTF). . . . New Jewish Agenda's feminist taskforce was heavily influenced by the work of many non-Jewish feminists of color. . . . NJA sent a delegation to the UN Decade for Women Forum in 1985 in Nairobi. . . . In 1985, NJA published and widely distributed a pamphlet called "Coming Out/Coming Home" about homophobia and gay rights within the Jewish community. They also spearheaded anti-homophobia work which included the development of workshops mobilizing the Jewish community to take part in many gay rights events. . . . In April 1986, the Brooklyn and Manhattan chapters of NJA sponsored the first New York community-wide conference on Lesbian and Gay Jews. . . . The work of the Feminist Taskforce covered ground that overlapped with many of the other campaigns, and the FTF housed both the Gay/Lesbian Working Group and the AIDS Working Group. AIDS was always on the NJA agenda, especially as an issue to promote within Jewish communities.

Also of tremendous significance, on Mother's Day 1988 (once again, tell me the motivations are pure), the Feminist Taskforce convened a conference in Philadelphia with a panel discussion led by Adrienne Rich, poet and author of "Compulsory Heterosexuality and Lesbian Existence"; from her Wikipedia entry:

> Rich considers how one's background might influence their identity. She furthers this notion by noting her own exploration of the body, her body, as female, as white, as Jewish and as a body in a nation. . . . She recounts her growth towards understanding how the women's movement grounded in the Western culture is limited to the concerns of white women to the verbal and written indications of Black United States citizens. Such professions have allowed her to experience the meaning of her whiteness as a point of location for which she needed to take responsibility.

---

[45] Try telling me one of the primary motivations isn't anti-Christian, anti-White animus.

It should be obvious that the central issue here is less to do with the political than it is the extension into politics of meta-political warfare on the complementary essences of men and women and on the essence of unique civilizations as reflective of a natural, divine order and an absolute Truth. At the risk of being overly-reductive, it does indeed hew along the lines of good-versus-evil, darkness-versus-light. It could not be clearer—organizations such as "Mother's Ruin" and so-called feminist conferences convening on Mother's Day, to say nothing of the New Jewish Agenda's founding conference on Christmas or, as Cnaan Lipshiz glowingly reported for the *Jewish Telegraphic Agency* of the "festive launch" of the Eighteen:22 organization:

> The scene last week at the Hotel Schloss Leopoldskron in Salzburg was a highlight of a three-day conference for some 70 young Jewish lesbian, gay, bisexual and transgender activists from around the world. They gathered to launch an international Jewish gay organization called Eighteen:22—a reference to the passage in Leviticus prohibiting gay sex. . . . At one of this Alpine city's finest hotels, an Argentinean Jew in a priest's vestments is waltzing with a Jewish transgender woman from New York. . . . The Salzburg conference, which was organized by Eighteen:22 founder Robert Saferstein as part of the Connection Points program of the Charles and Lynn Schusterman Family Foundation, was no solemn affair. . . . Hannah Elyse Simpson, a Jewish transgender woman from New York . . . wore a painted beard as a tribute to Conchita, the transgender Austrian whose victory at the 2014 Eurovision Song Contest highlighted Austria's embrace of gays. This year Vienna unveiled (ironic given the sheer volume of veiled Muslims the city's harboring) gay-themed stoplights at central pedestrian crossings.

Yes, very ironic indeed given that the Jewish role in importing those Muslims is so outsized. I'm not sure how anyone could believe this is based on some sort of "equality" or "compassion" rather than intentional malice given the obvious implications of the naming of the organization and the scene described. It is a fundamental inversion of everything natural and decent, to say nothing of the divine through divinity and the life-giving power of motherhood and the transcendent powers of masculinity and femininity respectively. The explicitly-Jewish organization Eighteen:22 echoes the Jewish pornographer Al "Christ Sucks" Goldstein in its clear contempt for Christianity and Gentiles more broadly and in its determination to undermine the host societies and transform them into something wicked, decadent, and broken.

Eighteen:22 is extremely well-connected: eJewishPhilanthropy, *Sh'ma Now: A Journal of Jewish Ideas*, Keshet, the Charles and Lynn Schusterman Family Foundation, Friday Night Lights ("world class, experiential events for gay Jewish professionals that offers new access points into the Jewish community and fosters long-term involvement in both Jewish and LGBTQ life"), et cetera. Their fellows include (with current or former "credentials"):

- Justine Apple: Executive Director of Kulanu Toronto, voice of the Jewish LGBT community
- S. Bear Bergman
- Rebecca Fox: Wellspring
- David Gee: KeshetUK

- Yelena Goltsman: Founder and co-president of RUSA LGBT, an organization formed in 2008 to establish a social network for the Russian-speaking LGBTQ community in the New York area and beyond
- Eli Nassau: Nassau founded Guimel, the first openly LGBT Jewish initiative in Mexico in 2012
- Sarah Weil: Women's Gathering Jerusalem; Queer Israel
- Gustavo Michanie: Jewish Argentine Gays
- György "Gyuri" Hámori: Resident of Moishe House Budapest since May 2014 and works at the Herzl Center Budapest and the Israeli Cultural Institute as an Educational Coordinator. Gyuri received a Masters in Philosophy and Bachelors in Philology from the University of Szeged in Hungary. Gyuri . . . has worked and volunteered for a variety of NGOs and organizations across Europe, including the European Volunteer Service in Málaga, Spain and The City is for All activist group in Budapest, Hungary

Eighteen:22 operates along the exact same lines and for the same exact purposes as the Open Society Foundations, the European Union, the United Nations, and the US State Department, all essentially indistinguishable as reflections of corruption, the marshaling of the disintegrative and corrosive death-forces against those of light and life.

# Transforming Our World

*"Anyone who has managed to get through the last two or three weeks is suddenly aware of how fast history can move. Sometimes, though, we don't notice it moving— until we sit down before an image of ourselves (a poster, a piece of architecture, a play) that has always been accepted as standard and just isn't any more."*
— Walter Kerr

On June 9th, 2015, the July issue of *Vanity Fair* featuring the "stunning and brave" Caitlyn né Bruce Jenner hit the newsstands, and two-and-a-half weeks later the Supreme Court ruled that the fundamental right to marry is guaranteed to same-sex couples by both the Due Process Clause and the Equal Protection Clause of the Fourteenth Amendment to the United States Constitution in *Obergefell v. Hodges*. Seamlessly melded, just like that, "trans" was poised to take over.

As we've covered, though, this had been positioned to occur behind the scenes for years prior. The agenda had been gradually picking up a head of steam, especially following the concerted efforts of the 1990s, but it is telling that of the "799 different institutional grantmakers invest[ing] more than $771 million in LGBTQ issues between 1970 and 2010," 86% of that sum was collected between 2000–2010, per Funders for LGBTQ Issues' "Forty Years of LGBTQ Philanthropy 1970–2010" report. Internationally, there were significant victories in that decade, including gay marriage legalization in the Netherlands (2000), Belgium (2003), Canada and Spain (2005), South Africa (2006), Norway (2008), Sweden (2009), and Argentina, Iceland, and Portugal (2010). Over the full forty-year period 1970–2010, we learn that the top donors to LGBTQ causes by dollar amounts are as follows, via Zelermyer:

| By Dollars | City | Total Dollars |
| --- | --- | --- |
| Anonymous Funders | ------------------------ | $ 90,089,279 |
| Arcus Foundation | Kalamazoo, MI | $ 77,935,323 |
| Gill Foundation | Denver, CO | $66,319,272 |
| Evelyn and Walter Haas, Jr. Fund | San Francisco, CA | $46,601,406 |
| Ford Foundation | New York, NY | $46,123,135 |
| H. van Ameringen Foundation | New York, NY | $25,296,700 |
| Pride Foundation | Seattle, WA | $22,503,848 |
| Horizons Foundation | San Francisco, CA | $21,704,359 |
| Tides Foundation | San Francisco, CA | $18,137,374 |
| California Endowment | Los Angeles, CA | $16,344,343 |

The Arcus Foundation was founded by heir to the medical device and technologies supply company Stryker Corporation fortune Jon Stryker. Stryker, who is homosexual, donates tens of millions of dollars to LGBT causes through his Foundation and through conditional donations to his alma maters Kalamazoo College and UC Berkeley; many of these causes also have a "diversity" component. *Forbes* puts Stryker's total donations to various "social justice" causes at $550 million, although some of that total has also gone to protecting apes.

In 2019, Stryker donated $2 million in the name of Audre Lorde to Spelman College for the creation of a chair in Queer Studies, the first of its kind at a Historically Black College or University. Jon's sister Ronda is the Vice Chair of Spelman College, a trustee of Kalamazoo College, and a member of the Harvard Medical School Board of Fellows, in addition to being on the Stryker Corporation's Board of Directors. Pat Stryker, another of Jon's sisters, has worked closely with homosexual "activist" and financier Tim Gill. Regarding Jon Stryker's "activism" and connections, Jennifer Bilek expands:

> Prior to 2015, Stryker had already built the political infrastructure to drive gender identity ideology and transgenderism across the globe, donating millions to small and large entities. These included hundreds of thousands of dollars to ILGA . . . and Transgender Europe. . . . In 2008 Arcus founded Arcus Operating Foundation, an arm of the foundation that organizes conferences, leadership programs, and research publications. At one 2008 meeting in Bellagio, Italy, 29 international leaders committed to expanding global philanthropy to support LGBT rights. At the meeting, along with Stryker and Ise Bosch, founder of Dreilinden Fund in Germany, was Michael O'Flaherty—one of the rapporteurs for the Yogyakarta Principles on the Application of International Human Rights Law in Relation to Sexual Orientation and Gender Identity (principles outlined in Indonesia in 2006). With the Yogyakarta Principles, the seeds were planted to bring in and attach gender-identity ideology to our legal structures. O'Flaherty has been an elected member of the United Nations Human Rights Committee since 2004. Out of the Bellagio meeting, Arcus created MAP, the LGBT Movement Advancement Project, to track the complex system of advocacy and funding that would promote gender identity/transgenderism in the culture. Simultaneously, the LGBTI Core Group was formed as an informal cross-regional group of United Nations member countries to represent LGBTI human rights issues to the U.N. Core Group members funded by Arcus include Outright Action International and Human Rights Commission. These initiatives promote gender identity and transgenderism by training leaders in political activism, leadership, transgender law, religious liberty, education, and civil rights.

Arcus has also worked with the ACLU to undermine Christian religious liberty exemptions as a form of resistance to their agenda; there was a 2014 grant of $100,000 to support "communications strategies to convince conservative Americans that religious exemptions are 'un-American'" and a $600,000 grant the year prior to support the ACLU's Campaign to End the Use of Religion to Discriminate. That same year, the Foundation launched a new Social Justice Initiative which has placed a heavy emphasis on "reaching out to faith communities around the world to build cultural acceptance for LGBT people." In 2014, Arcus gave $75,000 to Faithful America to "promote greater media visibility for Christians who denounce the abuse of religious-freedom arguments to oppose full equality" for LGBT people. Arcus has also given hundreds of thousands of dollars to various groups to "counter the narrative of the Catholic Church" and "to support pro-LGBT faith advocates to influence and counter the narrative of the Catholic Church and its ultra-conservative affiliates." This is not particularly necessary anymore, as the Catholic Church's leadership is very much in line with the globalist agenda.

Arcus has also expanded its operations to Europe, with an office in the UK and extensive financial support for ILGA-Europe. Their International Social Justice Program Coordinator is Adrian Coman, who was formerly Program Director with the International Gay and Lesbian Human Rights Commission (which is now OutRight Action International), where he designed and implemented the organization's strategy at the United Nations; OutRight Action International holds consultative status with the United Nations Economic and Social Council (ECOSOC).

Adrian Coman was also the Acting Director and Program Associate of the Baltic-American Partnership Fund at the Open Society Institute. From 1997–2002, he was the Executive Director of ACCEPT, a Romanian NGO "working for LGBT equality." Coman also served on the board of ILGA-Europe. Jay Michaelson, Vice President of Social Justice Programs, joined Arcus the same year as Coman. Michaelson is the founder and Executive Director of Nehirim, a national Jewish LGBT organization, and he holds a PhD in Jewish Thought from the Hebrew University of Jerusalem.

In the spring of 2011, the University of California-Berkeley's College of Environmental Design (CED) announced a gift of $1 million from Jon Stryker that, combined with a match from the William and Flora Hewlett Foundation, created a $2 million endowed CED chair named the Arcus Chair in Gender, Sexuality, and the Built Environment. The chair is named for the Arcus Foundation in honor of the long-standing relationship between Stryker and the university that began in 2000 with the gift from the foundation that launched the CED's Arcus Endowment, "a unique fund that has supported a wide array of critical and creative activities at the intersection of lesbian, gay, bisexual, transgender, and queer (LGBTQ) issues and architecture, city and regional planning, and landscape architecture."

Susan Stryker (no relation to Jon Stryker), "an openly lesbian trans woman," and Victor Silverman, whose "scholarly work encompasses a diversity of topics including US, international politics, labor, Jewish, queer, and environmental history," received funds to complete research for the documentary film *Screaming Queens: The Riots at Compton Cafeteria*. Among Susan Stryker's many "accomplishments" are a postdoctoral research fellowship in human sexuality studies at Stanford sponsored by the Social Science Research Council and the Ford Foundation, and the establishment in 2013 of the Transgender Studies Initiative at the University of Arizona where "she" focused on "hiring faculty of color." As C. Grieg Crysler writes of Berkeley's CED:

> Other initiatives include an LGBTQ heritage map for walking tours of Seattle, Washington. The maps were produced by cultural geographers of queer space Larry Knopp (University of Washington at Tacoma) and Michael

Brown (University of Washington at Seattle) in collaboration with the North-west Gay and Lesbian History Museum Project. . . . In 2006, the endowment shifted its resources towards creating a scholar-in-residence program. The first scholar, Annmarie Adams, was resident in 2008. Adams, a graduate of UC Berkeley's M.Arch. and Ph.D. programs, is currently the William C. Macdonald Professor at the School of Architecture at McGill University. During her residency, she initiated an interdisciplinary seminar on sexuality and space entitled Sex and the Single Building, attended by students from CED and a wide cross-section of campus departments. She also completed a research project on the Weston Havens house, a seminal example of mid-century Bay Area modernism now owned by CED. Her Havens house re-search was published in the spring 2010 issue of *Buildings and Landscapes;* a second project, begun in Berkeley in 2008, on gender-variant children and their bedrooms, was recently featured in the German journal *FKW///Zeitschrift fur geschlechterforschung und visuelle kultur*. In September 2010, Adams became the director of the McGill Institute for Gender, Sexuality, and Femi-nist Studies, where she continues to draw upon insights gained during her year as the Arcus scholar-in-residence. The New York architect and Yale University professor Joel Sanders also completed a residency in the spring of 2010. He delivered a public lecture and taught an intensive interdepartmental seminar, both entitled "Human/Nature: Gender Sexuality and the Landscape Architecture Divide," that explored how the design approaches and codes of professional conduct that separate architects and landscape architects are rooted in cultural conceptions about gender and sexuality. Research con-ducted at Berkeley formed the basis of his forthcoming book *Groundworks: Between Landscape and Architecture* (co-edited with Diana Balmori) . . . re-leased by Monacelli Press in the fall of 2011. Over the years, the Arcus En-dowment has also sponsored an annual lecture as part of the Department of Architecture's spring lecture series. Past speakers have included Alice T. Friedman, Professor of Architectural History at Wellesley College and author of *Women and the Making of the Modern House*, and Henry Urbach, Curator of Architecture and Design at the San Francisco Museum of Modern Art.

Speaking of modern art and the intentional creation of an era of intense ugliness Frances Stonor Saunders writes, "If any official institution was in a position to cele-brate the collection of Leninists, Trotskyites and heavy drinkers that made up the New York School, it was the CIA." The New York School was, as John Q. Publius describes it:

A heavily-Jewish and homosexual 'avant-garde' heir apparent to the kind of work the now-institutionalized Frankfurt School (which was first housed in America at Columbia University in 1935) had been conducting a generation prior. The 'New Left' of the 1960s and 1970s blindly followed the urging of the Jewish Adorno to resist the 'authoritarian personality.'

Regarding Adorno, Publius writes:

The advent of the atonal and harsh [can be traced to] Thedor Adorno's Theory of Modern Music with the explicit goal of producing degeneracy and mental illness via an auditory medium (Adorno found himself along with Max Horkheimer in Hollywood by the late 1930s).

Continuing with Frances Stonor Saunders:

Because Abstract Expressionism was expensive to move around and exhibit, millionaires and museums were called into play. Pre-eminent among these was Nelson Rockefeller, whose mother had co-founded the Museum of Modern Art in New York. As president of what he called "Mummy's museum", Rockefeller was one of the biggest backers of Abstract Expressionism (which he called "free enterprise painting"). His museum was contracted to the Congress for Cultural Freedom to organise and curate most of its important art shows. The museum was also linked to the CIA by several other bridges. William Paley, the president of CBS broadcasting and a founding father of the CIA, sat on the members' board of the museum's International Programme. John Hay Whitney, who had served in the agency's wartime predecessor, the OSS, was its chairman. And Tom Braden, first chief of the CIA's International Organisations Division, was executive secretary of the museum in 1949. . . . In 1958 the touring exhibition "The New American Painting", including works by Pollock, de Kooning, Motherwell and others, was on show in Paris. The Tate Gallery was keen to have it next, but could not afford to bring it over. Late in the day, an American millionaire and art lover, Julius Fleischmann [Jr.], stepped in with the cash and the show was brought to London. . . . Julius Fleischmann was well placed for such a role. He sat on the board of the International Programme of the Museum of Modern Art in New York—as did several powerful figures close to the CIA.

Fleischmann, Jr. was also the president of the CIA-funded Farfield Foundation.

The CIA and the Ford Foundation have long had a very cozy relationship, as we will see with the subsidizing/promotion of a particular kind of feminism soon, but as James Petras explains:

In the field of painting and theater the CIA worked with the [Ford Foundation] to promote abstract expressionism against any artistic expression with a social content, providing funds and contacts for highly publicized exhibits in Europe and favorable reviews by "sponsored" journalists. The interlocking directorate between the CIA, the Ford Foundation and the New York Museum of Modern Art lead to a lavish promotion of "individualistic" art remote from the people—and a vicious attack on European painters, writers and playwrights writing from a critical realist perspective.

For Publius:

Despite the rhetoric that such "art" is more democratic—perhaps because anyone can do it—it is clearly not the purpose of this "elite"-driven project, one that aligns almost exactly with Jewish sensibilities and that of the Jewish neo-aristocracy of the neo-liberal establishment. Representative would be that of Nigerian Chris Ofili's *Holy Virgin Mary* from the collection of the Jewish Charles Saatchi described as "a carefully rendered black Madonna decorated with a resin-covered lump of elephant dung. The figure is also surrounded by small collaged images of female genitalia from pornographic magazines," or that of "insider" and philo-Semite Andy Warhol who, as Lasha Darkmoon writes, "seems to have put his considerable charm to work with Henry Geldzahler, curator of the Metropolitan Museum of Art—an influential Jew who happened, like Warhol, to be homosexual."[46]

Just so happened . . . what a coincidence!

Circling back to the Arcus Foundation, according to Influence Watch, it has assets in excess of $179 million, and they disburse funding to a number of other organizations in addition to those we've covered thus far. Returning to Jennifer Bilek:

> The lineup of Arcus-supported organizations advancing the cause is daunting: Victory Institute, the Center for American Progress, the ACLU, the Transgender Law Center, Trans Justice Funding Project, OutRight Action International, Human Rights Watch, GATE, Parliamentarians for Global Action (PGA), the Council for Global Equality, the U.N., Amnesty International, and GLSEN. The Sexuality Information and Education Council of the U.S. (SIECUS), in partnership with Advocates for Youth, Answer, GLSEN, the Human Rights Campaign (HRC) Foundation, and Planned Parenthood Federation of America (PPFA), has initiated a campaign using a rights-based framework to inform approaches in reshaping cultural narratives of sexuality and reproductive health. Sixty-one additional organizations have signed a letter supporting an overhaul of current curriculums. These programs and initiatives advance gender identity ideology by supporting various faith organizations, sports and cultural associations, police department training and educational programs in grade schools, high schools (GLSEN, whose founder was brought to Arcus in 2012 as board of directors, has influenced many K-12 school curricula), and universities and medical institutions—including the American Psychological Foundation (APF). Arcus funds help APF (the leading psychology organization in the United States) develop guidelines for establishing trans-affirmative psychological practices. Psychologists are "encouraged" by those monies to modify their understanding of gender, broadening the range of biological reality to include abstract, medical identities. Concurrently, Arcus drives gender identity ideology and transgenderism in the marketplace by encouraging businesses to invest in LGBT causes.

Abstract painting, abstract identities, abstractions of money—we can see how the framework for the next evolution of the system, a wholly abstract and digitized dystopia, is being laid by the ruling class. This is all inter-connected; consider also the systemic overhaul along critical race theoretical lines. Both the gender ideology and the critical race theoretical ideology are both spawned from critical theory.

---

[46] Publius, *Plastic Empire*, 174.

The Arcus Foundation also supplied funding to the Division of Adolescent and School Health of the Centers for Disease Control and Prevention (CDC) to conduct a meta-study of other research conducted on transgender or "gender variant" youth, which concluded that, "Novel recruitment strategies for transgender/GV youth . . . are needed to confirm these protective relationships and identify others." Translation: they need test subjects to experiment on. It is not a coincidence we have seen so many pharmaceutical companies and people involved in big pharma, biotech, and the like involved in this project. The internationalist aspect is also vital, as the ultimate aim of the project is a fully-integrated and -controlled planet with no barriers— a global open society, in short.

OutRight Action International—with its consultative UN status and with funding from Arcus, the Horizons Foundation, the Ford Foundation, and the Open Society Foundations—is a perfect bridge organization. In 2019, OutRight worked with UN Women as part of a panel called "Gender Diversity: Beyond Binaries." Sort of self-defeating for UN Women to be attacking sexual dimorphism, but that's not what this project is about in the same way that UN Women was never designed to advocate for women's best interests.

OutRight was founded in 1990 by the Jewish Julie Dorf ("I went to Jewish day school until I was kicked out in fifth grade for being rude to my rabbi. My report card comments said, 'Beware of her feminist tendencies'"). OutRight's staff includes:

- Kevin Wanzor, Operations Manager, previously worked in global health PR, researching and assessing social and epidemiological studies related to HIV/AIDS, malaria and other infectious diseases.
- Daina Rudu\u0161a is OutRight's Senior Communications Manager responsible for media relations and raising the organization's profile, based in New York. She joined the team in February 2019 after almost three years at ILGA-Europe, the foremost European-level LGBTIQ organization. She has also worked at leading international development organizations CARE International UK and the Bill & Melinda Gates Foundation.
- Elise Colomer-Cheadle is Director of Corporate Engagement at OutRight Action International. . . . Elise has over 20 years experience working in the nonprofit industry connecting businesses to causes. Her past roles include Senior Director of Development overseeing institutional, special events and individual giving at SAGE, Associate Director & Director of Latin America Programs at the New York City Bar Association's Cyrus R. Vance Center for International Justice, and Business and Partnerships Officer at the United Nations Office for Project Services where she co-established and co-managed one of the UN's first units for partnerships with the private sector. . . . She holds a Master of Science in Administration of International Organizations from Columbia University School of Social Work.
- Damon Clyde is the Senior Development Officer for Institutional Giving at OutRight Action International. . . . He came to OutRight from the British Council, where he developed partnerships with donors based in the United States to support the Council's international programs on social

entrepreneurship, women's and girls' empowerment, youth civic engagement and LGBTIQ issues. Prior to that Damon worked at the EastWest Institute, a global nonprofit promoting peace and security. Damon started his international career as a U.S. Peace Corps Volunteer in Kyrgyzstan. While in the region, he also served as a consultant for the Asian Development Bank and UNHCR. . . . Damon holds . . . a Master of International Affairs degree from Columbia University.

- Kennedy Carrillo is the Regional Sexual and Development expert of Out-Right Action International, based in Belize. . . . After serving as Executive Director of the National AIDS Commission of Belize for 4 years Kennedy went on to establish MC Consultancy: Sexual Health and Development where as lead consultant with a group of social consultants she has been providing technical support to organizations both nationally and regionally in: Research, Strategic Planning, Policy Development, Curriculum Development, Monitoring and Evaluation and Training in several aspects of Sexual Health and Development. Over the past years she has gained extensive experience working in the Caribbean region providing technical support to key entities such as the Pan Caribbean Partnership for HIV, CARICOM, UNAIDS, USAID, the Global Fund, Caribbean Vulnerable Communities Coalition and CariFLAGS among others. Presently, Kennedy serves is the Caribbean Liaison Officer for the Latin American and Caribbean Regional Platform, of the Communities, Rights and Gender Special Initiative of the Global Fund.

OutRight's current Executive Director is Jessica Stern, whose biographical description on their website informs us that:

At OutRight, she has supported the legal registration of LGBTIQ organizations globally, helped secure the mandate of the United Nations Independent Expert on Sexual Orientation and Gender Identity, and advanced the UN LGBTI Core Group. She has provided expert opinions to governments globally, regional human rights institutions, and UN mechanisms, including UN Women where she serves as a member of the LGBTI Reference Group. Her writing has been cited by the Indian Supreme Court in its seminal judgment decriminalizing same-sex relations and featured in *The Oxford Handbook of Women, Peace and Security (2019)*. She is frequently quoted by the media, including by The New York Times and The Guardian. She is an adjunct associate professor at Columbia University's School of International & Public Affairs.

Stern states that, "There is nothing more feminist than standing for transgender rights." In context, I'm inclined to agree.

The Ms. Foundation for Women[47] was founded in 1972 by Jewish feminists Gloria Steinem and Letty Cottin Pogrebin along with actress Marlo Thomas and Pat

---

[47] All the way back in their 1977 Annual Report, Johnson & Johnson is listed as a donor; their 2019 Annual Report lists the following among their donors: the Ford Foundation, the NoVo Foundation, the

Carbine, an editor and publisher of *Ms.* magazine. Among the credited co-founders of the magazine are included Steinem, Pogrebin, and Nina Finkelstein; another co-founder was Elizabeth Forsling Harris, described in her *Washington Post* obituary as having done "crucial advance work for President John F. Kennedy's fateful November 1963 visit to Dallas." The obituary also informs that Harris "helped found a shopping cable network with Neiman-Marcus stores" and was at one time on the Board of the Planned Parenthood Federation of America. Suzanne Braun Levine was managing editor of *Ms.* from 1972–1988; she and Steinem remain close. As Nina Reyes writes for *The New York Times* regarding the Levine's daughter's wedding:

> Joanna Braun Levine and Yigit Bora Bozkurt were married Sept. 15 [2018] at Wave Hill in the Bronx. Gregg M. Rubin, a friend of the couple who became a Universal Life minister for this event, officiated, with Gloria Steinem, the writer and activist and a friend of the bride's family, leading a ceremony that incorporated Jewish and Turkish wedding traditions.

The Spring 1972 issue featured an illustration of the Hindu goddess Kali done by the Jewish Miriam Wosk. Steinem settled on the name *Ms.* which was being popularized by the Jewish feminist Sheila Michaels as a way to "not be defined by any relationships to men." As Caroline Davies writes in *The Guardian*, "Michaels had first seen 'Ms.' on an address label on a Marxist magazine posted to a Manhattan housemate and initially thought it was a typo." Also in the Spring 1972 issue, the magazine splashed the bold pronouncement "We have had abortions"[48] across two pages with "53 American women invit[ing] you to join them in a campaign for honesty and freedom," among them Barbaralee D. Diamonstein, Pogrebin, Steinem, the Jewish critic Susan Sontag, the Jewish writer and director Nora Ephron, the Jewish feminist Susan Brownmiller, the Jewish Irma Lazarus, lesbian tennis player Billie Jean King, the Jewish historian Barbara Tuchman (her father was the banker Maurice Wertheim and her mother was the daughter of Henry Morgenthau, Sr., ambassador to the Ottoman Empire and major donor to Woodrow Wilson—his son, who studied at Cornell, devised the Morgenthau Plan to essentially permanently cripple a defeated Germany after World War II via de-industrialization and other means[49]), and the artist Nancy Grossman, who's best-known for her wood sculptures covered with leather S&M-looking gear, which Grossman states is a challenge to gender identity. As Robert C. Morgan wrote in 1998 for *Sculpture Magazine*, "Grossman's father was a devout Jew, while her mother enforced Roman Catholicism on the children, thus creating a conflict."

The write-up was authored by Jewish Women's Foundation in New York Hu-

---

WK Kellogg Foundation, Morgan Stanley, S&P Global, Comcast NBCUniversal, Erika Karp and Sari Kessler, HBO, New York Life Insurance, and Planned Parenthood.

[48] Deepening these connections, Cecile Richards, former President of Planned Parenthood Federation of America and the Planned Parenthood Action Fund, serves on the Ford Foundation Board of Trustees.

[49] As Kevin MacDonald writes in the Preface to the first paperback addition of *The Culture of Critique*, "Both [Felix] Frankfurter and Morgenthau were strongly identified Jews and effective advocates of Jewish interests within the Roosevelt Administration. Morgenthau actively promoted Zionism and the welfare of Jewish refugees (e.g., Bendersky 2000, 333ff, 354ff). Both supported U.S. involvement in the war against Germany, and Morgenthau became well-known as an advocate of extremely harsh treatment of the Germans during and after World War II."

manitarian Award-winner Barbaralee D. Diamonstein, now Diamonstein-Spielvo-gel, who claimed that the repeal of "archaic and inhuman laws" banning abortion should be repealed "to save lives and spare other women the pain of socially-im-posed guilt"; her husband Carl Spielvogel is a prominent businessman, former am-bassador to Slovakia, former fellow at The Center for Business and Government at the John F. Kennedy School of Government-Harvard University, a member of the Council for the Study of Europe at Columbia University, mega-donor to the US Hol-ocaust Memorial Museum, was appointed in 1995 to serve on the US Broadcasting Board of Governors (now the US Agency for Global Media, which includes Voice of America and Radio Free Europe), set up the Colin Powell Fellowship Program at Baruch College to "encourage outstanding graduates to seek career opportunities at the State Department," was on the Board of Trustees of Mt. Sinai Hospital, and is a member of the Council on Foreign Relations.

*Ms.* is today wholly owned and published by the Feminist Majority Foundation (recipient of Open Society and Ford funding) of which the Jewish Peg Yorkin, de-fender of the Jewish rapist Roman Polanski, is co-founder and Chair. It has rather suspicious beginnings, as the magazine *Off Our Backs* reported in July 1975:

> The famous *Ramparts* exposures of 1967 of CIA subsidy of domestic groups had named [the Independent Research Service] . . . as a CIA front group. We now have documentation that Gloria Steinem knowingly worked for this CIA-financed group on a fulltime basis for a period of at least three years (1959–1962) as its founder and director; that her association with this lasted as late as 1968–69 when according to her own listing in *Who's Who in Amer-ica* she was still a member of the Independent Research Service's Board of Directors; that she never disclosed this group was CIA financed until after the information was already exposed by *Ramparts* magazine and after the *New York Times*, in the wake of the *Ramparts* story, named her as co-founder.

Steinem and her connections, including Ford Foundation President Franklin Thomas[50] pressured Random House into editing out of one of their titles the explo-sive findings regarding the Steinem-CIA connections. Nevertheless, Nancy Borman boldly exposed the machinations in 1979:

> At Random House on March 15, 1976, *Feminist Revolution* was just another Women's book in production. . . . That afternoon, an unannounced visitor appeared in the citadel of the free press. A presumably angry Gloria Steinem asked to see Random House president Robert Bernstein. She was there to hand-deliver a letter from her attorney threatening to sue for libel unless the chapter on the CIA was removed from the book. No one knows what Steinem and Bernstein said in their private meeting, and it may have been just coinci-dence that, within weeks Random House was blitzed with similar threats from other people and groups mentioned in the CIA chapter: Clay Felker, Women's Action Alliance, Warner Communications, Franklin Thomas, the

---

[50] Columbia University alumnus, was romantically-involved with Steinem for several years and would go on to marry a descendent of Franklin D. Roosevelt.

Overseas Education Fund of the League of Women Voters . . . which conducts international seminars for women in Asia and Latin America . . . identified in a 1975 article in *Counterspy* as allegedly helping the CIA obtain dossiers on individuals and women's groups in those regions . . . and Katherine Graham. But, in any case, publication of *Feminist Revolution* was delayed nearly 3 years; the printing run was cut to 12,500, despite 13,000 advance orders; and when the book was finally released . . . the chapter on Gloria Steinem and the CIA had been deleted in its entirety. . . . Without anyone saying how they had heard about the book, or specifically what they felt should be changed, a flurry of letters arrived at Random House from some of the city's most powerful law firms on behalf of several people and groups involved in the Steinem/CIA chapter [such as] Women's Action Alliance, a tax-exempt information-gathering organization founded by Gloria Steinem in 1971. WAA's attorney, Jeanne Drewson, of Paul, Weiss, Rifkind, Wharton and Garrison [Roberta Kaplan's old firm], said in her letter that permission to reprint a WAA form letter was denied. . . . Warner Communications, which invested $1 million in *Ms.* (virtually 100% of the capital although they took only 25% of the stock). Redstockings cited the Warner deal as an example of the "curious financing" of *Ms.* Warner was also represented by Paul, Weiss, Rifkind, Wharton and Garrison. . . . Clay Felker then publisher of *New York* magazine . . . had attended the World Youth Festival in Helsinki and had edited the Independent Research Service's *Helsinki Youth News*, a CIA-funded daily newspaper.

Further, as John Q. Publius documents in the brilliantly-named chapter "Sic Transit Gloria Steinem" in his book *Plastic Empire*:

Through a series of transactions, Kinney eventually became Warner Communications with [the Jewish Steven] Ross as co-CEO from 1969 to 1972. In 1972, Ross became the sole CEO as well as President and Chairman. As these things are all inter-connected, it should not surprise the reader to learn that with funding from Warner Communications, Gloria Steinem's *Ms.* magazine was launched as a monthly in the summer of 1972. . . . [Felker] accompanied Steinem to the Helsinki World Youth Festival in 1962, where she linked up with Samuel S. Walker, Jr., of the CIA-funded Free Europe Committee [originally the National Committee for a Free Europe], whose best-known project would be Radio Free Europe. Felker eventually became the editor of *Esquire* magazine, where he published many of Steinem's pieces. A few years after Felker [along with the Jewish Milton Glaser] started *New York* magazine, he hired Steinem as contributing editor, and Felker had actually first published *Ms.* magazine as a *New York* magazine insert in 1971 before providing the funds for the magazine's first standalone issue in January 1972 [which was actually labeled the Spring 1972 issue].[51]

The connections do not stop there. John McCloy, World Bank President from 1947–1949, was Chairman of the Board of the Council on Foreign Relations from 1953–

---

[51] Publius, *Plastic Empire*, 158–160, 166.

1970; in 1958 McCloy was named the Chairman of the Ford Foundation having already been on the Board of Trustees. Richard Bissell frequently met with Allen Dulles at the CIA while working for the Ford Foundation before ultimately leaving Ford for the CIA. In 1953, Dulles and Frank Wisner, one-time head of the Office of Policy Coordination, the section of the CIA responsible for propaganda like Radio Free Europe, were instrumental in engineering Operation Ajax to remove the democratically-elected Iranian Prime Minister Mohammad Mossadegh. Publius continues:

> Frank Wisner . . . replaced Allen Dulles as the CIA's Deputy Director of Plans and worked with Richard Bissell in establishing the Lockheed U-2 spy plane program; Bissell succeeded Wisner as Deputy Director of Plans after his [September] 1958 nervous breakdown [Bissell's tenure officially began January 1st, 1959]. When Wisner "recovered," he was first sent to London and then British Guiana before retiring in 1962. He committed suicide three years later.[52]

Bissell was also involved in the planning of the Bay of Pigs debacle; MK Ultra was launched in April 1953 on the order of CIA Director Allen Dulles and run by the Jewish Sidney Gottlieb. From 1946–1950, Dulles was also President of the Council on Foreign Relations, which was so instrumental in laying the intellectual foundations for the Marshall Plan and NATO, and he was at the forefront of urging the US to become embroiled in what became the Second World War as America could not, in his view, afford to remain isolationist in the increasingly-interdependent world, a world he and his compatriots were actively creating.

Earlier in his career, Dulles had insisted that he had identified *The Protocols of the Elders of Zion* as a forgery and tried in vain to make the US State Department issue a public announcement on it. Later, at Dulles's request, President Dwight D. Eisenhower, who prior to becoming president had chaired the Council on Foreign Relations' Study Group on Aid to Europe from 1948–1951 and was a member of the National Committee for a Free Europe along with Allen Dulles and Cecil B. DeMille (who had been recruited by Wisner and Dulles), demanded that Senator Joseph McCarthy cease and desist from issuing subpoenas against the CIA for his inconvenient findings regarding compromised agents, particularly Jewish ones. Documents emerging in 2004 revealed that the CIA had, on Dulles's direction, broken into McCarthy's Senate office and intentionally fed him disinformation in order to discredit him.

A huge percentage of post-World War II senior officials in the US government were drawn from the ranks of intelligence/espionage and/or the Council on Foreign Relations. Paul Labarique provides additional useful context:

> H. Rowan Gaither Jr . . . created the Rand Corporation thanks to the bank guarantees of the Ford Foundation. . . . The council of administration moved the director of the Marshall Plan, Paul G. Hoffman, to the position of president of the [Ford] Foundation. . . . Gathered around [Hoffman] were Rowan Gaither, Milton Katz, his former assistant in the administration of the Marshall Plan (ECA) and Robert M. Hutchins. . . . As of January 1st, 1952 the

---

[52] Ibid., 161–162.

team was reinforced by another consultant from ECA, Richard M. Bissell Jr. On July 15th, 1952, the budget the Ford Foundation has devoted to international projects was close to US 13,8 million dollars, that is to say, half of the amount allotted for national programs. . . . Eisenhower designated John Foster Dulles as his Secretary of State. His brother Allen Dulles, is named to head CIA where he takes the toughest stand regarding USSR, developing the "rollback" strategy in Central Europe. These nominations are a new camouflage for the projects of Hoffman, [George F.] Kennan, [Shepard] Stone, McCloy and Milton Katz, that continue multiplying contacts for liberal intellectuals. . . . The Ford Foundation favors financing social sciences on top of humanity and medicine. It also fosters university and academic exchanges, as well as institutional creations: it finances the Center of European Sociology of Raymon Aron and the network of planners of Bertrand de Jouvenel. Its presence is so discreet that, according to a memo drafted by Shepard Stone after a trip to Europe in 1954, the Foundation enjoys a great acknowledgment in Europe "even within the circles of the extreme left of the British Labor Party, the German SPD and among numerous leftist intellectuals in France. . . ." At the university level, the Ford Foundation financed, in 1959, St Antony's College in Oxford, specialized in Humanities. . . . In France, the Maison des sciences de l'homme, under the direction of Gaston Berger, received one million dollars in 1959 for the creation of a social science research center defended by university professors just like Fernand Braudel. . . . On May 6, 1953, the Council on Foreign Relations organizes a seminar, with Ford Foundation funding, devoted to relations between the USA and the USSR. Attending the seminar are: John J. McCloy [CFR Chair and former President of the World Bank and former US high commissioner for Germany], Henry L. Roberts (Research Secretary), John Blumgart (Rapporteur), Henry L. Roberts (banker/investor), Robert Amory (CIA), Robert Bowie (Department of State), McGeorge Bundy (Harvard), Merle Fainsod (Harvard), George S. Franklin Jr. (CFR), Howard Johnson (Ford Foundation), Devereux C. Josephs, J. Robert Oppenheimer (Institute for Advanced Study, Princeton), Dean Rusk (President of the Rockefeller Foundation), Shepard Stone and Henry M. Wriston (President of the Brown University).

The aforementioned Paul G. Hoffman (University of Chicago) was the first administrator of the United Nations Development Program (UNDP) from 1966–1972 and was President of the Ford Foundation from 1950–1953. He was also the first administrator of the Economic Cooperation Administration, where he led the implementation of the Marshall Plan from 1948–1950, succeeded by William Chapman Foster (MIT, Board member of the Johns Hopkins School of Advanced International Studies); Hoffman called on the countries of Western Europe to work towards greater union and to integrate their economies within a large single European market in a profoundly consequential address on Halloween 1949 at a meeting of the Council of the Organization for European Economic Cooperation (OEEC), with its first Secretary-General the French Robert Marjolin a one-time Rockefeller Foundation scholarship recipient:

[The task] is to move ahead on a far-reaching program to build in Western Europe a more dynamic, expanding economy which will promise steady improvement in the conditions of life for all its people. This, I believe, means nothing less than an integration of the Western European economy. . . . The substance of such integration would be the formation of a single large market within which quantitative restriction on the movements of goods, monetary barriers to the flow of payments and, eventually, all tariffs are permanently swept away. . . . In the absence of integration, nations would each separately try to protect their dollar reserves. They would attempt to earn dollars from each other by restricting imports. *The vicious cycle of economic nationalism would again be set in motion* (emphasis added). . . . Unless individual countries accept the necessity for some coordination of domestic financial policies, the prospects for eliminating even the most restrictive types of controls over international trade will be dim indeed. . . . Another essential of your plan, I believe, is that it should provide means for necessary exchange rate adjustments, subject, of course, to the general supervision of the International Monetary Fund.

Also of major significance, as his *New York Times* obituary states, as administrator of the UNDP he identified mineral lodes in Argentina, Chile, Somalia, and Panama, and "One of Mr. Hoffman's more spectacular contributions to the quality of life in the underdeveloped world was a project to rid North Africa and parts of Asia of their immespovial locust plagues by means of cross-border air patrols and insecticide aids." Hoffman would eventually marry Anna Rosenberg, described by the Jewish Women's Archive thusly:

During the 1920s Rosenberg gained experience in politics and philanthropy. A speech she made advocating women's suffrage brought her to the attention of Jim Hagan, a Tammany district leader. Rosenberg became active in Manhattan's seventh Assembly District Democratic Party Organization. . . . During the New Deal, Rosenberg moved into government administration, holding increasingly important roles. . . . In 1944 she served as President Roosevelt's personal representative in Europe and recruited many of the workers for the Manhattan Project to construct the atom bomb. In 1945 Truman sent her to the European theater to study military manpower problems. From 1946 to 1950 she was a member of the American Commission to UNESCO and, from 1944 to 1947, a member of the advisory board of the Office of War Mobilization and Reconversion. . . . Rosenberg reached the peak of her government career in the 1950s. In 1950 George Marshall called on Rosenberg to serve as assistant secretary of defense in charge of military manpower requirements, a position that involved procurement, utilization and policymaking. Rosenberg's nomination ran into trouble when rumors spread about her supposed un-American activity and Communist Party membership. . . . Jewish groups, the Anti-Defamation League among them, raised questions over Rosenberg's treatment. They pointed to her thirty years of loyal service[53] and claimed her detractors were "a rogues' gallery of antisemites. . . ." In 1953

---

[53] Loyal service to who?

Rosenberg returned to her firm and continued to work for nearly thirty years. Her son, Thomas, was a business partner. Respected by labor and management, she numbered among her clients the American Hospital Association, *Encyclopaedia Britannica,* Studebaker, the Rockefeller brothers, John Hay Whitney, Marshall Field and Mary Lasker. . . . Rosenberg's activities included numerous Jewish causes.

This explicit awareness of her Jewish identity and its informing of her activities is a central feature with not just Rosenberg but most of the Jewish "activists" and figures we've discussed and will discuss.

The current President of the Ford Foundation is Darren Walker, Vice President of foundation initiatives with the Rockefeller Foundation from 2002–2010, a member of the Council on Foreign Relations, and a former Board member of the Arcus Foundation alongside Cathy J. Cohen (University of Chicago) and Catherine Pino (Carnegie Corporation, Columbia University, La Raza, the Congressional Hispanic Caucus Institute, National LGBT Chamber of Commerce—NGLCC, the LGBTQ Victory Fund, the Hetrick-Martin Institute, Nielsen).

The Arcus Foundation is also a major donor to Human Rights Watch, founded in 1978 under the name Helsinki Watch to "monitor" the USSR's compliance with the Helsinki Accord by Jews Robert L. Bernstein and Aryeh Neier, National Director of the ACLU from 1970–1978 and President of George Soros's Open Society Foundations from 1993–2012. Human Rights Watch's Executive Director is the Jewish Kenneth Roth. Other major donors to Human Rights Watch include Goldman Sachs Gives, the Sandler Foundation, the Annenberg Foundation, The Atlantic Philanthropies, the Dutch Postcode Lottery, the Carnegie Corporation of New York, the Ford Foundation, the Gill Foundation, the Omidyar Group, the Oak Foundation, the MacArthur Foundation, MAC AIDS Fund, the Royal Bank of Canada, Jeffrey Katzenberg, Akin Gump Strauss Hauer & Feld LLP, and—surprise, surprise—the Open Society Foundations.

Instead of focusing on genuine human rights abuses and tragedies, Human Rights Watch and Amnesty International have supported national-level legal gender recognition campaigns in a number of countries including the Ukraine, Norway, the Netherlands, and Ireland. If, as the saying goes, one puts their money where their mouth is, genuine human rights abuses are evidently less important than sex changes and Pride parades. The entire ruling class, in fact, has become fixated on anything broken, deviant, and Other, creating a civilization in negative. Care for children now involves literally retarding them with hormone blockers, pulling them away from their family and friends, disfiguring them with hormonal and cosmetic procedures, and subjecting them to public humiliation, forcible sterilization, and even castration. This is treated as not just a positive, but something that should be celebrated.

The Annenberg Foundation, funders of Human Rights Watch, is the family foundation of the Jewish Annenberg family. They connect with the Jewish-globalist network (and sorry Heron Greenesmith, but that includes Soros and the Open Society Foundations) at a number of different points. The Weingart Foundation strives for "meaningful policy and systems change that advance racial, social and economic equity." It was founded in 1951 by the Jewish Ben Weingart and his wife and has granted close to $1 billion in its existence. Its current Chair, Aileen Adams, is married to the Jewish Geoffrey Cowan, whose "activism" extends all the way back to the 1960s Freedom Summer. His influence is probably best felt through his stint as the dean of the University of Southern California Annenberg School for Communication and Journalism (1996–2007), where he expanded the endowment and helped launch the Norman Lear Center, named after the Jewish TV writer and producer and "social activist" Norman Lear and founded and directed by the Jewish Marty Kaplan (Harvard, Stanford).

The Annenberg School for Communication and Journalism was established through the support of Walter Annenberg; in 2010, Cowan was named the first President of the Annenberg Foundation Trust at Sunnylands where the estate of the Jewish ambassador and publishing magnate Walter Annenberg[54] would be converted into "a venue for important retreats for top government officials and leaders in the fields of law, education, philanthropy, the arts, culture, science and medicine" to "promote world peace and facilitate international agreement." It is for all intents and purposes a Jewish organization, with trustees including his daughter Wallis and three of her children, including Charles Annenberg Weingarten, namesake of USC's Charles Annenberg Weingarten Program on Online Communities. Wallis is on the USC Board of Trustees along with the Jewish Marc Benioff of Salesforce. Cowan is also on the Advisory Board of the Harvard Kennedy School's Shorenstein Center on Media, Politics, and Public Policy. *Journalist's Resource*, a project of the Shorenstein Center, published an uncritically positive piece supporting "gender confirmation surgery" in 2019, which cites the views of a number of beneficiaries and drivers of the transgender agenda.

Looking at the Weingart Foundation's 2016 IRS 990 Form, in addition to a huge number of "diversity" and "social justice"-oriented groups and organizations—such as Doctors Without Borders, CAIR, Soros's Central European University, La Raza, the National Immigration Law Center, the New Venture Fund, the Aspen Institute,[55] and more—those centered on or affiliated with the LGBTQ agenda receiving Weingart donations included the ACLU, Planned Parenthood, the Children's Hospital of Los Angeles, and the Liberty Hill Foundation, which in turn also funds the GSA Network. It should be noted here that the Weingart Foundation also donated hundreds of thousands of dollars to Catholic Charities. Friends of the Israel Defense Forces and the Jewish Federation of Greater Los Angeles also received tidy donations.

The Arcus Foundation funds LGBTQ research at USC's Annenberg School and the US National Endowment for the Humanities funds USC Libraries' "Cold War Queer: The Pre-Stonewall LGBTQ Digitization Project." Also at USC, Vicki Callahan and SCA Research received funding from Kings College London for "Women in Transmedia: A Gender Diverse Industry" and the Jewish Jeremy Goldbach has received significant funding for a number of separate studies including: "A longitudinal investigation of minority stress in a diverse national sample of sexual minority adolescents" by the National Institute of Mental Health, "Improving Acceptance, Integration and Health among LGBT Service Members" by the US Department of

---

[54] His second wife was the niece of the Jewish co-founder of Columbia Pictures Harry Cohn.
[55] ADL CEO Jonathan Greenblatt is an alumnus; the Aspen Institute has partner institutes in Prague, Madrid, Berlin, Paris, Kiev, Bucharest, Mexico City, Tokyo, New Delhi, and Rome. Greenblatt is also a member of the Council on Foreign Relations.

Defense, and "Measuring Stress among Racially & Ethnically Diverse Sexual Minority Adolescents" by the National Institute of Child Health and Human Development.

The United Nations Development Program (UNDP) funds USC's Department of Preventative Medicine's "Strengthening Regional and National Legislative Environments to Support the Enjoyment of Human Rights of LGBT People and Women and Girls affected by HIV and AIDS in Sub-Saharan Africa" helmed by Sofia Gruskin. From USC's Keck School of Medicine profile of Gruskin we learn that:

> Gruskin's work, which ranges from global policy to the grassroots level, has been instrumental in developing the conceptual, methodological and empirical links between health and human rights, with a focus on HIV/AIDS, sexual and reproductive health, child and adolescent health, gender-based violence, non-communicable disease and health systems. Her current partners include the World Health Organization, United Nations Development Programme, Global Fund to Fight AIDS, Tuberculosis, and Malaria, Open Society Foundations and local organizations and universities in Brazil, India and Vietnam. Gruskin sits on numerous boards and committees including the PEPFAR Scientific Advisory Board and the technical advisory group for the High-Level Working Group on the Health and Human Rights of Women, Children and Adolescents, jointly initiated by the Office of the UN High Commissioner for Human Rights and WHO.

Gruskin is a Columbia University alum and was at Harvard from 1993–2010. We will return to the Keck School of Medicine later.

The Rights-Oriented Research and Education Network for Sexual and Reproductive Health, housed at USC, features the following collaborators in addition to USC: Sree Chitra Tirunal Institute for Medical Sciences and Technology (India), Monash University Sunway Campus (Malaysia), Sexual and Reproductive Health Matters, Institute of Tropical Medicine (Antwerp, Belgium), University of the Witwatersrand (South Africa), Johns Hopkins School of Public Health, and the University of São Paulo School of Public Health (Brazil). Sexual and Reproductive Health Matters is both a journal and a charity and a company limited by guarantee in England. Marge Berer (University of Bristol Law School) is the founder and was the editor of the journal *Reproductive Health Matters* from its founding until April 2015, when she left to become the Coordinator of the International Campaign for Women's Right to Safe Abortion. Berer is Jewish.

From 2015–2018, Reproductive Health Matters was run by Shirin Heidari, now Senior Research Fellow at the Graduate Institute of International and Development Studies in Geneva, and principal investigator of a multi-country research project on sexual and reproductive health and rights in forced displacement. She is also Senior Technical Consultant on Gender at the World Health Organization (WHO) Gender, Equity, and Human Rights unit. Before joining Reproductive Health Matters, she oversaw the Research Promotion Department of the International AIDS Society and was the editor of the *Journal of the International AIDS Society*. She received her doctorate degree from Karolinska Institute (Sweden) in 2001, where she continued as an HIV researcher until she moved to Geneva in 2007. She has been a Board member of Amnesty International-Sweden and is the founding chair of the Gender

Policy Committee of the European Association of Science Editors (EASE). She is the lead author of the Sex and Gender Equity in Research (SAGER) guidelines and has given a TEDx Talk encouraging "gender sensitive research and scholarly communication." She is also the founding president of GENDRO, an association with the mission to "advance gender-sensitive research and data analysis."

GENDRO's Treasurer Olivia Mettler has, according to her biography, "18 years of financial experience in multinationals and international non-profit companies" and is a member of the Board of the International AIDS Society. Board member Bernard Kadasia was employed by the International AIDS Society (IAS) as Deputy Executive Director and Director of Policy and Advocacy, Research Promotion, and Communications, and since 2012 has been:

> The President of the Geneva-based Alliance for Health Promotion, an international NGO in Official Relations with the World Health Organization. The Alliance has official UN ECOSOC Status. Mr. Kadasia is also a member of the Supervisory Board of North Star Alliance. North Star Alliance provides quality healthcare across Africa to mobile populations and the communities they interact with.

Former Board member Emily T. Blitz, per her GENDRO website biography was:

> The director of public health focused conferences with twenty years of experience in public relations, multicultural team leadership and stakeholder engagement. She has intimate knowledge of all programmatic and logistical aspects involved with implementing conferences and events for 25 to 25,000 participants. Ms. Blitz has worked for UNAIDS, UNICEF, Gavi – the vaccine alliance, the International AIDS Society, World Heart Federation and the International Union against Tuberculosis and Lung Disease. Ms. Blitz is passionate about health and development issues, particularly HIV, TB, NCDs, vaccines, sustainable agriculture, women's health and children's rights.

On April 9th, 2019, GENDRO and its Gender Health and Evidence Network were officially launched in an event "Making Sex & Gender Dimensions Count in Health Research and Programmes." The event was organized in collaboration with: the Global Health Center and the Gender Center, both of the Graduate Institute of International and Development Studies in Geneva; the Global Fund to fight AIDS, Tuberculosis, and Malaria (typically shortened to just "the Global Fund"); and the World Health Organization, and with the support of Geneva Think Tank Hub and Foraus.

Shirin Heidari, together with Veronica Magar from the WHO's Gender, Equity and Rights Unit opened the session, and were followed by a panel discussion consisting of: Anuradha Gupta, Deputy CEO of GAVI; Carole Presern, Head of the Office of Board Affairs at the Global Fund; Avni Amin, WHO Chief Scientist at the Department of Reproductive Health and Research; and Francelina Romao, Health Counsellor, Permanent Mission of Mozambique to the United Nations Office at Geneva. GENDRO's Gender, Health, and Evidence Network "is a think tank dedicated to convene actors in Geneva and facilitate joint actions toward improving integration of sex and gender in health research and data analysis" featuring "individuals from academia, UN agencies, and other international and civil society organisations."

In 2019, Reproductive Health Matters changed its name to Sexual and Reproductive Health Matters (SRHM). It is currently helmed by Julia Hussein as Editor-in-Chief and Eszter Kismödi as Chief Executive. With quoted descriptions sourced from their website, Sofia Gruskin is on the Board of Trustees alongside such figures as Sapna Desai ("Based in India, she currently works with the Population Council on research focused on women's health and health systems"), Jane Cottingham ("From 1994–2009 she worked at the World Health Organization in Geneva as Technical Officer and then Team Coordinator on Gender, Reproductive Rights, Sexual Health and Adolescence at the Department of Reproductive Health and Research, with a particular brief to bring gender and human rights perspectives into the research, policy and programmatic work of the Department"), and Michael Mbizvo ("director of the Population Council's office in Zambia and a senior associate in the Reproductive Health program. . . . Mbizvo joined the Population Council after serving as director of the Department of Reproductive Health and Research at the World Health Organization (WHO/HQ)"). Editor-in-Chief Julia Hussein has worked with various NGOs, universities, funding agencies, governments, and the United Nations, has chaired clinical trial study committees, and was on advisory committees for the Partnership for Maternal and Newborn Health at the World Health Organization and PATH. PATH's partners include GlaxoSmithKline, Pfizer, Novo Nordisk, and Johnson & Johnson.

Eszter Kismödi has been a senior consultant with United Nations agencies, including UNAIDS, UNHCR, UNDP, and OHCHR, and international organisations, such as the World Association for Sexual Health, and international NGOs, such as CREA, where she served as Advocacy Director. Between 2002 and 2012, she was the Human Rights Adviser at the Department of Reproductive Health and Research of the World Health Organization. Kismödi is a Board Member of Durex's Global Advisory Board for Sexual Health and Wellbeing, a member of the WHO's Global Advisory Board on Elimination of Mother and Child Transmission of HIV and Syphilis, and a Board Member of GATE (Global Action for Trans Equality). Previously she served as a member of WHO's Ethics Review Committee and SRHM's Editorial Advisory Board. She has been a Visiting Scholar at Harvard Law School and is currently a Visiting Fellow at the Global Health Justice Partnership of Yale Law School and Yale School of Public Health.

The aforementioned Population Council, discussed in connection to Sexual and Reproductive Health Matters (SRHM) and Sapna Desai, was founded in 1952 by John D. Rockefeller III with funding from the Rockefeller Brothers Fund. The Population Council predominantly researches HIV/AIDS and "reproductive health," conducting biomedical research to develop contraceptives and how:

> Reproductive and immunological processes serves not only as the basis for the development of new contraceptive methods that reach out to both men and women, but also for new hormone therapies and AIDS-prevention products. The council is involved in a collaboration with industry partner ProMed Pharma.

The Population Council and partners recently launched the first clinical trial to test the safety and efficacy of the Nestorone and Testosterone (NES/T) gel.

Previous presidents of the Population Council include Frank W. Notestein (Cornell University, founding director of the Office of Population Research at Princeton, and the first director-consultant of the Population Division of the United Nations), George Zeidenstein (Harvard, Ford Foundation, the International Center for Research on Women—"Some of its priorities include the economic empowerment of women, the prevention of HIV/AIDS among women and girls . . . and increasing food security for vulnerable women"), and Bernard Berelson (University of Chicago, Columbia University, former head of the Center for Advanced Studies in the Behavioral Sciences set up by the Ford Foundation at Stanford). Berelson was one half of the notorious 1969 Jaffe Memo:

> The 1969 Jaffe Memo [from the Jewish then-Vice President of Planned Parenthood Frederick Jaffe to the president of the Population Council, Bernard Berelson] evidences the designs to limit white population growth through "social constraints" and other measures which include (and yes, these are directly from the memo): "encourage increased homosexuality; postpone or avoid marriage; alter image of ideal family size; encourage women to work or require women to work and provide few child care facilities; fertility control agents in water supply; reduce/eliminate paid maternity leave or benefits; child tax; tax married more than single; payments to encourage sterilization, contraception, and abortion; compulsory sterilization of all who have two children except for a few who would be allowed three; discouragement of private home ownership."[56]

Most of that should sound pretty familiar—it describes the present. The rest is surely coming.

The current Population Council President is Julia Bunting, a former director at the International Planned Parenthood Federation (IPPF). While with the UK Department for International Development (DFID), Bunting oversaw the UK government's international development policy on HIV and AIDS; maternal, newborn, and child health; sexual and reproductive health and rights; and population. She worked on DFID's International Statistical Capacity Building Program, collaborating with partners including the World Bank, the International Monetary Fund, and the Organization for Economic Co-operation and Development (OECD) to "improve the analysis and use of data for decision-making—both at the national level and globally."

Bunting was a lead catalyst of the 2012 London Summit on Family Planning. This event brought together the UK government, the Bill and Melinda Gates Foundation, UNFPA, USAID, national governments, donors, NGOs, the private sector, and the research and development community to "support the rights of women and girls to decide whether to have children and, if so, when and how many." Bringing these efforts in line with the UN's Millennium Development Goals was a central component of the discussion. One of the primary commitments (this word is underscored on the summit overview's Zero Draft document dated April 20th, 2012) "The Summit seeks . . . from the global community" is: "Manufacturers need to engage with funders and procurers in new and expanded partnerships to make a greater range of quality contraceptive products available, affordable and accessible to people in

---

[56] Publius, *Plastic Empire*, 117.

the poorest countries."

Other Board and staff members have ties to organizations such as the MacArthur Foundation, the Global Health Council, the Council on Foreign Relations, USAID, the Global Fund, the Gates Foundation, the US Fund for UNICEF, PATH, Harvard, the Pan American Health Organization (PAHO), Merck for Mothers, the World Health Organization (WHO), the World Bank, the National Institutes of Health, Johns Hopkins, and the International Contraceptive Access Foundation, Helsinki, Finland, a public–private cooperation with Bayer AG.

On their website, the Population Council states that:

> In the developing world, governments and civil society organizations seek our help to understand and overcome obstacles to health and development. And we work in developed countries, where we use state-of-the-art biomedical science to develop new contraceptives and products to prevent the transmission of HIV. . . . We use research to identify the world's most critical challenges to health and development and to improve the lives of those often overlooked—including young women and girls, adolescents, and key populations at risk of HIV.

James Sailer is Executive Director of the Population Council's Center for Biomedical Research (CBR), which conducts research and develops new methods of contraception, HIV prevention, and other STD prevention. Sailer leads and provides strategic direction to the Council's product development program, and supervises a staff of scientists, fellows, and operations professionals at CBR's laboratories on the campus of Rockefeller University.

Through DREAMS, "an ambitious partnership to reduce HIV infections among adolescent girls and young women," the Population Council, with funding from the Gates Foundation, is utilizing real-time data to inform the current and future scale-up of girl-centered programs in ten sub-Saharan African countries. As part of USAID's Evidence Project, Population Council researchers identified opportunities to expand the role of the private sector to provide "family planning" in Egypt and are now generating evidence on scalable interventions to reach people ages 18–34. Since 2012, the Population Council has been the lead evaluator of the effectiveness of self-help groups—small groups of women who gather to learn skills and support each other—and the integration of health and nutrition programming in the eastern state of Bihar in India. Based on the Population Council's findings, the government, together with the World Bank, is now scaling up the intervention, reaching almost seven million women.

The Population Council has received funding from a number of sources integral to this project: Bayer, the American Jewish World Service, the World Health Organization, the World Bank, UNAIDS, the University of California-San Francisco (UCSF), UNDP, UNICEF, UNESCO, UNFPA, the Research Triangle Institute International, Rockefeller Philanthropy Advisors, PATH, AmazonSmile, PayPal Giving, the Oak Foundation, the Charles Stewart Mott Foundation, the NoVo Foundation, McKinsey, the Elton John AIDS Foundation, the Ford Foundation, the Goldman Sachs Philanthropy Fund, DFID, SIDA, the Norwegian Agency for Development Cooperation (NORAD), EngenderHealth, the Gates Foundation, the Microsoft Matching Gifts Program, the MacArthur Foundation, the WK Kellogg Foundation, the Henry M. Jackson Foundation for the Advancement of Military Medicine, the Magee-Women's Research Institute and Foundation (MWRIF), the Los Angeles Biomedical Research Institute at Harbor-UCLA, the International Labor Organization (ILO), the International Rescue Committee (IRC), HRA Pharma, the William and Flora Hewlett Foundation, Fondation des Amis de Médecins du Monde, the Harvard T.H. Chan School of Public Health, USAID, the CDC, the National Institutes of Health (NIH), the International Planned Parenthood Federation (IPPF), and the Sackler Institute for Nutrition Science.

Surely all of this is a coincidence, though, right, and there's no malevolent global conspiracy? If only. Whether transgender ideology specifically, or more broadly all the various LGBTQ, anti-racist, feminist, etc. factions that compose the intersectional behemoth, the powers-that-be of the modern liberal order are without a doubt transforming the world and the ways in which peoples view these topics globally.

# Case Studies: Ireland and South Africa

Given that the entire basis of this project is to "open up" closed societies and incorporate them into the growing globalist Blob—George Soros himself stated that South Africa was the perfect target for his efforts back in the late 1970s—it is worth considering how two closed societies in South Africa and Ireland were "opened up" to ready acceptance of the LGBTQ agenda in record time. Ireland legalized gay marriage the same year as the United States, 2015, and most of its "progress" has been the result of international astroturfing largely from corporate influence and in the "philanthropic" sphere from The Atlantic Philanthropies, which spent over €63 million from 2004–2012 to advance "human rights" in the nation. Much of Atlantic Philanthropies' funding was funneled into "activist" organizations such as the Gay and Lesbian Equality Network (GLEN) and MarriagEquality and its predecessor, two of the primary organizations that pushed for the passage of the Civil Partnership Act in 2010 and a public referendum on civil marriage.

Another recipient of major Atlantic donations was Transgender Equality Network Ireland (TENI); their pressure paired with litigation brought by Free Legal Advice Centres (FLAC) eventually led the government to create the Gender Recognition Advisory Group, designed to "make recommendations on how to proceed toward legal frameworks for gender recognition for transgender people." TENI's Strategic Plan 2020–2023 shows support from Bank of America and the Social Innovation Fund and its manager Aisling Redmond of Rethink Ireland ("It's time to back big ideas and sustainable solutions. It's time to create the inclusive Ireland we all want to be part of."), which itself receives government funding and support from Twitter, Bank of America, State Street, and more.

FLAC's long-standing representation of Lydia Foy was absolutely crucial; in 1993, Foy had written to the Registrar of Births and Marriages in order to acquire a new birth certificate with a female name and showing the sex as female. This request was denied, and in 1996, Foy sought out FLAC, who readily accepted the case and issued legal proceedings to have the birth certificate changed. There was no precedent in Irish law; the closest thing to a legal precedent was *Corbett v. Corbett* (1970) in the UK, but this was not encouraging from Foy and FLAC's perspective: the divorce between transgender model April Ashley and Arthur Corbett was allowed to be annulled as Ashley was not biologically female. The first Foy case was eventually dismissed in 2002 on the grounds that only clerical errors may cause an alteration of the original birth certificate, however the visibility of the case and the media's coverage proved to be a boon to their cause.

The Atlantic Philanthropies first began pushing Ireland in this direction in 1999 with a pair of relatively small donations, one to enable Lesbians Organising Together (LOT) to commission a research study "which will review the implementation in secondary schools of those aspects of the Relationships and Sexuality Education programme (RSE) which refer to sexual orientation," and another "to enable Gay Community Health Development to develop a position paper on what is the most appropriate model to combat discrimination on the basis of sexual preference in secondary schools in Ireland." The year following another €17,000 went to LOT to devise an "activism" action plan, and in 2002 a whopping €342,000 went to "enable Gay Community News to become a high quality, self-sustaining paper."

In 2005, GLEN received a massive infusion of cash—€2.1 million—to launch their same-sex legislative campaign, and another smaller donation of €80,000 went to another organization "to improve the access of co-habiting couples to their rights by providing support for the KAL Advocacy Initiative which seeks the establishment of civil partnership legislation in Ireland." €285,000 arrived in 2007 for a Supreme Court challenge, and €400,000 came the year following for MarriagEquality. In the meantime, FLAC had persisted, and their efforts and those of other organizations eventually came to fruition in 2015 when the Constitution of Ireland was amended to permit marriage "to be contracted by two persons without distinction as to their sex" following a successful public referendum in May. Two months later, the Gender Recognition Act was passed, taking effect in September of 2015. Foy received the first Gender Recognition Certificate and a new birth certificate, and while it is tempting to view this saga as a triumph for justice and human rights, FLAC shortly thereafter began pushing for legal recognition of alternate gender identities for minors. The slippery slope is often a logical fallacy, but as regards homosexuality and the transgender agendas that has proven to not be the case, with the slippery slope being tragically very real.

As a source of external pressure, FLAC had also appealed to the European Court of Human Rights (ECtHR) in Strasbourg. Where once Foy had filed with the Court in the 1990s and had the case dismissed, the Court a decade later was willing to conclude that on the basis of several other cases, mostly from the UK, and its more "progressive" mindset that using Article 8 of the European Convention on Human Rights (ECHR) as its basis—which states that "everyone has the right to respect for his private and family life, his home and his correspondence"—the failure of a state to alter the birth certificate of a person to their "preferred gender" would be in violation of this Article, and thus the member states of the Council of Europe are legally bound to recognize self-determined gender identity. This has profoundly disturbing long-term implications. What's more, the ECtHR has used the ECHR as a basis for stating that full gender reassignment should be considered and covered as "medically necessary."

Concurrent with their activities in Ireland, Atlantic had been infusing LGBTQ organizations in South Africa with similar amounts of money and for similar aims, such as 6.8 million rand in 2004 to the Lesbian and Gay Equality Project for "its litigation, advocacy and coalition-building activities" and almost 3.3 million rand in 2007 "providing start-up costs to organisations representing transgendered and intersexed people, to strengthen advocacy around service delivery for this community." The leg-work in South Africa had already paid off in November 2006, however, when same-sex marriage was legalized. As we can see, the following year Atlantic was already pushing transgenderism.

In both Ireland and South Africa, the strategy was the same: targeted pressure campaigns and the false impression of surging "grassroots support" through the creation or expansion of numerous organizations advocating concurrently for the same ends.[57] In South Africa, as it appeared grassroots support was materializing, as in Ireland, a third vector of pressure was introduced: domestic media. 6.3 million rand arrived in South Africa in 2011, for example, with the stated intention to "increase the visibility of gays and lesbians in mainstream culture and to promote social diversity," which was spread out over multiple organizations.

With enough momentum built-up in Ireland, no further financial support from The Atlantic Philanthropies for LGBTQ organizations was deemed necessary even for a few years before their successes in 2015—the foundation had already been laid and the general public sufficiently propagandized.[58] Atlantic, founded by Cornell graduate and Duty Free Shops founder Chuck Feeney, which has provided over $8 billion in grants over the course of its existence since its founding in 1982, announced it would shut down for good at the end of 2020. Not to worry, however, there are plenty more organizations to carry the torch.

In South Africa, as an early going-away present, The Atlantic Philanthropies announced in 2012 that it was dedicating 33.5 million rand to cover five years of operating costs for The OTHER (Openness, Tolerance, Humanity, Equality, Rights) Foundation, which would be a central node in the globalizing efforts of the LGBTQ agenda. OTHER's purpose is to "defend and advance the human rights and social inclusion of homosexual and bisexual women and men, as well as transgender and intersex people in southern Africa." Its headquarters is in Johannesburg, but it also operates in Angola, Botswana, Lesotho, Madagascar, Malawi, Mauritius, Mozambique, Namibia, Seychelles, Swaziland, Zambia, and Zimbabwe. OTHER's CEO Neville Gabriel was the Chairman of the Open Society Initiative for Southern Africa and the Chairman of the Open Society Foundations' Africa Regional Advisory Committee. Former trustee Carla Sutherland is a central figure in the institutionalization of the LGBTQ agenda; she led the Ford Foundation's Education and Sexuality program in East Africa, helmed the Arcus Foundation's international Sexual Orientation and Gender Identity program, and was an Associate Research Scholar at the Center for Law, Gender, and Sexuality at Columbia University Law School.

OTHER's Research Officer is Samuel Shapiro, a former national organizer and

---

[57] For example: "LGBT Diversity was a key vehicle and deliberate strategy of Atlantic's to support increased cohesiveness within and across LGBT communities. There was more direct contact, networking and information-sharing among the groups, and an increase in the promotion of each other's work. A network made up of 12 LGBT organisations, LGBT Diversity successfully delivered a new regional and local community development programme across Ireland. Representatives of these organisations, together with local partners, clarified their purpose, developed governance systems, carried out financial management, made decisions, managed conflict, and aligned national, regional, and local voices. A large number of two- or three-organisation partnerships began to deliver innovative projects, like BeLonGTo's transgender specific support group, IndividualiTy, for young transgender people, and LGBT NOISE's solidarity campaign, 'SolidariTy: I'm for Transgender Rights.'" From "Catalysing LGBT Equality."

[58] By this time TENI had "developed close working relationships with the Health Service Executive (HSE), focusing on developing transgender treatment initiatives. TENI's advocacy has ensured that transgender health issues are dealt with separately from LGB health issues. TENI's development worker is a member of the HSE Transgender Health Working Group. Resulting advances include improved guidelines and training for HSE staff about treatment options such as surgery and hormone therapy."

senior researcher for Equal Education, "the social justice campaign for equitable and good quality education in South Africa," which is funded by the Open Society Foundations, the Sigrid Rausing Trust, the Ford Foundation, The Atlantic Philanthropies, and Comic Relief, among others. The Joint Fund to Promote and Advance Constitutionalism in South Africa (Constitutionalism Fund – CF), is listed as a separate funder on their website as well; it is "a collaboration between The Atlantic Philanthropies, the Ford Foundation and The Open Society Foundations, with a combined investment of US$25 million to be spent on grantmaking over a ten to twelve year period."

In 2016, OTHER established PLUS. The LGBTI+ Business Network, which is designed to reflect and enable the "growing desire by the business sector at large to tap into LGBTI markets." Aided in their endeavors are Shell, EY, Anglo-American, and Norton Rose Fulbright. In 2018, Anglo-American ZA launched the Real You LGBT+ Colleague Network as part of its Inclusion and Diversity strategy; they also have the WoMINE women's network in South Africa as well as analogs in Chile, Brazil, and the UK. Anglo-American has established "inclusion and diversity" networks in Singapore and Australia, and in the UK they also have a Real You network as well as their women's network and a disabilities network. Anglo-American also states that it is committed to the United Nations Global Compact and the UN Guiding Principles on Business and Human Rights. Anglo-American is partnered with UN-AIDS and has stated its commitment to the UN's Sustainable Development Goals 2030.

Naturally the ubiquitous Open Society Foundations have been very active in South Africa; from the Open Society Foundations' "Transforming Health: International Rights-Based Advocacy for Trans Health" (this is a long excerpt but an essential one):

On November 27–28, 2010, the South African-based organization Gender Dynamix hosted an historic two-day medical conference on transgender health in Cape Town that brought together transgender activists and community members, government officials, and medical experts from South Africa and other areas of the continent. The meeting was the first of its kind in Africa, and provided an opportunity to establish research and advocacy priorities in developing a rights-based approach to the delivery of health care to transgender people in South Africa and across the continent. . . .

Health professionals at the conference, including plastic surgeons, sexologists, general practitioners, and counselors, discussed the provision of health services that respected the rights of transgender people and evaluated possible strategies to expand such practices within the health system. The Open Society Initiative for Southern Africa and the Open Society Public Health Program's Sexual Health and Rights Project provided funding for the conference as part of their efforts to support the development of rights-based approaches to transgender health across the world. . . .

The U.S.-based Center of Excellence for Transgender Health [at the University of California-San Francisco, or UCSF], in partnership with the Open Society Foundations and organizations in Peru, South Africa, and Kyrgyzstan, is working on a similar project to develop national culturally competent protocols for transgender health. These protocols are intended to be largely universally applicable, with substantial segments that can be adapted to different country settings. The ultimate goal of this project is to train medical providers in each country to provide appropriate and comprehensive care to trans individuals. . . . Gender Dynamix (GDX) is the first African organization solely focusing on the trans community. Based in Cape Town, South Africa, GDX provides resources, information, and support to trans people; their partners, families, and employers; and the public. . . . As part of its mission to work toward a society where everyone is free to choose and express their own gender, GDX undertakes activities such as international HIV/AIDS awareness activities; working with hospitals around improving care for trans people; documenting and reporting human rights abuses against trans people; organizing the first South African trans health conference; documenting discrimination and violence against trans people in employment, education, public accommodations, health care, identity document policies, policing, and commenting on the WPATH Standards of Care and the GID diagnosis in the DSM. The 2010 South African Trans Health and Research Conference brought together trans community representatives, researchers, representatives from the Department of Health, health care providers, medical aides, traditional healers, and other stakeholders, including WPATH. The conference focused on six broad areas: general health services; hormones and surgeries; sexual health and HIV/AIDS; sexuality, pleasure, and reproductive capacities; indigenous and traditional knowledge and language; and depathologization. A major theme for the work of GDX is the degree to which a lack of attention to the needs of trans people overlaps with and exacerbates structural inequalities such as racism, poverty, and the broad lack of sufficient health care services in South Africa. . . .

The Open Society Public Health Program and the Center of Excellence for Transgender Health at the University of California, San Francisco, are convening the "International Partnership for Advancing Transgender Health" seminar on October 2–8, 2011 in Austria as part of the Salzburg Medical Seminars International. The seminar launch[ed] a multi-year partnership with the organizations TIG (lead organization) and Labrys (supporting partner)[59] in Kyrgyzstan, RED TRANS in Peru, and Gender DynamiX in South Africa. The partnerships aim to establish and implement culturally appropriate guidelines on transgender health care. Ultimately, groups plan to cultivate trained networks of medical care providers who can offer high quality transgender health care and who will participate in the dissemination of best practices regionally. Salzburg Medical Seminars International is part of the Austrian-American Foundation, funded by the Open Society Foundations and the Aus-

---

[59] "Kyrgyz Labrys . . . is working with the government of Kyrgyzstan to issue a progressive protocol guiding trans people, providers, and government ministries through a formal process of legal and medical transition. In order for trans people to change their identity documents and access transition-related care, this protocol relies on in a diagnosis of GID and completion of the course of care outlined in the WPATH standards. In the context of Kyrgyzstan, this represents a positive step forward, since most medical professionals and government officials in Kyrgyzstan—as in many other countries—still refuse to recognize the existence of trans people, let alone their need for a clear pathway to medically necessary services, legal recognition of their true gender, and protection from discrimination."

trian Ministry for Science and Research, offering post-graduate medical educational trainings for highly qualified health professionals from around the world.

The Open Society Foundations funds and trains "activists" all over Africa in countries like Kenya[60] and, indeed, all over the globe. Society Foundations Community Youth Fellow Adél Ónodi, for example, became the first "trans woman" to be featured as the cover model for *Elle* Hungary.

The fingerprints of the Open Society Foundations are all over the LGBTQ agenda; crucially, we can see how Open Society trial runs of particular projects have proven successful and have been replicated across the globe. Three other examples, via *The Washington Times*:

- The Los Angeles Gay and Lesbian Community Center: Their Leadership Lab was published in the journal *Science* this spring [2016], that evaluated the impact that door-to-door canvassing can have on reducing transphobia. It's being used as a national model.
- Streetwise and Safe: With the purpose of supporting a "national project focused on increasing safety for LGBTQ youth during interactions with law enforcement and developing advocacy skills to engage debates around discriminatory policing practices."
- Stake: A group that's looking to promote diversity in the courts for people within the LGBT community.

As far back as ProPublica lists Open Society tax returns, we can see huge donations to advance the LGBTQ agenda, such as an award amount of half-a-million dollars in September 1999 to the National Lesbian and Gay Community Funding Partnership to study the "chronic pattern of underfunding of lesbian, gay, bisexual, and transgender programs in this country" and $100,000 to GLSEN in July 2000, as well as the Tides Center, large and frequent donations to the Tides Foundation, the Regents of the University of California, and the Trustees of Columbia University.

President of the Open Society Foundations Patrick Gaspard was the US Ambassador to South Africa from 2013–2016; according to the Open Society Foundations' website:

Gaspard has had a dynamic career at the intersection of government, political campaigns, and social justice movements. He was the White House director of political affairs, the executive director of the Democratic National Committee, and the national political director for Obama for America in 2008.

---

[60] "Activists in Kenya have primarily used strategic litigation to address the issue of gender marker change. The Open Society Foundations initially supported a legal consultative forum to train lawyers on trans* issues. Several of the lawyers participating in this initial forum have worked closely with trans* organizations to launch strategic litigation." From Frazer, Somjen and Erin Howe, "Growing Trans* Funding and Strategy: A report from the field in 2013," 2015. Arcus Foundation and Open Society Foundations: New York, NY. Commissioned by GPP Trans* Working Group in collaboration with Arcus Foundation and Open Society Foundations.

Global Board members of the Open Society Foundations have ties to Chatham House, the European Council on Foreign Relations, the University of Chicago, Harvard University, the International Chamber of Commerce, the World Economic Forum, the World Bank, the United Nations, and more.

# Networks and Frameworks

By now it should be readily apparent that this project is a conscious undertaking by the ruling class and that it connects to the various other agendas being implemented by the Establishment such as mass migration/"diversity," so-called climate change, and the like. All are pieces and they all serve a function in consolidating power at the top and subjugating the whole of humanity under the banner of the insidious One World government. Before we consider all the implications, however, we must fully map out the infrastructure of the LGBTQ agenda in order to best understand how it feeds into the whole and how everything ties together.

The weaponization of an untold number of aggrieved and propagandized "activists" is absolutely central to this agenda in much the same way that the color revolutions playbook is executed. In many instances, the "surge" of "grassroots" activism takes many forms and with the color revolutions it is a precursor to regime change. It doesn't matter necessarily what aspect of supposed inequality or repression these "activists" are protesting prior to the catalyzing event (almost always a disputed election), especially as we have seen that the system is forever linking the various causes, but rather that they are contributing to general unrest in order to sow the requisite chaos preceding consolidation (see the work of Yuri Bezmenov for more).

In January 2012, "activists" in Sweden initiated the ALLOut social media campaign and began pressuring "LGBT-friendly politicians" to publish statements confirming their opposition to forced sterilization. "Trans activists" were invited on a major national morning TV program, with the host "unable to fathom why any party would want to retain forced sterilization." Hundreds of organizations from all around the world supported the ALLOut pressure campaign. Once again, as with conversion therapy, we see the most extreme and rare aspects of trans "opposition" positioned as the norm to galvanize public support; these hundreds of organizations were surely coordinated to pressure the Swedish government to virtue-signal and generate the impression that there is wide-spread international consensus on "progressive" issues. Opposition to forced sterilization *is* actually mainstream, but it's the people opposing forcing transgenderism and the attendant surgical procedures, hormones, and/or puberty blockers on children.

It's the illusion of consent that makes the shadow system run, and social media is a vital component in this way, in addition to its usefulness as a grooming tool, creating the false impression of any number of things, from what's "trending" to the illusion of a mass of "activists." The censorship aspect is also crucial: call a "transwoman" a man, get banned.

In the kabuki theater of politics, despite overwhelming objection to the project, the Polish "trans politician" Anna Grodzka proposed the Gender Accordance Act which deliberately avoids the terms transgender and intersex and is "inclusive of anyone whose gender assigned at birth differs from their gender identity." It's not about passing this piece of legislation into law because who cares when the EU will dictate terms anyway, but rather signaling to the outside machinery that here is a point to seize upon and direct efforts. Poland has been savaged by the Establishment media for its "LGBT-free zones" and surface refusal to accept throngs of thirty-year-old men who are supposedly "refugees." The reality is somewhat different, as the country is importing wage-depressing labor from the Third World to fill its "shortage" the same way every industrialized nation is, one way or another.

As with every arm of the system, the initiatives designed to advance this project are implemented at the highest levels—the UN, the EU, et cetera—and in individual municipalities or singular entities like universities, and everything in between. As one high-level example, the European Union Instrument for Democracy and Human Rights (EIDHR) Funding Program dispenses funds to a number of LGBTQ organizations such as the London-based Micro Rainbow International. The LGBTI Equal Rights Association for the Western Balkans and Turkey (ERA) is yet another astroturf organization supported by the European Union. It has a whopping 65 member organizations scattered throughout Turkey, Albania, and the former Yugoslavia.

Vienna is one such city that has readily embraced the entire globalist platform, from importing and catering to huge numbers of migrants to pushing the LGBTQ agenda. In 1998, Vienna established the Vienna Anti-Discrimination Agency for Same-Sex and Transgender Lifestyles (WASt); its main objective is "to tackle prejudices and discrimination directed towards LGBT people. . . . As well as holding public discussions, workshops and speeches, the agency held 31 trainings at different educational institutions within Vienna." The City of Vienna supports projects that in particular achieve one or more of the following objectives: measures to combat and sustainably (there's that buzzword again) reduce existing discrimination based on sexual orientation or gender identity; lesbians, gays, bisexuals, transgender, and intersex people who are affected by discrimination are supported; reduction of homophobia and prejudice against lesbians, gays, bisexuals, and transgender and intersex people; promotion of participation; support of associations and initiatives; increase in diversity. Funding from the "Queer Small Project Pot" takes into account "the lively need for project-oriented funding in the field of sexual orientation and gender identity." Funding for projects of up to 5,000 euros is possible from the pot in individual cases. Some of these projects for 2019 included Visibility Matters: Celebrating LGBTIQ Africans by Afro Rainbow Austria and the YOUNG Trans* and INTER* Camp.

EuroPride, a pan-European event "dedicated to LGBTIQ pride" is hosted by a different European city every year. In 2019, it was Vienna, and its sponsors were the City of Vienna, Stonewall, Billa, Merkur, Penny Markt, BIPA, OBB, HOSI, ADEG, Wien Energie, and Different Together. "We are more than our borders. We are more than the languages we speak and the colour of our skin. We are more than our gender and who we want to love." The accompanying EuroPride Conference is described:

The largest LGBTIQ conference in Austrian history [which takes] place under the patronage of the Austrian president Alexander Van der Bellen ... highlighting various aspects of the European LGBTIQ movement, from business and labour market to the struggle for human rights.

EuroPride debuted in London in 1992, where it was held again in 2006 and 2012. In 2020 it was scheduled to be in Thessaloniki. Next up: Copenhagen 2021 and Belgrade 2022. So brave.

The Time is Now Project initially convened in Belgrade to plan out a three-year partnership with organizations in Serbia, Macedonia, Kosovo, Turkey, Bosnia and Herzegovina, and Albania. The project is led by The Helsinki Committee for Human Rights of North Macedonia and the LGBTI Equal Rights Association for Western Balkans & Turkey (ERA). The overall objective of this action is to:

Advocate and improve protection of human rights and fundamental freedoms of LGBTQIs in the Western Balkans and Turkey, by promoting, supporting and achieving a more dynamic and influential LGBTQI movement that takes an active role in shaping public debates on democracy, human rights, social and economic inclusion and rule of law, and has capacities to influence policy and decision making processes.

In 2019, IGLYO was incorporated to design and deliver a series of capacity building trainings as part of the project.

Trans-Gayten, the trans arm of Gayten-LGBT in Serbia, has been working with sex change/gender reassignment surgeons and providers using the WPATH Standards of Care. According to the Open Society Foundations:

The application of the standards has historically been too rigid to take into account the reality of individual trans people's lives. In particular, the medical team expected that their trans patients should be heterosexual after transition and required them to go through a standard course of transition that included genital surgery. ... The team also had a monopoly on the provision of transition-related services in Serbia.

Trans-Gayten succeeded in convincing the government to loosen the requirements for completing a course of transition-related treatment, so "trans people in Serbia no longer have to undergo sex reassignment surgery in order to legally change their name and sex on identity documents." Evidently, referrals from Trans-Gayten's trans support group are now accepted and a pledge to heterosexuality, should one call it that, is no longer required. Trans-Gayten also encourages "trans cultural competence and continued training in the latest surgical techniques for the members of the medical team." So trans is a culture now.

The Council of Europe's LGBT pilot project is, according to the Open Society Foundations, "another example of effective collaboration with trans activists." Four of the six countries involved in the project (Albania, Serbia, Latvia, and Poland) committed to developing "ideal draft laws" by the end of 2013 and these were teed-up to be introduced in parliament.

Anna Kirey, who was born in Russia but grew up in the Ukraine, was a founding member of Labrys, an LGBT organization founded in 2004 in Bishkek, Kyrgyzstan. Kirey is now a research fellow at Human Rights Watch in New York, focusing on "LGBT issues in Eastern Europe and Central Asia." She talks about using the United Nations' treaty body processes to "highlight human rights violations against trans people in Ukraine." Similarly, as part of the multi-pronged and global approach to advancing this agenda, per the Open Society Foundations' "License to be Yourself" report, "In Kenya activists are building pressure for change through strategic litigation and advocacy, while support for changing Ukraine's regressive legal gender recognition regulations has been found at the UN level."

In 2013, the Global Fund for Women financed a meeting in the Ukraine of dozens of "activists" working on "trans human rights," resulting in the Trans* Coalition, consolidating "trans activists" from the former Soviet sphere, including members from Armenia, Georgia, Kazakhstan, Kyrgyzstan, Moldova, Russia, and the Ukraine. Legal gender recognition was one of its primary "advocacy" goals and its initial focus was to be on Armenia, Kazakhstan, and the Ukraine. There is clearly almost zero popular support for this agenda in these places, and it's obvious why: it's "elite"-driven and purely manufactured, and it has nothing at all to do with "equality" and everything to do with social reengineering, population control, and profit. It's "caught on" to the degree that it has in the West to some extent partly due to biological predispositions to openness, tolerance, and a more "liberal" default by disposition from evolutionarily-evolved traits, but also due to a sustained multi-generational propaganda campaign, extensive subversion, proximity to the locus of control, and the presence of a hostile and alien "elite" derived primarily from or reliant upon it at the center of the globalist system.

In 2013, the American Jewish World Service (AJWS) and Global Action for Trans Equality (GATE) with Strength in Numbers Consulting Group surveyed hundreds of LGBTQ organizations in order to better coordinate organization and facilitate increased funding. This was inspired as an extension of the first such endeavor in 2005 when Funders for LGBTQ Issues previewed their debut report on global LGBTQ funding and grantee organizations for sixty assembled grant-makers and international policy and program specialists at the Open Society Foundations' New York headquarters.

Using the data collected by Strength in Numbers Consulting Group, GATE, and AJWS earlier in 2013, in December, ten donors came together to form the Global Philanthropy Project's (GPP) Trans* Working Group: American Jewish World Service, Arcus Foundation, Astraea Lesbian Foundation for Justice, East African Sexual Health and Rights Initiative (UHAI-EASHRI), The Foundation for AIDS Research (amfAR), Hivos, Mama Cash, Open Society Foundations, Urgent Action Fund (UAF), and Wellspring. The goal was to "increase the size of the pie" in GPP's words and network and coordinate funding and services of the network the Working Group would draw together and expand. A 2015 follow-up and re-analysis of the 2013 data included 38 key donor organizations surveyed: American Jewish World Service; Arcus Foundation; Astraea Lesbian Foundation for Justice; Bulgarian Fund for Women; Calala Women's Fund/Calala Fondo de Mujeres; The Calamus Foundation, Inc.; David Bohnett Foundation; Dreilinden gGmbH; Dutch Ministry of Education, Culture and Sciences; Elton John AIDS Foundation; Evelyn & Walter Haas, Jr. Fund; filia.die frauenstiftung; Ford Foundation; Foundation for AIDS Research (amfAR)—GMT Initiative; Freedom House; Fund for Global Human Rights; Fundación

Fondo de Mujeres del Sur (FMS); German Ministry for Economic Cooperation and Development; Gill Foundation; Global Fund for Women; Global Fund to Fight AIDS, Tuberculosis and Malaria; Groundswell Fund; Heinrich Böll Foundation; Hivos; Horizons Foundation; Human Rights Campaign Foundation; Levi Strauss Foundation; Mama Cash; Open Society Foundations; Pride Foundation; Red Umbrella Fund; Sigrid Rausing Trust; Susan G. Komen; Trans Justice Funding Project (Tides Foundation as fiscal agent); UHAI EASHRI (East African Sexual Health and Rights Initiative); Urgent Action Fund—Africa (INWF Member); Urgent Action Fund for Women's Human Rights; Urgent Action Fund—Latin America.

GATE, which bases its mission on "intersectional, decolonial and collective practices" receives its funding primarily from the Arcus Foundation, the American Jewish World Service, the Astraea Lesbian Justice Foundation, and the Open Society Foundations. GATE's Executive Director is Mauro Cabral Grinspan, who is primarily responsible for lobbying for Argentina's "landmark" transgender legislation in 2012 where:

> All persons have the right . . . to the recognition of their gender identity; to the free development of their person according to their gender identity; to be treated according to their gender identity and, particularly, to be identified in that way in the documents proving their identity in terms of the first name/s, image and sex recorded there. . . . Gender identity is understood as the internal and individual way in which gender is perceived by persons, that can correspond or not to the gender assigned at birth.

The gender identity law also mandates coverage of all medical costs related to what are increasingly being referred to as "gender affirmation" surgeries. In essence, sex changes/gender reassignments became institutionalized as a legal human right.

GATE's Project Coordinator is the Jewish Max Appenroth and their Board of Directors includes major figures in the institutionalization of transgenderism from or based out of Venezuela, Iceland, Australia, Switzerland, the United States, South Africa, and Zimbabwe. Kitty Anderson of the Board co-founded Intersex in Iceland and worked with the Minister of Health to draft "gender identity legislation" very similar to that of Argentina's, which passed in 2019. GATE has coordinated with WPATH on transgender conferences and with a number of other organizations to establish Trans Advocacy Week at the United Nations.

In 2017, the Global Philanthropy Project (GPP) partnered with the International Lesbian, Gay, Bisexual, Trans, and Intersex Association (ILGA)-Europe on an LGBTQ fundraising primer for Europe and Central Asia; one of their primary sources was Lydia Guterman of Arabella Advisors. Guterman has previously worked for the Open Society Foundations and has an MPH from the Joseph L. Mailman School of Public Health at Columbia University. Some of their "success stories" include the Sarajevo Open Center in Bosnia, the Russian LGBT Network, PINK Armenia, Kyrgyz Indigo, Prague Pride, Transgender Network Switzerland, Campaign Against Homophobia (KPH—Poland), LIG (France), COC Netherlands' Bob Angelo Fund, Female Oxygen (Denmark), and Stonewall (UK). Their October 2018 follow-up placed clear emphasis on the need for increased activism and LGBTQ funding in Europe and Central Asia.

GPP Senior Program Officer for Knowledge and Learning Ezra Berkley Nepon has been involved with both LGBTQ and Jewish activism. Nepon is a member of Jewish Voice for Peace, and served as a Philadelphia Chapter Steering Committee member from 2013–2018; Nepon also authored *Justice, Justice Shall You Pursue: A History of New Jewish Agenda*. GPP's members include: the Ford Foundation, the Open Society Foundations, the Wellspring Philanthropic Fund, the International Trans Fund, the Oak Foundation, the Arcus Foundation, Dreilinden, the OTHER Foundation, the Astraea Lesbian Foundation for Justice, the Horizons Foundation, Mama Cash, Hivos, the Sigrid Rausing Trust, the American Jewish World Service, and more. It is a veritable who's who of LGBTQ funders.

The American Jewish World Service (AJWS) was founded in 1985 in Boston, and has donated close to $400 million to "social justice" causes in its existence; its website states that "AJWS funds constellations of organizations that are working on the same issues—both within countries and across borders." Most of these issues seem to center on "climate change," feminism, and LGBTQ causes.

Jewish Congressman Jerrold Nadler has been vociferous in his support for the AJWS. In turn, an open letter dated April 8th, 2016 signed by more than fifty "activists and leaders from the Lesbian, Gay, Bisexual, and Transgender (LGBT) Jewish community" supporting Congressman Jerry Nadler in his re-election campaign for Congress cites his "years of dedication and hard work championing issues of concern to both the LGBT and Jewish communities" (see Appendix A for the full list of signatories):

New York's 10th Congressional District, as you well know, is the home to the largest number of members of the Jewish community, and likely the largest number of members of the LGBT community in any Congressional District in the country. . . . Before it was remotely fashionable to support LGBT equality, while you were in the NYS Assembly, you sponsored critical bills banning discrimination against AIDS patients in funeral home care and price-gouging on AIDS drugs. Once in Congress, your comprehensive bill to fight AIDS, the *AIDS Cure Act*, led you to receive the first-ever political endorsement of an Act Up chapter. Since then, you have been an original sponsor of every major piece of LGBT rights legislation, and personally authored the landmark *Uniting American Families Act* (for same-sex, permanent partner immigration rights) and the *Respect for Marriage Act* (to repeal DOMA), and the *Father Mychal Judge Act* (the first ever law to knowingly grant a federal benefit to a gay partner). You have used your leadership as a Founding Member and Vice Chair of the LGBT Equality Caucus, and a top member of the House Judiciary Committee, to help craft and lead key strategies to beat back the Federal Marriage Amendment and other hateful anti-gay legislative efforts. You won the first-ever LGBT-related appropriation not earmarked for the fight against AIDS for the NY LGBT Center. You authored and led the congressional *amicus briefs* in the key marriage-equality related cases that were heard by the Supreme Court *Windsor* and *Obergefell*. . . . You were one of only a handful of pro-LGBT members to vote against the *Employment Nondiscrimination Act* because it wasn't trans-inclusive. Similarly, on issues of concern to the Jewish community, you have of course also been a key Congressional champion. You have been a life-long, deeply committed supporter of a safe, secure and democratic Israel, at peace with its neighbors. . . .

You have always been a clarion voice in the domestic and global fight against anti-Semitism.

In the AJWS's 2019 Annual Report, we see that the Klarman Family Foundation, the Pritzker Pucker Family Foundation, the Horowitz Family Foundation, the Foundation for a Just Society, and others all made huge donations of at least $1 million during their fiscal year 2019 (May 1st, 2018–April 30th, 2019). Its current President and CEO Robert Bank:

> Joined AJWS in 2009 as its Executive Vice President to both grow and deepen the organization's impact in championing the rights of the world's poorest and most oppressed people. As a human rights attorney, activist and experienced organizational leader, Robert has dedicated his professional life to fighting for the rights of women, people of color, immigrants, LGBT people and people living with HIV/AIDS. Prior to joining AJWS, he served in New York's municipal government and in the leadership of GMHC—one of the leading organizations in the world engaged in combatting HIV/AIDS. In 2008, he played an instrumental role in the campaign to overturn the ban on HIV-positive people entering the United States and becoming U.S. citizens. Robert has received the Wasserstein Public Interest Fellowship from Harvard Law School.

Current Executive Vice President Amy Pasquale spent over a decade with American Express and is a Columbia University alum with a Masters in Psychology. Shari Turitz, Vice President for Programs, was previously the Director of Programs for George Soros's Open Society Foundations' Public Health Program and is another Columbia alum. Margo Bloom, Vice President for Development, is a Columbia University alumnus, the former Senior Division Director of Development at NYU Langone Medical Center, the former Director of the National Museum of American Jewish History in Philadelphia, and has nearly two decades of experience leading Jewish communal organizations. Stuart Schear, Vice President for Communications and Marketing at AJWS, is yet another Columbia alum; he also previously managed the TV interview operation for the Clinton White House, was Vice President for Communications at Planned Parenthood Federation of America, and had a leading role with The Atlantic Philanthropies.

In 2016, the American Jewish World Service (AJWS), the Astraea Lesbian Foundation for Justice, and Global Action for Trans Equality (GATE) surveyed 455 groups from across the globe working on "trans issues" in order to continue to better coordinate organization and facilitate increased funding. Also in 2016, GATE, AJWS, and Astraea did the same thing regarding "intersex issues." They were aided in their intersex and transgender endeavors by the International Trans Fund, another grant-making organization that dispenses funds to transgender "activists" and organizations. The International Trans Fund's grantees include (this is a lengthy selection but it is worth including so that the reader may understand the breadth and the at-once dangerous and farcical nature of these "causes"—and these are just some of the ones in the West, to say nothing of those being funded across the rest of the globe):

- Queerstion Media (Sweden): Queerstion Media was founded in 2016. Their mission is to amplify the voices, celebrate and increase visibility of transdiverse people of color in Sweden and Sub-Saharan Africa. . . . Virtual Queerstion Magazine is a one-stop information hub, community building platform and alternative space for advocacy, data collection and archiving of trans*diverse narratives from Sweden to Sub Saharan Africa
- Alliance of Trans* Activists of Russian LGBT Network: Alliance of Trans* Activists of Russian LGBT Network was founded in 2016 and unites activists from 12 regions of Russia. . . . The organization's goal is to improve the current situation for trans people and protect trans rights in Russia. They aim to ease the process for legal gender name change and seek to fill the gaps in information within service providers around trans issues. . . . They plan to support trans groups emerging in the region with no or limited experience in activism and organizational development through trainings and meetings
- Irish Trans Student Alliance: The Irish Trans Student Alliance (ITSA) was formed in 2013 in Ireland and is a peer-support group for students and young people (18–30) who are trans, gender variant, intersex, questioning or exploring their gender identity
- Institute Transfeminist Initiative TransAkcija (Slovenia): Their mission is to address the needs of transgender and gender non-conforming persons holistically, aiming for justice for people of all genders. They work to address human rights, develop and enhance the transgender and gender non-conforming community, address legal and systemic erasure of transgender and gender non-conforming persons from legislative and social structures, raise visibility and awareness of trans issues, support transgender people and enable the empowerment of trans lives
- Traveschile (Chile): A trans feminist group formed in 1999
- Trans(forming) (United States): Formed in 2007 in Atlanta, United States. It is a grassroots intergenerational membership based organization led by and for trans, gender non-conforming and intersex people of color who were female assigned at birth. They are one of the oldest racial justice trans organizations that are working towards the liberation of communities and transforming institutions of oppression in society. They work mostly around civil rights for trans, gender non-conforming and intersex people of color. . . . They will also enhance the Transforming Prison Project, which supports trans and gender non-conforming people in prisons in Georgia with medical support and advocating for a change of policies relating to trans prisoner's rights
- Trans Coalition in the Post-Soviet Space: Trans Coalition is a post-soviet trans network formed in 2013 by trans activists from Kazakhstan, Kyrgyzstan, Moldova, Russia, Ukraine and other countries
- T-Action (Russia): T-Action was formed in 2014 as a response to the deteriorating situation of transgender people in Russia. T-Action's mission is to work to increase the capacity of transgender people [and] to empower the T-community. . . . T-Action will . . . deliver trainings on trans sensitivity to lawyers and journalists and give consultations on HIV and sexual health with express testing for trans people

- Ouest Trans (France): They will continue to develop support groups, organize a symposium on trans health rights and build a network of healthcare providers by facilitating a training on healthcare with medical specialists from Paris that work with trans persons
- Gender Minorities Aotearoa (New Zealand): Gender Minorities Aotearoa (GMA) was founded in 2014 and is a cross cultural, transgender led organization. GMA's mission is to create a credible, consistent, evidence-based, and trans-led national organization that is inclusive of sex workers, HIV+ trans people and/or Maori
- Cólectivo Intercultural TRANSgrediendo (CIT) (United States): Founded in 2008 and is led by trans Latinx immigrants, many of whom are sex workers, in Queens, New York
- Trans Intersex and Allies (TIA) (Bulgaria): TIA was formed in 2015 from a social media campaign where they made information related to trans issues accessible in Bulgaria
- ASTT(e)Q – Action Santé Travesti(e)s et Transsexuel(le)s du Québec (Canada): ASTT(e)Q was founded in 1998 by a group of HIV+ trans women in Montréal, Canada
- Greek Transgender Support Association (GTSA): GTSA uses a volunteer-run structure and provides activities that are free of charge: supporting trans people as well as parents of trans children, providing legal counseling and support to victims of discrimination and racist violence, providing support of LGBTI refugees, assisting victims of extreme poverty, cooperating with other NGOs on projects about trans prisoners and sex workers and raising awareness on health issues. . . . During this grant period, the GTSA will engage in the following activities:
  1) Organize events, workshops, street actions for both International Transgender Day of Remembrance (TDoR), as well as for International Transgender Day of Visibility (TDoV)
  2) Conduct an educational seminar in collaboration with other organizations to improve the law on legal recognition of gender identity as well as other trans rights laws
  3) Training seminar for the depathologization of gender identity
  4) Travel to islands where LGBTI refugees are located, in order to reach them and for the best possible strengthening and upholding of their rights
  5) Support trans people in need as well as outreach and empowerment of trans prisoners
  6) Conduct a campaign against transphobia
  7) Streetwork to reach trans sex workers to provide information and testing
- RARICA Now! (Canada): RARICA Now! was founded in 2017 and aims to coordinate collaboration and build a social justice movement amongst transgender refugees at the local, provincial, national and international level to enhance the collective capacity to advocate for refugees' rights and access to basic services. They advocate for changes to Canadian policy and legislation that will promote the health and wellbeing of

transgender refugees and ensure equal rights, awareness, education, advocacy, and access to culturally relevant support services for trans refugees
- Trans Black and People of Colour (TBPOC) in Europe: A strategy meeting for trans black and people of colour based in Europe will be organised in 2019 by a group of trans black and people of colour, including some with migration and sex worker background, as well as with disabilities. In Europe, all LGBT or trans funded organizations are led by white people. The lack of intersectional perspective from the European trans movement leaves trans people of color, migrants, sex workers and disabled [and] marginalized

The Jewish Rebecca Fox of the Wellspring Philanthropic Fund is on the International Trans Fund's Steering Committee; Fox has also been on the Board of Jews for Racial and Economic Justice. Fox was one of a number of representatives of funders for the transgender agenda present at a major 2015 conference in Istanbul as a follow-up to a 2013 conference in Berlin connecting these funders, which included the Open Society Foundations, the US State Department, and a number of these other foundations and institutions we've discussed.

Amnesty International and USAID were involved with the 2013 Berlin conference and Dreilinden has also featured prominently. GPP and members Dreilinden and the Open Society Foundations co-sponsored the March 2020 conference in Berlin "German Philanthropy's Role in the Global LGBTI Funding Landscape." Chloe Schwenke of Freedom House and formerly of USAID, the World Bank, and the Inter-American Development Bank was also present in 2013, as was the Jewish Kimberley Zieselman (a Boston Children's Hospital alum) of Advocates for Informed Choice. The Australian Department of Foreign Affairs and Trade and the Dutch government both made financial commitments. GATE figured prominently in both the 2013 and 2015 conferences in addition to the 2019 Trans Pre-Conference in Africa and the other initiatives discussed. The State of Trans Funding project for 2019 represents the joint efforts of AJWS, Astraea, the Global Philanthropy Project (GPP), and GATE; the report's copyediting was done by the Jewish "queer activist" Mark "MaxZine" Weinstein.

The International Trans Fund's 2019 Trans Pre-Conference at CFCS VII was funded by the Ford Foundation, the American Jewish World Service, and the Arcus Foundation. The goal was to create a Pan-African Task Force to advance transgenderism across the continent. Present at the conference was a panel with representatives of funders and supporters of groups in Africa including the US State Department, the Open Society Foundations, Open Society Initiative for East Africa (OSIEA), American Jewish World Service (AJWS), UHAI-EASHRI, and the Astraea Lesbian Foundation for Justice. The Astraea Lesbian Foundation for Justice also launched the Intersex Human Rights Fund in 2015 to support organizations, projects, and campaigns led by "intersex activists." The Intersex Fund is primarily supported by Kobi Conaway and Andrew Owen, the Arcus Foundation, the Global Equality Fund, the Open Society Foundations, and the Wellspring Philanthropic Fund.

Recent years have seen additional funding to the International Trans Fund from GiveOut and the Levi Strauss Foundation, in addition to the Open Society Foundations, the American Jewish World Service, the Ford Foundation, and the Arcus

Foundation.

GiveOut is a registered charity in England and Wales focused on LGBTQ causes. Staff and trustees' ties evidence a deep involvement in business and finance, globalist institutions, and governmental and globalist organizations such as the United Nations, Baker McKenzie, Amnesty International, the Boston Consulting Group, the Gates Foundation, the Elton John AIDS Foundation, Standard Chartered, BNP Paribas, ILGA, the Urgent Action Fund, the All-Party Parliamentary Group on Global LGBT+ Rights, and the Cicero Group.

Sarah Gunther joined Astraea in 2013 after serving as the Director of Africa Programs at American Jewish World Service (AJWS), where she "oversaw grantmaking to grassroots organizations pursuing sexual rights, natural resource rights, and civil and political rights in Africa. Sarah also played a key role in developing AJWS's global sexual rights strategies with a focus on LGBTQI rights, trans justice, and sex worker rights." Gunther exemplifies the kind of over-lap between these organizations in terms of (re)cycling personnel. Another example is Roz Lee, formerly Director of Programs of Stonewall Community Foundation, "where [she] created a Racial Equity Initiative to support organizations led by and for LGBT people of color," formerly the Arcus Foundation Director of Social Justice Initiatives Program, and former Officer for the Jewish Funds for Justice. Today Lee is Vice President of Strategy and Programs at the Ms. Foundation for Women.

Once again exhibiting the linked nature of neo-liberal globalism, Luxembourg Prime Minister Xavier Bettel, who is homosexual, used his platform at the 2019 UN Climate Action Summit in New York to claim that everyone has a duty to "fight hate speech." Luxembourg's Deputy Prime Minister Étienne Schneider is also homosexual; unsurprisingly, the Minister of Justice announced that "anti-LGBT" motives will soon be considered as aggravating circumstances in an upcoming law reform. Kosovo is yet another country that has now established hate crimes and hate speech penalties "on grounds of sexual orientation and gender identity" in its new Criminal Code.

Speaking of hate speech, in October 2019, the German government increased punishments for "online hate speech" supposedly to "combat right-wing extremism," but we all know it is blanket censorship to suppress any criticism of the regime. Looking at "LGBTI-funded projects" from 2010, we see that the German Embassy was instrumental in providing funding for Serbian Pride; in fact, the Embassy dispensed funds for numerous projects in Serbia. As we have seen, Serbia has been the object of intense focus by the Establishment, presumably because breaking it open would create a domino effect in the Balkans and provide a forward operating base for astroturfed "activism" in the region and further east. This has in some ways already come to fruition, not on a deep cultural level, but with Belgrade as an "activist" hub to train and deploy these faux-revolutionaries as part of the color revolutions model.

German bilateral grant-makers to global "LGBTQ causes" include the Federal Ministry of Health (BMG), the Federal Ministry of Economic Cooperation and Development (BMZ), and the Foreign Office (AA). The BMZ has a specific LGBTI segment for NGOs. According to research prepared for Hivos, "LGBTI grantmaking" in Germany had tripled from 2008 to 2010, largely driven by state actors and bilateral funders. This research authored by Arn Thorben Sauer on behalf of

(Trans)Gender & Diversity Consulting in Berlin found that for what are called po-litical foundations, the Heinrich Böll Foundation, affiliated with the Green Party, was "the clear leader not only in terms of spending, but also in its inclusion of LGBTI issues as an official and deliberately chosen part of its gender strategy." The Foun-dation's by-laws provide for a quota of women and immigrants on all the Founda-tion's bodies and among its fulltime staff.

The Rosa Luxemburg Foundation, named after the Jewish communist,[61] followed in spending amount, and for 2010 it was explicitly focused on a slew of projects in Poland, including "anti-discrimination" films for teachers and various "Campaigns against Homophobia." Next was the Friedrich Ebert Foundation, where the state ac-tors and multilaterals insist that the internationalist framework of "human rights" which includes the Council of the European Union's LGBT-Toolkit[62] and the Yog-yakarta Principles be integrated into any kind of development aid or cooperation. This seems to suggest that Third World countries receiving aid from this medium will have the expectation of integrating the prevailing LGBTQ framework into offi-cial policy, a "gay version" along the lines of what the IMF and the World Bank do with their conditional lending.[63]

The Yogyakarta Principles are the product of a 2006 meeting where a group of LGBTQ activists and functionaries convened in Yogyakarta, Indonesia with the ex-press purpose of drafting a new legalistic and ideological framework tailored specif-ically for the globalist multi-lateral approach, eyeing the UN as its ultimate vehicle. The resultant "set of international principles relating to sexual orientation and gender identity" were dubbed the Yogyakarta Principles: "a universal guide to human rights which affirm *binding international legal standards with which all States must com-ply*" (emphasis added).

With Yogyakarta touted as the new Magna Carta, Yogyakarta signatories includ-ing Mauro Cabral Grinspan and Stephen Whittle unveiled their "binding interna-tional legal standards" as a global charter in March 2007 at the United Nations Hu-man Rights Council in Geneva; later that year, the charter was presented at the ILGA-Europe conference in Vilnius, Lithuania (the "Rainbow Flag" event was banned by the mayor) and once again before the UN, this time in New York and co-sponsored by the governments of Argentina, Brazil, and Uruguay. Despite the fact that the Principles were not adopted by the UN, they did influence a proposed dec-laration on sexual orientation and gender identity in 2008, as Piero A. Tozzi writes:

> A statement promoted by the government of France and issued jointly in De-cember by 66 United Nations (UN) member states on "sexual orientation and gender identity" advances an agenda set forth in a highly controversial 2006

---

[61] Their website states that "the EU must turn away from nationalism" and their publications feature such titles as "Feminise Politics Now!" They also state, tellingly, that "social justice, the right to freedom of movement and global social rights are interconnected."

[62] In 2013, the "protection of LGBTI human rights" officially became part of EU foreign policy, when the Foreign Affairs Council of the European Union adopted the Guidelines to Promote and Protect the Enjoyment of All Human Rights by Lesbian, Gay, Bisexual, Transgender and Intersex (LGBTI) Persons. The Guidelines is a comprehensive legally binding document which provides instructions to EU institu-tions and member states and prioritizes actions around combatting "discriminatory laws and policies, LGBTI-phobic violence, and the promotion of equality and non-discrimination."

[63] The IMF also focuses heavily on "increasing women's labor force participation" under the guise of "gender equality."

document called the "Yogyakarta Principles." The Yogyakarta Principles claim to govern "application of international human rights law in relation to sexual orientation and gender identity." Proponents assert the Yogyakarta Principles bind States to new legal standards even though the Yogyakarta document is the creature not of governmental agreement but of homosexual pressure groups and UN bureaucrats. . . . The original draft of the French statement debated internally among European Union (EU) nations explicitly referenced the Yogyakarta Principles, but Ireland, Malta and Poland insisted the reference be removed. Despite the deletion from the final version of the French statement, Dutch Foreign Affairs Minister Maxime Verhagan, one of the effort's principal spokesmen, explicitly linked the statement to the Yogyakarta Principles. At a subsequent UN meeting on "Human Rights, Sexual Orientation and Gender Identity," Verhagan said his government endorsed the Yogyakarta Principles and called upon "all other states to embrace these Principles" as well. Human Rights Committee member Michael O'Flaherty likewise explicitly appealed to the Yogyakarta Principles to define the terms "sexual orientation" and "gender identity" that appeared in the French-led statement. The Principles define "sexual orientation" as "each person's capacity for profound emotional, affectional and sexual attraction to, and intimate and sexual relations with, individuals of a different gender or the same gender or more than one gender," and "gender identity" as "each person's deeply felt internal and individual experience of gender, which may or may not correspond with the sex assigned at birth, including the personal sense of the body (which may involve, if freely chosen, modification of bodily appearance or function by medical, surgical or other means) and other expressions of gender, including dress, speech and mannerisms." Critics point out that provisions in the Yogyakarta Principles that ostensibly affirm freedom of opinion and expression "regardless of sexual orientation or gender identity" actually restrict free speech, as they call upon the state to "Ensure that the exercise of freedom of opinion and expression does not violate the rights and freedoms of persons of diverse sexual orientations and gender identities." They cite curbs on Christian preachers' right to opine on the sinfulness of homosexual acts by Canada and Sweden as harbingers of what to expect if the Yogyakarta Principles are ever implemented more broadly.

A committee re-convened in 2017 and added more insanity to the measures they expect all governing bodies to comply with; the resultant Yogyakarta Principles Plus 10 (YP+10) aimed to "document and elaborate . . . a set of Additional Principles and State Obligations. . . . YP+10 should be read alongside the original 29 Yogyakarta Principles. Together, these documents provide an authoritative, expert exposition of international human rights law as it currently applies to the grounds of sexual orientation, gender identity, gender expression and sex characteristics." The YP+10 document supplements the original 29 Yogyakarta Principles and, in fact, derives its *raison d'être* from preambular paragraph 9 of those Principles:

Acknowledging that this articulation must rely on the current state of international human rights law and will require revision on a regular basis in order to take account of developments in that law and its application to the particular lives and experiences of persons of diverse sexual orientations and gender identities over time and in diverse regions and countries.

"The past was alterable. The past never had been altered. Oceania was at war with Eastasia. Oceania had always been at war with Eastasia." The Yogyakarta Principles mandate that states must:

- Embody the principles of equality and non-discrimination on the basis of sexual orientation and gender identity in their national constitutions
- Take all necessary legislative, administrative and other measures to fully respect and legally recognise each person's self-defined gender identity
- Take all necessary legislative, administrative and other measures to ensure that procedures exist whereby all State-issued identity papers which indicate a person's gender/sex—including birth certificates, passports, electoral records and other documents—reflect the person's profound self-defined gender identity

This is exactly in line with the aims and tactics laid out in the Open Society Foundations' May 2014 "License to be Yourself" Report:

Human rights arguments, particularly self-determination and freedom from forced sterilization, have been particularly effective in Europe as a way to counter reliance on the views of medical experts.[64] The WPATH Board has explicitly supported the approach taken in the Argentinean law. It has provided advice to courts and governments in Ontario in Canada, South Korea and Ireland arguing that legal gender recognition should not require a diagnosis, medical treatments, or that a trans person has lived for a set period in their preferred gender role.... [Strategies] include focusing on the emergence of gender identity more broadly as a prohibited ground of discrimination and the values of human dignity and personal autonomy underpinning the European Convention on Human Rights. . . . In a number of countries activists established a legal experts group early on to help develop alternative legal proposals. This became a chance to give basic Trans 101 education to a group that was in a strong position to influence future debates. It has also enabled activists to adapt progressive overseas initiatives to their domestic legal framework. In Ireland, the Public Interest Law Alliance provided such pro bono legal drafting expertise. Strategic litigation has been important in many countries, and pivotal in some including the United Kingdom, Germany, Sweden, Argentina, and Ireland. Critical decisions, including by the European Court of Human Rights, have played a role in forcing governments to act.

---

[64] In other words, fully marginalize legitimate scientific expertise in favor of "self-definition," meaning you can be whatever you want to be as long as you remain within the confines that have been prepared for you. Of course, many "medical experts" on the ground level are partisan hacks and ideologues as we've seen; most of the senior officials and experts are not neglecting science but are rather using this ideology as cover for their own agenda.

That's the operative word there: *forcing.*

Some of the additions to the Yogyakarta Principles from 2017 include the following; they are worth excerpting at length to illustrate not just their utter insanity, but to provide the reader with an illustration of exactly what the ruling class has in store if and when these principles are universally adopted by the Establishment in full, beyond what has already been put into practice:

- Ensure sensitivity training of judicial and law enforcement officers and other public officials on issues relating to sexual orientation, gender identity, gender expression and sex characteristics;
- Identify the nature and extent of attitudes, beliefs, customs and practices that perpetuate violence, discrimination and other harm on grounds of sexual orientation, gender identity, gender expression and sex characteristics, and report on the measures undertaken, and their effectiveness, in eradicating such harm;
- Ensure that human rights violations are vigorously investigated and, where evidence is found, those responsible are prosecuted and, if convicted, punished as appropriate;
- Ensure access to effective complaints procedures and remedies, including reparation, for victims of violence, discrimination and other harm on grounds of sexual orientation, gender identity, gender expression and sex characteristics.
- Everyone has the right to legal recognition without reference to, or requiring assignment or disclosure of, sex, gender, sexual orientation, gender identity, gender expression or sex characteristics. Everyone has the right to obtain identity documents, including birth certificates, regardless of sexual orientation, gender identity, gender expression or sex characteristics. Everyone has the right to change gendered information in such documents while gendered information is included in them.

STATES SHALL:
A. Ensure that official identity documents only include personal information that is relevant, reasonable and necessary as required by the law for a legitimate purpose, and thereby end the registration of the sex and gender of the person in identity documents such as birth certificates, identification cards, passports and driver licenses, and as part of their legal personality;
B. Ensure access to a quick, transparent and accessible mechanism to change names, including to gender-neutral names, based on the self-determination of the person;
C. While sex or gender continues to be registered:
   i. Ensure a quick, transparent, and accessible mechanism that legally recognises and affirms each person's self-defined gender identity;
   ii. Make available a multiplicity of gender marker options;
   iii. Ensure that no eligibility criteria, such as medical or psychological interventions, a psycho-medical diagnosis, minimum or maximum age, economic status, health, marital or parental status, or any other third

party opinion, shall be a prerequisite to change one's name, legal sex or
gender;

iv. Ensure that a person's criminal record, immigration status or other status is not used to prevent a change of name, legal sex or gender.

STATES SHALL:
A. Guarantee and protect the rights of everyone, *including all children, to
   bodily and mental integrity, autonomy and self-determination* (emphasis
   added);
B. Ensure that legislation protects everyone, including all children, from all
   forms of forced, coercive or otherwise involuntary modification of their
   sex characteristics

Except they aren't advocating for this last part: normal people are. These are the
people stating that children have the right to "self-determine" their gender and that
the courts can overrule parents on these procedures, even taking children from their
parents for "human rights abuses." Remember: human rights are what they say they
are. Per the Open Society "License to be Yourself" report, "Strategic litigation has
been critical in countries in both Europe and Latin America and increasingly these
human rights arguments are being reiterated in submissions to United Nations and
other human rights mechanisms."

Following "strategic lobbying by activists," the US implemented a policy that no
longer requires any medical treatment as a pre-requisite for changing gender on passports. The Australian government adopted similar changes and went further by introducing "progressive Government Guidelines on the Recognition of Sex and Gender." In Hong Kong, a campaign has been launched for the introduction of a new
Gender Recognition Ordinance. In December 2019, the Ministry of Social Affairs in
Austria lifted the lifetime ban on homosexuals who want to donate blood, and in
2018, the Constitutional Court ruled that gender markers in civil registers and IDs
must reflect "an individual's own self-determined gender identity."

We see with the Yogyakarta Principles document what the ruling class ultimately
intends for universal codification of these "rights," adopted piecemeal thus far; the
YP+10 Principles also include a directive to:

• Remove any barriers that may hinder timely access to affordable and quality abortion services
• Ensure that "gender identity" is used as a legitimate claim for asylum and
  exempt these people from "invasive" procedures, as well as respect their
  right to privacy
• Develop and implement affirmative action programmes to promote public
  and political participation for persons marginalised on the basis of sexual
  orientation, gender identity, gender expression or sex characteristics
• Ensure that gender affirming healthcare is provided by the public health
  system or, if not so provided, that the costs are covered or reimbursable
  under private and public health insurance schemes
• Ensure that the detention of asylum seekers is avoided
• Ensure that HIV status is not used as a pretext to isolate, marginalise or

exclude persons of diverse sexual orientations, gender identities, gender expressions or sex characteristics
- Prevent the disclosure of HIV status
- Ensure access to HIV medication
- Ensure that legal provisions, including in customary, religious and indigenous laws, whether explicit provisions, or the application of general punitive provisions such as acts against nature, morality, public decency, vagrancy, sodomy and propaganda laws, do not criminalise sexual orientation, gender identity and expression, or establish any form of sanction relating to them
- Repeal other forms of criminalisation and sanction impacting on rights and freedoms on the basis of sexual orientation, gender identity, gender expression or sex characteristics, including the criminalisation of sex work, abortion, unintentional transmission of HIV, adultery, nuisance, loitering and begging
- Ensure that associations which seek to promote human rights related to sexual orientation, gender identity, gender expression or sex characteristics can seek, receive and use funding and other resources from individuals, associations, foundations or other civil society organisations, governments, aid agencies, the private sector, the United Nations and other entities, domestic or foreign
- Provide access to medical care and counselling appropriate to those seeking asylum, recognising any particular needs of persons on the basis of their sexual orientation, gender identity, gender expression or sex characteristics, including with regard to reproductive health, HIV information and therapy, hormonal or other therapy, and gender affirming treatment
- Take positive measures, including affirmative action measures, to overcome specific challenges to the enjoyment of the freedom of association of groups that are marginalised and made vulnerable on grounds of sexual orientation, gender identity, gender expression or sex characteristics

This document is absolutely dystopic and outlines *exactly* where we are going. This isn't some "laugh-it-off" ridiculousness despite its preposterousness as the neo-liberal axis uses all of the means at its disposal to depose obstinate regimes, including military intervention, and actively grooms, abuses, and mutilates children, as we've seen. A civilization that fails to protect its most vulnerable, especially its children, is doomed to oblivion. No amount of propaganda should be able to sway us otherwise. This monstrous regime cannot be allowed to continue to operate with impunity simply because it claims to be democratic and puts a rainbow flag on everything.

The so-called Enlightenment made man the center of the universe, a premise no less ridiculous than the not-long-discarded geocentric theory. When man is the center of the universe, he *is* God—his *own* God—and his possibilities are limitless, or at least man perceives them that way. If Man is God, He is created in His own image—or any image He wants to create. We see this near-boundless arrogance embodied in the utopianism of Progress, an increasingly queer (double entendre intended) entropic Progress that is revealing itself as in actuality an accelerator of dissolution and decay. In the ultimate paradox, this hyper-individualist/narcissistic utopia renders everyone a widget, a number, part of a data set in the architects' network.

Indeed, the word utopia is derived from the Greek *ou-topos*, meaning "no place" or "nowhere." Is that not the essence of this globalized project—everywhere becomes nowhere, everything becomes nothing?

For Pawel Leszkowicz and Tomasz Kitlinski, who write in their chapter of *A Critical Inquiry into Queer Utopias*, part of Palgrave Macmillan's Critical Studies in Gender, Sexuality, and Culture series (try arguing critical theory isn't institutionalized):

> An analysis of other crucial and current aspects of queer European policy such as transgender rights and LGBTQ refugees and migrants . . . require[s] a . . . very necessary! text. . . . Queer rights visual campaigns create a utopian queer space that aims to transform the complex system of inequalities and prejudices that exist in various European countries. It is a vision of an imagined equal society of sexual diversities.

Imagined. Not real.

Unsurprisingly, their touchstones of "evidence" (meaning unproven/provable theories used as evidence) include the writings of Lee Edelman, Judith "Jack" Halberstam, and Hannah Arendt. Telegraphing precisely what "progress" means, Abi McIntosh writes for *The Independent*, "replacing one of the most recognizable lesbian celebrities on television [Ellen DeGeneres] with another white man is a step in the wrong direction for equality." Equality now defined, as the oppositional ideology of intersectionality increasingly rules the day, we are seeing with increasing frequency incidents like the Hebrew Immigrant Aid Society's Greek branch along with another NGO supporting a "trans woman" migrant's bid to force the government to alter the name and gender registration on "her" residence permit and travel document. In 2011, Austria denied refugee status to "Yasar, a Turkish trans woman." Vienna-based NGO TransX organized protests and asked people to send letters to the government to stop the deportation. In the end, the government caved and Yasar was released from detention.

The Swedish Migration Agency declares that it will give asylum to people who "are persecuted in their homeland due to sexual orientation and gender." The Church of Sweden holds Rainbow Masses, which "aim to mirror every person's equal worth, also from an LGBTQ perspective." Malin Strindberg, priest at the Rainbow Mass, says: "Most priests are wise enough to understand that homosexual love is worth every bit as much as any other kind of love." Only once the already-ludicrous idea of "equality" has been warped beyond all recognition into a genocidal weapon are such sentiments not only entertained by people, but become the default accepted opinion. For many reasons, not least of which include the survival of the Swedish people, homosexual love insofar as it exists is *not* "worth every bit as much as any other kind of love." Such "wisdom" is indicative of the late-stage decadence and decline of an exhausted and unnatural liberalism, weaponized against its adherents. Furthermore, only out of the cosmic energy as reflected in race such as in the mind of Franz Kafka could the grotesque absurdities we are confronted with today find form.

The Yogyakarta mandates get progressively weirder, too, like the right to use the internet regardless of gender or sexual orientation or ensuring no one who is trans or homosexual live in poverty as "poverty is incompatible with respect for . . . equal rights." These are actually not out of step with the UN's Sustainable Development Goals (emphases in the text, sourced from the Council of Europe):

> The UN 2030 Agenda envisages *"a world of universal respect for human rights and human dignity, the rule of law, justice, equality and non-discrimination"*. It is grounded in the Universal Declaration on Human Rights and international human rights treaties and emphasises the responsibilities of all states to respect, protect and promote human rights. There is a strong emphasis on the empowerment of women and of vulnerable groups such as children, young people, persons with disabilities, older persons, refugees, internally displaced persons and migrants. The Agenda's 17 Sustainable Development Goals (SDG), and their 169 targets, aim at eradicating poverty in all forms and *"seek to realize the human rights of all and achieve gender equality."*

Bear all of this in mind as we progress; we will see what that *really* looks like, although the reader should already have a pretty good indication. UN Women is one of three UN agencies that sent representatives to join NGOs like OutRight Action International and GATE for the informal briefing of the Yogyakarta Principles plus 10 in March 2018.

Other Yogyakarta principles basically mandate that people be able to use whatever public restrooms they want as "The Right to Sanitation," and another states that people should be able to compete in sports against whatever gender they identify as. There is also a "Right to Cultural Diversity": "Ensure the right to practice, protect, preserve and revive the diversity of cultural expressions of persons of all sexual orientations, gender identities, gender expressions and sex characteristics on the basis of the equal dignity of and respect for all." Unless you're White, straight, Christian, and/or otherwise normative and *especially* if you are exceptional in some capacity. The necessity of propaganda is also articulated:

- Ensure inclusion of comprehensive, affirmative and accurate material on sexual, biological, physical and psychological diversity, and the human rights of people of diverse sexual orientations, gender identities, gender expressions and sex characteristics, in curricula, taking into consideration the evolving capacity of the child
- Develop, implement and support education and public information programmes to promote human rights and to eliminate prejudices on grounds of sexual orientation, gender identity, gender expression and sex characteristics
- Ensure inclusion of comprehensive, affirmative and accurate material on sexual, biological, physical and psychological diversity, and the human rights of people of diverse sexual orientations, gender identities, gender expressions and sex characteristics, in teacher training and continuing professional development programmes.

"Accurate" being determined by these ideologues. "Everyone has the right to freedom of opinion and expression, regardless of sexual orientation or gender identity"—unless of course you speak out against the forceful sterilization of a three-year-old, that is. In which case, you are guilty of a hate crime and human rights abuses, the kinds of which could find you dying in a jail cell of mysterious—but *totally* natural—causes. If this sounds hyperbolic, remember what happened to Slobodan Milošević.

The human rights committee of the Council of Europe has been used as another vehicle to combat "homophobia" and advance this particular form of "human rights" which essentially mandates access to hormones and sex changes, and allows people to edit their gender né biological sex at will. The Council of Europe's Sexual Orientation and Gender Identity Unit is now training police officers to "recognize and combat anti-LGBTQ hate crimes," very similar to what the Yogyakarta Principles recommend and which the Anti-Defamation League does with law enforcement officers in the United States.

The Council of Europe published a comprehensive manual in May 2017, "Policing Hate Crime against LGBTI persons: Training for a Professional Police Response," on which the training of officers from Bulgaria, France, Georgia, Greece, Italy, Lithuania, Moldova, Poland, Portugal, Serbia, Spain, Sweden, and the UK thus far has been based. There is also apparently something called the European LGBT Police Association which has been involved in the training. Their website links to a guide produced by Stonewall and the Paul Hamlyn Foundation among others "challenging homophobia in primary schools."

ILGA-Europe also provides a "training police officers on tackling LGBTI-phobic crime" toolkit, a general recognizing "anti-LGBT hate crime" manual, and a handbook on "monitoring and reporting homophobic and transphobic incidents." The European LGBT Police Association features affiliates in Greece, the UK, Finland, Austria, Italy, Spain, Norway, Sweden, Belgium, Switzerland, Ireland, the Netherlands, Serbia, France, and Germany.

The European Union, like member state Germany and many others, has taken it upon itself to vigorously monitor (read: suppress) speech on the internet regarding not just "migrants" but "hate speech targeting sexual orientation and . . . gender identity." What, exactly, constitutes hate speech is, as usual, in the eye of this particular beholder and their agenda. On October 3rd, 2019, the Court of Justice of the European Union (CJEU) issued a judgment declaring that host providers such as Facebook can be compelled to "proactively remove content and comments from their sites that have previously been determined to be illegal." The following month, the LIBE Committee in the European Parliament organized a hearing on "Media Freedom, Freedom of Expression and Combating hate speech online and offline," with ILGA-Europe among the other organizations expressing concern at "the rise in LGBTI phobic hate speech across Europe." Always rising, always a crisis that stultifying layers upon layers of legal proceedings and committees and bureaucracies can tackle.

According to ILGA-Europe's 2020 Annual Review, the enshrinement of the LGBTQ agenda and its intersectional nature has permeated the highest levels of the supra-governmental European governing bodies, including aspects of their foreign policy (the report was produced using funds from the European Union itself, which is not at all incidental and especially when considering that ILGA-Europe remains committed to not just "LGBTI asylum seekers," but "rainbow families in the asylum system" and "issues concerning intersectionality"):

On 12 February [2019], the European Parliament adopted a resolution on the backlash in women's rights and gender equality in the EU. The resolution addresses the current "visible and organised effort at the global and at the European level against gender equality and women's rights," whose targets are among others LGBTI people's human rights. The European Parliament points out how this backlash was especially visible in 2018 around the topic of the Istanbul Convention, whose adoption has opened doors for *violent hate speech* [emphasis added—violent speech?] targeting LGBTI people in particular, and expresses concerns about the rise of LGBTI-phobic hate speech. . . . On 18 December [2019], the European Parliament adopted a resolution on "Public discrimination and hate speech against LGBTI people, including LGBTI free zones", following a debate in the European Parliament on public discrimination and hate speech against LGBTI people, which was held in plenary in Strasbourg on 26 November. The resolution expresses deep concern at the growing number of attacks against the LGBTI community coming from the State, State officials, Governments at the national, regional and local levels, and politicians in the EU. It recognises that such attacks have seen a rise in violence against LGBTI people, with hate crimes motivated by homophobia and transphobia on the rise across the EU while responses from authorities too often remain inadequate. It reiterates a call on the Commission to adopt an EU LGBTI strategy and a comprehensive, permanent and objective EU mechanism on democracy, rule of law and fundamental rights that includes the protection of LGBTI rights. . . . The European Commission's Enlargement Progress Report 2019, published in May and covering 2018, recommended a number of steps regarding the improvement of LGBTI rights across the region of the Western Balkans. These included addressing insufficiencies regarding adoption and implementation of anti-discrimination laws inclusive of SOGI, investigation of hate crimes, access to justice, access to healthcare, trans rights, intersex rights, tackling negative public attitudes towards LGBTI people, adoption of laws on registered partnership and legal gender recognition. . . . On 20 March [2019], in the final meeting this legislative term of the EU High-Level Group for Countering Racism, Xenophobia and Other Forms of Intolerance, the European Commission presented the Staff Working Document: Countering Racism and Xenophobia in the EU (2019), setting out three priorities for future work, each led by a working group: recording and data collection practices, including reporting of hate crime; training and capacity building for national authorities, aimed at ensuring effective implementation of national law on hate crime and hate speech; and developing and implementing hate crime victim support systems and services. . . . Ahead of the European Parliament elections, 23–26 May [2019], over 1650 candidates across all EU Member States signed ILGA-Europe's ComeOut pledge. After the elections, 225 MEPs from eight different political groups signed the ComeOut pledge, strengthening the support in numbers and geographical and political diversity. . . . On 14 February [2019], the European Parliament adopted a Resolution on the future of the LGBTI List of Actions (2019–2024), calling on the European Commission to ensure strong follow-up to the European Commission LGBTI List of Actions 2014–2019, including by adopting a comprehensive and coherent EU LGBTI Strategy. On 23–

24 September [2019], the Finnish Presidency of the EU organised a High-level conference on advancing LGBTI equality in the EU: from 2020 and beyond. The two-day meeting included speeches from Commissioner Jourova and the Finnish Minister for Nordic Cooperation and Equality and the Minister for Education, Culture and Science, The Netherlands, high-level panels as well as eight thematic workshops on priority areas identified for the conference, as input to the EC work plan and follow-up of the list of actions for LGBTI rights. . . . In the European Parliament resolution of 14 March [2019] on the human rights situation in Kazakhstan, two references to LGBTI rights were made, regarding equality and non-discrimination. On 26 March, the European Parliament adopted a report on the new comprehensive agreement between the EU and Uzbekistan . . . The report specifically addresses LGBTI rights issues, by asking the Council and the Commission to "encourage the authorities to decriminalise consensual sexual relations between persons of the same sex and foster a culture of tolerance for LGBTI people."

The European Parliament's LGBTI Intergroup "consists in monitoring the work of the European Union; monitoring the situation of lesbian, gay, bisexual, transgender and intersex (LGBTI) people in EU Member States and beyond; and liaising with civil society groups to relay their concerns at the European level." It is the largest of the European Parliament's twenty-seven Intergroups because human rights and the rest of the tired rhetoric. It also clearly telegraphs the priorities of the European Parliament.

Criminal proceedings were initiated against a pair of individuals for "anti-LGBT" social media posts in Latvia in 2019. In November 2018, the Swedish parliament took the second of two necessary decisions to include trans as a protected class in the reality-defying Freedom of Speech Act's regulation on "hate speech." This is not an outlier but a central pillar of cracking down on dissent. Norway is working to implement its LGBTI Action Plan, which will include police training, and accepted a UPR recommendation from the UN "to combat anti-LGBT hate crimes, hate speech and discrimination." The Oslo police district also organized a public discussion during Pride to publicly apologize for "contributing to anti-LGBT attitudes, discrimination and violence in Norway's past." A new "action plan against racism" was published in December 2019, and includes the creation of a national competency center regarding hate crimes.

In yet another example of the assault on national sovereignty, "the European Parliament adopted a resolution on discrimination and hate speech against LGBTI people, including LGBTI-free zones, calling on Poland to revoke resolutions attacking LGBTI rights, including local bills against 'LGBT ideology.'" Another resolution to revoke resolutions. It's a never-ending stream of repetition designed to wear down any resistance and indoctrinate the masses.

There has been significant push-back on the LGBTQ agenda in Poland:

In March [2019], Poland's ruling Law and Justice (PiS) party leader Jarosław Kaczyński said that the Warsaw mayor's support of LGBT people was an attack on children and families. The Church and other conservative circles used similar rhetoric. In the following months, more than 80 towns declared that they are "LGBT-free zones" or "free from LGBT ideology". Lublin city presented awards to local officials opposing "LGBT ideology". According to LGBT activists, these actions supported the nationalist-conservative party, which continuously used anti-LGBT rhetoric in the lead-up to the autumn elections. The government referred to the election as an ideological war. On 17 July [2019], the conservative Gazeta Polska newspaper launched a campaign enclosing "LGBT-free zone" stickers in its weekly edition. The editor said their point was not to incite hatred, but instead to demonstrate that they would be subject to censorship for printing anti-LGBT views. The conservative government stated they would not sanction the paper, to protect freedom of speech. Several public figures condemned the campaign, including the US Ambassador and Warsaw's deputy mayor, Paweł Rabiej, who likened it to the Nazi era. LGBT activist Bart Staszewski brought the case to the Warsaw District Court, which placed an injunction on the stickers on 25 July. It is uncertain if the stickers will be banned permanently. On 2 August, the Krakow Archbishop Marek Jedraszewski called the LGBT movement a "rainbow plague."

Over at the United Nations, 2019 saw a strong condemnation of Estonia for insufficient hate crime and hate speech protections for LGBT people, and the usual hysteria regarding "trans violence" in Tajikistan, Kazakhstan, Poland, and the UK. As part of the Universal Periodic Review (UPR), North Macedonia came under fire and was compelled to withdraw school textbooks that "stigmatise LGBTI people." The reader should by now notice the consistent and constant use of the same words and phrases. This is part of the normalization strategy of propaganda, of "priming" the population. Terms can then be linked—think of "inclusive" or "sustainable" for example—to other arms of the agenda, all feeding into the globalist maw.

In 2019, Slovakia accepted the UN UPR recommendations to "combat anti-LGBTI hate speech." The UN uses its influence to pressure countries to make concessions to this particular agenda, not least of which included Cyprus's adoption of an action plan on "racism." According to IGLYO's 2018 LGBTQI Inclusive Education report:

In the school year 2014–2015, some schools took part in a pilot project based on the Code of Conduct Against Racism and Guide for Management and Recording of Racial Incidents (2000). They were advised to treat intimidating incidents based on some aspect of the victim's diversity (i.e. sexual orientation, gender identity) as racist violence. The pilot implementation of the Code and Guidelines was actively supported by the Authority against Discrimination on the Ombudsman Office and Human Rights and the UN High Commissioner for Refugees. In this protocol, the identity of individuals in relation to their sexual orientation is embodied. According to anti-racist policies of the Ministry of Education and Culture, violent incidents on the basis of gender diversity, gender identity or sexual orientation are defined as racist and are treated with the appropriate sanctions. There is also a special mention on homophobia and transphobia; hostility, discrimination, or disgust against LGB people, or individuals expressing their gender identity. In March 2017, the Cyprus Police signed a memorandum of Cooperation for the Protection and Promotion of Human Rights with 12 NGOs including KISA, ACCEPT-

LGBT and Hope for Children.

Per ILGA-Europe's 2020 Annual Review:

North Macedonia accepted recommendations [from the UN] to investigate and prosecute anti-LGBTI hate crimes; Norway accepted a recommendation to combat anti-LGBT hate crimes, hate speech and discrimination, but noted a recommendation on adding gender identity and expression (GIE) to the hate crime section of the Penal Code. Bosnia and Herzegovina was recommended to train law enforcement and the judiciary on combating anti-LGBT hate crimes, hate speech, and discrimination. San Marino was recommended to ban anti-LGBT hate crimes. . . . At the 63rd session of the Commission on the Status of Women in March in New York, the LBTI Caucus, including activists from Ukraine, Sweden, France and the Netherlands, created strong visibility on SOGIESC issues by organising several side events, addressing the UN Secretary General and providing recommendations in meetings with governments for their negotiations. This contributed to some strong language in the final adopted text, such as on multiple and intersecting forms of discrimination, diverse needs of families, 'all women and girls' and structural barriers like discriminatory laws and policies, negative social norms and gender stereotypes . . . The CEDAW recommended Austria to ensure substantive and procedural protection against discrimination on the basis of sexual orientation in the private and public sector. It recommended Serbia to address discrimination on the basis of SOGI in the new gender equality legislation, and to speedily adopt it. The CESCR recommended Kazakhstan to combat discrimination against LGBT persons and adopt comprehensive anti-discrimination legislation that includes SOGI. The CRC recommended Italy to prevent discrimination and, if needed, take affirmative action for the benefit of LGBT children and children of LGBT parents. As part of the UPR, Cyprus accepted recommendations to combat discrimination and violence against LGBTI people; Portugal accepted two recommendations to combat discrimination and exclusion on the basis of sexual orientation; Bosnia and Herzegovina and Kazakhstan received similar recommendations. Italy was recommended to renew its National LGBT Strategy. San Marino was recommended to ban discrimination on the basis of gender identity. Slovenia was recommended to combat anti-LGBTI prejudice, stereotypes, discrimination, and hate crimes, and to put in place awareness raising campaigns. . . . The CESCR recommended Kazakhstan to guarantee an enabling environment for NGOs, especially LGBT groups by allowing them to freely register. . . . As part of the UPR, Norway agreed to guarantee the right and access to healthcare for trans people. Slovenia was recommended the same. . . . As part of the UPR, Cyprus accepted and Albania noted recommendations to adopt gender recognition legislation. Slovenia was recommended the same. . . . The CEDAW recommended Austria mandate sex education that aims to eliminate barriers of lesbian, bisexual and trans women to sexual and reproductive rights. The CEDAW also urged Serbia to enhance access to family planning services and artificial insemination for LBTI persons. . . . Last June [2018], the World

Health Organisation depathologised trans identities by removing all trans related diagnoses from the chapter on mental health disorders of ICD-11, into
a new chapter on Conditions Related to Sexual Health.

Council of Europe leadership has also chimed in, condemning the Bulgarian government for spreading "misinformation" and Armenia and Poland for politicians' "hate
speech." As you can see, it is a constant and unrelenting barrage.

According to a 2018 comparative analysis by the European Commission into
"Trans and intersex equality rights in Europe," significant inroads have already been
made with EU secondary law containing reference to trans identities, and the Court
of Justice of the European Union:

> Has been willing to employ a progressive interpretation of sex equality stand-
> ards, thus creating a baseline obligation for Member States in relation to trans
> non-discrimination. However, the Court has looked at most cases through the
> lens of 'gender reassignment', resulting in a highly medicalised picture of
> trans populations. Consistent references to the fact that claimants have under-
> taken a process of surgical transition frames trans equality as contingent upon
> medical interventions.

The European Union Agency for Fundamental Rights (FRA) states that, "On 28 November 2008 the EU adopted a framework decision relating to hate speech and hate
crime motivated by racism and xenophobia (OJ L 328/2008). The EU needs to consider adopting similar legislation to cover homophobic and transphobic hate speech
and hate crime so that LGBT persons can be protected in all Member States." FRA
is financed by European Union funds allocated to it on an annual basis by the European Union budgetary authority, so this uniform adoption is probably inevitable. As
we've seen, many member states have already taken similar measures and still more
are in various stages of coercion.

The Director of the FRA, by the way, is Michael O'Flaherty, former member of
the UK Foreign Office's advisory bodies on
freedom of expression and the prevention of
torture, the Irish Department of Foreign Affairs' human rights advisory committee,
major figure in international "human
rights," former senior official in the UN including Secretary of the UN Committee on
the Elimination of Racial Discrimination
and UN human rights advisor for implementation of the Dayton Peace Agreement,
and rapporteur for the development of the
Principles and State Obligations on the Application of International Human Rights
Law with regard to Sexual Orientation and
Gender Identity: the Yogyakarta Principles.

This is an actual flier from the Publications Office of the European Union:

## Boas Constrictor

Gender theory is characterized by Encyclopedia.com as having "replaced or challenged ideas of masculinity and femininity and of men and women as operating in history according to fixed biological determinants. In other words, removing these categories from the realm of biology." We've discussed much of the baseline for this fiction, but it is worth considering the other tangled roots, most notably the deeply-flawed work of Margaret Mead and her Noble Savage-esque depictions of Samoan culture and sexuality/"gender roles." In her *Coming of Age in Samoa* (1928), Samoa was portrayed as an untouched Eden where its people knew no sexual inhibitions, and where Samoan maidens sought to acquire as many lovers as possible. Mead claimed that neither sex possessed a notion of "romantic love as it occurs in our civilization, inextirpably bound up with ideas of monogamy, exclusiveness, jealousy and undeviating fidelity."

Mead had studied under the Jewish anthropologist Franz Boas and his protégé Ruth Benedict (considered the originator of the idea of cultural relativism) at Columbia University, where she attained her master's degree in 1924. It is believed that Mead and Benedict were romantically involved (or at least sexually involved, if their relationship resembled Mead's portrayal of the Samoan source material). Benedict co-published an "anti-racism" pamphlet in 1943 *The Races of Mankind* for the US Army during World War II with fellow Boasian acolyte, communist, and Columbia University professor the Jewish Gene Weltfish ("The world is shrinking. Thirty-four nations are now united in a common cause—victory over Axis aggression, the military destruction of fascism. . . . All the peoples of the earth are a single family and have a common origin"). The central thesis is that racial differences/disparities are the consequence of cultural rather than biological factors.

One of Benedict's star pupils was the Jewish Ruth Landes (né Schlossberg), who wrote extensively on gender, race, and sexuality, putting forth the now-familiar litany of Boasian and other critical-theoretical postulations that have supplanted hard evidence for generations at this point. In *City of Women* (1947), Landes writes that the female-centric sphere of candomblé in Brazil was a source of empowerment for blacks and "passive homosexuals." Before Margaret Mead left for Samoa, she carried on an affair with another Jewish Boasian acolyte in Edward Sapir.[65] As proto-Bidens, both of Mead's sisters married Jews. This is a common phenomenon we shall and have seen, of Gentiles marrying Jews and "inextirably binding up," to borrow from Mead, their interests. Paul G. Hoffman and Anna Rosenberg would be another example, and Kamala Harris and Douglas Emhoff is another.

The Boas school was no exception, and for its Jews, regarded their project as not merely informed by their predominantly Jewish identities but, as with Freudian psychoanalysis, as an active undermining of white Gentile culture and solidarity. As Ira Bashkow writes in "The Boas Circle vs. White Supremacy" published in the *History of Anthropology Review*:

> [Madison] Grant's most troublesome critic was the anthropologist Franz Boas, an assimilated Jew who had immigrated to the US from Germany and taught at Columbia University. Boas regularly belittled Grant's racial theories as "Nordic nonsense" and, in publication after publication, he upended the conceit that they had any basis in science. Grant's book was "dogmatic" and "dangerous," Boas wrote presciently in the *New Republic*. Its racial fear-mongering rested on fallacies, starting with the concept of race itself. Grant's categories, which included Nordic, Mediterranean, Hindu, Negro, and Jew, were ill-defined, overlapping, historically fickle, and internally heterogeneous. They primarily reflected the habits of perception and classification that people learnt growing up. Race, Boas liked to point out, was very much in the eye of the beholder.

Where is the evidence for Boas's claims? There isn't any; this is the familiar smug attack on a fixed position through critique based on theory sans evidence. At best we could say that Grant's racial categories are certainly internally heterogeneous, but that does not undermine the broad concept of race—even in people like Bashkow's own modern rhetoric, race is treated with even greater fixity than that of white theorists one hundred years ago and is certainly uniform. Consider, for example, that "black" is treated as a global monolith, even when there is considerable admixture. Secondly, though we understand that there are various hybridizations of race that resist absolutes—quite like most things—that does not categorically eliminate the biological reality of race. Culture does not explain racial differences; race explains cultural differences. Where does culture come from, then? Trees? The air? It is clear to see the ideological and ethnic bent of the Boasian School:

---

[65] For more on this milieu, the reader is encouraged to see Chapter Two of Kevin MacDonald's *The Culture of Critique* to learn how without any hard scientific evidence—indeed in defiance of decades of dis-confirming research—"The Boasian revolution in anthropology had triumphed, and theorists who believed that race was important for explaining human behavior became fringe figures."

Boas became close to the pioneering feminist sociologist Elsie Clews Parsons, a Barnard graduate and Wall Street heiress who—after Columbia cut the Anthropology Department's funding—paid Boas's secretary's salary and sponsored field research trips for his female graduate students. . . . Each one in this circle was in some way an outsider, like Boas himself. . . . In 1934 [Ruth Benedict] published one of the greatest anthropological statements of all time, *Patterns of Culture*, the source of the term "cultural relativity. . . ." What might repulse an American—she gave as examples homosexuality and women falling in trance—are in another society given positive meaning as routes to special gifts and supernatural power. . . . Boas wrote in his introduction that "the relativity of what is considered social or asocial, normal or abnormal is seen in a new light." Clearly, here was a point of view congenial to those who felt out of kilter with their own social world. . . . Margaret Mead was another such figure. Though a child of privilege, she was small and frail and felt out of place at her first midwestern college, so she transferred in 1920 to Barnard, where she found herself in a new group of "freethinking, adventurous women," some of them lesbian, "half of them Jewish, and all equally acquainted with Bolshevism and the poetry of Edna St. Vincent Millay." This was New York in the Jazz Age, culturally vibrant and sexually liberating. Mead and her girlfriends marched in support of the Amalgamated Clothing Workers and the Italian immigrant anarchists Nicola Sacco and Bartolomeo Vanzetti. . . . [Zora Neale] Hurston enrolled as an anthropology doctoral student at Columbia, with Boas her mentor, and, equipped with a Guggenheim Fellowship, she set out for new research in Jamaica and Haiti. This led to her most famous novel, *Their Eyes Were Watching God*.

With the modern framework of race in place and the foundation for "Whiteness" and White culture as derived from its own unique biological inheritance in particular suitably eroded, gender and sexuality would not be far behind.

Though by the late nineteenth century the ruling class of Britain had already been deeply Judaized (see Andrew Joyce's "Free to Cheat: 'Jewish Emancipation' and the Anglo-Jewish Cousinhood," which describes conditions remarkably similar to those that occurred later in the United States), concerns over the flood of Jews entering Britain led to the 1905 Aliens Act; although the Our Migration Story website laments the fact that "anti-Semitic prejudice was widespread in the debates of the time [as] poor Jews were said to bring crime, bad labour conditions, anarchism, dirt and disease into the country" (the site partners with the deeply subversive Runnymede Trust so this is unsurprising),[66] they may have been on to something, at least if the American experience is any indication.

---

[66] This "race equality think tank," run almost exclusively non-native Britons, publishes pieces such as "Home Office failing LGBTQI asylum seekers," which favorably quotes the UK Lesbian and Gay Immigration Group, which is supported by the Barrow Cadbury Trust, the Tudor Trust, AB Charitable Trust, the Wakefield & Tetley Trust, LGBT+ Future Programme, the Trust for London, the Sigrid Rausing Trust, and Lloyds Bank Foundation. The AB Charitable Trust lists "migrants and refugees" as one of its primary focus areas, and disbursed £1.137 million to those ends in 2019-20. "Refugees" and asylum seekers, along with LGBT people, are considered "communities of interest" by the Tudor Trust. The Barrow Cadbury Trust is part of the Migration Exchange, which "aims to work together to improve the lives of migrants and receiving communities in the UK by informing public debate on migration and creating welcoming communities." Other major funders in the Migration Exchange include the Esmée Fairbairn Foundation,

While the first half of the twentieth century especially saw Jewish interests viewed as synonymous with communism, there was a significant infatuation in the 19th century with anarchism. Emma Goldman and her lover/partner-in-crime Alexander Berkman are illustrative. Though Goldman was a co-conspirator, Berkman made the failed attempt on Henry Clay Frick's life that saw him imprisoned. Berkman and Goldman—both immigrants—had become attracted to anarchism after the Haymarket affair in 1886 and through the writings of Jewish anarchist Johann Most. In 1889, Berkman, Goldman, Modest Stein, and Helene Minkin (who would go on to marry Most) all moved in together to form a sort of commune; Berkman and Stein were members of the explicitly-Jewish anarchist group the Pioneers of Liberty, which was known for its Yiddish-language publications.

The Pioneers were vehemently anti-religious and yet clung tightly to their Jewish identity. The YIVO Institute for Jewish Research states that:

> Yiddish-speaking Jewish anarchists were one of the pillars of the U.S. anarchist movement before World War II. . . . Yiddish-speaking anarchists played a pivotal role in unions like the International Ladies' Garment Workers' Union (ILGWU), while the Yiddish anarchist newspaper the *Fraye Arbeter Shtime* (*The Free Voice of Labor*) was the largest and longest-lasting U.S. anarchist publication and formed a significant part of the Yiddish cultural landscape. In the 1930s a second generation of bilingual Jewish anarchists emerged, including Sam and Esther Dolgoff, and Audrey Goodfriend, whose influence is still felt in today's anarchist movement.

Throughout her life and "career," Goldman was arrested numerous times for incitement to riot and illegally distributing information about birth control; Goldman was an outspoken homosexual advocate and corresponded with Magnus Hirschfeld. Goldman also took Spanish anarchists up on their invitation to join them in Barcelona during the Spanish Civil War. The 1970s saw a revival in interest in Goldman's work driven by Jewish feminist Alix Kates Shulman's two books on Goldman: the biography *To the Barricades* (TY Crowell, 1971) and *Red Emma Speaks: An Emma Goldman Reader* (Random House, 1972).

The influence of and intersection with Jewish identity and involvement in subversive activities—or "activism" if you're feeling polite—intersects with the Jewish-driven influence of critical theory, as Anna Elena Torres explicates in an interview with *Jewish Currents*:

> Looking at these specific cultural forms might also connect Yiddish anarchism with recent thought on decolonizing anarchism, which critiques more "universalizing" aspects of European anarchism, as in the brilliant work of Macarena Gómez-Barris and J. Kehaulani Kauanui. Yiddish anarchism was invented by refugees who theorized from their experience of border crossing—how does that history relate to anticolonial anarchisms and indigenous

the Joseph Rowntree Charitable Trust, the Migration Foundation, Unbound Philanthropy, the Trust for London, the Sigrid Rausing Trust, the Oak Foundation, the Paul Hamlyn Foundation, and the Open Society Foundations.

critiques of the state. . . ? Taking seriously the particularities of Yiddish anarchist culture could be a move towards also considering the particularities
of Indigenous and First Nations and Maroon and PoC movements and their
ongoing relationships to the state. . . . There's an intriguing figure named
Rabbi Dr. Yankev-Meyer Zalkind. He was called *der go'en anarkhist*, the
anarchist sage. He had a deep education at the Volozhin yeshiva, where his
chevrusa was the poet Hayyim Bialik. . . . Looking at Zalkind's life can tell
us a lot about these convergences of religiosity and anarchism. From ads in
Yiddish newspapers, we know he gave public lectures framing the Talmud
as a proto-anarchist ethical tradition with no state power behind it. He definitely represents a strain of Yiddish anarchism rooted in textual tradition, in
defiance of antisemitism and Christian hegemony.

This defiance of Christian hegemony, with "white" implied here and often explicitly
stated by many Jews themselves, is the through-line that connects all Jewish radical
politics be they anarchism, communism, or Cultural Marxist-informed neo-liberalism. With increasing success with each one of these listed "-isms," they have also
been vehicles to advance Jewish interests and attain power, and in many instances
the radical fringe actually served to reinforce the well-positioned Jews who came to
shape the globalist agenda that evolved into neo-liberalism. "Rabbi and psychotherapist" Howard Cooper inadvertently reveals this interplay as well as the pronounced
role of Jews in communist insurrections through his favorable review of *A Specter
Haunting Europe* by Paul Hanebrink that supposedly "debunks" Judeo-Bolshevism:

Readers of the Jewish Chronicle are approaching a significant anniversary.
In the spring of 1919, the JC's long-standing editor, Leopold Greenberg,
wrote two articles on the relationship between Jews, Bolshevism and Communism. They provoked a furore. The Russian revolution of October 1917,
with its extensive Jewish presence in high-profile posts, had been followed
by the spread of revolutionary fervour to Germany in 1918 under the leadership of Rosa Luxemburg and Karl Liebknecht (both of Jewish descent), and
the establishment of the Hungarian Soviet Republic in early 1919 under the
control of Béla Kun (born Béla Kohn). While Greenberg lamented the havoc
Bolshevism was causing in Europe, he recognised that London's impoverished East End Jews might see an attraction in Bolshevism as a legitimate
response to oppression and discrimination. And he suggested that the utopian
ideals of communism might be experienced by some Jews as "consonant"
with the Jewish longing for a transformed, more equal, society. This was a
red rag both to bullish British conservatives, long suspicious of the potential
treachery of Russian Jewish immigrants, and to the great and good of the
British Jewish community (Lionel de Rothschild, Sir Israel Gollancz, Claude
Montefiore), who publicly dissociated themselves "absolutely and unreserv-
edly from the mischievous and misleading" doctrine of Bolshevism.

Global capitalism, though, well . . . that's another story! Indeed, as Jerry Z. Muller
writes in 2010's *Capitalism and the Jews*, "Capitalism has been the most important
force in shaping the fate of the Jews in the modern world. . . . The anti-Semitic context . . . led Jews to downplay the reality of their economic achievement—except in

internal conversations." And conservatives, well, look no further than "A Conservative Defense of Transgender Rights" from December 2016 in *National Review*, long known to purge any legitimate voices such as Revilo P. Oliver from its ranks. There is a reason conservatism and its static defense have been invariably crushed for generations, and this includes its built-in susceptibility to subversion.

Intense in-group favoritism is a central feature of any of these movements; even "conservatism"-as-transformed into neo-conservatism is a Jewish vehicle. I had earlier in this book introduced modern "art" and atonal music as harbingers of this era of intense ugliness. As with Boasian anthropology and the like, Kevin MacDonald explicates for *The Occidental Observer*:

> It's not surprising that Jewish attitudes would be reflected in what counts as fine art and whose work gets promoted. As [Brenton] Sanderson notes in his essay on Tristan Tzara and the Dada movement, there was a "Jewish intellectual substructure of many of these twentieth century art movements . . . manifest in their unfailing hostility toward the political, cultural and religious traditions of Europe and European-derived societies." Given this reality, it is not difficult to envision Jewish critics championing Jewish artists or non-Jews like Jackson Pollock whose work can be seen as advancing this hostility toward the culture of the West. Nor is it difficult to imagine Jewish art dealers promoting such artists (e.g., Sidney Janis promoting Mark Rothko whose fame had nothing to do with any recognizable talent but was inextricably linked to his being a member of a Jewish sub-culture). The same goes for Jewish art museum curators (e.g., Katherine Kuh promoting Rothko), Jewish collectors (e.g., Charles Saatchi promoting Damien Hirst), and Jewish critics (Clement Greenberg promoting Jackson Pollock).

The more Judaized or "user friendly" as former ADL National Director Abe Foxman put it the more nakedly awful it becomes for Europeans in particular. For Johannes Volkelt:

> The demoralization of our attitude and sentiment toward life itself is even more portentous than our declining recognition of artistic form. It is a mutilated, deformed, moron humanity which glowers or drivels at us through expressionist pictures. All they suggest is profound morbidity. . . . The soul is exhausted by its ceaseless chasing after nothing.

There is no higher purpose, simply to demoralize and luxuriate in abject awfulness—of form *and* content. Past that, the deep antipathy many Jews feel toward White Gentiles is reflected in the consistent and intensifying daily antagonisms directed from positions of power.

Warren J. Blumenfeld, author of *Warren's Words: Smart Commentary on Social Justice* (Purple Press); editor of *Homophobia: How We All Pay the Price* (Beacon Press); co-editor of *Readings for Diversity and Social Justice* (Routledge) and *Investigating Christian Privilege and Religious Oppression in the United States* (Sense); and co-author of *Looking at Gay and Lesbian Life* (Beacon Press), created a presentation for the World Congress of GLBT Jews: Keshet Ga'avah entitled "Heterosexism and Anti-Jewish Oppression: Making the Links": "When looking over this history, we find many clear and stunning connections between historical representations of Jewish people and lesbian, gay, bisexual, and trans* (LGBT) people." In "'Straight Pride' makes less and less sense the more you think about it," the perpetually-aggrieved and clearly ideologically-motivated Blumenfeld writes:

> The legislative council of the small town Emo, Ontario (population 1,333) voted by a margin of 3 to 2 to turn down a resolution recognizing June as "Pride Month." Voting against the measure were two councilors and town Mayor Harold McQuaker who said that it would be unfair because there is no "Straight Pride. . . ." So, would it be likewise unfair to commemorate October each year as LGBTQ History Month in the United States, or mid-September through mid-October as Hispanic Heritage Month, or November as Native American Heritage Month, or February as Black History Month, or March as Women's History Month, or May as Asian Pacific Islander American Heritage Month? Well, every month and every day is straight, white, Christian, male, pride, heritage, and history month and day. And why is that? It is because in our patriarchal, heterosexist, white-supremacist, Christian-centric North America, white, heterosexual, Christian males' lives matter more than any other. They are afforded an entire array of socially constructed privileges held back from all others based solely on the chance of their birth.

That must be why they're vilified in the media and on college campuses, attacked with impunity, and *dis*-privileged through college acceptance and hiring quotas like Affirmative Action, right?

In another piece, Blumenfeld proclaims that "cultural imperialism must end," but then turns around and whines about the entirety of the globe not accepting the artificial constructs of his ethno-religious/racial and ideological allies. Using an occupied Germany as an example of how to erase nationalist predilections and instill guilt, Blumenfeld states that, "the US needs to teach the Confederacy like Germany teaches Nazism." For Blumenfeld, part of the model to emulate is that of the BRD, which "from its inception has mandated a 'denazification' campaign to eliminate the promotion, production, and the nostalgia of a bygone era" including the banning of symbols and imprisonment for questioning the officially-sanctioned narrative of "historical events." Blumenfeld writes:

> German students read Jewish authors such as Thomas Mann, Hannah Arendt, Kurt Weill, Anne Frank, Elie Wiesel, and others. They watch documentaries and dramatizations, like the celebrated TV miniseries *Generation War*, portraying young people caught up in the brutalities of war. Students travel to former concentration camps to learn firsthand the loss of all human and civil rights, the enslavement and murder of Jews, homosexuals, Roma, Jehovah's Witnesses, people with disabilities, communists, the so-called "work shy" vagrants (unemployed and homeless) and others. . . . German schools do not deeply examine the actual military events of the war in consideration that to emphasize the war itself may incite positive attitudes of Nazi territorial expansionism.

Yes, to do so would reveal a great many truths obscured by the propaganda post-1945 and might actually instill the *volk* with a sense of pride over the revolution it took the entire aligned forces of capitalism, communism, and cowardice to crush.

Echoing the same position as Blumenfeld, Carlos Fraenkel writes in the *Boston Review*:

> Traditional anti-Semitism . . . is alive in other ways in the AfD—for example, in the historical revisionism of AfD leaders such as Björn Höcke, who want to restore German national pride by dismantling one pillar of postwar German political culture: remembering and doing penance for the Holocaust.

As Rachel Adler writes, "I wrote an article exploring a feminist approach to Holocaust theology." This one sentence is far more revealing than Adler likely realizes. It *is* a theology, a way to bind Jews in perpetual grievance, but also a cudgel to prevent a strong sense of racial or national consciousness among the peoples of Europe. This multi-generational guilt trip at the base of a mythologized event is absolutely vital to both Jewish hegemony and the new religion of Democracy such as it is, especially as any alternatives to the current trajectory are drowned out by the incessant propaganda. There *are* alternatives and there *is* more to life, alternatives that could bring us much closer to a political ideal that is in harmony with nature and reflective of the order of the metaphysical and cosmic plane. One may yet take a "feminist approach to Holocaust theology" or adopt a "queer lens" and be absolutely in keeping with the intended reverberations, but breaking from the paradigm to focus on one's kith and kin while respecting nature and universal order is strictly *verboten*. The Illinois Holocaust Museum and Education Center has hosted at least one event celebrating "Jewish LGBTQ+ historical figures," for example, and who can forget Yonah Bex Gerber's *Jewish Telegraphic Agency* classic, "As a queer Jew, learning Anne Frank was bisexual was a game changer" from June 2019?

The "gay history" Schwules Museum in Berlin—where "lending requests have come from as close as the German Historical Museum in Berlin and as far away as from the United States Holocaust Memorial Museum in Washington, D.C."—held its first exhibit in 1986, and used a grant received from the Senate of Berlin in December 2009 "to put more emphasis on lesbian and transgender people." In Anina Falasca, Miriam Goldmann, and Martina Lüdicke's 2013 "Are there gay Jews?" Question of the Month in the Context of the Exhibition "The Whole Truth" for the Jewish Museum Berlin:

> In the exhibition *The Whole Truth*, homosexuality is only mentioned peripherally in the context of Aviv Netter's meshugge parties and his golden calf. Currently, the Schwules Museum is showing the exhibit *lesbian. jewish. gay.* The subject of homosexuality in Judaism would have fit very well in *The Whole Truth*. Ad hoc, I'd display the flags and buttons with a rainbow and a Star of David that the Israeli Embassy distributed at this year's Christopher Street Day parade. A few months ago, the Jewish newspaper *Jüdische Allgemeine* published a long article on the title page and printed a photo of this flag. I think that's a great idea.

Schwules's expansion was made possible with funding from sources such as the European Regional Development Fund and the German Class Lottery Foundation Berlin, also known as the Lotto Foundation Berlin. Schwules is commonly considered the first "gay history" museum, and crystallized around the work of Andreas Sternweiler, Wolfgang Theis, and Manfred Baumgardt, along with Homosexual Action West Berlin co-founder Manfred Herzer; in J. Edgar Bauer's "On Behalf of Hermaphrodites and Mongrels: Refocusing the Reception of Magnus Hirschfeld's Critical Thought on Sexuality and Race," Herzer is favorably connected with the work of Magnus Hirschfeld:

> A relevant exception in this regard is the way sexuality historian Manfred Herzer has shortly approached the "doctrine of sexual intermediaries" as the "key concept" of his thought. While assessing and setting in historical perspective Herzer's interpretive contentions, the present study foregrounds Hirschfeld's Darwinian-inspired, non-essentialist naturalism as the ontic support for *the new sexual and race regime he envisaged* (emphasis added). By conceptualizing the potential in-finitization of sexualities and races, Hirschfeld was envisioning an unprecedented path toward the Messianic—albeit a-theological—goal of intra-historic liberation.

Herzer was also part of the group that convened in the apartment of Hans-Günter Klein in 1982 to form the Magnus Hirschfeld Society. Klein's research generally focused on Jews like Gideon Klein, Viktor Ullmann, and the Mendelssohn family. Klein was friends with the Jewish associate of Hirschfeld's Kurt Hiller, an openly gay communist and former Chairman of Hirschfeld's Scientific Humanitarian Committee. The Magnus Hirschfeld Society has been instrumental in publicizing the work of on-again, off-again Hiller associate the Jewish Eva Siewert. The Magnus Hirschfeld Society has received funding from the Astraea Lesbian Foundation for Justice, the Lotto Foundation Berlin, and the New Synagogue Berlin Center Judaicum.

According to a 2020 letter penned by the Board of the Jewish Community of Warsaw, "We have observed politicians . . . cynically undertake to foment hostility and hatred towards LGBT persons. We Jews—the descendants of Holocaust survivors—cannot and will not remain indifferent to words that would dehumanize LGBT persons." Interesting that the Holocaust would be cynically invoked every time a Jewish individual or group finds something objectionable or inconvenient. German Foreign Minister Heiko Maas has said that attempts by some Polish communities to introduce what are being characterized as "LGBT-free zones" were "incompatible with European values." Would these be Dave Rubin's much-vaunted Judeo-Christian values? As Carlos Fraenkel writes:

> Conservatives propose that immigrants should be assimilated to a German "Leitkultur"—the core values of German history and culture (whatever these may be). Critics stress the chauvinistic character of this proposal. An acrimonious debate over Leitkultur has been going on since the late 1990s. A day after *yarmulke*-wearing Germans staged a protest in solidarity with [Adam] Armoush and German Jews, the conservative governor of Catholic Bavaria, Markus Söder, decreed that every government office in his state must display

a crucifix "as an expression of Bavaria's historical and cultural heritage and a visible acknowledgment of the fundamental values of Germany's political order." Söder's goal was to signal that Islam doesn't belong in Germany—a slap in the face for the hundreds of thousands of Turkish migrant workers, the *Gastarbeiter*, who, since the 1960s, have done the jobs that Germans did not want and helped rebuild the country's economy [how were they jobs the Germans didn't want if it was in response to a "labor shortage" as the narrative holds? Surely beggars can't be choosers.]. But such state-sponsored *symbolic violence* (emphasis added) does not only affect Muslims. Although the Islamophobic imagination in Germany typically portrays Islam as alien to "Judeo-Christian civilization," the hyphen in "Judeo-Christian" is a hypocritical sleight of hand. For Christians, the cross signifies redemption through Christ's death, but for Jews it evokes two thousand years of persecution as supposed Christ-killers (a charge first made in John's Gospel and only dropped from official Christian teaching after the Holocaust). . . . Germany has done an impressive job building a culture of remembering the Holocaust. Now is a good time to complement it with a culture of pride in more than seventy years of stable liberal democracy. These are values that existing German citizens and those who aspire to become new ones can celebrate together as they underpin the political and social space they share. . . . But there is an urgent need to discuss the complex causes that lie behind the rage fueling anti-Semitism—*while insisting that Jew-hatred is always misdirected* (emphasis added). This debate must involve a reckoning with the ways in which the West, and Germany in particular, contributed to the problems in the regions where refugees come from: the legacies of colonialism and European anti-Semitism.

How does European anti-Semitism create refugees in Palestine, I wonder? With this passage not only do we have the admission here that there is a two thousand-year grievance against Christians and that the Jewish default is for mass importation of aliens into Western nations, but that Jews are blameless in their efforts to undermine their host societies as "Jew-hatred is always misdirected" and German history and cultural are smugly dismissed ("whatever these may be"). Fraenkel has no issue replacing Germans with Turks or other Muslims because, "As historian Mark Cohen has shown in a meticulous comparative study, up to modern times, Jews in general fared much better under Muslim rule than they did under Christian rule." This partially explains some of the efforts of organizations such as HIAS and IsraAID to support the literal ferrying of Muslims into Europe.

IsraAID—which is funded by the UNHCR and UNICEF, the Lisa and John Pritzker Family Fund, Kathy Levinson and Naomi Fine of the Lesbian Equity Fund, the Sheryl Sandberg and Dave Goldberg Family Fund, Airlink, Airbnb, Blueprint Healthcare, the Consulate General of Israel in San Francisco, Laura and Gary Lauder, the Jewish Federations of North America (JFNA), and B'nai B'rith International, among others—states of their recent endeavors:

The BRÜCKENBAU (Bridgebuilding) program offers support and empowerment for women, LGBT+, children, and other vulnerable groups in refugee shelters in Frankfurt, in partnership with the Integration Ministry and ZWST

- the Central Welfare Board of Jews in Germany. BRÜCKENBAU reached more than 2,600 refugees in 2018 and won the Chancellor's Integration Prize.

We see Fraenkel's "ideal" in action through IsraAID and the Central Welfare Board of Jews in Germany, all part of this "reckoning" for Germany and the West for historical grievances in virtually every instance wildly distorted from the reality, but that is the usefulness of controlling every institution and of producing propaganda. This is the essence of the "liberal democracy" Fraenkel believes should be celebrated, not the core essence of the Germanic peoples and their wonderful heritage. Guilt for a war they didn't initiate must replace their ethnic pride before they themselves are ultimately replaced.

While Jennifer Bilek does an excellent job cataloguing some of the major players behind the advancement of the transgender ideology in her 2018 piece, "Who Are the Rich, White Men Institutionalizing Gender Ideology?" for *The Federalist*—including George Soros, Jennifer Pritzker and the Pritzker family, Martine Rothblatt, David T. Rubin, Loren Schecter, and Mark Hyman—not all of the people behind the advancement of the transgender agenda are men and none of those I just named are actually white: they are Ashkenazi Jews.

It may be easy to bemoan the "old white men doing X" as a common cultural scapegoat, but there is no reason for Bilek to frame the perpetrators this way other than that white men are acceptable whipping posts, and thus the framing presumably runs some sort of interference. Despite proving her worth as a true journalist and not an ideologue in speaking truth to power, she nevertheless accepts the cultural frame and compounds one kind of injustice while trying to uncover another; the rightful anger we feel toward those responsible for pushing the extremely harmful transgender ideology on children especially is projected on to white men as a group, when one actually finds a relative dearth of them—especially straight ones—among the culprits here. The truth must be confronted directly regardless of how inconvenient or uncomfortable it may be. For the ruling class, however, this must never be allowed to occur. As we can see with the theology of the Holocaust, guilt—and especially guilt transference—is a supremely powerful talisman.

As David Adler wrote for the *Boston Review* in 2018:

In reality, the Jewish community already receives extensive—disproportionate, in fact—protection from the British government. Theresa May's government currently commits £13.4 million each year to protect Jewish schools, compared to just £2.4 million that the government spends on its 'hate crime action plan' to provide protection for places of worship for all other religions.

Is this because Jews are such prominent targets or something else? Were up to one million of them groomed and raped on the basis of their race and religion? Similarly, and in the same publication, Carlos Fraenkel disingenuously insists that due to "far-right extremism": "As Angela Merkel reminded Germans: heavily armed police officers protecting Jewish institutions have regrettably always been part of the postwar German cityscape." I thought Fraenkel believed that guilting Germans for the Holocaust should be complemented by "a culture of pride in more than seventy years of stable liberal democracy"? Is this a central feature of "liberal democracy"? What does that communicate to us? Is there more to the story?

## The Emperor's New Penis

*"I want it to be super Jewy! I want it to be really, really Jewy. . . . Feminists, gay people, trans people—and Jews. There's a lot of Jewish writers, but the old adage is 'Write Jewish, Cast British.' You're supposed to write the Jewish anxieties, but then take out any references to Tu Bishvat and make sure that the actors look WASP-y. So I think I'm gonna subvert that."*

– Jill Soloway, creator of Transparent

A 1931 survey of the Mandate of Palestine based on the population figures of the British Mandatory Government's census to determine prevalence rates of mental illness found slightly higher rates of insanity (the official term used) among Jewish men than Christian men, and both were higher than Muslim men. Jewish women were three times more likely than Muslim women to be classed as insane. A second survey of psychiatric morbidity was carried out by Prof. L. Halpern in 1936 in Palestine and found that endogenic psychoses (schizophrenia, manic-depressive psychoses, and paranoia) formed 79% of all Jewish cases.

Emil Kraepelin's postulate that Jews suffer from divergent patterns of mental illness (and quite possibly incidence rates as well) from Europeans in particular, and as the evidence seems to suggest other groups, may be supported by the isolation of mutations in the NDST3 gene more prevalent in Ashkenazi Jews, but much more work needs to be done. Treating this is a hypothesis for now, recall also the connection between homosexuality and transgenderism—and the higher percentages among Jews than Gentiles—and mental illness and the picture becomes clearer. Kraepelin's other views have proven prescient: "I have always believed that the most valuable and indispensable characteristics of the female sex would be seriously endangered if women were rigorously incorporated into the bustle of the working world," and "Any dominant influence of the Jewish spirit on German science, such as sadly came to be increasingly evident, seemed to me to pose a very grave danger indeed." We are living the results of this now, and not just in the sciences but in media, academia, finance, and the torn remnants of "culture."

The American Library Association's Rainbow Round Table publishes the Rainbow List, "its list of top LGBT titles aimed at children . . . [which] represent all reading levels from birth to 18, and run the gamut from science fiction to gritty short stories, realistic fiction to graphic novels, and even a picture book bending gender roles." *Queerty* states that for their 2014 list, "they may want to add *The Purim Su-*

*perhero,* billed as the first LGBT-inclusive Jewish children's book written in English." Keshet sponsored a national writing contest for the creation of "an educational Jewish book for kids that featured LGBT humans." The author of *The Purim Superhero* and winner of Keshet's contest, Elisabeth Kushner, spent nine years as a librarian at a Jewish Day School.

Teen novelist Norma Klein grew up in New York among "extremely liberal left-wing Jews" where "Freud had replaced God in whom [her] father had decided early on he didn't believe." Klein writes of the thought process of one of her characters in 1983's *Beginner's Love*: "There aren't very many Jewish babies. . . . I could probably sell it for a year's tuition at Yale." Interestingly, in her memoir, Eryn Loeb was struck not by lines such as these with Klein, but rather by what she called the "pervasive Jewishness" of Klein's work. It focuses entirely on:

> Secular Jews . . . often professors or writers, friendly progressive types who . . . . all own *The Joy of Sex* and are happy to discuss its contents with their precocious, introspective offspring. . . . There are affairs, divorces, abortions, ardent feminists, gay characters and lots of sex—all portrayed with Klein's distinctive casualness and honesty at a time when nearly all of these things were destined to stir up controversy.

According to Arielle Kaplan ("Arielle Kaplan (she/her) makes content for horny Jews. Brooklyn based, she hosts Alma's weekly Torah series, And God Was Like, co-hosts Oral History, a podcast on seductresses from Cleopatra to Jessica Rabbit, and moonlights as a sex influencer as Whoregasmic on Instagram. Find her bylines on Salty Magazine, Kveller, The Nosher, and JTA") writing for *Alma* in February 2019:

> There are a few things you need to know about Mikaela Straus: She loves Juuling, eating pickles, and Amanda Bynes. She partook in a diverse Gap ad campaign featuring Muslims and Jews (she's the latter). She stans Barbara Streisand and Ruth Bader Ginsburg. She wrote a song called "Pussy Is God," and her stage name is King Princess. Oh, and she is your newest favorite queer Jewish pop icon. . . . In "Pussy Is God," Straus says, "You know that it's god baby, when you're around her, I've been praying for hours, she's god and I've found her." These lyrics are Straus' attempt at illustrating that homosexuality and religion aren't oil and water. "I think if there's a space for religions and sexuality to intersect, there can be some comedy about it because there is something extremely fucked up and fun about being the antithesis of a belief system," Straus told *Harper's Bazaar*.

Kaplan also favorably quotes bisexual Jewish comedienne Gaby Dunn:

> I, Gaby, am bisexual and non-monogamous. . . . There's just stuff that's so inherently Jewish, like hand motions, or a way of talking, or being so loud. . . . And the way that our parents guilt and stuff . . . it's so dark. You know, my girlfriend's parents aren't like, "I guess I'll just lay here and die and your grandmother survived the Holocaust for no reason!" It's SO intense!

So I tell my girlfriend just to ignore her 'cause she's gonna lay on the floor and talk about the Holocaust.

Also in *Alma*, Emily Burlack writes favorably about TV program *grown-ish* and actress Emily Arlook:

On the show, Nomi is a freshman who hasn't yet come out to her family, but is extremely vocal about her sexuality at college. The visibility of bisexual characters on television is *so* important, and Nomi is definitely a step forward in terms of representation. Emily spoke to us about what playing Nomi has meant to her, her own Jewish upbringing, and why kugel is her absolute favorite Jewish food.

For Arlook: "I'm still very, very connected in my culture."

Though not Jewish, in 2018 Bruce/Caitlyn Jenner was honored with a "Champion of Israel and LGBTQ rights" award during the sixth annual World Values Network gala in New York. The organization is headed by Rabbi Shmuley Boteach and aims to annually "recognize individuals who honor human rights and defend the protections and values of democracies like Israel." Boteach's daughter Chana runs a "kosher sex shop" in Tel Aviv. Jenner's "stunning and brave" reveal on the cover of *Vanity Fair* was shot by the Jewish Annie Leibovitz. Leibovitz, who states that, "I'm not a practicing Jew, but I feel very Jewish," was lovers with the Jewish Susan Sontag (born Susan Rosenblatt), who stated that, "The white race *is* the cancer of human history."

UK Chief Rabbi Jonathan Sacks wrote the foreword to Rabbi Chaim Rapoport's *Judaism and Homosexuality: An Authentic Orthodox View*. In September 1991, Sacks called for a Decade of Renewal which should be based on five central values: "love of every Jew, love of learning, love of God, a profound contribution to British society, and an unequivocal attachment to Israel." Peter Fox writes that, "For me, being gay and Zionist are one and the same." According to Dan Bilefsky writing in *The Independent*:

Rabbi Lisa Grushcow, the first openly gay rabbi of a large synagogue in Canada . . . edited a seminal book on Judaism and sexuality, works to improve ties between Canadian Jews and Muslims; and counsels lesbian, gay, bisexual and transgender Jews from Newfoundland to Mexico . . . while Judaism has a long history of trailblazers in gay and gender equality – the first female rabbi, Regina Jonas, was ordained in Berlin in 1935, and the Reform movement formally endorsed the ordination of gay clergy in 1990 – Grushcow is playing a leading role in breaking what she calls the "stained glass ceiling" in Canada, where senior female rabbis remain rare. . . . "Being a divorced and lesbian rabbi and mom deepened my understanding of human experience," she adds. "It broadened who I can relate to. . . ." "God doesn't make mistakes," she counters that the Talmud, an ancient Jewish text, did not limit gender to male or female. "In the Jewish tradition, we aren't born who we become," she says. Her time in liberal New York, she says, emboldened her with a strong sense of acceptance. "You can't go 10 city blocks in New York without running into a lesbian rabbi," she says.

In 2015, the New York Public Library published a piece by Amanda Seigel, Jewish Division, Stephen A. Schwarzman Building "Celebrating Transgender Jews":

> The *Forward* recently honored 13-year-old Tom Sosnik, who came out as transgender to his Jewish day school class this year, while the *Forverts* and the *New York Post* interviewed Abby, a young Hasidic transwoman. *Haaretz* wrote about a young Moshe's transition to Miriam, and Keshet shared parents' stories of their children's transitions and community reactions. Writer and executive producer Jill Soloway (child of a transgender parent) received accolades for the television series *Transparent*, about gender transition in a Jewish family. The *Jewish Journal* wrote about gender identity issues among Jewish Los Angelenos, while the *Huffington Post* devoted a section to transgender Jews, as did the *Forward*. The Union for Reform Judaism officially welcomed transgender people with a resolution, and the *New York Jewish Week* wrote about reactions in the transgender Jewish community. The *Jewish Telegraphic Agency*, the *Times of Israel* and *Haaretz* wrote about Mai Peleg's life and her will. *The Daily Mail* and *Tablet* interviewed Yiscah Smith about her religious and gender journey. . . . Did you know that the Talmud recognizes many different gender categories? Dr. David Teutsch of the Reconstructionist Jewish movement writes about transgender ethics with a nuanced understanding of gender identity in rabbinic texts. *Balancing on the Mechitza: Transgender in Jewish Community*, edited by Noach Dzmura, is a groundbreaking collection on transgender and gender identity issues in Jewish law and community. Dzmura also directs Jewish Transitions, an organization that encourages Jewish communities to celebrate the sacred in every gender. The organization Keshet works for the full equality and inclusion of LGBT Jews in Jewish life, with resources such as "TransTexts: Exploring Gender in Jewish Sacred Texts," created by pioneering transgender rabbis Reuven Zellman and Elliot Kukla. The Union of Reform Judaism recently published its Resolution on the Rights of Transgender and Non-Gender-Conforming People.

As Laura Paull writes in a 2017 profile of Rabbi Dev Noily, "who may be the first rabbi in the country to adopt [the pronoun they]'s use":

> Rabbi Elliot Kukla, who in 2006 became the first out transgender male to be ordained, at Hebrew Union College-Jewish Institute of Religion in Los Angeles, continues to use the pronoun "he." So does Rabbi Reuben Zellman, director of music at Congregation Beth El in Berkeley, the first openly transgender student accepted to rabbinical school in 2003 and the second to be ordained (Hebrew Union College, 2010). Jhos Singer, maggid and congregational leader at the Renewal congregation Chochmat HaLev in Berkeley, is a married trans male like Zellman and Kukla and also uses "he." Newly ordained Rabbi Gray Myrseth, who will be replacing Noily as Kehilla's school director in July, identifies as nonbinary and transmasculine and uses the pronouns "they" and "them". . . . "The Bay Area Jewish community has a long history of being a center of gender diversity," noted Jacob Klein, who

works in the San Francisco office of Keshet, a national organization that advocates for full LGBTQ equality and inclusion in Jewish life. "From early projects with local bases like TransTorah, Jewish Mosaic and Nehirim, to progressive institutions like Keshet, Kehilla Community Synagogue and the Graduate Theological Union, to the DIY self-made scenes of the East Bay Jewish queers, the Bay Area is rich with people rethinking and re-creating our understandings," said Klein, who uses "they". . . . Rabbi Becky Silverstein, education director at the Pasadena Jewish Temple and Center, uses a feminine first name and the masculine pronoun. Hired in 2014, he is the first openly trans rabbi at a Conservative congregation in California, and believes he is one of the first trans-identified rabbis affiliated with the Conservative movement overall.

Brandeis University graduate and "out Orthodox lesbian" Sarah Weil states that "I went on a journey. Like any good Reform Jew I was an atheist," she relates with a sarcastic wink. She continues:

The notion of God that I grew up with was superficial, materialistic, childish and Christian. . . . Part of our Judaism was atheism because the notion of God seemed ridiculous, because God wasn't an important part of Judaism anyway. Judaism was about the family, about the community, about Tikkun Olam and social justice.

For people like Weil, Barbara Kay writes:

Tikkun olam is shorthand for the Judaization of political progressivism. For liberal Jews have always experienced a deep yearning to melt into the left's universalist, 'brotherhood of man' vision. That yearning has made leftism a magnet for Ashkenazi Jews ever since the Enlightenment freed them from the ghettos of Europe. Diaspora Jews could for the first time choose between continued attachment to Jewish peoplehood as their primary cultural identity and attachment to complete secularism with a view to 'disappearing' their Judaism altogether via a universalist ideology [ultimately they chose to embrace universalism for everyone else while retaining Jewish particularism]. . . . The whole 1960s counter-culture was dominated by secular Jews—Saul Alinsky, Jerry Rubin, Abby Hoffman, David Horowitz . . . but radical movements always boast a high Jewish cohort. . . . It is an indisputable fact that Jews were extremely disproportionately represented in the Communist movement and held high positions in the Soviet Union. . . . Those groups who promote tikkun olam most assiduously as their mission spend the bulk of their time championing such causes as gender rights, healthcare, abortion rights and racism.

Sarah Weil prefers the term queer over gay since she feels that "gay" is too narrow a term "and does not allow her the kind of gender and sexual fluidity that she needs":

If gay and lesbians uphold the binary gender norms of our society, then queer challenges those norms on a fundamental level. I like to identify as queer because I don't fit into the traditional gender and sex categories that gay and lesbian identities uphold. I not only tend to think outside the box, but I live outside it as well.

Other prominent Jewish individuals or groups living outside the box and active in promoting the LGBTQ agenda include: intersex anti-apartheid "activist" and ANC member Sally Gross; Emma Sulkowicz, the part-Jewish infamous "Mattress Girl" from Columbia University whose parents are both Manhattan psychoanalysts and who now evidently identifies as "non-binary"; the Southern Jewish Resource Network for Gender & Sexual Diversity (SOJOURN); JQ Youth; the Institute for Judaism, Sexual Orientation & Gender Identity at Hebrew Union College-Jewish Institute of Religion (HUC-JIR); Abbie Goldberg (former Williams Institute visiting scholar and professor of psychology at Clark University); Barnes-Jewish Hospital of St. Louis; Jeanna Eichenbaum; Naomi Zeveloff; Sarah Marian Seltzer; Mimi Lemay; Havi Fisher; Eshel; Nadin Mayblum-Boaz; Laurie Frankel; Moriah Levin; Koach Baruch Frazier; Galia Godel; Gila Goldstein; Gavriel Ansara; Moving Traditions; Tzelem; Rabbi Margaret Wenig; Rabbi Emily Aviva Kapor; Rafi Daugherty ("I am a single transgender man having my first baby"; as *The Jewish News of Northern California* writes, "After eight hours of labor, Daugherty was holding his 7-pound, 10-ounce daughter: Ettie Rose, named, in the Jewish tradition, for Daugherty's maternal grandmother and great-grandmother . . . he's been warmly welcomed by Colorado's progressive Jewish community"); Sawyer Goldsmith; Stav Strashko; Chen Arieli; the Union for Reform Judaism; Ady Ben-Israel; and Hannah Gladstein. Recapping the sheer volume of Jewish involvement, Julie Gruenbaum-Fax writes:

This month [May 2015] alone, there are at least two significant trans events in the L.A. Jewish community. JQ, along with New York-based Eshel, is sponsoring "TransTorah: A Family Journey," at The Jewish Federation of Greater Los Angeles on May 3, part of the Jewish Wisdom and Wellness Conference sponsored by Cedars-Sinai and the Kalsman Institute of Hebrew Union College. On May 5, the Sandra Caplan Community Bet Din will hold a daylong conference for rabbis titled "In God's Image: Transgender Folk in the Conversion Process. . . ." The Mishnah and Gemara recognize four genders that are neither male nor female, where people have various combinations of anatomy from both genders or neither, either by nature or by injury. The rabbis debated their status, but the very fact that they are acknowledged undermines the whole idea that there are only two choices, says Rachel Biale, a San Francisco-based author and activist. . . . Rabbi Len Sharzer, a professor of bioethics at the Jewish Theological Seminary who was a plastic surgeon before he became a rabbi, said he hopes to present a new halachic treatise, or teshuvah, by early 2016 that will expand that recognition to include transgender people who have not had surgery, as many opt not to have the highly invasive and imperfect procedures. . . . More than 30 leaders from nine L.A.-area day schools participated in a daylong workshop last November about sexual identity and orientation. The program was organized in part by Conservative Temple Beth Am's Rabbi Yechiel Hoffman, its director of education and a trained educator for Keshet, a Boston-based Jewish LGBTQ advocacy and educational organization, which sponsored the programing.

The workshop launched a yearlong program to foment cultural change. "The issue tends not to be one of outright homophobia, but of creating environments that are less hetero-normative, and making institutions more welcoming and embracing to students and faculty and families who identify as LGBT," said Catherine Bell, national program director at Keshet. . . . A year ago, the Los Angeles Jewish Federation, in partnership with JQ and IJSO, sponsored a similar workshop for Jewish communal professionals. Nearly 50 front-line Jewish professionals—executive directors, social workers, rabbis, mental health professionals—attended, focusing both on issues of sexual orientation and sexual identity. . . . Yiscah Sara Smith, who lived much of her life as a male Judaic studies teacher at Orthodox institutions in the U.S. and Israel, recently published "Forty Years in the Wilderness: My Journey to Authentic Living. . . ." Rabbi Ed Feinstein of Conservative Valley Beth Shalom said he has helped several families struggling as their young-adult children transitioned.

Even more Jews who have been central to the LGBTQ agenda under the guise of "LGBTQ rights," range from "queer theorist" Eve Kosofsky Sedgwick (Cornell, Yale) to Harvey Milk (one of the first openly gay men elected to public office as a member of the San Francisco Board of Supervisors and a noted gay rights activist) to Bella Abzug and Ed Koch, the first members of the US House of Representatives to introduce legislation in 1974 in "an 'Equality Act' which would have added 'sex, marital status or sexual orientation' to the protected classes specified in the Civil Rights Act of 1964." Koch, "a fervent supporter of Israel," was also the Mayor of New York from 1978 to 1989.

In the Netherlands, then-Amsterdam mayor Job Cohen became the world's first public official to legally wed same-sex couples in April 2001. The homosexual Barney Frank, among many other things, was instrumental in getting the Employment Non-Discrimination Act passed and employed transgender legislative assistant Diego Sanchez. In 2008, as Kilian Melloy wrote:

Marisa Richmond, long a veteran of election-year politics and conventions and a professor of history at Middle Tennessee State University, won't be the only transgendered member of the convention; the DNC's chairman, Howard Dean, has also appointed Diego Sanchez to a committee. . . . In a Mar. 26 article, the *Washington Blade* reports that Richmond has been active in politics—she worked on Ted Kennedy's presidential campaign in 1980—longer than she's lived as a woman, having made the M-to-F transition in 2001 when she was 42 years old. . . . The article reported that Richmond is a delegate for New York's Sen. Clinton though she's not insistent on Hillary for President. . . . Added Richmond, "She and Obama are actually identical. . . ."[67] Sanchez, appearing on a radio show called The Radical Trannies, said to host Ethan St. Pierre, "It's certainly a wonderful obligation and nothing that I would've guessed two years ago. . . ." Though last year's maneuvering from Democratic Congressman Barney Frank to get approval for a federal hate crimes bill involved the highly controversial splitting of the bill into two

---

[67] How do you like that?

measures, one to cover gays, lesbians, and bisexuals and the other to be pursued at a later date and include transgendered individuals, Sanchez was optimistic that the Democratic party was ready to welcome the voices of the transgendered.

Indeed it was. The Jewish Barbra Siperstein was another transgender person active in the Democratic National Committee around this time: "I would encourage as many transgender people to engage in the party as possible," Siperstein said. "Most of us are stealth." When Siperstein died, New Jersey Governor Phil Murphy ordered that flags be lowered to half-staff. "There always have been people who felt or acted as if they were the other sex," stated the Jewish former Kinsey Institute trustee, professor, and "gender historian" Joanne Meyerowitz, graduate of the University of Chicago and Stanford University.

Just as we should be dosed-up on oxytocin in order to be sufficiently lubed-up for our sodomization by the Third World's collective phallus,[68] so, too, must we, men in particular, become "receptive [to] penetrative sex toy use" in order to "challenge straight male homohysteria, transhysteria, and transphobia" according to a recent study entitled "Going in Through the Back Door," which actually turned out to be a hoax (more on this in a second). Certainly our immigration/refugee policy rams plenty of unwanted objects up our "back-door," but did you know that, according to the study's author "M. Smith":

> To date, very little research literature exists concerning receptive penetrative anal eroticism in straight men. Of particular interest are its impacts upon other factors relevant to masculinities, sex roles, and the study of sexualities. Several co-constituted features of masculinity are likely to be relevant to straight-male anal sexuality, including masturbatory play with penetrative sex toys. Specifically, this study seeks to explore, "Do men who report greater comfort with receptive penetrative anal eroticism also report less transphobia, less obedience to masculine gender norms, greater partner sensitivity, and greater awareness about rape?" This study uses semi-structured interviews with thirteen men to explore this question, analyzed with a naturalist and constructivist grounded theory approach in the context of sexualities research and introduces transhysteria as a parallel concept to Anderson's homohysteria. This analysis recognizes potential socially remedial value for encouraging male anal eroticism with sex toys.

This brilliant piece of satire was actually accepted by the journal *Sexuality & Culture*, but in a supremely disturbing twist, the mockery is based on "legitimate" scholarship, proof positive that this school of "thought" is itself parodic, and may well have already crossed the threshold to being beyond parody.

I thought the term "homohysteria" was used due to the fact that "homophobia" (a term coined by Jewish psychologist George Weinberg) is a criminal offense in a number of countries, but it's actually "the fear of being thought homosexual because of behavior that is typically considered gender atypical," a concept explored by "pro-feminist scholar" Eric Anderson, who specializes in "adolescent men's gender and

---

[68] See Marsh, et al., "Oxytocin-enforced norm compliance."

sexualities" at the University of Winchester, and whose "seminal" studies include "Relaxing the straight male anus: Decreasing homohysteria around anal eroticism" (February 2017) with Jonathan Branfman and Susan Stiritz, and "Generational Masculinities" (November 2017). "Relaxing the straight male anus":

> Examines the practice and perception of receptive anal eroticism among 170 heterosexual undergraduate men in a US university. We analyze the social stigmas on men's anal pleasure through the concept of homohysteria, which describes a cultural myth that the wrongdoing of gender casts homosexual suspicion onto heterosexual men. For men's anal eroticism, this means that only gay, emasculated or gender deviant men are thought to enjoy anal pleasure. We suggest, however, that decreasing homohysteria has begun to erode this cultural 'ban' on anal stimulation for straight men. Our data finds self-identified straight university-aged men questioning cultural narratives that conflate anal receptivity with homosexuality and emasculation. We also show that 24 percent of our respondents have, at least once, received anal pleasure. These results suggest that cultural taboos around men's anal pleasure may be shifting for younger men and the boundaries of straight identity expanding. We call for further research to clarify how anal erotic norms are shifting among men of different racial, geographic, socioeconomic, and age demographics, and to determine how these shifts may foster more pluralistic and inclusive views of gender and sexuality.

Branfman and Stiriz—both Jewish—in addition to working with the homosexual Anderson co-published "Teaching Men's Anal Pleasure: Challenging Gender Norms with 'Prostage' Education" in October 2012, which states that:

> To help students critique sex/gender norms, sexuality educators should address men's anal pleasure. Men's anal receptivity blurs accepted binaries like male/female, masculine/feminine, and straight/queer. By suppressing men's receptivity, the taboo against men's anal pleasure helps legitimize hegemonic sex/gender beliefs-and the sexism, homophobia, and male dominance they encourage. Conversely, by deconstructing men's anal taboo and creating a new language of anal pleasure-"prostage" (pro-STAHJ)-educators can help students challenge restrictive gender norms.

This is what passes for research in higher education these days. Branfman is at Ohio State University, and his work "converses with masculinity studies, queer studies, queer of color critique, and Jewish studies."

Queer studies is a manufactured discipline not based on any kind of hard science, much like Freudian psychoanalysis, Boasian anthropology, and the critical theory of the Frankfurt School. Not coincidentally, all of these "disciplines" were created by Jews, and spread and ultimately institutionalized by Jews in dramatic disproportion. All have been instrumental in the corruption of the academy and, consequently, the very framework with which we discuss—or do not discuss—issues of sexuality, race, et cetera. As Edwin L. Rubin explicates in the article "Jews, Truth, and Critical Race Theory":

Critical race theory, radical feminism, and gay legal studies constitute a major force in modern legal scholarship. . . . The charge of anti-Semitism also raises an interesting issue about the role of Jews in legal academics. This field, like the motion picture industry, is one in which Jews have played a leading role, but have tended to de-emphasize their particular identity. In focusing on anti-Semitism, [Daniel] Farber and [Suzanna] Sherry invite consideration of the specific role of Jews, as Jews, in legal scholarship.

As we've discussed with Elena Kagan at Harvard, I've decided to take them up on their invitation. This acceptance will surely be called "anti-Semitic," however, as anything that is not glowing praise inevitably is.

The initial de-emphasis of Jewishness highlighted in Rubin's passage is part of the public front related to both crypsis and the desire to not have the alienness of the concept compounded by the alienness of the person. In-facing and in private correspondence, most of the progenitors of these concepts did not just identify as Jews first and foremost, but believed their Jewishness to inform their conceptual framework (see Kevin MacDonald's *The Culture of Critique*). Most still do, but they are less bashful about it given Jewish preeminence.

A prime example would be that of Dana Nessel, who, from "setting up a hate crimes division, fighting for LGBTQ rights and helping immigrants, Dana Nessel says she stands up for people like her grandparents who fled the Holocaust." Beyond trite and totally disingenuous, but as Josefin Dolsten continues, from *The Times of Israel* article "How Judaism inspires the first openly gay politician in Michigan state office":

Dana Nessel has spent much of her career challenging the state and federal government to advance progressive causes. In 2015, the Jewish attorney successfully argued in a case to overturn Michigan's ban on same-sex marriage. The lawsuit, in which Nessel represented a lesbian couple looking to jointly adopt their foster children, was later combined with others in that year's landmark Supreme Court case Obergefell v. Hodges, which legalized same-sex marriage. . . . Nessel is passionate about what she calls defending immigrants from federal overreach, an issue that she links to her family history. . . . Nessel also has established a hate crimes division in the attorney general's office. She said its goal is "to fight against hate crimes and the many, many hate organizations that exist in our state now and that have proliferated under frankly, I think, the auspices of the Trump administration. . . ." [Nessel] traces many of her values back to Judaism.

As with the vast majority of the Jews we've covered in this book, Nessel's "activism" and behaviors are explicitly informed by her Jewish identity.

The origins of "anti-hate" legislation—which is very much in the eye of the beholder and with "hate speech" is obviously antithetical to free speech, designed as it is to suppress criticism—can also be traced to the Jewish milieu, from *Fundamina*:

As the Civil-Rights Movement gained momentum, civil-society organisations such as the Anti-Defamation League and the Southern Poverty Law Centre began compiling statistical reports to establish the number and frequency of crimes motivated by prejudice, bias and bigotry [similar to what we encountered in the Introduction with the "epidemic of violence" against "trans" people, debunked by Wilfred Reilly]. In 1981 the Anti-Defamation League, concerned by the rise in crimes motivated by racial and ethnic bias and prejudice in the United States of America, particularly anti-Semitic crimes [of course!], and the fact that media exposure, education and law enforcement were ineffective, drafted a model hate-crime statute which recognised racial, religious and ethnic biases. . . . The model statute was intended to influence state legislatures and the Federal government to enact hate-crime laws. The Anti-Defamation League's model hate-crime statute had the desired effect since a number of state legislatures in the United States of America subsequently enacted laws based on the model statute. Shortly after the drafting of the Anti-Defamation League's model hate-crime statute in 1981, the states of Oregon and Washington passed similar laws. . . . Since the enactment of the Hate Crimes Statistics Act in 1990 a number of federal hate-crime laws have been passed in the United States of America. Contemporary hate-crime laws recognise a wide spectrum of victim characteristics that includes race, ethnicity, religion, disability, gender and sexual orientation. These hate-crime laws include the Hate Crimes Sentencing Enhancement Act of 1994 and the Matthew Shepherd and James Byrd Junior Hate Crimes Prevention Act of 2009. To date, over forty-five American states and the District of Columbia have enacted hate-crime statutes based on the Anti-Defamation League's model statute. The American trend to enact hate-crime laws has had some international impact, particularly in Western democratic countries. In 1998 the United Kingdom passed the Crime and Disorder Act which is the British equivalent of a hate-crime law and in 2003 France passed its first hate-crime law, which is commonly referred to as la loi Lellouche.

The Jewish role in this system is integral and indeed defines its characteristics perhaps more than any other single factor. In fact, without the Jewish role, which has seen neo-liberalism become by-and-large the particular vehicle to advance Jewish group interests and for some number enact strange and perverse revenge fantasies on the Gentile population, the system would not actually exist. Its very genesis, adoption, and propagation can all be traced to primarily Jewish or Jewish-connected (Margaret Mead, Ruth Benedict, Paul G. Hoffman, et cetera) figures. As with the perpetually-rising tide of "anti-Semitism" and its usefulness, the trans hysteria functions very similarly.

We can see the various offshoots of critical theory as they influence education and intersect with politics and culture, Judaism, and Jewishness, and the Jewish tendency toward terraforming their environs to better reflect "openness" versus tradition and what the Jewish psychoanalysts would frame as "repression," typically as a result of Christian and/or Western mores. The situating of educators as indoctrinators of an extreme agenda is not a new phenomenon, either, as Kevin MacDonald writes:

[Alfred] Adler, the leader of "far left" psychoanalysis . . . wanted to immediately politicize teachers as radicals. . . . The apex of the association between Marxism and psychoanalysis came in the 1920s in the Soviet Union, where all the top psychoanalysts were Bolsheviks, Trotsky supporters, and among the most powerful political figures in the country. . . . This group organized a government-sponsored State Psychoanalytical Institute and developed a program of "pedology" aimed at producing the "new Soviet man" on the basis of psychoanalytic principles applied to the education of children. The program, which encouraged sexual precocity in children, was put into practice in state-run schools.[69]

You could substitute 1920s for 2020s and that passage would still be 100% true.

This is a long-standing trend not just limited to Elena Kagan at Harvard or the Jewish commissars running the pre-World War II Soviet Union; for the academic year 1968–69, 15–20% of the faculty at the following universities was Jewish: Berkeley, Chicago, Harvard, Columbia, Michigan, Pennsylvania, Princeton, and the City University of New York. In 1971, 25% of all Ivy League professors were Jewish.[70] According to Chaim Seidler-Feller, today's leading institutions typically have around a 20% Jewish faculty. Every single major university press now publishes a line of Judaica. We also should not forget that the Frankfurt School found its American home at Columbia, and that all of these specifically-named institutions have been instrumental in the advancement of the LGBTQ agenda, not to mention other "social justice" endeavors; the University of Michigan hosts a Bohnett Leaders Fellowship and has *ninety-three* full-time diversity and equity staff, twenty-six of whom earn six figures.

The product is something like Hector Carrillo and the Jewish Amanda Hoffman seeking to change the definition of "heterosexual" in order to make it more "elastic" and "inclusive" of same-sex desire:

> We present findings from interviews with 100 such men, whom we recruited while they were seeking sex with men online, and examine the logics that allow them to maintain an identity as straight. Our sample is somewhat unique in that it included men across a wide age range (from 18 to 70), and also because many of our participants are white adult US men who are married or in stable relationships with women. Based on their patterns of sexual interpretation, we discuss how these men make their same-sex desires and behaviours consistent with a primary self-identification as straight. We argue that, in the process of maintaining identities as straight men, they change the definition of heterosexuality, in effect turning it into a considerably elastic category that is perceived as fully compatible with having and enacting same-sex desires.

Notice the singling-out of hetero-normative White men.

With "diversity" (racial, sexual, etc.) as a necessary component of the entire terraforming of the West, "elastic" eventually begets abolition: Hoffman spiritually

---

[69] MacDonald, *The Culture of Critique*, 114.

[70] Regarding presidents, deans, and high-level administrators, in 2011, of the twenty-four senior administrators of the Ivy League colleges and universities, twenty were Jews or were married to Jews. Richard Levin was president of Yale from 1993-2013, Harold Shapiro was president of Princeton from 1988-2001, and David J. Skorton was president of Cornell from 2006-2015, and the current presidents of Penn, Harvard, Princeton, and Yale are Jews as well. Three of Harvard's four most recent presidents Neil Rudenstine, Larry Summers, and Lawrence Bacow are Jews, and the other, Drew Faust is married to one. Princeton had a string of seven straight Jewish provosts from 1977-2012. Four of Harvard's last five provosts have been Jewish.

handing off to Noel Ignatiev in essence. Additionally, as with immigration/"diversity," the LGBTQ set requires a certain number of willing collaborators like Carrillo and Eric Anderson to advance the agenda and provide cover, and these collaborators in turn are recipients of various rewards from their masters, not least of which is a pat on the head for a job well done. Spiritually, there is little to no divergence between homosexual interests and Jewish interests, with ideological cousins in the weaponized and aggrieved Outer Party serving their spiritual role as forces of dissolution and decay as well.

With all of these examples we can see the intersection of Jewishness, Jewish in-group favoritism, the institutions they've coopted, the targeting of children, and radical agendas—for our purposes here specifically that of the LGBTQ agenda, althlough as we've seen the radical agenda is all linked—reflected in innumerable examples. Consider the Jewish Martin Duberman's efforts to establish a center for lesbian and gay studies at Yale University in 1985; in 1991, he left for the City University of New York, where he founded its Center for Lesbian and Gay Studies. Yale was still to become a hub for gay and lesbian studies, however, as Mark Alden Branch writes:

> In 1993, an alumnus gave money to fund research projects in the field, and the provost appointed a faculty committee to administer what became known as the Fund for Lesbian and Gay Studies. That committee developed the Pink Book, a listing of courses relevant to lesbian and gay studies, and established a small lending library. . . . In 1994 . . . the committee began to oversee a series of one-year visiting professorships. . . . The visiting professorship, which actually resides in the women's and gender studies program, is but one of the programs coordinated by the Kramer Initiative. In just its first year, the Initiative [became] a nexus for gay and lesbian academic, social, and political activity, largely due to the efforts of executive coordinator Jonathan D. Katz. . . . Katz studies the influence of sexuality and sexual relationships among gay mid-century artists such as Robert Rauschenberg, Jasper Johns, and Cy Twombly. He is also a veteran political activist and a founder of the 1990s gay activist group Queer Nation.

The Jewish Jonathan D. Katz is also the co-founder of the Harvey Milk Institute, named after the Jewish homosexual Harvey Milk, portrayed by Sean Penn in the major motion picture *Milk* (2008). According to the *Washington Post*, "Harvey Milk's fight for social justice was fueled by Jewish tradition." Katz received his PhD from Northwestern University, another central fixture in the LGBTQ agenda.

Jonathan Ned Katz was one of these visiting professors at Yale; Ned Katz's *Love Stories: Sex Between Men Before Homosexuality* makes the claim that Abraham Lincoln's relationship with his friend Joshua Speed had an "erotic current."[71] The Kramer Initiative is the Larry Kramer Initiative for Lesbian and Gay Studies, which ran

---

[71] Further for Mark Alden Branch: "[Larry] Kramer has seized on such scholarship to declare that Lincoln was 'unequivocally gay,' though he acknowledges that 'I don't need as much proof as William Bennett is going to need. . . .' Kramer believes that uncovering gay history will do more good in terms of increasing public acceptance of homosexuality. 'The more historical figures we can legitimately 'out,' the more seriously we'll be taken,' he says."

from 2001–2006 on the back of a $1 million donation from the Jewish Arthur Kramer, co-founder of the law firm Kramer Levin, to be named after his brother Larry, co-founder of the Gay Men's Health Crisis and catalyst for and co-founder of ACT UP. ACT UP, as you'll recall, was a willing participant in at least one march alongside NAMBLA.

Indeed, the Jewish role in promoting not just the LGBTQ agenda—and the inextricability of Judaism and Jewishness itself from transgenderism and homosexuality in the words of Jews themselves and in their actions, which have been plainly illustrated in this book—but mass immigration, anti-white rhetoric, crony capitalism, and the corrosive array of other proclivities, activities, and policies is dramatically outsized. It must be acknowledged that the neo-liberal system and all its excesses and the group interests of Jews are now virtually identical. If we were to consider the Jewish role in neo-liberal economics (see Chapter Four of John Q. Publius's *Plastic Empire*), especially at the "margins" of ethical behavior, or that of pornography (also revealed in *Plastic Empire*), such a thesis becomes even more apparent and inescapable.

An objective analysis of media and entertainment would reveal the same (see Chapter Three of Publius's *Plastic Empire*), and all three intersect and are essential to the neo-liberal system overall as it brings us to the precipice of the next evolution/mutation of globalism. It is impossible to truly separate each of these elements as they are all deeply inter-connected and reinforce each other, as we have seen at numerous junctures in this book. Despite their villainization in the mainstream media and in Hollywood, it is clearly not Evangelical Christians pushing this rot. Indeed, as Daniel Boyarin, Daniel Itzkovitz, and Ann Pellegrini write:

> While there are no simple equations between Jewish and queer identities, Jewishness and queerness yet utilize and are bound up with one another in particularly resonant ways. This crossover also extends to the modern discourses of antisemitism and homophobia, with stereotypes of the Jew frequently underwriting pop cultural and scientific notions of the homosexual. And vice versa. . . . To bring the matter to a sharper point: there may just be something queer about the Jew.

The claim is that homosexuality and "queerness" are not just inextricable from Judaism but from "the Jew" as the authors put it; extending the thesis of Boyarin, Itzkovitz, and Pellegrini, Elon Gilad states: "Let us begin at the very beginning of the Kingdom of Judah, with King David, who many suspect was gay. Or at least bisexual," and as Ofri Ilany writes, "Homosexual passion and its realization constitute a layer in Judaism itself. Sodom, after all, is also located in Israel." That's not all that's located in Israel, but that is a topic for another book, and it's quite grim (hint: it has to do with sex and organ trafficking). For Ilany, "Homosexuality is part of Jewish tradition":

> Intimate relations between men existed in Jewish communities and apparently were also common. Historian Yaron Ben-Naeh has shown in his research that despite the explicit biblical prohibition, in Jewish communities in the Ottoman Empire same-sex relations were rather common. This is indicated by dozens of sources. Moreover, until the modern era, *grown men who*

*had a need for the favors of youths did not have a negative image in Jewish society* (emphasis added). . . . Homosexuality is an integral part of the history of the Jewish people and Jewish tradition. . . . Hans-Joachim Schoeps, a Prussian Jewish historian and theologian . . . was a pioneer of the campaign to cancel the prohibition on homosexuality in Germany [in the 1970s]. Since the prohibition on homosexuality often relied on the prohibition in Leviticus 18, Schoeps wanted to make clear the context in which this prohibition was promulgated. He argued that priestly male sacred prostitutes were common in biblical Israel, as in other Semitic cultures. Schoeps concluded that such sacred prostitutes were active even in the Temple in Jerusalem, based especially on Deuteronomy 23:18, "There shall be no harlot of the daughters of Israel, neither shall there be a sodomite of the sons of Israel" – where the Jewish Publication Society translation (and others) uses "sodomite" for the word qadesh, the feminine form of which, qdesha, is a holy prostitute. (German translations use a cognate for "whore".)[72] Only in the period of Josiah's reform, when the cults of foreign gods were uprooted, was sacred male prostitution prohibited. And since the cult was so popular among the people, it was necessary to make the prohibition in a particularly stringent way and the cult is now considered an abomination. However, Schoeps stresses that the prohibition in Deuteronomy relates to a pagan cult of this sort, not to the sexual act itself. . . . Jiří Mordecai Langer argued that "brotherly love," i.e. *love of a man for a man, is in fact the deepest basic urge in Judaism* (emphasis added), at the basis of the commandment of "love thy fellow man as thyself. . . ." Like Schoeps after him, Langer concluded that the harsh prohibition of sexual relations between men constitutes proof that the tendency toward it was common among Jews. He also argued that an erotic relationship, while not actualized in the form of intercourse, is what connects yeshiva students to one another and to their rabbi.

Lovely.

The Jewish Diane Ehrensaft holds the view that transgenderism is a form of rebellion against restrictive Gentile mores. Perhaps, but these "restrictions" did not allow for the horror show of modernity. Pandora's Box has been open for some time now, but it goes beyond mere "rebellion," although that is part of it. This deviance is inextricable from the very essence of "Jewishness" *by these authorities' own admission.* Just as homosexuality is part-and-parcel of Judaism by its own intellectuals' and religious leaders' admission, so, too, is transgenderism; for Rabbi David J. Meyer:

From the beginning of our Torah's imaginings of the creation of humankind, gender diversity was part of the Divine plan. . . . It is remarkable that a sacred text which is likely more than two thousand years old considers the circumstances of gender identity outside the assumed binary distinctions of male and female. . . . The sages explain the unusual language as meaning that God created the first human being as an androgynous person, containing both male

---

[72] This difference speaks volumes.

and female characteristics simultaneously. . . . In fact, and strikingly, our Jewish legal tradition identifies no fewer than six distinct "genders," certainly assuming as normative the male and female, but including as well designations which we now refer to as "intersex" identities. . . . I would suggest, based on the study of these legal texts that the Jewish understanding of gender is neither binary nor even a grid into which every person must be forced to fit. Rather, we see gender diversity as a spectrum, truly a rainbow of possibilities for reflecting the Image of God.

From Northwestern University's Weinberg College of Arts and Sciences website:

The past few years have come to be labeled a "transgender moment" because of the increasing visibility of transgendered individuals in law, the media and popular culture. One of the artistic productions that both responds to and is responsible for this moment is *Transparent*. . . . The family is more authentically and accurately Jewish than any other characters in the history of television. At different points the show forces a provocative intersection of Jewish and trans/gender identity that both analogizes the individual subcultural experiences and even fuses them. One of the characters, Ali, is hard at work on a Gender Studies thesis that is interested in connecting Jewishness and gender fluidity. . . . It is not surprising that several Jews have made significant contributions to transgender theory. Magnus Hirschfeld advocated for transgender rights in 1920's Germany. Isaac Bashevis Singer's short story Yentl the Yeshiva Boy about a girl who cross-dresses to study in Yeshiva is far more provocatively transgendered than the better known Oscar winning film *Yentl* made by Barbara Streisand in the 1980's. Judith Butler has noted her early background in the study of Jewish ethics as a contributor to her fundamental re-imagination of gender as performance in her groundbreaking *Gender Trouble* [*Feminism and the Subversion of Identity*]. Further back in history, the Talmud and other works of rabbinic literature regularly treat intersex phenomena as legal categories and at times consider the possibility of three genders on this basis.

*The New York Times* published a piece entitled, "Is God Transgender?" by New York rabbi Mark Sameth, whose cousin Paula Grossman, an elementary school music teacher in New Jersey, "came out as transgender" in 1971, where Sameth states that "the Hebrew Bible, when read in its original language, offers a highly elastic view of gender":

The four-Hebrew-letter name of God, which scholars refer to as the Tetragrammaton, YHWH, was probably not pronounced "Jehovah" or "Yahweh," as some have guessed. The Israelite priests would have read the letters in reverse as Hu/Hi—in other words, the hidden name of God was Hebrew for "He/She."

The following is the official position on transgenderism from the Reconstructionist Rabbinical College, via David Teutsch:

The dominant approach to gender in Western society has its origin in Christian thought that understands both sex and gender as binary. In that understanding, everyone is either male or female, and gender and sex are identical. The Talmud contains hundreds of references to other categories. . . . The Talmud recognizes that sex organs do not necessarily make people purely male or purely female. The Talmud also recognizes that an individual's gender orientation does not necessarily match his or her sex organs. This perspective is underlined by the Mishna: "The androgynos is like a man in some ways and like a woman in some ways, like both a man and a woman in some ways, and like neither a man nor a woman in some ways." (Bikurim 4.1). . . . The other biblical prohibition is of castration. Of course, this is irrelevant for female-to-male transgender people. Most male-to-female transgender people do not have "bottom surgery," in which case it is not an issue for them either. Contemporary Jewish bioethicists treat vasectomy as an equivalent of castration, so for those who would allow vasectomy, voluntary castration should be treated similarly [!]. . . . The mitzvah of healing is not limited to health professionals; it is incumbent upon every Jew. Supporting transgender people in who they are is part of that mitzvah.

Ah yes, the mitzvah.

Orthodox Rabbi Shmuly Yanklowitz declared that "the Jewish values of justice, equality, and dignity" led him to support gay rights and same-sex marriage. The National Jewish Committee supported the movement to allow homosexuals into the Boy Scouts of America. According to Prizmah: Center for Jewish Day Schools, "For people who will later identity as transgender, research indicates that most are aware from as early as 2–3 years of age that their gender identity does not match their biological sex, or social expectations about their gender role." Westchester Jewish Community Services started TransParentcy "to help trans youth and their parents or guardians deal with an often hostile world." TransParentcy runs Pride Camp, a week-long summer program where young people "learn leadership and communications skills." What else they're learning or doing I cannot say, but I have my suspicions.

The LGBT Network Chief Executive Officer David Kilmnick is homosexual and Jewish. Operating in Long Island and Queens, the LGBT Network's supporters include Walmart, Capital One, Enterprise Holdings, Tito's Vodka, and National Grid, among others. On March 3rd, 2020, Kilmnick and New York State Senator Brad Hoylman—also homosexual and Jewish—held a press conference to call for the immediate passage of bill A4744/S1478 that would require all New York State schools to teach LGBT history.

In 2017, the Senior Rabbi of the Spanish and Portuguese Sephardi Community Joseph Dweck claimed that "the entire revolution of feminism and even homosexuality in our society . . . is a fantastic development for humanity." According to Galia Godel, Manager of LGBTQ Initiatives at the Jewish Family and Children's Service of Greater Philadelphia, transgenderism and Judaism are "not mutually exclusive—they're not at odds at all. All of the Jewish communities that I have been a part of and that I've worked with in my position at JFCS have been so excited to be trans-affirming and to support the members of their community." According to "bisexual Jewish violinist" and author Shira Glassman, "My Judaism and queerness do not stand in opposition."

Jewish newspaper *The Forward* has sponsored an "ongoing series looking into the lives of transgender Jews." Alex Borinsky states in *Tablet* magazine article "Putting the Pieces Together" ("Since I came out as transgender, I've never felt more Jewish"): "Back in the queer-experimental-theater-ecology-Marxist-feminist part of my life in New York, I'd occasionally get a craving for some Judaism." Minus the ecology, that's about as Jewish as one might get, so where Borinsky is *missing* the Jewishness there, or perhaps feels that this milieu is not Jewish *enough*, well. . . . I guess that's where the "trans" aspect comes in:

> So why, after a lifetime of alienation from Jewish contexts . . . why do I finally feel a deepening sense of connection to Jewish community. . . ? I encountered Rabbi Eliot Kukla and Reuben Zellman's rereading of Deuteronomy 22:5 ('a sacred obligation to present the fullness of our gender as authentically as possible'). I discovered Joy Ladin's beautiful book, *The Soul of the Stranger*. And ever since then, it's been the language of Judaism, refracted through trans experience.

For April Baskin and Idit Klein:

> We are troubled by how the struggles for LGBTQ rights and Black liberation are often viewed as separate, unrelated movements. . . . Marsha P. Johnson and Sylvia Rivera, both trans women of color, led the fight at the Stonewall Inn. And yet, they are often omitted from the story of Stonewall and excluded from the traditional canons of Black and Latinx American history. As Jewish colleagues of different racial and cultural backgrounds, we understand the power of our own histories and the shared responsibility we have to work for justice.

Google agrees, as they note in their "Diversity and Inclusion" stories page from 2020:

> Google is a committed supporter of the Marsha P. Johnson Institute (MPJI) and its mission to end violence against all trans people across the U.S. In addition to defending and protecting the lives of Black trans people, MPJI is also expanding its COVID-19 relief efforts for trans communities. As part of our ongoing commitments to advance racial justice, Google.org recently made a donation to MPJI, which will expand the organization's relief work.

According to the MPJI's website, founder and Executive Director Elle Hearns:

> Was a co-founding member and former strategic partner of the Black Lives Matter Network. . . . Elle has delivered keynotes and talks at The Movement for Black Lives inaugural convening, Harvard University, Columbia University, the Schomburg Center for Research in Black Culture, The Public Theatre, and The National Lawyers Guild.

Digital Media Manager Eva Reign previously worked at Condé Nast's LGBTQ+ platform, *them.* as Assistant Editor. Advisory Board member Jonathan Lykes is a

University of Chicago alumnus, and Advisory Board member J Mase III is described thusly:

A Black/trans/queer poet & educator that has worked in the US, UK, and Canada on LGBTQIA+ rights and racial justice in spaces such as K-12 schools, universities, faith communities and restricted care facilities. He is founder of awQward, the first trans and queer people of color talent agency. His work has been featured on MSNBC, Essence Live, Everyday Feminism, Black Girl Dangerous, NPR, Blavity, the New York Times, Buzzfeed, the Root, the Huffington Post, TEDx and more.

The Anti-Defamation League of B'nai B'rith "filed amicus briefs in a number of cases urging courts to hold a ban on marriage equality unconstitutional, and has been a strong voice advocating against measures to deny that fundamental right," in their own words. In 2013, according to the *Jerusalem Post*, the ADL "brought together a number of religious and Zionist organizations in what it is calling a 'broad coalition in support of marriage equality,'" including the Central Conference of American Rabbis, the Women of Reform Judaism, Hadassah: The Women's Zionist Organization of America, Truah: Rabbis for Human Rights-North America, and the Women's League for Conservative Judaism.

Alice Rothchild agrees that revolutionary/subversive activity is a congenitally Jewish trait, and implicitly acknowledges that Jewish crypsis is a major part of their ability to maintain power without being "outed" as the primary instigators of subversion:

After decades of anti-Semitism, we have successfully joined White America in a big way; we can pass. We can go to medical school, join the country club, live in any neighborhood, marry almost anyone's daughter with a minimum of fuss. As we crawled out of the Jewish ghettos . . . [and] moved to the suburbs, we flexed our liberal-minded political muscles.

This has obviously had profoundly destructive consequences.

This admission of power, method, and motive is typically absent in mainstream publications, but one may find it in abundance when reading Jewish publications or listening to in-group conversations. As Jane Eisner writes:

From the debate over a nuclear deal with Iran, to the emergence of transgender identity in synagogues and on screen, to the groundbreaking acceptance of marriage equality, American Jews are playing a starring role. . . . Beyond the never-ending presidential race the boisterous debate over the Iran deal found Jews negotiating (Wendy Sherman), opposing (Chuck Schumer), supporting (Jerry Nadler) and otherwise shaping the most serious foreign policy development of the year. Our influence goes well beyond politics. The legal framework to support same-sex marriage, which Evan Wolfson developed as a law student 30 years ago, was ratified at the highest level when the Supreme Court ruled in favor of marriage equality. . . . Another human rights issue—ensuring that transgender Americans do not suffer discrimination—was championed in a Jewish day school by a remarkable bar mitzvah boy

(Tom Sosnik), on the high-fashion runway (Hari Nef) and in the acclaimed television show "Transparent" (director Jill Soloway and actor Jeffrey Tambor).

Of the twenty-five groups joining the ADL's amicus brief in *Obergefell v. Hodges*, thirteen were explicitly Jewish in nature. Following the Supreme Court's decision, Rabbi Jonah Pesner stated that he hoped it would serve as a catalyst for the next letter in the LGBT acronym and energize a "bipartisan effort to end discrimination in the workplace" for transgendered persons.

Abroad, Kochava Lilit is described as:

A queer and disability rights activist who absolutely loves being autistic, ADHD, and Jewish. Their culture and heritage is an inextricable part of their activism and identity. Kochava has performed at the Melbourne Writes' Festival [and] spoken about queer rights and culture at the United Nations.

Yet another activist-identitarian is the head of Transgender Victoria in Australia, the "Jewish transwoman" Sally Goldner, who collaborated with the Open Society Foundations on their "License to be Yourself" report. In it, Goldner outlines the specific strategies undertaken to gain a greater foothold in Australia:

All of these policy changes depended on the basic groundwork we did with politicians. It had to start with 'Trans 101,' explaining our lives, before we could begin to propose any policy changes. We worked with a cross-party group of politicians called the Federal Parliamentary Friends of LGBTI. Rainbow Labour [an LGBTI organization affiliated with the Australian Labour Party] pushed hard for these changes too. Our main community allies were from LGBTI organizations such as the National LGBTI Health Alliance and the Australian Coalition for Equality. . . . Transgender, gender-diverse, and intersex activists worked really well together. One of the best things we did was a June 2012 roundtable organized by the National LGBTI Health Alliance, with some federal government funding. The key outcome of the roundtable was the Diversity in Health Report which was published in November 2012. Identity recognition was one of the report's priority areas. What we stated in the report is pretty much what we got in the guidelines. . . . The passport policy change was a toe in the water. The guidelines were based on the same theory: self-defined, affirmed gender dignity.

Perhaps this is a somewhat basic or obvious point, but unless one is de-constructing whiteness, race is *not* subject to the same arbitrary "self-definitions," definitions which for many "trans" people change daily or even hourly. Indeed, for all but Whites, race is encouraged to be a supremely deep and definitive source of identity, which I do not disagree with, but rather acknowledge that it applies to *all* races and ethnicities. This encouragement is in the context of weaponized identitarianism within the West as a means to fracture the host society and abroad as a tool of aggrievement (see: militant Islam), but this a stepping-stone to the ultimate aim of de-racinating *everyone*.

Nevertheless, race/ethnicity and sex are in fact reflections of something far more significant than self-perception and/or self-deception and cannot be summarily dismissed by the fictive efforts of "scholars" and "activists" pushing against nature. Where the regime has been wildly successful is in harnessing particular energies to suit its needs. This is manifested in useful functionaries like the apparently-mixed Leda Fisher ("my family always emphasized the Jewish value of *Tikkun Olam*"), who wrote in *The Dickinsonian* piece "Should White Boys Still Be Allowed to Talk?" (February 2019) in an astounding lack of self-awareness: "White boys spout the narrative of dominant ideologies and pretend they're hot takes instead of the same misleading garbage shoved down our throats by American institutions from birth." My goodness, just a modicum of self-reflection would do Fisher a world of good—or not, as such naked hate-mongering has been incentivized by the ruling class.

Then there is Raffi Freedman-Gurspan, a Lencan Indian from Honduras, who was adopted by Massachusetts Jews, converted to Judaism, transitioned to female, and worked for the Obama administration as Outreach and Recruitment Director in the White House Office of Presidential Personnel and as White House LGBT liaison. Freedman-Gurspan seems to have captured the spiritual essence of Judaism in such a way that is almost trans-racial. It could also simply be the reflection of cosmic oppositional forces; in the modern world we have been conditioned to neglect the metaphysical, whereas most cultures throughout human history understood the competing forces of chaos and order, good and evil. Intentionally undermining morality, nature, and hierarchy will invariably produce dis-harmony and chaos, where the most wicked acts are not just permissible but celebrated.

Would that we were done with the Jewish role in what are framed as "LGBTQ rights," but we are not even close. Yet more central figures include (along with relevance and/or major positions once or currently held):

- Allen Ginsberg, poet and prominent supporter of "relations" with young boys
- Ben Schatz, left his position as the Executive Director of the Gay and Lesbian Medical Association to become a drag queen
- Homosexual actor/hate-crime-hoaxer Jussie Smollett is half-Jewish
- Arnie Kantrowitz, author, "activist," and co-founder of the Gay and Lesbian Alliance Against Defamation (GLAAD—originally named The Gay and Lesbian Anti-Defamation League); partner Lawrence D. Mass was a co-founder of the Gay Men's Health Crisis (GMHC) and wrote *Confessions of a Jewish Wagnerite: Being Gay and Jewish in America*:

  > While researching what would become the first feature article on the epidemic that later became known as AIDS, the author had the first confrontation of his adult life with overt anti-Semitism, an incident he was completely unprepared to deal with psychologically. As AIDS spread, and every sexually active gay man was forced to confront his own mortality, the need to understand the even greater depths of fear touched by the incident became urgent, and Mass began to face the reality that his life had been dominated by internalized anti-Semitism, even as he came to grips with his gay identity.

- Jeanne Manford, founder of Parents and Friends of Lesbians and Gays (PFLAG)

- Leonard Bernstein, "married homosexual" composer and musician, Harvard, raised money for HIV/AIDS research and "awareness"
- Lesléa Newman, lesbian author of *Heather Has Two Mommies*: In December of 1989, Newman and her Jewish friend Tzivia Gover, "a new lesbian mom," first published the book through Gover's desktop publishing business; the book was re-printed by Sasha Alyson, who created the imprint "Alyson Wonderland" to publish children's books that depicted families with lesbian and gay parents
- S. Bear Bergman, "trans man," author, artist, founder of a Flamingo Rampant, which is "focused on making celebratory, inclusive picture books for LGBT2Q+ children and families"; co-edited with the Jewish Kate Bornstein *Gender Outlaws: The Next Generation*; is married to J. Wallace Skelton, described as:

  An educator, activist, and writer based in southern Ontario. His work focuses on lesbian, gay, bisexual, transgendered, transsexual, 2-spirited, intersexed, queer and questioning (LGBTT2IQQ) individuals, their communities and related issues – with a particular focus on youth.

  Skelton describes himself thusly: "I still find it helpful to identify myself here as queer, trans, Jewish, a parent, and fat."
- Asaf Orr, the National Center for Lesbian Rights Transgender Youth Project staff attorney, UCSF Child and Adolescent Gender Center Clinic attorney
- "Activist" Carmen Elmakiyes Amos, who defines herself as "Mizrahi, woman, lesbian, religious"
- Half-Jewish homosexual critic David Ehrenstein ("As everyone knows Whites feel no guilt about America's racist history whatsoever.")
- Transgender Chair in English at Stern College for Women at Yeshiva University Joy Ladin (who announced "her" decision to transition after attaining tenure; in 2012 published *Through the Door of Life: A Jewish Journey Between Genders* and in 2018 published *The Soul of the Stranger: Reading God and Torah from a Transgender Perspective* (Brandeis University Press)
- Maggid Jhos Singer "has been on the pulpit since 2000, and with his wife, Julie Batz, is currently one of the congregational leaders at Chochmat HaLev in Berkeley. He is also the Maggid for the Jewish Community Center of San Francisco." From July 2012's "A Memoir of Gender Transition" from *Tikkun*[73] ("a quarterly interfaith Jewish left-progressive magazine" published by Duke University Press): "My transition story is similar to Ladin's in many ways—both of us are Jewish and transitioned in our forties while raising young children and in a committed relationship."
- Eric Marcus, author of *Making Gay History* (which won the American Library Association's Stonewall Book Award, "given annually to English-language books of exceptional merit relating to the gay, lesbian, bisexual, and transgender experience") and is co-producer of a Holocaust podcast
- Evelyn Torton Beck, "a child survivor of the Holocaust," editor of 1982's *Nice Jewish Girls: A Lesbian Anthology*; as a founding member of the National Women's Studies Association, she helped start its Jewish and lesbian caucuses

---

[73] Features such articles as "The New Abolitionism: The Struggle to End Deportation," "Creating Sanctuary: Faith-Based Activism for Migrant Justice," and "Away With All Borders: The Immigration Mess."

and has written extensively about homoeroticism in Franz Kafka's work and about Frida Kahlo's bisexual identity

- Lesbian producer Ilene Chaiken (*The L Word, The Handmaid's Tale, Empire* featuring actor Jussie Smollett)
- Robert Raben, former Principal Deputy Assistant Attorney General under the Clinton Administration, Counsel to Congressman Barney Frank, and founder and President of The Raben Group LLC
- Dana Beyer, the first transgender candidate for State Delegate in the Maryland House of Delegates and Vice President of Equality Maryland
- Anne Kronenberg, Harvey Milk's 1977 campaign manager and former Director of Policy and Planning at the San Francisco Department of Public Health; co-founder of the Harvey Milk Foundation; the Harvey Milk Foundation's major sponsors/donors include: Levi's, Salesforce, Facebook, Apple, Stolichnaya Vodka, Desmond Tutu, the Kennedy Family, Dolores Huerta, and the US State Department
- Scott Wiener, co-sponsor of the proposal to re-name San Francisco International Airport the Harvey Milk San Francisco International Airport; Wiener introduced a bill in California as State Senator so that it would no longer be a felony to knowingly expose a sexual partner to HIV (or give HIV-positive blood) without prior notification in the State of California as Wiener believed the existing law was "irrational and discriminatory"; we discussed his other work earlier
- Alan Klein, co-founder of ACT UP and spokesperson for GLAAD ("I was heavily involved in the GayStraight Alliance at Ithaca College, actually. I worked with an out professor there named Marty Brownstein, who really was an inspiration to me at the time"); co-founder of Queer Nation and one of the "Obsessive Jews"; per his biographical description for The Obsessive Jews:

> Klein co-founded one of the nation's first public relations firms to cater to LGBT and social justice clients. He has provided strategic communications services to some of the nation's most notable nonprofits and corporations, including AT&T, Rolling Stone, HBO, Comedy Central, NRDC, Housing Works, Lambda Legal, and GMHC. Klein has galvanized public opinion by placing cutting-edge issues on front pages and in primetime. Klein served as the first national communications director and spokesperson for GLAAD. He played a pivotal role in Ellen DeGeneres' coming out, and subsequent media frenzy, by helping to orchestrate international coverage. He also brought the crisis of anti-LGBT violence to national attention by co-creating and co-producing "The Anti-Violence Campaign," the first-ever anti-gay violence television ad campaign, chaired by celebrities including Susan Sarandon, John Waters, Harvey Fierstein and Lou Reed. Most recently, Klein helped to raise awareness of the plight of LGBT Russians suffering under Vladimir Putin's regime.

- Tamara Cohen, from the Jewish Women's Archive:

> Is a Jewish feminist writer, activist and educator. She currently works as the Director of Lesbian, Gay, Bisexual and Transgender Affairs at the University of Florida and the once-a-month Spiritual Leader of the

Greater Washington Connecticut Coalition for Jewish Life. In 2004, Cohen directed a national study of Jewish women and feminism for Ma'yan: The Jewish Women's Project, a program of the JCC in Manhattan for whom she worked as Program Director for many years. While at Ma'yan, she worked in partnership with the Jewish Women's Archive to create the first Women of Valor posters. Cohen has also worked as an educator with Jewish women in the former Soviet Union through Project Kesher. She has served on the boards of Joshua Venture, Brit Tzedek V'Shalom, and Jews for Racial and Economic Justice. She is the editor of the Ma'yan feminist Haggadah, *The Journey Continues*, as well as an author of numerous articles and poems on Jewish women's spirituality and feminist approaches to text. Cohen holds a M.A. in Women's History from Sarah Lawrence College and a B.A. in Women's Studies and English from Barnard College. She currently lives in Gainesville, Florida, with her partner, Gwynn Kessler.

- Mike Moskowitz, an Orthodox Jewish rabbi and "advocate for transgender rights," scholar-in-residence for trans and queer Jewish studies at Congregation Beit Simchat Torah; Moskowitz's 2018 talk at Tufts University was sponsored by Jewish Queer Students at Tufts (JQUEST) and organized with the help of Tufts' Jewish Chaplain, Rabbi Dr. Naftali Brawer, and Keshet, according to JQUEST Chair Eli Rosmarin
- Moises Kaufman, writer of *The Laramie Project*, "I am Venezuelan, I am Jewish, I am gay, I live in New York. I am the sum of all my cultures"
- Betty Berzon, founder of what's now known as the Society for the Psychological Study of Lesbian, Gay, Bisexual and Transgender Issues
- Claude Cahun, a "genderqueer and Surrealist art icon": "Masculine? Feminine? It depends on the situation. Neuter is the only gender that always suits me"
- Rabbi Allen Bennett, born Allen Blumenstein in Ohio, claims to be the first openly gay rabbi in the United States, officiated Harvey Milk's funeral
- Abby Stein, transgender rabbi, author of Becoming Eve: My Journey from Ultra-Orthodox Rabbi to Transgender, and member of the Women's March 2019 Steering Committee:

As a young child in an isolated Hasidic Jewish community, transgender activist and writer Abby Stein collected newspaper clippings of organ transplants—'heart, lung, kidney, hands and legs. My idea was that I will collect them all, I will go to a doctor and have him do a full body transplant.

Stein—along with Linda Sarsour, Ilhan Omar, Jewish Voice for Peace Action, transgender Arizona Democratic Party Vice-Chair and "activist" Brianna Westbrook, and Mari Lynn "Bob Bland" Foulger of the Women's March—was a major supporter of viciously-anti-white "activist" and Massachusetts 4th Congressional District Democratic Congressional candidate Ihssane Leckey
- Tony Kushner, playwright and "activist" whose work "address[es] homophobia, AIDS, and racism through a dramatic lens"
- Gloria Allred, attorney: in 1983, represented "lesbian activists" Deborah Johnson

and Zandra Rolón in their lawsuit against a restauranteur who denied them service in a couples' booth; in 1995 represented eleven-year-old Katrina Yeaw in *Yeaw v. Boy Scouts* in a suit to determine whether the Boy Scouts had the right to exclude girls from membership; in 2012, represented Jenna Talackova, a "transgender woman" who was challenging a disqualification from the Miss Universe Canada pageant for not being biologically female—Talackova was subsequently given a reality TV show by E! Canada called *Brave New Girls*, a title that conveys much more about the reality of the situation than perhaps the network realizes[74]

- Sheldon Andelson (not to be confused with Sheldon Adelson), described by the Associated Press as "a prominent gay leader and fund-raiser for such politicians as Sen. Edward Kennedy and former Vice President Walter Mondale"; from the AP's December 30th, 1987 obituary:

> Andelson, a member of the University of California Board of Regents, died Tuesday night as family members gathered at his side at his Bel-Air mansion, once called the 'gay White House' because it had hosted scores of senators and presidential hopefuls. . . . A multimillionaire, lawyer, patron of the arts, and founder and chairman of the West Hollywood-based Bank of Los Angeles, Andelson was perhaps best known for his political activities. He raised huge amounts of money for liberal politicians at lavish parties he threw at his Bel-Air home and West Hollywood restaurant, Trumps. . . . [He was] a director in the B'nai B'rith Anti-Defamation League.

The Andelson Collection at the University of California-Santa Barbara Library is named in his honor. Located in the Ethnic and Gender Studies Library, "the Collection supports the teaching curriculum and research interests of faculty and students in gay, lesbian, bisexual, transgender and studies across the disciplines."
- Rinat Brodach, *Making the Cut* contestant and fashion designer of "gender-free" clothes
- Janet Weinberg, "LGBTQ activist" and same-sex partner of Roz Richter, Associate Justice of the New York Appellate Division of the Supreme Court, First Judicial Department, former Executive Director of Lambda Legal Defense & Education Fund, recipient of the Benjamin Cardozo Award from the Jewish Lawyers Guild ("The Jewish Lawyers Guild hosts its annual dinner where it confers awards to jurists who exemplify the qualities of Benjamin N. Cardozo and Golda Meir"—hard pass)
- Lesbian "activist" and author Amy Siskind, who was the first female Managing Director at Wasserstein Perella & Co.; "anti-hate vigil" organizer; #MeToo supporter
- Annette Eick, lesbian writer especially active during the Weimar period in Germany

---

[74] Allred refused to represent Maria Farmer against fellow Jew Jeffrey Epstein and was also mentioned along with her daughter Lisa Bloom as alleged suppressing the victims of another fellow Jew Harvey Weinstein in the 2019 book *She Said: Breaking the Sexual Harassment Story that Helped Ignite a Movement*.

- Miriam Ben-Shalom, openly lesbian sergeant in the US Army and the first President of the Gay, Lesbian, and Bisexual Veterans Association (now called American Veterans for Equal Rights)
- Aryeh Lev Stollman, homosexual neuroradiologist at Mount Sinai Hospital in New York City and author ("At the heart of *The Far Euphrates* lie the vexed questions raised by the Holocaust and its legacy")
- Australian singer Troye Sivan ("Sivan's music videos frequently feature LGBTQ relationships between the characters"), did a joint interview for *Vogue* with then-partner Jacob Bixenman as a "prominent queer couple" in 2019
- Bi-sexual English DJ Samantha Ronson
- Jonathan Rauch, Brookings Institution fellow, *The Atlantic* contributing editor, and same-sex marriage advocate who states: "I am an unrepentantly atheistic Jewish homosexual"
- Fritz Klein, sexologist, "the Jewish Alfred Kinsey," founder of the *Journal of Bisexuality* and the American Institute of Bisexuality
- Laurie Frankel, author of the novel *This Is How It Always Is*, a story of a Jewish family raising a transgender child
- Abigail Weissman, founder of Waves therapy, described as a:

> Jewish, queer, and trans-identified psychologist [who] has extensive experience and training in working with queer, trans and Jewish populations. She has served on the board of directors and has run a trans inclusive women's chavurah (group) at a San Francisco LGBTQIQA-focused synagogue in San Francisco and has presented at Transkeit, a Jewish trans and queer conference

- Asher Gellis, co-founder and Executive Director of JQ International, a Los Angeles-based "programming and advocacy group for LGBTQ Jews," which partners with and/or is funded by the Jewish Federation of Greater Los Angeles, the Jewish Community Foundation of Los Angeles, the Jewish Venture Philanthropy Fund, and UpStart ("bring bold Jewish ideas to light")[75]
- Eunice Lipton, "feminist art historian" and author of *French Seduction: An American's Encounter with France, Her Father, and the Holocaust*, described as her

---

[75] "At UpStart our vision is a more just, vibrant, and inclusive future. That vision means a future that is safer and more equitable. . . . First, we want to say unequivocally that Black lives matter and that we are committed to building an anti-racist Jewish community . . . In the next fiscal year, we will: Allocate targeted funds in our budget and increase dedicated staff time to advance Diversity, Equity, and Inclusion (DEI) and anti-racist work. Codify a regular rhythm for mandated anti-racism training, prioritized in line with other mandated training for both the staff and Board. Engage in a facilitated process to identify UpStart's core Diversity, Equity, and Inclusion (DEI) priorities, 3–5 year outcomes and milestones, and strategies to achieve them. Emphasize hiring consultants or consulting firms who are led by Black, Jews of Color, or People of Color to facilitate UpStart's anti-bias trainings and to develop our ongoing strategy. Maintain an ongoing portfolio of initiatives to advance DEI and racial justice, including the codification of equitable hiring and compensation policies and practices, developing interventions for core programs to attract and support a diverse and representative pool of participants, and integrating equity more firmly into our decision-making frameworks. Invest in ongoing staff learning around implicit bias and anti-racism."

Passionate attempt to reconcile opposing characteristics in French culture and society. An amalgam of history and personal narrative (as was the author's wonderful study of Manet's model in *Alias Olympia*), *French Seduction* scrutinizes both what is so enticing and so repellent about France.

- *Queer Spawn Diaries* by Nava EtShalom and Chana Joffe Walt, "two young Jewish women right out of college who co-produce a web and radio project by and for the grown children of lesbian, gay, bisexual, and transgendered (LGBT) parents"
- Rena Newman, self-described:

  (they/them), a genderqueer Jew from Chicago, Illinois . . . involved in gender advocacy work . . . specifically centered around education about transgender identities. I came out publicly as genderqueer in the summer of 2015, during my time as a fellow on the Bronfman Youth Fellowship. Throughout my journey as a Jew, a young educator, and a member of the transgender community, I've found there's much work to be done in Jewish spaces. As Jews we are familiar with an experience of otherness, of being an outsider. . . . Being inclusive of transgender identity fulfills *mitzvot* of community; it is a necessary part of welcoming the stranger.

- Rabbi Sharon Kleinbaum: "I never wanted to be simply a female rabbi. I want to be a part of a Judaism that is transformed by feminism."
- Cartoonist Hilary Price: "Being Jewish, feminist, gay—it all informs my work."
- Leroy Aarons, founder of the National Lesbian and Gay Journalists Association
- Rabbi Jane Litman, who, from *Lilith* magazine:

  Has led mikveh rituals with people at various stages of gender transition—which, she reports, were extremely powerful. Litman says that, for her, the rituals were 'closest to a conversionary mikveh . . . it's a chance to let go of the past, to let go of the pain of what it is to be in a wrong presenting-gender body, to allow mikveh to heal some of that and to welcome the future, while taking in the present moment. Conversion is a rebirthing ceremony, and this is a similar rebirthing.

- Rachel Zolf, "an out Jewish lesbian" poet
- David Mamet, author and playwright, who wrote the following lines for the character Ricky Roma in *Glengarry Glen Ross*:

  You think you're queer? I'm going to tell you something: we're all queer. You think you're a thief? So what? You get befuddled by a middle-class morality? Get shut of it. Shut it out. You cheat on your wife? You did it, live with it. You fuck little girls, so be it.

From a 2011 *Slate* interview by John Gapper:

We return to politics and I suggest that his intellectual journey from liberalism to neoconservatism has been traveled before by Jews such as Irving Kristol and Norman Podhoretz. This triggers a long reflection on his own Zionism and how he thinks Israel has been betrayed by the American left. 'The speeches that Charles Lindbergh made and Oswald Mosley made in the 1930s are the same speeches that are being made today, only slightly more politely: "The Jews are bringing us to war. Perhaps we should give their state away." The liberals in my neighborhood wouldn't give away Brentwood to the Palestinians but they want to give away Tel Aviv. . . . Does he believe that anyone who disputes Israel's land claims and believes in reallocation of territory to the Palestinians is anti-Semitic. . . ? 'Yes!' he exclaims. 'Of course! I mean you Brits. . . . Whatever education I have comes from reading your writers and yet, time and time again, for example reading Trollope, there is the stock Jew. Even in George Eliot, God bless her. And the authors of today. . . . I'm not going to mention names because of your horrendous libel laws but there are famous dramatists and novelists over there whose works are full of anti-Semitic filth. There is a profound and ineradicable taint of anti-Semitism in the British. . . . There is a Jewish state there ratified by the United Nations and you want to give it away to some people whose claim is rather dubious.'"

Mamet must be unfamiliar with the Balfour Declaration.

- Jill Soloway, creator of *Transparent*; according to her Wikipedia page:

    Identifies as nonbinary and gender non-conforming, using gender-neutral singular they pronouns. On June 26, 2020, Soloway announced a preference to be referred to as Joey rather than Jill. . . . Around 2011, [her father] came out as transgender.

- Jay Blotcher, documentarian and "activist":

    Through a Boston-based Jewish adoption agency, he was brought home on June 30, 1961, by Malvin 'Sonny' Blotcher and Elaine 'Lolly' Blotcher to Randolph, Massachusetts, where he grew up. His parents also adopted his sister, Andrea, from a woman in Augusta, Maine. Both Jay and Andrea were raised in a Jewish household and attended Temple Beth Am Hebrew School. Lolly and Sonny Blotcher were deeply immersed in Temple activities and would eventually serve as presidents, respectively, of the Sisterhood and Brotherhood groups, as well as volunteers for numerous Temple events.

- Fran Lebowitz, "author, public speaker, and chain smoker . . . the 'modern-day Dorothy Parker,'[76] has been an atheist since the age of seven, but describes her

---

[76] According to Wikipedia, the Jewish Parker "reported in 1937 on the Loyalist cause in Spain for the Communist magazine *The New Masses*. At the behest of Otto Katz, a covert Soviet Comintern agent and operative of German Communist Party agent Willi Münzenberg, Parker helped to found the Hollywood

Jewish identity as 'ethnic or cultural or whatever people call it now.'"

- Rebecca T. Alpert, *Lesbian Rabbis: The First Generation*
- Judy Dlugacz, according to *Autostraddle*:

> Bonnie J. Morris, in her book *The Disappearing L* wrote that 'this move-ment of woman-identified music began with Jewish leadership.' Young lesbian activist Judy Dlugacz founded Olivia Records in 1973, an inde-pendent record label that sold over one million albums by women artists for female fans, creating a network for lesbians to meet each other and bond over the soothing soul-sounds of lesbian folk-rock music. Jewish artists associated with Olivia include Alix Dobkin, who said during a set at Michfest, 'Jews and lesbians have much in common: we were never meant to survive.' In 1990, Olivia began its transition to Olivia Travel with a 'concert on a cruise.' Now it's the premier travel company for the lesbian community and the longest-running lesbian company in the world! Dlugacz is also a political activist and philanthropist who served on Obama's 2012 re-election campaign's LGBT Leadership Council.

- Susan Gottlieb, according to *Autostraddle*:

> Introduces herself as 'the All-American Jewish Lesbian Folksinger,' was a key figure in the 1970s/80s Los Angeles punk scene as well as the elec-tropunk and Queercore movements. She was a founding member of That's Nervous Gender, a proto-industrial synth-punk group comprised of two gay Chicanos and one androgynous Jewish lesbian, which she left to join post-punk new wave band Catholic Discipline. These days she's doing more visual art and exhibits at the Craig Kull Gallery in Santa Monica. . . . Of visiting an LGBT synagogue while on tour, she said, 'It was great, I felt a sense of family being away from my own family but singing the same tunes and saying the same prayers. You can be a Jew anywhere in the world—it's great that you can find a community.'

- Robin Ochs, editor of The Bisexual Resource Guide and *Getting Bi: Voices of Bisexuals Around the World*
- Amy Bloom, according to Combined Jewish Philanthropies of Great Boston:

> Has a children's book, *Little Sweet Potato*, about appreciating one's self and finding a community that takes all kinds. Her first book of nonfic-tion, *Normal: Transsexual CEOs, Crossdressing Cops and Hermaphro-dites with Attitudes*, is a staple of university sociology and biology courses. She has written for magazines such as *The New Yorker*, *The New York Times Magazine*, *Vogue*, *The Atlantic Monthly*, *Slate*, and *Salon*.

---

Anti-Nazi League in 1936, which the FBI suspected of being a Communist Party front. The Hollywood Anti-Nazi League's membership eventually grew to some 4,000 strong. According to David Caute, its often wealthy members were 'able to contribute as much to [Communist] Party funds as the whole Amer-ican working class.'"

Bill Gladstone writes:

> A new sub-genre of Jewish literature seems to be emerging in which the subjects move or have moved across North America in a northwesterly direction. We saw it earlier this year in Michael Chabon's novel *The Yiddish Policeman's Union*, about an alternate postwar history in which a Jewish homeland is established not in Israel but in Alaska. The literary compass again points north by northwest in Amy Bloom's intriguing second novel, *Away*, about a Russian immigrant to New York about 1924 who needs to get to Siberia in a hurry and sets off for Alaska with the intent of crossing the Bering Strait on foot. Lillian Leyb, the 22-year-old Russian-Jewish protagonist, has survived a pogrom in her town of Turov and has come to New York with a broken heart, having lost her husband, parents and—she believes—little daughter Sophie. Driven, resourceful, compliant and willing to do whatever is necessary to survive in America, Lillian soon finds work as a seamstress in the Goldfadn Theatre and becomes the mistress of Meyer Burnstein, a matinee idol of the Yiddish stage who is secretly homosexual. She also has an affair with Meyer's father and becomes pregnant.

Susan Weidman Schneider writes in *Lilith*:

> Bloom, whose 1994 *New Yorker* report on female-to-male transsexuals broke new ground, continues, '[O]ur mistake is thinking that the wide range of humanity represents aberration when in fact it represents just what it is: range. Nature is not two little notes on a child's flute; Nature is more like Aretha Franklin: vast, magnificent, capricious—occasionally hilarious—and infinitely varied. . . .' Clearly, this is a moment in the Zeitgeist when 'transgender' is on our radar screen. And Jewish transgendered people are beginning to go public with their experiences. Margaret Rothman, coordinator of gay, lesbian, bisexual and transgender services at San Francisco's Jewish Family and Children Services, says 'Half of my GLBT speakers bureau is transgender—they're dying to talk. . . .' Jews crossing gender boundaries are becoming increasingly vocal. . . . Many transgender Jews feel very strongly about finding their place in the Jewish community and spiritual solace in Judaism.

- Billy Eichner, comedian, "activist," and "part of the Jewish LGBTQ community"
- Hari Nef, per Hillel Ontario:

> The model, Hari Nef, was born Harrison Jacob Neff to her Jewish parents in Philadelphia. Nef is the first transgender woman who was signed by one of the biggest model agencies, IGM Models. But more importantly for the LGBTQ community, the model has been a very active LGBTQ supporter, and is said to be leading today's transgender revolution.

- Dana International, per Hillel Ontario:

Sharon Cohen, also known as Dana International, had her biggest success [in] 1998, when she won the Eurovision song contest for Israel. With eight albums and three compilation albums, the Israeli singer and songwriter is amongst Israel's most successful musicians. Sharon Cohen, born Yaron Cohen, came out as transgender at the early age of 13. With her win at the Eurovision Song Contest, Dana International fought the negative reactions she first received when Israel announced that they would send a transgender singer to represent them at this major annual European event. Since then, Dana International has become an LGBTQ icon and is internationally known for her success.

- Harvey Fierstein, actor (*Mrs. Doubtfire, Mulan, Hairspray*) and gay spokesman
- Matt Nosanchuk, described by Peter Rosenstein as having:

Extensive experience working in senior policy and communications roles in the Obama and Clinton administrations, on Capitol Hill, and at high-profile NGOs. He served in several senior roles in the Obama administration: at the White House as Director of Outreach for the National Security Council, and as President Obama's liaison to the American Jewish community; and in senior positions at the Departments of State, Justice, and Homeland Security. Earlier in his career, he served in the Clinton administration as the point person at the Department of Justice on a range of significant policy and legislative priorities. He has worked on Capitol Hill as U.S. Sen. Bill Nelson's counsel, and as Special Minority Counsel on the House Judiciary Committee. For his work to further LGBT rights, he received the American Bar Association's Stonewall Award and the Attorney General's Distinguished Service Award.

- Sarah Schulman, co-founder of MIX: NY LGBT Experimental Film and Video Festival, the US Coordinator of the first LGBT Delegation to Palestine, the Co-Director of the ACT UP Oral History Project, author of *Israel/Palestine and the Queer International*, and co-founder of Lesbian Avengers; Vikki Reich writes of the Lesbian Avengers:

In my years with the Minneapolis Lesbian Avengers, we defaced anti-choice billboards, participated in visibility actions at schools, constructed a giant paper machè bomb piñata filled with lube and dental dams [and] helped plan the first of many Dyke Marches.

- Rabbi Debra Kolodny, per *Autostraddle*:

Editor of *Blessed Bi Spirit: Bisexual People of Faith* and has served in directorial, executive and advisory positions at ALEPH: Alliance for Jewish Renewal, the National Religious Leadership Roundtable, Nehirim and Binet USA. Following the legalization of same-sex marriage, she carried the torch for queer faith leaders to use the resources gathered in that fight and devote them towards new struggles—specifically, towards Black

Lives Matter. Along with Muslim and Christian leaders, she organized a queer clergy retreat in Portland in 2015.

- "Emmy-award winning comic and TV writer Judy Gold is very lesbian and very Jewish" according to *Autostraddle*
- John Singer (Faygele ben Miriam) attempted to get the first same-sex marriage license in Seattle in 1971 with, as Eli Sanders writes, "another man, Paul Barwick, whom he'd met recently at a meeting of the Seattle chapter of the Gay Liberation Front." From Sanders's 2012 *Tablet* profile:

  Upon his arrival in Seattle in 1970, by way of New York and, briefly, San Francisco, he immediately began stirring up a brand of trouble that was way beyond the confines of its cultural moment. He was propelled by conviction, no doubt, but also by the stacks of unfiltered Camel cigarettes he chain smoked ("If you gave him a filtered cigarette, the first thing he'd do was break the filter off," Barwick said), and by a likewise unfiltered personality. It seemed to combine the sex drive and irrepressible humanity of Allen Ginsberg (another gay New York Jew); the bravery and timing of Harvey Milk (another gay New York Jew, who started his work on the West Coast two years after Faygele); the fury of Larry Kramer (yet another gay New York Jew, whom Faygele once denounced for taking too long to come out of the closet); and the politics of Woodie Guthrie (another New Yorker, if not a Jew, whose guitar, emblazoned with the phrase "This Machine Kills Fascists," seems the likely inspiration for the phrase Faygele painted across the Dodge van he drove from Seattle to New York and back several times: "Faggots Against Fascism"). Also key to the mix: the feminism of his radical mother, Miriam (although Faygele, when discussing that part of his politics, preferred to talk about his "effeminism").

- Rebecca Walker, from her *Autostraddle* profile:

  The daughter of legendary writer Alice Walker and New York lawyer Mel Leventhal, Walker is the author of the NY Times Bestseller *Black, White, and Jewish*. . . . At 22, she introduced the concept of Third Wave Feminism to the world in an article for *Ms.* Magazine.

- Gertrude Stein, who wrote *QED*, posthumously-published, credited as being one of the first "coming out" novels to be published in the United States
- Michael Kors, for 2019's Pride month, the fashion designer launched "#MKGO Rainbow," a collection "dedicated to supporting the LGBTQ+ community"
- Lionel Blue, believed to be Britain's first openly homosexual rabbi and author of *Godly and Gay*, Blue states that he became a Marxist after prayer failed to strike Oswald Mosley dead
- Rebecca Sugar, creator of the cartoon *Steven Universe*, which prominently features "LGBTQ themes"; it received a GLAAD Media Award for Outstanding Kids & Family Program
- Maayan Jaffe-Hoffman writes for the *Jewish News Syndicate*:

In an article published by *Ha'aretz*, teen Tom Chai Sosnik (formerly Mia), who had a bar mitzvah and Jewish naming ceremony at his school after coming out as a boy, says, "Being trans doesn't make you unclean; it doesn't make you weird or different. People that are trans are just doing what we all should be doing: they're embracing who they really are." Louis Bordman—senior director of the URJ (Union for Reform Judaism) Eisner and Crane Lake Camps, which have welcomed several transgender teens—adds, "I would hope that a transgender child would be bar/bat mitzvah as the gender that they identify. . . ." In an article that ran on MyJewishLearning.com, Britt Rubenstein, mother of Lily (once a boy), talks about her daughter's transition, which occurred around the time of his/her bar/bat mitzvah. . . . Lily's story is becoming more common. Casey Cohen, communications director for Camp Tawonga in Groveland, Calif., says, "We want all kids to connect to Judaism and spirituality in a way that is personal and meaningful for them." To that end, Tawonga is launching the "Beyond the Bimah" program in the fall of 2016. . . . "In talking to trans families, they want their child to have an individualized journey as a human being. It is coming at it from a Jewish lens, without a focus on being a man or a woman, but a person," says Jamie Simon-Harris, Camp Tawonga's associated executive director.

- Idalia Friedson, Advisory Board of the Quantum Alliance Initiative at the Hudson Institute and a fellow in the Hineni 2018–2019 program, which focused on "empowering LGBT Jews to be leaders in their community"
- Ann Kaner-Roth, Executive Director of Project 515 and co-founder of Minnesotans United for All Families; as Jessie Van Berkel writes for the *Star Tribune*: "She was involved in her synagogue at a young age . . . and a principle of Jewish life is to repair the world. . . . She also started a monthly gathering of women working in social policy and was an active member of Shir Tikvah synagogue in Minneapolis."
- David Schneer, Louis P. Singer Endowed Chair in Jewish History at the University of Colorado Boulder; from his university biography:

> Called a 'pathbreaking' scholar by the *Frankfurter Allgemeine Zeitung*, Shneer's research focuses on 20th century European, Russian, and Jewish history and culture. . . . He is currently working on . . . *Art is My Weapon: The Radical Musical Life of Lin Jaldati*, examines Yiddish musical culture's role in European history from 1933 through 1989 through the life and work of Lin Jaldati, a Dutch-Jewish Yiddish-singing cabaret singer, who survived the Holocaust and was the last person to see Anne Frank alive. After the war, she moved to East Germany and became the Yiddish diva of the Communist world until her death in 1988. . . . His other books include *Queer Jews*. . . . Shneer has taught or been a scholar-in-residence at the University of California campuses at Berkeley and Davis, and at the University of Illinois, the National Yiddish Book Center, the University of Wisconsin, the U.S. Holocaust Memorial Museum, serving as the Pearl Resnick Fellow, and the Graduate Theological Union in Berkeley. He currently serves on as co-editor-in-chief of *East European Jewish Affairs* and on the editorial boards of *Journal of Jewish Identities*, the Association for

Jewish Studies' magazine *Perspectives*, and for the book series Border-lines with Academic Studies press. He serves as consultant to numerous Jewish agencies on questions of contemporary Jewish identity, and has served on the board of directors of the Association for Jewish Studies. He has won prestigious fellowships from the Social Science Research Council, Hadassah-Brandeis Institute, the International Research and Exchange Council, and the U.S. Holocaust Memorial Museum. In his broader work, Shneer co-founded *Jewish Mosaic*, the first national Jewish LGBT organization, which merged with Keshet in 2010, and was education director of Congregation Sha'ar Zahav, the LGBT outreach synagogue of the San Francisco Bay Area, from 1997 through 2001. His work with the Jewish non-profit world includes consulting with organizations around issues of integrating post-Soviet Jews into Jewish communal life, having served as co-chair of Limmud Colorado, vice-chair of Keshet, and working with Facing History and Ourselves, a global non profit dedicated to fostering a democratic, human-rights oriented education in high schools.

- Caryn Aviv, about whom Sharon Udasin writes in "When Jacob Has Two Mommies" from 2009:

  The Posen lecturer in secular Jewish culture for the Center for Judaic Studies at the University of Denver is the co-author of a newly released synagogue survey on "Diversity and LGBT Inclusion," which she presented at a meeting of more than 50 Jewish community leaders, professors and congregants—many of them clad in rainbow-patterned yarmulkes—at The JCC in Manhattan.

- Denice Frohman (no relation to the Sausage King of Chicago), described thusly by *Autostraddle*:

  Self-declared 'NuyoJewricanqueer' Denice Frohman is the 2013 Women of the World Poetry Slam Champion, 2014 CantoMundo Fellow, 2013 Hispanic Choice Award winner, 2012 Leeway Transformation Award recipient . . . performed at The White House in 2016. . . . Her work has appeared on ESPN, in the *Huffington Post*, and garnered over 7.5 million views online. . . . Her work looks at intersections of race/ethnicity, gender, sexuality and the "in-betweenness" that exists in us all, drawing from her experience as a queer woman from a Puerto Rican and Jewish background, in an aim to "disrupt traditional notions of power, and celebrate the parts of ourselves deemed unworthy."

- Warren Hoffman, Executive Director for the Association for Jewish Studies in New York where he leads the largest membership organization of Jewish Studies scholars, teachers, and students in the world; has taught at multiple universities; wrote *The Passing Game: Queering Jewish American Culture* and *The Great White Way: Race and the Broadway Musical*
- Robin Tyler, activist and "comedienne"; her first album, *Always a Bridesmaid,*

*Never a Groom*, was distributed by Judy Dlugacz's Olivia Records; Tyler authored "My Big Fat Jewish Lesbian Wedding" for the *Huffington Post*:

> Gloria Allred filed the first lawsuit in the California Supreme Court same-sex marriage case on Feb. 24, 2004, on behalf of me and Diane and a gay couple—Rev. Troy Perry and his husband, Phillip Ray de Blieck, whom he had married in Canada . . . there we were, plastic champagne glasses for sparkling cider, plastic plates, plastic forks, and beautiful flowers donated to us by Regent Media, which owns the Advocate and HereTV. Right before the ceremony, Michael Libow, the most famous real-estate agent in Beverly Hills, sang a cappella. . . . Four men held the chuppah, a canopy under which a Jewish wedding ceremony is performed. They were Steve Krantz, founder of Jews for Marriage Equality, and regional director of the Southern Pacific Region of PFLAG (Parents and Friends of Lesbians and Gays); Terry Leftgoff, our friend who founded the Santa Barbara Gay and Lesbian Business Association; our attorney Mike Maroco and our fabulous friend Bill Rosenthal, an openly gay Los Angeles city councilman. Of course, they all wore yarmulkes.

- Steph Loehr, aka Ferocious Steph, a transgender Jew who identifies as a deer (I'm serious), is an administrator on the gaming platform Twitch as part of their "Safety Advisory Council," and is listed as a "Professional Community Leader" with the ADL where she is described as "Transgender, and an advocate for authenticity, challenging herself and others to find and express truth through vulnerability."
- Vicky Osterweil, self-described "queer Jewish anarchist" who is also transgender and wrote the book *In Defense of Looting*; Osterweil's writing is regularly featured in *The New Inquiry*, founded by Mary Borkowski, Jennifer Bernstein, and Rachel Rosenfelt
- Eva Kotchever, Polish lesbian émigré, friend of Emma Goldman; ran Eve's Hangout (also known as Eve Adams' Tearoom) a "haven for lesbians, but also for migrants" in the mid-1920s before her deportation for obscenity for her collection of short stories Lesbian Love and for disorderly conduct
- Marla Brettschneider, in the 1980s served in Israel as Coordinator for the student activist group the Progressive Zionist Caucus; per her biographical write-up:

> Is Professor of Political Philosophy and Feminist Theory at the University of New Hampshire with a joint appointment in Politics and Women's Studies. She is founder of the UNH Queer Studies Program as well as the Social Justice Leadership Project. Brettschneider also teaches in the UNH Race and Ethnicity Program. Brettschneider has served in different capacities within activist organizations, including as Executive Director of Jews For Racial and Economic Justice in New York City. She writes and lectures widely in diversity democratic theory and Jewish diversity politics, including in feminist, queer, race, Jewish, and class-based critical theories. Brettschneider is an award-winning author, having published four other academic journal special issues, three edited book volumes, and is working to complete her sixth single author book. Some of her award-

winning works include: *Jewish Feminism and Intersectionality*; *The Family Flamboyant: Race Politics, Queer Families, Jewish Lives*; and *The Narrow Bridge: Jewish Views on Multiculturalism* with a forward by Cornel West.

In describing a "photograph of my family of choice at our home in the Bronx" for the Jewish Women's Archive, she writes:

> We are an adoptive, multi-racial, two mom family with a mix of Jews birthed, raised, and by choice. One key feminist insight this artifact expresses is the feminist notion that the personal is political. Jewish feminists are queering our worlds. . . . I also chose this artifact because it expresses the core political orientation of my Jewish identity. In this photo, my partner – rabbi and professor – Dawn Rose, our children Paris Mayan and Toni Louise Brettschneider/Rose, and I stand on our terrace with a banner. The banner was the standard issue of United for Peace and Justice (UFPJ), the organizers of the march protesting the Republican National Convention in New York City, August 29, 2004. UFPJ was co-founded by Leslie Cagan, a radical Jewish lesbian and partner to Melanie Kaye/Kantrowitz, a Jewish lesbian feminist writer and activist.

## TERF Wars

*"Sex is fucking and gender is everything else."*

– Kate Bornstein[77]

Lesbian and gay, or "queer," studies first began to proliferate on college campuses in the 1970s. In the spring of 1970, UC Berkeley began to offer courses in what would become known as queer studies, followed by a few Midwestern universities in the fall. One professor, Louis Crompton, served as a faculty advisor to the University of Nebraska's Gay Action Group, setting the foundation for the ubiquitous LGBTQ-rainbow-ally groups that are such a fixture on campuses today. This is crucial as part of its rapid institutionalization, along with the fact that academia in general had become far more Leftward-oriented in the preceding decades as well as the fact that critical theory had pretty well infected a great number of disciplines and departments by this time. In 1974, Crompton co-founded the Gay and Lesbian Caucus of the Modern Language Association (MLA), the preeminent authority in the humanities for higher education. Virtually every college student will have encountered the MLA citation style from their English or Composition courses and the APA citation style from the corrupted APA we discussed earlier.

The City College of San Francisco was offering gay literature courses in 1972, and "Gay and Lesbian Literature" arrived at UCLA in 1976, taught by Peter Thorslev, who "argues brother-sister incest was 'made sympathetic' or even 'idealized' as 'a metaphor for human perfectibility' in Byron and Shelley."[78] More recently, the Gender Studies Program at UCLA has sponsored courses with lesbian and gay content, among them the "Introduction to Lesbian, Gay, and Bisexual Studies," first taught in 1992 by Daniel Calder, professor of English, and Linda Garnets, lecturer in psychology and (then) women's studies.

Trans studies as a discipline, insofar as we can call it that, started to crystallize in the late 1980s and early 1990s at approximately the same time as the next mutation in critical theory, "intersectionality," defined by Merriam-Webster as, "the complex, cumulative way in which the effects of multiple forms of discrimination (such as

---

[77] Jewish transgender author, "performance artist," "activist," and former "high-ranking lieutenant in the Sea Org (which the Church of Scientology describes as a 'fraternal religious order, comprising the church's most dedicated members')," diagnosed with borderline personality disorder
[78] Lambert, *Unclean Lips*, 233.

racism, sexism, and classism) combine, overlap, or intersect especially in the experiences of marginalized individuals or groups." By the 2000s, intersectionality was *de rigueur* and was out of the academy and into the "activist" scene. Returning to Karen Zelermyer:

> Intersectionality for LGBTQ grantmakers meant recognizing interdependencies and common concerns in the wider progressive movement, including commitments to labor, immigrant, economic and reproductive justice [note: they do not care about labor whatsoever, as the commitment to mass immigration and the "movement" slavishly doing the bidding of global capital displays]. Pride at Work was founded as an official constituency group of the AFL-CIO as a way for the LGBTQ and labor movements to partner. . . . Women's foundations have been particularly instrumental in bridging the reproductive justice and LGBTQ movements, investing close to $2 million in this work between 2007 and 2010. The Arcus, Ford and Overbrook foundations awarded the Lesbian, Gay, Bisexual & Transgender Community Center of New York City $510,000 for Causes in Common, a coalition between reproductive rights and LGBTQ freedom movements.

In a sad irony for the numberless feminists who've punted on a meaningful life, it's now come to the fact that they're campaigning for men masquerading as women and vice versa if they're not doing the bidding of global capital and conflating empowerment with being either a cog in the corporate machine or becoming glorified prostitutes. By 2008, these feminists had their own special label: TERFs (Trans-Exclusionary Radical Feminists).

Returning to the institutionalization of "trans studies" in academia, a lot of scrounging was needed to create a canon; without anything of self-evident value, "foundational" texts were established out of the Jewish transgender Sandy Stone's "The Empire Strikes Back: A Posttranssexual Manifesto," the Jewish communist lesbian Leslie Feinberg's *Stone Butch Blues* and *Transgender Warriors*, the Jewish Judith Butler's work on "gender performativity" (and all the world's a stage!) and the un-coupling of sex and gender, and the Jewish Jack/Judith Halberstam's *Female Masculinity*.[79] Not a Shakespeare in the bunch, but when you're manufacturing a discipline out of thin air, you'll take what you can get. Subsequent "research" is no less preposterous, but really quite dangerous with the seriousness with which it is taken.

The key transitionary figure here in incorporating sexuality, specifically homosexuality, as vital to feminism is the Jewish Gayle Rubin, co-founder of Samois—a "lesbian-feminist BDSM organization based in San Francisco" from 1978 to 1983—and author of "The Traffic in Women: Notes on the 'Political Economy' of Sex" (1975), which relies on theories of Claude Lévi-Strauss, Jacques Lacan, and Sigmund Freud, and considers "the part of social life that is the locus of the oppression of women, of sexual minorities, and of certain aspects of human personality within individuals. I call that part of social life the 'sex/gender system,' for lack of a more

---

[79] Halberstam studied at UC Berkeley and the University of Minnesota, and was a Professor of American Studies and Ethnicity, Gender Studies, and Comparative Literature and the Director of The Center for Feminist Research at USC before becoming a tenured professor at Columbia University.

elegant term," although this does not reject the biological basis of sex but rather acknowledges the social factors that do in fact shape certain expectations. This is not wrong as such, but it paved the way for the un-coupling of biology from reality.

The un-coupling of sex and gender is given its firm ideological (but obviously fallacious) basis in the work of Judith Butler, whose "Performative Acts and Gender Constitution: An Essay in Phenomenology and Feminist Theory" (1988) published by the Johns Hopkins University Press advances the thesis that gender is "performative," based on the *theories* of the Sartre milieu, Simone de Beauvoir,[80] and Sigmund Freud. For Butler, there is a major difference "between sex, as biological facticity, and gender, as the cultural interpretation or signification of that facticity." By situating her work in the feminist stream, we can see that the undermining of gender in fact undermines feminism as a vehicle for (in theory) representing women's interests; Butler claims that without a critique of sex, the feminist strategy for "contesting constructions of binary asymmetric gender and compulsory heterosexuality" will be ineffective. Butler's 1990 work *Gender Trouble: Feminism and the Subversion of Identity* favorably cites the work of Monique Wittig (co-founder of Parisian lesbian group the Red Dykes and partner of Jewish filmmaker and author Sande Zeig) in claiming that lesbianism is the one recourse to the constructed notion of sex.

Now we are in the realm of multitudinous genders (plus sexualities) as opposed to the female sex, and the late-1980s theories of intersectionality ("the interconnected nature of social categorizations such as race, class, and gender as they apply to a given individual or group, regarded as creating overlapping and interdependent systems of discrimination or disadvantage") including race could be brought into the fold, which then begets white privilege (the Jewish Paula S. Rothenberg[81] is responsible for the "seminal text" *White Privilege*: "People of color are not racist because they do not systematically benefit from racism") and white fragility.[82] There is a very

---

[80] For Butler: "When Simone de Beauvoir claims, 'one is not born, but, rather, becomes a woman,' she is appropriating and reinterpreting this doctrine of constituting acts from the phenomenological tradition. In this sense, gender is in no way a stable identity or locus of agency from which various acts proceed; rather, it is an identity tenuously constituted in time-an identity instituted through a stylized repetition of acts."

[81] From the jacket of Rothenberg's *Invisible Privilege: A Memoir about Race, Class, and Gender*: "Through recollections of her childhood in an upper-middle-class Jewish family and her college years in the sixties, she tells us how she discovered that the world she took for granted as 'everyday life' was in fact riddled with privilege. Reviewing the social upheaval of the seventies that challenged fundamental assumptions about gender roles, race relations, and even the nature of the family, Rothenberg tells how she gained a new understanding of what it meant to be an educator and activist. She shares personal events surrounding the publication of Race, Class and Gender to offer an insider's perspective on the culture wars, and brings her story into the 1990s with a cogent discussion of hate speech and the controversy over 'political correctness.' She also offers a hard-hitting critique of current teaching practices and a response to critics of multiculturalism and feminism, as well as a look at how de facto segregation continues in American education in the form of tracking. Both deeply personal and broadly social, this memoir will capture the interest of anyone who cares about the future of education, race relations, feminism, and social justice."

[82] From Andrew Joyce's review of Robin DiAngelo's *White Fragility: Why It's So Hard for White People to Talk About Racism* (2018): "My first action on picking up a copy of *White Fragility* was to turn to the bibliography. I knew what I'd see, and it was a gratifying and familiar feeling to see so many names from my research on Whiteness Studies. They were almost all there, protruding from the page like shunned relatives at a family reunion — Noel Ignatiev, George Lipsitz, Ruth Frankenberg (described in *White Fragility* as 'a premier white scholar in the field of whiteness studies'), Michelle Fine, Lois Weis, along with helpful co-ethnics like Thomas Shapiro, David Wellman, Sander Gilman, Larry Adelman, and Jay Kaufman. These are DiAngelo's mentors and intellectual forbears, and I could tell, scanning through this

clear through-line despite the tensions that exist between the various off-shoots, dating back to the original aims of feminism in the first place. The present iteration of feminism actually marginalizes real women who believe feminism should reflect real women's interests. Whether many of these feminists are correct in what, exactly, those interests are is another story: most of the time it involves parroting the Establishment's talking points for the day.

Without the leg-work of the preceding generations, however, the grotesque spectacle that is Jonathan/Jessica Yaniv would not exist. Yaniv is infamous for many reasons, not least of which include initiating over a dozen complaints to the BC Human Rights Tribunal for Vancouver-area salons' declining to perform a Brazilian wax on "her" testicles, complaints which were, in showing that the modern world is itself grotesquely parodic, met with deep seriousness, as one tribunal member wrote: "Waxing can be critical gender-affirming care for transgender women." Yaniv has claimed responsibility for getting hundreds of real women permanently banned from Twitter, including prominent names like Meghan Murphy, founder of *Feminist Current*.

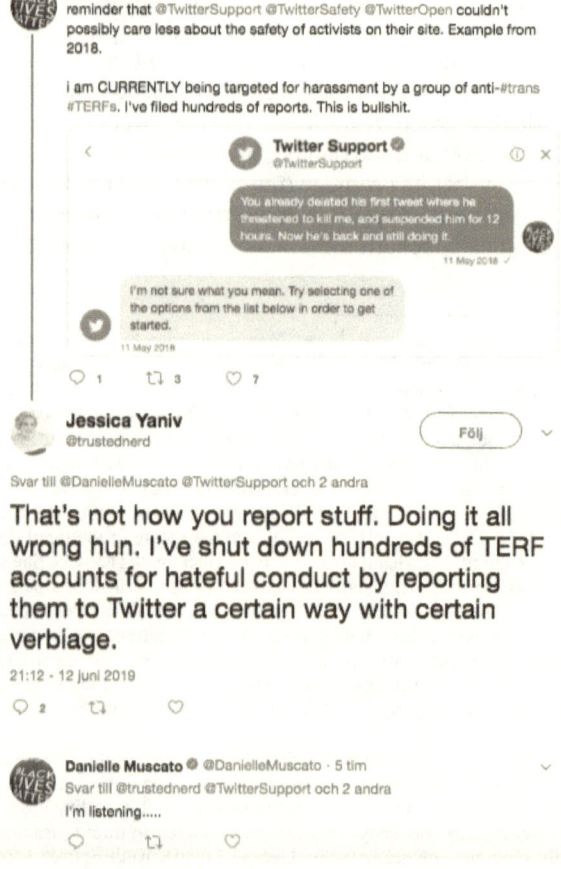

---

list of names and works, that *White Fragility* was sure to boast very many references to 'fellow Whites,' and streams of inducements to abandon White ethnic interests."

Meanwhile Rachel McKinnon, who the reader will recall from earlier in this book, remains on the platform after tweeting, "I'm more specific and want them [cis people] to die in a grease fire." Yaniv's tweets also include an open invitation to an "interesting event" which included *topless* swimming for "all-bodied" children with *no parents allowed*.

Yaniv is also the subject of numerous allegations of harassment, including allegations of sexualized online communication with teenage girls, at least one of whom has contacted a national tip-line for reporting the sexual exploitation of children. The preposterous nature of the anti-reality regime does not preclude tragedy, however. In fact, as we might expect, it is just the opposite.

While books are banned left and mostly right by Amazon and TERFs are booted off Twitter for acknowledging the existence of biology, historical fiction like *Female Husbands* by Jen Manion, author of "Transgender Children in Antebellum America" is promoted heavily; the rear jacket features glowing praise from "trans" author and "activist" Susan Stryker, the Jewish Joanne Meyerowitz, and Harvard University President Emeritus[83] Drew Faust (now on the Goldman Sachs Board of Directors), who married her Jewish doctoral advisor Charles E. Rosenberg. For the Jewish Women's Archive, "For many feminists, LGBTQ advocacy is an integral part of feminist responsibility. In 1972, feminist writer Joan Nestle helped launch the Gay Academic Union, and in 1973, she co-founded the Lesbian Herstory Archives."

Whereas Danya Ruttenberg, author of *Yentl's Revenge: The Next Wave of Jewish Feminism*, states that, "The 'trans' movement has, in a way, taken some of feminism's work and pushed it even further. If a culture that thrives in part on gender oppression loses its concrete anchor on 'gender,' the system as a whole must shift" (thus invalidating the objective and provable existence of women in the same way "whiteness" is rendered "conceptual" and "a construct"), Lidia Falcón, founder of the Feminist Party of Spain, refers to the transgender lobby as "pimps and children buyers," and correctly stated that the legal gender recognition law was imposed on Spain by the "gay lobby." Regarding the former claim, in 2019 the Swedish newspaper *Svenska Dagbladet* published an explosive exposé where journalists had set up a fake account of a 14-year-old boy on a dating site and received over 100 propositions within just a couple of days including that of a senior official at the Ministry for Foreign Affairs and "a key person in the Pride community."

According to drag queen Marti Gould Cummings's TEDx Talk, "Drag is a leadership role model for everyone—kids, too. . . . Drag to me is about action, political activism—doing the work . . . it takes a village to raise a child, well drag is a part of that village." With the nuclear family targeted for oblivion, Cummings' words may prove prescient. Cummings is part of a drag queen makeover show called *Dragged*; as Katie Dupere describes one of their episodes:

> Long Island women are known for being unapologetically bold and larger-than-life—and so are drag queens. Combine the two together and you have an unstoppable, feminine force. . . . When it comes to a drag name, Russell

---

[83] Preceded at Harvard by Jewish Presidents Neil Rudenstine and Larry Summers, and succeeded by the Jewish Lawrence Bacow (MIT), who "hung a mezuzah on the front of the president's residence at Tufts, an eminent Boston university that he served from 2001 to 2011, and participated in events at the campus Hillel" (*Jewish Telegraphic Agency*).

turns up the Long Island inspiration, choosing the name Shawna Tova. The name is a play on the traditional Jewish greeting of 'shana tova,' which is used during Rosh Hashanah and translates to 'good year'. . . . With over-the-knee boots, a flouncy skirt and a smoky, gemmed-eye look, this queen serves Long Island femininity. . . . As if you'd expect anything else from Long Island's newest Jewish drag queen."

A grotesque facsimile of femininity to be sure, but nothing about this is "feminine" or true to the essence of womanhood.

The UN Committee on the Elimination of All Forms of Discrimination against Women has expressed its "concern at specific health problems experienced by transgender women." Why is the UN Committee on the Elimination of All Forms of Discrimination against Women worried about biological men? Because in this odious system up is down and black is white. The UN Committee on the Elimination of Discrimination against Women has urged the UK to "combat hate crimes against trans people, ensure effective investigation and prosecution." Hate crimes can constitute something so frivolous as "misgendering" someone. Trans/feminism is a clear fault line not just on the left, but through the fabric of reality.

There is no question that the primary bankrollers of feminism have always viewed the ideology of feminism as highly useful for a variety of reasons, ranging from women as wage depressors and tax cattle to weaponizing them against men and the structure/strictures of traditional society. Without getting too far into the weeds on the various internal conflicts and aims of feminism, its mainstream form has always been that which is most advantageous to the ruling class's designs, *not* any ideals of equality, despite many adherents' best intentions. The same applies for causes racial, immigrational, and, of course, LGBTQ as they intersect with the One World, one position inversion of reality, where the ruling class tries to force reality to suit the ideology.

In September 2019, the Flemish government amended the Flemish staff regulations stating that mothers are now "gender neutral" and employees will have a total of twenty days of leave for exams and counseling related to "trans healthcare." In February 2019, members of the Orivesi municipal council in Finland proposed a motion that children should only be taught about two genders, but ultimately it was concluded that this would be discriminatory and the motion was dismissed. The Finnish Institute for Health and Welfare's Action Plan for the Prevention of Violence against Children 2020–2025 includes a specific chapter on "sexual and gender minority children and youth."

In October 2019, Rainbow Families Croatia held a successful crowdfunding campaign for its second coloring book for pre-school children entitled "My Rainbow Family's Fun Day Out." In June 2019, in a campaign coordinated by the magazine *Žmonės*, ten Lithuanian brands released their logos in rainbow colors to support Baltic Pride, with the "please clap" campaign as we expected receiving a "Baltic Best" advertising award. In October 2019, Lithuanian national broadcaster LRT aired an online documentary called *Spalvos* ("Colors"), including segments glamorizing "same-sex parenting."

In France, both the Ministry of National Education and the Inter-ministerial Delegation to Racism and Antisemitism (which has now been extended to "the fight against LGBTphobia")[84] have funded "civil society projects informing the public of SOGIE-based violence." From 2013–2014, a program called "ABCD de l'égalité" was piloted by the Moroccan-born Najat Vallaud-Belkacem, who was then-Women's Rights Minister, with the aim of "combat[ting] gender stereotypes and promot[ing] gender equality, starting from preschool." So-called LGBTphobia has been included in civic education since 2015. The National Assembly has now dispensed with gender altogether and voted in favor of amending the School of Trust Bill, mandating schools replace "mother" and "father" on official forms with the terms "parent one" and "parent two."

The perversion/destruction of the family and anti-natalism for whites are just aspects of the overall aim, however. The desired end result is as the Jewish Marxist-feminist Shulamith Firestone declared in her 1970 book *The Dialectic of Sex: The Case for Feminist Revolution* that—in addition to the idea that we should look to technological developments to "free women from childbirth" which she likened to "shitting a pumpkin"—"the end goal of feminist revolution must be . . . not just the elimination of male privilege but of the sex distinction itself: genital differences between human beings would no longer matter culturally," then "the tyranny of the biological family would be broken," "unobstructed pansexuality" would reign, and "all forms of sexuality would be allowed and indulged [including pedophilia]. . . . Unless revolution uproots the basic social organization, the biological family . . . the tapeworm of exploitation will never be annihilated." This is what the Judaized "Queer Utopia" looks like.

Ideologically, the one thing that binds all of these disparate causes is animus for traditional Western cultures and societies and the Whites who created them. Perhaps nothing so clearly evidences this ugly truth as the recent glorification of Thierry Paulin, a gay, black, HIV-positive, transvestite serial killer in France. Originally from Martinique, Paulin's attempt at a military career was frustrated by criminal inclinations such as menacing and robbing an elderly woman in her own grocery store in 1982. Paulin eventually became a drag performer at Paradis Latin in Paris, and soon after met drug addict Jean-Thierry Mathurin, an immigrant from French Guiana. The two became lovers, sold drugs, and committed an escalating series of crimes; the two committed a spate of murders at the tail end of 1984, using the victims' stolen money and goods to finance a lavish lifestyle of partying and cocaine.

Eventually the pair broke up and Paulin committed still more murders before spending a year in prison for attacking his cocaine dealer with a baseball bat in the fall of 1986. In prison, Paulin contracted HIV and went on a last hurrah rampage and partying binge after his release before being positively identified by an elderly woman who had miraculously survived one of his attacks. Paulin was apprehended and confessed to everything, also implicating Mathurin. All told, Paulin claimed to have murdered twenty-one elderly French women before succumbing to AIDS-related complications in prison in 1989 before his trial date. Mathurin was convicted of seven murders and one attempted murder, yet he only served a little over twenty years in prison, having been released in 2009. Paulin told police, "I only tackled the weakest of them." Some of the victims had been beaten to death, some had their heads stuck into plastic bags, and one was forced to drink drain cleaner. Still, the more of these people the merrier for the ruling class.

---

[84] See Appendix B for the list of measures.

## Case Study: Cruel Britannia

*"We have always been kin: kin in blood, kin in religion, kin in representative government, kin in ideals, kin in just and lofty purposes; and now we are kin in sin, the harmony is complete, the blend is perfect."*

– Mark Twain

BBC Radio 4's Today ran a feature on "trans kids" as part of their news item on Obama's letter instructing American schools to allow "transgender students" to use the bathroom of their choice on May 13th, 2016. Ten days later, on the evening of May 23rd, BBC Radio 4 followed up: "This episode of Analysis won't attempt to deconstruct gender, nor will it try to define exactly what gender is and where it comes from: what it will do is explore the concept of non-binary." The Director of the Tavistock and Portman NHS Foundation Trust's Gender Identity Development Service (GIDS), a "highly specialised clinic for young people presenting with difficulties with their gender identity," stated that non-binary may include some hormones but no surgery, "challenging . . . pre-conceived ideas of 'this is male, this is female.'" The Director, Polly Carmichael, was interviewed by *Vice* later that year with a smug dismissal of concerns over Carmichael's work as "tabloid scare stories" and that:

> Dr. Polly Carmichael helps children as young as three experiencing gender dysphoria. . . . In 1989, when the clinic opened, it got two referrals over the whole year. In the year 2015/16, it had more than 1,400—double the year before. The waiting list for her clinic has risen from up to 18 weeks to nine months.

On December 8th, 2011, the UK government officially launched its first ever "transgender action plan." The plan committed government departments including the Department of Health and Social Care, the Department for Work and Pensions, the UK Border Agency, and the Government Equalities Office, among others, "to work actively towards promoting human rights and equality in the lives of trans people." The NHS's position on transgenderism is: "We now believe that gender identity is on a spectrum, with male at one end, female at the other and a 'diversity' of gender identities in between. These can include male and female, non-binary or even agender (no gender)." The NHS links to something called Tranzwiki, which is "a comprehensive directory of the groups campaigning for, supporting or assisting trans and gender non-conforming individuals, including those who are non-binary and non-gender, as well as their families across the UK." It has been developed by the Gender Identity Research and Education Society (GIRES) to "support the trans community but its content is determined by a broad range of stakeholders."

GIRES, which provided the funding for WPATH to translate its standards of care into numerous other languages, is funded in large part by the National Lottery Community Fund (also known as the Big Lottery Fund)[85] and they have a charitable donation deal with AmazonSmile. Additional funding comes from LGBT "catalyst and connector" organization The National LGB&T Partnership, which is a Sector Strategic Partner of the Department of Health and Social Care, Public Health England, and NHS England, "collaborating with a wide range of organisations as part of the Health and Wellbeing Alliance," which also includes "diversity"-centric Race Equality Foundation and Friends Families and Travellers which focuses on gypsies. Its other partnering organizations include Yorkshire MESMAC, Stonewall Housing, Metro Charity, LGBT Foundation, London Friend, LGBT Consortium, the Health Equality and Rights Organization (HERO), Birmingham LGBT, and ELOP (East London's LGBT Center). The National LGB&T Partnership has a close working relationship with the National LGBT Health Adviser, which is an official position in the NHS.

The "charity" Mermaids, which advocates for the introduction of sex hormones to children, was part of a group of organizations establishing a five-year project in 2019 to "reduce discrimination in key public services" funded by the National Lottery Community Fund; founding partners included Stonewall, All About Trans, the Gender Identity Research and Education Society (GIRES), and Gendered Intelligence. Stonewall states that:

> The UK is miles behind countries like Ireland, Malta, Norway and Argentina who have already done away with medical tests and bureaucracy, and have a system based on self-declaration. There are no down-sides, for example when Ireland did it, nobody else was affected.

They also state that "the age to access gender recognition" should be lowered.

Starbucks created the winning entry to the 2019 Channel 4 Diversity in Advertising Award "focusing on the representation of LGBT+ individuals in advertising" with their #whatsyourname campaign in conjunction with Mermaids. Additionally, Starbucks has made a "limited edition Mermaids Cookie." Amazon has also partnered with and donated to Mermaids, and a £500,000 grant in February 2019 from the National Lottery Community Fund went to Mermaids specifically as well. Other donors include the BBC's Children in Need, the Department for Education, the Tudor Trust, the Henry Smith Charity, and the Paul Hamlyn Foundation. Alexandria Ocasio-Cortez and Chelsea Manning appeared on an online stream of a man playing a Nintendo game, which raised hundreds of thousands of dollars for this "charity." "Trans model" Munroe Bergdorf, LGBTQ adviser for the Labour Party, is also a Mermaids patron; according to Bergdorf:

---

[85] Another National Lottery charitable arm, the National Lottery Heritage Fund has "invested" (its word) "over £5 million across the UK in sharing stories of LGBT+ (lesbian, gay, bisexual, trans and others) heritage, creativity, activism and much more" over the past several decades.

Honestly I don't have energy to talk about the racial violence of white people any more. Yes ALL white people. Because most of ya'll don't even realise or refuse to acknowledge that your existence, privilege and success as a race is built on the backs, blood and death of people of colour. Your entire existence is drenched in racism. From micro-aggression to terrorism, you guys built the blueprint for this shit.

Feminist bookstore The Second Shelf in London, which only sells books by female authors, announced it will donate to Mermaids every time someone purchases a book by JK Rowling. Mermaids' trustee and treasurer Stephen Ellis is also the COO for the Commercial Banking Markets business at Lloyds Banking Group. Mermaids' Paul Devlin is a Non-Executive Director and Trust Chair in the NHS, which as Douglas Murray recounts in *The Madness of Crowds* is essentially an assembly line for gender reassignment/sex change surgeries.

Then we have this little horror story regarding the UK's National Health Service (NHS) *The Mail on Sunday* reported in 2014:

Children as young as nine will be given controversial drugs on the NHS to prepare them for sex-swap surgery. . . . The drugs, known as hypothalamic blockers, stunt the development of sexual organs so less surgery is required if a child chooses to change sex after reaching adolescence. Monthly injections into the stomach suppress the production of testosterone and oestrogen. In girls that halts the menstrual cycle and the development of breasts. In boys, they stop facial hair growing and voice changes. Doctors at The Tavistock And Portman NHS Foundation Trust in North London have just completed a three-year trial involving 12- to 14-year-olds, assessing the 'psychological, social and physical benefits and risks involved. . . .' The clinic was first given public funding in 2009. . . . Because the trial was deemed such a success, medics have decided to make the drugs more widely available – and to much younger children. Supporters of the injection treatment say the drugs give children who are confused about their gender a much-needed 'window' before they take on too many masculine or feminine features. . . . The best-known brand of blocker is Gonapeptyl, which costs £82 per dose, and possible side-effects include depression, rashes, asthma and ovarian cysts. . . . One particularly influential campaign group is the Gender Identity Research and Education Society (GIRES), founded in 2010 by Bernard and Terry Reed, whose adult daughter is a transsexual. The group's influence extends to giving policy advice to the NHS, the Association of Chief Police Officers, the Crown Prosecution Service, the Department for Children, Schools and Families, and the Home Office. . . . There are now about 150 transgender support groups in Britain. Those diagnosed with gender dysphoria can be prioritised by local councils for housing as 'vulnerable people. . . .' So, is NHS right to offer this treatment to 9-year-olds? Yes, says Susie Green chair of Mermaids.

In "honor" of LGBT History Month 2019, Schools OUT UK collaborated with the Proud Trust ("Home of LGBT+ Youth"; Stephen Whittle is a patron, as are lesbian actress Alicia Eyo and Ben Copperwheat, who has "created textile collections and brand direction for Gucci, Calvin Klein, Tommy Hilfiger, Peter Som, Edun, Pret A

Surf, Victorinox Swiss Army, Stephen Burrows, 3.1 Phillip Lim, DKNY, and Daryl K; his work is commissioned by personalities and organizations like Beyoncé and Blue Ivy, Boy George, Liza Minnelli, Pat Cleveland, Isabella Blow, and David Collins Studio") to produce a "Peace, Reconciliation and Activism Resource and Education Pack." The project was funded by the UK Government Equalities Office, the Paul Hamlyn Foundation, the Tudor Trust, and the Co-op Foundation.

The Co-op Foundation announced on its website its commitment in June 2018 to the #iwill campaign:

> To get six out of 10 young people involved in social action like campaigning, fundraising or volunteering by 2020. . . . The #iwill Fund is made possible through investment from the National Lottery Community Fund and Department for Digital, Culture, Media and Sport. £1m from the #iwill Fund is being matched by £1m from the Co-op Foundation. We've already funded 10 projects – including the Proud Trust.

The #iwill Fund is an England-wide joint investment that brings together £40 million in funding, creating a central investment pot.

The foreword to the 2019 activism packet (which celebrates the work of Magnus Hirschfeld) was written by Phyll Opoku-Gyimah, pictured holding up a black power fist and wearing a Black Panthers-style beret. Opoku-Gyimah writes:

> As LGBT+ people our activism must be intersectional, so that we can remove these barriers of oppression and the barriers to participation for all LGBT+ people and people who like us, are also pushed to the margins of our society. . . We must reflect on the way we amplify ours and others voices to eradicate and dismantle structural and systematic LGBTphobia, but also racism, sexism and misogyny too. We must work to erase the discrimination against disabled people, organise against the poverty young people face on a day-to-day basis and stop the hate fuelled at Muslim people.

No word on the up to one million girls systematically groomed and raped by Muslims in the country, nor of the ruling class's tacit support for it.

"Activism examples" from the packet include ACT UP (which invited NAMBLA to march with them in 1994), UK Black Pride, Black Lives Matter, Mermaids, Muslims for Progressive Values, Never Going Underground, and #StandByYourTrans and #LwiththeT.

Labour MP Zarah Sultana states with pitch-perfect NPC programming that, "Trans women are women, trans men are men, and trans rights are human rights. The whole Labour movement should be clear about this." LGBT+ Labour is a "proud supporter" of the Black Lives Matter "movement," by the way, stating that "there is no LGBT+ liberation without black liberation" and that they "believe it is the role of white people, and those whose ethnicity puts them in closer proximity to whiteness to use their privilege to amplify black voices and advocate for change." With this spectrum, black being the antithesis of white. Are you seeing how this works? As Tim Dams wrote in *Variety*:

U.K. TV channels and radio stations are changing their programmes to mark "Blackout Tuesday", following George Floyd's death in police custody. Channel 4-owned 4 Music said it will pause its output once an hour throughout the day, and cease activity on its other platforms. "This a day to pause business as usual, take the time to reflect on recent events, and start a meaningful conversation around how to actively support and achieve progress for the whole black community," said 4Music on Twitter today. ITV daytime show "This Morning" briefly went dark today, showing a black screen with the words "Black Lives Matter". Host Phillip Schofield read out the message: "ITV say 'We stand in solidarity with our black colleagues, storytellers and viewers around the world because #BlackLivesMatter #BlackOutTuesday.'" Meanwhile, ViacomCBS's UK services MTV, BET, Comedy Central and Paramount Network will go dark across their platforms, including linear broadcast, at 7pm BST on Wednesday for 8 minutes and 46 seconds – the length of time it took for George Floyd to die.

Rothschild & Co seeks to amplify this change with its official networks; its UK Balance & Inclusion Committee has supported the creation of: the Rothschild & Co Women's Network; the LGBT Network; and the Ethnic Minorities Network. "The Committees work in conjunction with management to represent the interests of our employee communities." In October 2019, the UK Ethnic Minorities Network hosted a "fireside chat with a well-known author in celebration of Black History Month. The discussion focused on race, identity, and belonging in the UK [do they ever talk about anything else?]. The event was open to all internal colleagues and selected external networks." Once again showing the "intersectional"—oppositional would be more appropriate—nature of this project, per their website:

Rothschild & Co is a member of Stonewall, Britain's best practice forum on sexual orientation in the workplace which acts as a thought leader for our work in the LGBTQ space in the UK. We have an active network who also participate in a broader City network called the Interbank Forum, where members can collaborate on events and share ideas to promote LGBTQ inclusion in the industry. In 2019, the UK Graduate Recruitment Team launched its Horizon Women and Pioneer programmes. The team welcomed 40 sixth form students (67% female) from 36 different diverse UK schools. This year the UK Graduate Recruitment team have selected Bright Network as their Early Careers Media Partner. Bright Network helps companies attract a diverse range of candidates, from traditionally underrepresented groups. Their mission is to connect the next generation with the opportunities, insights and advice needed to succeed as the workforce of tomorrow. This is achieved by raising the profile of Rothschild & Co on the Bright Network website and at specific diversity events attended by undergraduates from a range of universities and subjects. Through this connection we connect with 200,000 Bright Network student members, of which 76% are state educated, 59% are female, 26% STEM, 40% BAME and 85% study outside London. During the next recruitment season we will participate in events for Women in Leadership, Black Heritage Future Leaders and the LGBT + Proud to B.

I am not a woman, nor do I play one on television, but I would imagine it is positively infuriating to continually see your sex grouped in the oppositional army, in much the same way it would be for any member of these groups who object to the globalist project to see their identities weaponized to produce such abjectly awful outcomes.

Allies of the globalist axis recruiting (importing) these "BAME folks" into the country in the first place has been particularly enriching, depending of course on who you are: HIV treatment consumes £1 in every £200 spent on the NHS in England, for a £606 million figure—and this HIV figure does not include money spent on testing. Since 2012, all HIV-positive patients have been able to receive anti-retrovirals for free from the NHS, but what's more, according to *The Daily Mail*, a mere 44% of HIV patients were born in the UK (not all of whom will be actual Britons), 35% come from Africa, and the remaining 21% were born in other parts of the world. How do you like that?

The reality necessitates propaganda; according to the Open Society Foundations' "License to be Yourself":

> In 1998, the producers of the long-running British soap opera Coronation Street created a trans character, Hayley. Trans activists in Press for Change applauded the move but criticized the original scripts for depicting clichéd and ill-informed stereotypes of trans women. Activists' offer to provide background advice was accepted and a trans community member went on to create a back story for Hayley and her partner Roy. During the gender recognition campaign this brought important timely debates, such as Hayley and Roy being unable to marry, into millions of people's homes.

Press for Change works closely with Transgender Europe, the Scottish Transgender Alliance, the Equality and Human Rights Commission, and the Gender Recognition Panel.

Trans Media Watch (TMW) seeks to "improve media coverage of trans people in order to foster social acceptance and civil recognition for trans persons." TMW, in conjunction with Channel 4, created the memorandum of understanding regarding media coverage and presentation of trans people, which pledges to remove all "transphobic" content and prevent negative coverage; very clearly this amounts to censorship and propaganda. Speaking of censorship, under the provisions of the Hate Crime and Public Order Bill in Scotland:

> Part 1 makes provision relating to the aggravation of offences by prejudice. It provides that a criminal offence is aggravated if either: the offender evinces malice and ill-will towards the victim based on the victim's membership of a group defined by reference to a listed characteristic, or the offence is motivated (wholly or partly) by malice and ill-will towards any such group. The listed characteristics are age, disability, race (and related characteristics), religion, sexual orientation, transgender identity and variations in sex characteristics. Part 2 creates offences of stirring up hatred against a group of persons based on the group being defined by reference to a listed characteristic. It also creates offences of possessing inflammatory material with a view to communicating the material in circumstances where there is an intention to

stir up hatred or it is likely that hatred would be stirred up. The listed characteristics are the same as those in Part 1.

The University of Leicester's Centre for Hate Studies "bridges the gap between academic research and professional practice" and has conducted "a tailored programme of work with LGB and T communities in Leicester and Leicestershire with the aim of encouraging greater levels of reporting." The National LGBT Hate Crime Partnership is "a unique partnership of LGBT voluntary and community organisations from across England and Wales that has come together to tackle and prevent homophobic, biphobic and transphobic (HBT) hate crime and incidents." Both serve the purpose of quite literally policing Wrongthink, as "hate crime and incidents" involve *perceived* bias, which can occur online as well.

Stop Hate UK is yet another organization dedicated to bludgeoning the population into submission; supporting, funding, and/or partnering organizations include the Anne Frank Trust UK, Migration Yorkshire, the Ministry of Justice, West Yorkshire Police, Lloyds Bank Foundation of England and Wales, the National Holocaust Centre and Museum, North Yorkshire Police, and many more.

Returning to TMW's propaganda efforts, they also worked with the BBC in establishing the Trans Comedy Award. Trans Media Action, which is now called All About Trans, was launched in 2011 as a joint initiative between Channel 4, the BBC, and TMW; its purpose is to "positively change how the media understands and portrays trans people" and to "promote trans voices in the media." It currently receives most of its funding from the Paul Hamlyn Foundation and the Esmée Fairbairn Foundation; its most visible member, Paris Lees, has been given major platforms on BBC Radio One and Channel 4, and in the pages of *Vogue*, *Vice*, and *The Guardian*, among other outlets. Lees produced a documentary called *The Hate Debate* which gave way to *My Transgender Punk Rock Story* interviewing Laura Jane Grace né Thomas James Gabel of anarcho-punk band Against Me! These documentaries were clearly targeting a young audience and were instrumental in "introducing the teenage audience to trans concepts of identity both within and outside of the binary." It's *so* punk rock to serve as a spokesperson for the globalist Establishment's agenda. Anarchy in the UK!

The "charity" Gendered Intelligence's members include "Radical Transfeminists," and they've worked with the Football Association "to develop guidance around the practical inclusion of all trans people in football." They created a "trans history" display at the Science Museum with funding from the National Lottery Heritage Fund, oversaw the creation of the *Transvengers* web comic put together by teenagers as young as thirteen for the Institute of Sexology exhibition at the Wellcome Collection, and they've also produced plays and "circus productions." The whole damn planet is a circus production with these people.

There is a veritable plethora of other organizations, many of which focus on "youth" and/or some variant of intersectionality. YPAS offers "a range of support and therapeutic services for children aged 5–15 years, young people aged 16–25 years and their families in Liverpool." The UK Lesbian & Gay Immigration Group (UKLGIG):

Supports LGBTQI+ people through the asylum and immigration system [and] provide[s] legal advice and psychosocial support to people who are claiming asylum [with] a monthly legal advice meeting for LGBTQI+ people who are making partnership applications.

The X2Y LGBT Youth Group runs two LGBT+ youth groups, one for 11–17-year-olds and another for 18–25-year-olds that meet in the center of Wolverhampton on a weekly basis.

Out of the Can LGBT Youth Group is an LGBT youth group for young people aged between 13–19 years old. xQ Enterprises Ltd (Extraqueericular.com) focuses on: "BME/Black People, LGBT+ People, and Non-UK Residents." *Transgender Love* is a "documentary following six trans men and women in Scotland as they struggle to find love and maintain existing relationship," aired on BBC Scotland and BBC One. Success Capital is:

A proudly African and unapologetically LGBTIQ+ Youth led, managed and serving organisation that links grassroots experiences with global and regional mechanisms. . . . Success Capital's work is centered on three pillars: a) participatory decolonized knowledge production, b) peer to peer systemic knowledge sharing and c) supporting variant forms of civic action and participation.

The Rainbow Reading Group is an LGBT Reading Group, organized by the Croydon Area Gay Society (CAGS) in conjunction with Croydon Library. The list is basically endless.

In February 2020, the British Library in London hosted a "suitable for all ages" event called *Marvellous and Mischievous: Literature's Young Rebels*, which featured "sensory storytellings for under 3's," the Jewish Michael Rosen reading "his most rebellious stories and poems," and *three* separate Drag Queen Story Times. An image from official UK Drag Queen Story Hour Twitter account (rainbow-colored, of course) is shown right:

Drag Queen Story Hour UK
@DragStoryHourUK

Love has no age!

2:15 AM · Jul 26, 2020 · Integromat

Also in February 2020, Scottish Member of Parliament Mhairi Black and a drag queen performer going by the moniker Flow Job visited Glencoats Primary School in Paisley to read to four- and five-year-olds, and when this was met with parental outrage, Black took to Twitter to declare that (sic):

You just know that the people pretending to be livid that a drag queen read a book in a school in my mentions rn are also the people who run out to buy their kids the latest Grand Theft Auto on release day. Your homophobia is transparent.

Drag "performer" Ivy Adamas was set to visit the Dunbar Grammar School at approximately the same time before Richard Lucas of the Scottish Family Party learned of the scheduled performance and notified the headteacher of the nature of Adamas's performances, prompting a cancelation: "Of concern are the blood-stained dress, foul language, graphic sexual vulgarity ('I want to eat your d&*%' etc.), overtly sexual movements (such as masturbatory motions), crude fake female genitals, and the extraction of a condom from his mouth." Was it that the school did not look into Adamas, or that Lucas publicized the material of Adamas's performances?

The Jewish Museum in London in 2016 featured Through a Queer Lens, described:

> The first comprehensive series of photographic portraits of Jewish LGBTQ (Lesbian, Gay, Bisexual, Trans and Queer) people. The twenty portraits, by fine art photographer Ajamu, feature well-known faces including Yotam Ottolenghi and Rabbi Lionel Blue as well as leading artists, activists and entrepreneurs. The exhibition celebrates the diversity of Jewish and LGBTQ people living in the UK.

In addition to KeshetUK, other prominent Jewish LGBTQ organizations in the UK include: the Jewish LGBT+ Group; Imahot v'Avot, "a social group for families who have one or more parent who identify as Jewish and Lesbian, Gay, Bisexual, Transgender, Queer, or Questioning (LGBTQQ)"; and Laviot, "a community of queer, Jewish women which fills a gap in the social landscape." With funding from the National Lottery Heritage Fund and hosted by Liberal Judaism, an associated member of the World Congress of GLBT Jews: Keshet Ga'avah, Rainbow Jews— "a pioneering project that records and showcases Jewish lesbian, gay, bisexual and transgender (LGBT) history from the 1950s to today"—took form. Additional support was provided by the London Metropolitan Archives and homosexual Jewish lecturer at the University of Portsmouth Searle Kochberg.

In 2018, the World Congress of GLBT Jews: Keshet Ga'avah "supported equality language in the United Nations International Crimes Against Humanity Treaty" and the year following supported the United Nations mandate to "address violence and discrimination on the basis of sexual orientation and gender identity." As Luna Lara Liboni writes regarding the 2018 conference held in Rome:

> The main theme of the congress —"Minorities Alone – Strong Together"– recalls the importance of the dialogue and cooperation among minorities in the fight against stigma and discrimination experienced by LGBT people and Jews in Europe and in the rest of the world. . . . As for antisemitism, it has now been confirmed that the holocaust survivor Mireille Knoll was brutally murdered in France due to an antisemitic attack. . . .[86] A whole panel was then dedicated to the importance of the cooperation between Jewish and Muslim LGBT activists and communities.

According to President Goldy Goldberg, "To truly proclaim our support for both our Jewish and LGBTQI+ families, we must raise our voices in tikkun olam and support

---

[86] By a Muslim immigrant.

the 'Black Lives Matter' movement." Speaking about Vice President Gustavo Michanie:

> [He] works tirelessly as an activist for the Diversity and Inclusion Cause in Argentina and has been working for more than 15 years in the creation and operation of JAG (Jewish Argentine Gays). . . . In 2014, JAG was acknowledged and included in the most representative Jewish Institution of Argentina, DAIA (Argentine Delegation of Israel Associations), and in November 2018, Gustavo was elected as a member of its Board.

Officer-at-Large in the Western Hemisphere Ian M. Brown is an active duty US Army Major and serves as the Headquarters and Headquarters Company Commander in the US Army Cyber Command. They have member organizations across the US as well as in Mexico City, Buenos Aires, Winnipeg, Sydney, Rome, Berlin, London, Paris, and Amsterdam. Another Officer-at-Large for the Western Hemisphere, Laura Weinstein is described as:

> A prominent Colombian trans activist who has been working for 22 years to defend and guarantee the rights of LGBT people in Bogotá, Colombia, focusing primarily on the Trans population. Passionate about equal rights and justice for all, Laura also fights for women rights, the rights of Afro descendent people, family, LGBT childhood, and protecting the lives of human rights leaders. She is the Executive Director of GAAT, a Group of Support and Action for Trans People as well as founder and member of the Trans Aquelarre Trans network. Laura is a representative for Trans People before The National Board dealing with HIV, Sexual and Reproductive Health and she worked as a consultant for the Urgent Action Fund. Through her affiliations and efforts, decree 1227 of 2015 was passed, which modifies the law that regulates the civil registry in Colombia so that Trans people can have their names, sex and identification number written down according to their needs.

Urgent Action Fund Board member Mariam Gagoshashavili conducted "grassroots queer feminist organizing" in the country of Georgia before re-locating to the United States and has an MA in Gender Studies from George Soros's Central European University.[87] Another Board member, Ruth Baldacchino, is described as:

> A trans, queer and feminist activist from Malta with extensive experience in community organising, international LGBTIQ activism and LGBTIQ research. Their human rights work started with the Malta LGBTIQ Rights Movement. Ruth is currently ILGA World Co-Secretary General and has served on a number of boards including the International Lesbian, Gay, Bisexual, Transgender, Queer & Intersex Youth and Student Organization (IGLYO), ILGA World and ILGA-Europe.

---

[87] From the "Central European University" Wikipedia entry: "CEU was founded in 1991 by hedge fund manager, political activist, and philanthropist George Soros, who provided the university with an $880 million endowment, making the university one of the wealthiest in Europe. A central tenet of the university's mission is the promotion of open societies." The University was not allowed to continue operations in Hungary due to subversive activities and subsequently re-located to Austria.

Baldacchino helms the Intersex Human Rights Fund at the Astraea Lesbian Foundation for Justice and further:

> Worked on trans, intersex, migrants integration in Malta and co-developed an education policy for trans, gender diverse and intersex children in Malta, making Malta the first country in Europe to publish a comprehensive education policy focusing specifically on trans and intersex children.

In Malta, from ILGA-Europe's "Annual Review 2020":

> In April [2019], MGRM [Malta LGBTIQ Rights Movement] issued its report of the 2017 Malta National School Climate Survey, partnered with GLSEN and Columbia University, finding an urgent need for a safe and affirming learning environment for LGBTI students. The report also highlights the positive impact of supportive staff, inclusive policies and curricula. The SOGIGESC Unit is working with the Directorates of Education on a pilot intra-curricular programme with two volunteer middle schools, the plan [is] to extend the program to all middle schools. . . . In July [2019], the Equality Act and Human Rights and Equality Commission Act were tabled in Parliament. The Act reached the Committee stage, but is expected to be adopted in 2020. *The Equality Act aims to ensure legal certainty and elevate the principle of equality to a right in itself, and make it applicable to all spheres of life* (emphasis added). The Bill also implements the Twelfth Protocol to the European Convention into national law. Once passed, the Equality Act will provide for anti-discrimination measures outside of employment on a range of grounds including sexual orientation, gender identity, gender expression and sex characteristics, as well as providing for cases to be brought on intersectional grounds [so they are literally codifying intersectionality into law]. . . . On 7 January [2019], the government presented Malta's new guidelines Transgender Healthcare Services, an outcome of lengthy consultations with civil society and other key stakeholders. . . . Care will be provided by a multidisciplinary team, including pediatric experts to ensure that the needs of trans children and youth are met. . . . Malta's first Gender Wellbeing Clinic, which opened in 2018, has been successfully running and providing services to trans people, including counseling, hormone therapy and other gender affirming healthcare. . . . The Ministry for European Affairs and Equality instructed the police to refer to individuals in gender neutral terms in their media reports, to avoid misgendering trans people or exposing their gender assigned at birth without their consent. . . . As part of Malta's second LGBTIQ Equality Strategy and Action Plan (2018–2022), the government launched the All Welcome campaign in June. This campaign encouraged businesses to register through the Equality Ministry and attend an information session, to receive a sticker they can post by their entrance to show that they are LGBTI-friendly. The reaction from the community was mostly negative.

So once again, we see popular support for these initiatives is simply not there. People understand that this is being forced upon them and has nothing to do with "equality" in the sense that it is generally understood. We also see the insistence on sexualizing and pushing transgenderism on children, and the disingenuousness of including intersex, and again and again we see support at the highest levels of government, "philanthropy," education, et cetera for transgenderism, the sexualization and mutilation of children, the obliteration of family, tradition, and decency, and everything else under the noxious umbrella of this project including wholesale population replacement. This is made even more galling by the flat tone with which these measures are described and the euphemisms used.

Returning to the UK's own brand of intersectional hell, Living Free UK "supports and validates the lived experiences of LGBT Africans, Asylum Seekers and Refugees through our interventions and events throughout the year." The Baring Foundation, based out of London, has committed itself to "empowering LGBTI communities in sub-Saharan Africa" and other LGBTQ and "human rights" causes; of central importance to their International Development program is to facilitate and provide funding from UK sources to sub-Saharan African groups advancing the LGBTQ agenda. They also do this work domestically; in 2017, the Baring Foundation provided a grant to Stonewall for a "dedicated post to advocate for the mainstreaming of the UK Department for International Development's (DFID) LGBT approach across its new funding programme, UK Aid Connect." Through UK Aid Connect, "DFID wants to bring . . . together in coalitions that address key development challenges in the following priority thematic areas" including "promoting sexual and reproductive health and rights, disability inclusion, . . . building open societies, . . . [and] addressing lesbian, gay, bisexual and transgender inclusion."

Among the recent Baring Foundation grants are included LGBTQ-specific grants and a variety of other neo-liberal causes and organization grants, especially those pertaining to feminism and mass migration. In 2020, grants included £50,000 over two years to All Out "to support activities to foster empowerment for queer African women"; £25,000 to Pan Africa ILGA; £100,000 over three years to Social, Health and Empowerment Feminist Collective; and £130,000 over three years to Gender Dynamix in South Africa.

Some of the Baring Foundation's 2019 grants included: £10,000 "to enable ISDAO to support the attendance of West African trans activists at the International Conference of AIDS and STIs in Africa (ICASA) taking place in Kigali in December 2019"; £25,000 "to support the Global Feminist LBQ Conference in Cape Town, South Africa"; and £40,000 to Gender Dynamix. In 2018, the Baring Foundation granted £35,000 over six months to the OTHER Foundation, £40,000 over two years to the Kaleidoscope Trust, £30,000 to All Out, £105,000 over three years to Synergia, £20,000 over eighteen months to the Astraea Lesbian Foundation for Justice, £25,000 to Pan Africa ILGA, and £60,000 over three years to Global Dialogue "to develop and implement a UK based LGBTI donor community with and for existing and future donors, tailored to their passions and needs supporting equal rights and quality of lives for LGBTI people globally."

Baring has also dispensed hundreds of thousands of pounds to develop and support the operations of Initiative Sankofa D'Afrique de L'Ouest, "the first West African Lesbian, Gay, Bisexual, Trans* and Queer (LGBTQ) Activist-Led Fund dedicated to strengthening and supporting a West African movement for gender diversity and sexual rights." The Baring Foundation has also dispensed funds to the Human Dignity Trust, which has "mobilised more than £12 million of pro bono technical legal assistance to support local activists, civil society organisations and decriminal-isation efforts across five continents." The Baring Foundation financed the Human Dignity Trust's "Injustice Exposed: The Criminalisation of Transgender People and its Impacts," a 136-page report insisting that trans and "gender diverse" people are being "criminalized," which, evidently "fuels the HIV epidemic in the trans commu-nity." I'm not so sure about that.

The Baring Foundation collaborates with the Legal Education Foundation and the Esmée Fairbairn Foundation on its Strengthening Civil Society program initia-tives; the Esmée Fairbairn Foundation is "committed to social change" and has dis-pensed £45.4 million over hundreds of "social change" grants. Their endowment is over £1 billion and also encompasses other arms of "activism." They have a number of "diversity"- and immigration-focused grants and partnerships with various organ-izations such as: the Immigration Law Practitioners' Association to cover "the costs of the Strategic Legal Fund which supports efforts to uphold and promote the rights of vulnerable migrant children and young people"; Global Dialogue, "towards the co-ordination and activity costs of the Migration Exchange network"; Operation Black Vote; the Scottish Refugee Council; Refugee Action; Migrant Voice; City of Sanctuary; Migrants Law Project; Asylum Support Appeals Project; Funders for Ra-cial Equality; Equality and Diversity Forum; Islington Law Center; and Women for Refugee Women. Regarding the LGBTQ agenda specifically, they've granted funds to the following among many others:

- Tonic Housing: an investment towards an LGBT+ older persons housing community
- HERe NI: towards work to support lesbian and bi-sexual women in North-ern Ireland and influence policy and practice to protect their rights and increase their visibility
- New Family Social: towards core costs to raise the profile of LGBT adopters/fosterers and enable the development and dissemination of best practice to reduce prejudice within the adoption/fostering systems and so-ciety

The Esmée Fairbairn Foundation has also given the Paul Hamlyn Foundation over £1 million, and the Paul Hamlyn Foundation and Esmée Fairbairn Foundation work in partnership on projects such as the Act for Change Fund; this particular partner-ship works jointly with the National Lottery Community Fund and is matched by their managed and co-funded #iwill Fund. For more about this Fund, its website in-forms that:

The #iwill Fund launched in November 2016 to support the #iwill campaign's goals in England, aiming to make social action part of life for as many 10 to 20 year-olds as possible by the year 2020. . . . The #iwill Fund is managed by The National Lottery Community Fund and overseen by a Leadership Board that's made up of representatives from Government, The National Lottery Community Fund and Step Up To Serve (the charity coordinating the #iwill campaign). . . . When people are in the lead, communities thrive and this funding through DCMS [the Department for Digital, Culture, Media and

Sport] and The National Lottery Community Fund supports young people to make a difference in their community.

CEO Rania Marandos, like Pete Buttigieg, is a McKinsey alumnus. Another #iwill project involves the Jewish Lads and Girls Brigade, which are:

> Jointly investing £1.8 million into this three year project, where JLGB plan to expand and develop their existing Evolve programme in order to build a self-sustaining, community-wide, collective impact project that supports young people who face intrinsic barriers to participation. This work will be underpinned by an online platform that provides training, social action opportunities, awards, and qualifications in a trusted and culture sensitive way.

Evolve's funders include the Jewish Youth Fund and the Maurice Wohl Charitable Foundation, which "gives charitable grants intended to bring about change in key areas in the UK, with a particular focus on the advancement of medical sciences, Jewish community welfare and Jewish education."

The Paul Hamlyn Foundation, named after its founder the publishing magnate Paul Hamlyn who "was a migrant, fleeing persecution in Nazi Germany" (read: Jewish),[88] spends huge sums on organizations committed to mass immigration into the UK as well as weaponizing "diversity" for those non-Britons already on the Isles against the native British.[89] They support the Migration Exchange network, Right to Remain, and Asylos, among many others, and help fund the University of Oxford's Centre on Migration, Policy and Society (COMPAS). The Foundation also provides hundreds of grants to groups in India and they have a "teacher development fund" for the UK. They have also collaborated with Lankelly Chase, Tudor Trust, Lloyds Bank Foundation for England and Wales, and City Bridge Trust, among other organizations. Total expenditures "in furtherance of our charitable purpose" in 2018/19 was £37.4 million and the Foundation has over six hundred active grants; at the end of 2018/19, total funds held amounted to £771.27 million.

There are huge numbers of these LGBTQ and LGBTQ-supporting organizations in the UK, but let's take a look at just a few more of them and their mission statements. One is called Deaf Lesbian, Gay, Bisexual, Transgender, Intersex, Queer and Asexual. House of Rainbow (HOR) "fosters relationships among Black, Asian, Minority Ethnic (BAME), Lesbian, Gay, Bisexual, Transgender, Intersex, Queer (LGBTIQ+) individuals, people of faith and allies in order to create a safer and a more inclusive community." Hidayah is described as:

> A nationwide organisation for LGBTQI+ Muslims. [They] run social and support groups in Manchester, London, Newcastle, Glasgow and Leeds to date. [They] also campaign for the visibility of LGBTQI+ Muslims and work

---

[88] As a not-insignificant side note, Hamlyn is far from the only Jewish "refugee" to arrive in Britain around this time and come to dominate the publishing world. Also included are George Weidenfeld, Andre Deutsch, and Ernest Hecht.

[89] "Diversity in our organisation is not a 'nice to have' – it is a business imperative, and our newly established staff Equality and Diversity Group will help us keep that realisation live." From their Trustees and Financial Statements 2018-19 Report.

on educational projects and research to highlight the voices of LGBTQI+ Muslims in the U.K.

The Inclusive Mosque Initiative:

> Is dedicated to creating safe and inclusive places of worship and spiritual practice, to the promotion of inclusive Islamic principles, and to centering and uplifting the voices and experiences of marginalised people within our communities. To us, that means having a critical awareness of the dynamics of power and privilege, and working against racism (including anti-black-ness, Islamophobia, anti-Semitism), homophobia, gender-based discrimina-tion, poverty, ableism, and environmental damage and all the ways these in-tersect. In particular, we express solidarity with immigrant, refugee, disabled, working-class and poor, Black and brown people, and we are critical of the State violence enacted on these communities through excessive surveillance, police brutality, the prison industrial complex, national borders, poverty and the Prevent duty, to name a few.

You read it here, folks: national borders are considered state violence. I think we can all see the direction all of these organizations are pointing, and as stated with the Yogyakarta Principles and the Black LGBTQ+ Migrant Project, this is in direct keeping with the United Nations' 2030 Agenda for Sustainable Development (the Sustainable Development Goals), the Green New Deal, and the Paris Agreement. It is also in keeping with the various linkages of "racism" and "inequality" to COVID-19 and again, this is because they are all of a piece.

Though not centered on the UK, a prime example would be the National Black Trans Advocacy Coalition, supported in part by AIDS United, ViiV Healthcare, the Human Rights Campaign, Borealis Philanthropy, the ACLU-Texas, Jordan Samuel Skin, and Gilead Sciences' COMPASS Initiative:

> In 2017, Gilead launched its COMPASS (COMmitment to Partnership in Ad-dressing HIV/AIDS in Southern States) Initiative, a 10-year, $100 million partnership with community-based organizations working to combat the HIV/AIDS epidemic in the Southern United States.

Another example is the National Queer and Trans Therapists of Color Network; il-lustrative are two members of its Advisory Board:

- Violeta Donawa: Violeta is a spirit, human, and black woman and femme invested in deep soul work, intergenerational trauma, and generative heal-ing. . . . Violeta [graduated] in December 2019 from the University of Michigan School of Social Work with an MSW focused on Interpersonal Practice and Mental Health. . . . In her personal and professional life, she has co-facilitated some of these conversations in community spaces, at universities and invited talks, and at the United Nations in Geneva, Swit-zerland. When Violeta is not in deep Sagittarian thought about holistic and integrated health, she is usually on the phone with her mom, cacklin' with other Black folx, or resting as resistance.

- Anjali Alimchandani: Ph.D., MPP, (pronouns: she/her) is an Indian American, cisgender, queer-identified psychologist, currently working in both the Homeless Patient Aligned Care Team and the Transgender Care Team at the Greater Los Angeles VA Medical Center (GLA VA), as well as in private practice. She completed her Ph.D. in Counseling Psychology at New York University in late 2015 and a Masters in Public Policy (MPP) at Harvard University in 2006. Her clinical and research passions include the provision of culturally responsive, justice informed psychotherapy for marginalized populations facing a multitude of complex mental and social health issues (PTSD, complex trauma, substance use disorders, psychosis, etc.), intersections of oppression with trauma and other mental health issues, contributing factors to resiliency within oppressed groups, and the intersections of psychology practice with social justice advocacy. In addition to helping develop the transgender care team services at the GLA VA, Anjali has provided multiple trainings/presentations on client-centered care for transgender and gender nonconforming (TGNC) individuals to psychiatry, psychology, and primary care staff members and residents/trainees at GLA VA, and is invited annually lecture on this topic for first-year medical students at the University of California, Los Angeles (UCLA) David Geffen School of Medicine. She held a Health Sciences Assistant Clinical Professor position at UCLA Geffen School of Medicine in 2018–2019 and is an Adjunct Assistant Professor position within the Marriage and Family Therapy (MFT) program at the University of Southern California (USC). Prior to coming to the field of psychology, Anjali worked in a variety of fields aimed at social justice promotion, including public policy/human rights advocacy, domestic violence prevention/response, international development, and direct social services with refugee and 'at-risk' youth. Her commitment to healing justice began in the wake of recognizing that in the context of structural oppression, healing, in and of itself, is a form of activism, that psychological healing and resilience are integral to building community-driven sustainable social justice movements, and that healing compassionate justice can liberate us all.

Founder and Executive Director Erica Woodland, who evidently uses "masculine pronouns":

> Is a black queer/genderqueer facilitator, consultant and healing justice practitioner born and raised in Baltimore, MD. He is also a Licensed Clinical Social Worker committed to working at the intersections of movements for racial, gender, economic, trans and queer justice and liberation. . . . From 2012–2016, Erica served as the Field Building Director for the Brown Boi Project, a national gender justice organization transforming the way communities of color experience gender. He has a private practice in the San Francisco Bay Area, where he provides psychotherapy and clinical supervision. In 2017, Erica was awarded the Ford Public Voices Fellowship and had his work featured in Role Reboot, Yoga International, and Truthout. Also, in 2017, Erica was awarded the Robert Wood Johnson Foundation Culture of Health Leaders Fellowship.

The Ford Public Voices Fellowship, sponsored by the Ford Foundation:

> Went far beyond media—as we envisioned. Fellows amplified critical social justice movements at key moments, led demonstrations, brought hidden information to the public eye, and framed headline news. Fellows came together to discuss and collaborate on some of the most difficult conversations of our age, from some of the most important vantage points. They brought vital movements—Black Lives Matter, Marriage Equality, and the Transgender movement, among others—into the public conversation in poignant ways. With Ford's support, The OpEd Project is also working on a larger impact evaluation project tracking the "S&P 500 of Voice," including how the media landscape has shifted to include significantly more underrepresented voices since our founding in 2008. This project is being conducted in partnership with MIT Media Lab.

The OpEd Project's Public Voices Fellowship is a national initiative first piloted at Yale, Stanford, and Princeton Universities, and is now:

> Rolling out in partnership with top universities and foundations across the nation. . . . Each Public Voices Fellowship is customized for approximately 20 women and underrepresented thought leaders at each institution. Fellowships last one year and in most cases lead to ongoing partnerships.

In addition to those sponsoring fellowships, we also see Columbia University, Massachusetts General Hospital, Cornell University, the Center for Global Policy Solutions, Northwestern University, and Yale's Program on Climate Change Communication also represented.

Returning to the UK and queerdom specifically, the appropriately-named Mother's Ruin's "mission is to facilitate radical and robust queer performance platforms in regional spaces." UNIQUE is:

> A voluntary organisation supporting Trans people in North Wales and West Cheshire. Trans people – from closet Cross-dressers to Transsexuals following Gender Reassignment Surgery – often need reassurance and support from others with similar experiences. One of Unique's prime aims is to help Trans people accept themselves and find acceptance from others.

Trans-Staffordshire "work[s] with the police to reduce hate crime, with NHS sexual health teams and offer[s] telephone support if people need it." TPSG Hull Dragons is for 13–19-year-olds (sic):

> Questioning Your Gender, Wanting to transition, Transitioning, Non Binary, Inter-sex, Transsexual, Gender Queer, Transgender, Family or Ally? Doesn't matter what Colour of the rainbow or shade of grey. . . . TPSG Hull Tiger Cubs is a peer support group for parents, family & siblings of Trans & Non Binary + children aged 12 years and under.

Freedom Youth "is a gender, sexuality and identity project working with those aged 11–25." LGBT Youth Scotland is "Scotland's national charity for LGBTI young people, working with 13–25-year-olds across the country." LGBT+ Service Nottinghamshire provides "specialist one-to-one, group and counselling services for young people aged 11–25 and their families across Nottinghamshire." Feeling good about the future yet? This is the "progressive" agenda after all. If you support the system, this is what you support.

Stonewall Cymru was established in 2003 with support from the Welsh Government (which has declared Wales a "sanctuary nation," a decision endorsed by the United Nations) and Stonewall GB. Pride in Prison & Probation (PiPP) is the LGBTI+ staff support network within Her Majesty's Prison & Probation Service (HMPPS). Micro Rainbow CIC "run[s] safe houses exclusively for homeless LGBTI asylum seekers and refugees."

Pride in Diversity was established in 2017 and its debut event in Harrogate was attended by organizations such as the North Yorkshire Police, who apparently had the time off from investigating all those grooming gangs, and the NHS. Over the Rainbow is an NHS Initiative in Dorset; Communi-T Trans Group is "a social group for trans people and . . . welcoming to anyone who is on the trans spectrum." Mosaic LGBT+ Young Persons Trust runs a summer camp for ages 13–19, a drag academy, and "London's only club nights for under 18s under Pride Prom and Homoween brands."

The Diversity Trust is "an organisation proud to be led by Trans and Non-Binary people who work across our organisation to advance social and legal equality." Their website features such articles as "Need new ideas for your business? Hire more autistic staff!"[90] Their September 2020 webinar featuring Nikki Hayfield, a qualitative researcher and Senior Lecturer in Social Psychology at the University of the West of England-Bristol, centered on "a brief history of bisexuality and pansexuality and how they might challenge the binaries of sex and sexuality."

The Diversity Trust works with companies, businesses, and organizations on a wide-range of projects including "accessibility audits, project management and on the design and delivery of equality, [and] diversity and inclusion training and consultancy." Trainings include the now ubiquitous unconscious bias training, plus: Transgender Awareness Training; It's About Race – Challenging Racial Bias and Racism in Practice; Equality, Diversity & Inclusion; Black, Asian and Minority Ethnic (BAME) Talent and Leadership Development; and Diversity in Practice – Working with Lesbian, Gay, Bisexual and Trans (LGBT) Communities. They also "produce powerful short films to promote equality, diversity and inclusion." Recent clients or partners include the Devon Partnership NHS Trust; Bristol, North Somerset, and South Gloucestershire Clinical Commissioning Group of the NHS; West of England Works (funding has come from the European Union and the National Lottery Community Fund); NHS Somerset Clinical Commissioning Group; UWE Bristol; Loughborough College; NHS South West Clinical Networks; Avon & Somerset Constabulary; Bath Spa University; Amicus Foster Care; Bristol Grammar School; Creative Youth Network; Stand Against Racism & Inequality (SARI); University Hospitals Bristol NHS Foundation Trust; University of Exeter; and on it goes.

---

[90] All they need to do is go on 4chan, it's not that difficult.

Next, we have from the *Jewish News* on July 5th, 2018, "Pride in London: Ten LGBT Jews inspiring change":

As founder of oral history projects Rainbow Jews, Twilight People and Rainbow Pilgrims, Shaan [Surat Knan] has secured Lottery Heritage funding to bring the lives and lessons of LGBT+ Jews and LGBT+ people from a range of cultures to tens of thousands of people across the UK. Shaan works for Liberal Judaism and through the Rainbow Pilgrims project has campaigned for the repeal of anti-gay laws in the Commonwealth. Shaan says: "It's perfectly fine to be trans and a person of faith. Don't let anyone tell you the opposite. . . ." [Rabbi Elli Tikvah Sarah] has included work at the Women's Research and Resources Centre collective, which created the Jewish feminist magazine, *Shifra*, and being assistant editor of Women's Studies International Forum. Before moving to Brighton, where she's been rabbi for 18 years, she was director of programmes for the Reform Synagogues of Great Britain and the Sternberg Centre's deputy director. . . . Isabella [Segal] is a pioneering trans activist and role model. As head of forensic accounting at Nyman Libson Paul and the partner responsible for diversity and inclusion at the firm, Isabella has advocated and advanced the visibility and inclusion of trans people within the business community. This was recognised in 2014 and 2015, with Isabella appearing in the Top 100 LGBT lists of OUTstanding, an LGBT professional networking and campaigning group. . . . Isabella is an ambassador for Transformation Diversity & Inclusion and gives talks for Diversity Role Models on homophobia and transphobia in schools. . . . Elliot [Jebreel] is now a civil servant and has worked in the Department for Work and Pensions, and at the Treasury. He also sits as a magistrate on the Central London bench. . . . Peggy Sherwood MBE was recognised in 2017 for her service to the Jewish community and for championing inclusion after 15 years as President of the Jewish Gay and Lesbian Group (now the Jewish LGBT+ Group), the longest such established group in the world. . . . Rabbi Mark Solomon was the first UK Orthodox rabbi to come out as gay, having studied for the rabbinate at the Lubavitcher Yeshivah Gedolah in Melbourne, Kfar Chabad in Israel, and Jews' College, London. Rabbi Solomon is currently the rabbi for Liberal Jewish communities in Edinburgh and Leicester. . . . Natalie [Grazin] is a coach and organisational consultant, formerly at McKinsey, and works with clients in senior management and clinical roles across the NHS. Natalie deploys her skills to develop the impact and leadership of a range of Jewish charities, including JW3 and UJIA. Before joining McKinsey, Natalie worked with the International Partnership for Innovative Healthcare Delivery and The Health Foundation. . . . As head of operations at the Faith & Belief Forum (formerly 3FF), Hannah [Taylor] spearheads projects tackling prejudice and building bridges across communities during times of increased violence and polarisation in the UK. Previously, Hannah worked at the Institute for Strategic Dialogue specialising in the use of social media to influence attitudes, tackle intolerance and inspire social change. This included leading the Nothing Holy about Hatred initiative tackling homophobia with and within faith communities. With a background in equality and diversity, particularly in relation to faith, interfaith and LGBT issues,

Hannah is also a trustee for the LGBT Consortium. . . . As chief executive of UK Jewish Film, Michael [Etherton]'s commercial and creative skills have expanded UK Jewish Film onto the international stage, producing and programming film festivals in Geneva, Hong Kong, Zurich, Montreal and Tel Aviv. He has also established major year-round partnerships in London and across the UK, expanding the programme to more than 450 additional films annually. Michael has recently overseen a National Lottery-funded educational outreach programme and has launched a new FilmLab programme to inspire and support work from a new generation of filmmakers. A champion of diversity in the arts, Michael is musical director of Mosaic Voices, chairman of the Young Actors Theatre, Islington, and a fellow of the Royal Society of Arts.

The Sigrid Rausing Trust is another major "charity" supporting "social justice" and LGBTQ "causes," such as George Soros's Central European University's Roma program, the Open Society Foundations' SolidarityNet,[91] Labrys in Kyrgyzstan, the Aegis Trust (UK),[92] the Human Dignity Trust, the ACLU, the Astraea Lesbian Foundation for Justice, Bail for Immigration Detainees (UK), the Media Diversity Institute (MDI), the Migrants' Rights Network (UK), Minority Rights Group (UK—with consultative status at the UN ECOSOC), the New Israel Fund, the Feminist Fund in Poland, the European Roma Rights Center,[93] the feminist Women's Initiatives Supporting Group in Georgia, Women's Link Worldwide in Spain, Women's Human Rights Training Institute in Bulgaria, Cape Town Holocaust Center in South Africa, European Network Against Racism in Belgium, Human Rights Watch, Asylos, FeMale in Lebanon, Hope Not Hate (UK), Safe Passage (UK), Southall Black Sisters (UK), Roma Pavilion in Italy, Refugee Youth Project (UK), Polish Society of Anti-Discrimination Law, Information Centre about Asylum and Refugees in the UK, the Jewish Museum in London, and the No Borders Project/Social Action Center in the Ukraine, which "protects the rights of minority groups . . . by challenging xenophobia and discrimination." They've also dispensed funds to the University of York (UK), the London School of Economics, St. Antony's College-Oxford, University of Warwick (UK), the University of Cape Town (South Africa), University of the Western Cape (South Africa), and University College London.

The Sigrid Rausing Trust granted £325,000 from 2011–2015 to the Organization for Refuge, Asylum, and Migration (Offices in Minneapolis, Minnesota and Berlin, Germany):

---

[91] "The SolidarityNet Foundation was set up in 2013 by OSF [the Open Society Foundations] to address the needs of Greek society in the face of the economic crisis. It aims to deliver medical, legal and employment support to the most vulnerable Greek citizens through a series of 'Solidarity Centres', initially in Athens and Thessaloniki. These centres will also make grants to local NGOs in order to strengthen Greek civil society."

[92] "The Aegis Trust, established by the UK Holocaust Centre, is a research and advocacy organisation focused on war crimes, genocide, and crimes against humanity. The Trust supported its Wanted for War Crimes project, which seeks to bring cases against those suspected of committing war crimes, genocide, and crimes against humanity on the basis of universal jurisdiction and advocates reforming UK domestic laws to make prosecutions of such crimes more feasible."

[93] Sigrid Rausing dispensed £1,981,500 from 1998-2013.

Founded in 2008, the Organisation for Refuge, Asylum and Migration (ORAM) is the only international migrant rights organisation focusing exclusively on lesbian, gay, bisexual, transgender and intersex refugees. ORAM's work includes research, public education, policy advocacy, direct legal representation and resettlement, and their publications bring public attention to LGBTI refugee protection issues worldwide. ORAM's advocacy encompasses NGOs, inter-governmental organisations, governments and community groups. Their educational efforts include lectures, reports and presentations to the public.

Other major donors to ORAM include the Tides Foundation, the Arcus Foundation, the Open Society Foundations, the Office of the United Nations High Commissioner for Refugees, and the US Department of State Bureau of Population, Refugees, and Migration. Other LGBTQ- and/or -intersex specific Sigrid Rausing grantees include:

- ACCEPT Association (Romania): "It undertakes strategic litigation, advocates for legislative changes to uphold the rights of LGBT people, and provides direct services to the LGBT community such as legal and psychological counselling for victims of discrimination and hate crimes. It also provides training for professionals including police, judges, magistrates, social workers and teachers, and organises community events such as the annual Bucharest Pride and LGBT History Month." ACCEPT has also received funding from EEA Grants (from the governments of Iceland, Liechtenstein, and Norway) as project promoter of: "Creating a complementary set of educational, training and advocacy measures for better fighting the homophobic phenomenon within Romanian high schools. An innovative research on the attitudes and perceptions of high-school students regarding LGBT issues will be conducted. 540 high school students will form educational clubs in 9 high schools, following a semester of anti-discrimination training. They will also manage pro-democratic and inclusive activities within the LGBT History Month 2016. In addition, 54 teachers will be trained to implement the new curricula within the partner high schools and to better respond to homophobic cases."
- Campaign Against Homophobia (KPH—Poland)
- Coalition of African Lesbians (South Africa)
- OUT (South Africa): "Founded in 1994, OUT provides direct health services to the lesbian, gay, bisexual and transgender (LGBT) community in South Africa including a clinic and psychosocial services. It also engages in research, advocacy and trains mainstream government officials."
- Council for Global Equality (US): "Founded in 2008, it is a coalition of 22 US-based human rights and LGBT organisations working together to promote the inclusion of LGBT rights in US foreign policy. Council members seek to ensure that those who represent the US—in Congress, in the White House, in US embassies and in US corporations—use the diplomatic, political and economic leverage available to them to oppose human rights abuses directed at individuals because of their sexual orientation, gender identity or gender expression." Sigrid Rausing has dispensed at least £585,000 to the Council for Global Equality since 2013.

- Aswat— Palestinian Feminist Queer Movement for Sexual and Gender Freedoms: "Aswat – Palestinian Gay Women was formed in 2003 to support Arab lesbian and transsexual women's rights in Israel and the Occupied Territories. Aswat provides a safe environment for sexual minorities and strengthens their voice in Arab and Palestinian society."
- Insight (Ukraine): "Insight is a Ukrainian non-profit organisation established in 2008. Based in Kyiv, its main aim is to represent and promote LGBT rights at national and international levels. Though working with all community members, the organisation has a particular emphasis on women and trans people. It undertakes advocacy for anti-discrimination and hate crime legislation, campaigns and takes cases to establish better protection for legal gender recognition." At least £212,000 has been granted to Insight by Sigrid Rausing to date. Their 2019 publication "Human Rights of LGBIQ Women in Ukraine" was given technical and financial support from the UN Women CEDAW in Action! Project financed by Global Affairs Canada, the department in the Government of Canada that manages Canada's diplomatic and consular relations, encourages Canadian international trade, and leads Canada's international development and humanitarian assistance. In 2013, "trans activists" from Insight and Human Rights Watch participated in the UN Human Rights Committee's periodic review of Ukraine's compliance with the International Covenant on Civil and Political Rights (ICCPR). Insight is also mentioned by the Open Society Foundations as a partner in their May 2019 publication "An Essential Legal Right for Trans People": "Trans activists and allies around the world are advocating for their rights by introducing or changing national laws or regulations. The Open Society Foundations provide financial support to trans-led or LGBT organizations that promote progressive, rights-based processes for legal gender recognition. Our partners include: Transgender Europe; . . . Transgender Education & Advocacy, a Kenyan organization that is pressing courts to allow name and gender change on passports, national ID cards, and academic certificates; Insight, a Ukrainian organization that engages with ministerial bodies, the Office of the Ombudsman, and other civil society allies to reform the draconian process for changing name and gender; . . . The Coalition "Sexual and Health Rights of Marginalized Communities" in Macedonia; . . . [and] Organizando Trans Diversidades, a Chilean community-led organization."
- Gays and Lesbians of Zimbabwe
- Initiative for Equality and Non-Discrimination (INEND—Kenya)
- Jamaica Forum for Lesbians, All-Sexuals and Gays (J-FLAG)
- Mawjoudin (Tunisia)
- National Gay and Lesbian Human Rights Commission (NGLHRC—Kenya)
- OII-Europe
- Labris (Serbia)
- Legebitra (Slovenia)
- Parliamentarians for Global Action
- Pembe Hayat (Turkey)
- Stonewall
- African Men for Sexual Health and Rights: "African Men for Sexual Health and Rights (AMSHeR) is a regional coalition of MSM/LGBTI-led organisations and other groups which work to protect LGBTI people from human rights violations,

and address the vulnerability of gay and bisexual men, male-to-female transgender women, and other men who have sex with men, to HIV. AMSHeR is made up of 25 organisations from 20 African countries. In addition to its move-ment-building, health and human rights activities, it works to strengthen and de-velop community structures' capacity to implement quality programmes and sound strategies for the protection of the rights of LGBTI people, and increased access to health services for men who have sex with men."

- LGBTI Support Center of the Macedonian Helsinki Committee (North Macedo-nia): "The LGBTI Support Centre began as a programme of the Macedonian Hel-sinki Committee in 2010 and was upgraded to a support centre in 2012. Their activities are organised around three main areas: advocacy to improve the legal and social standing of LGBTI people, community development, and public rela-tions. They offer free legal aid, monitor legislation and implementation of inter-national standards accepted by Macedonia, prepare shadow reports, and lobby local and international decision-makers. They also run support groups for gay men, lesbians, trans people and parents with LGBT children; hold film nights, political debates, arts festivals for the wider public; produce media articles; and conduct media monitoring."

- PINK Armenia: "Public Information and Need for Knowledge (PINK) Armenia is a Yerevan-based LGBT organisation established in 2007. Its activities include HIV prevention for men who have sex with men (MSM) and youth, provision of legal support for LGBT people, sex workers and people living with HIV, and advocacy for anti-discrimination and hate speech protection. It also publishes an online magazine, 'As You', which provides information not found in the main-stream media about civil society, health, human rights, gender and sexuality."

- SIPD (Uganda)

- The OTHER Foundation (South Africa)

- GenderDoc-M (Moldova): Sigrid Rausing dispensed £344,000 from 2007–2017; from the Open Society Foundations' "Transforming Health: International Rights-Based Advocacy for Trans Health": "The major drivers behind the creation of this support group were the lack of legal and social recognition for trans people in Moldova, which contributes to high rates of attempted suicide and other phys-ical and mental health concerns; a lack of medical professionals qualified to pro-vide transition-related care; and the lack of an established legal protocol through the Moldovan Vital Statistics Records Service for allowing trans people who have transitioned to obtain appropriate identity documents in their true name and gender. The group has helped several trans people change their identity docu-ments and has partnered with the Moldovan Ministry of Health to create a work-ing committee tasked with developing a protocol for resolving the legal issues facing trans people in obtaining identity documents and accessing transition-re-lated medical services that are covered by health insurance. In addition to the legal and psychosocial support it provides to trans people, the Transgender Sup-port Group organizes information sessions for various groups of professionals who come into contact with trans issues, including social workers, medical pro-viders, journalists, and police officers. The group also engages in international network building for trans advocacy. In 2010 it organized a meeting called 'Ad-dressing the Challenges Faced by Transgender Individuals in the Post-Soviet Re-gion,' which included participants from Moldova, Ukraine, Georgia, Kazakhstan,

Kyrgyzstan, Russia, Poland, the United Kingdom, and representatives of the LGBT advocacy organization ILGA-Europe. A major future area of advocacy for the group is helping Moldovan surgeons receive training abroad in transition-related surgical techniques."

- Sarajevo Open Center (Bosnia): "Sarajevo Open Centre (the Centre) was founded in 2007, and today is a feminist organisation that works to defend and promote the rights of lesbian, gay, bisexual, transgender and intersex (LGBTI) persons and women. It provides direct services such as legal and psychological counselling for victims of discrimination and hate crimes. It advocates at national and European level for legislative changes to uphold the rights of women and LGBTI people under Bosnia and Herzegovina's constitution and international obligations. It also provides trainings for the police, judges, civil servants, social workers, psychologists and psychiatrists. The Centre organises community events in Sarajevo such as the annual Merlinka LGBTI film festival."
- Transgender Equality Network Ireland (TENI)
- Transgender Europe (TGEU)
- UK Lesbian and Gay Immigration Group (UKLGIG): "Founded in 1993, the UK Lesbian and Gay Immigration Group (UKLGIG) supports lesbians, gay men and transgender people to gain fair and equal treatment under UK immigration law. It supports gay asylum seekers through the legal process, and provides them with emotional support through its telephone helpline and regular meetings. UKLGIG also campaigns to change the way the UK Border Agency deals with asylum claims from LGBT people."
- UHAI-EASHRI (Kenya)
- Transitioning Africa: "Transitioning Africa is a new transgender rights umbrella organisation founded through the collaboration of three African transgender and intersex groups – Gender Dynamix (Cape Town), Trans and Intersex Africa (Soshanguve Township, Gauteng, South Africa) and Support Initiative for People with Atypical Sexual Development (SIPD – Kampala). Transitioning Africa aims to form a platform for the three organisations to engage in regional work and facilitate collaboration with other groups, with the ultimate aim of building a strong network of African trans and intersex organisations."
- Transgender Legal Defense Project/Transgender People Legal Aid Project (Russia): "The Transgender Legal Defense Project is a group of professional lawyers and paralegals established in 2012 which works for the advancement of LGBTI people's rights in former Soviet countries. The project focuses on legal gender recognition issues, providing legal services, educating transgender people and pushing for human rights-based procedures for changing documentation through strategic litigation."
- ILGA-Europe: In addition to the Sigrid Rausing Trust, ILGA-Europe also receives major funding from Freedom House, the Arcus Foundation, the Rights Equality and Citizenship (REC) program (2014–2020) of the European Union, COC Nederland, the Government of the Netherlands, and RFSL (the Swedish Federation for Lesbian, Gay, Bisexual, Transgender, Queer and Intersex Rights). They have received funding from the Open Society Foundations in the past. I was able to locate a $450,000 grant from May 2012.

The Sigrid Rausing Trust has also granted funds to the Urgent Action Fund-Africa (2005–2015: £841,000) and the Urgent Action Fund-US (2007–2009: £240,000). The Urgent Action Fund, in its own words, "is led by an activist Board of Directors, who represent communities around the world. Urgent Action Fund's decision-making is grounded in an international, feminist framework." Its Board of Directors is chaired by Patricia Viseur Sellers, who served as Prosecutor and Legal Advisor for Gender at the International Criminal Tribunal for the former Yugoslavia. Jewish Treasurer Paulette Meyer operates out of San Francisco and is and has been involved with a number of feminist and "social justice" projects such as Bend the Arc: A Jewish Partnership for Justice. Her husband David A. Friedman "has been active in many Bay Area non-profits, within . . . [the] Jewish Community and in the social justice and economic development arenas. David is a past trustee of the UC Berkeley Foundation, and past chair and trustee of The San Francisco Foundation."

Goldman Sachs has also been active in promoting the LGBTQ agenda in the UK and beyond; we will return to them later, but as one example in the UK, Goldman Sachs's employee health coverage benefits also include those for gender dysphoria which seems to go beyond what the NHS provides as it is highlighted in their benefits package. Laura Holleman, Goldman Sachs Managing Director, was honored at the 2018 London Out & Proud Corporate Counsel Award Reception—sponsors included White & Case, Baker McKenzie, and Cleary Gottlieb—for:

> Her work with the LGBT Network at Goldman Sachs. . . . Laura frequently engages in LGBT outreach events with law firms, schools, and other businesses and LGBT organizations such as Stonewall, providing advice and guidance on establishing and enhancing Ally Networks. She is also a mentor for a number of LGBT lawyers in London. Having been part of the original effort of the Goldman Sachs LGBT network to enhance the transgender pillar, she regularly attends events in support of the transgender community.

Speaking of Stonewall—whose corporate partners include the Premier League, Adidas, Asos, Absolut, eBay, Sky Sports, Aviva, Barclays, and Prudential—John Q. Publius relates the following appalling manifestation of neo-liberalism as it intersects with their annual "LGBT-inclusive employers list":

> MI5 – the United Kingdom's domestic counter-intelligence and security agency – was the fourth-most "LGBT-inclusive" employer in the entire country in 2019. So instead of preventing people from being run over, stabbed to death, or maimed with nail bombs in the name of the jihad, MI5 is concerned with whether or not it has enough homosexuals and transgenders in its ranks. The gross failure and incompetence at all levels of the security apparatus, including the police, will soon become clear; also featured on the list were: the National Assembly for Wales and the Newcastle City Council, tied at number five (it emerged recently that a massive grooming gang had been operating with impunity in Newcastle); the Welsh Government (#8); the Ministry of Justice (#12); the Royal Navy and Royal Marines (#15); the Cheshire Constabulary (#18); Lancashire Constabulary (#36); the British Army (#51); Sheffield City Council (#61); the Royal Air Force (#68); Leeds City Council

and the Scottish Government (#72, tie); Sunderland City Council (#76); Sussex Police (#81); MI6— the foreign intelligence service of the government of the United Kingdom (#86); Northumbria Police (#88); Nottingham City Council (#95); and the National Crime Agency (#100). Cheshire Fire and Rescue clocked in at #4 on the 2018 list along with the House of Commons (#23), the Home Office (#38), Tyne and Wear Fire and Rescue Service (#59), and Police Scotland (#90).

Flying a rainbow flag and confiscating butter knives and garden tools is clearly a much greater priority than stopping the industrial-scale rape perpetrated by grooming gangs or the myriad attacks on the British populace. Further, in displaying the intersection of systemic collapse, societal decay, and dereliction of duty and standard with Pride, we find the London Borough of Tower Hamlets at #12 on this list. As of June 2017, Tower Hamlets was the second-most densely-populated local authority in the UK, home to the largest Bangladeshi population in the country, 43% of residents were born outside the UK, 38% of the residents were Muslim, and more than two-thirds of all Tower Hamlets residents were classed as "belonging to minority ethnic groups." Tower Hamlets is also one of the most dangerous boroughs in London.

Grenfell Tower, in North Kensington, is a microcosm of this phenomenon, unable to maintain even:

> Basic maintenance and fire safety protocols. . . . Grenfell Tower . . . went up in a massive conflagration on June 14th, 2017 and burned for sixty hours, resulting in the deaths of seventy-two people and injuries to several hundred others. It was the worst residential fire in the United Kingdom since World War II. The fire spread so rapidly because the building's exterior did not comply with building regulations. An alternative cladding with better fire resistance was refused due to cost-cutting. The building was designed under the assumption that a full evacuation would never be necessary. There was no centrally-activated fire alarm and only a single central staircase. There was only one entrance and exit, and the building's fire doors would not close or seal properly. Most of its corridors were filled with garbage and many exits had been blocked by mattresses and other discarded items. For at least twelve years prior to the fire residents had complained about a lack of proper maintenance and fire safety equipment. In 2012, an official recorded that the fire-fighting equipment had not been checked in four years, and most of the fire extinguishers were expired. When one of the residents posted about this online, they were threatened with legal action. In June 2016, an independent assessor identified forty serious fire safety issues in the Tower that required immediate attention but were never addressed. . . . Of course, many of the residents bear some responsibility for clogging exits and hallways with mattresses and other detritus, and generally treating their living space as a garbage dump; in a dark harbinger of the Shape of Britain to Come, Grenfell Tower's residents were primarily poor, non-white recent immigrants to the country.

It's all a far cry from the Britannia that once was.

# Men Are From Mars, Women Have a Penis

Based out of the Netherlands, Mama Cash, "helps to build the partnerships and networks needed to successfully defend and advance women's, girls', trans and intersex people's human rights globally"—apparently because the "human rights" of each group are all the same. Mama Cash has three major donor-advised funds and also partners with the Swedish International Development Cooperation Agency (SIDA), the Dutch Postcode Lottery, the Dutch Ministry of Foreign Affairs, the Channel Foundation, the Arcus Foundation, the Ford Foundation, the Levi Strauss Foundation, the NoVo Foundation, the Bill and Melinda Gates Foundation, the Oak Foundation, and the Sigrid Rausing Trust. Mama Cash also partners with the Open Society Foundations, the Oak Foundation, the Levi Strauss Foundation, the Elton John AIDS Foundation, and the American Jewish World Service to finance the Red Umbrella Fund, "the first global fund guided by and for sex workers." Since 1983, Mama Cash has distributed at least €60 million in grants to women's, girls', trans and intersex groups "who make their demands loud and clear," as well as connecting these "activist" groups to each other and other donors. Once again, we see feminism as an essential tributary to this package of "human rights," to say nothing of "girl's groups" and sex workers/sexuality. Disturbing? Definitely. Copacetic for the ruling class? Absolutely.

Also based in the Netherlands, Hivos is headquartered in The Hague and is a partnership between various stakeholders, financial institutions, governing bodies, governments, and NGOs. Their ideal is to create "an open society" and they operate on a truly global scale. Some of the principal partners in the network include: the Dutch Ministry of Foreign Affairs, the Open Society Foundations, the UK's Department for International Development (DFID), the Ford Foundation, the Omidyar Network, the European Union, the Hewlett Foundation, the Swedish International Development Cooperation Agency (SIDA), CamASEAN, Oxfam Novib, the Asian Development Bank, the Norwegian Agency for Development Cooperation (NORAD), Triodos Bank through the Hivos Triodos Fund (providing microfinancing and other kinds of loans), USAID, and more.

One of Hivos's most effective campaigns was a partnership with advertising agency M&C Saatchi "to change the common narrative of LGBTI" through the creation of "an innovative campaign to tackle stigma and discrimination against LGBTI people and sex workers." This linking of LGBTQ and sex workers seems to be a common thread. Hivos is also a part of Dgroups, "a partnership of international development organisations working together towards a common vision: A world where every person is able to contribute to dialogue and decision-making for international development and social justice." These are some of the largest such organizations in the world, including a number of outgrowths of the United Nations such as its Capital Development Fund and the Food and Agriculture Organization (FAO).

COC Nederland/Netherlands is very bullish on the gay-straight alliance (or what is now in the United States the GSA Network, the Gender and Sexualities Alliance Network) chapters in schools because "participating in a GSA positively influences students' social attitudes" and "the presence of a GSA in a school makes LGBT issues more visible in school activities." The National Institute for Public Health and the Environment independently assessed COC's study of GSAs and stated that it was "well substantiated," highlighting their effectiveness. Effectiveness at what? Conditioning children, presumably.

Founded by Nico Engelschman in 1946, COC is considered the oldest continuously-existing explicitly-LGBTQ organization in the world. Engelschman had been a member of the revolutionary socialist party RSAP as part of the leadership of its youth-group, the Leninist Youth Guard, prior to World War II. Just as with the Mattachine Society in the United States and the Soviet connection to Magnus Hirschfeld's work, we see a consistent connection with the communist ideology and a potent means to undermine healthy expressions of nationalism particularly among European peoples with the modern foundations of the LGBTQ agenda. Although we must now consider this basis as it has mutated into Cultural Marxism, the words of Leszek Kołakowski prove very helpful in understanding the tactics:

> Lenin laid the foundation for the tactics which were soon to become binding on Communist parties: the right course was to support any movement tending to overthrow the system at any point, for any reasons and in the interests of any class: liberation in colonial countries, national or peasant movements, bourgeois national uprisings against the big imperialists. This was a generalization of the tactics he had been preaching in Russia for years: to support all claims and all movements against the Tsarist autocracy, so as to exploit their sources of energy and seize power at the critical moment. The victory of the Marxist party was the final aim.[94]

Obviously in the present context we are talking about global capitalism preparing the world for a return to some sort of digitized feudalism rather than communism, but as we are dealing with a Cultural Marxist framework, Kołakowski highlights the use of "activists" and other pressure points/interest groups/grievances: use whatever means necessary to attack and fracture the enemy, in this case cohesive and homogeneous societies.

COC Nederland International is supported by the Dutch Ministry of Foreign Affairs. In September 2011, COC Nederland in conjunction with VU University Amsterdam, the Hungarian Helsinki Committee, and the European Council on Refugees and Exiles (ECRE) and with funding from the Dutch Ministry of the Interior and Kingdom Relations and the European Refugee Fund, Sabine Jensen and Thomas Spijkerboer produced the report "Fleeing Homophobia: Asylum Claims Related to Sexual Orientation and Gender Identity in Europe" to help provide an intersectional

---

[94] Kołakowski, *Main Currents of Marxism, Vol. II*, 471–472.

framework to mass migration and European population replacement. Apparently, "the human rights for LGBTI individuals is frequently denied in the asylum practice of European States," with the thin at best rationale a precursor to documents like the Open Society Foundations' "License to be Yourself: Responding to National Security and Identity Fraud Arguments" we discussed earlier in this book. According to Funders for LGBTQ Issues, "Immigration rights greatly affect trans people. . . . While only 1 in 500 detainees identifies as trans, a staggering 1 in 5 victims of sexual abuse in immigration detention is trans." What does that say about the people they're bringing in?

Still, RainbowHouse Brussels wants more, launching with InQlusion the Q-Asyl'Home project "to train social assistants, caseworkers and inhabitants of asylum centres on SOGIESC issues and improve services for LGBTI asylum seekers." In August 2019, Belgium's inaugural POC* Pride was held in Antwerp, and that same month, a similar group called Black Pride Ireland, "dedicated to the nurturing and uplifting of queer black people in Ireland," was established.

Half a world away, Aleph Melbourne, "a social, support and advocacy group for same-sex attracted, trans and gender diverse, and intersex people (and allies) who have a Jewish heritage, living in Melbourne, Australia," traces their values to Judaism and links to various organizations such as the Refugee Action Collective, the Asylum Seeker Resource Center, the Australian GLBTIQ Multicultural Council, and a slew of other Jewish and/or LGBTQ groups, once again evidencing the inextricably linked nature of "social justice" with Jewishness and Judaism.

Immigration Equality, "the [US]'s leading LGBTQ immigrant rights organization," was founded in 1994 as the Lesbian and Gay Immigration Rights Task Force by Suzanne Goldberg, Noemi Masliah, and Lavi Soloway. If you guessed that they are all Jewish, you'd be correct. If you guessed that they have received funding from the Open Society Foundations, you'd also be correct. One of their major projects was campaigning to lift the ban on HIV-positive aliens' entry into the United States.

Since the lifting of the HIV ban took effect in January 2010, Immigration Equality has worked to ensure as many HIV-positive people are granted asylum as possible. According to their website, they've "won asylum for over 1,000 LGBTQ and HIV-positive immigrants while maintaining a 99% success rate." In 2009, the Immigration Equality Action Fund, a 501(c)(4) organization devoted to federal lobbying, was created. Immigration Equality's primary sponsor is Marriott, but they also receive funding from a slew of Jewish law firms and notorious globalist firms like Ropes & Gray and DLA Piper (employer of Kamala Harris's husband) as well as Deutsche Bank. Their Pro Bono Network features WilmerHale, ViacomCBS, Barclays, 3M, Bank of America, Deloitte, Deutsche Bank, MetLife, and once again a preponderance of Jewish law firms, many of them immigration law firms.

The National Center for Transgender Equality is similar; in the 2013 paper "Our Moment for Reform: Immigration and Transgender People" with input from UCLA's Williams Institute, the Center for American Progress, the Sylvia Rivera Law Project, Immigration Equality, and the National Immigrant Justice Center, among others, and using the Center for American Progress's "Living in Dual Shadows" report as a springboard, "the issues affecting LGBT undocumented people in the United States" is evidently of grave concern. Why? Throw a few darts at the "social justice" dartboard: "fleeing desperate poverty compounded by gender-based discrimination" (in the same Third World countries whose populations are flooding en masse into the West); and also:

> This combination of being transgender and undocumented means trans immigrants have a double minority status that creates barriers to housing, health care, and economic security and exposes them to heightened risk of discrimination, negative health outcomes, and violence.

*Ad nauseum*. Therefore: no borders for you and complete compliance with the coming One World tyranny.

This intersectional and explicitly anti-white, moral perversion forms the core of similar organizations and missions, from the National Queer Asian Pacific Islander Alliance to the Transgender Law Center to the Foundation for a Just Society to Borealis Philanthropy.

One of the central "issues" of the Foundation for a Just Society is "LGBTI migration." It has dispensed over $133 million in grants to LGBTQ and other "social justice" organizations including the American Jewish World Service, the Astraea Lesbian Foundation for Justice, Borealis Philanthropy, the Coalition of African Lesbians, Front Line Defenders, Funders for LGBTQ Issues, the Groundswell Fund, Human Rights Watch, the Initiative for Strategic Litigation in Africa, the International Rescue Committee (IRC)-run by the Jewish David Miliband, the LGBTQ Racial Justice Fund, Mama Cash, MAP, NEO Philanthropy, the National Immigration Law Center, Queer African Youth Network, the SPLC, the Transgender Law Center, UHAI-EASHRI,[95] Urgent Action Fund, Women's Refugee Committee, and COMCAVIS Trans in El Salvador, which also receives support from the American Jewish World Service, USAID, UNDP, ILGA-Latin America and Caribbean, and UNAIDS:

> UNAIDS brings together the efforts of 11 United Nations organizations— UNHCR, UNICEF, WFP, UNDP, UNFPA, UNODC, UN Women, ILO, UNESCO, WHO and the World Bank—and works closely with global and national partners to end the AIDS epidemic by 2030 as part of the Sustainable Development Goals.

Following along these ideological lines, The Diversithon, a Wikipedia editing event "held in a social and supportive setting to celebrate diversity" for LGBT+ History Month and Black History Month 2019 held at the University of Edinburgh through the "combined efforts" of the participating groups such as UncoverED— "a collaborative and decolonising research project, funded by Edinburgh Global, which aims to situate the 'global' status of the University of Edinburgh in its rightful imperial and colonial context"—produced a number of entries such as that of Clara Marguerite Christian, who was:

---

[95] Supporting and/or collaborating organizations include: ViiV Healthcare, the American Jewish World Service, the Arcus Foundation, the Red Umbrella Fund, the Elton John AIDS Foundation, the Ford Foundation, the Astraea Lesbian Foundation for Justice, Comic Relief, the Sigrid Rausing Trust, and the Dutch Ministry of Foreign Affairs.

The 1st black woman to study at the University of Edinburgh. Her university experience speaks to the 'double jeopardy' (sic) of 'navigating both race and gender within whiteness,' embodying 'the simultaneous invisibility and hyper-visibility' of being a black woman in Edinburgh during the 1910s.

This farcical trash masquerading as scholarship is just academic jargon that doesn't mean anything. In fact, nothing in this framework means anything, which is a large part of the problem. Plus, despite being itself conquered and colonized, much like Ireland, Scotland is somehow an exporter of colonial atrocities; this is ahistorical, but precisely due to the skin color of Scots and Irish.

The ideological impetus for The Diveristhon was provided by 2015's "Queering Wikipedia" by Rachel S. Wexelbaum ("There are people who want to be recognized as Jewish, and Jewish folx who want to know who the other Jewish folx are in society. Also a significant number of Wikipedia editors are Jewish and proud, just FYI."), et al.:

> To increase the diversity of voices, genders, and cultures among its contributors and editors, the Wikimedia Foundation has made it a strategic goal to recruit and foster more women, people of colour, and other underrepresented individuals—including LGBT+ populations. . . . the Wikimedia Foundation recognizes that the majority of its Wikipedia contributors and editors are disproportionately male, under 22 years old, and (most likely white and straight) from "the Global North". They also admit that Wikipedia's coverage is skewed toward the interests, expertise, and language skills of the people who created it.

Increasingly, we are seeing the framework constructed of whiteness and maleness as synonymous with heterosexuality, meaning—especially since the prevailing orthodoxy believes "whiteness" to be an artificial construct—that heterosexuality is as well. From such "scholarship" as Eric Anderson's "Generational Masculinities," we now know, evidently, that:

> Whereas I once (2008) theorized that a 'one-time rule of homosexuality' existed for men in the 1980s and 1990s, so that any sexual activity with another male socially coded him as homosexual, a 2017 special edition of the journal Sexualities documents the ways in which heterosexuality is also expanding to include a more expansive set of same-sex sexual behaviours (McCormack, 2017). Heterosexual men are, for example, engaging in male-male-threesomes (Scoats, Joseph, & Anderson, 2017), enjoying their own anal eroticism (Branfman, Stiritz, & Anderson, 2017) and having sexual intercourse with other men without having it question their own sexual identity as straight (Carrillo & Hoffman, 2017; Savin-Williams, 2017). Thus, it is evident that inclusive masculinities are not just about how males act towards each other, or what artistic, athletic, aesthetic, entertainment, occupational, or other aspects of social life they are culturally permitted or thwarted from engaging with; it is also about what sexual and semi-sexual behaviours they are culturally permitted to engage in.

So evidently one may "identify" as straight while having sexual intercourse with other men. To quote Ice-T, "I got news for you: that means ya gay."

The DC Area Educators for Social Justice is but one of a litany of indoctrination nodes metastasizing like cancerous tumors across the US (and world). It is a project of Teaching for Change ("Building Social Justice, Starting in the Classroom") that describes itself as:

> A network of educators who seek to strengthen and deepen social justice teaching. We are [a] community of mutual support for educators to collaborate on curriculum, professional learning, and activism. We challenge systems of oppression through anti-bias, anti-racist, and multicultural education . . . to create a more just and equitable world.

Mandatory struggle sessions in public "school" when? Its primary grant sources are identified as the Communities for Just Schools Fund and the Taste of Salt Fund.

I could find very little on the Taste of Salt Fund, but it is listed alongside such donors as Lockheed Martin, Team Fannie Mae, Amazon, AT&T, the World Bank Group, the IMF Matching Gift Fund, and the Anne Frank House for the DC-area Friendship Place, which makes me rather suspicious. The Communities for Just Schools Fund is housed at the New Venture Fund and currently includes support and participation from: the Arcus Foundation, The Atlantic Philanthropies, the Ford Foundation, the Open Society Foundations, and the WK Kellogg Foundation, among others. The Youth Transition Funders Group (YTFG)—a "network [that] provides a unique space for diverse funders to come together to explore cross-cutting issues affecting all vulnerable youth"—publicized this fund in a press release on their website in July 2015.

The YTFG's Steering Committee includes representatives of the Conrad N. Hilton Foundation (a major funder of HIV/AIDS-related philanthropy), Casey Family Programs (as John Q. Publius writes of the BLM-adjacent Casey Family Programs, "In 2007, after the Ford Foundation published 'Why We Can't Wait,' ABFE, Casey Family Programs, Ford, and the Open Society Foundations hosted a National Funders' Dialogue on Black Males in Seattle to 'discuss grantmaking for black males'"), the Annie E. Casey Foundation, the Redlich Horwitz Foundation, and the Zellerbach Family Foundation. Youth Justice Work Group Lead Consultant Carrie Rae Boatman served as the Senior Policy Associate for Juvenile Justice Reform at the Annie E. Casey Foundation and has also served as a grant-making consultant to The Atlantic Philanthropies, the Ford Foundation, and the Open Society Foundations. Suspicions confirmed.

On its website, the DC Area Educators for Social Justice provides reading lists for children under umbrellas such as the Elementary Book List—Organized by Guiding Principles of Black Lives Matter, Gender Identity, and LGBTQ. Under Lessons for Early Childhood and Elementary, recommended lesson plans center on topics such as Introduction of Transgender and Nonbinary Identities with I Am Jazz— which is recommended for pre-K through second grade—and Exploring Gender Stereotypes with Role Plays, which is recommended for kindergarten through second grade. In the latter, "Children will use creative, dramatic expression to consider not only the roots of gender stereotypes, but also their consequences and strategies for counteracting them. Queer Affirming, Trans Affirming, Collective Value." The lesson plan links to further resources from Gender Spectrum, GLSEN, and NOW (the National Organization for Women).

The lesson plan was created by the Southern Poverty Law Center's (SPLC) Teaching Tolerance project, which also includes guidelines on "confronting white nationalism" and immigration. The Teaching Tolerance Gender and Sexual Identity page leads off by favorably quoting Joel Baum, Jewish Director of Advocacy with the Child and Adolescent Gender Center Clinic at UCSF and Senior Director of Professional Development at Gender Spectrum, and lesbian Kim Westheimer, Director of Strategic Initiatives at Gender Spectrum, who also directed the launching of the Human Rights Campaign Foundation's Welcoming Schools Program, created in 2007 to "foster LGBT inclusion in elementary schools."

Westheimer's biography states that "gender has been a recurring thread in her work: whether encouraging students to examine their own gender stories or developing systemic approaches to build inclusive PK – 12 schools." Some of Westheimer's other credentials include participating in a 2005 panel discussion in Boston around a screening of *HINEINI: Coming out in a Jewish School* and sitting on the Board of American Friends of the Parents Circle-Families Forum, which does "critical work to increase dialogue and understanding among Palestinians and Jewish Israelis." Alongside Westheimer on the Board include former IDF Major Oz Benamram and Howard Sumka, who is:

> Minister Counselor in the Senior Foreign Service with the U.S. Agency for International Development. From 2006–2010, he was based in Tel Aviv as director of USAID's Mission to the West Bank and Gaza overseeing programs for Palestinian economic development and state building. He had previously been director of the USAID Missions to Albania and to Bosnia-Herzegovina.

The DC Area Educators for Social Justice also links to Rethinking Schools:

> The preeminent publisher of social justice education materials in the United States. Our quarterly magazine has subscribers in all 50 states, all 10 Canadian provinces, and around the world. Our books are used in teacher education programs, by social organizations and teachers' unions, and by classroom teachers everywhere.

They push "climate justice" and Black Lives Matter and rely heavily on the work of the Jewish Howard Zinn. Additionally, according to the Our History description from their website:

> Although our primary work is advocacy through publication, Rethinking Schools has always supported education activism. Rethinking Schools editors were instrumental in launching a community struggle in Milwaukee to establish La Escuela Fratney in 1988 as Wisconsin's first two-way Spanish-English bilingual program—a school characterized by robust parent involvement and multicultural-antiracist curriculum. Rethinking Schools editors were founding members of the National Coalition of Education Activists (NCEA),

an important multi-racial organization of parents, community activists, and educators united to defend and transform public schools. Although NCEA no longer exists, Rethinking Schools has been active in supporting regional gatherings like the Northwest Teaching for Social Justice Conference (in Seattle and Portland), Teachers 4 Social Justice (in San Francisco), the Cross-Border Conference on Teaching for Social Justice (sponsored by the British Columbia Teachers Federation and the Surrey Teachers Association), the Chicago Teachers for Social Justice Curriculum Fair, and other national gatherings, including the Teacher Activist Group network. For several years, Rethinking Schools collaborated with the San Francisco-based human rights organization Global Exchange to lead educator tours to the U.S.-Mexico border, as part of a "From the World to Our Classrooms" project. We have also collaborated with the National Education Association on week-long "Power of the Pen" writing retreats for teachers from around the country.

Of the "kid-friendly" Black Lives Matter "guiding principles" authored by Lalena Garcia and reproduced by the DC Area Educators for Social Justice, we see that key planks include those of "Queer Affirming," "Transgender Affirming," "Diversity," and "Globalism," all presented very favorably and deceptively in such a way that lends itself to easy indoctrination of children. Parent organization of the DC Area Educators for Social Justice, Teaching for Change links to lesson plans such as its own Challenge Islamophobia initiative and the Zinn Education Project, which is a collaboration between Teaching for Change and Rethinking Schools. Teaching for Change funders include or have included the Tides Foundation, the Open Society Foundations, the Fannie Mae Foundation, the WK Kellogg Foundation, the DC Mayor's Office on Latino Affairs, Capital One, and the Target Foundation.

The DC Area Educators for Social Justice also claims inspiration from the work of Teachers for Social Justice, NYCoRE, and NW Teachers for Social Justice. NW Teachers for Social Justice's Northwest Teaching for Social Justice Resources Fair, an extension of their annual conference, has in the past featured participants such as Rethinking Schools (a co-sponsor), GLSEN, Haymarket Books, and the Washington State Holocaust Education Resource Center. Its 10th Annual Northwest Teaching for Social Justice Conference (2017) was sponsored by Rethinking Schools, the Oregon Writing Project at Lewis & Clark College, the Portland Association of Teachers (which represents more than 4,000 professional educators in the Portland Public School system), and Social Equality Educators:

> A rank and file organization of activist educators in Seattle. We seek to transform education in terms that empower students, teachers, and the communities that our public schools serve. As NEA members, we understand that the educators' union has a vital role to play in creating an equitable education system.

Teachers for Social Justice, stylized Teachers 4 Social Justice:

> Condemns all forms of systemic violence caused by policing that continues to disproportionately impact Black lives and perpetuate the trauma of white

supremacy. . . . We must struggle for liberation in solidarity with our school communities . . . in support of the movement to abolish police and prisons.

What are they liberating themselves from other than rational thought and reality?

Teachers for Social Justice, along with Rethinking Schools, NYCoRE, and more, are represented in the "grassroots" national coalition called Teacher Activist Groups (TAG). NYCoRE hilariously links New York Governor Andrew Cuomo and New York City Mayor Bill DeBlasio with President Donald Trump by stating, "we are particularly frustrated by Cuomo, DeBlasio, and Trump's legislation and action" and condemning neo-liberalism—which I actually agree with. Their proposed "systemic changes," however, revolve around things like NYQueer, which is:

A working group of the New York Collective of Radical Educators (NY-CoRE) that focuses on gender and sexuality as they relate to school communities. We believe that educators of all age groups can and should address issues of gender and sexuality in the classroom.

In other words, exactly what the neo-liberal Establishment supports. A for effort, gang.

Through a Soros Justice Fellowship, Olga Tomchin has started an immigration detention project at the Transgender Law Center. The project will "advocate for the human rights of transgender people in immigration detention, particularly undocumented trans women of color." Giselle Ariel Bleuz of the *Huffington Post's* "10 Trans Filmmakers You Should Know" received a Soros Justice Fellowship to "build the capacity of transgender and gender nonconforming people to produce and distribute media addressing the ways the criminal justice system impacts their communities" through the Global Action Project:

At Global Action Project youth make media, grow their leadership, and create innovative stories that promote and amplify movements for social justice from low-income, new immigrant, TGNC (trans and gender non-conforming) and LGBQ (Lesbian, Gay, Bisexual and Queer) communities.

CeCe McDonald received a Soros Justice Fellowship to "create a curriculum for grassroots education that builds community support and power for transgender women, particularly transgender women of color" at the Barnard Center for Research on Women (despite the fact that McDonald is a biological male). Yessica Gonzalez Rodriguez received a Soros Justice Fellowship "to end the practice of holding transgender and gender nonconforming people in immigration detention centers" through the TransLatin@ Coalition. These followships are training programs for weaponized and aggrieved "activists" to plug into the system and push it further in the direction of the Soros camp and their allies. The Soros Justice Fellowships:

Strongly encourage applications for projects that demonstrate a clear understanding of the intersection of criminal justice issues with the particular needs of low-income communities, communities of color, immigrants, LGBTQ people, women and children, and those otherwise disproportionately affected by harsh criminal justice policies, as well as applications for projects that cut across various criminal justice fields and related sectors, such as education, health and mental health, housing, and employment.

Another major organization active in promoting the LGBTQ agenda is Funders for LGBTQ Issues, founded in 1982. It is "a network of more than 75 foundations, corporations, and funding institutions that collectively award more than $1 billion annually, including approximately $100 million specifically devoted to LGBTQ issues." They work closely with the Evelyn and Walter Haas, Jr. Fund, and they facilitate grants from PFLAG, TD Bank, the Astraea Lesbian Foundation for Justice, and the Open Society Foundations, to name just a few. Their Board of Directors includes representatives from the Foundation for a Just Society, Borealis Philanthropy, the Women's Foundation of California, and the Wellspring Philanthropic Fund. Their National Director of Philanthropic Outreach is Rebecca Wisotsky, formerly of the Audre Lorde Project and the Astraea Lesbian Foundation for Justice. In 2011, Wisotsky "was a fellow in the Selah Leadership Program, a national network of progressive Jews who work for social justice, where she is still an active network member." Ben Francisco Maulbeck, former CEO of Funders for LGBTQ Issues, is described as "a leader for LGBT rights, racial equity and social change." He is a Harvard Kennedy School alumnus. Funders for LGBTQ Issues Treasurer Kristine Stallone, whose resumé includes CFO for the Arcus Foundation and Vice President for Finance and Administration with the American Jewish World Service.

Karen Zelermyer, former Chair and CEO of Funders for LGBTQ Issues and former Deputy Director at and major donor to the Astraea Lesbian Foundation for Justice, was on the Board of Jews for Racial and Economic Justice, which receives funding from, among others, the New York Community Trust, the Wellspring Philanthropic Fund, and the Nathan Cummings Foundation, which was, returning to Sean Cooper for *Tablet* in 2020:

Established in 1949 by Nathan Cummings, the founder of the Sara Lee Corporation. . . . The foundation was endowed with $415 million by Cummings upon his death, in 1985. . . . Not long after her arrival in New York, Stosh Cotler [of Bend the Arc] was added to a short list of rising Jewish activists compiled by Ronit Aviv, a Jewish executive who was part of the Jewcy network, who'd been asked by a consultant working with a New York Jewish family foundation seeking to build a visionary new project for Jewish professionals. The project was the brainchild of the consultant, a labor activist in his 40s named Simon Greer, and Rachel Cowan, a Reform rabbi from the Upper West Side of Manhattan and civil rights activist who became the program director for Jewish life at the Nathan Cummings Foundation. . . . Built from the ground up with the latest in corporate efficiency tactics borrowed from the business world, the program's graduates, as a uniformly trained corps, could go back out into the professional world to leverage their own organizational resources toward supporting the network's shared mission. Just as Cowan saw in Greer a bold new voice in New York activist circles, Greer had seen something of his own ambition and promise in the newly arrived Stosh Cotler. Eager to immerse herself in the center of the Jewish power dynamic which Cotler had viewed from afar in the Pacific Northwest, she accepted Greer's invitation to what would be the first iteration of the training program, a retreat administered by the California-based Rockwood Leadership Institute, a premier incubator for nonprofit business executives. . . . The prototype of sorts for the Selah program, Rockwood itself was founded in 2000 by a man named Robert Gass, a Harvard graduate who'd become a sought-after leadership guru and professional network node to a political-left subset of the Ivy League educated C-suite class. . . . Among the organizations that paid fealty to Gass and his methods was the Obama White House. During President Obama's first term in office, five senior leaders in his administration trained at Rockwood; during his reelection campaign, Obama gave his national field director, Jeremy Bird, the benefit of personal coaching from Gass himself. . . . As a fierce advocate for new technologies, free market competition, and disruptive social movements, Gass bestowed a set of organizational ideals and common language that scattered from the halls of the White House into a close-knit professional network of like-minded alumni. Operating within bureaucratic strata galvanized by principles of transformational leadership and corporate cultural practice, Gass' disciples have carried the Obama doctrine into powerful offices that are likewise run and operated on the premise of wide-scale social change carried out according to technocratic principles. Ken Zimmerman, Rockwood graduate and liaison for Obama's transition team, now directs the U.S. programs for George Soros' Open Society Foundations. Sara El-Amine, the executive director of Obama's issue advocacy shop, Organizing for Action, and also a Rockwood alum, is now a senior director of the Chan Zuckerberg Initiative.

The Nathan Cummings Foundation has donated millions of dollars to Bend the Arc, with Simon Greer the key figure, growing what would become Bend the Arc before leaving to head the Nathan Cummings Foundation. The Nathan Cummings Foundation also provides funding to the ADL and slew of "progressive" causes, many of them BLM-adjacent.

Returning to Karen Zelermyer, her Spring 2015 peers on the Board of Jews for Racial and Economic Justice included Rusty Stahl (Ford Foundation alum and founder and Executive Director Emeritus of Emerging Practitioners in Philanthropy, where Wisotsky is a Steering Committee member), Audrey Sasson (formerly of the American Jewish World Service), Jennifer Hirsch (Professor and Deputy Chair for Doctoral Studies in the Department of Sociomedical Sciences at Columbia University's Mailman School of Public Health with research focusing on gender, sexuality, and reproductive health and US-Mexico migration and migrant health), and Rebecca Fox of the Wellspring Philanthropic Fund and former Board member of Funders for LGBTQ Issues.[96] Audrey Sasson is now their Executive Director.

Further evidencing that this agenda is nothing but a whacky conspiracy theory, Sean Cooper writes:

---

[96] Fox is also an alumnus of Bend the Arc: A Jewish Partnership for Justice's Saleh Leadership Program designed for Jewish social justice leaders working in Jewish and secular organizations. Rebecca Wisotsky, Rusty Stahl, and Audrey Sasson are also alumni, and they were all part of the same cohort to boot. Maureen Greenwood-Basken of Wellspring is also an alum.

Since the time of Simon Greer's start of what would become Bend the Arc, the organization has never been more powerful or more influential. . . . Greer explained to one reporter that he'd "spent a lot of time building a relationship with George Soros," adding, in the third person, that the "Soros people think Simon's totally reliable, easygoing, humble." If he's an ally to George Soros, the billionaire investor and philanthropist who made a fortune in futures markets and famously turned a $2 billion profit for his hedge fund when he shorted the pound sterling, Greer also became something of a mentor to his son, Alex, who described Greer, in 2012, as part of his inner circle of personal advisers. In 2015, after Greer had already left Nathan Cummings, Alex Soros formalized his involvement with Bend the Arc by taking a board director seat on the organization's first political action committee, which he personally funded. . . . As Soros explained in the mid-'90s to one reporter, "this whole interest in universal ideas is a typical means to escape from the particular," a reference to his Jewish identity. "I am escaping the particular. I think I am doing exactly that by espousing this universal concept." In his creation of what would become Bend the Arc, Greer championed these same universalism principles in the name of a Judaism that would seek to transcend its own specificity to achieve what he estimated to be a more powerful universalism.

As we have seen, that last point about transcending its own specificity is only so much sophistry; the aim is for everyone else *except* Jews to embrace universalism, "equality," and, ultimately, sameness.

The Open Society Foundations also figures prominently among the major donors to the Astraea Lesbian Foundation for Justice, which also include the American Jewish World Service, the Ford Foundation, the Oak Foundation, the Arcus Foundation, the Amy Mandel and Katina Rodis Fund, Dreilinden, the Laughing Gull Foundation, Macy's, the Horizons Foundation, Gilead Sciences, the Foundation for a Just Society, the NoVo Foundation, the Sigrid Rausing Trust, Wells Fargo Advisors, the Tegan & Sara Foundation, Morgan Stanley Global Impact Funding Trust, Mama Cash, Naomi Sobel and Becky Silverstein, Emily Rosenberg and Darlene de Manincor, the Philip and Muriel Berman Foundation, the East African Sexual Health and Rights Initiative (UHAI-EASHRI), the PayPal Giving Fund, the OTHER Foundation, Karen Zelermyer and Tami Gold, the Tides Foundation, the Levi Strauss Foundation, RBC Wealth Management, Jason Reitman, the Shlenker Block Fund at the Houston Jewish Community Foundation, Erika Karp (the self-described "Jewish lesbian" founder and CEO of Cornerstone Capital), the Jewish Communal Fund,[97] the Jewish Community Federation and Endowment Fund,[98] the Gill Foundation, Kathy Levinson of the Lesbian Equity Foundation,[99] Martine and Bina Rothblatt, Ellen Page,

---

[97] Established in 1972, it is one of the largest Jewish donor advised funds (DAFs) in the country, managing $1.8 billion in charitable assets.

[98] "The Federation's $1.8 billion Endowment Fund serves as a trusted advisor for philanthropic services by aligning donors' personal and financial charitable goals with Jewish values."

[99] From her website: "As part of her civil rights work, Ms. Levinson has held prominent positions in the Democratic Party, including memberships in the California Democratic Central Committee, the Jefferson Trust, and the Gay and Lesbian Leadership Council. She was appointed as a co-chair of the National Finance Committee for President Obama's re-election campaign in early 2011. Ms. Levinson also supports the activities of several Jewish organizations, and she held the position of President of the Board of

Funders for LGBTQ Issues, and Susan Rosenberg.

The Jewish Susan Rosenberg was sentenced to 58 years in prison on weapons and explosives charges after being apprehended with her accomplice in 1984 while unloading 740 pounds of dynamite and weapons from a car into a storage locker in New Jersey; Rosenberg was also being sought as an accomplice in the 1979 prison escape of cop-killer Assata Shakur. Her sentence was commuted by Bill Clinton, whose daughter Chelsea is married to the Jewish private equity figure Marc Mezvinsky, on his last day in office at the same time the Jewish Marc Rich was pardoned; Rich fled the country after being indicted on 65 criminal counts, including income tax evasion, wire fraud, racketeering, and conducting illicit deals with Iran during the US Embassy hostage crisis and Carter's oil embargo. Regarding Rich's pardon, via his Wikipedia page:

In a February 18, 2001 op-ed essay in *The New York Times*, Clinton (by then out of office) explained why he had pardoned Rich, noting that U.S. tax professors Bernard Wolfman of the Harvard Law School and Martin Ginsburg of Georgetown University Law Center had concluded that no crime had been committed, and that Rich's companies' tax-reporting position had been reasonable. . . . Clinton also cited clemency pleas he had received from Israeli government officials, including then-Prime Minister Ehud Barak [a known Jeffrey Epstein associate]. Rich had made substantial donations to Israeli charitable foundations over the years, and many senior Israeli officials, such as Shimon Peres and Ehud Olmert, argued on his behalf behind the scenes. Many leading figures of the Jewish world such as Abraham Foxman, the head of the Anti-Defamation League (ADL), whose organization had received over $250,000 from Rich over the years also wrote to President Clinton for Rich's pardon. Among other leading Jewish leaders writing to Clinton were Shlomo Ben-Ami, Israel's former foreign minister; Michael Steinhardt, a philanthropist and CEO of Steinhardt Associates; and Rabbi Irving Greenberg, chairman of the United States Holocaust Memorial Council, which oversees the U.S. Holocaust Memorial Museum. Although none of the figures other than Foxman were investigated for their support of Rich's pardon. Clinton later claimed on more than one occasion that Jewish pressure contributed to his decision to pardon Rich. He stated in an interview with *The New York Times* that "Israeli officials of both major political parties and leaders of Jewish communities in America and Europe urged the pardon of Mr. Rich." He made similar comments off camera to CNBC's Geraldo Rivera that "Israel did influence me profoundly." Speculation about another rationale for Rich's pardon involved his alleged involvement with the Israeli intelligence

---

the Gideon Hausner Jewish Day School. She spent five years assisting the Albert L. Schultz Jewish Community Center in Palo Alto, California, and sat on the board of the Jewish Community Federation of San Francisco. Currently, Ms. Levinson serves as a Managing Director for the Golden Seeds, a national network of angel investors dedicated to investing in early stage companies founded and/or led by women. She also sits on the Advisory Council of Illuminate Ventures, an early stage venture capital firm based in the San Francisco Bay Area, as well as on the boards of several of private companies and non-profit organizations. Kathy Levinson studied economics at Stanford University . . . Levinson also completed a Harvard University School of Business MBA in Professional Management Development program in 1988. . . . Ms. Levinson is also a graduate of the prestigious Wexner Heritage Foundation, which focuses on strengthening Jewish leadership throughout North America and Israel."

community. Rich reluctantly acknowledged in interviews with his biographer, Daniel Ammann, that he had assisted the Mossad, Israel's intelligence service, a claim that Ammann said was confirmed by a former Israeli intelligence officer. According to Ammann, Rich had helped finance the Mossad's operations and had supplied Israel with strategic amounts of Iranian oil through a secret oil pipeline. The aide to Rich who had persuaded Denise Rich to personally ask President Clinton to review Rich's pardon request was a former chief of the Mossad, Avner Azulay. Another former Mossad chief, Shabtai Shavit, had also urged Clinton to pardon Rich, who he said had routinely allowed intelligence agents to use his offices around the world.

Following her release, Susan Rosenberg immediately landed on her feet when she was hired by the American Jewish World Service (AJWS) as Communications Director and today she is the Vice Chair of the Board for Thousand Currents, the umbrella organization for Black Lives Matter, which is itself along with BLM-adjacent organizations, just another Establishment creation, underwritten by the Ford Foundation, the Open Society Foundations, and the like. According to *Politico*, in late 2015:

> Some of the biggest donors on the left plan to meet behind closed doors . . . with leaders of the Black Lives Matter movement and their allies. The meetings are taking place at the annual winter gathering of the Democracy Alliance major liberal donor club, which runs from Tuesday evening through Saturday morning and is expected to draw Democratic financial heavyweights, including Tom Steyer and Paul Egerman. . . . The DA, as the club is known in Democratic circles, is recommending its donors step up check writing to a handful of endorsed groups that have supported the Black Lives Matter movement. . . . The Democracy Alliance was created in 2005 by a handful of major donors, including billionaire financier George Soros and Taco Bell heir Rob McKay. . . . Endorsed beneficiaries include the Center for American Progress think tank, the liberal attack dog Media Matters and the Democratic data firm Catalist, though members also give heavily to Democratic politicians and super PACs that are not part of the DA's core portfolio. . . . The Democracy Alliance last year voted to endorse a handful of groups focused on engaging African-Americans in politics — some of which have helped facilitate the Black Lives movement.

Thousand Currents receives major donations from organizations like the MacArthur Foundation, Apple, the International Planned Parenthood Federation (IPPF), the JP Morgan Chase Foundation, the Horizons Foundation, the Clif Bar Family Foundation, the Rita Brandeis Memorial Fund at the Tides Foundation, and the Morgan Stanley Global Impact Funding Trust.

Genre Pluriels is yet another of these seemingly-infinite LGBTQ organizations. Based in Belgium, it derives significant institutional support from various cultural institutions, the city of Brussels (as part of the Rainbow Cities Network), L'Institut pour l'égalité des femmes et des hommes, and RainbowHouse-Brussels. RainbowHouse-Brussels features such member organizations as Genre Pluriels, Fat Positivity, the Network of European LGBTiQ Families Associations, Balkan

LBGTQIA+, Lesborama* 2020,[100] Rainbow Cops Belgium LGBT Police (a member of the European LGBT Police Association), and Transkids:

> As part of the Pride Festival. . . . Transkids will offer 3 events not to be missed: "Le Fabuleux Weekend", the first gathering reserved for transgender children and teenagers aged 6 to 18. 48 hours of activities and workshops to help them fully live their identity. Two editions of 'L'Atelier Très Très Très Dégenreant!' where all children aged 6 to 12 are invited to create stories to deconstruct gender stereotypes. They will then be used to design a book that will serve as an educational tool.

The All Genders Welcome campaign is "an awareness campaign by the RainbowHouse for companies and municipalities in Brussels, with the support of the Brussels Capital Region and the Fédération Wallonie-Bruxelles." Brussels, which proudly proclaims itself the "second-most cosmopolitan city on earth," identifies key "focus areas" as: Developing awareness-raising projects on the topics of homophobia and transphobia, aimed at citizens; Strengthening the fight against homophobic and transphobic incidents (hate speech and crimes); Providing training courses on LGBT issues for the Brussels police departments; Financial support of projects developed by Brussels LGBT organisations; Contribution to and implementation of the Federal Action Plan against Homophobia and Transphobia 2016/2019; and Being an inclusive employer of LGBT staff.

In addition to partnering with RainbowHouse and the organizers of Pride, Brussels Capital Region collaborates with the Brussels municipalities, Unia (Interfederal Centre for Equal Opportunities), the Institute for the Equality of Women and Men (L'Institut pour l'égalité des femmes et des hommes), the French Community Commission (COCOF), the Flemish Community Commission (VGC), the Common Community Commission (COCOM), Brussels Gay Sports, Rainbowcops, Cavaria, Merhaba (LGBT youth), Omnya (LGBT youth), Basta (LGBT youth), Identités du Baobab (urban film festival), and Genres d'à Côté (urban film festival).

Esch-sur Alzette in neighboring Luxembourg partners with Centre d'Information Gay et Lesbien (CIGALE) and Rosa Lëtzebuerg (Rosa Luxemburg) *asbl* and lists its priorities as "visibility" and "LGBT refugees." It is, like Brussels, part of the Rainbow Cities Network, whose members work with similar associations and have similar missions. For example, Reykjavík's description of activities through the Rainbow Cities Network:

> External training and counselling is provided by the National Queer Organisation through a service contract with the city. Additionally there is a focus on gender neutral facilities, trans children within the school system and a special focus on LGBT+ people and domestic violence. . . . A long

---

[100] "Lesborama* returns from March 4th to 7th 2020 with 7 screenings of lesbian, bi-, trans- and feminist fictions and documentaries as well as an exhibition, with this year a special focus on the community and its precious allies who support us and make our lives more enjoyable. This sixth edition of Lesborama* will take you on a road-trip to the sea, from a photo exhibition to a Lady on fire, from free and happy clitoris to an African-American lesbian club, from joyful gender transitions to reflections on consent"

term project that has recently been established is called Reykjavík Rainbow Certification. Through the project all staff, including division leaders and management, and all units within the City of Reykjavík will be able to apply for the certification which can be obtained through LGBT+ sensitive training.

The Rainbow Cities Network encompasses: Reykjavík, Iceland; Esch-sur Alzette, Luxembourg; São Paulo, Brazil; Kotor, Montenegro; Aarhus, Denmark; Bergen, Norway; Bruges, Belgium; Leuven, Belgium; Mexico City, Mexico; Oslo, Norway; Amsterdam, Netherlands; Berlin, Germany; Brussels Capital Region, Belgium; Cork, Ireland; Geneva, Switzerland; Hanover, Germany; Munich, Germany; Ljubljana, Slovenia; Paris, France; Vienna, Austria; Zurich, Switzerland; Rotterdam, Netherlands; Mannheim, Germany; Nuremburg, Germany; Ghent, Belgium; Barcelona, Spain; Bern, Switzerland; Cologne, Germany; Frankfurt, Germany; and Hamburg, Germany.

The German Agency for International Cooperation (GIZ) has sponsored LGBTQ-centric projects in Belize, Haiti, Jamaica, Kenya, Colombia, Madagascar, Serbia, Suriname, South Africa, Russia, Poland, the Ukraine, Nicaragua, Honduras, Guatemala, El Salvador, Turkey, and Tanzania.

In Colombia, Proyecto Colombia Diversa (PCD) has received funds from the Swedish International Development Cooperation Agency (SIDA) and the Canadian International Development Agency (CIDA). The German BMZ and AA have made overtures to SIDA and Hivos "to suggest a common LGBTI strategy" and in order to amplify their impact and reach. Research authored by Arn Thorben Sauer on behalf of (Trans)Gender & Diversity Consulting in Berlin also mentions the possibility of the "pro-LGBTI governments" leveraging their power (since they tend to be the wealthiest and most connected in Europe) to influence LGBTQ policy in the various supra-governmental or international governing bodies/organizations.

Within the country of Germany, in Brandenburg, an action plan was adopted in 2017 for the "acceptance of gender and sexual diversity, for self-determination and against homo- and transphobia." The federal program "Demokratie leben" supports nine pilot projects that encourage the acceptance of "same-sex lifestyles, reduce prejudice and hostility towards LGBTI people and address violence on grounds of sex or gender, gender identity and sexual orientation." As IGLYO reports:

In Saarland (state of the Federal Republic of Germany) there exists – supported by resources of the federal republic – a school-project. The LSVD-Saar ('Lesbian and Gay Federation in Germany') deliver classes in school with gay and lesbian young people to talk about their sexuality with the students. The government also issued the Policy of sexual education in schools which contains a section on the diversity of sexual identity and orientation.

Further, from IGLYO's 2018 LGBTQI Inclusive Education report:

The framework curriculum 2017/2018 for Brandenburg explicitly stipulates on the interdisciplinary competence development (area: education for acceptance and diversity; area: gender mainstreaming as well as area: sexual education/education for sexual self-determination) as well as developing concrete guidelines for teachers in Brandenburg. . . . The State of Berlin, for instance, states that all schools should designate a person responsible to provide support to teachers and LGBTQI learners. In the senate department for education in Berlin there is a central ombudsperson for anti-discrimination. . . . The state of Berlin has published several materials as part of the local action plan for sexual and gender diversity. . . . The state government of Lower Saxony, for instance, gives annual financial support to a civil society organisation named "SCHLAU" which serves as an umbrella organisation for providing queer educational services. In addition, 10 Lower Saxon municipalities support queer educational projects on a local level. For its part, the state government of Berlin financially supports civil society organisations like Bildungsinitiative QUEERFORMAT, Migrationsrat Berlin, Lesben- und Schwulenverband Berlin-Brandenburg, ABqueer, Jugendnetzwerk Lambda Berlin-Brandenburg to implement the local action plan by providing further trainings and educational materials for teachers and school workshops for students. . . . To disseminate knowledge in the field of counselling, the Federal Ministry for Family Affairs, Senior Citizens, Women and Youth funded the following publications. The flyers which translate as 'Girl? - Boy? - Your transgender child' and 'Female? - Male? - Your intersex child,' both issued by the registered association Queer Leben e.V., aim at informing relatives of transgender and intersex children but also qualified medical and psychological staff and further occupational groups alike.

Dreilinden, based in Germany, is another name we've seen continually crop up. Dreilinden, which states that "LGBTI Rights are Children's Rights" based on the writings of Kirsten Sandberg (former Acting Supreme Court Justice in Norway, former Chair of the United Nations Committee on the Rights of the Child, former Visiting Fellow at the University of Chicago, and Professor of Law at the University of Oslo) and other sources, provides both grants and manages investment fund portfolios intersecting with "climate change," investment in microfinance institutions to aid in equatorial migration into the West (much like the World Bank and USAID), feminism, and "LGBTQIA* communities." From their December 2019 document "Beyond Gender Lens Investing":

On our journey to scope and size the queer investment universe, we started looking around the impact investment space to see how we could build on already existing approaches and frameworks. Luckily we didn't have to look very far as our friends at Criterion Institute (and many others) have already done fantastic work in a related field—gender lens investing (GLI)! GLI connects well to the way we want to approach queer impact investing. . . . Queer businesses and businesses catering to the queer communities face identical challenges. We have seen great results in countries with queer chambers of commerce (e.g. FMELGBT in Mexico). . . . Queer communities face certain challenges that are systemic and need to be addressed through legal, policy and grassroots initiatives. We do not accept these shortcomings of the status quo and will keep supporting projects that drive grassroots change.

Dreilinden is also part of several LGBTQ networks such as the GPP, Tides' Equality Without Borders, LGBTI-Plattform für Menschenrechte der Hirschfeld-Eddy-Stiftung (Berlin), and Regenbogen-Philanthropie. The LGBT Platform, founded as Network Rainbow Philanthropy in 2009 and financed by Dreilinden, is coordinated by the Hirschfeld Eddy Stiftung, also known as the Hirschfeld Eddy Foundation (HES),[101] which "meets once per year and is committed to informing about international LGBTI issues, connecting German development aid actors, [and] increasing LGBTI funding and networking internationally." The Hirschfeld Eddy Foundation with an unnamed "external agency" sponsored "activists" from thirteen African countries to travel to Germany, and they sponsored projects in Nigeria and Nicaragua.

Dreilinden has sponsored a number of "Rainbow Conferences," where NGOs meet and identify "action areas" to focus their efforts. The most recent concentrated on Russia. Their recent grantees include:

- Erasmus University of Rotterdam: The Dreilinden Fellowship for LGBTI students in Work and Globalization at the International Institute of Social Studies
- Astraea Lesbian Foundation for Justice
- Amadeu Antonio Stiftung (Berlin) for Gender Fachstelle: National networking and lobby hub regarding gender sensitive right-wing extremism prevention
- OII Europe
- Insight Ukraine
- Tides
- OutRight Action International
- Queer Montenegro
- The Initiative for Strategic Litigation in Africa (ISLA)-South Africa: A feminist and Pan-African organisation that aims to contribute to the development of jurisprudence on women's human rights and sexual rights on the continent

In late 2019, Dreilinden commissioned iGravity and Federacion Mexicana de Empresarios LGBT+ to "scope out the queer investment universe" in Poland, Slovakia, Mexico, and South Africa and create an "impact investment" LGBTQ action plan and to "incubate a queer investment practice." One strategy that was deemed particularly promising was establishing and expanding "queer chambers of commerce," with the ideal being that of the United States.

Dreilinden's investment portfolio is diverse and is patterned after the increasingly-prevalent/centralized "philanthropic capitalism" favored by the ruling class. The amplification effect cannot be understated, and their partners include some of the wealthiest and most powerful people on the planet. As one example, their "Sarasin Sustainable Properties—European Cities" is a product of Catella Real Estate AG (Munich) in cooperation with Bank J. Safra Sarasin AG (Switzerland). The Bank J. Safra Sarasin is a Swiss private bank, founded in 1841 and headquartered in Basel.

---

[101] The human rights foundation of the Lesbian and Gay Federation in Germany, named after Magnus Hirschfeld and FannyAnn Eddy, founder of the Sierra Leone Lesbian and Gay Association.

It is owned by the Safra Group; in 2013, Safra Group acquired Bank Sarasin & Co. Ltd and merged it with its Bank Jacob Safra Switzerland subsidiary. The Safra Group, based out of Brazil, is an extensive network comprised of banking and financial institutions, industrial operations, real estate, and agribusinesses. The Safra Group is run by Joseph Safra (net worth: $24.7 billion) and the Safra family. They are Jewish.

Dreilinden's investments also intersect with projects of the World Bank, the United Nations, the Rockefeller Foundation, and Credit Suisse, among others. Another of their affiliated projects is the Media Development Investment Fund (MDIF), "a fund structure that includes private equity, debt and hybrid funds. With a current portfolio of more than $100 million, all of our funds provide financing to independent media in countries where access to free and independent is under threat." Reading between the lines, what this means is that they are going to seed money to "independent" media that will toe the legacy media's line on all things globalist, including LGBTQ, providing the illusion of "open dialogue" and "plurality" so central to the maintenance of this system.

# Transgender, Inc.

*"You see I can't always get through to you*
*So I go for your son. . . .*
*Right now*
*I think I'm gonna plan a new trend*
*Because the line on the graph's getting low*
*And we can't have that*
*And you think you're immune*
*But I can sell you anything."*

– Joe Jackson, "I'm the Man"

If you're not on board with the project, as for example the UK's Core Issues Trust is not, Barclays—a major London Pride sponsor—like Chase Bank (see: Martina Markota), is more than happy to close your bank account. In 2017, JP Morgan Chase announced it would be giving $1 million to be split equally by the Southern Poverty Law Center and the Anti-Defamation League to "fight hate." Around the same time, homosexual Apple CEO Tim Cook announced he would be giving $1 million each to the SPLC and ADL for the same reason. These organizations are attack dogs going after any person or group whose message contradicts that of the Establishment apparatus from TERFs to conservative Christians to academics and pediatric organizations. The alternatives are diminishing, too, with thousands of small businesses in the United States shut down for good due to the imposition of otherwise half-assed coronavirus measures.

Barclays and JP Morgan Chase are totally on board with the blanket censorship and the rigorous enforcement of orthodoxy, and they put their money where their mouths are. The current Interbank LGBT Forum Committee consists of members of the LGBT Networks from the following organizations in addition to those of JP Morgan Chase and Barclays: Accenture, Bank of America-Merrill Lynch, Bloomberg, BNP Paribas, BNY Mellon, Citigroup, CME Group, Credit Suisse, Deloitte, Deutsche Bank, EY, Goldman Sachs, HSBC, IG, Lloyds Banking Group, Macquarie, Moody's, Morgan Stanley, NatWest, Nomura, Refinitiv (jointly owned by the Blackstone Group which has a 55% stake and Thomson Reuters; CEO David Craig was a partner at McKinsey and is a leader on the World Economic Forum's Digital Disruption Innovation Group on digital identities and federated ledgers (Blockchain) and also sits on the WEF AI and Automation in Financial Services steering committee), Rothschild, Royal Bank of Canada, Societe Generale, State Street, and UBS.

In the UK, the Interbank LGBT Forum also supports Corporate and Social Responsibility initiatives, encouraging its members to support "LGBT community initiatives across the Greater London area," for example. It has sponsored a special film screening at the London Lesbian and Gay Film Festival/BFI Flare and has previously sponsored the Pride 10k. In 2015, Interbank was the main sponsor of Positive East's Red Run which took place at the end of November and has kept sponsoring the event since. The HIV-focused fundraiser includes other sponsors such as Gilead Sciences and ViiV Healthcare.

The Interbank LGBT Forum supports trans*formation:

> trans*formation is a new, thrice-yearly networking evening for professionals who identify as trans* and their friends and supporters. It seeks to connect and inspire trans* professionals in a safe and welcoming environment and, as its name suggests, work to achieve a real transformation in the standing, openness and wellbeing of trans* professionals and the companies for which they work. Traditional LGBT networks have been a good start for this group, but this initiative has been launched and led by, trans* professionals to meet that community's unique needs and aspirations.

They speak at Inside & Out, "an annual recruitment event aimed at LGBT graduates to improve knowledge and awareness of roles in the investment banking industry."

NatWest was the founding partner of the British LGBT Awards; 2020 category partners and sponsors included Nestlé, HSBC UK, Network Rail, MI5, Johnson & Johnson, Deutsche Bank, Tesco, IKEA, and Sky. 2015 LGBT+ Diversity Champion nominees included: Captain Hannah Winterbourne, "the senior transgender representative on the Army's LGBT committee. From the start, Hannah has been a vocal and visible role model for other transgender soldiers and her recent engagement in media projects (including the 'all about trans' video series, an interview in The Sun and appearance on the Lorraine Show)"; Robert Kerse, "the Executive Director of Resources of Circle housing, the third largest affordable housing provider in the UK"; and Steven Cox, Executive Director, Public Sector, UK & Ireland Fujitsu, "Steven regularly attends Stonewall roundtable discussions, on topics such as Straight Ally programmes. Steven actively encourages Fujitsu staff participation in London and Manchester Pride events (marching with Stonewall in 2014, and plans for Fujitsu to march as a company)." The institutional support—nay, imperative—for advancing this agenda could not be clearer. Soon it will be so that any dissidents will be uniformly denied service and forced to comply, starve, or go off the grid.

KPMG works with Stonewall and in 2014 established "diversity target zones" which:

> Encapsulated [their] ambition to become a more representative workforce. They focused on: Gender; Ethnicity; Disability and Sexual Orientation. . . . As part of [their] Fairer Futures campaign, [they] set new inclusion, diversity and social equality targets to achieve by 2022. In support of [their] leading work on social mobility, [they] are exploring setting a socioeconomic back-

ground target and [they] have also increased [their] support for Black Heritage talent, as [they] want to drive a significant increase in representation. . . .
[They] are a signatory of the [UK] government and Business in the Community's Race at Work Charter, which commits businesses to improving recruitment and career progression of BAME (Black, Asian and Minority Ethnic)
employees and are a signatory of the Women in Finance Charter.

KPMG is a sponsor of organizations such as Out Leadership and PFLAG. PFLAG's
other corporate sponsors include Verizon, WilmerHale LLP, Walmart, Oreo, Sub-
aru, Calvin Klein, UPS, Bank of America, American Airlines, Merck, Hallmark,
Major League Baseball, Dow, Nike, Facebook, Bloomberg, Citi, and GlaxoSmithKline.

The aforementioned Race at Work Charter includes such signatories in addition
to KPMG such as: MI5, MI6, the NHS, the Department for Education, the Home
Office, JP Morgan Chase, BlackRock, Barclays, the Bank of England, the Bank of
Ireland, Anglo-American, Bain & Company, the British Army, Boots UK (a pharmacy chain that also sells cosmetics and other products, similar to a Walgreens in
the US), HSBC UK, the Royal Mail, the House of Commons, the House of Lords,
the Royal Air Force, the Royal Navy, Channel 4, the City of London Corporation,
Deutsche Bank, National Grid, the National Assembly for Wales, the European Bank
for Reconstruction and Development, NatWest Group, *Financial Times*, Nestlé UK
& Ireland, National Police Chiefs Council, Unilever, UK Government Investments,
the Ministry of Defence, the Ministry of Justice, the Welsh Government, McDonald's, Lloyds Banking Group, Saatchi & Saatchi, Her Majesty's Treasury, the Scottish Government, Hilton, PepsiCo, the Royal College of Veterinary Surgeons, the
Human Tissue Authority, and the London Borough of Tower Hamlets.

The World Bank is here to remind us of the costliness of "exclusion," whether it
be "gender minorities" as the UK Baring Foundation calls them or the Roma, with
whom George Soros seems to have a particular obsession; from a *New York Times
Magazine* feature published in 2018 penned by Michael Steinberger:

Soros's efforts on behalf of one group in particular, the Roma, seem especially germane right now. In June, the new Italian interior minister, Matteo
Salvini, the head of the far-right League party, commissioned a census of the
country's Roma. As an "answer to the Roma question," as he menacingly
phrased it, Salvini vowed to expel all non-Italian Roma and added, "Unfortunately, we will have to keep the Italian Roma." Even in the age of Trump,
his words were shocking, but he has refused to disavow them or back down.
Improving the status of Europe's estimated 10 to 12 million Roma has been
a major priority for Soros and the O.S.F. since the early 1990s. The organization has contributed more than $300 million to projects combating discrim-
ination against the Roma and providing them with greater education, employment and civic opportunities.

EEA Grants has dispensed funds to Positive Voice in Greece to "reach out," along
with the Hellenic Liver Patient Association Prometheus, to Roma with HIV/AIDS
and Hepatitis B and C, but the ulterior motive is not "inclusion" or however they've
decided to frame it: it's actually "to link people with HIV/AIDS with the public

health system, and to collect and analyze statistical data regarding HIV/AIDS and hepatitis B and C per community and geographical area." Positive Voice is funded heavily by big pharma; their supporters include Gilead Sciences (which has also donated extensively to Prometheus), AbbVie, Roche, Mylan, Janssen, Bristol-Myers Squibb, Abbott Hellas, AHF (AIDS Healthcare Foundation)-Europe, Elpen, Merck Sharpe and Dohme, ViiV Healthcare, and GlaxoSmithKline. Oh yeah, and the Open Society Foundations has also dispensed funds to Positive Voice.

The World Bank states in their 2013 document, "Inclusion Matters": "Segregation can restrict the free movement of talent and resources, resulting in productivity losses to an entire economy. One study found that exclusion of the ethnic minority Roma cost Romania 887 million euros in lost productivity." Once again we see here the centrality of dismantling any obstacles or restrictions. The dream here for the ruling class is a thin layer of unfathomably wealthy persons at the top making money from fractional reserve banking and interest, a small bureaucratic class as mid-level functionaries, and a mass of favela-dwelling deracinated and compliant mocha-consumers to cycle in and out of the workforce semi-regularly. Feminists and LGBTQ persons especially make for fantastic cultural commissars *and* consumers in their own right, and are nestled perfectly in that bureaucratic niche.

Goldman Sachs's Lloyd Blankfein states, "Equality is not only a civil rights issue, but also an important business issue for Wall Street and the broader business community." The cultivation of and motivations behind catering to this "market" are probably best illustrated in John Q. Publius's *The God that Failed: Liberalism and the Destruction of the West*, which makes apparent—as with feminism and "diversity"—the economic impetus to market to and cultivate the extant consumer habits of this group; it also has other benefits which extend to the social and the political. This is part and parcel of neo-liberalism, and helps clarify why these NGOs, financial institutions, corporations, and the like insist on enfolding "migrants' rights," "reproductive rights," and appeals to "people of color" in their LGBTQ branding/"activism." Furthermore, the free movement of people and goods into targeted areas has been absolutely central to the neo-liberal project, and anything that greases the skids, removes impediments, and serves as a revenue stream in its own right is going to be valued very highly. Further, for Publius:

> Frank Browning's research of contemporary gay culture found that the homosexual group often used consumption venues and activities to express their hostility and anger toward straight society. This has significant ramifications regarding homosexuals as a revolutionary vanguard and as ruthlessly effective enforcers of Establishment orthodoxy; after all, they are clear beneficiaries of the current system and would not want their privileged position jeopardized. Many LGBTQ people are being unconsciously manipulated as well. The reader must understand the various rainbow identities as a market share, because businesses certainly do. They cultivate it, market to it, and commodify it. The media's incessant wailing about "Donald Trump's America" and the "erasing of trans identities" is actually extremely useful from a business perspective for, as Junghyun Kim writes, "Compensatory consumption refers to a goal-directed behavior that may resolve psychological threats (e.g., social exclusion, identity threats, etc.) by consuming products/brands reinforcing a desired self-view (Lisjak et al. 2015; Kim and Rucker 2012; Lee and Shrum

2012)." Consumers not functionally oriented are significantly affected by the symbols encountered in the identification of goods in the marketplace (Levy, 1959). Grubb and Grathwohl (1967) specified that self-concept is valuable to the individual, and behavior will be directed toward the protection and enhancement of self-concept (Sirgy, 1982), ie-the individual "seeing themselves" represented in or by some facet of the product. Goffman (1951) suggested that products possess symbolic properties, which are somehow congruent with an individual's self-concept (Kates, 1998).[102]

This passage plus the conspicuousness of the consumerist/hedonistic bacchanalia that are these various Prides belie the notion that somehow all of this has to do with "equality." I suspect there are more than a few people who would be diagnosed with narcissistic personality disorder among this crop.

Publius focuses more on the profit-motive—and that is absolutely central to the issue—but he touches on another, perhaps even more vital feature in what we are witnessing as the consequence of hyper-plastic, deracinated consumers who double as political "activists" wholly within the realm of the material. Identity is here *indistinguishable* from brands, consumer products, moral posturing, sexuality, visibility through social media, and "activism," what Publius calls Connected Consumers. They are totally plugged-in to the Matrix, if you like. As Publius writes in *Plastic Empire*:

> Even better for increased profits, Goldenberg et al. (2009) found that social hubs (or highly connected individuals/Connected Spenders) "speed up idea diffusion and adoption processes for virtual goods shared between online users, meaning all of these things tie together, reinforce, and even amplify each other." Consumers tend to utilize emotion-focused coping strategies when avoidance motivations are activated (Han, Duhachek, and Rucker 2015; Duhachek, Agrawal, and Han 2012).

The means of escape for the alienated individual have been pre-planned by the system as a tributary to eventually empty back into the revenue stream or the "inevitable tide of progress," whichever characterization you prefer. Really, it's both—though "progress" is not what I would call the forces of dissolution and decay acting on our civilization and across the globe. The Connected Consumer is forever plugged into an omnipresent, pervasive and invasive system in totality, which is informed by the interests, disposition, and morality (or more appropriately lack thereof) of the ruling class and the "elites" who comprise it, and they are making every effort to ensure that extrication from this system becomes impossible.

The convergence of interests have colluded to ensure "inclusivity" in what is often a precursor to military intervention in the more intractable instances but in many cases is done in tandem with other arms of the Establishment such as the intelligence agencies and NGOs to exert pressure both from within and without on non-compliant regimes and/or more "closed," traditional societies. Prime examples abound in the post-Soviet sphere and the Middle East, where the entire range of measures have been employed to one degree or another; a less overtly coercive method of corporate

---

[102] Publius, *The God that Failed*, 271–272.

and financial pressure applied on behalf of the LGBTQ agenda can be observed with Taiwan.

The first Pride was held in Taipei City in 2003, and the participants wore masks to obscure their identities. Today, Taipei City holds the second-largest Pride parade in Asia after—you guessed it!—Tel Aviv. This is the product of sustained pressure from Western governmental sources looking to further draw Taiwan into its orbit as well as the multi-nationals and financial institutions. In the lead-up to the November 24th, 2018 referendums in Taiwan in which "marriage equality" and "inclusion of LGBTQ issues in school curricula" were to be voted on, the Taiwan Tongzhi (LGBT) Hotline Association, the Human Rights Campaign (HRC), and Out & Equal Workplace Advocates organized a mass campaign to secure major signatories such as Open for Business, IBM, Dow Chemical, Oracle, JP Morgan Chase, HP, Microsoft, Google, EY, Deutsche Bank, Airbnb, and Air Canada. Despite the overt pressure campaign, the HRC claimed that it was actually "American exporters of hate" who were able to force the referendum and not have it imposed by judicial fiat, and that "anti-equality forces sowed fear and misinformation to derail the progress towards marriage equality." Sounds like someone has been reading their Anti-Defamation League press releases!

Nevertheless, the Establishment was ecstatic as same-sex marriage was legalized. "We congratulate the Marriage Equality Coalition Taiwan and all the advocates who worked tirelessly to bring same-sex marriage to Taiwan," said Jean Freedberg, HRC Director of Global Partnerships. Google, Airbnb, Deutsche Bank, EY, Mastercard, Microsoft, and the Taiwan-based O-Bank Co all lauded the decision and stated that there would be innumerable benefits of same-sex weddings, such as "increased productivity, greater labor mobility and less stress in the workplace over perceived discrimination."

According to 2016 research from Credit Suisse (the same Credit Suisse that tweeted out on the International Day Against Homophobia, Transphobia, and Biphobia (IDAHOT) 2019: "Today, Credit Suisse employees around the globe are wearing purple to make a visible stand against homophobia, biphobia and transphobia, helping to create a diverse and inclusive workplace," so hardly unbiased), the performance of a basket of 270 companies that supported LGBT+ policies was on average 3% higher than that of the MSCI All Country World Index, which measures global stock movements. "We value diversity, inclusivity, respect, equality and non-discrimination, as well as seek to protect these values within our company and while working with our business partners," said Patrick Pan, enterprise public lead at Microsoft Taiwan.

Jean Freedberg, HRC Director of Global Partnerships has been very busy; HRC Global visited Taiwan in 2015 to celebrate the largest-ever LGBTQ Pride event in Taipei City where then-Presidential candidate Tsai Ing-wen announced her support for "marriage equality." That same year, HRC co-hosted a special briefing on Capitol Hill organized by Freedom House to welcome the State Department's first Special Envoy for the Human Rights of LGBTI People, Randy Berry; Freedberg addressed those gathered by stating:

> HRC is pleased to co-host this important event. The Obama Administration has taken a strong leadership position in pushing back against bigotry in the

world, and we must continue to pursue every avenue to help LGBT people who are being targeted simply for who they are or who they love.

Other sponsors of the briefing included the Council for Global Equality, Advocates for Youth, RFK Human Rights, and the American Jewish World Service in cooperation with the Congressional LGBT Equality Caucus.

The year prior, Freedberg was part of an American delegation to Germany to attend the Organization for Security and Cooperation in Europe (OSCE) Conference on Anti-Semitism. Using a report authored by Human Rights First and the ADL, the delegation addressed how "the majority of states are still falling short . . . in fighting hate crimes and discrimination against Jews and all vulnerable communities." The conference commemorated the tenth anniversary of the 2004 Berlin Declaration which "urged OSCE participating states to reject anti-Semitism and to monitor and combat it through legislation and education."

"The Participating States of the OSCE gather to assess their action over the last decade against the backdrop of a stunning escalation of anti-Semitism across the region that has shocked the conscience of the world," said Stacy Burdett, Government and National Affairs Director of the Anti-Defamation League and co-chair of The Leadership Conference on Civil and Human Rights' task force on human rights. Continuing:

> We have come together to demonstrate that Jewish communities must not face these threats alone. Working together, NGO coalitions can help create political space for more effective government action against anti-Semitism and all forms of bigotry and hate crime which are also rising in the region.

As always, evidently. Burdett and Freedberg were joined by such "luminaries" as then-Southern Poverty Law Center (SPLC) President Richard Cohen, Hadar Susskind (Bend the Arc: Jewish Action and the Bend the Arc Jewish Action PAC), and Linda Kamm, who has served on the boards of several Jewish organizations, including the American Jewish World Service.

The HRC was also instrumental in lobbying Congress to repeal the ban on HIV-positive immigrants. On March 25th, 2013, they engineered a viral campaign on social media using a red version of their "equality flag" logo to signal support for the *United States v. Windsor* court case; Smirnoff, the HBO program *True Blood*, and Beyoncé all signaled their support. For what it's worth, Beyoncé's Ivy Park clothing line, which bills itself as embodying a "woman-power ethos," is made in Sri Lankan sweatshops where seamstresses make 54 cents an hour—super empowering! The reader may also be interested to learn that the Ivy Park line is actually a joint venture between Beyoncé and retail billionaire Philip Green, who is Jewish.

Some of the HRC's various "equality" and "visibility" award-winners speak volumes about whose interests they actually serve: Monsanto, Michael "Mike" Bloomberg, the Boston Consulting Group, Goldman Sachs, Credit Suisse, and Boeing. HRC's corporate partners include Pfizer, Citibank, Accenture (which according to the most recent tax returns I could locate received over $1.5 million from the Open Society Foundations for IT support in 2017), American Airlines, Nationwide, Mitchell Gold + Bob Williams, UPS, Target, J. Crew, Lyft, Microsoft, Apple, Google, Amazon, Intel, Coca-Cola, Northrop Grumman, Nike, Lexus, Deloitte, Capital One,

Williams Sonoma/Pottery Barn, Diageo/Smirnoff, Carnival Cruises, Chevron, Nordstrom, British Petroleum, EY, Mastercard, MGM Resorts, Cox Enterprises, US Bank, Shell, PNC, Whirlpool, Morgan Stanley, Macy's, Lincoln Financial, IBM, Hyatt, Hershey, and Goldman Sachs. Other partnerships include the Open Society Foundations, the New Venture Fund, and the JP Morgan Chase Foundation.

The Human Rights Campaign (HRC) was founded in 1980 and counts Elizabeth Birch of Apple, Joe Salmonese of pro-abortion group EMILY's List, and former Clinton White House aide Chad Griffin among its former leaders. It is currently helmed by New York Governor Andrew Cuomo's former legal counsel Alphonso David. The HRC has been active in pressuring academic institutions to "disavow" researchers who do not agree with the transgender line. The Human Rights Campaign and its Foundation have combined revenues of nearly $70 million, but do not fund many outside organizations. Of the few, the National Center for Transgender Equality and Muslims for Progressive Values are numbered. Cornell University's library holds all of their archived documents. Cornell University has received donations from the Open Society Foundations.

Jewish homosexual Fred Hochberg, former Chairman and President of the Export-Import Bank of the United States, fall 2017 resident fellow at the University of Chicago Institute of Politics, and MBA from Columbia University is a former Board member and Co-Chair of the Human Rights Campaign. While with the Small Business Association, Hochberg "helped to lead aggressive outreach to minority, women, and gay and lesbian-owned businesses across the nation." Hochberg is the founder of the David Bohnett LGBTQ Leadership Fellows Scholarship:

> The LGBTQ Victory Institute,[103] in collaboration with The David Bohnett Foundation, has sent over 150 outstanding LGBTQ leaders to the Harvard Kennedy School's Senior Executives in State and Local Government program since 2002, and connects these alumni to opportunities for further leadership development.

Kyrsten Sinema, the "first openly bisexual US Congressperson" is a former recipient of a David Bohnett LGBTQ Leadership Fellows Scholarship. Hochberg's "partner" Tom Healy went to Harvard and Columbia and is a member of the Council on Foreign Relations. Hochberg is also on the Trustee Advisory Board for the Center for American Progress; the Jewish Winnie Stachelberg, Executive Vice President for External Affairs at CAP was with the HRC for eleven years. Stachelberg, per CAP's website, "has been instrumental in shaping policy victories such as the repeal of 'don't ask, don't tell' and the passage of the Equality Act in the U.S. House of Representatives."

---

[103] "Through our training programs, we are identifying and preparing a diverse pipeline of future LGBTQ leaders to advance equality . . . Thousands of successful LGBTQ leaders are training alumni, including Colorado Governor Jared Polis, former Houston Mayor Annise Parker, Ohio State Senator Nickie Antonio and Virginia Delegate Danica Roem." They also have projects and/or campaigns in the Balkans, Colombia, the Dominican Republic, Guatemala, Honduras, El Salvador, and Nicaragua. Additionally: "Three South African trainees began working for political parties . . . The first trans woman appointed to a Lok Adalat—a dispute redressal system in India—is a political leadership fellow . . . Two of the three newly elected trans women in Brazil are past conference participants . . . Two of the three newly elected trans women in Brazil are past conference participants." From the Victory Institute's 2018 Annual Report "Because America Needs Us."

The David Bohnett Foundation, the foundation of its homosexual namesake, has disbursed funds to LGBTQ organizations and institutions promoting the LGBTQ agenda, including: the ACLU Foundation of Southern California, American Jewish Committee, the American Jewish World Service, the Aspen Institute, Amnesty International, the Astraea Lesbian Foundation for Justice, Black Lesbian and Gay Pride, the Brookings Institution, the Brain Mapping Foundation, the Biden Foundation (Advancing LGBTQ Equality: YMCA Equity and Inclusion Initiative), Cedars-Sinai Medical Center, the Center for American Progress, Columbia University, Cornell University, the Elton John AIDS Foundation, Drag Queen Story Hour, Harvard University, Immigration Equality, Movement Advancement Project (MAP), the Liberty Hill Foundation, the Human Rights Campaign Foundation, the National Center for Lesbian Rights, the National Center for Transgender Equality, Planned Parenthood-Los Angeles, UCLA, the Transgender Law Center, UCSF, USC, University of Chicago, and the Black AIDS Institute.

The Black AIDS Institute is funded by Walgreens, ViiV Healthcare, Amazon Studios, the CDC, Paramount Pictures, AIDS United, Gilead Sciences, Bank of America, the David Geffen Foundation, Gucci, GlaxoSmithKline, Lambda Legal, the Howard Brown Health Center, Merck, amfAR-The Foundation for AIDS Research, Janssen Pharmaceuticals, the Planned Parenthood Federation of America, and the Human Rights Campaign, among others.

As another example of weaponizing the LGBTQ "community" for political activism, the Human Rights Campaign documents their 2018 election strategy:

Our historic victories were no accident. Rather, they were the result of a bold two-year campaign undertaken by HRC and our allies. In 2017–2018, HRC endorsed more than 480 pro-equality candidates in 70 races across 44 states, including more women and people of color than ever before. We helped elect more than 150 LGBTQ people to office and doubled the number of LGBTQ people serving in the U.S. Senate. . . . We deployed 150 staff to more than 70 key races across 23 states, with staff on the ground in more than three-quarters of the House races that flipped from red to blue. We registered more than 32,000 voters in all 50 states and helped turn out 7 million LGBTQ voters and millions more allies. HRC's Equality Votes PAC spent $3.4 million to drive turnout in priority HRC Rising states and other key races, running six-figure ad campaigns in Georgia and Florida and reaching 4.6 million people through tested digital advertising. HRC also raised $1.6 million directly for endorsed candidates. In 2018, we saw the full power of HRC Rising, our largest grassroots expansion ever, in which we spent $26 million to energize and mobilize pro-equality voters and candidates across America, particularly in six key states—Arizona, Michigan, Nevada, Ohio, Pennsylvania and Wisconsin. We placed 35 full-time staff in these priority states for more than a year—helping to elect or re-elect pro-equality U.S. senators in every single one.

On August 9th, 2007, HRC and Logo TV (ViacomCBS's LGBTQ channel) co-hosted a forum for Democratic presidential candidates to discuss LGBTQ issues. Jazz Jennings received a Youth Trailblazer Award in 2014 from Logo TV. The Establishment is trying to create a "halo effect" around "trans" to make it seem cool and appealing—not to mention "stunning and brave." The most obvious example is of course Caitlyn (né Bruce) Jenner, but another of the most visible transgender persons in the world and star of a hit television show which glamorizes the transgender lifestyle is Jazz Jennings.

Jazz's story is designed to recruit and groom children. Jazz is very probably a victim of Munchausen syndrome by proxy. Jazz was apparently diagnosed with gender dysphoria at age five, and the following year the Jennings family was making the rounds on television shows. The documentary *I Am Jazz: A Family in Transition* premiered in 2011 on the Oprah Winfrey Network; Jazz was inked to a spokesperson deal by Johnson & Johnson in 2015 for Clean & Clear's "See the Real Me" campaign which shared "the trials of growing up transgender."

Adding to and capitalizing on the "halo" effect of "trans" is Slay Model Management, founded in 2015 and specializing in "gender queer and transgender models." In 2016, Slay was the subject of an Oxygen Network series called *Strut*, which shows "the challenges its models faced in the fashion industry, fighting to overcome gender and beauty stereotypes." So challenging, in fact, that its models have appeared on the covers of *Vogue, Speigel, Forbes, Purple, Attitude, Gay Times, Vogue Germany,* and *Vogue Italia*; have appeared on *Pose, Project Runway, America's Next Top Model, America's Next Top Model: All-Stars, The Bold and the Beautiful, Law and Order: SVU*, and Netflix's *Next In Fashion*; have presented at the Grammys; have been on the catwalk for New York Fashion Week; and have done major campaigns for I Am Vodka, Diesel, Katy Perry's fragrance INDI, Barney's, and The Eva Mendes Collection for New York & Company.

Transgender model and "YouTuber" Nikita Dragun has a cosmetics line called Dragun Beauty, which is "all about empowering beauty lovers of all shapes, skin tones and sexualities as we journey along the road to self-discovery; unleashing the fantasy within." This is a very similar strategy to Rihanna's Fenty Beauty and to MAC Cosmetics' VIVA Glam line. This aspect of the LGBTQ agenda has been picking up steam lately, but it has been going on for some time, as Caroline Lowbridge wrote for *BBC News* in September 2019:

> African-American transgender model Tracey Norman, who later changed her last name to Africa . . . enjoyed a successful career, with her work including a high-profile campaign for Clairol cosmetics. . . . Back in the UK, a closeted transgender women called Caroline Cossey had been climbing the ladder of the fashion industry under the name Tula. "Cossey worked as a model from 1975 to 1981, appeared in magazines such as Australian Vogue and Harper's Bazaar and did extensive work as a model," says [Susan] Stryker. . . . Jay McCauley Bowstead, a lecturer at the London College of Fashion, believes social media has "provided a space through which more diverse representations can emerge." Brands and magazines can now look old-fashioned, he argues, if they do not mirror the diversity seen on social media. . . . He names Chella Man and Krow Kian as two prominent transgender male models. "Someone like Chella Man did actually pose for The Gap, the American brand. You can't get much more mainstream," he says. . . . "Also in the United States you have very popular television shows like Orange is the New Black, that has the trans actress Laverne Cox on it, and she's been incredibly outspoken and an advocate for trans people," [says Elspeth] Brown. . . . [Paris

Lees] was speaking at Fortune's Most Powerful Women conference, where she was announced as a brand ambassador for hair care brand Pantene. Lees, who grew up in the Nottinghamshire town of Hucknall, is the first transgender woman to be appointed by Pantene. However, she is far from the only transgender person to model for a mainstream brand, with transgender men and women including Valentina Sampaio, Chella Man and Andreja Pejić being hired by the likes of Victoria's Secret, Gap and Make Up For Ever. . . .
April Ashley is thought to have been the first successful transgender model. Born George Jamieson in Liverpool in 1935, she had gender reassignment surgery in 1960 at the age of 25, and her striking looks led her to grace the pages of Vogue magazine.

Circling back to Jazz, another project of "hers" was the co-authoring of a transgender children's book with the Jewish Jessica Herthel. The Jewish Anti-Defamation League promotes the book on its website, where it can be purchased. It is recommended by the ADL for ages 4–8. The Jennings family is also Jewish—the name Jennings being a prime example of crypsis. The Jennings family runs the TransKids Purple Rainbow Foundation where among other things they provide resources to receive funding for sex change operations, linking to the Jim Collins Foundation and Point of Pride Annual Transgender Surgery Fund. Counselor, sex therapist, and member of the Florida Department of Health's Transgender Community Task Force Deborah Eve Grayson works with the Foundation; she is Jewish. The Human Rights Campaign and several smaller groups are also involved with this Foundation.

The Human Rights Campaign plays a crucial role in all of this; their Foundation's Corporate Equality Index "sets the standard for LGBTQ inclusion in the workplace, leading to incredible growth in LGBTQ-friendly policies, benefits and practices." Stonewall does something similar in the UK as both a pressure tactic and a way to incentivize the ready acceptance and implementation of their agenda as "suggested policy aims," which include: "fully inclusive, globally applicable nondiscrimination policies and/or codes of conduct," "inclusive diversity training," "at least one health care plan with transgender-inclusive coverage," and "at least three efforts of public commitment to the LGBTQ community, including recruitment, marketing, advertising and public policy weigh-in."

Already in the UK, "gender reassignment" became a separate protected characteristic under the Equality Act of 2010, meaning that transgender individuals are "protected against discrimination in the workplace." According to the Equality and Human Rights Commission:

> The Equality Act says that you must not be discriminated against because:
> - of your gender reassignment as a transsexual. You may prefer the description transgender person or trans male or female. A wide range of people are included in the terms 'trans' or 'transgender' but you are not protected as transgender unless you propose to change your gender or have done so. For example, a group of men on a stag do who put on fancy dress as women are turned away from a restaurant. They are not transsexual so not protected from discrimination
> - someone thinks you are transsexual, for example because you occasionally cross-dress or are gender variant (this is known as discrimination by

perception)
- you are connected to a transsexual person, or someone wrongly thought to be transsexual (this is known as discrimination by association)

The HRC Foundation also has a Buying for Workplace Equality Guide, "a tool to help consumers stand with the LGBTQ community by buying from companies that support inclusive workplaces and practices." The HRC has international employer rating indexes such as Equidad MX (Mexico) and Equidad CL (Chile, in partnership with Fundación Iguales, Chile's largest LGBT advocacy group), with Equidad Peru in the works. In December 2018, the HRC announced a partnership with Presente— Peru's largest LGBTQ advocacy group to these ends. In May 2018, the HRC also partnered with IBM to launch a series of business workshops in Colombia, Chile, Peru, Argentina, and Mexico "to share best practices and develop action steps to create more welcoming workplaces for LGBT employees." Indeed, much of HRC's work centers on exporting the LGBTQ agenda to other countries:

HRC's Global Partnerships in Innovative Advocacy offers capacity-building and strategic planning to help strengthen selected LGBTQ advocacy organizations around the world. This year [2018] we conducted workshops on issues such as gaining national non-discrimination protections, relationship recognition, fundraising strategies and building coalitions for equality with advocates in Georgia, Myanmar, Kyrgyzstan and Uruguay. HRC's Global Partnerships in Pride provides sponsorship and in-kind support to select Prides and related events in places where visibility can make a difference. This year we supported Prides in Bulgaria, Sri Lanka, Greece, eSwatini, Jamaica, Cambodia, Botswana and Pakistan. . . . HRC's Global Fellows are established and emerging LGBTQ leaders and allies who come to Washington, D.C. for professional development opportunities and training. Global Fellows work alongside HRC staff and LGBTQ and human rights activists to gain new ideas and tools, share what's happening in their country's equality movement, and make new connections. This year [2018] Global Fellows came from China, Turkey and Vietnam.

The HRC and its Foundation also focus on "advancing LGBTQ equality and other social justice issues" at historically-black colleges and universities (HBCUs), including with the HBCU Program, given additional financial resources by the Coca-Cola Foundation and the David Bohnett Foundation. A recent initiative has seen the creation of the LGBTQ HBCU Alumni Network, and:

In July 2018, HRC held our second HBCU Diversity and Inclusion Leadership Briefing for University Presidents and Senior Executives, a day-long meeting for school administrators to discuss LGBTQ-inclusive practices and policies. Twelve HBCUs were represented, including five HBCU presidents and Michael Lomax, CEO and president of the United Negro College Fund, along with HRC staff, representatives from major employers, and HBCU alumni who serve on HRC's Parents for Transgender Equality Council.

The HRC produces materials for "creating LGBTQ-inclusive schools" and runs an annual conference called Time to THRIVE targeting educators and councilors all the way down to the kindergarten level in partnership with the American Counseling Association and the National Education Association (NEA), with AT&T, BBVA Compass, and Toyota as presenting sponsors. The HRC has also teamed-up with the NEA to run an annual Jazz and Friends National Day of School and Community Readings hosting school and community readings of the Jazz Jennings-Jessica Herthel pro-trans children's book *I Am Jazz* and others geared toward "gender-expansive youth of color," including *Julián Is a Mermaid* by Jessica Love and *They, She, He Easy as ABC* by Maya and Matthew Smith Gonzalez. NEA President Lily Eskelsen García says, "This unequivocal message of love, support, and inclusion for our transgender and non-binary students is not only right but, unfortunately, necessary in light of outright hostility towards them from people like Betsy DeVos." Another manufactured bogeyman to put alongside Donald Trump and Mike Pence.

The HRC Foundation in partnership with the Equality Federation Institute runs an annual Municipal Equality Index, essentially the same thing as their Corporate Equality Index and their Healthcare Equality Index, which we will get to later. The Municipal Equality Index shows, says HRC President Alphonso David:

> These inclusive and welcoming cities are standing up to the unrelenting attacks on the LGBTQ community by the Trump-Pence administration, and sending a clear message that the fair and equal treatment of our community, our families and our neighbors is a true American value.

The Equality Federation's Co-Chair Kellan Baker is the Centennial Scholar in the Department of Health Policy and Management at the Johns Hopkins Bloomberg School of Public Health, where he is pursuing a doctorate in health services research with a focus on transgender health and economic evaluation. Kellan is also a current Health Policy Research Scholar with the Robert Wood Johnson Foundation. Previously he was a Senior Fellow at the Center for American Progress, where he worked on LGBT health and data collection policy at the federal and state levels.

In March 2018, HRC aired two #LoveYourNeighbor videos as television ads in the northeastern Mississippi media market with a grant from Toyota and additional support from Levi Strauss & Co. The HRC Foundation has worked with the University of Connecticut in the past on "comprehensive LGBTQ youth surveys" aimed at creating more "welcoming and inclusive" schools. In July 2018, the HRC Foundation released a new Coming Out guide for Asian and Pacific Islander Americans, in partnership with the National Queer Asian Pacific Islander Alliance, and has been vociferous in its support for DACA. The HRC supports full illegal alien amnesty and seeks to link a number of "social justice causes" together in amplifying coalitions, a tactic a great many of these organizations employ for synergistic potential. The HRC has its Spanish-language hub Recursos en Español de HRC, to "offer more resources to Spanish-speaking members of the LGBTQ community" and to "elevate our message of inclusion to give the Latinx, LGBTQ, immigrant and allied communities an opportunity to share their stories, advocate for justice and learn more about LGBTQ issues."

The HRC Foundation has also hosted a National Rainbow Seder at its Washington, DC headquarters and has published an "LGBTQ guide" for Jews called "Coming Home to Judaism and To Self." Denise Eger, "the first openly LGBT president of the Central Conference of American Rabbis" and member of HRC's Religion Council states, "This guide underscores the reality that being LGBTQ and being Jewish are not mutually exclusive."

We cannot escape the persistent and consistent intersections of Jews and Judaism both in the specific context of the LGBTQ agenda and in the broader globalist system and wealth accrual. There is far more commonality between the HRC and Goldman Sachs, for example, with not just their goals but the pressure tactics often employed to realize these goals than anyone unfamiliar with the state of play is apt to realize. Jewish Goldman Sachs CEO David Solomon declared from Davos in January 2020:

> "Starting on July 1st in the U.S. and Europe, we're not going to take a company public unless there's at least one diverse board candidate, with a focus on women," Solomon told CNBC Thursday. He didn't mention Asia. . . .[104] The mandate is the latest in a series of signals that non-diverse boards and management are unacceptable. BlackRock Inc. and State Street Global Advisors are voting against directors at companies without a female director. Public companies with all-male boards based in California now face a $100,000 fine under a new state law. . . . "It's what big investors are looking for these days," said Fred Foulkes, a management professor at the Boston University Questrom School of Business. "If the board has all white males, that's a big negative. . . ." JPMorgan Chase & Co. doesn't have a similar policy to the new Goldman Sachs rule, but since 2016 has had a director advisory service that works to help companies find diverse candidates for their board, the company said in a statement.

Diverse means quite simply not a white male. Presumably it will be actual white males, not Ashkenazi Jews pretending to be "fellow whites" who get the axe. For the women and "diverse" (direct translation: non-white) hires, this is tokenism pure and simple, but apparently no one minds. Merit: meet "equality." Something's gotta give. BlackRock and State Street Global Advisors are voting against directors at companies without a female director because merit obviously matters in this system, the same way JP Morgan Chase has a "director advisory service" that finds "diverse candidates" for their Board.

Goldman Sachs runs the LGBT+ Possibilities Summit, "an interactive multiday program for LGBT+ undergraduate college freshmen and sophomores." They have a litany of such programs, all geared toward recruiting non-straight white males, unless of course they happen to be "fellow whites." Goldman Sachs publishes an annual "diversity and inclusion" report, and in the EMEA (Europe, Middle East, Africa, which they're trying to meld into one) 2019 report, we learn about the Gender Pronoun Initiative, which "Aims to educate our people on gender identity and pronoun use as an effective tool for building an inclusive environment. It offers employees several channels to self-identify their pronouns, should they choose," and Out In The Open – Being LGBT+ in the Workplace," which "articulates why being open about one's sexual orientation and gender identity is important in the workplace,

---

[104] Who could *possibly* guess why?

raises awareness of the challenges faced by LGBT+ professionals and provides ally best practices." There's a whole lot more like that, apparently because "what happens between two consenting adults behind closed doors is no one else's business." Remember that line?

Anyway, Goldman Sachs boldly proclaims: "Being diverse is not optional; it is what we must be." This is eerily reminiscent of the half-Jewish Wesley Clark's statement or that of the Jewish Barbara Lerner Spectre's comments on the future multi-cultural Europe:

> I think there's a resurgence of anti-Semitism because at this point in time Europe has not yet learned how to be multi-cultural, and I think we're [Jews] going to be part of the throes of that transformation, which must take place. . . . Europe is not going to be the monolithic societies that they once were in the last century. Jews are going to be at the center of that. It's a huge transformation for Europe to make. They are now going in to a multi-cultural mode, and Jews will be resented because of our leading role.

Should you mention that leading role, however, that's "anti-Semitic."

Early in this book, we discussed the cult-like nature of the transgender agenda, especially among many of its prominent "activists," and how they groom and prey on the vulnerable, such as children and the mentally ill. The cultish quality is in some instances either directly tied to cults or at the very least derived from cult practices. Straight Inc., introduced by Jenn Smith as a copycat successor to the tactics employed by Synanon, was founded by the Jewish Mel Sembler "from the ashes of The Seed—an earlier program suspended by the U.S. Senate for tactics reminiscent, said a senator, of Communist POW camps," as John Gorenfeld describes it. You'd be hard-pressed to find a more vile human being than Sembler. Gorenfeld elaborates:

> For 16 years, Sembler, with his wife Betty, directed the leading juvenile rehab business in America, STRAIGHT, Inc., before seeing it dismantled by a breathtaking array of institutional abuse claims by mid-1993. Just one of many survivors is Samantha Monroe, now a travel agent in Pennsylvania, who told *The Montel Williams Show* this year [2005] about overcoming beatings, rape by a counselor, forced hunger, and the confinement to a janitor's closet in "humble pants"—which contained weeks of her own urine, feces and menstrual blood. . . . Although prosecutors closed the clinics, six-figure settlements sucked it dry, and state health officials yanked its licenses after media reports of teen torture and cover-up, Sembler himself escaped punishment. As one of the preeminent and hardest-working GOP fundraisers, Sembler has received the honor of living during the George W. Bush presidency at the Villa Taverna, the official residence for the U.S. ambassador, which has the largest private garden in Rome. . . . He's come home, but still wafting across national drug policy is the influence of his STRAIGHT, which has legally changed its identity to the Drug Free America Foundation (director Calvina Fay denies it's the same organization but the name change is listed in Florida corporate filings), subsidized by tax dollars . . . with an advisory board that includes the likes of Gov. Jeb Bush and his wife Columba, and Homeland Security Director of Public Safety Christy McCampbell. A more

pressing issue is that former overseers of Sembler's company, true believers in the STRAIGHT model, are still running spin-off businesses that treat teens with the old methods.

Though the Bushes are no longer officially affiliated, this 2005 snapshot is illustrative; currently the aggressively anti-white "conservative" Ana Navarro sits on the Advisory Board. Additionally, as Jenn Smith reports, "The Drug Free America Foundation [is] still operating, and . . . gets much of its funding from the pharmaceutical industry that is also funding and supporting transgender research and activism."

People like Sembler don't just have significant influence over the political process anymore, they *are* the power structure, and with their control comes the ability to turn entire societies into Jonestowns, someday the whole world if they get their way.

Sembler is on the Board of NorPAC, which funds and supports political candidates who "demonstrate a genuine commitment to the strength, security, and survival of Israel." Sembler was close friends with Robert Pritzker and they served on the Board of the American Enterprise Institute (AEI) together. As Kevin MacDonald writes, AEI:

> Received $50,000/year from Purdue from 2003 "until recently"—~$800,000 total—pocket change for a family that walked away with at least $11 billion. The original "research" touting the non-addictive properties of Oxycontin and based on 38 subjects was performed by R. K. Portnoy of the Metropolitan Jewish Health System . . . in 2004 the *New York Times* published an article by AEI writer Sally Satel, presumably Jewish, opposing jail sentences for doctors who over-prescribed opioids after running it past a Purdue lobbyist. And in 2007 the *Wall Street Journal*, a major neocon media outlet, published another article by Satel in which she called Oxycontin a "godsend" and lamented that it [is] not being prescribed enough. Satel is intimately associated with the AEI as a Resident Fellow. She is typical of our new elite and its involvement in elite institutions and media. . . . A good example illustrating these connections is Richard Perle. Perle is listed as a Resident Fellow of the AEI [2004], and he is on the boards of directors of the *Jerusalem Post* and the Hollinger Corporation, a media company controlled by Conrad Black. Hollinger owns major media properties in the US (*Chicago Sun-Times*), England (the *Daily Telegraph*), Israel (*Jerusalem Post*), and Canada (the *National Post*; fifty percent ownership with CanWest Global Communications, which is controlled by Israel Asper and his family; CanWest has aggressively clamped down on its journalists for any deviation from its strong pro-Israel editorial policies). Hollinger also owns dozens of smaller publications in the US, Canada, and England. All of these media outlets reflect the vigorously pro-Israel stance espoused by Perle. Perle has written op-ed columns for Hollinger newspapers as well as for the *New York Times*.

Purdue is Purdue Pharma, owned by the Jewish Sackler family, who specifically targeted white people—primarily veterans and the elderly. Purdue Pharma's former President and Chairman Richard Sackler stated at the OxyContin launch party that,

"The prescription blizzard will be so deep, dense, and white." It is also worth noting here how the lockdowns imposed by governments in response to COVID-19 (or ostensibly in response to the pandemic) greatly exacerbated opioid and drug abuse and had a directly-deleterious effect on a great number of people's psychological well-being.

Finally, we cannot escape the central role of the seemingly-ubiquitous Open Society Foundations, which positively cite a claim that children "understand their gender identity as early as age two" and refer readers in their November 2015 report "Trans Children and Youth" to a Canadian site Gender Creative Kids which provides "resources for gender creative kids and their families, schools and communities" with the "kids" in question as young as three. TD Bank and the Province of Quebec are among its financial supporters—and speaking of opioids, what was then the Open Society Institute awarded a grant amount of $150,000 in January 1997 to the University of Wisconsin Research and Sponsored Programs to fund "A Resource Program to Address Barriers to Availability of Opioids for Pain Relief," which not only echoes "addressing barriers to healthcare" for "trans" people and others, but predicts the corrosive and malign effects as well as reveals the intent. Still any doubts as to the irredeemably corrupt nature of the ruling class?

# Gross Domestic Products

*"Fourth grader Jacob Lemay socially transitioned when he was 5 years old and has since become a beacon for the acceptance of trans youth. Jacob's mother chronicled his transition in the memoir* What We Will Become: A Mother, a Son, and a Journey of Transformation, *and in October, he asked then-presidential candidate Sen. Elizabeth Warren (D-MA) how she would support trans youth in schools. In a profile on NBC Nightly News with Lester Holt, Jacob's parents described their family's path to embracing his gender identity. His father noted the importance of trans youth having access to gender-affirming medical care, saying, 'He's becoming educated on what future choices he'll need to make. And that's one of the reasons why he is, you know, taking a puberty blocker so that we know he's had years to think this through.'*

– Alex Paterson,
"On Trans Day of Visibility, watch these five stories of incredible trans youth,"
*Media Matters for America*, March 31st, 2020)

Robert Pritzker was mentioned in connection to Mel Sembler and AEI, and he is not the only member of the Jewish Pritzker family we are going to see or have seen; we have already been introduced to Illinois governor J.B. Pritzker (his nephew) and a child from his first marriage Jennifer Pritzker, born James Pritzker, a major financier of transgender clinics, causes, and foundations. With a net worth of close to $2 billion, Jennifer Pritzker is able to make a massive impact; the entire Pritzker fortune is estimated to be approximately $29 billion, and they fund both transgender and pro-immigration "causes" and groups lavishly. Robert's brother Jay (University of Chicago and Northwestern University alumnus) created the Hyatt Hotels chain after the purchase of the flagship Hyatt House in 1957. Today, Thomas Pritzker is the Executive Chairman of the Board of Directors.

Thomas Pritzker is also on the Board of Trustees of the University of Chicago along with prominent Jewish figures David M. Rubinstein (Carlyle Group) and Kenneth M. Jacobs (Lazard); he founded Bay City Capital (biotechnology) and Reliant Pharmaceuticals, the latter of which was acquired by GlaxoSmithKline. The Dean of the University of Chicago Pritzker School of Medicine, the Jewish Kenneth S. Polonsky, is also the President of the University of Chicago Medicine health system, is an honorary fellow of the Royal College of Physicians of Ireland, and was the Chair of the Department of Medicine at Washington University in St. Louis.

Thomas Pritzker is also the Chairman of the Board of Trustees of the Center for

Strategic and International Studies (CSIS) think tank; the Jewish William S. Cohen, Chairman and CEO of the globalist Cohen Group is also on the CSIS's Board, along with figures such as Henry Kissinger, Stanley Druckenmiller (former Managing Director at Soros Fund Management), William K. Reilly (formerly President of the World Wildlife Fund and later Chairman of the Board; former Director of the Rockefeller Task Force on Land Use and Urban Growth), and Joseph S. Nye, Jr. (Harvard, National Intelligence Council, Trilateral Commission). Brian Katz:

> Is a fellow in the International Security Program at the Center for Strategic and International Studies (CSIS). His research agenda focuses on the intersection of intelligence, national security, and technology, including the integration and implications of emerging technologies; adapting intelligence to the future of counterterrorism; and the role of intelligence in policymaking, strategy, and military operations. He also frequently writes on Middle East security issues, counterterrorism, nonstate actors, and proxy warfare. Mr. Katz served as a visiting fellow at CSIS from 2018–2019 through the Council on Foreign Relations International Affairs Fellowship program. He joined CSIS after a decade of service in the U.S. Government at the Central Intelligence Agency (CIA) and Department of Defense. At the CIA, Mr. Katz served as a military analyst for the Middle East, South Asia, and Eastern Europe, including multiple overseas tours. From 2016 to 2017, he served as country director for Syria in the Office of the Secretary of Defense, where he provided policy and strategy advice to senior officials on the Syrian conflict and U.S. military and counterterrorism efforts against the Islamic State and Al Qaeda. Mr. Katz is also an officer in the U.S. Navy Reserve currently serving with U.S. European Command. He holds a B.S. in economics from Duke University and an M.A. in international relations and strategic studies from the Johns Hopkins University School of Advanced International Studies. He is a previous Center for a New American Security Next Generation National Security Fellow and a recipient of the Secretary of Defense Medal for Exceptional Civilian Service and two National Intelligence Medals.

Also from the CSIS website, (in what will become particularly significant later in this book):

> CSIS is pleased to introduce *Reset the Table*, a project targeting today's challenges to global food security and calling for renewed U.S. leadership at the table. *Reset the Table* aims to bring in new information, new themes, and new voices to find solutions to today's challenges. . . . Global food security is impossible without an integrated set of robust climate policies. . . . A United Nations (UN) report by the Intergovernmental Panel on Climate Change (IPCC) sounded the alarm that the world is moving toward irreversible damage by climate change that could place the future of food and the livelihood of millions in peril.

Gigi Pritzker's husband Michael Pucker is a member of Lurie Children's Hospital's Board of Directors; the Pritzker Pucker Foundation is their "charitable" foundation. The Pritzker Pucker Foundation has donated to the American Jewish World Service, the Ann and Robert H. Lurie Children's Hospital of Chicago, Barnard College at Columbia University and Columbia University directly, the Anti-Defamation League (ADL), the ACLU, Keshet, Northwestern University, Planned Parenthood, Stanford University, USC, UNICEF, and the University of Chicago.

Daniel Pritzker (Northwestern University) runs the Jay Pritzker Foundation, which has donated to the ADL, the Hebrew Immigrant Aid Society (HIAS, a mass immigration NGO), the SPLC, and the Tides Foundation. Donald Pritzker attended Harvard and the University of Chicago, and Anthony Pritzker received his MBA from the University of Chicago. UCLA's Institute of the Environment and Sustainability offers a Pritzker Emerging Environmental Genius Award with funds for the award made possible as part of a $20 million gift to UCLA from the Anthony and Jeanne Pritzker Family Foundation. Anthony "Tony" Pritzker is also on the Board of Advisors for the Institute, which counts Chevron and BlackRock among the active members of its Corporate Partners Program.

Nick Pritzker (University of Chicago), Board member of vaping company JUUL Labs, also co-founded Tao Capital, which invested in JUUL and the synthetic DNA company Twist Biosciences. Companies in their portfolio with accompanying classification include:

- Alternative Transportation: Tesla (TSLA), Uber (UBER), SpaceX, Proterra, Turo, Ouster, Bird, The Boring Company
- Alternative Energy: SolarCity (SCTY), Enlighted (Siemens)
- Technology: DeepMind (GOOG), MJ Freeway (KERN), IonQ, Crossbar, Illumio, Zenefits, ironSource, BitTitan, Snow, RapidDeploy, Premise, Skupos, Holo
- Healthcare: Foundations Recovery Network (UHS), Twist (TWST), CareZone (WMT), PointClickCare, Zymergen, Verge, Activ Surgical, 908D, Encodia, Enspectra, Truvian, Scale Biosciences
- Education: DreamBox, Newsela, Panorama
- Sustainable Food & Agriculture: Granular (DWDP), Ripple, Myco, Apeel, Greenlight Bio, The Kitchen, Midwestern BioAg, Revolution Foods, Soylent, Eatsa, Benson Hill, FoodMaven, TemperPack, Dig Inn, Meati
- Consumer: Harry's (EPC), Warby Parker, PAX, JUUL, 100 Thieves, Cometeer, United Record Pressing
- Real Estate & Hospitality: Buildium (RP), Sonder, Raken, Porch, Revinate, Atlantica Hotels, multi-family and commercial

Nick Pritzker is Co-Chair of the Clean Energy Trust. Also, per a June 2002 press release from the University of Chicago:

The Pritzker family of Chicago, widely known philanthropists whose many business ventures include the Hyatt Hotel chain, has announced that it is making a gift of $30 million to the University of Chicago. The gift is part of the University's recently announced $2 billion fund-raising campaign, The Chicago Initiative, and it will specifically support the University's Biological Sciences Division and its Pritzker School of Medicine, which was named for the family in 1968. The Pritzker Foundation, whose board includes Robert

Pritzker, Thomas Pritzker, Nicholas Pritzker and Penny Pritzker, is making this gift on the occasion of the 100th anniversary of the founding of Pritzker and Pritzker, which is the family law firm. Thomas Pritzker said . . . "We have long supported the University of Chicago and the medical school that bears our name and we chose to make this new gift for two reasons. The first is our longstanding pride in the University's advancement of human knowledge, especially in medical research and the training of many of the nation's leading physicians and scientists. . . ." In addition to their support for the Pritzker School of Medicine and the Biological Sciences, the Pritzker family has also provided substantial support for the University of Chicago Law School and the University's work in South Asian Studies and Astronomy & Astrophysics. Thomas Pritzker (J.D./M.B.A.'76) is on the Executive Committee of the Board of Trustees. Nicholas Pritzker (J.D.'75) serves on the Physical Sciences Division Visiting Committee; J.B. Pritzker serves on the Visiting Committee for the School of Social Service Administration; and Margot Pritzker serves on the Visiting Committee on the Visual Arts. Susan Pritzker and Cindy Pritzker are also members of the University's Women's Board, and Jay Pritzker was a Life Trustee of the University at the time of his death in 1999.

The John Pritzker Family Fund is a major supporter of Jewish organizations as well as the Department of Psychiatry at UCSF; Nancy Adler, according to her biographical description for the California Preterm Birth Initiative's Strategic Advisory Council:

Is the Lisa and John Pritzker Professor of Medical Psychology at UCSF, vice-chair of the Department of Psychiatry, and directs the Center for Health and Community. Her research examines the impact of risk perception on reproductive and sexual health decision making and identification of mechanisms by which socioeconomic status and other social determinants influence health. She directed the MacArthur Foundation's Research Network on Socioeconomic Status and Health and developed a widely used measure of subjective social status. She heads the national program office of the Robert Wood Johnson Foundation "Evidence for Action" grants program. A fellow of the American Psychological Society and the American Psychological Association, she was elected to the American Academy of Arts and Sciences and the National Academy of Medicine (NAM), which awarded her the David Rall Medal. She served on the Advisory Committee to the Director of National Institutes of Health, the Report Review Committee of the NRC/NAS and the NAM Council and Executive Committee. In 2017, she received the Medal for Distinguished Contributions in Biomedical Sciences from the New York Academy of Medicine.

Serving with Adler on the Strategic Advisory Board are Ann E.B. Borders (a maternal-fetal medicine specialist in the Department of Obstetrics and Gynecology at NorthShore University Health System, and a clinical associate professor at the University of Chicago Pritzker School of Medicine) and Lynne Benioff, Marc Benioff's[105] wife:

> She is a Distinguished Director of the Board of Overseers of the University of California, San Francisco Foundation, and serves on the boards of directors of the Rise Fund, UCSF Benioff Children's Hospitals, Common Sense Media, the Benioff Ocean Initiative and Forward. Ms. Benioff was appointed to the Presidio Trust board by President Barack Obama in 2015.

The Matthew Pritzker Company has invested in SpaceX, and Karen Pritzker (Northwestern University) with her husband has donated millions to the Yale University School of Medicine. She is the Chairman of the Board of the Colson Associates, a medical device conglomerate that generates approximately $500 million in revenue annually. The Pritzker Vlock Family Office's Managing Director is Elon Boms, who according to their website is:

> A seasoned investment professional. . . . Elon has led over 250 investments across a range of industries and geographies. Along with Karen Pritzker and Michael Vlock, Elon is the co-founder of LaunchCapital, a premiere seed stage investment fund with offices in Boston, New Haven and New York. In the last 10 years, Elon has helped raised over $2.5 billion dollars of capital for leading and emerging companies and has been involved in over $1 billion dollars of M&A transactions. Since 2008, Elon's firm recorded an IRR that places them in the top 10% of venture funds worldwide. He is currently managing a robust portfolio of leading technology, consumer, medical device and biotech including companies such as Valerion, award-winning Arccos Golf, Gelesis, Adimab, Pico Quantitative Trading, Snap, Spotify, and more.

Jason Gray is a Vice President of the Pritzker Vlock Family Office:

> In 2012 for President Obama's re-election campaign, Jason helped build the field organization from a staff of 5 to over 200 in a key battleground state. In 2016 for Hillary Clinton's presidential campaign, Jason managed a team across nine battleground states responsible for scaling the campaign organization, and led the launch and implementation of new nationwide voter contact programs. He holds an MBA with Distinction from Harvard Business School and BA & MA degrees summa cum laude from Brandeis University.

For Jennifer Pritzker, the flagship is the TAWANI Foundation, which focuses on "cultural institutions," education, and the military. Some of the recipients of TAWANI money include: the National Yiddish Book Center; Hebrew Union College; Birthright Israel Foundation; Tulane University (where 43% of the undergraduate student body in 2018 was Jewish according to the Official Hillel Guide to Jewish Life on Campus published by Hillel International); Doctors Without Borders; Loyola University-Chicago; the ACLU; the Williams Institute-UCLA; Lurie Children's Hospital of Chicago; University of Arkansas for Medical Sciences Foundation Fund;

---

[105] In 2009 named a Young Global Leader by the World Economic Forum (WEF).

the New Israel Fund; Amnesty International; Cornell University (20% Jewish undergraduate in 2018); Women's Business Development Center; the University of Chicago Medicine and Biological Sciences; YMCA Metropolitan Chicago; Oxfam (which recently came under fire for its volunteers engaging in large-scale rape across the countries they were supposed to be helping); SETI Institute; the American Jewish Historical Society; Democracy Now; NPR; and the United States National Holocaust Memorial Museum.

In 2018, TAWANI also gave $3.5 million to Norwich University in Vermont, on top of the $25 million donated by Jennifer Pritzker through TAWANI in 2013. Jennifer Pritzker, as Jennifer Bilek writes, is also part of the management committee of:

> Squadron Capital, an acquisitions corporation, with a focus on medical technology, medical devices, and orthopedic implants. Pritzker sits on the leadership council of the Program of Human Sexuality at the University of Minnesota, to which he also committed $6.5 million over the past decade. Among many other organizations and institutions Pritzker funds are Lurie Children's Hospital, a medical center for gender non-conforming children, serving 400 children in Chicago; the Pritzker School of Medicine at the University of Chicago; a chair of transgender studies at the University of Victoria (the first of its kind); and the Mark S. Bonham Centre for Sexual Diversity Studies at the University of Toronto.

The homosexual Robert Garofalo is the Head of the Lurie Children's Hospital Gender Development Program as well as Division Head of Adolescent and Young Adult Medicine and Potocsnak Family Professorship in Adolescent & Young Adult Medicine, plus Professor of Pediatrics at the Northwestern University Feinberg School of Medicine. The Gender & Sex Development Program at St. Lurie's (the Sex half is run by Earl Cheng, also a professor at the Northwestern University Feinberg School of Medicine) "specialists provide compassion and gender identity support development for children from *newborns* (emphasis added) to adolescents."

J.B. Pritzker has donated at least $1 million to Planned Parenthood, and Planned Parenthood Illinois Action endorsed J.B. Pritzker for governor during his campaign, a campaign that was described as essentially "pre-ordained" by the state's Democratic political machinery; former Governor Bruce Rauner told reporters in 2017, "He has rigged the system; he controls it. It's a Mafia protection racket."

Planned Parenthood stated in 2018 that "amid a dwindling US abortion rate, Planned Parenthood has moved to diversify its business model by getting into transgender hormone therapy." Diversify its business model. I thought they were only there to provide health counseling to "under-served communities"? I guess harvesting baby parts isn't lucrative enough, nor is the at least $2 billion from the government Planned Parenthood received from 2013–2017. Planned Parenthood is already the second-largest provider of "gender-affirming hormone therapy" in the United States.

J.B. Pritzker has also been a major donor to the Northwestern University School of Law, which has been instrumental in "transgender advocacy" among other "social justice" causes. J.B. Pritzker has significant investments in medical technologies and medical technology start-up incubators:

[J.B.] is co-founder of the Pritzker Group, a private investment firm that invests in digital technology and medical companies, including Clinical Innovations, which has a global presence. Clinical Innovations is one of the largest medical device companies and in 2017 acquired Brenner Medical, another significant medical group offering innovative products in the fields of obstetrics and gynecology. J.B. provided seed funding for Matter, a startup incubator for medical technology based in Chicago. He also sits on the board of directors at his alma mater, Duke University, where they are making advances in cryopreserving women's ovaries. . . . [J.B] put $25 million into an Obama administration public-private initiative totaling $1 billion for early childhood education. J.B. and his wife, M.K. Pritzker, donated $100 million to Northwestern University School of Law, partly for scholarships and partly for the school's "social justice" and childhood law work.

J.B. received his J.D. from Northwestern. Another major figure in the advancement of the transgender agenda is J.B.'s sister, Penny (Harvard, Stanford):

Penny Pritzker served on President Obama's Council for Jobs and Competitiveness and Economic Recovery Advisory Board. She was national co-chair of Obama for America 2012 and national finance chair of Obama's 2008 presidential campaign. . . . As Obama's secretary of commerce, Penny Pritzker helped create the National Institute for Innovation in Manufacturing Biopharmaceuticals (NIIMBL), by facilitating an award of $70 million from the U.S. Department of Commerce, the first funding of its kind. Obama made transgenderism a pet issue of his administration, holding a meeting at the White House (the first ever) for transgenderism. The administration quietly applied the power of the executive branch to make it easier for transgender people to alter their passports, get cross-sex treatment at Veteran's Administration facilities, and access public school restrooms and sports programs based on gender identity.

The US Department of Veterans Affairs sponsors transgender research on veterans as well; in 2019 a pair of studies were commissioned, one on hormone therapy and one on transgender veteran health care use and health outcomes. In the US Department of Health and Human Services' own words:

Since 2010, the U.S. Department of Health and Human Services (HHS) has been committed to advancing the health and well-being of all lesbian, gay, bisexual, and transgender (LGBT) communities through significant and cross-departmental coordination.

In April 2010, President Barack Obama asked Secretary of Health and Human Services Kathleen Sebelius to identify steps the Department of Health and Human Services could take "to improve the health and well-being of lesbian, gay, bisexual, and transgender ('LGBT') individuals and families." Sebelius set up a Department-wide LGBT Issues Coordinating Committee, which set in motion policy aims for 2011, 2012, and beyond. What emerged is as follows:

- In 2011, the Health Services and Resources Administration (HRSA) funded the "Enhancing Access to and Retention in Quality HIV Care for Transgender Women of Color" initiative. This 5-year, $3.2 million initiative will identify, evaluate, and disseminate successful strategies to improve engagement and retention in HIV primary care for transgender women of color living with HIV. Nine demonstration project grants were awarded in four cities: two in New York City, two in Chicago, two in Los Angeles, and three in the San Francisco Bay area. The University of California, San Francisco (UCSF) is serving as the Evaluation and Technical Assistance Center, leading the multisite evaluation and also providing technical assistance and capacity building to the demonstration sites and their medical provider collaborating organizations. All nine demonstration projects have implemented their identification, access, retention, and adherence interventions, with current enrollment in the multisite evaluation at 750 participants.[106]
- The National Institutes of Health ("NIH") will release a report that identifies the gaps and opportunities in its portfolio in light of the recommendations that the Institute of Medicine made in its 2011 report entitled *The Health of Lesbian, Gay, Bisexual, and Transgender People: Building a Foundation for Better Understanding.* This report will inform NIH and the greater research community about important areas in which to advance biomedical research on LGBT health.
- In September 2011, HRSA awarded a grant to the Fenway Institute to create a National Training and Technical Assistance Center to help more than 8,500 community health center sites improve the health of LGBT populations. . . . The new center will offer training and technical assistance based on *The Fenway Guide to LGBT Health*, the only clinical text book on LGBT health, published in collaboration with the American College of Physicians in 2008.[107]
- HRSA continues to improve workforce outreach and recruitment activities related to LGBT communities in the National Health Service Corps scholarship and loan repayment programs.
- Throughout 2011, various HHS agencies reached out to LGBT community-serving organizations through listserv messages, social media, stakeholder engagement, and conference exhibits to highlight funding opportunities that could benefit LGBT communities and to help these organizations understand how to apply for HHS competitive grants.
- HHS held two workshop sessions at the first ever White House Conference on LGBT Health to provide information about how to participate in the grant funding process.
- The Administration for Children and Families (ACF)'s Office of Refugee Resettlement identified LGBT refugees as a vulnerable population in need of targeted services. . . . ACF announced the creation of a first-ever training and technical assistance center to support the resettlement of LGBT refugees, which will be housed at the Heartland Alliance of Chicago.

---

[106] HHS LGBT reports, "Health Objectives."
[107] The Fenway Institute also leads "research projects" in Vietnam, Thailand, Brazil, and Zambia.

- In February 2012, HHS partnered with the White House Office of Public Engagement and Mazzoni Center to co-sponsor the first ever White House LGBT Conference on Health in Philadelphia. More than 300 people attended the event at Thomas Jefferson University. The conference included workshop sessions focused on LGBT aging, LGBT youth, substance abuse and mental health in LGBT communities, LGBT cultural competency, HIV/AIDS, transgender health, and health care reform.
- The HHS Office on Women's Health will fund pilot studies in five locations across the nation to identify and test effective and innovative ways of reducing obesity in lesbian and bisexual women.
- A number of Community Transformation Grant awardees under the Affordable Care Act have included LGBT communities among their target populations. The Centers for Disease Control and Prevention ("CDC") will work with these grantees, including by providing additional funds, to assess the impact of chronic disease prevention programs on these communities.
- NIH is strongly committed to the principles of equal employment opportunity (EEO), diversity, and inclusion. Because of this commitment, in 2013, the NIH established the SGM Portfolio in OEDI (previously known as the Lesbian, Gay, Bisexual, Transgender, and Intersex Special Emphasis Program). The SGM Portfolio strategist works to ensure that equal opportunity for SGM employees are present in all aspects of the agency's programs and services. OEDI offers SafeZone training to interested employees; SafeZone provides a new framework to help create inclusive and affirming workspaces within NIH for SGM communities.
- The US Government successfully sponsored a resolution at PAHO entitled, *Addressing the Causes of Disparities in Health Services Access and Utilization for LGBT persons,* which unanimously passed in the Fall of 2013. This resolution has opened up the Americas to a number of important dialogues on health and PAHO is currently in the process of producing a robust data-driven report on the barriers for LGBT persons to accessing health care in the Americas and their resulting health disparities. . . . We have also worked closely with the World Health Organization, the specialized agency of the United Nations concerned with international public health as well as its regional agency the Pan American Health Organization (PAHO) to address the health access needs of the LGBT population. In the Fall of 2012, together with Thailand, the United States successfully petitioned to have the topic of LGBT health challenges placed on the agenda of the May 2013 WHO Executive Board meeting.

"Transgender is an umbrella term for people whose gender identity is different from the sex they were assigned at birth," says Annette Verster, a technical officer in the HIV Department at the World Health Organization (WHO). WHO's Member States have committed themselves to providing universal coverage of health services in their efforts to achieve the UN's Sustainable Development Goals by 2030. "Reaching marginalized groups, such as transgender people, will be essential," Verster says.

Transgender people are one of five groups that are disproportionately affected by HIV globally, according to the WHO's Guidelines on HIV prevention, diagnosis, treatment and care for key populations released in 2014. The others are: people who inject drugs, men who have sex with men, sex workers, and prisoners. Citing a 2013 study published in *The Lancet* estimating the "HIV burden" among transgender women outside the United States where the authors found that data on HIV prevalence in "transgender women" were only available for fifteen countries, but of those, India had the highest prevalence with 43.7% of the 135 study participants HIV-positive, Verster says:

> These groups are defined as key populations for the HIV response because they are at increased risk of HIV infection. In addition, they are often marginalized, stigmatized and criminalized which affects their ability to access health services, including HIV prevention, testing and treatment. It is estimated that in low- and middle-income countries transgender women are around 49 times more likely to be living with HIV than other adults of reproductive age.

One thing the reader may notice is the significant emphasis on HIV/AIDS in these studies. This is not incidental, as according to the Children's Hospital of Philadelphia (CHOP), "Up to 1 in 4 young transgender women (YTW) in the US are living with HIV and globally transgender women are 50 times more likely than the average person to become infected with HIV." The emphasis on homosexual "men of color" intersects with demographic transformation in that Blacks, Hispanics, Asians, and Jews are more likely to identify as LGBTQ than are Whites.

In 2017, gay men and "other men who have sex with men" accounted for 18% of new HIV infections worldwide. According to the CDC, 44% of black "transgender women" in the US have HIV, as do 26% of Hispanic "trans women" and 7% of white "trans women." This is a very telling statistic for a host of reasons. Nevertheless, it makes sense why Janssen Therapeutics, owned by Johnson & Johnson, has announced that it will donate to "improving linkage to care and retention among young men who have sex with men (MSM) of color living with HIV" and "improving linkage to care and retention among transgender women and gender-noncomforming people living with HIV." From 2008 through March 2016, nine funding initiatives along these lines totaled over $3.6 million. Janssen has also funded a series of continuing medical education workshops developed by the Annenberg Center for Health Sciences at Eisenhower that trains physicians on providing "culturally competent HIV care for transgender persons." Janssen has also donated to the University of Chicago.

The World Health Organization, as we have seen, is not just central to this agenda, but is becoming increasingly important in the future direction and designs of the globalist agenda. The WHO is deeply enmeshed with the Establishment, and functions as a propaganda arm as well. If you were wondering why the WHO seems so susceptible to naked partisanship, it's because it is part of the globalist matrix; it receives funding from organizations such as the Bill and Melinda Gates Foundation, the Bloomberg Family Foundation, the IOM, the Open Society Institute Budapest Foundation, the Rockefeller Foundation, the European Commission, and the World Bank, so of course it is going to reflect the same interests and toe the same line. It is part of the United Nations orbit. The main objectives of the WHO Office at the UN (WUN) are to:

- improve, on behalf of all WHO, its engagement with the UN system;
- better position health in the debates and decisions of UN, inter-govern-mental bodies;
- anchor health in the global 2030 sustainable development agenda;
- strengthen WHO's effectiveness and leadership role in health as part of the UN humanitarian system;
- create and sustain effective networks and coalitions with the relevant UN agencies and other stakeholders, based on shared agendas for substantive work;
- contribute to a coherent and effective UN system at global, regional and country levels.

It's not about—it's *never* about—"global uplift" or a spirit of collaboration or anything like that. Its obscurantism and deliberate mis-direction became blatantly obvious during the onset of the panic over the coronavirus. The WHO is not a respectable organization based on advancing sound health care practice so much as it basically exists to use the patina of respectability to push a particular agenda. The World Health Organization in 2012 issued its official definition of transgenderism as:

Persons who identify themselves in a different gender than that assigned to them at birth. They may express their identity differently to that expected of the gender role assigned to them at birth. Trans/transgender persons often identify themselves in ways that are locally, socially, culturally, religiously, or spiritually defined.

This is not a medically-sound definition, to put it mildly.

In 2017, WHO funder the Rockefeller Foundation announced a grant to the Sylvia Rivera Law Project:

To guarantee that all people are free to self-determine gender identity and expression, regardless of income or race. . . . [The] grant to the Sylvia Rivera Law Project (SRLP) will support SRLP's advocacy, public education, and coalitional work to improve access to gender-affirming healthcare and identity documents and increase safety and security for the most marginalized transgender communities while growing the skills, leadership, and political power of trans, gender non-conforming, and intersex people. SRLP will increase access to gender-affirming healthcare for transgender New Yorkers; increase safety, security, and the ability to self-advocate for their rights for TGNCI immigrants, prisoners, and students; and increase access to safe and affirming legal and social services for trans, gender non-conforming, and intersex people. Juana Paola Peralta, Director of Outreach & Community Engagement at the Sylvia Rivera Law Project said, "In this hostile climate, where racist, transphobic, anti-immigrant, and anti-black rhetoric continues to place those most marginalized by intersecting systems of oppression at the greatest risk of harm and violence, it is a crucial moment for the Sylvia Rivera Law Project to increase our efforts to ensure that our community is aware of their rights and is able to advocate for themselves and to continue to resist.

We commend Rockefeller Foundation for standing in solidarity with LGBTQIA communities, especially trans and gender non-conforming people and people living in the south. We are excited to partner with RF to resource our communities and are honored by the show of support."

The globalist Establishment is uniform in its agreement on "gender affirming healthcare"—also known as medicalized conversion therapy—and its intersectional nature. With this in mind, Gilead Sciences' sponsorship of the National LGBTQ Task Force, for example, is not some altruistic gesture. There is serious money to be made.

In 2006, the Howard Brown Health Center based out of Chicago was selected to lead a joint effort to "provide services for LGBTQ seniors." With funding from the National LGBTQ Task Force, the initiative also combined the resources of the Council for Jewish Elderly Life, the Heartland Alliance, the Rush University Medical Center (which has received money from the Pritzker Pucker Family Foundation and features a slew of University of Chicago Pritzker School of Medicine alumni), and the Midwest Hospice and Palliative Care to create "a comprehensive program for seniors in the LGBTQ and disadvantaged communities." Children from twelve may receive "LGBTQ care" at the Howard Brown Health Center's Broadway Youth Center. In 1991, the Howard Brown Health Center was inducted into the Chicago Gay and Lesbian Hall of Fame for being "the Midwest's leading provider of support services to and for people living with AIDS and HIV disease, and an internationally recognized center for hepatitis and AIDS/HIV research."

While we're on the subject of the National LGBTQ Task Force, we might as well peek under the hood. Lo and behold, its Co-Chair Liebe Gadinsky is married to a Jewish man and there is a preponderance of Jews in prominent leadership positions and on staff, and as usual there's the insistence on enfolding all things anti-Western into the platform; from their 2015–16 Annual Report they proudly proclaim that they've roundly "Condemned US Immigration and Customs Enforcement (ICE) for its raids targeting undocumented immigrant families and children and called for the dire need of comprehensive immigration reform by Congress," and even though they celebrate the hijab to the heavens as a sign of empowerment (unless it's somewhere the neo-liberal order has targeted for "opening up" such as Iran, in which case it's oppressive), they celebrate defeating religious liberty in the context of mandates requiring doctors to perform "gender transition" surgeries. Also funding this organization are included the Art of Shaving, Coca-Cola, Wells Fargo, JP Morgan Chase, Planned Parenthood, GLAD, Morgan Stanley, the MAC AIDS Fund, the Johnson Family Foundation, the Arcus Foundation, the NoVo Foundation, the Ford Foundation, the Evelyn and Walter Haas, Jr. Fund, the New Venture Fund, and the Horizons Foundation.

One of their largest donors is the Jewish homosexual Andrew Solomon, who is also on the Board of Directors. Solomon has an interest, like George Soros, in contributing to and expanding awareness of "gypsy causes." He has worked to promote the LGBTQ agenda in Romania as well, is a Council on Foreign Relations member, and is on PEN America's Board of Trustees. His father was the CEO of Forest Laboratories, a pharmaceutical company, and was the founder of Hildred Capital Partners, a private equity firm focusing on the healthcare industry.

Returning to the US government's funding priorities under Obama, for 2014:

- The National Institutes of Health (NIH) will enhance LGBT health research through the launch of Health Inequity Exploration Research Supplements for existing research projects that expand the scientific knowledge base concerning health inequities in sexual and gender minority populations. To increase understanding of broad research needs relating to health needs and specific health concerns faced by members of the LGBT community, NIH will also release a strategic plan for sexual and gender minority health research, which aligns with the recommendations issued by the Institute of Medicine.
- In 2014, AHRQ awarded a three-year cooperative agreement to the University of Chicago to reduce healthcare disparities in racial and ethnic LGBT populations.

And over the course of 2015–16:

- [In 2015] the CDC began a four-year demonstration project (of up to $60 million) designed to improve outcomes for gay, bisexual, and other MSM of color. The HHS Office of Minority Health awarded over $2 million in grant funding to community-based organizations to address unmet needs of young racial and ethnic minority men who have sex with men participating in its HIV/AIDS Initiative for Minority Men (AIMM) program.
- The Special Projects of National Significance Program: "Enhancing Access to and Retention in Quality HIV Care for Transgender Women of Color" is a $3.2 million per year initiative which will identify, evaluate, and disseminate successful strategies to improve engagement and retention in HIV primary care for transgender women of color living with HIV.
- The HRSA HIV/AIDS Bureau funded the Resource and Technical Assistance Center for HIV Prevention and Care for Black Men who Have Sex with Men (Black MSM). The aim and purpose of this project is to compile and disseminate models of care and technical assistance strategies which increase the capacity, quality, and effectiveness of HIV/AIDS service for the Black MSM community in HIV clinical care, especially Black youth aged 13–24.
- In the spring of 2015, the Eunice Kennedy Shriver National Institute of Child Health and Human Development (NICHD), with contributions from the National Institute for Allergy and Infectious Diseases and the National Cancer Institute, supported a workshop to discuss research gaps related to the health care needs of transgender people. This meeting provided a venue for interdisciplinary scientists to meet and exchange ideas about the key issues and methodological challenges in conducting research in transgender health. The workshop area foci were: health disparities; gender identity development across the lifespan; clinical management of gender nonconforming children and adolescents; the safety and efficacy of transgender hormone regimens; and innovative research methods; and opportunities for collaboration. Six papers were published in the journal *Current Opinion in Endocrinology, Diabetes, and Obesity*, as a result of the workshop.

- In June 2015, ACF's Office of Refugee Resettlement (ORR) issued a letter to all state refugee coordinators, state refugee health coordinators, national voluntary agencies, and other interested parties to provide guidance on using Refugee Social Services funding for services to LGBT refugees and other ORR-eligible populations.
- Across the Department, HHS Divisions have taken steps to make it clear that all grantees should work to meet the unique needs of LGBT populations. For example, SAMHSA requires that grant applicants submit information about how they will serve LGBT populations. ACL is currently revising the guidance issued to state units on aging (SUAs) for preparing state plans on aging to encourage greater inclusivity of LGBT and other diverse populations in outreach activities and service provision.
- In May 2016 OCR published the final rule implementing Section 1557 of the ACA. . . . individuals must be treated consistent with their gender identity, including with respect to access to facilities such as patient rooms. Additionally, the rule prohibits categorical exclusions in insurance coverage for all health care services related to gender transition and denials and limitations in coverage for specific transition-related services. . . . The rule also prohibits the denial or limitation in health services ordinarily or exclusively available to individuals of one sex, to a transgender individual, based on the fact that the individual's sex assigned at birth, gender identity, or recorded gender, is different from the one to which such health services are ordinarily or exclusively available. . . . As this rule applies to any health program or activity that receives funding from HHS, or that HHS itself administers it means that foreign organizations that enter into contracts HHS to perform health programs or activities are likewise prohibited from discriminating on the basis of sex carrying out those programs or activities.
- In June [2016], Secretary Burwell announced the creation of a new position for a Senior Advisor for LGBT Health within the Office of the Assistant Secretary for Health (OASH).
- In October [2016], in recognition of the significant health disparities facing the LGBT population and the important role that research plays in identifying and helping to mitigate those disparities, the National Institutes of Health (NIH) officially designated sexual and gender minorities (SGM) as a health disparity population for research.
- The NIH Office of Equity, Diversity, and Inclusion (OEDI), along with the SGMRO, co-sponsored several events in 2016 to highlight Pride month at the agency. Events included panel discussions, trainings, and the "Telling Our Stories" film series.

From fiscal year 2008 through the first few months of fiscal year 2020, we see that the US Department of Health and Human Services dispensed over $123 million to transgender "causes" and research in listed accessible grants alone. Over that same time frame, we also see over $21.3 million granted by USAID, over $4.8 million from the Department of Justice, over $2.8 million from the Department of Housing and Urban Development ($12.8 million for "LGBT" in general), nearly $1 million from the Department of Defense, plus additional grants from the US State Department directly, the National Endowment for the Arts, the Department of the Treasury, the National Endowment for the Humanities, and, preposterously, NASA, among others. The Los Angeles LGBT Center alone has received at bare minimum $50 million from the US government since 2007. The NIH spends about $2,583 each year per person with HIV/AIDS versus $418 each year per person with cancer. Insane.

Callen-Lorde Community Health Center in New York City sponsors nurse practitioner fellowships and collaborates with the Columbia University Medical Center and Public Health Solutions. They are a hub of transgender research; in early 2018, they partnered with Johns Hopkins Bloomberg School of Public Health, Fenway Health, Harvard University T.H. Chan School of Public Health, the University of Miami, Emory University and Grady Memorial Hospital, Whitman Walker Health, and Boston Children's Hospital to study a cohort of 1,100 "transgender women and transfeminine people in the US" with financial backing from the National Institutes of Health (NIH).

Callen-Lorde and Fenway Health are also integral to the LEGACY Project, which will "examine how medical gender affirmation impacts quality of life, mental health outcomes, and HIV-related outcomes among 4,500 transgender and non-binary adult patients from Fenway Health and Callen-Lorde Community Health Center in New York City." The principal investigator is Sari Reisner and according to granting institution the Patient-Centered Outcomes Research Institute (PCORI):

> Transgender people are working as part of the research team to plan and guide the study. The team includes staff from the [UCSF] Center of Excellence for Transgender Health and the National LGBT Health Education Center. A community advisory board and a scientific advisory board are also helping the research team.

Christine Goertz, Chair of the PCORI Board of Governors, is a Professor in Musculoskeletal Research at the Duke Clinical Research Institute and Director of System Development and Coordination for Spine Health in the Department of Orthopaedic Surgery at Duke University. She is also the Chief Executive Officer of the Spine Institute for Quality and Adjunct Professor in the Department of Epidemiology, College of Public Health at the University of Iowa. Goertz received her Doctor of Chiropractic (DC) degree from Northwestern Health Sciences University in 1991 and her PhD in health services research, policy, and administration from the School of Public Health at the University of Minnesota in 1999. Goertz is a former member of NIH's National Advisory Council for Complementary and Integrative Health.

The Vice Chair is Sharon Levine, Associate Executive Director for The Permanente Medical Group of Northern California, a large multi-specialty group practice in Oakland within Kaiser Permanente's integrated delivery system. PCORI is funded through the Patient-Centered Outcomes Research Trust Fund (PCOR Trust Fund), which was authorized to be established through the Patient Protection and Affordable Care Act of 2010.

Returning to Penny Pritzker, Jennifer Bilek writes:

Penny has funded the Harvard School of Public Health and, with her husband through their mutual foundation, The Pritzker Traubert Family Foundation, are funding early childhood initiatives as well as providing scholarships to Harvard University medical students. The Boston Children's Hospital Gender Management Services wing physicians are all affiliated with Harvard Medical School. Penny Pritzker also sat on the board at Harvard.

The Pritzker Traubert Family Foundation's President is the Jewish Cindy S. Moelis (Stanford JD), a close friend of Michelle Obama's and wife of Robert S. Rivkin (Harvard, Stanford)—both were Obama administration appointees.

Harvard undergrad also produced transgender Jew Rachel Levine (Tulane Medical School, residency in pediatrics and fellowship in adolescent medicine at Mt. Sinai), who as Pennsylvania Secretary of Health famously relocated "her" 95-year-old mother from a nursing home after Levine publicly stated that such centers should begin accepting coronavirus patients discharged from hospitals. Levine naturally condemned the backlash as "transphobia."

The University of Chicago Pritzker School of Medicine hosts an annual LGBTQ+ People in Medicine Forum. Alongside the Pritzker School of Medicine, the University of Chicago also has a Center for the Study of Gender and Sexuality to produce the ideological framework of the transgender-industrial complex. The Baylor College of Medicine has hired a number of physicians from the University of Chicago Pritzker School of Medicine; the Pritzker School of Medicine has a number of "pathway programs" which target predominantly non-white candidates for a future career in medicine and/or research: "The program seeks students who come from disadvantaged backgrounds and/or who represent groups that are known to be underrepresented in health related sciences and medicine." The skeptic—provided they're not of the Michael Shermer variety—might read that as indoctrination and weaponizing of non-whites, and speculatively I'd imagine they'd be right.

Bob McLaughlin Dean of the School of Health Professions at Baylor College of Medicine (who has "spoken at conferences as the keynote speaker, educator workshops, and lay and professional groups on various topics including Motivational Interviewing, effective group leadership, sexuality, and gender identity development which constitutes a focus of his clinical practice") is a Board Member-at-Large for and co-founder of "charity" Gender Infinity: "With a growing body of volunteers now numbering over 100 per year, we continue the annual conference and added additional services, including a camp for transgender and gender expansive children started in 2018." The Tegan and Sara Foundation (named after its lesbian identical twin Canadian pop duo namesakes) is a partner.

The Jewish Mark Hyman (Cornell, UCSF) is the inaugural endowed Pritzker Foundation Chair in Functional Medicine at the Cleveland Clinic Lerner College of Medicine, and yet another Pritzker School of Medicine alum, David T. Rubin, is on the Advisory Board of Accordant/CVS Caremark. In 2015, CVS made the major acquisition of Target's department store pharmacies. As Jennifer Bilek writes, "Target, of course, is the site of a major social controversy about unisex bathrooms and is a corporate funder of the trans-pushing Human Rights Campaign activist group."

Speaking of the Human Rights Campaign, the HRC Foundation also has a

Healthcare Equality Index for reasons that are about to become very apparent. Among their "suggested policy aims" include hospitals providing explicit "gender transition guidelines" and "transgender-specific policies," and "offer[ing] trans-inclusive benefits." One of their primary partners is the Pharmaceutical Research and Manufacturers of America (PhRMA), whose stated mission is "advocacy for public policies that encourage the discovery of new medicines for patients by companies engaged in pharmaceutical and biopharmaceutical research." Lo and behold its leadership and Board of Directors includes senior management representing a veritable who's who of the pharmaceutical companies pushing the transgender agenda and profiting off of the transgender-industrial complex (see Appendix C for the full list).

Donors to the AIDS United "charity" also reveals a veritable who's who of the principal figures behind this agenda. The CDC, the Ford Foundation, the Health Resources and Services Administration (HRSA), and the Corporation for National and Community Service (CNCS) all donated at least $1 million in 2016 alone, for example. ViiV Healthcare, Gilead Sciences, and both Johnson & Johnson and Janssen all donated between $250,000 and $999,999, and other major donations came in from Barack Obama, the Human Rights Campaign Foundation, the National Minority AIDS Council, AZPAC - Match Program (AstraZeneca), the JP Morgan Chase Foundation, the American Academy of HIV Medicine, Walgreens, Merck, the New York Community Trust, Fenway Health, the Elton John AIDS Foundation, the Levi Strauss Foundation, the Elizabeth Taylor AIDS Foundation, Bristol-Myers Squibb, the H. van Ameringen Foundation, and the National Committee on US-China Relations.

The Executive Vice Chairs for the National Committee on US-China Relations are the Jewish Henry Kissinger and the Jewish Maurice R. "Hank" Greenberg, both of whom are members of the Council on Foreign Relations. Chair Carla Hills is a Council on Foreign Relations member, and per the website's biographical description:

> Ambassador Carla A. Hills is chair and chief executive officer of Hills & Company International Consultants, which provides advice to international firms on investment, trade, and risk assessment issues abroad, particularly in emerging market economies. Ambassador Hills served as United States Trade Representative from 1989 to 1993. As a member of President George H.W. Bush's cabinet, she was the president's principal advisor on international trade policy. She was also the nation's chief trade negotiator, representing American interests in multilateral and bilateral trade negotiations throughout the world. Ambassador Hills negotiated and concluded the North American Free Trade Agreement and also led the U.S. negotiations on the Uruguay Round of the World Trade Organization. During her tenure, the United States entered into a large number of trade and investment agreements with countries around the world. Earlier, Ambassador Hills served in the cabinet of President Gerald R. Ford, as secretary of the Department of Housing and Urban Development (the third woman to hold a cabinet position). She also served as the assistant attorney general in the Civil Division of the U.S. Department of Justice. Before entering government, Ambassador Hills co-founded and was partner in what is now the Munger, Tolles & Olson LLP

law firm. She also served as an adjunct professor at the University of California at Los Angeles Law School teaching antitrust law, and co-authored *The Antitrust Adviser* (McGraw-Hill, 1971). Her prior expertise in antitrust and federal civil matters informs her understanding of business. Over the years, Ambassador Hills has served on a number of corporate boards, including AIG, AT&T, Chevron, Corning Glass Works, Gilead Sciences, IBM, Time Warner, Trust Company of the West, and United Airlines. She is currently on the international advisory board of J.P. Morgan Chase. She also serves in leadership positions with not-for-profit organizations. She is chair of the International Advisory Board of the Center for Strategic and International Studies; co-chair of the Inter-American Dialogue; chair emeritus of the Council on Foreign Relations (after serving as co-chair until July 2017); honorary director of the Peterson Institute for International Economics; and executive committee member of the Trilateral Commission.

National Committee on US-China Relations President Stephen A. Orlins ("My mother was an immigrant to the United States. My paternal grandparents were immigrants to the United States. I grew up in a family where we were taught that, but for the American government and the American people, we wouldn't exist, we would have perished in Europe. They were European immigrants and Jewish immigrants") is a Harvard alumnus, worked for the US State Department and Carlyle Asia, and is a member of the Council on Foreign Relations. The Board is loaded with Jews and features ties to Johns Hopkins, the Brookings Institution, Columbia University, the Ford Foundation, Kissinger Associates, the US military and government, more Council on Foreign Relations, the Walt Disney Company, Sanofi, Bayer, high finance, and MIT. Cornerstone supporters include BlackRock, Blackstone, and the Carnegie Corporation of New York. Sanofi US is a corporate chair; benefactors include KPMG, JUUL Labs, Chevron, Amgen, and the Ford Foundation; and corporate leaders include Merck, McKinsey, KKR, PayPal, Walmart, and Gilead Sciences. Of additional relevance regarding China, two Jewish families, the Sassoons and the Kadoories, are generally credited with "opening up" the country.

Cedars-Sinai Medical Center in Los Angeles offers Genital Reconstructive Surgery Clinical and Research fellowships "with a primary focus on a comprehensive list of all available feminizing or masculinizing genital surgeries. . . . Fellows have access to an NIH-funded research laboratory." These procedures—and I am going to spare the reader the gruesome details here—explain why medical supply companies, prosthetics companies, hormone-producing labs, plastic surgeons, dermatologists, and the like are all invested in promoting transgender "hormone therapy" and surgery as not just a "viable option" but "medically necessary." Again, why do you think Gilead Sciences, Genentech, Abbott Laboratories, Bristol-Myers Squibb, and Boehringer Ingelheim are so invested in sponsoring transgender NGOs and "charities"?

The Yale School of Public Health is studying "an evidence-based intervention" for young gay and bisexual men at risk for HIV infection as well as examining "the intersection of physical health, mental health and stigma among lesbian and bisexual women, LGBT people in underserved areas and transgender women in prison" with these projects and others receiving funding from the National Institute of Mental

Health (NIMH), Yale's Fund for Lesbian and Gay Studies, and the Fogarty International Center at the National Institutes of Health.

On another side of the operation, transgender incubator and Patient Zero for the Frankfurt School's poisonous influence in the US Columbia University (24% of its undergraduates in 2018 were Jewish) hosts Cluster Q, Columbia Business School's LGBT Business Association, described as:

> An open and welcoming community for lesbian, gay, bisexual, transgender, and queer students, faculty members, and administrators. Cluster Q's membership is one of the largest and most diverse LGBT groups among the world's top business schools and also boast the largest representation of straight allies among all business schools.

Eat your heart out, Goldman Sachs!

The University of Pennsylvania, which has its share of Pritzker School of Medicine alums at its Perelman School of Medicine, announced that Sarah Wood, adolescent medicine fellow at the Children's Hospital of Philadelphia (CHOP), received a University of Pennsylvania Centers for AIDS Research Pilot Grant and NIH F-32 Award to study how social support networks can improve success with taking PrEP for young men-who-have-sex-with-men (YMSM) and young-transgender-women (YTM) at-risk for HIV infection. "Sarah's research interests include exploring the implementation science of biomedical HIV prevention, as well as identifying barriers to successful treatment for youth living with HIV." Wood had previously published these findings:

> As part of a larger study on how to improve HIV prevention and treatment for YTW [young-transgender-women] we used qualitative methods to explore attitudes and experiences with HIV Pre-Exposure Prophylaxis (PrEP). The newest option in the HIV prevention tool box, PrEP is a daily pill to prevent HIV infection that, if taken properly, is more effective than most vaccines. Among the 25 young women we interviewed for this study, one-third of participants had never heard of PrEP. Participants cited many reasons they thought PrEP was an important option for their community including that it could make their relationships with sexual partners better and help them to feel empowered. Despite overwhelmingly positive attitudes towards PrEP many participants didn't think they would be able to afford it, especially if they didn't have access to other gender-affirming treatments such as hormones. This study was recently accepted for publication in the *Journal of Adolescent Health*.

The CHOP Gender and Sexuality Development Clinic was established in 2014 and has "served" hundreds of minors in the subsequent years. These minors have also been given the guinea pig treatment:

> A qualitative, ethnographic study of patients seeking services at GSDC for children and youth aged 7–21 years old. The primary objective was to deter-

mine the ways in which medical and psychosocial treatments (including psychotherapy, puberty-blocking therapy, and hormone therapy) impact gender variant and transgender-identified children and adolescents.

They've also partnered with the Mazzoni Center[108] in evaluating children as young as *five*. Additionally:

> Together with the CHOP Social Work and Family Services Department and PolicyLab we collaborated with the University of Pennsylvania Student Legal Clinic for form a Medical Legal Partnership (MLP). MLPs are designed to bring lawyers to health care teams to improve the health and well-being of underserved populations. So far the MLP has served over 25 youth and their families. Our legal partners are also working on developing guides for addressing insurance coverage issues and the process of legal name change. Dr. [Nadia] Dowshen is working together with PolicyLab staff to design a robust evaluation and plan for disseminating this model to other clinics across the country which may also benefit.

Dowshen's fellowship in General Academic Pediatrics was at the Ann and Robert H. Lurie Children's Hospital of Chicago; she is an adolescent medicine specialist, Director of Adolescent HIV Services, and Co-Director of the Gender and Sexuality Development Clinic at CHOP. The other Co-Director, Linda Hawkins, states that, "A child begins to have an innate sense of their gender identity between ages 3 and 5."

Vanderbilt University Medical Center's LGBTQ Health Department is another prominent institution involved in the entrenchment and expansion of this insidious agenda. Its major figures include:

- Del Ray Zimmerman, Director of the Program for LGBTQ Health and Office for Diversity Affairs, and has been involved with GLSEN
- Shayne Sebold Taylor's expertise is in Adolescent LGBT Health; Taylor has published articles such as "The Gender Non-Conforming Child" and "The Gender Non-Conforming Child Version 2.0"
- Lea Davis was a postdoctoral fellow and research assistant at the University of Chicago
- Keanan Gottlieb studies dental health for LGBTQ patients
- Shawn Reilly is the Trans Buddy Coordinator and works with "trans youth" as well as serves as the Student Engagement and Leadership Chair for GLSEN Tennessee and is a founding member of the Tennessee Department of Health Transgender HIV Task Force
- RJ Robles is the former Trans Buddy Coordinator and "is a queer and transgender Latinx activist and member of Southerners on New Ground seeking to continue the strong legacy of trans people of color organizing

---

[108] The Mazzoni Center of Philadelphia is a major hub of LGBTQ activism on the East Coast; its major funders include: the Department of Justice, the CDC, the Department of Homeland Security, the Bristol-Myers Squibb Employee Giving Program, Vanguard, the United Way, Bank of America, Comcast, Gilead Sciences, and TD Bank.

in the South"
- Kristen Eckstrand, founding Co-Director, is also the founding chair of the Association of American Medical Colleges' Advisory Committee on Sexual Orientation, Gender Identity, and Sex Development, co-editing and authoring Implementing Curricular and Institutional Climate Changes to Improve Health Care for Individuals Who Are LGBT, Gender Nonconforming, or Born with DSD: A Resource for Medical Educators. Eckstrand also serves as the Vice President of Education for the Board of Directors of GLMA: Health Professionals Advancing LGBT Equality and is a member of the American Medical Association's LGBT Advisory Committee.

The founding Director of the Program for LGBTQ Health Jesse Ehrenfeld—who states, "I'm gay and Jewish"—is also the Secretary of the American Medical Association Board of Trustees and is a graduate of the University of Chicago Pritzker School of Medicine and the Harvard School of Public Health.

*Fortune Business Insights* has predicted that the HIV/AIDS medication market will reach $40.675 billion by 2026; the biggest companies in the industry also happen to be some of the largest donors to "transgender causes": Genentech/Roche, ViiV, Gilead Sciences, Bristol-Myers Squibb, Johnson & Johnson/Janssen, et cetera. The reality of the situation is quite a bit less rainbow-rosy than all the so-called philanthropic endeavors and bright commercial lies would have you believe, as we should expect at this point.

Pharmaceutical giant Bristol-Myers Squibb, which sells HIV drugs like Reyataz and Evotaz, and is studying several other treatments for the disease, has a significant interest in the transgender/homosexual/"diverse"/etc. populations both from an R&D perspective and from a sales perspective. All the way back in 1994, the FDA had approved for sale a second Bristol-Myers Squibb medication to treat HIV infection; the drug, d4T, was developed at Yale University's School of Medicine. Additionally, via *Fierce Pharma*:

Gilead Sciences used its monopoly on one critical component in HIV combo meds to stifle generic competition and keep prices high, a new lawsuit claims—and the Big Biotech did so with the help of combo partners Johnson & Johnson and Bristol-Myers Squibb. In a class action lawsuit, HIV and AIDS activists say Gilead teamed with Bristol-Myers, [Johnson & Johnson's] Janssen unit and Japan Tobacco to knock back competition to HIV cocktail meds. The companies agreed to stick with patent-protected ingredients in their fixed-dose combination drugs, rather than sub in low-cost generics, even after patents expired on the individual components. . . . The strategy forced much higher prices over time. . . . Even after exclusivity lapsed for some components of the meds—which are key to HIV treatment because they drastically reduce the number of pills patients need to take—Gilead's fixed-dosed-combination drug Complera sells for $35,000 per year, the plaintiffs say. A version using available generic components—plus Janssen's still-patent-protected Edurant—would cost half that, the suit alleges. . . . The lawsuit follows a string of headlines about Gilead's HIV business. . . . A California judge refused to dismiss a separate lawsuit claiming Gilead illegally delayed its next-gen HIV meds to milk as much revenue as possible from its current generation before the older drugs went off patent.

I wonder if it's also a coincidence that the Bristol-Myers Squibb Foundation and the Baylor International Pediatric AIDS Initiative used HIV-positive children in Botswana, Lesotho, Swaziland, Tanzania, and Uganda as test subjects while collaborating with the countries' respective ministries of health in establishing tertiary care centers in each country. The goals, as stated by Bristol-Myers and Baylor researchers were for each center to be, via *Health Affairs*:

> A resource for both training and clinical and operational research that would be relevant to the local context, for other potential funders and health care facilities throughout each country. Operational research can be defined as a process of identifying and solving program problems in the real world.

Sebastian Wanless, former Vice President of Research and Program Evaluation for the Baylor International Pediatric AIDS Initiative was hired by the Bristol-Myers Squibb Foundation as a private contractor to help write up their findings in *Health Affairs*. Researcher Mark Kline is a Professor of Pediatrics at the Baylor College of Medicine and the founder and President of the Baylor International Pediatric AIDS Initiative. Kline is principal investigator for the Baylor College of Medicine site of the Child Health Research Center Program, which is funded by the National Institutes of Health.

Let's consider the connections members of the Baylor College of Medicine have to the transgender-industrial complex and relevant previous experience, education, and/or training:

- Daniel Yoshor: Chair of Neurosurgery; BA from Yeshiva University, MD from the University of Chicago Pritzker School of Medicine, fellowship at the University of California-San Francisco (UCSF) Affiliate Hospitals, research supported by grants from the NIH and the Department of Veteran's Affairs
- Eugene Choi: Associate Professor of Surgery (Division of Surgical Oncology); BA from the University of Chicago, residency at the University of Chicago, MD from the University of Chicago Pritzker School of Medicine
- Sherise Desiree Ferguson: Assistant Professor of Neurosurgery; MD from the University of Chicago Pritzker School of Medicine, residency at the University of Chicago
- Martin Matzuk: Stuart A. Wallace Chair in the Department of Pathology and Immunology; undergraduate degree from the University of Chicago, MD and PhD from the Washington University School of Medicine
- Eli Mizrahi: Chair of the Department of Neurology; residency at the Stanford University School of Medicine
- John E. Wolf, Jr.: Chair of the Department of Dermatology; UCSF residency, Cornell University Medical College internship
- Todd Rosengart: Chair of the Michael E. DeBakey Department of Surgery; MD from Northwestern University

- Michael A. Belfort: Chair of the Department of Obstetrics and Gynecology and Obstetrician and Gynecologist-in-Chief at Texas Children's Hospital; adjunct clinical professor at Yale University School of Medicine
- Michael Coburn: Professor and Russell and Mary Hugh Scott Chair in Urology, holds the Carlton-Smith Chair in Urologic Education; BA Cornell University
- Donald T. Donovan: Chair of the Bobby R. Alford Department of Otolaryngology; fellowship from Columbia University Affiliated Hospitals
- Wayne Goodman: Chair of the Menninger Department of Psychiatry and Behavioral Sciences; former Chair of Mount Sinai's Behavioral Health System, BS from Columbia University, MD from Boston University School of Medicine, residency and fellowship at Yale University
- Thomas R. Hunt III: Chair of the Joseph Barnhart Department of Orthopedic Surgery; BS from Stanford University, fellowship at Hospital of the University of Pennsylvania
- Michael Y. Lee: Professor and Executive Vice Chair of the H. Ben Taub Department of Physical Medicine and Rehabilitation, residency at Northwestern University
- Jean Leclerc Raphael: Associate Professor of Pediatrics; Post-Doctoral Fellowship at Commonwealth Fund Harvard University Fellowship in Minority Health Policy, Residency at Boston Children's Hospital/Boston Medical Center, MD from Harvard Medical School
- D'Juanna White Satcher: Assistant Professor of Pediatrics; internship and residency at Boston Children's Hospital, MD from Harvard Medical School, MPH from Harvard School of Public Health

You get the idea. This is exactly how the Frankfurt School and Boasian acolytes coopted academia in their respective fields, and this is precisely what is happening today with the transgender-industrial complex.

The Kelsey Coalition estimates that the annual total medical bill for transgender surgeries in the US is over $1.3 billion. According to Johns Hopkins researchers, "gender-affirming surgeries" increased four-fold between 2000–2014.[109] In 2016, they had increased another 19% from the year previous. Additionally, there are now over fifty "gender youth clinics" in the US alone. As Robert Bridge writes:

Do the medical community and pharmaceutical companies have an incentive to promote risky hormonal treatment, together with the radical surgical procedures, to the public? Something similar is happening now in the United States with the deadly opioid epidemic. Big Pharma played no small part in getting these powerful painkillers to patients regardless of the safety hazards involved. According to The Kelsey Coalition, the situation with regards to hormone treatment is nearly identical. By way of example, the coalition cited Endo Pharmaceuticals, a pill manufacturer which lost millions of dollars in court settling opioid lawsuits. Today, as the Kelsey Coalition told RT, the company is now "focusing on their testosterone line of products." That may not sound like such a terrible thing, until it is realized that "almost every vocal

---

[109] Interestingly, whites were underrepresented in these surgeries relative to their population share.

pro-medicalization 'gender expert' in the US has an association with Endo Pharmaceutical as an advisor," the group claimed. The Kelsey Coalition specifically mentioned Dr. Joshua Safer, executive director of the Mount Sinai Center for Transgender Medicine and Surgery, New York, who speaks out on the purported benefits of puberty suppressors. Safer has reported that he'd received consulting fees from Endo Pharmaceuticals and that his wife is an employee of Parexel, the second largest clinical research organization in the world. At the same time, the organization that's writing the treatment guidelines for transgender patients, The World Professional Association for Transgender Health (WPATH), is run by the for-profit company Veritas. . . . Veritas sits on the advisory boards for a number of organizations, including Lipocrine Pharma, a company that produces hormones, with a particular focus on testosterone. . . . Veritas also sits on the Board of Intuitive Surgical, producers of robotic assisted surgical devices. This equipment has various medical usages, including the removal of the uterus, ovaries and vaginal canal, in preparation for the construction of the 'neo-penis' (artificial penis) for females transitioning to males. . . . So here we have WPATH, an organization that has an advisory role in determining what treatments are proven safe, being run by Veritas, a company that acquires large profits when pharmaceutical companies and surgeons implement expensive medicines and procedures provided by the very firms they represent. That certainly sounds like a conflict of interest.

Indeed it does.

Endo Pharmaceuticals is under the auspices of Endo International, an Irish-domiciled pharmaceutical company that generated over 93% of 2017 sales from the US healthcare system. Supprelin LA, a puberty-blocking implant that lasts about a year with a list price of $37,300 according to pricing data from ConnectureDRX, is manufactured by Endo. According to a February 2020 report from NPR, "Supprelin LA would cost around $95,000, plus the cost of implantation, the [OHSU Hospital in Portland, Ore., part of Oregon Health & Science University] billing department [said]." As *Forbes* reported in April 2007:

> In 1969, Dupont purchased Endo, before joining it together with Merck assets in 1990 to create a joint venture called Dupont Merck Pharmaceuticals Co. In 1994, Endo became a separate entity in the joint venture. Three years later, [Carol] Ammon and two colleagues led a management buyout of the Endo division, purchasing all of its generic products as well as 12 brands such as Percocet and Percodan, for $277 million.

The International Stop Trans Pathologization (STP) 2012 campaign and WPATH itself hold the position that not all trans people have gender dysphoria and that "gender nonconformity" is not a disorder. STP 2012 actually wants the removal of gender dysphoria from the DSM and the ICD completely; according to the Open Society Foundations, "the STP 2012 campaign also works to secure public coverage of trans-specific health care and for the recognition of trans identities as a human rights issue rather than a disease."

The Australian and New Zealand Professional Association for Transgender

Health, the New Zealand Sexual Health Society, and the New Zealand Society of Endocrinology all subscribe to the WPATH standards of care. WPATH Board member Jaime Veale is a Lecturer in Psychology at the University of Waikato in New Zealand; Veale states: "I also conduct research on the sexuality of transgender people, particularly on portrayals of transgender women's sexuality within psychology and medicine." The Australian Psychological Society, representing 24,000 professionals, stated its official position in 2019 that the disapproval of both parents for a child to have reassignment surgery should not inhibit that child from seeking out "reassignment" procedures and that hospitals should have the right to petition courts and "convince" the parents to change their minds.

On January 28th, 2020, WPATH and USPATH issued a joint statement in response to the "recent and troubling trend" of proposed legislation "denying evidence-based care for transgender people under 18 years of age":

> The World Professional Association for Transgender Health (WPATH) and its US chapter, the United States Professional Association for Transgender Health (USPATH), vehemently oppose the legislation being proposed in Florida (HB 1365), South Carolina (HB 4716), South Dakota (HB 1057), Colorado (HB 20-1114), and similar legislation in other states. These bills seek to deny evidence-based care for transgender people under 18 years of age and to penalize professionals who provide that medical care. These bills will punish practitioners of gender affirming care with revocation of their medical license, or up to 15 years in prison in some states. These bills will treat health care providers as if they committed manslaughter or arson.

Good.

It is also worth noting that in 2008, the Endocrine Society, with members in over one hundred countries, "approved" puberty blockers as a treatment for adolescents as young as twelve. The NPR report cited earlier was in the context of an eight-year-old. On May 24th, 2019, the Endocrine Society publicly "expressed major opposition to a rule proposed today by the Department of Health and Human Services (HHS) that would jeopardize transgender individuals' access to healthcare." Unsurprisingly, the Endocrine Society has a Committee on Diversity and Inclusion (CoDI):

> "The more opportunities the Endocrine Society has to include diversity and inclusion activities at our meetings and annual conferences, the more we will be at the leading edge around clinical care, innovation, and investigation," says Sherri-Ann Burnett-Bowie, Chair of the Committee on Diversity and Inclusion; assistant professor of medicine, Harvard Medical School; clinical investigator, Massachusetts General Hospital Endocrine Unit. . . . The minority health disparities of the endocrine disorders have been well documented: For instance, African American and Hispanic adults are almost twice as likely to be diagnosed with diabetes as non-Hispanic whites, according to the Office of Minority Health. In 2015, African American women were 60% more likely to be obese than non-Hispanic white women. One of the reasons attributed to the slow progress in eliminating these disparities is the corresponding disparity issue in the number of minorities with careers in medicine.

Notice "attributed," not *proven*. I can attribute anything—like the way Useful Idiots attribute motive such as "hate." These disparities—"inequalities," which will be rectified by ceding all sovereignty to the New Global Order—are *certainly* not due to genetic predisposition and/or lifestyle choice, right? Similarly, "Another 2016 report by the Association of American Medical Colleges found that despite efforts by U.S. medical schools to diversify their pool of applicants, one demographic, black males, has remained unchanged for nearly 40 years," is easily explained once again by biological disparities, a frank discussion of which is rendered impossible in "polite society" by the full force of the Establishment and its phalanx of diversity-cherishing, pluralistic and freedom-loving liberals.

# Trans America: World Police

*"Every parade is a gay pride parade now, which may explain why South Bend no longer celebrates the Fourth of July. There was no celebration in South Bend this summer because America in any coherent sense worth celebrating has ceased to exist. . . . America has become a gay disco."*

— E. Michael Jones

The US government has been an essential extension of the neo-liberal/globalist axis since at least World War I, having been occupied from the inside through collusion between Jewish interlopers and those of extant capital willing to play ball. No analysis of the globalized push for the rainbow regime would be complete without considering its role in subsidizing numerous NGOs, applying strategic pressure, and even going so far as to deploy its military and intelligence services for the express purpose of breaking down any barriers to the One World, Indivisible project. We have covered quite a bit of this already, but unfortunately there is more.

The Johannesburg Pride proclaims, "Pride has no borders." Indeed, it has no boundaries, either, and given that the Harvey Milk Foundation has received support from the US State Department, it is little wonder that when Czech President Václav Klaus called for the ban of Pride in Prague in 2011, the Foundation marshaled its resources and "answered the call for help" alongside the US Embassy and Martina Navratilova "in direct response to the government-sponsored hate speech." In 1981, Navratilova granted an interview to Steve Goldstein of the *New York Daily News* "coming out" as bisexual, but she asked him to table it until she was ready to "come out" publicly. The interview was released anyway, causing Navratilova and her then-girlfriend the Jewish Nancy Lieberman to grant a responding interview to the *Dallas Morning News*. Navratilova has since identified as a lesbian. The US Embassy has helped sponsor Prague Pride since 2011; 2020's Prague Pride was funded by the Open Society Foundations, the US Embassy, Tides, the European Union, and Vodafone, among others.

The Harvey Milk Foundation has been very active in providing "on the ground support" in countries like Hungary, Turkey, and Italy. Their website features numerous photographs of co-founder and President Stuart Milk with various US ambassadors. In 2014, per the Foundation's website:

The Harvey Milk Foundation, a global organization that promotes Harvey Milk's legacy through human rights education and global outreach efforts, announced. . . . Ambassador Nancy Brinker and her son, Eric Brinker, will join Stuart Milk, nephew of the late civil rights leader Harvey Milk and co-founder of the Harvey Milk Foundation on October 9, 2014 in Budapest, Hungary for a reception hosted by the US Embassy to honor the work of the Harvey Milk Foundation. The reception with community and civil society leaders will include remarks by Former Ambassador Brinker, Mr. M. André Goodfriend, the Chargé d'Affaires, a.i. of the U.S. Embassy Budapest and Mr. Milk. . . . The Harvey Milk Foundation works to promote the celebration of diversity across the globe and has supported LGBT advocates on the ground in Hungary. This work has included Milk serving as the keynote speaker for the annual Pride March in both 2011 and 2013, holding panel discussions, and a LGBT film series. In 2012, Milk brought Hungarian LGBT rights advocates to the U.S. Capital for substantive briefings with Congressional leadership and to participate in a White House LGBT rights forum and East Wing reception. In 2013, with the support of the U.S. Embassy in Budapest, Milk met with religious and civil society leaders and held discussions following an exclusive viewing of the 2009 Academy Award winning film, MILK. Stuart Milk and Nancy Brinker will be joined by Eric Brinker, her son who is openly gay.

The Jewish Nancy Brinker is on the Foundation's Leadership and Advisory Board, and is the founder of the breast cancer charity Susan G. Komen, named after her sister. In light of the previous information, however, it becomes unsurprising to learn that what is supposed to be a breast cancer research charity has donated large sums of money to mass immigration NGOs and to LGBTQ causes; according to Funders of LGBTQ Issues, they donated nearly $1 million to LGBTQ causes in the US South alone in 2011–12. D'Feet Breast Cancer, Inc. is another charity ostensibly working to find a cure, and yet they, too, seem more concerned with the LGBTQ agenda instead.

The other members of the Harvey Milk Foundation's Leadership and Advisory Board include, per their website including positions currently or formerly held:

- Commissioner Nicole-Murray Ramirez, San Diego; Presiding Officer International Court System; has chaired and served on the boards of the Task Force, HRC, EQCA, and has led three LGBT rights marches
- Mechthild Rawert, MP Deutscher Bundestag; Vice Chairman of the SPD district Tempelhof-Schöneberg
- Hon. Raymond Buckley, former member of the House of Representatives and Chairman of the New Hampshire Democratic Party; Vice Chair, National Democratic Committee
- Bruce Cohen, founding Board member of AFER and Academy Award winner for Best Picture – *American Beauty*; produced *MILK* and has been a leading activist and voice for equality throughout the US
- Michael Colby, Deputy Director, Boston Redevelopment Authority; former Executive Director National Stonewall Club; HMF Founding Member
- Tom Dyer, Esq. CEO Watermark Publications, one of the Southeast's

most influential business leaders and a major builder of LGBT collaboration in Central Florida

- Rob Epstein, won the Academy Award for his direction and production of both *The Times of Harvey Milk* and *Common Threads: Stories from the Quilt.*
- Enemencio Gomez, Principal, Global Translations LLC; Senior Interpreter; Bailey Faculty; a leading voice of inclusion for the American Caribbean and a leading voice of cultural acceptance in Texas and the Southwest US
- Dr. Trish Hatch, Director, Center for Excellence in School Counseling, San Diego State University; Assistant Professor San Diego State University
- Dr. Timothy Patrick McCarthy, Professor on Public Policy and Director of the Human Rights and Social Movements Program at the Carr Center for Human Rights Policy at Harvard University, Kennedy School
- Audrey Milk, Harvey's sister-in-law and PFLAG member

The Harvey Milk Foundation and counsel Miriam Richter spearheaded a partnership with the US Post Office to release a Harvey Milk Forever stamp. In 2010, Richter founded and led the effort to establish domestic partnership benefits in municipalities and cities in the Southeast including legislative same-sex partnership benefits for Broward County and the City of Fort Lauderdale. According to Marvin Glassman:

> 11% of Broward Jewish households who have at least one member identify as lesbian, gay, bisexual, or transgender (LGBT). . . . It is the largest Jewish community in Florida and the eighth largest American Jewish community. . . . 93% stated that they were involved in Jewish activity.

Richter has been a participant in round table forums held by the US Justice Department, the US Department of Labor, and the White House. The Harvey Milk Foundation has also partnered with the Anti-Defamation League (ADL) on its "Imagine a World Without Hate" initiative.

Andrea Banfi, Italian "human rights activist," has been leading the Harvey Milk Foundation's work in Italy since 2008, when Banfi "organized a seven city speaking tour with Equality Italia that had Stuart Milk meeting not only leading Italian civil rights leaders, but advancing human rights at all levels in the government." In 2014, the Harvey Milk Foundation sponsored a UK short film competition co-sponsored by Schools OUT UK ("we at Schools OUT UK welcome the overdue review of Sex and Relationships Education and the commitment to making it mandatory in schools and inclusive of LGBT+ people") centered on the life of Milk and at least two British LGBT figures pre-provided. The youngest age category was 6–11. As Jennifer Kates writes:

> In recent years, the U.S. government has paid increasing attention to the health and human rights of lesbian, gay, bisexual and transgender (LGBT) individuals around the world, utilizing both multilateral and bilateral channels [as well as "once-removed" channels like the Harvey Milk Foundation

and various other NGOs and think tanks], including through a 2011 Presidential Memorandum on "International Initiatives to Advance the Human Rights
of Lesbian, Gay, Bisexual, and Transgender Persons" and diplomatic engagement at the United Nations (UN) and World Health Organization (WHO)...
. To explore opportunities and challenges facing the U.S. government in this
arena, the Kaiser Family Foundation convened two roundtable discussions
(in October 2013 and March 2014) of high-level experts working on global
LGBT health and rights as well as those working more broadly on global
health. Participants included representatives from the U.S. government, multilateral institutions, non-governmental organizations, think tanks, and academia.

The Active Citizens Fund Bulgaria has a total value of €15.5 million provided by
donor countries Iceland, Liechtenstein, and Norway, with the Open Society Institute
– Sofia (OSI – Sofia), in consortium with the Workshop for Civic Initiatives Foundation (WCF) and the Trust for Social Achievement Foundation (TSA), selected by
the Financial Mechanism Office in Brussels as Fund Operator. The program will run
until 2024 and will contribute to (among other objectives):

> The achievement of the common objectives of the EEA FM and the Norwe-
> gian FM. . . . The aim of the Active Citizens Fund is "Strengthened civil so-
> ciety, active citizens and empowered vulnerable groups." The Fund will sup-
> port the long-term sustainability and capacity of the civil sector, strengthen-
> ing its role in promoting democratic participation, active citizenship and hu-
> man rights. . . . In the framework of the calls for project proposals, initiatives
> of civil society organizations will be supported, which contribute to. . . . Em-
> powering vulnerable groups; gender equality and prevention of gender-based
> violence [and] increasing the commitment of citizens to environmental pro-
> tection / in connection with climate change.

Bilitis, a major Bulgarian NGO that describes its mission "at the level of civil society
. . . to spread the values of feminism of diversity and to overcome heteronormative
structures, including gender stereotypes," is a grantee of the Active Citizens Fund;
Bilitis has also received funding for various projects from Mama Cash, the Astraea
Lesbian Foundation for Justice, the European Commission, the International Trans
Fund, ILGA-Europe, the PlanetRomeo Foundation, the Rosa Luxemburg Foundation, and the US Embassy in Sofia. In a disgusting display of cultural appropriation,
the US Embassy stated in its 2017 "Statement in support of Sofia Pride":

> The anniversary of Sofia Pride this year is under the motto "Let's banish prej-
> udice." The goal is to unite the LGBTI community through mummery, one
> of the most popular traditions in Bulgaria. Tradition and diversity do not con-
> tradict each other: colored mummers will be a symbol of overcoming preju-
> dices against LGBTI people, clearly showing that they are part of a whole.
> By signing this statement, we encourage Bulgarians to join the Sofia Pride
> procession and to accept LGBTI people as equal citizens, without prejudice
> or discrimination, and to promote equality to the LGBTI community.

Would you like to guess what tribe the American Ambassador signatory Eric Rubin belongs to? Other signatories included the Israeli Ambassador, the UNHCR Representative for Bulgaria, and the UNICEF Representative for Bulgaria. In July 2018, according to the US Embassy in Berlin:

[Homosexual] Ambassador [Richard] Grenell and Embassy Berlin were proud to take part in Berlin's 40th Christopher Street Day (CSD) parade. This year marked the embassy's seventh time marching, and the Ambassador's 25th Pride (his first was the March on Washington in 1993). The Embassy and Ambassador Grenell hosted a series of activities to communicate U.S. support for human rights during Pride season in Berlin, including flying the Pride flag, displaying a large banner on the side of Chancery building (which read "Unsere Botschaft heißt Liebe"), and an afternoon reception at the Chancery. Plus, of course, participation in Berlin's famous parade, which attracted a million spectators this year, where the embassy had a float.

Despite the opposition of the Belarussian government to the LGBTQ agenda specifically and neo-liberalism and its mutating next step more broadly, on one of the many "holidays" pertaining to the LGBTQ set, the International Day Against Homophobia, Transphobia, and Biphobia (IDAHOT) in 2019 saw a number of neo-liberal-aligned embassies in Minsk, including those of the UK, US, Sweden, and Israel, fly the rainbow flag, which was condemned by Belarus's Ministry of Interior.

This is in keeping with US foreign policy, however, as then-Acting Under Secretary for Public Diplomacy and Public Affairs and State Department Spokesperson Heather Naubert stated in 2018:

As we approach Pride Month and the International Day Against Homophobia, Transphobia, and Biphobia this year, we will again ask our embassies to sponsor events that are appropriate to their country context and organized in close collaboration with local civil society organizations. Alongside many of the partners assembled here tonight, we are also proud to support the Global Equality Fund, which provides civil society organizations with the resources they need to combat violence and discrimination.

Is flying a flag within the confines of a sovereign nation in defiance of both governmental and cultural attitudes "appropriate to their cultural context"? No, but neo-liberalism, for all of its ideological nonsense regarding "diversity" is a soul-crushing force of homogeneity.

The Global Equality Fund (GEF) was established in 2011 by the US State Department in collaboration with "a growing and diverse international coalition of governments, companies, non-governmental organizations (NGOs), and foundations." Its ability to "operate in restrictive environments" makes it a perfect vehicle to undermine sovereign nations' judicial and political processes with the purposes of furthering the LGBTQ agenda under the guise of "human rights" and "democracy." Through various methods, from funding massive propaganda campaigns in Europe to funding strategic litigation and "advocacy coordination training" in Africa, the GEF is able to advance the LGBTQ arm of the neo-liberal agenda through more covert means but with the full support of the co-opted US government and others.

The GEF is active in over 90 countries and has significant partnerships with USAID and the governments of Argentina, Australia, Canada, Chile, Croatia, Denmark, Finland, France, Germany, Iceland, Italy, Montenegro, the Netherlands, Norway, Sweden, and Uruguay, as well as the Arcus Foundation, FRI: the Norwegian Organization for Sexual and Gender Diversity, the MAC AIDS Fund, Deloitte, Royal Bank of Canada, Hilton Worldwide, Bloomberg LP, Marriott International, the Human Rights Campaign, Out Leadership, and the John D. Evans Foundation. The homosexual Evans serves on the US State Department's Fine Arts Committee and the US State Department's Global Equality Fund. Through the John D. Evans Foundation, he is committed to "social justice, AIDS vaccine research, environmental protection, technological innovation, education and the arts to improve mankind."

Out Leadership's featured speakers at previous conferences have included Lloyd Blankfein of Goldman Sachs, "transhumanist"/transgender Martine Rothblatt (United Therapeutics), Mark McCombe (BlackRock), Sally Susman (Pfizer), Fabrice Houdart (United Nations, Office of the High Commissioner for Human Rights), Rachel Lynn Golden (who provides "LGBTQ+ affirming, intersectionally-informed and trauma-informed therapy"), and Angelica Ross, transgender CEO of TransTech Social Enterprises, "a firm that helps employ transgender people in the tech industry." Clients include SC Johnson and Deutsche Bank.

"Biogenetics is poised to be the investment of the future," says Jewish transhumanist Martine Rothblatt, investor in biogenetics and transplants and founder and Chairman of the Board of United Therapeutics, a major biotechnology company. 1996 was a big year for Rothblatt, who both founded United Therapeutics and had a "sex change." In 2019, Rothblatt was named to Business Insider's list of the most powerful LGBTQ+ people in tech. Rothblatt finances the SpacePAC, a political action committee for son Gabriel, a "technoprogressive political activist and transhumanist." According to Rothblatt's blog *Mindfiles, Mindware and Mindclones*, there is a "coming age of our own cyberconsciousness and techno-immortality." If it looks like this, count me out.

Parliamentarians for Global Action (PGA), "an international non-profit network of more than 1,300 legislators in 143 Parliaments worldwide," is financed by the GEF, the UNSCAR, EU, a number of governmental ministries and agencies, the Sigrid Rausing Trust, the Oak Foundation, the Arcus Foundation, Pew Charitable Trusts, the Stewart R. Mott Foundation, and the Open Society Foundations, among others. Through its partnerships such as with the Global Equality Fund, PGA endeavors to advance:

> Human rights and the rule of law, democracy, human security, nondiscrimination and gender equality. Through its geographically-diverse membership and its commitment to human rights, PGA has been able to bridge cultural and national divides to frame the discussion of LGBTI rights as a human rights issue encouraging parliamentarians to address the needs and challenges of this community. PGA promotes its vision to create a "rules-based international order for a more equitable, safe and democratic world" by mobilizing parliamentarians to become human rights champions through peer-to-peer information sharing and an improved understanding about equality and non-discrimination. As part of this effort, and in collaboration with the United

Nations Development Programme (UNDP), PGA is developing a Parliamentary Handbook on Human Rights, Sexual Orientation and Gender Identity, a tool with key information about human rights and concrete actions to raise awareness, examine, and reform legal frameworks to address the needs of LGBTI persons.[110]

Human rights of course being whatever arbitrary nonsense the ruling class decides.

Furthermore, if sex changes and deviant sexualities, to say nothing of pedophilia which arrives with the blessing of people like "gay icon" Larry Brinkin and his child porn stash, are "human rights," then the framework has been established for intervention along the lines of "human rights abuses," which involves the direct use of force. Obviously this is a last resort, but consider the fate of Yugoslavia at the hands of the globalist establishment. Also consider that after toppling the regimes in Afghanistan and Iraq, the United States mandated gender quotas for members of parliament in the two countries' new constitutions. Who's to say the probably-inevitable military action in Iran doesn't include a clause for a minimum number of transgender parliamentarians in the interests of "queering" one of the last bastions of strong national particularism?

"Gendered" considerations *always* precede the introduction of homosexuality and "trans" in the blueprint of societal break-down employed by the neo-liberal regime. The US State Department explicitly states that:

> Per the Women, Peace, and Security Act of 2017 and subsequent U.S. Strategy on Women, Peace, and Security, it is a U.S. government-wide priority to expand and apply gender analysis, as appropriate, to improve the design and implementation of U.S. government-funded programs.

According to the Organization for Security and Cooperation in Europe (OSCE), "gender equality is an international legal obligation." The OSCE states that:

> The UN Human Rights Council has emphasized this in resolutions on "Protection against violence and discrimination based on sexual orientation and gender identity" and "Human rights, sexual orientation and gender identity." Integrating a gender perspective in policing is crucial for countries to make progress towards these commitments.

As John Q. Publius writes:

> In late 2019 the United Nations placed strict gender quotas on a British Army "peacekeeping force" sent to Mali to "contain extremist activity" as part of its Uniformed Gender Parity Strategy 2018–2028, Department of Peace Operations – war is peace after all – that mandates quotas for female personnel in the name of equal opportunity. Forty-four French soldiers have died in the Sahel region as "peacekeepers" since 2013 and for what? Meanwhile their home country is being transformed beyond all recognition. Other salient

---

[110] "Global Equality Fund Annual Report 2015," 13.

points from the Uniformed Gender Parity Strategy "to ensure that the uniformed component of United Nations peacekeeping is diverse and inclusive of women, reflecting the communities the United Nations serve" include: OMA/Police Division to coordinate with the military/police component in each mission to include in their gender strategy and action plan relevant goals and actions to support the implementation of the Uniformed Gender Parity Strategy and ensure that all staff are appropriately trained; Training on overt and unconscious gender bias made available to staff involved in recruitment and selection boards, based on UN developed materials; Deliver annual Military Gender Advocate of the Year Award and the International Female Police Peacekeepers Award; Give priority during selection to officers from contributing countries that nominate at least 30% women candidates; [and] Update calls for nomination to include an option to not accept nominations which contain only male candidates. . . . . NATO offers four "gender perspective" courses aimed at adopting a gender theory perspective in military affairs and "apply[ing] a Gender Perspective in scenarios of patrolling, checkpoints and engagement with the local population in a culturally sensitive manner." The preposterousness – and dangerousness – of this requires no comment, but it suggests the priorities of the Establishment.[111]

On September 29th, 2015, twelve entities (ILO, OHCHR, UNAIDS Secretariat, UNDP, UNESCO, UNFPA, UNHCR, UNICEF, UNODC, UN Women, WFP, and the WHO) released a joint statement calling for "an end to violence and discrimination against lesbian, gay, bisexual, transgender and intersex people." They are content, evidently, to visit violence on others during their "peacekeeping" missions, however. It doesn't end there—not even close.

By incorporating "gender equality" into its Sustainable Development Goals (SDGs), "advancing gender equality is thus necessary to support national development processes within the SDGs' framework" for the UN. The WHO lists "health security" as a priority, and given the linkages discussed in this book, who's to say that doesn't include military or "policing" intervention to ensure "necessary" sex changes and the like? As a precursor, the UN states that:

The Women, Peace and Security Agenda, made up of nine UN Security Council resolutions, reaffirms the important role of women in peace and security and stresses the importance of expanding their role to ensure equal participation and full involvement in security and peacebuilding efforts. A range of UN Security Council resolutions on peacekeeping and international police deployments similarly require the inclusion of a gender perspective, call for more women police to be deployed, and recognize the need to address gendered security needs, with particular reference to conflict-related sexual violence.

So "gender equity/equality" means more white women being deployed to combat situations, the globalist hegemony sending more of its janissaries forth as grist for the mill. This is unconscionable and is yet another feature of this vile, oppressive,

---

[111] Publius, *The God that Failed*, 283–285.

and anti-reality system, and even if it *was* for some kind of women's equality, melding that into the transgender agenda—which has been the next outgrowth of the "gay rights/liberation" and "women's rights/liberation" movements *in tandem*—has nothing at all to do with women, other than those who wish to become men or some other selection on the made-up continuum. That any of this is taken with not just seriousness but is mandated shows the power of propaganda and the power of the system in implementing it.

According to a "Gender and Security Toolkit" document entitled "Policing and Gender" published by the Geneva Center for Security Sector Governance (DCAF), OSCE/ODIHR, and UN Women with support from Switzerland, Sweden, and the UK's DFID, authored by Lisa Denney, a Research Associate with the Overseas Development Institute (ODI):

> Policing that advances gender equality is citizen-oriented. It serves the needs and interests of all the community, paying attention to groups that have been historically marginalized, such as women, girls and LGBTI people [told you].
> . . . Representations of police, including in the media, government communications and recruitment campaigns [must] reflect diversity and the contributions of women and LGBTI people. Policing is not associated with a hypermasculinized culture, but rather with a respectful and inclusive culture that values gender diversity as well as diversity of age, ethnicity, race, religion, region, class and other identity markers. . . . Training to ensure understanding of non-discrimination policies and codes of conduct is a routine part of in-service training. A culture of zero tolerance in relation to sexual and gender-based discrimination, harassment, bullying and abuse exists across the police service.

Much of this "gender equality" policing action therefore takes the form of wearing-down host societies in order to enable the LGBTQ agenda space to operate and get in a foot-hold. Additionally, we see the situating of age (probably as a construct of sorts to justify pedophilia along with the idea of one having been "born this way"), queerness, trans, etc. as *an inevitable extension of feminism*, and as always part-and-parcel with "diversity" and "civil/human rights." Further in the same document, we see the "de-masculinizing" of men and the "empowerment" of women through, in this case, also de-emphasizing "stereotypically" female traits:

> The organizational culture of the police cultivates and is characterized by positive masculinities – that is, the culture does not replicate ideas of men as intrinsically aggressive, strong or dominant. Positive masculinities, rather, emphasize that care, compassion and respect are not innately feminine.

In the interests of creating a police force that will function (insofar as it can function with these operating principles—consider that "selection criteria are focused on the skills and competencies required in modern policing – not those that are associated with stereotypes of what policing involves; images of police that emphasize militarized security functions over community interaction and other policing tasks can reinforce masculine stereotypes and deter those who do not identify with such stereotypes from applying," and affirmative action is taken as a given—"Affirmative action policies need to be carefully communicated to both the police service and the community") more as an occupying army of quantity over quality and will certainly further the aims of the globalist police state:

> Achieving a diverse and representative police service that draws on the highest quality of candidates possible requires active measures to recruit women and LGBTI people, as well as other underrepresented groups. Women and LGBTI people from minority backgrounds or with disabilities may experience double discrimination and therefore require additional support in recruitment processes. . . . Uniforms should accord with cultural and social expectations about gender, but also be operationally effective and provide choices that do not reinforce stereotypes. . . . Headscarves should be included as an option [and] where relevant, allowing female police [to] be accompanied by a male relative for any travel or training so that cultural norms do not prevent them from attending [male chaperones—super empowering!]. . . . The numbers of LGBTI people in international police deployments are unknown, but increasing the representation of LGBTI people within deployments could similarly challenge discriminatory attitudes and provide role models in host countries [in other words we're going to occupy your country and give you homosexual and transgendered "role models" to look up to while they put a boot on your neck and bomb your country to pieces]. There are important "do no harm" considerations around potential heightened risks to LGBTI officers in contexts where homophobic and transphobic attitudes are prevalent [but importing people from these countries en masse is "progressive," apparently]. This challenges the UN, other peacekeeping organizations and Police Contributing Countries to consider how they can protect their deployed officers from GBV, including homophobic and transphobic violence. The UN is consulting with its LGBTI staff association, UN-GLOBE, to work towards a fair process that recognizes and responds to these risks. . . . Standard operating procedures: articulating clear guidelines for all police operations, including but not limited to the investigation of hate crimes and GBV. Standard operating procedures should integrate a gender lens in all investigations (including interviews and interrogations); searches (of persons and property); arrest and escorting of prisoners; arrests at borders; intelligence and data collection and analysis; [and] using appropriate identifiers (him/her/they) in interactions with people of diverse gender identities and expressions.

"What are your pronouns?" ze asked before being pumped full of lead!

This will clearly not be an effective occupying force, but it will be ideologically-motivated and unsympathetic to the communities it patrols—*not* protects. That works in its favor. However, in what is the major Achilles heel of the hegemony of the Last Man (or Woman, or Whatever), quality is not a pre-requisite and is in fact to be denigrated; this is explicitly-acknowledged in this document as well: "In Liberia, for instance, the push to recruit more women into the police [was] driven by the need to meet a 20 per cent target. Some recruits were unable to read or write. This poses obvious problems in performing basic policing functions." Ya think?

In 2017, "conservative" Nikki Haley, America's UN ambassador, issued a statement reaffirming the country's commitment to "non-discrimination" and denouncing the Chechen authorities who have "arbitrarily detained, tortured and killed gay men in concentration camps, thus evoking Nazi Germany's persecution of LGBT people." Rather rich when you consider that the American government and its neoliberal allies *back* many of the most savage regimes on the planet and is, in many ways, itself the worst of the lot. In 2004, John Laughland wrote of the American and allies' position on Chechnya:

> The leading Russian critics of Putin's handling of the Beslan crisis are the pro-US politicians Boris Nemtsov and Vladimir Ryzhkov - men associated with the extreme neoliberal market reforms which so devastated the Russian economy under the west's beloved Boris Yeltsin - and the Carnegie Endowment's Moscow Centre. Funded by its New York head office, this influential thinktank - which operates in tandem with the military-political Rand Corporation, for instance in producing policy papers on Russia's role in helping the US restructure the "Greater Middle East" - has been quoted repeatedly in recent days blaming Putin for the Chechen atrocities. The centre has also been assiduous over recent months in arguing against Moscow's claims that there is a link between the Chechens and al-Qaida. . . . This harshness towards Putin is perhaps explained by the fact that, in the US, the leading group which pleads the Chechen cause is the American Committee for Peace in Chechnya (ACPC). The list of the self-styled "distinguished Americans" who are its members is a rollcall of the most prominent neoconservatives who so enthusiastically support the "war on terror". They include Richard Perle, the notorious Pentagon adviser; Elliott Abrams of Iran-Contra fame; Kenneth Adelman, the former US ambassador to the UN who egged on the invasion of Iraq by predicting it would be "a cakewalk"; Midge Decter, biographer of Donald Rumsfeld and a director of the rightwing Heritage Foundation; Frank Gaffney of the militarist Centre for Security Policy; Bruce Jackson, former US military intelligence officer and one-time vice-president of Lockheed Martin, now president of the US Committee on Nato; Michael Ledeen of the American Enterprise Institute . . . now a leading proponent of regime change in Iran; and R James Woolsey, the former CIA director who is one of the leading cheerleaders behind George Bush's plans to re-model the Muslim world along pro-US lines. . . . It compares the Chechen crisis to those other fashionable "Muslim" causes, Bosnia and Kosovo - implying that only international intervention in the Caucasus can stabilise the situation there. In August, the ACPC welcomed the award of political asylum in the US, and a US-government funded grant, to Ilyas Akhmadov, foreign minister in the opposition Chechen government, and a man Moscow describes as a terrorist.

It's not like the US has given safe haven to terrorists before, right? Perhaps the reader will recall the ethnically-Chechen Tsarnaev brothers, inexplicably allowed into the United States, the surviving brother having his death sentence vacated on appeal due to "prejudice" in the original trial. Judge O. Rogeriee Thompson wrote that "for even the most heinous of offenses, our system of justice demands vigorous protection." That's not a justice system, that's a cruel farce. Add that to the protection of certain classes and the consistent persecution of dissidents in the West for decades—though never identifying them as dissidents, but rather hiding under rhetorical cover—this "justice system" is actually designed to punish and incarcerate its opponents. It's more than that, though; what this signals more than anything is open warfare by the "elites" against (ostensibly) their own people, in keeping with the moral degradation and corruption of the times.

Simply put: only in this environment is Transgender Europe's existence for one and its featuring at its European Transgender Council in 2018 organizations like Trans*sexworks considered normal for another. The Trans* Visible Project—co-led by Emy Fem, "a sex positive sex worker, workshop leader, performer, consultant and international activist . . . as a queer sex worker, escort, domme, and actress in feminist porn, she has numerous personal connections to the theme sex work"[112]— is funded as a model project in a federal program by the Federal Ministry for the Family, Seniors, Women, and Youth. Pretty sick.

The aforementioned Global Equality Fund (GEF) is an integral part of the web of "international aid" devoted specifically to "LGBTQ causes." Transgender Europe (TGEU) receives or has received funding from the GEF in addition to the US State Department, the Federal Foreign Office of Germany, the European Commission, the Council of Europe, the Open Society Foundations, the Arcus Foundation, the Government of the Netherlands, and Heinrich Böll Stiftung (the Heinrich Böll Foundation), among others. TGEU states on their website that, "Intersectionality is a key approach in our decision-making processes and actions" and that they also take a "decolonial approach." TGEU partners with ILGA-Europe, ILGA World, and GATE, among other organizations.

According to the GPP and Funders for LGBTQ Issues' 2015–16 Global Resources Report, the GEF was the third-largest government or multilateral funder of international aid for LGBTQ issues, just ahead of the European Commission, the Government of Denmark, and the World Bank. The GEF and the US government's data is woefully incomplete, as the report acknowledges: "The most notable gap in this edition of the Global Resources Report is the lack of data from the U.S. Government and incomplete data on grants awarded through the Global Equality Fund." This general lack of detail means that the sums of money referenced in this book in the form of grants, aid, and other means from the US and its allies are probably very conservative. Indeed, per the report, "If the U.S. Government has continued to provide LGBTI funding at a similar level in 2015–2016, and the Global Equality Fund continued to award grants at a similar level in 2016, then that would constitute approximately $29–34 million in missing grants data." And that is just in terms of straightforward donations or grants.

Following the paper trail of US government funding to the incubating/metastasizing tumors of transgenderism as best as we can shows in stark relief once again that not only does support for this agenda go all the way to the top, but that none of these institutions are operating in isolation and that there is nothing organic about it.

---

[112] For Fem: "Sex work is a voluntary consensual service that offers sexual and intimate encounters over an agreed period of time for a fee. As such, it is often perceived as disturbing by those who only want to locate sexuality in the heteronormative, patriarchal organized family context . . . Sex work is feminist work."

A further consideration of US government funding priorities and government contracts reveals many of the major players in the advancement and propagation of this cruel and unusual project (sadly this is a small sample done for illustrative purposes and it is by no means exhaustive; year ranges are not all calendar year as some are fiscal for the organization(s) in question):[113]

- City of Houston: $6.1 million for HIV prevention and care over four years (2015–2019) from the CDC—not coincidentally, Houston had a lesbian mayor (Annise Parker) at the initial receipt of the grant; Parker is on the Board of Directors of the Holocaust Museum Houston and is CEO and President of the LGBTQ Victory Fund, the founders of which claim inspiration from pro-abortion EMILY's List
- Ann & Robert H. Lurie Children's Hospital of Chicago: $3.7 million over five years (2011–2016) from the NIH for "HIV prevention intervention for young transgender women"
- Wits Health Consortium, the University of the Witwatersrand, South Africa: $11 million over five years (2018–2023) from USAID for "providing appropriate services for key populations, including sex workers and transgender people," looking at "clinical interventions"
- Johns Hopkins University: $3 million over two years (2017–2019) from the NIH to lead the American cohort "to study HIV acquisition among transgender women in high risk areas"; $2.8 million over five years (2018–2023) from the NIH for "validation of stigma metrics for marginalized men"; $2.3 million over five years (2017–2022) from the NIH to lead the American cohort studying "HIV acquisition among transgender women in high risk areas"
- Howard Brown Health Center: $1.6 million over five years (2017–2022) from the CDC for a "targeted HIV prevention project for young transgender persons of color and their partners"
- UCLA: Over $828,000 from the NIH over two years (2017–2018) for a "US transgender health population survey"; over $857,000 from the Department of Defense over two years (2015–2017) for "improving acceptance, integration, and health among LGBT service members"
- University of Pennsylvania: $2.3 million over five years (2018–2023) from the NIH for "increasing engagement and improving HIV care outcomes via stigma reduction in an online social networking intervention among racially diverse young men who have sex with men and transgender women"
- Stanford University: $1.5 million over five years (2018–2023) to study "sex hormones on neurodevelopment: controlled puberty in transgender adolescents" from the NIH
- Boston Children's Hospital: $732,000 from the NIH in 2017 for "family environment, social support, and health in transgender youth"; almost $233,000 for the same 2015–2017
- Fenway Health: Over $567,000 from the Department of Justice over two years (2011–2013) for "domestic violence and sexual assault services for lesbian, gay, bisexual, and transgender people of color"; $2 million from the CDC in 2008 for

---

[113] As a side note, a number of US government-funded studies grouped both "transgender women" and "men who have sex with men" together, which telegraphs quite a bit about what's going on here.

an "LGBT national tobacco control network"; almost $839,000 over five years (2010–2015) from the NIH for "LGBT health" and research

- Long Island Gay and Lesbian Youth Inc. (New York): $600,000 over three-and-a-half years (2014–2018) from the Department of Justice for "technical assistance for LGBT centers"
- United Nations Development Program: $500,000 over two years (2016–2018) from USAID for "strengthening actions in favor of the lesbian, gay, bisexual, transgender, and intersex community in Guatemala"; $2.5 million in 2014 for "Being LGBT in Asia"; $1.6 million in 2016 for "Being LGBT in Africa"
- Helsinki Committee for Human Rights in Bosnia: $40,000 in 2019 from the US State Department to establish a "safe environment" for the LGBT population
- LGBT Open Center in Sarajevo: $32,000 from USAID in 2014
- Centar Za Mlade Kvart (Bosnia): almost $23,000 in 2017 from the US State Department to "empower the position of LGBT population"
- Charitable Foundation Gender Z (Ukraine): Almost $16,000 from the US State Department in 2017 for "training school psychologists on counseling LGBT teens and their families"
- Pravozakhysny LGBT Tsentr Nash Svit (Ukraine): $18,000 in 2017 from the US State Department to "document hate crimes against the LGBTI community [and] improve legal instruments to counteract hate crimes"
- Centro de Orientacion e Investigacion Integral: $5.4 million from the CDC over five years (2015–2020) for "strengthening clinical services for men who have sex with men, transgender, and bisexual populations living with HIV/STI in the Dominican Republic"
- Nijiiro Diversity NPO (Japan): $20,000 over two years (2019–2021) to "implement a camp empowering LGBT families and youth to encourage being a change marker to enhance LGBT inclusion in Japan"
- US Department of Defense: $887,000 for a "transgender multidisciplinary medical diagnostic team" (2017)
- Feminist Press, Inc.: $55,000 from the National Endowment for the Arts in 2016 "to support the digitization of classic LGBT titles"
- Sentient Research (California): Almost $460,000 for a one-year grant (2018) from the CDC for "transgender HIV"
- Family Health International (North Carolina): Nearly $150,000 over a two-month period in 2012 from USAID for "HIV prevention services for men who have sex with men and transgender"
- Edutech, Limited (Maryland): Nearly $150,000 over a three-month period in 2012 from the Department of Health and Human Services for "enhancing engagement and retention in quality HIV care for transgender women of color"
- University of Minnesota: One-off 2012 grant for $1,000 from the VA for "off-site consultation for transgender training from University of Minnesota physicians"
- San Francisco State University: A one-year (2012) grant of $99,999 from the Department of Health and Human Services for "practitioner guidance for lesbian, gay, bisexual, and transgender youth in multiple service sectors"
- Rescue Social Change Group LLC (California): $11 million over three years 2015–2018) from the FDA for an "LGBT young adult tobacco education campaign extension"

- Inicitativa Inakost (Slovakia): $4,000 from the US State Department in 2019 to organize the first annual Slovak LGBT Awards
- Drustvo Informacijski Center Legebitra (Slovenia): $4,000 from the US State Department in 2017 "to build a support network for older LGBT people in order to increase the tolerance among the wider community"
- Rainbow Mission Foundation (Hungary): $3,400 from the US State Department for a Budapest Pride in 2010
- Centro Boliviano Americano De Santa Cruz de la Sierra (Bolivia): $12,500 from the US State Department in 2018 to "organize and execute a tech camp focused on finding technological solutions to daily challenges found by GBV, TIP and LGBT-related NGOs"
- University of Southern California: Almost $134,000 from the National Archives and Records Administration for an "LGBT Civil Rights and Social Equity Movement" cataloging project
- Northwestern University: $2 million over five years (2014–2019) from the NIH in "HIV prevention research in LGBT youth"
- American Bar Association Fund for Justice and Education: $300,000 over three years (2015–2018) from the Department of Justice for an "LGBT legal capacity building program"
- NGLCC Foundation: $2 million from USAID over seven years (2013–2020) for "promoting LGBT equality" in Latin America
- The Astraea Lesbian Foundation for Justice: $3.8 million in 2019 "to advance the rights of sexual minorities worldwide" from USAID
- Shanghai Pride (China): $4,360 from the US State Department in 2017
- Sofia Pride (Bulgaria): $3,000 from the US State Department in 2011
- Museo Nazionale del Cinema (Italy): $2,300 from the US State Department for the annual LGBT+ Lovers Film Festival in 2019
- Eesti LGBT Uhing (Estonia): $1,500 from the US State Department to feature a speaker from GLSEN in November 2019
- Humsafar Trust (India): $18,000 from the US State Department for 2019–2020 "to conduct a three-day film festival in Mumbai to celebrate US Pride Month and showcase American films and documentaries on LGBT themes"
- LGBT Center-Ulaanbaatar (Mongolia): $18,000 in 2010 from the US State Department to produce a multi-media pressure campaign for the passage of a "non-discrimination" law
- Pertubuhan Pembangunan Kebajikan and Persekit (Malaysia): Nearly $21,000 from the US State Department in 2017 for "non-discrimination" initiatives and LGBTQ healthcare guidelines
- Botswana Network on Ethics Law and HIV/AIDS: $25,000 in 2012 from the US State Department "to support a civil society-led information and awareness raising campaign regarding LGBT rights"
- Heartland Alliance International: $562,500 from the Department of Health and Human Services' Administration for Children and Families over three years (2011–2014) for an "LGBT refugees and asylees national resource center"
- IGLHRC: $500,000 from USAID in 2015 for "increasing access to justice for LGBT communities in Indonesia"
- The Arab Foundation for Freedoms and Equality (Lebanon): Over $145,000 from the US State Department in 2016 for "media advocates for LGBT"

- Pride in Action (Jamaica): $150,000 over five-and-a-half years (2014–2020) from the Inter-American Foundation for an LGBT resource center for young people and university students as "an incubator for budding activists and LGBT initiatives"
- SSG Advisors LLC (Vermont): $2 million over two years (2017–2019) from USAID for HIV services to "key populations [which] includes people who inject drugs, men who have sex with men, transgender persons, sex workers and prisoners. Also included in the definition are discordant couples, migrant populations, and youth." Okay then.
- Sisters Foundation (Thailand): $20,000 from the Department of Defense in 2019 that "affirms surveillance for antimicrobial susceptibility of gonorrhea in transgender women support services." I told you they're using these people as guinea pigs.
- The Urban Institute: $2.8 million over three years (2013–2016) from the Department of Housing and Urban Development for "a task order to do a pilot for an estimate of housing discrimination against LGBT people"[114]

As insane as it is, that list is just a small sample.

USAID and the Elton John AIDS Foundation collaborated on the Deep Engagement Fund to "support access to health care by LGBTI people in Uganda, Kenya and Mozambique." The partnership has also initiated an Emergency Response Fund administered by the International HIV/AIDS Alliance. USAID is deeply committed to "advancing LGBTI inclusive development," following, per Rajiv Shah, "a groundbreaking Presidential Memorandum [from] President Barack Obama direct[ing] USAID and all federal agencies engaged abroad to ensure that the United States promotes and protects the rights of LGBT people." By "integrating LGBT issues in USAID's work," they will "support and mobilize LGBT communities" through methods generally similar to the GEF, although in what is a major boon to the pharmaceutical companies, USAID puts more emphasis on the HIV/AIDS health care aspect, stating in their "LGBT Vision for Action" document that transgender individuals have astronomical HIV prevalence rates and that male homosexuals are nineteen times more likely than the general male population to have HIV. This is connected in the usual vague and ill-defined manner to "stigma" and "discrimination," not that they don't wear condoms or that they re-use needles. In their own words, these are some of the policies and projects advanced by USAID:

> USAID-supported HIV research on the burden of the disease, needs assessments, evaluations, and operations research used to design effective program models of targeted prevention, care and treatment services for populations at highest risk have included gay men and other MSM and transgender persons for over 20 years. These efforts have expanded with increased funding over the last decade as part of the President's Emergency Plan for AIDS Relief (PEPFAR). . . . An innovative approach to operationalizing LGBT integration has been taken by USAID field missions that develop LGBT inclusive Mission Orders (MOs) that establish responsibilities and outline the processes

---

[114] All of these numbers can be verified at usaspending.gov.

and procedures for protecting and promoting the human rights of LGBT persons in mission operations and through programming. In some cases, these MOs are standalone documents that focus exclusively on LGBT issues whereas in others, they are addressed along with gender, diversity, and/or disability in a single inclusive development Mission Order . . . with USAID support: (a) the Colombian National Police barred discrimination including on the basis of sexual diversity and gender identity and subsequent dialogues in eight cities aimed to prevent human rights violations by the police, (b) in a major step forward, the Colombian Constitutional Court extended partnership benefits on inheritance and property rights to same-sex couples and recognized de facto civil unions, (c) the Government of Colombia's implementation of the Victims and Land Restitution Law ensured that the Victims Unit provides support to LGBT armed conflict victims as well as access to historical memory initiatives to *ensure reparation to the LGBT community* (emphasis added) and (d) other work has focused on self-protection and legal remedies for transsexual women in the region, who are often exposed to severe human rights violations. . . . USAID/Nicaragua has historically integrated DRG across its PEPFAR-funded HIV/AIDS activities not only to address the health-related needs of MSM and transgender communities and organizations, but also to provide them with training in legal advocacy and financial and institutional strengthening. USAID/Nicaragua is also supporting the nascent LGBT rights movement through an integrated program supported jointly by the offices of Democracy and Governance, Health, and Education, which provides LGBT CSOs with institutional strengthening and technical training and the opportunity to develop and implement short term, high impact advocacy projects through a sub-grants mechanism. . . . The "Being LGBT in Asia" activity will result in a first-of-its kind joint analysis undertaken by USAID and UNDP together with grassroots LGBT organizations and community leaders to understand the challenges faced by LGBT persons in seven countries in Asia. The project is based on a multi-sectoral analysis that integrated attention to health, DRG and other sectors, while drawing on donor collaboration, innovative and participatory methodologies, and multimedia and social media technologies to support the empowerment and education of both stakeholders and development partners. . . . The Europe and Eurasia Bureau in Washington has produced Testing the Waters: LGBT People in the Europe and Eurasia Region, a comprehensive overview of the situation that LGBT people face. . . . The document includes specific sectoral recommendations as to key entry points for programming designed to meet the needs and be inclusive of LGBT people and CSOs, and is expected to result in better-targeted, culturally-sensitive development programming in the region. . . . USAID policies, guidance, and strategies are inclusive of LGBT concerns. Key examples include the USAID Policy Framework; USAID's Country Development Cooperative Strategy (CDCS) Guidance; USAID's Project Design Guidance; USAID Automated Directives System (ADS); the USAID Gender Equality and Female Empowerment Policy; USAID's Strategy on Democracy, Human Rights and Governance (DRG); the U.S. National Action Plan on Women, Peace and Security; USAID's

Global Health Strategic Framework; USAID's Policy on Youth in Development and others. *Even in the most restrictive country environments, USAID has successfully incorporated LGBT stakeholders and concerns into the analyses that feed into inclusive development objectives and intermediate results* (emphasis added) in USAID field missions' CDCSs, Regional Development Cooperation Strategies, Project Appraisal Documents, budget requests, Operational Plans and Program Performance Reports.[115]

In their "Suggested Approaches for Integrating Inclusive Development Across the Program Cycle and Mission Operations," the authors indicate that USAID's "inclusive development" approach is in line with that of the World Bank and the United Nations, and that the UN's Sustainable Development Goals are integral to USAID "assistance." In a very curious move in what may perhaps be a prolonged textual Freudian slip, the authors state that:

Countries with inequality between different ethnic, religious, or regional groups are more likely to experience violent conflict. Excluded groups tend to have significant economic and political grievances, which can result in challenging authority with violence. . . . Marginalized ethnic groups are three times more likely to initiate conflict against the state compared to included groups that have central political representation.

Perhaps they ought to consider this in their sustained attacks on white people. Conflict does also sow chaos, though, which is vital for the creation of a situation that "necessitates" greater central control.

The USAID authors then outline the six domains in which USAID and its partnering organizations work to influence and/or implement their "inclusive development" approach:

1.  Laws, policies, regulations, and institutional practices
2.  Cultural norms and beliefs
3.  Roles, responsibilities, and time use
4.  Patterns of power and decision making
5.  Access to and control over assets and resources
6.  Personal safety and security.

With an emphasis on "increasing integration of marginalized groups as a strategic priority for all programs," the goal is to erode any distinctions or preservation mechanisms in place both within the host society in question and as a protectant from external influence in order to produce what Kerry Bolton characterizes as *homo globicus*, the neo-liberal equivalent of the New Soviet Man.

Personal safety and security are of course desirable, but in practice what this looks like is a one-off or distortion of some law or policy is made into a propaganda vehicle to bring outside pressure on the host society in question without regard to context, nuance, or, indeed, whether the situation in question was motivated by

---

[115] "LGBT Vision for Action," USAID.

"hate" or even occurred the way it is or was portrayed (a la Matthew Shepard, Stephen Lawrence, Rodney King, Tawana Brawley, Trayvon Martin, et cetera). In fact, most of the totems of "hate crimes" dating back to at least Leo Frank have been lies or at the very least grossly distorted.

Still, rainbow-clad NATO's mission is to ensure that the regime's "values" are "upheld" and white nationalism—any nationalism, sans Israel and maybe China—is suppressed by whatever means necessary. A further look at the *modus operandi* of NATO is evidenced by Susan Corke, Senior Fellow at the German Marshall Fund of the United States[116] and Director of Transatlantic Democracy Working Group's prepared statement for the House Foreign Affairs Subcommittee on Europe, Eurasia, Energy, and the Environment, US House of Representatives, on November 13th, 2019, entitled "Democracy and the NATO Alliance: Upholding our Shared Democratic Values," where populism is conflated with authoritarianism simply because leaders listen to their constituency and do not impose this fringe and frankly psychotic agenda, as in Corke's words this is "not a passive project":

> As we grapple with this era of authoritarian resurgence which threatens the stability and values of the transatlantic alliance, it is important to humbly take stock of how we arrived here. . . . [In 2010] there were valid issues and concerns with how the establishment and so-called elites handled the drivers of discontent – the financial and refugee crises. . . . The European refugee crisis was full blown by 2015 and bolstered far right forces and their fearmongering. Antisemitism and xenophobia were on the rise [!]. Europe faced an existential identity crisis, torn between nationalist and integrationist forces, which was galvanizing political upheaval. The sense of democratic inevitability that Europeans had taken for granted since the fall of the Berlin Wall has been shattered. . . . Since Russia's meddling in the U.S. Presidential election of 2016, Russia has continued its attack on Western elections and we can expect that it will only increase. . . . The emergence of self-styled illiberal states across Europe presents a challenge to Western collective action in an era of authoritarian resurgence. Far-right populist parties, many with illiberal tendencies, have gained a toehold or the majority in 23 of 28 EU member states' parliamentary systems.

The NGO the National Endowment for Democracy (NED), helmed by former member of the Governing Council of the American Jewish Committee Carl Gershman, is predominantly-funded by the US government, and provided at least twenty separate grants to organizations in or focused on Serbia alone in 2019, with the goal of furthering so-called "Euro-Atlantic integration," "democratic reform," "media freedom

---

[116] Which receives funding from USAID, the Open Society Foundations, the Klarman Family Foundation, the Sandler Foundation, Robert Bosch Stiftung, the William and Flora Hewlett Foundation, the Charles Stewart Mott Foundation, the European Commission, the John Pritzker Family Fund, the US Mission to the EU, the US Mission to NATO, the US State Department, the World Jewish Congress, Raytheon, Wells Fargo, Boeing, Airbus, the RAND Corporation, NATO, McKinsey Global Institute, Google, JP Morgan Chase, Lockheed Martin, the European Council on Foreign Relations, the European Investment Bank, Bayer AG, and the Democracy Fund—itself founded by Pierre Omidyar, helmed by Joe Goldman (former Public Service Fellow at Harvard University's John F. Kennedy School of Government), and a funder of the Center for American Progress, the Center for Strategic and International Studies (CSIS), the University of Chicago, the Trustees of Columbia University, and MIT.

and pluralism," and other Open Society-esque initiatives. Eastern Europe is very high on the priority list for the NED and other arms of the Establishment for expanding "post-1989 progress"; organizations in or focused on the Ukraine received over sixty separate NED grants in 2019 for these types of initiatives and over eighty separate grants were dispensed to Russian or Russian-focused organizations' "democratic" initiatives in 2019; other target countries in Eastern Europe included Croatia, Slovenia, Montenegro, the Czech Republic, Poland, Bulgaria, Hungary, Bosnia, Kosovo, Albania, Moldova, North Macedonia, and Belarus. These are "closed" societies that must be "opened up" by whatever means necessary, including ensuring that a multitude of "independent media" outlets all echo the official line of the US State Department providing the illusion of plurality and consensus in manipulating and gaslighting the host population as well as providing a fake impression to the "outside world" that the people of, say, Belarus, are clamoring for Drag Queen Story Hour, Pride parades, student loan debt, and HIV-positive migrants from Waziristan or even outside intervention to protect "democracy," a la Syria, Iraq, Afghanistan, Iran, and, indeed, the Ukraine.

Part of this manufacture of consensus or plurality also includes seeding money out to grantees in multiple countries and/or multiple grantees in one country focused on one "issue" or region to create the impression of international and/or "grassroots" pressure, when it really is originating from the same source; as regards "democracy" in the Ukraine, a couple of examples from 2019 would be NED grant recipients such as Arnika—Citizens Support Center based out of the Czech Republic that will "train and guide the coalition [of Ukrainian civic initiatives] as it develops an action plan to mobilize citizens to monitor and hold governments accountable," Chatham House ("The London-based think tank will examine Ukraine's vulnerabilities to foreign malign influence and propose strategies and policy recommendation to state institutions and civil society to increase resilience"—good bit of gaslighting there), and the European Institute for Democracy (EID) in Poland, that will "increase the skills of new political leaders" in the Ukraine. The EID is also or has also been funded by the Ministry of Foreign Affairs of Poland, the British Embassy in Warsaw, the British Embassy in Kiev, the US Embassy in Warsaw, the National Democratic Institute (NDI), the Westminster Foundation for Democracy, and Freedom House.

In 1992, the Westminster Foundation for Democracy (WFD) was established in the UK patterned after the National Endowment for Democracy (NED), although it has a more explicitly-governmental character through its direct working relationship with the Foreign and Commonwealth Office as opposed to the NED's plausible deniability. Westminster is a member of the European Partnership for Democracy and its major partners include the World Bank, the Organization for Security and Cooperation in Europe (OSCE), the UNDP, the Norwegian Ministry of Foreign Affairs, the European Union, and GIZ. Among its many subversive projects spreading neoliberal "democracy"—and we will look at a couple of examples—Westminster is also deeply committed to "LGBT+ inclusion." Their efforts are often of the "intersectional" variety, encompassing the usual pablum of "marginalized groups" with all the buzzwords. The use of repetition is vital for effective propaganda.

One representative case study would be Kyrgyzstan; with funding from the Foreign and Commonwealth Office and the UK Department for International Development (DFID), WFD Kyrgyzstan works to astroturf "grassroots" support for "liberal democracy" through various local councils, mobilizing a "network of women city councilors," and using media as a dissemination vehicle of propaganda. For example, funding of radio programming "challenging negative dominant discourse about women's participation in decision making-processes and increasing public support for women candidates" advances the feminist agenda, and "sustainable media sector reform . . . as part of the consortium of European NGOs" advances neo-liberal "democracy." Further, these "reforms" would "support efforts to eradicate hate speech." Their work in North Macedonia is focused on enhancing the presence of disabled people in "the policy making process," and in Bosnia it involves using women as a grievance group to advance "gender responsive policies" and the creation of "more inclusive democratic institutions." We do not need to imagine what this looks like: Americans, Canadians, Britons, Swedes, Germans, Australians, New Zealanders, and many others are already living it, and it only gets worse the more "open" the society.

DFID, like the World Bank, like so many other of these organizations and governing bodies, is committed to this process of "inclusive development." For DFID, what this looks like is access to abortions, "positioning LGB&T as a core development issue," increasing engagement with non-state and state actors alike, "include[ing] homophobia in DFID's ongoing work on social norms (behaviour change group)," and "building new relationships (with civil society and the private sector for example) for indirect influence on decision-makers and on society." In their own words, here is what DFID is "doing on LGBT inclusion":

1. We regularly assess partner governments' commitment to human rights through the Partnership Principles—agreed principles for providing financial aid to countries.
2. We work with the FCO to build support for LGBT rights internationally, working through institutions such as the UN, EU, Council of Europe and the Commonwealth.
3. We raise concerns about LGBT rights at the highest levels. Whether this is done in public or in private is guided by the context.
4. We fund specific programmes that support LGBT people, often using health as an entry point for raising awareness, tackling violence, harassment and exclusion, and challenging discriminatory laws.
5. We fund work that can indirectly support LGBT rights, through strengthening the rule of law, improving access to justice, building capacity on human rights and supporting an enabling environment for civil society groups.

The UK government is at present co-chair with the Argentinian government of the Equal Rights Coalition (ERC) launched in July 2016 under the leadership of Uruguay and the Netherlands at the Global LGBTI Human Rights Conference in Montevideo; "the ERC advances the human rights of LGBTI persons and promotes inclusive development in both member and non-member countries. With 42 member states, the ERC advances its agenda by engaging with civil society organisations and multilateral agencies." Already, it has forty-two member nations: Albania, Belgium, Costa Rica, Ecuador, Germany, Luxembourg, Ireland, the Netherlands, Portugal, Sweden, the US, Uruguay, Switzerland, Serbia, New Zealand, Israel, Malta, Greece, Cyprus, Estonia, Argentina, Cape Verde, Australia, Canada, the Czech Republic, Finland, Iceland, Italy, Mexico, Slovenia, North Macedonia, the Ukraine, Austria,

Chile, Denmark, France, Honduras, Lithuania, Montenegro, Norway, Spain, and the UK. The ERC works with its partners on: International and regional diplomacy; LGBTI inclusion in the UN's 2030 Agenda for Sustainable Development; Coordination of donor funding; National laws, policies and practices.

Their collaborating network of organizations includes Akahatá, Creating Resources for Empowerment in Action (CREA), OTD Chile, Kaleidoscope Trust, COC Nederland, RFSL (the Swedish Federation for Lesbian, Gay, Bisexual, Transgender, Queer and Intersex Rights), Council for Global Equality, Canadian HIV/AIDS Legal Network, Colectivo Hombres XX, Rainbow Railroad (Canada), OII Australia, ILGA World, Equitas (Canada), Egale Canada, Dignity Initiative, Human Rights Watch, the Office of the United Nations High Commissioner for Human Rights (OHCHR), UNAIDS, UNDP, OutRight Action International, Pan Africa ILGA, Synergía, Stonewall, the United Nations Population Fund (UNFPA), and the World Bank.

The Executive Director of Synergía is Stefano Fabeni: Columbia University; Advisory Board member of Akahatá; former Executive Director of Heartland Alliance for Human Needs and Human Rights' Global Initiatives for Human Rights unit; the conceiver, coordinator, and director of the Center of Research and Legal Comparative Studies on Sexual Orientation and Gender Identity's (CERSGOSIG) EU-funded project CERSGOSIG-InformaGay; and former consultant and legal expert for members of the Italian Parliament, institutions, consultancy firms, and NGOs across Europe, as well as for the World Health Organization.

Freedom House, which we've seen come up quite a bit, is helmed by the Jewish Michael Abramowitz; per their website:

> Initially, the mission of Freedom House was to counter isolationism, a powerful force promoted by the America First Committee. At the time, ninety percent of American citizens were opposed to involvement in the European war. . . . The leaders of Freedom House argued that Hitler posed a grave threat to American security and values. . . . Freedom House supported the Marshall Plan, the Universal Declaration of Human Rights, and the Atlantic Alliance. . . . Freedom House worked closely with Thurgood Marshall, Roy Wilkins, and other prominent civil rights leaders. Bayard Rustin, a leading adviser to Dr. Martin Luther King, Jr., was an active member and leader of the Freedom House Board of Trustees. . . .[117] A second cause was the struggle against McCarthyism. . . . Responding to growing strife in Africa, Freedom House sent study missions to Zimbabwe and South Africa led by Bayard Rustin. It also sent missions to assess conditions in Central America during the 1980s, as part of an ongoing project to support centrist democratic forces under siege from the Marxist left and the death squad right. . . . Freedom House has earned a reputation for taking on freedom causes in some of the most difficult environments, such as Venezuela, Cuba, Zimbabwe, Ethiopia, Egypt, Russia, Belarus, Ukraine, and Kazakhstan. . . . [In 1995] Freedom House Budapest office begins work on cross-border networks to support

---

[117] Rustin worked alongside Ella Baker a co-director of the Citizenship Crusade in 1954, and before the Montgomery Bus Boycott he helped organize a group called "In Friendship" amongst Baker, George Lawrence, and Stanley Levinson of the American Jewish Congress.

democratic reform through Central and Eastern Europe and begins Cuba de-mocracy programs. . . . [In 2004] during the Ukrainian elections, Freedom House assists in coordinating the first ever large scale regional civic monitor-ing effort mobilizing 1000 representatives from reform-oriented monitoring groups.

Primary funding for Freedom House comes from USAID and the US State Depart-ment in addition to the MacArthur Foundation and the Ford Foundation, the Euro-pean Union, and the governments of Canada, the Netherlands, Norway, and Sweden.

At present, in the European context, Freedom House is very focused on Moldova and the Ukraine. Freedom House works with policy-makers in the Organization for Security and Cooperation in Europe (OSCE), the Parliamentary Assembly of the Council of Europe (PACE), the European Parliament, various UN bodies, and the US Congress to "seek international accountability for impunity for rights violations." Freedom House is actively committed to its initiative Expanding Allies for LGBT+ Rights in the Ukraine.

More broadly, Freedom House is part of the Dignity for All consortium which:

Provides emergency assistance; security, opportunity, and advocacy rapid re-sponse grants (SOAR grants); and security assessment and training to human rights defenders and civil society organizations under threat or attack due to their work for lesbian, gay, bisexual, transgender and intersex human rights.

The consortium is led by Freedom House, with support from Akahatá, Creating Re-sources for Empowerment in Action (CREA), Synergía, the Arab Foundation for Freedoms and Equality, OutRight Action International, UHAI-EASHRI, and ILGA-Europe. Funding is provided by the Global Equality Fund (GEF). Via Dignity for All support, ILGA-Europe states that it has been able to support:

Various initiatives requiring emergency intervention; such as preparations for the Pride event in Kiev (2014), providing assistance and support to Georgian activists (2014) . . . and providing reactive support to Russian activists fol-lowing the introduction of restrictive legislation.

So apparently holding a Pride event in the Ukraine is considered an emergency.

The Heartland Alliance for Human Needs and Human Rights was at one time a part of the Dignity for All consortium with Freedom House, ILGA-Europe, and com-pany; Heartland has played a prominent role in the refugee resettlement racket in the United States. The Hebrew Immigrant Aid Society (HIAS) is also central to "refu-gee" re-settlement in the United States and in Europe; HIAS-Ukraine, a member of ECRE, partners with Kiev-based NGO Right to Protection. The Hungarian Helsinki Committee, which is another member of ECRE, is like Heartland Alliance similarly positioned at the nexus of "refugee" re-settlement and the LGBTQ agenda.

The Arab Foundation for Freedoms and Equality, also part of the Dignity for All consortium, is funded by ViiV Healthcare, Heinrich Böll Stiftung, the European Un-ion, the Arcus Foundation, the Global Equality Fund, Freedom House, the Interna-tional Women's Health Coalition, the US-Middle East Partnership Initiative (MEDI), the Open Society Foundations, and Hivos. Heartland Alliance International was involved with the project in its early days.

The initial strangeness of ViiV Healthcare's involvement with the Foundation is explained by the fact that one of its primary focuses is on HIV/AIDS care and support and public health. ViiV Healthcare's Positive Action Community Grants "address HIV/AIDS disparities," and it also donates to "patient-based initiatives designed to support communities affected by HIV" in countries like the UK, Greece, Latvia, Portugal, Serbia, Croatia, and the Czech Republic. In 2015, for Nicole Gray:

> Viiv announced it would be providing funding of £2 million per year to support various programs in Africa focused on the needs of MSM (men who have sex with men) and transgender individuals. Viiv also stepped up its funding for children through the Positive Action for Children Fund (PACF), which supports 34 community-based organizations in 16 sub-Saharan nations.

UHAI-EASHRI, another member of the Dignity for All consortium, is funded by the Global Equality Fund, the Swedish International Development Cooperation Agency (SIDA), ViiV, the American Jewish World Service, and the Astraea Lesbian Foundation for Justice, among others.

Benetech, "a nonprofit social enterprise organization that empowers communities with software for social good," is the lead organization for "Increasing the Capacity of Local Human Rights Defenders to Document Violations against LGBT Individuals and Communities in Southern Africa" project funded by the Global Equality Fund.[118] Iranti-Org out of South Africa, which recently launched an LBTIGNC (lesbian, bisexual, transgender, intersex, and gender non-conforming) Media Makers Network to support "activist"-produced media in Southern Africa, and Hivos also joined the project.

The LGBTI Global Development Partnership was established in 2013 as a joint effort of USAID, SIDA, the Astraea Lesbian Foundation for Justice, the Swedish Federation for Lesbian, Gay, Bisexual, Transgender and Queer Rights (RFSL), the National LGBT Chamber of Commerce (NGLCC), Olivia Companies (a travel agency for lesbians founded by the Jewish Judy Dlugacz), and the Arcus Foundation. The LGBTQ Victory Institute and the Williams Institute at UCLA are sub-awardees of Astraea under the Partnership.

The LGBTQ Victory Institute and Serbian advocacy group Labris trained 19 LGBTI leaders from all over the Balkans in 2014, helped to organize four Civil Society Forums throughout the region with the support of Labris, Subversive Front (Macedonia), Open Mind Spectrum Albania (OMSA), and the Center for Social Group Development (CSGD) Kosovo, and partnered with LGBTI human rights foundation Hirschfeld-Eddy-Stiftung to organize a Regional Conference in Serbia in 2015. The LGBTQ Victory Institute partners with trainees in Albania and North Macedonia to "increase LGBTI political participation in the Balkans and continue to provide post-training assistance in their efforts to use political participation as a tool to achieve equality."

The November 2014 "Conference to Advance the Human Rights of and Promote Inclusive Development for Lesbian, Gay, Bisexual, Transgender, and Intersex (LGBTI) Persons"—"made possible through the generous support of the U.S.

---

[118] The US State Department lists a direct grant to Benetech from 2011 for almost $683,000.

Agency for International Development (USAID), the Bureau of Democracy, Human Rights, and Labor at the U.S. Department of State (DRL), and the Royal Norwegian Embassy"—hosted by USAID and the US State Department with support from the Council for Global Equality, convened:

> Representatives of over 30 governments, eight multilateral institutions, and 50 civil society organizations from over 50 countries to discuss challenges and opportunities in advancing the human rights of, and inclusive development for lesbian, gay, bisexual, transgender and intersex (LGBTI) persons around the world. This conference followed two prior conferences where government and nongovernmental groups came together for similar discussions in 2011 and 2013 in Stockholm and Berlin, and reflected growing support for LGBTI equality, both financial and political.

We've touched on the Berlin conference and the Istanbul conference of 2015 earlier.

A joint communiqué supporting the proposed measures was signed by such entities as the Government of Israel, the US, the UK, Canada, Australia, the Nordic countries, UNAIDS, the EU, and UNDP. These proposals echo what we've discussed, such as:

- Data should be disaggregated for L, G, B, T, and I populations
- Bilateral and multilateral funding agencies should enact policies and procedures to ensure that neither they nor those funded to implement programs (contractors and subcontractors, grantees and sub-grantees) discriminate on the basis of sexual orientation, gender identity, gender expression, or bodily diversity
- Civil society advocates and organizations should be actively involved, alongside private foundations and other funding agencies, in shaping donor strategies and structures to maximize effective coordination of responsive funding.

The opening speakers at the conference stated that:

> The dialogue over homosexuality and LGBTI issues was marked by: populist arguments of traditional culture against supposed Western cultural values; politically manipulated 'moral panics'; the surrogacy of the human rights of LGBTI persons for larger geo-political competitions, or a 'global culture war'; and juxtaposition of an authentic natural desire for rights against equally authentic insecurities.

Interestingly enough, this is exactly right, although also exactly inverted to serve their agenda.

The role of multilateral organizations in "promoting the human rights of LGBTI persons" was outlined by representatives from UNDP, UNAIDS, the World Bank, the Inter-American Commission on Human Rights, and the Pan-American Health Organization (PAHO). World Bank member countries apparently believe the World Bank should do more to "emphasize the link between human rights and development outcomes, e.g., the example in which the World Bank froze a major health sector project in Uganda in response to the Anti-Homosexuality Act." The World Bank, the Global Fund, and UNAIDS in particular often work with the US government on "LGBT rights," as witnessed with the actions toward Uganda and Nigeria, for example. A collaborative economic survey conducted by USAID and UCLA's Williams Institute claimed that "abuses of [LGBTQ] human rights are likely to have a harmful effect on a country's level of economic development," and the American Jewish World Service and Global Action for Trans* Equality (GATE) presented material suggesting a number of "activist" groups that are believed to be "under-funded."

Supporting organization the Council for Global Equality seeks:

> To ensure that those who represent our country—including those in Congress, in the White House, in U.S. embassies and in U.S. corporations—use the diplomatic, political and economic leverage available to them to oppose human rights abuses that are too often directed at individuals because of their sexual orientation, gender identity or gender expression.

Senior Director and co-founder Julie Dorf is described on their website:

> Also founded and directed the International Gay & Lesbian Human Rights Commission (IGLHRC, now OutRight Action International) from 1990 to 2000. . . . She has bridged her activist career with philanthropy, serving as the Director of Philanthropic Services for Horizons Foundation, a San Francisco Bay Area foundation for the lesbian, gay, bisexual, and transgender community; and as an independent consultant for WPATH, Open Society Institute, Global Fund for Women, Arcus Foundation, Astraea Foundation, and Fenton Communications/J-Street Project. Julie is currently the lead advisor to the Equality Without Borders individual donor initiative. She also serves on the board or advisory boards of PowerPAC, Human Rights Watch's LGBT Rights Program, Horizons Foundation, OutRight Action International, and the Northern California Finance Committee of J-Street. She holds a B.A. from Wesleyan University in Russian and Soviet Studies. Julie has written, spoken, and advocated extensively on social justice issues ranging from reparations for gay victims of the Nazis, Jewish-Palestinian relations, and marriage equality.

Member organizations of the Council for Global Equality include the Open Society Foundations, Freedom House, the HRC, GLSEN, the LGBTQ Victory Institute, the NCLR, the National LGBT Chamber of Commerce, the Center for American Progress, Amnesty International, GLAAD, Human Rights Watch, the ADL, the National Center for Transgender Equality, the American Jewish World Service, and more.

Eva Kolodner, the Eastern Region Director of Development at the American Jewish World Service, producer of the film *Boys Don't Cry*, and formerly of the International Rescue Committee (IRC) and the Reproductive Health Access Project, is married to GLSEN's Executive Director Eliza Byard, also on the Gill Foundation's Board of Directors. GLSEN, by the way, has received funding from Bear Sterns, the Ford Foundation, the Arcus Foundation, MTV Networks, Goldman Sachs, the Evelyn and Walter Haas Jr. Fund, Kevin Williamson, Morgan Stanley, Disney, Merck (which has partnered with the UNHCR), the United Federation of Teachers, HBO, Bloomberg, Kramer Levin Naftalis & Frankel LLP, Steven Spielberg, The Atlantic Philanthropies, NEA Health Information Network, and many more. GLSEN's corporate partners are Target, Hollister, and Wells Fargo.

USAID has given the Astraea Lesbian Foundation for Justice millions of dollars. In turn, Astraea has donated to LGBTQ organizations in the US and across the globe including the GSA Network, the LGBTQ Victory Institute, the Black LGBTQIA+ Migrant Project, Iranti-Org, Aswat, Labris (Serbia), Labrys (Kyrgyzstan), Intersex Danmark, IntersexUK, Intersex Iceland, Trans Aid (Croatia), Radical Queer Affinity Collective (Hungary), Trans-Fuzja Foundation (Poland), XY Spectrum (Serbia), the Lesbian Organization Rijeka (LORI—Croatia, conducts educational training aimed at school psychologists and teachers in five schools in Rijeka and two in Opatija), the Larry Chang Foundation (Jamaica), ILGA World, Insight (Ukraine), Institute Transfeminist Initiative TransAkcija (Slovenia), Intersex Human Rights Australia, Intersex Trust Aotearoa New Zealand, Association of Russian-Speaking Intersex People (Russia), Lesbianas Independientes Feministas y Socialistas (Peru), Bilitis Resource Center Bulgaria, and Gayten-LGBT (Serbia), among, as we have seen, many others.

USAID's Office of Gender Equality and Women's Empowerment, similar to NATO's "gender perspective" courses aimed at adopting a gender theory perspective in military affairs and "apply[ing] a Gender Perspective in scenarios of patrolling, checkpoints and engagement with the local population in a culturally sensitive manner," apprises us that:

> All USAID staff are required to complete Gender 101: Gender Equality at USAID and USAID's Counter Trafficking in Persons Code of Conduct: Accountability and Action within 12 months of hire. USAID has several other training courses available: Gender 102: Putting ADS 205 into Action, Gender 103: The Roles and Responsibilities of Gender Advisors and POCs, Disability Inclusive Development 101, LGBTI 101: LGBTI Inclusion in the USAID Workplace, LGBTI 102: LGBTI Integration in USAID Programs, and Indigenous Peoples Programming at USAID.

In the geo-political and military spheres, NATO plays a central role in the globalist project as we have seen, and it is also fully committed to spreading the gospel of tolerance at gunpoint. Rose Gottemoeller, former Deputy Secretary General of NATO, tweeted her support for "#IDAHOT2017" (International Day Against Homophobia, Transphobia, and Biphobia, which "aims to coordinate international events that raise awareness of LGBT rights violations and stimulate interest in LGBT rights work worldwide"), stating that "NATO is committed to diversity and inclusion— these values make us stronger and safer." I'm sure Slobodan Milošević would agree if he was alive.

Dylan P. White, Acting Deputy Spokesperson for NATO certainly does, tweeting his support for this "holiday" in 2019: "#LGBT+ people deserve dignity, inclusion, and freedom from fear. We are everywhere: doctors and teachers, CEOs and aid workers, artists . . . and NATO officials too." Both Gottemoeller's and White's tweets featured images of themselves holding a bright rainbow NATO flag and beaming. White followed up with a tweet celebrating the fact that NATO "was a world leader on same-sex marriage. The organization extended equal benefits to same-sex couples in 2002."

As if the spectacle couldn't get any more grotesque, while not exactly the same thing, the reader will recall that the "gender equity" precursor was enforced "democratically" when after toppling the regimes in Afghanistan and Iraq, the United States mandated gender quotas for members of parliament in the two countries' new constitutions. In its increasing aggression toward the Russian sphere, James Kirchick inadvertently sums NATO's mission up perfectly: "One suspects that if Russia were a place where Pride parades were allowed, its quarrels with the United States, and ours with it, would diminish." I would imagine so.

Dylan P. White is right: they "are everywhere," and if you don't like it, first come the condemnations, boycotts, and economic sanctions; then more covert means of subversion, very possibly coup attempts and/or color revolutions; then finally, tons of NATO or Coalition of the Willing bombs, Establishment-backed proxies and/or boots on the ground. In "celebrating" its "first ever LGBTQI event at NATO," the European Organization of Military Associations and Trade Unions (EUROMIL), the Permanent Representation of Belgium to NATO, and the Joint Delegation of Canada to NATO co-hosted a panel discussion on "Integrating LGBTQI Perspectives in Allied and Partner Armed Forces" at the NATO Headquarters in Brussels in June 2019. From EUROMIL's website:

> The panel discussion was organised as a side-event taking place in the framework of the Annual Conference of the NATO Committee on Gender Perspectives (NCGP) as part of the continued efforts to strengthen and support gender mainstreaming, inclusivity and diversity initiatives. . . . The aim of the side-event was to provide a forum where lead nations and actors working on integrating diversity and inclusion perspectives in the defence sector could share experiences, lessons learned, and best practices in promoting Lesbian, Gay, Bisexual, Transgender, Queer and Intersex (LGBTQI) rights, equality and inclusion. . . . In recent years, LGBTQI inclusion has also started to be considered as a matter of operational effectiveness. Diversity and inclusion are critical if defence organisations want to survive and prosper in a security environment in constant evolution. . . . As an international organisation based on common values (values of individual liberty, democracy, human rights and the rule of law), NATO should lead by example, by promoting LGBTQI rights and by acting towards inclusive armed forces. International organisations should also collaborate on this issue. Identified best practices include leadership, training, code of conduct, support networks and mentors, antidiscrimination policies, recognition of same-sex relationships, recognition of transgender identity, including and protecting personnel abroad (including those serving in multinational missions). . . . An inclusive defence sector is a more effective defence sector!

It is not, but that's not what's at issue here. The presumption is that superior technology and lavish funding can simply overpower any resistance. Ask the US military how that's going in Afghanistan.

The entire military-industrial complex is nevertheless a central feature of the neoliberal system and is totally on board with the "diversity and inclusion" project.

Northrop Grumman and Lockheed Martin have sponsored Human Rights Campaign (HRC) annual dinners/galas, and Northrop Grumman has sponsored Pride parades, has a Pride in Diversity Alliance (PrIDA) employee resource group, and has been the presenting sponsor of the Out & Equal Workplace Summit which focuses on "LGBT inclusion." Raytheon has a Gay Lesbian Bisexual Transgender Allies employee resource group and in 2005 was the first in the defense industry to achieve a perfect rating from the Human Rights Campaign.

The Jewish Amanda Simpson—coming out of the military-industrial complex (Simpson began "transitioning" while with Raytheon)—was re-posted to the Pentagon in mid-2011 from the Department of Commerce and departed in January 2017. Simpson is now Vice President for Research and Technology at Airbus Americas. While with Raytheon, Simpson was on the Boards of the Raytheon Women's Network; the Lesbian, Gay, Bisexual, Transgender, Queer and Allies RAYPRIDE; and Raytheon's "diversity council." Triple-threat! Simpson has also been on the Boards of Out and Equal Workplace Advocates and the National Center for Transgender Equality. Given these considerations and others, the Army's adoption of the "Army of One" marketing slogan makes a lot of sense in this choose-your-own-adventure/reality so long as it aligns with the aims of the ruling class.

In the UK, the British Ministry of Defense hosted a reception in a Thameside pavilion at the House of Commons on January 9th, 2020, "to pay tribute to LGBT service personnel." Three days later, to mark twenty years since "the landmark ruling allowing military personnel to serve as openly lesbian, gay or bisexual (LGB), buildings across defence [were] lit in celebration" including Edinburgh Castle with bright rainbow colors and with the hoisting of the rainbow flag. Various US embassies globally fly the rainbow flag, from South Korea (which in 2020 was also accompanied by a Black Lives Matter banner) to Switzerland.

BAE Systems, a British multinational defense, security, and aerospace company, also supports the LGBTQ agenda; in May 2017, they launched their LGBT Allies program across all UK locations, and it sponsors Pride parades in Blackpool, Surrey, and Portsmouth. BAE Systems supplies Saudi Arabia with arms and services, and though the country has harsh penalties for homosexuality, the Establishment has been covertly undermining its domestic affairs in favor of "liberalizing" for years. At the same time, because BAE Systems is so committed to an agenda of inclusivity, their sales allow bombs to fall indiscriminately on school buses filled with children in Yemen and render the infrastructure so damaged finding clean water is borderline impossible, via Dan Sabbagh for *The Guardian*:

> Britain's leading arms manufacturer BAE Systems sold £15bn worth of arms and services to the Saudi military during the last five years, the period covered by Riyadh's involvement in the deadly bombing campaign in the war in Yemen. . . . Andrew Smith of CAAT said: "The last five years have seen a brutal humanitarian crisis for the people of Yemen, but for BAE it's been business as usual. The war has only been possible because of arms companies and complicit governments willing to support it." Thousands of civilians have been killed since the civil war in Yemen began in March 2015 with indiscriminate bombing by a Saudi-led coalition that is supplied by BAE and other Western arms makers. . . . The Saudi military is BAE's third largest customer

overall, after the US Department of Defence and the UK's Ministry of Defence. In 2019, revenues from the Pentagon – the world's largest buyer of arms – accounted for £6.5bn, while in the UK, where BAE builds and maintains ships for the Royal Navy, the figure was £3.9bn.

I wonder if the people prancing around waving dildos at these Prides have any concern about that. The most terrible injustices are committed under the auspices of "tolerance" and "diversity," the rhetoric and the reality becoming more egregiously diametrically opposed—the more "open" and "inclusive" the rhetoric, the more savage and violent the means of suppression and advancement of this project more broadly, via the US Department of Defense in 2019:

> The many different backgrounds of those who serve in the military make room for diversity, which makes the country strong, Illinois Sen. Tammy Duckworth said at the celebration of Lesbian, Gay, Bisexual and Transgender Pride Month in the Pentagon Center Courtyard. . . . Duckworth was joined by retired Air Force Brig. Gen. Wayne Monteith and by Stuart Milk, renowned global LGBT human rights activist and nephew of slain civil rights leader Harvey Milk. "Bigotry has no place downrange. . . . It weakens our forces and imperils our nation," said Duckworth, an Army wounded warrior from the Iraq War. . . . In September [2019], the Navy will begin building the USNS Harvey Milk. . . . "Equality, justice and the celebration of all of us needs to be seen as a basic human rights issue," [Stuart Milk said].

As with Richard Branson of Virgin calling for a boycott of Uganda for its "anti-homosexuality" legislation, JP Morgan Chase and Deutsche Bank have urged employees to boycott hotels owned by the Sultan of Brunei over the country's gay sex punishment. As hypocrites, they're happy to do business with Saudi Arabia, though; as Charles Riley wrote for CNN Business in 2019:

> JPMorgan has done business with Saudi Arabia recently. It was one of several banks, including Goldman Sachs, Morgan Stanley and HSBC that managed a $12.5 billion bond sale for state-owned oil giant, Saudi Aramco, in early April. . . . The head of JPMorgan's investment bank, Daniel Pinto, appeared on stage at a finance conference in Riyadh last week. . . . The event [was] attended also by the CEOs of HSBC and BlackRock.

## 50 Shades of Gay, Starring the United Nations

*"All the world's a cage and we are animals pounding at the glass*
*Housebroken, declawed, unaware of the threat*
*Bull hooks that keep us in line while cameras flash*
*And we play while the trespassers plot to collect on their debts."*

– Every Time I Die, "Organ Grinder"

In July 2013, the Office of the United Nations High Commissioner for Human Rights (OHCHR) launched UN Free & Equal – "an unprecedented global UN public information campaign aimed at promoting equal rights and fair treatment of LGBTI people." As then-High Commissioner for Human Rights Navi Pillay said:

> Our campaign on behalf of marginalized communities will meet resistance, even opposition. We must not be discouraged. We must stay engaged. Let us keep voicing our concerns, let us keep finding new allies, sharing good practice and standing fast alongside local human rights defenders on the front lines of this struggle.

Those present at the initial meeting included then-US Secretary of State, John Kerry; the foreign ministers of Argentina, Brazil, Croatia, the Netherlands, and Norway; the French minister for development cooperation; senior officials from Japan, New Zealand, and the European Union; as well as the executive directors of Human Rights Watch, Kenneth Roth, and OutRight Action International, Jessica Stern. According to their website:

> In 2017, UN Free & Equal reached 2.4 billion social media feeds around the world. . . . A number of celebrities have been named as campaign "Equality Champions" – including U.S. singer Ricky Martin, South African musician Yvonne Chaka Chaka, Bollywood actress Celina Jaitly, Brazilian pop star Daniela Mercury and her wife Malu Verçosa Mercury, U.S. hip-hop duo Macklemore and Ryan Lewis, and the band fun. Other prominent supporters – many of whom have taken part in campaign events – include South African Archbishop Emeritus Desmond Tutu, tennis legend Martina Navratilova, U.S. basketball champion Jason Collins, Indian actor Imran Khan, U.S. actor Zachary Quinto, and musicians Melissa Etheridge, Sara Bareilles and Rachel

355

Platten. . . . In 2019, UN partners at the national level included the International Organization for Migration (IOM), the Office of the United Nations High Commissioner for Refugees (UNHCR), the United Nations Children's Fund (UNICEF), the UN Development Programme (UNDP), the United Nations Educational, Scientific and Cultural Organization (UNESCO), the United Nations Food and Agriculture Organization (FAO), the United Nations Office on Drugs and Crime (UNODC), the United Nations Population Fund (UNFPA), UN Women, the International Labour Organization (ILO), UNAIDS, and the World Health Organization (WHO). . . . [In 2019,] we advocated for the rights of trans people on Trans Day of Visibility and the need to ensure justice and protection for the LGBTI community on International Day against Homophobia, Biphobia and Transphobia. We called on our allies to protect LGBTI and other kids from bullying on Spirit Day and celebrated their courage with an unprecedented video series featuring prominent African supporters of LGBTI equality. . . . More than 270 companies have signed up as supporters of the standards and the UN Human Rights Office has developed a toolkit aimed at activists who engage with the private sector.

From the United Nations' Free & Equal Campaign:

Major recent Free & Equal campaigns have targeted Cambodia, Cape Verde, Brazil, the Gambia, the Dominican Republic, Guatemala, Mongolia, Haiti, Sri Lanka, Peru, Timor Leste, Uruguay, and Vietnam, as well as a sub-regional campaign covering Costa Rica, El Salvador, Honduras, and Panama, and Serbia and the Ukraine. In Serbia, the propaganda took the following form:

In late 2018, the team translated the UN Human Rights Office-produced Standards of Conduct for Businesses on Tackling Discrimination against Lesbian, Gay, Bi, Trans, & Intersex People into Serbian and launched the document at an event in Belgrade. . . . The campaign also created a public information campaign around the standards in Serbia, including a video showing the positive impact that inclusion and diversity efforts have had at local company Hemofarm. . . . Three big Serbian corporations publicly endorsed the Standards of Conduct in 2019 and numerous additional businesses took part in LGBTI related events such as Pride Parade. Free & Equal Serbia also focused on de-pathologizing trans identities. The national legal system does not recognize transgender identities, and in the health care system being trans is still classified as a mental disorder. Free & Equal Serbia has sought to facilitate discussion between government partners, civil society organizations, trans activists and other expert participants about how to change the current regulations, allowing the trans community to become active participants in shaping a part of the legal framework that impacts their lives. Free & Equal Serbia has also actively appealed to public opinion through a series of public information activities. These included an exhibit documenting the lives of trans people in Serbia at the Belgrade Youth Centre.

For the Ukraine:

> Ensuring the protection of LGBTI events is the responsibility of the National Police and Free & Equal Ukraine has over the past two years worked with LGBTI activists and international police officers to train the National Police in how to safeguard the LGBTI community. In 2019, four training sessions for 80 mid-ranking and junior police officers have taken place. Participants report that the trainings have been helpful and relevant, not just in terms of technical learning outcomes, but also as a door-opener, helping police officers and LGBTI activists to get to know one another face to face – and discuss several of the same questions that were brought up in the 100 Questions online video series. Both the police trainings and online advocacy will continue in 2020.

Free & Equal was also a partnering organization with the LGBT Center of Ulaanbaatar, Mongolia's Equality and Pride Days 2020 along with the EU and the Government of Canada among other entities, and about which the US Embassy in Ulaanbaatar tweeted its support. The US Embassy put out a press release in support of the 2015 event as well, with the Embassy providing several films for the film festival and Embassy Public Diplomacy Officer Richard Roberts speaking at the opening concert and participating in what the Embassy described as a march, not a parade. This is a *very* important distinction and communicates to us exactly the nature of these projects.

As a case-in-point, the Asia Foundation was another co-sponsor of the LGBT Center's 2020 Equality and Pride Days. The Asia Foundation "addresses critical issues affecting Asia in the 21st century—governance and law, economic development, women's empowerment, environment, and regional cooperation." The "Committee for a Free Asia" was founded in 1951 as a CIA front, and it changed its name in 1954 to the Asia Foundation. Its purpose was—and frankly clearly still is—as described by Emma Best, to serve as a "propaganda machine and a front for covert activities including psychological warfare."

The original founding officers of the Board included: T.S. Peterson, CEO of Standard Oil of California (now Chevron); J.D. Zellerbach, Chairman of the Crown Zellerbach Corporation; university presidents including Grayson Kirk from Columbia, J.E. Wallace Sterling of Stanford, and Raymond Allen from UCLA; Pulitzer Prize-winning writer James Michener; Paul G. Hoffman, the first administrator of the Economic Cooperation Administration, where he led the implementation of the Marshall Plan from 1948–1950; and several major figures in foreign affairs. Its first President Robert Blum was with the OSS during World War II and followed the intelligence service's transformation after the war, eventually becoming assistant to Secretary of Defense James Forrestal. Blum was also chief of the US Special Technical and Economic Mission to Cambodia, Laos, and Vietnam, and was the Assistant Deputy for Economic Affairs at the Paris Office of the US Special Representative in Europe for the Mutual Security Agency, which replaced and superseded the Economic Cooperation Administration and the Marshall Plan with the Mutual Security

Act in October 1951. John McCloy was the US High Commissioner for Occupied Germany from September 1949 through July 1952.

To put this last position in context, as with references to the Marshall Plan and the US's immediate post-World War II "initiatives" in Europe, we're looking at the actions of a conquering army, even of its supposed allies. With a temporarily-crippled Europe over the barrel, the US dictated terms and dismantled the colonial empires to open them up to trade, as well as priming the globe for the onset of "international law" with the UN and its affiliates. The traditional cultures of Europe were consciously ear-marked for destruction at the hands of the neo-liberal Establishment, both the "winning" and defeated nations' people alike brought under the dominion of a wicked and decadent globalism. Seventy-odd years later, we are living the consequences, even in far-flung Mongolia.

Returning to the Asia Foundation, its current President David Arnold was the President of American University in Cairo and from 1984 to 1997 worked for the Ford Foundation, serving as its first program officer in the field of governance and then for seven years as the organization's representative in India, Nepal, and Sri Lanka. Current donors to the Asia Foundation include DLA Piper, the AmazonSmile Foundation, Google, Facebook, Gilead Sciences, the Omidyar Network, the Tides Foundation, the NBA franchise the Golden State Warriors (majority owner Joe Lacob is Jewish), the Rockefeller Foundation, the Carnegie Corporation of New York, the Ford Foundation, Goldman Sachs, and the Estée Lauder Companies.

The Asia Foundation's governmental and multilateral supporters are as follows: Asian Development Bank; Australian Department of Foreign Affairs and Trade; British Embassy in Afghanistan; Canada Fund for Local Initiatives; Department for International Development (DFID—United Kingdom); European Commission/European Union; Foreign and Commonwealth Office (United Kingdom); GIZ (Germany); Global Affairs Canada; International Development Research Center[119]; International Labor Organization (ILO); Italian Agency for Development Cooperation; Korea Development Institute (School of Public Policy); Korea International Cooperation Agency; Millennium Challenge Corporation; New Zealand Embassy in Timor-Leste; New Zealand Ministry of Foreign Affairs and Trade; Royal Netherlands Embassy, in China and Indonesia; Stockholm Environment Institute; Swiss Agency for Development and Cooperation; Swedish International Development Cooperation Agency; United Nations Children's Fund (UNICEF); United Nations Environment Program (UNEP); United Nations Economic and Social Commission for Asia and the Pacific (UNESCAP); USAID; United States Department of State; US Embassies in Cambodia, Indonesia, Japan, Korea, Laos, Malaysia, Mongolia, Nepal, Myanmar, Pakistan, Philippines, Singapore, and Thailand; The World Bank.

The UN has also convened "activists" and representatives of big business to form

---

[119] "The International Development Research Centre is a public corporation created by the Parliament of Canada to help researchers and communities in the developing world find solutions to their social, economic, and environmental problems. IDRC connects people, institutions, and ideas to ensure that the results of the research it supports and the knowledge that research generates, are shared equitably among all its partners, North and South . . . Poverty is a deeply rooted problem in both developing and developed countries. IDRC's experience has shown that the components of complex issues like global poverty cannot be usefully separated; social, environmental, and economic factors remain inextricably linked. By themselves, traditional disciplines, like economics, are inadequate in confronting many of the challenges developing countries face. To deal with the tangled nature of development issues, IDRC has pioneered new approaches for delivering its program of research support."

the basis of the report "Minding the corporate gap: how activists & companies can work together to tackle LGBTI discrimination." The United Nations has enlisted "private sector partnerships" with companies like the Gap, Kenneth Cole Productions, and H&M:

> UN Free & Equal celebrated Pride with Gap Inc. In 2019, Gap Inc.'s largest and most comprehensive collection of Pride-themed t-shirts, other Pride-themed accessories, and e-gift cards were sold online and in stores around the world with proceeds going to support UN Free & Equal. Gap Inc. brands Athleta, Banana Republic, Banana Republic Factory, Gap, [and] Gap Factory joined the partnership. Employees also joined LGBTI advocates at Pride marches across the U.S. and around the world honoring the 50th anniversary of the Stonewall Riots as well as Gap's 50th birthday. During Pride Month, Gap Inc. invited out Olympic skier and medalist Gus Kenworthy to an employee townhall where he spoke on the significance of living authentically. During the year, Gap Inc. employees also attended high-level UN LGBTI Core Group meetings at UN headquarters in New York. . . . A groundbreaking partnership with Kenneth Cole Productions and UN Free & Equal continued into 2019. KCP released its most expansive Pride Collection—including footwear, t-shirts, caps, underwear, and sunglasses—pegged to World Pride in New York City and the 50th Anniversary of the Stonewall Riots. Kenneth Cole created and led an impactful, trailblazing campaign with Broadway's award-winning musical "The Prom," which received a Silver Clio Award in the category of "Live Entertainment: Partnerships and Collaborations." This holistic campaign included a special edition Kenneth Cole t-shirt, which was sold at The Prom's theater and on KC.com and had proceeds go to UN Free & Equal. It also included events, such as in-theater talk backs and intimate in-store performances, which garnered the participation of UN diplomats from around the world as well as Mr. Kenneth Cole. KCP employees also joined OHCHR staff and diplomats at marquee UN events promoting LGBTI equality. . . . UN Free & Equal teamed up with H&M to help launch the company's 2019 Pride collection. With over 30 pieces – including gender neutral options and the UN Free & Equal logo – the partnership raised both awareness and funds for UN Free & Equal for the second year in a row. The collection was featured in H&M stores in more than 50 countries globally and promoted through celebrity champions including actress and advocate Laverne Cox; actor Rickey Thompson; and influencer Shannon Beveridge. A dazzling kickoff bash was also held in May at the House of Yes in Brooklyn, New York.

Major employers *love* this stuff, and the more all-encompassing the better. As Antonio Zappulla (Open for Business's Board of Trustees, CEO of the Thomson Reuters Foundation, founder of Openly, "the world's first platform dedicated to fair, accurate and impartial coverage of LGBT+ stories with global distribution through the Reuters wire"), writes for the World Economic Forum:

> In the words of the UN, the fight against homophobia is now, more than ever, a 'development imperative.' By forging an internal culture of inclusion that

transcends national policies yet is aware of them, companies have a tremendous opportunity to leverage their global influence to shape socio-economic progress.

In 2017, the United Nations published the Standards of Conduct for Business, which Open for Business uses as its template to leverage the private sector against any countries or areas that are reticent to "open up," perhaps giving new meaning to the idea of an "open society." Most relevant to our discussion here is Point Five: Act in the Public Sphere where "businesses are encouraged to use their leverage."

Open for Business, launched in 2015 at the Clinton Global Initiative in the context of its Annual Summit, agrees. Open for Business is described as:

> A coalition of leading global companies dedicated to LGBT+ inclusion. Our task is to present the business rationale on global LGBT+ inclusion: successful, enterprising businesses thrive in diverse, inclusive societies and the spread of anti-LGBT+ policies runs counter to the interests of business and economic growth.

In 2019, Open for Business sent a delegation of executives to meet with the Vatican's Secretary of State and subsequently, per Open for Business's website:

> Secured initial support from the Catholic Church—the Secretary of State of the Vatican welcomed the conversation, condemned all forms of violence against all persons around the world and signalled his intention to look for common ground to collectively move the conversation forward . . . a new report aimed at framing a continued dialogue with the Vatican on LGBT+ rights . . . has been shared with His Holiness Pope Francis. . . . [Open for Business is] working with the International Bar Association to secure a statement from the Vatican supporting the decriminalisation of same-sex acts in close to 70 countries around the world.

Open for Business's coalition partners also "share a deep-rooted commitment to diversity and inclusion in their own workplaces." These include GlaxoSmithKline, Google, Deutsche Bank, Tesco, Microsoft, KPMG, Barclays, Virgin, LinkedIn, and more. Open for Business works closely with numerous LGBTQ organizations such as UN Free & Equal, the National LGBT Chamber of Commerce (NGLCC), Stonewall, the Human Rights Campaign (HRC), and the UK Parliament's All-Party Parliamentary Group on Global LGBT+ Rights, whose:

> Membership includes parliamentarians of all parties from both the House of Commons and House of Lords, united in a common aim to improve rights for LGBT+ people globally. We work with major UK-based LGBT+ charities and human rights organisations to identify political priorities on LGBT+ issues, and we advocate in the UK Parliament for positive change in the lives of LGBT+ people.

Open for Business's Executive Director Kathryn Dovey previously worked for the OECD, and former fellow Tisha Cromwell was with GlaxoSmithKline prior to her fellowship. Open for Business's Research Advisory Board and Board of Trustees are as connected as it gets, previously or currently affiliated with/employed by: McKinsey; American Express; the Thomson Reuters Foundation; Bloomberg Television; OutRight Action International; the University of Oxford; the Australian Centre in Sex, Health and Society at La Trobe University; HEC Paris; the Williams Institute at UCLA; Hivos; Brunswick Group; and the World Economic Forum.

Research Advisory Board member Suen Yiu Tung has spearheaded and chaired a number of international conferences in collaboration with the European Union and the UNDP, and previously served as a consultant and data analyst for the UNDP Being LGBT in Asia program. Board of Trustees member Dinah McLeod began her career as Social Protection Specialist at the World Bank, where she worked on "community-based financing and social infrastructure projects for marginalised and vulnerable groups"; held senior sustainability roles with the Overseas Development Institute (ODI), BT, Novartis, and Allianz; holds a Master's degree in Public Administration from Princeton University's Woodrow Wilson School as well as a BA from Columbia University; and was a Policy Advisor at the UK Prime Minister's Strategy Unit.

Research Advisory Board member Vivienne Ming's biographical blurb for Open for Business's 2019–2020 Impact Report informs us that:

> Ming's work on 'The Tax of Being Different' calculated a financial cost of not being a straight white male, and she speaks frequently on her AI-driven research into inclusion and gender in business. Previously a visiting scholar at UC Berkeley's Redwood Center for Theoretical Neuroscience, Dr. Ming is currently a faculty member of Singularity University focusing on cognitive neuroscience and she co-founded Socos Labs, an independent think tank exploring the future of human potential. She sits on boards of numerous companies and nonprofits including StartOut, The Palm Center, Cornerstone Capital, Platypus Institute, Shiftgig, Zoic Capital, and SmartStones. . . . Ming found when she was Evan Smith, a talented, aspiring male student who graduated with honors in his field from Carnegie Mellon University, people looked at her and judged her potential based on her sex: male at the time.

Felicity Daly, former Executive Director of the Kaleidoscope Trust and current researcher at the Institute of Commonwealth Studies, School of Advanced Study, University of London for the "Strong in Diversity, Bold on Inclusion" project funded by the UK Aid Connect program is also on Open for Business's Research Advisory Board. The Kaleidoscope Trust "work[s] with parliamentarians, government ministers, officials and policy makers to try to effect real change in the lives of LGBT communities around the world. With [its] base in the UK [it] urge[s] the British government and Commonwealth stakeholders to use their influence in support of the rights of LGBT people." Its current Executive Director is Phyll Opoku-Gyimah, co-founder and Executive Director of UK Black Pride. The Kaleidoscope Trust "has joined a group of organisations to deliver the LGBT stream of the Department for International Development's [DFID] flagship UK Aid Connect programme."

Open for Business has disseminated materials to "activists" across the globe, and their Local Influencer Program has various regional initiatives dedicated to undermining targeted societies, such as the East Africa Program centered on Kenya, and various projects in the Asia, where:

> Our coalition partners have had two roundtables of business leaders in Hong Kong, have built a self-sustaining network focused on disseminating LGBT+ inclusion best practices in Singapore, partnered with the Economist and UNDP on Executive Dialogues in India, and partnered with IBM in Japan, Korea, and the Philippines. Additionally, we have worked with civil society organizations in Taiwan to build business support for marriage equality and in China to translate our reports into Simplified Chinese. . . . We are currently helping to encourage our coalition partners to support a viewpoint put forward by the American Chamber of Commerce in Japan outlining the business benefits of marriage equality.

In Eastern Europe, Open for Business states that, "We are partnering with Google and a foundation partner to construct a data-driven economic case for LGBT+ rights in Eastern Europe. The initiative is run by our Program Lead based in Berlin and focuses on Poland, Hungary, Romania, and Ukraine." For the Caribbean Local Influencer Program:

> We are partnering with Virgin Atlantic to develop the first quantitative view on the impact of LGBT+ discrimination on the Caribbean's economy, with a special focus on the tourism and travel industry. Our work is led by Phil Crehan,120 a respected researcher with experience investigating the socioeconomic impacts of LGBT+ discrimination around the world with the World Bank.

Facebook's Data for Good is also involved.

Open for Business has also worked with the UK Embassy in Washington, DC, the Commonwealth Heads of Government Meeting in London, the US State Department, Bloomberg, the Open Society Foundations, LinkedIn, Microsoft, Brunswick Group, EY, the UN Consultation on Engaging the Private Sector on LGBT+ Issues in Berlin, the United Nations General Assembly, McKinsey, American Express, the Federation of Indian Chambers of Commerce and Industry (FICCI) in New Delhi, the Equal Rights Commission, and the Beijing LGBT+ Center in China. The Free & Equal campaign of the United Nations was named the Open for Business Strategic Partner of the Year in its 2019–2020 Impact Report.

On the NGO side of things, Open for Business receives substantial support and funding from Tides and the Tides Advocacy Fund, the Oak Foundation, the Arcus Foundation, Dreilinden, and Frontline AIDS. Frontline AIDS also partners with the BBC Radio 4 Appeal and M&C Saatchi, and is funded primarily by ViiV, Gilead

---

[120] Additionally, Crehan has worked on the SecureNutrition Platform in addition to the Global Agriculture Food Security Program. With these projects, he has promoted the link between agricultural development, food security, and nutrition. The Gates Foundation was among the inaugural donors to the Global Agriculture and Food Security Program (GAFSP) along with several governments.

Sciences, GIZ, DFID, Comic Relief, the Elton John AIDS Foundation, the Ministry of Foreign Affairs of the Netherlands, the Swedish International Development Cooperation Agency (SIDA), the SPIDER Center, and the Global Fund to Fight AIDS, Tuberculosis, and Malaria (typically just called the Global Fund).

SPIDER is "an independent centre focusing on the digitalisation of international development. We bring together actors in development to promote human centered technology for the achievement of Sustainable Development Goals (SDGs)." SPIDER states on its website that, "A gendered analysis is encouraged to address the specific needs, reflect the lives of, and respond to the social realities of men, women, minority groups in their use of technology as well as their input into its design." Their work is essential in facilitating the supposedly necessary "global partnerships" and networks to deal with the very crises the Establishment has either created or greatly exacerbated, and to ensure continued progress toward the UN's SDGs.

Barbara Rothschild sits on the Advisory Board of the Oak Foundation; recent Oak Foundation grants have gone to a joint project between the Swiss National Youth Council and Milchjugend to make youth associations in Switzerland "more inclusive for LGBT youth," the Boston Children's Hospital, the University of Maine System, the Tides Center, the Center for Effective Philanthropy, Røde Kors (supports a health clinic for "undocumented migrants" in Denmark), the Refugee Survival Trust ("to reduce destitution and homelessness in Glasgow among asylum seekers"), NEO Philanthropy, the New York Foundation, the New Venture Fund, the European Programme for Integration and Migration (EPIM), the Regents of the University of California, Columbia University, the Danish Refugee Council, Mama Cash, the Refugee and Migrant Centre (supports asylum seekers, migrants and refugees in Wolverhampton and Birmingham, UK), the Heartland Alliance, the True Colors Fund, the Center for Popular Democracy, the US Committee for Refugees and Immigrants, the Tides Foundation, the Proteus Fund, Rockefeller Philanthropy Advisors, the Regents of the University of California, UNICEF, Amnesty International, Women's Refugee Commission, Human Rights Watch, the European Network on Statelessness,[121] and the Platform for International Cooperation on Undocumented Migrants.

According to Igor Suran of Parks, "founded on the principles of Rosa Parks nonviolent powerful protest, works to enact change through encouraging private companies to recognize their ability to be champions of change for the LGBT community in Italy," showing how deep the (anti-) cultural imperialism's rot has set in:

> Businesses are identifying diversity efforts as critical means of their operations. . . . Businesses have the ability to enact social change in areas where cultural values might not align with diversity efforts. Businesses have the unique ability to shift cultural understandings because they control so much of a country's livelihood. Parks helps companies understand that they are essential agents of social change. . . . Signalling the support of LGBTQ employees can attract firms internationally, as an environment of inclusion is something many companies around the world value and *require* (emphasis added).

---

[121] Primary donors are the Open Society Foundations, the Oak Foundation, the Sigrid Rausing Trust, and the UNHCR.

For Óscar Muñoz, the co-founder of REDI (Red Empresarial por la Diversidad e Inclusión LGBTI), "the LGBTI business network in Spain":

> The creation of REDI was inspired by the experience of similar international entities, such as Stonewall in the United Kingdom, Out & Equal in the USA, Parks in Italy, PROUT AT WORK in Germany, etc. REDI soon became the most active network/forum in Spain regarding LGBTI D&I at the workplace and, in February 2018, was established as a non-profit organization including some of the most important Spanish companies as well as many international companies located in Spain. . . . Our main goal is to foster an inclusive and respectful environment in organizations where talent is valued, regardless of their identity, gender expression and sexual orientation, *therefore contributing to the social 'normalization' and the eradication of socio-cultural prejudices* (emphasis added).

We know this is totally organic and "grassroots" because as Stephen Golden, Hong Kong-based Asia-Pacific head of global leadership and diversity at Goldman Sachs, said in an interview with Ignites Asia in May 2014, "It's really senior leadership that sets direction." Golden said that, before the International Day Against Homophobia and Transphobia (IDAHOT), Goldman Sachs's Asia-Pacific management committee, as well as its Chairman, wore something purple, the official IDAHOT color, to show their support. Goldman Sachs also has what it calls "MD allies," who are senior managing directors in every division of the company who are very supportive of the company's LGBT network and are probably making sure their employees have not just the requisite fifteen pieces of flair, but "voluntarily" go above and beyond! "When our employees see that their senior leaders are doing this, then they know it's important to the firm and to the company," Golden says.

It's also very important to the self-styled masters of mankind at the United Nations. According to the United Nations' 2016 "Living Free and Equal" document:

> States have a duty to protect, respect and fulfil the human rights of all persons regardless of their gender identity, including those who have non-binary gender identities, such as gender identities that are neither 'man' nor 'woman'. . . . States should legally recognize and protect the rights of those with non-binary gender identities, including: hijra, muxe, waria, transpinoy, meti, third gender, two spirit, fa'afafine, khwaja sira, and gender queer.

For Ban Ki-moon, former Secretary-General of the United Nations, a major proponent of the Green New Deal, and a *Foreign Policy* Top 100 Global Thinker for his role in the ratification of the Paris Agreement on climate change:

> There are 17 Sustainable Development Goals all based on a single, guiding principle: to leave no one behind. We will only realize this vision if we reach all people regardless of their sexual orientation or gender identity. . . . Ending marginalization and exclusion of LGBT people is a human rights priority – and a development imperative.

Former UN High Commissioner for Human Rights Zeid Ra'ad Al Hussein stated, "If we are to achieve faster global progress towards equality for lesbian, gay, bi, trans, and intersex people, businesses will not only have to meet their human rights responsibilities, they must become active agents of change." Achim Steiner, Administrator of the UNDP[122] said:

> Justice and protection for all are central to driving progress on the 2030 Agenda for Sustainable Development and the Sustainable Development Goals. Enacting and enforcing non-discriminatory laws and policies, repealing punitive laws and ensuring access to justice for all are critical to delivering on the commitment to leave no one behind.

In December 2017, the United Nations Development Program (UNDP) completed the development of 51 LGBTI Inclusion Index indicators in five strategic inclusion areas for "development efforts that are inclusive of LGBTI people." The support of the Swedish LGBTQ NGO RFSL, OutRight Action International, and ILGA were instrumental for the completion of these consultations, which were done in partnership with the World Bank. ILGA has UN Economic and Social Council consultative status.

Over the course of 2020, OutRight Action International launched the COVID-19 Global LGBTIQ Emergency Fund with founding partners Microsoft, Gilead Sciences, Calvin Klein, and the Dunn Family Charitable Foundation, which focuses on "poverty alleviation and social justice globally." Other contributors to OutRight's COVID fund include the Open Society Foundations, Salesforce, the Wellspring Philanthropic Fund, the Horizons Foundation, Visa, Warner Music Group, PepsiCo, and the Council for Global Equality. We can see how everything is consciously being linked under the auspices of a nebulous "justice" that somehow only benefits these major stakeholders. They can fly to Davos in their private jet, but you have to live in a pod next to forced "diversity" and eat plants and bugs. It's the only way to stop the apocalypse you know!

In 2017, the UNDP, in partnership with Global Action for Trans Equality (GATE) and Organization Intersex International (OII) Australia, carried out two "global capacity building webinars on advancing the rights and inclusion of intersex people." Two more, one in Spanish were planned for 2018. With financial support from USAID, UNDP launched the "Being LGBTI in the Caribbean" project, which includes Barbados, the Dominican Republic, Haiti, and Jamaica.

As a founding co-sponsor of the Joint UN Programme on HIV/AIDS (UNAIDS), UNDP convenes the work on "removing and reforming punitive laws and policies that block effective responses to HIV promoting enabling legislation, access to justice, and eliminating discrimination in healthcare settings, co-convenes with UNFPA the work on empowering key populations (including gay and bi men and trans people) to access HIV prevention." In 2016–2017 UNDP partnered with other UN entities, particularly UNFPA, the UNAIDS Secretariat, the World Health Organization

---

[122] UNIC Nairobi, in collaboration with the Israeli Embassy, organized an event on January 27th, 2010 to "honour the Victims of the Holocaust. Guest speakers included Mr. Ezra Pakter, a Holocaust survivor; Israeli Ambassador Jacob Keida; German Ambassador Margit Hellwig-Boette; and Dr. David Silverstein, who represented the Jewish community. UNON Executive Director General Achim Steiner delivered the Secretary-General's message for the day."

(WHO), and UN Women on "advising countries against the adoption on homo- and transphobic laws and policies in five countries."

"Discrimination against any group is not only morally wrong, it stands in the way of sustained, balanced, and inclusive economic growth," said former World Bank President Jim Yong Kim (Harvard Medical School). "By emphasizing that LGBTI exclusion affects everyone, we can hopefully help countries realize that putting an end to discrimination will bring a wide range of benefits," explained Maria Beatriz Orlando, Lead Social Development Specialist. "Saying no to homophobia is in their best economic interest. And it's the right thing to do."

Sponsors of San Francisco Pride's 2020 "celebration," which was held digitally, concur. As we see from their website—after learning that Black Lives Matter and Black Trans Lives Matter—the event's sponsors included: Genentech, Gilead Sciences, Bud Light, Kaiser Permanente, Facebook, Hilton, a pair of TV stations, and Salesforce.

Member organizations in Pride in Diversity—"the national not-for-profit employer support program for LGBTQ workplace inclusion specialising in HR, organisational change and workplace diversity, Pride in Diversity publishes the Australian Workplace Equality Index (AWEI), Australia's national benchmarking instrument for LGBTQ workplace inclusion from which Top Employers for LGBTQ people is determined"—include: Goldman Sachs, the Australian Federal Police, the Australian Government Department of Defence, Bloomberg LP, HSBC, Zurich Financial Services Australia, Visa Australia, JP Morgan Chase, Vanguard Investments Australia, ING, Deutsche Bank, Citi Australia, BNP Paribas, Sodexo, Victoria Police, Amazon, Lockheed Martin Australia, Thales, Eli Lilly, Pfizer, Novartis, Bayer, Johnson & Johnson, and AstraZeneca, among many others.

In what will surely meet the approval of the Log Cabin Republicans, the National LGBT Chamber of Commerce (NGLCC) in the United States is absolutely massive. Their website states that:

> Through the NGLCC Supplier Diversity Initiative, our corporate partners have spent hundreds of millions with Certified LGBT Business Enterprise® companies throughout their supply chains. The NGLCC is available as a resource to any corporation in its efforts to achieve full inclusion.

Its founding corporate partners are JP Morgan Chase, Wells Fargo, IBM, Motorola, Travelport, American Airlines, Aetna, EY, Intel, and Wyndham Worldwide. Their other corporate sponsors are a veritable who's-who from Coca-Cola to Johnson & Johnson to Goldman Sachs to Disney to Major League Baseball. They have affiliated chambers in thirty US states and Washington, DC. They have also partnered with global chambers in Australia, Brazil, Canada, Uruguay, South Africa, Mexico, Jamaica, Italy, India, Ecuador, Colombia, Costa Rica, the Dominican Republic, and the Scandinavian LGBT Chamber of Commerce, which also partners with the American Chamber of Commerce in Sweden, the US Embassy-Stockholm, the International Gay and Lesbian Travel Association, the Canadian Gay and Lesbian Chamber of Commerce, and East Meets West, a network of LGBTI professionals based out of Vienna. Their network, in turn, encompasses Austria, Russia, Kosovo, Romania, Poland, Czech Republic, Bulgaria, Hungary, Slovenia, Slovakia, Bosnia, Serbia, Croatia, Albania, Macedonia, and the Ukraine. "Diversity and inclusion is at the heart of our culture," says Liz Sullivan, an executive vice-president at T-Mobile. Indeed, and the entire corporatocracy is on board. The reason there is so much commonality is that the beneficiaries are all the same, and it truly means a One World government, functioning through a series of interlocking networks ultimately feeding into the whole.

Goldman Sachs has a number of "Affinity Networks" such as: The Goldman Sachs Women's Network ("Enhances the experience of women professionals at the firm through programs that foster greater interaction among peers, as well as the broader community"); The Firmwide Black Network ("Aims to enhance professional development and advancement opportunities for Black employees, and advises senior business leaders on issues of importance to the firm's Black community"); and The Lesbian, Gay, Bisexual and Transgender Network ("Advocates for maintaining a work environment that respects, welcomes and supports lesbian, gay, bisexual and transgender professionals, and enables them to perform to their fullest potential and contribute to the greater goals of the firm"). Some of Goldman Sachs' major partners in these efforts include beyond those we've discussed (and this list is unfortunately not exhaustive):

- *The Economist*
- Out for Australia, "an organisation that seeks to support and mentor aspiring LGBTIQ professionals as they navigate their way through the early stages of their careers." Their partners include JP Morgan Chase, Accenture, Baker McKenzie, Pricewaterhouse Coopers, and Deloitte.
- Bright Network UK
- Code First Girls UK to advance women in tech; it crows on its website that 53% of its membership is BAME. Other partners include Bank of America, Google, and private equity firm KKR & Co. Inc.
- EmployAbility UK, which works with Amazon, Bloomberg, Google, and Nat-West, among others.
- Diversity Council Australia
- Investing In Ethnicity UK, whose founding partners are Moody's, Lloyds, HSBC UK, and the Bank of England.
- IT for S-H-E in Poland, whose partners include Citi, Ericsson, Facebook, Nat-West, Tom Tom, Google, Intel, and Procter & Gamble, in addition to Goldman Sachs.
- The Lord Mayor's Appeal Charity, London
- Pink News
- Stonewall
- Powerlist: Britain's most influential people of African and African-Caribbean heritage; sponsors include Linklaters, Pricewaterhouse Coopers, and JP Morgan Chase
- Women of The Square Mile: Their website states that is brought to you by the world's largest conference series dedicated to driving gender diversity in the Financial Services sector; listed companies that get involved are included Credit Suisse, the Bank of England, Barclays, Ernst and Young, NatWest, *The Telegraph*, Deutsche Bank, and the Royal Bank of Scotland, plus UN Women. HSBC was 2019's headline sponsor.

- Women in Banking and Finance UK, with branches in Bristol, London, Edinburgh, Glasgow, Birmingham, and Manchester. Its July 2020 virtual seminar co-hosted with Moody's entitled "The Economic Impact of the COVID-19 Crisis and What it means for women" featured speakers Laura Perez, Moody's Chief Credit Officer in the EU, and Elise Badoy, Deputy Head of Research for Europe Middle East and Africa at Citi. Prior to Citi, Badoy worked at Goldman Sachs from 1999 to 2009.
- Disability Forum UK: "Our research report shows the benefits of global organisations making disability inclusion an integral part of their corporate strategy, drawing on evidence and case studies from leading global organisations." Its partners are: Accenture, Allianz, State Street, Shell, the BBC, Barclays, American Express, Kingfisher, HSBC, BT, Bank of America, Atos, EY, Unilever, Sainsbury's, Cisco, Deloitte, the Department for Transport, the Department for Work and Pensions, Lloyds, KPMG, Enterprise Rent-a-Car, Environment Agency, the Royal Mail, RBS, PricewaterhouseCoopers, the National Crime Agency, Microsoft, the Ministry of Justice, Microlink PC, the Home Office, Anglo-American, GlaxoSmithKline, Her Majesty's Revenue and Customs, and NHS Scotland.

As yet another example evidencing the truly global nature of this project—and its global uniformity—Amsterdam Pride's 2020 sponsors included Booking.com, PricewaterhouseCoopers, ING, Philips, Heineken, Google, Uber, Netflix, Salesforce, and PostNL. Across the globe, in 2016, Freshfields Tokyo co-founded (with Goldman Sachs, Linklaters and Morrison Foerster) an LGBT Lawyers and Allies Network (LLAN), which "aims to promote LGBT+ equality in Japan, specifically focusing on same-sex marriage. . . . We are proud to express our support for the UN LGBTI Standards of Conduct for Business."

In Georgia, the World Bank carried out numerous focus group discussions with the LGBTQ "community" across the country. In Nepal, the World Bank contributed resources to a project "with a focus on creating SOGI-sensitivity tools in schools." The World Bank Country Partnership Framework for Uruguay includes SOGI-specific entry points in the portfolio. Country diagnostics in the Western Balkans and Thailand incorporated "LGBTI exclusion as an integral challenge to larger development outcomes." The World Bank is now working with the Thai government to, in its words, "strengthen awareness on their commitment to safeguard marginalized groups—particularly LGBTI people." The conditional grant "seeks to build a South-South learning platform among countries in Southeast Asia to promote LGBTI inclusion." Are you seeing how all this works?

Since 2011, the World Bank has convened numerous events on "sexual orientation and gender identity (SOGI) inclusion in development—particularly by advancing the link to poverty and larger development goals." In 2014, a World Bank/IMF shareholder meeting was convened to meet with over a dozen prominent LGBTQ "leaders." In 2016, the World Bank created the position of Advisor on Sexual Orientation and Gender Identity (SOGI) issues, responsible for promoting lesbian, gay, bisexual, transgender, and intersex (LGBTI) inclusion throughout the work of the World Bank. According to the World Bank's press release, advisor Clifton Cortez:

Has more than 20 years of professional experience working in developing countries with the UNDP and USAID, focusing on health, HIV, and sustainable development – including the important intersection of sexual orientation, gender identity, and development. Most recently, he managed UNAIDS partnerships, in which he played a key role in UNDP leadership addressing the broader governance, law, and human rights challenges faced by LGBTI people. . . . The creation of a senior-level position for LGBTI builds on the World Bank efforts to develop a coordinated, strategic approach to inclusion and gender equality. The Bank has established a multi-sectoral Task Force to spearhead work in this area, and is adding staff to monitor the environment for LGBTI persons in countries around the world. . . . The Bank has launched several LGBTI data-collection and research initiatives this year [2016], and is working with the United Nations on a coordinated research agenda. In addition, the World Bank was the first international financial institution to offer health insurance for same-sex couples, and has offered Domestic Partner benefits to same-sex couples for over 10 years.

In 2016, along with the creation of this new position, the World Bank enacted a Presidential Directive to be implemented alongside its new framework; the Directive "specifically demarcates discrimination based on SOGI as contributing toward vulnerability, and thus places a responsibility on staff to ensure vulnerable groups (including LGBTI people) are not negatively impacted by lending." The World Bank is essentially making conditional grants on the basis of "anti-discrimination" as a way to force change upon impoverished nations looking to the institution.

The UN's ability to provide the patina of respectability of this incredibly harmful agenda and its ability to marshal force and dispense resources is of vital importance to the process of centralized globalization. The multi-lateral approach, be it through the hybrid system of philanthropic capitalism, the Global Equality Fund, the United Nations, or any of these other multitudinous organizations allows for the synergistic and amplifying nature of the Establishment agenda, be it LGBTQ or mass migration. The process of globalization is one that operates on numerous fronts simultaneously, and its expansion is hastened along whichever lines ultimately prove most advantageous. The endless layers of bureaucracy, which are intentionally overwhelming, are essential for the smoke-and-mirrors and for drowning people in Newspeak and wave after wave of NPC cultural commissars.

The individual occupied Western governments are useful in the interim stage before national sovereignty is ultimately done away with under one global government banner run by the well-positioned and powerful, with the US taking the lead for the simple fact that it's Ground Zero for so many these various industrial complexes, has the most well-funded and largest military presence, and of course was the destination of choice to be colonized by global Jewry. If the final planned One World government is in fact helmed the UN or some other yet-created entity remains to be seen, but whatever flag it waves, it'll be run by the same cabal of bankers, string-pullers, senior officials, and the like we've covered extensively in this book. It is clear that the aims of the occupied governments, the NGOs, the multi-nationals, and the supra-governmental globalist entities like the EU and the UN are exactly the same, they simply approach the furtherance of their goals through different means and mechanisms to create pressure on multiple fronts.

Very obviously the Establishment sanctions this project, whether it be the slew of aforementioned examples or the more obscene anecdotal examples like the prisoner serving a life sentence for murder in California receiving a state-funded sex change, as the Associated Press reported in January 2017:

> A 57-year-old convicted killer serving a life sentence has become the first U.S. inmate to receive state-funded sex-reassignment surgery, the prisoner's attorneys confirmed. . . . California prison officials agreed in August 2015 to pay for the surgery for Shiloh Heavenly Quine, who was convicted of first-degree murder, kidnapping and robbery for ransom and has no possibility of parole. Quine's case led the state to become the first to set standards that will allow other transgender inmates to apply to receive state-funded sex-reassignment surgery. It also prompted a federal magistrate to require California to provide transgender female inmates housed in men's facilities with more female-oriented items such as nightgowns, scarves and necklaces. "For too long, institutions have ignored doctors and casually dismissed medically necessary and life-saving care for transgender people just because of who we are," said Kris Hayashi, executive director of the Transgender Law Center, which represents Quine and other transgender inmates.

The *modus operandi* of intersectionality and the terminal preposterousness of late-stage decline decadence is by now well-understood; the sociopathic "elites" heavily recruit through multiple vectors for their intersectional army to bring about their post-modern dystopia.

For example, the LGBTQ Victory Institute has since 2015 awarded Victory Empowerment Fellows, "a program designed for LGBTQ leaders of color and/or trans leaders . . . who have been identified to lead the LGBTQ community as elected officials or other public servants." Isaiah Levinson wrote for the LGBTQ Victory Institute's blog on June 11th, 2020:

> As we enter this year's Pride month, Black LGBTQ leaders are fighting for intersectional police reform solutions as Black Lives Matter protests advocate across the nation against police brutality and violence. . . . Shannon Hardin, Columbus City Council President [declared] racism a 'public health crisis.'

Levinson describes the LGBTQ Victory Institute's Open Society Foundations-esque training of intersectional "activists":

> Executive Secretary of the International Youth Parliament Thokozile Nhlumayo will join the Youth African Leaders Initiative (YALI) for its 2021 class of Mandela Washington Fellows. In the six years since its creation, the Fellowship has trained over 4,000 Sub-Saharan African activists through Leadership Institutes at American universities and professional development experiences, culminating in D.C.-based Fellow Summits. . . . Another previous South Africa Victory Institute trainee, Mpho Buntse, joined the Mandela Fellowship for its 2018 cohort. Now the National Spokesperson of the South African ruling political party's Women's League LGBTI+ Desk launched earlier this year, Mpho boasts a long history of LGBTQ activism. Both Mpho and

Thokozile marked the importance of their time with Victory Institute in attaining both the Fellowship and their career achievements. In 2017, Mpho joined Victory for its World Leaders Conference in Washington, D.C., marking his first trip to the United States. At this Conference, Mpho developed his queer organizing skills and his understanding of U.S. politics, enabling him an easier transition during his Philadelphia placement with the Fellowship. He and Thokozile joined Victory Institute for its LGBTQ Political Leadership Institute in South Africa in 2017 and 2019 respectively. The Institute trained them with "a hybrid of innovative content" featuring networking and elected official engagement education. Thokozile emphasized the Leadership Institute's development of her communication and organization skills, both of which played "a vital role in [her] political career to help [her] become a competent politician" and "understand how to engage with different political systems." She consistently uses the knowledge she gained with Victory Institute in her position with the International Youth Parliament to increase the organization's membership and political impact, abilities she will further develop during the Mandela Fellowship.

Levinson crows about victories in Europe such as in May 2020, "the northeastern French town of Tilloy-lez-Marchiennes marked a significant achievement in the country's history when it elected Marie Cau as its mayor, the first town in the nation to do so." Stéphanie Nicot, co-founder of France's National Transgender Association, said the election showed that "our fellow citizens are more and more progressive." Is it "fellow citizens" or the ruling class's unceasing and all-encompassing campaign to transform society in its disgusting image?

In 2008 the UN Human Rights Committee urged Ireland to "recognize the right of transgender persons to a change of gender by permitting the issuance of new birth certificates," citing the rights to privacy, equality, and recognition before the law. If you can retroactively change your sex "at birth," you can change anything in history essentially.

Since 2009, "activists" in Norway, Germany, Sweden, Belgium, Ireland, Australia, and Scotland have made submissions raising legal gender recognition issues to the United Nations' Universal Periodic Review (UPR). The UN High Commissioner for Human Rights has recommended that states "facilitate legal recognition of the preferred gender of transgender persons." In 2011, the UN Committee on Economic, Social and Cultural Rights called on Germany to enact measures to protect the "personal integrity and sexual and reproductive health rights" of transgender and intersex individuals. In 2013, "trans activists" from the Ukrainian NGO Insight and Human Rights Watch participated in the UN Human Rights Committee's periodic review of Ukraine's compliance with the International Covenant on Civil and Political Rights (ICCPR).

In 2016, UNESCO organized "an international ministerial meeting to catalyse responses by its Member States to violence including bullying based on sexual orientation and gender identity/expression in education" on the International Day Against Homophobia and Transphobia (IDAHOT). In 2013, with support from the Government of the Netherlands, UNESCO launched the three-year project "Education and Respect for All: Preventing and Addressing Homophobic and Transphobic Bullying in Educational Institutions" in the regions of Asia-Pacific, Southern Africa,

Latin America, and the Caribbean. With the support of UNESCO, the International Lesbian, Gay, Bisexual, Transgender, Queer & Intersex Youth and Student Organization (IGLYO) organized in Brussels in January 2018 for a follow-up meeting to the Call for Action for European countries. In 2018, UNESCO worked with the Council of Europe to develop a European version of the Out in the Open report, and the year prior, at the invitation of UNDP and the World Bank, UNESCO chaired the expert working group on education for the development of an "international LGBTI Inclusion Index."

From 2011–2016, the IOM LGBTI Focal Point provided training on:

> Working with persons of diverse sex, sexual orientation and gender identity in the humanitarian context to nearly 1,500 staff members of IOM and 25 other organizations and entities, including UNHCR, other UN agencies, government representatives and NGOs, in 18 countries in the Americas, Europe, Africa, the Middle East and Asia.

The training sessions were between one and three days in length and included such topics as terminology, global issues, communication, creating safe spaces, conducting interviews, operational protection, resettlement, and travel and transit for LGBTQ migrants and refugees.

In 2015, the IOM appointed an LGBTI Focal Point who handles "programmatic and personnel questions related to migrants and staff members of diverse sex, sexual orientation and gender identity from throughout the organization." The LGBTI Focal Point is also the IOM's representative to UN-GLOBE:

> Advocating for the equality and non-discrimination of LGBTI staff in the UN system and its peacekeeping operations. . . . We will introduce proposals for inclusive workplaces for transgender and intersex staff members. . . . We will introduce proposals for inclusive workplaces for staff members with HIV/AIDS.

The IOM has made several policy changes related to LGBTQ staff issues, including on the provisions on rotation, recognition of spouses and partners in same-sex relationships (IN/225), and the inclusion of gender identity as a category protected by the Standards of Conduct (IN/15, Rev. 1).

In December 2016 and August 2017, the IOM and UNHCR held joint "training of trainers" sessions for 46 staff members from around the globe to deliver the training package. Since those Training of Trainer sessions, the certified IOM trainers have provided LGBTQ training for more than 300 staff members in ten countries with continued training for the IOM, UNHCR, and operating partners.

In 2017, the IOM hired its first Diversity Officer under the division of Human Resources Management. The Diversity Officer's portfolio includes: gender and geographical balance in the workforce and other diversity-related concerns, including improving the workplace for persons of diverse ability, sexual orientation, and gender identity.

For the International Day Against Homophobia, Transphobia, and Biphobia (IDAHOT) in recent years, the IOM has undertaken a wide range of activities, including a multi-agency panel discussion in Geneva, training sessions and global information dissemination to staff through a staff advisory and other means. The Director General released a video message to all staff members and the general public on "IOM and Working with LGBTI People in the Humanitarian Context" and the organization also produced an article for partners on the IOM's LGBTQ-related work and printed diversity and inclusion, "safe space workplace" and "LGBTI ally" posters, buttons, stickers, and bookmarks distributed to regional offices and digitally to staff worldwide.

UN Women states that:

LGBTI people's inclusion in economic and human development and the full realization of their human rights are strong imperatives for UN Women's engagement within the context of its mandate on advancing gender equality and women's empowerment. Therefore, UN Women works across its normative, UN coordination and operational roles to develop programming and advocacy that integrate LGBTI people's rights and perspectives, and has continued to expand its work on LGBTI issues.

UN Women has developed an internal Guidance Note on strengthening of programming and "advocacy" on the "rights and empowerment" of LGBTQ people, framed by "international human rights standards and the Agenda 2030." "Advocacy" and "advocate," like "activist," are increasingly being used in the business world as well ("activist investor," "customer advocate"), exhibiting further linkage.

UN Women states that it "integrates issues related to the human rights of LGBTI peoples into our work on civil society mobilization, especially given the intersectional lens of the [Sustainable Development Goals] SDGs." In its own words:

In addition to co-signing the Joint UN Statement, UN Women continues to issue public statements during IDAHOT, and during International Human Rights Day. UN Women's Executive Director regularly meets with the LGBTI caucus. UN Women aims to ensure that all civil society meetings convened by UN Women have intersectional representation, including from LGBTI groups, not just in the global meetings but also in the regional and country level meetings. UN Women also ensures that LGBTI voices are part of the formal mechanism of its Civil Society Advisory Groups at the global, regional and country levels; UN Women integrated its advocacy work on LGBTI rights into various forums of the 62nd session of the Commission on the Status of Women held in March 2018, where UN Women partnered with some LGBTI groups on flagship side events on Leaving No One Behind, which specifically had the marginalization of LGBTI people as a key focus area, and the Youth Dialogue, where Youth LGBTI civil society activists and leaders also played a key role.

For IDAHOT 2017, UN Women Pakistan together with several ambassadors and UN representatives signed an Op-Ed in Pakistan's major English language newspaper advocating for "transgender rights," which obviously are synonymous with women's rights, bigot!

The World Health Organization has been focusing heavily on key populations for

HIV: young men who have sex with men, young people who inject drugs, young transgender people, and young people who sell sex, as primary foci. This aspect of their extensive research dovetails with the role of big pharma *and* the cultivation of these particular population groups. Indeed, in the UN's own words, "Issues affecting LGBTI children (and the children of LGBTI parents) are cross-cutting and relevant to all areas of UNICEF programming, especially social inclusion, protection, health, HIV, and education." UNICEF's mandate is to "support the realization of the rights of all children," which they perversely interpret to include their "work *on* LGBTI children—and those who are perceived as LGBTI" (emphasis added).

One 2016 report from the United Nations lamented the fact that in 2013, "44 countries still impose restrictions on the entry, stay or residence of people living with HIV," and "60 per cent of Governments in 2012 reported the existence of laws and policies that present obstacles to effective prevention, treatment, care and support for people living with the human immunodeficiency virus (HIV)," again exhibiting the intersectional nature of this project and its luxuriating in spreading all that is defective and broken.

As we can see, even the containment of infectious diseases has been pathologized in order to avoid "discrimination," recently shown in addition to the litany of diseases ranging from HIV to the bubonic plague (yes, seriously) with the spread of the coronavirus, which was also enabled by the insistence especially in the United States, of economics over health and of course compounded by the ever-changing and contradictory press and "expert" organizations like the WHO, the woeful inadequacies of the American health care system, and the outsourcing of manufacturing and production to China and elsewhere. There are certainly other compelling interpretations of these events regarding its intentionality, but wherever one stands on it, the ideological and economic aspects worked in synergy, and when the virus turned out to be something quite different from the narrative, it was employed as a means of global policing and population control and a set-up to the World Economic Forum's "Great Reset." What is being communicated to us is that communicability is fine in all cases but where it has been greatly-exaggerated by the ruling class.

Furthermore, as we heard earlier from Columbus City Council President Shannon Hardin, racism is another public health crisis, as the AIDS Healthcare Foundation (AHF) also proclaimed, and they were not alone. For the record, the AHF's President and co-founder is Michael Weinstein, "born in Brooklyn's Bensonhurst neighborhood to a family of left-wing Jews." We also learned that the coronavirus itself is somehow racist! Together, they become still more lethal, and combined with climate change, these threat-multipliers know no bounds! People chucking used needles on the street on top of mounds of feces[123] in places like San Francisco is fine, though, as is anarchy, as long as it's communists (so long as they don't protest Wall Street or the WTO) and other "protected classes" doing the rioting/looting.

Nearly 1,300 public health and infectious diseases professionals, plus many other requisite stakeholders, including representatives from USC, UCLA, Harvard Medical School, Cornell University, Columbia University, the University of Chicago, and

---

[123] Speaking of feces, if you read Bill Gates's blog, you'll find several articles on how he is investing in technology to extract "clean drinking water" from human excreta. Add this to the maggots you'll be forced to eat in your little hovel surrounded by the Dinka tribe in Portland, Oregon while the developers get rich. You'll be allowed to watch Netflix, though.

Northwestern University signed off on the following open letter justifying Black Lives Matter protests' proliferation and incitement by the media at precisely the moment citizens were becoming genuinely furious with the draconian laws and the crippled economy, as well as while major financial institutions like BlackRock were involved in seismic backroom-dealing and consolidation that make the bailouts/incest of the Great Recession's "recovery" look like peanuts (and note how once again there are numerous references in the letter that align exactly with the UN's SDGs):

> White supremacy is a lethal public health issue that predates and contributes to COVID-19. . . . On April 30, heavily armed and predominantly white protesters entered the State Capitol building in Lansing, Michigan, protesting stay-home orders and calls for widespread public masking to prevent the spread of COVID-19. Infectious disease physicians and public health officials publicly condemned these actions and privately mourned the widening rift between leaders in science and a subset of the communities that they serve. As of May 30, we are witnessing continuing demonstrations in response to ongoing, pervasive, and lethal institutional racism set off by the killings of George Floyd and Breonna Taylor, among many other Black lives taken by police. A public health response to these demonstrations is also warranted, but this message must be wholly different from the response to white protesters resisting stay-home orders. Infectious disease and public health narratives adjacent to demonstrations against racism must be consciously anti-racist, and infectious disease experts must be clear and consistent in prioritizing an anti-racist message. . . . Black people suffer from dramatic health disparities in life expectancy, maternal and infant mortality, chronic medical conditions, and outcomes from acute illnesses like myocardial infarction and sepsis. Biological determinants are insufficient to explain these disparities. They result from long-standing systems of oppression and bias which have subjected people of color to discrimination in the healthcare setting, decreased access to medical care and healthy food, unsafe working conditions, mass incarceration, exposure to pollution and noise, and the toxic effects of stress.[124] Black people are also more likely to develop COVID-19. Black people with COVID-19 are diagnosed later in the disease course and have a higher rate of hospitalization, mechanical ventilation, and death. COVID-19 among Black patients is yet another lethal manifestation of white supremacy. In addressing demonstrations against white supremacy, our first statement must be one of unwavering support for those who would dismantle, uproot, or reform racist institutions. . . . As public health advocates, we do not condemn these gatherings as risky for COVID-19 transmission. We support them as vital to the national public health and to the threatened health specifically of Black people in the United States. . . . This should not be confused with a permissive stance on all gatherings, particularly protests against stay-home orders [so what, the virus takes a break when people are protesting "systemic racism"?]. Those actions not only oppose public health interventions, but are also rooted in white nationalism and run contrary to respect for Black lives. Protests against systemic racism, which fosters the disproportionate

---

[124] No evidence is provided to support this.

burden of COVID-19 on Black communities and also perpetuates police violence, must be supported.

Of course, then the virus has a greater chance to spread in such settings, and disproportionately affect blacks, to say nothing of self-loathing whites and various subnor-
mals protesting a fiction.

Then there was the Feminist Alliance for Rights' call for a "feminist COVID-19
policy," which included yet again the same demands in line with the UN's SDGs.
There is in fact a link to the UN's 2030 Agenda (the SDGs), and their staff's resumés
include the Office of the High Commissioner for Human Rights (OHCHR), Columbia University, the UN High Commissioner for Refugees (UNHCR), and the Asia
Foundation (recall who is behind the Asia Foundation and working with and for it,
and its CIA roots).

Speaking of the CIA, regarding Allen Weinstein's comments in 1991 that, "A lot
of what we do today was done covertly 25 years ago by the CIA," about the National
Endowment for Democracy, well, the CIA is still doing its thing, too; the CIA and
the Office of the Director for National Intelligence (ODNI) hosted the first IC (Intelligence Community) LGBT Summit in 2012,[125] and for Corey Lynn:

> That same year, [the CIA] became a corporate sponsor of STEM at an LGBT
> national conference held in Chicago. This is especially interesting, because
> the Clinton Global Initiative, along with AbbVie (producer of Lupron puberty
> blockers), Takeda Pharmaceutical Company (teamed with AbbVie in puberty
> blockers), Microsoft, and others got involved with STEM in Chicago that
> following year, in 2013. . . . That is an interesting combination of organiza-
> tions, LGBT, CIA, and puberty blocker manufacturers all involved with
> STEM in Chicago. Curious.

This is about power and control by the so-called "elite," but it goes even deeper and
darker than that in its all-encompassing constriction and malevolence.

---

[125] From Intelligence.gov: "The annual IC LGBTA Summit has roots in ANGLE—the Agency Network
of Gay and Lesbian Employees—the IC's first LGBTQ+ employee resource group, formed at [the] CIA
in 1996 . . . IC LGBTA Summits have been hosted by CIA, NGA, NSA, NRO, DIA, and FBI in 2017 . . .
Among their other accomplishments to date, IC Pride has formed the first IC-wide transgender working
group, partnered with ODNI [Office of the Director for National Intelligence] to develop agency policy
guidance for the inclusion of transgender and gender nonconforming employees, and developed an ally
training module for IC executive leaders, which they delivered in the Washington, DC, area as well as to
Military Combatant Command Headquarters and Military Intelligence Centers."

# Conclusion

*"Inconspicuous, slow, yet implacable persecution, both economic and cultural: the systematic suppression of all possibilities for the vanquished, without it 'showing,' the merciless 'conditioning' of children, all the more horrible that it is more impersonal, more indirect, more outwardly 'gentle,' the clever diffusion of soul-killing lies; violence under the cover of non-violence."*

– Savitri Devi

Throughout this book, we have explored the "violence under the cover of non-violence" that is the Transgender-Industrial Complex, as it pertains both to transgenderism and all its connected "movements." We have followed the money, identified the culprits, and still, there are more questions, more dots left unconnected. This is a behemoth so vast and insidious that its breadth cannot be fully described in this work, but I do hope the reader takes these findings as a whole and is able to come to this conclusion: the LGBTQ agenda is not grassroots but a propaganda machine that works in tandem with many other facets of the Jewish liberal world for evil purposes—the whole monster is anti-national, anti-white, anti-Christian, anti-natal. We have seen time and again who exactly is pushing and funding this and why. In this last chapter, I will present even more findings to support that end, but there is much more out there.

On its website, the World Health Organization (WHO) lists WPATH, GATE, Transgender Europe, and the UCSF Center of Excellence for Transgender Health under "Useful Links." UCSF's Center of Excellence for Transgender Health (Trans CoE) was founded in 2009 with a mission to:

> Advance health equity for trans and gender non-binary communities. . . . The Center of Excellence for Transgender Health (CoE) envisions a safe and affirming world, free from all oppressions, where trans and gender non-binary communities are healthy and thriving.

It is housed in UCSF's Department of Medicine, Division of Prevention Science along with the UCSF Prevention Research Center and the UCSF Center for AIDS Prevention Studies, the latter of which collaborates with the Transgender Center of Excellence along with UCSF Transgender Care ("a multidisciplinary program consisting of experts in transgender medicine and surgery at UCSF Medical Center") and Pacific AIDS Education and Training Center, which is itself supported by the Health Resources and Services Administration (HRSA) of the US Department of Health and Human Services (HHS).

UCSF is one of the most significant universities/hubs for the transgender agenda. We've seen quite a bit of its involvement already, but unfortunately not all of it. In 2007, on the back of a $25 million donation from the Lisa and John Pritzker Family

Fund, UCSF announced the formation of the Pritzker Center specializing in child and adolescent mental health services, combining and expanding the programs and services of San Francisco General Hospital Medical Center and the specialty clinics, training, and research of UCSF's Langley Porter Psychiatric Institute (LPPI) into one cohesive program and building, with Tipper Gore Chair of the Center's leadership council. The project went through the early development stages but appears to have stalled. Still, over $51 million went to UCSF from the Lisa and John Pritzker Family Fund in fiscal year 2015, in addition to donations of over $30 million from the Bill and Melinda Gates Foundation and over $124 million from The Atlantic Philanthropies, so central to the LGBTQ agenda in Ireland.

Fiscal year 2018 saw approaching $23 million go to UCSF from the Gates Foundation. Also in fiscal year 2018, the Helen Diller Foundation awarded a massive $500 million to UCSF. The Foundation sponsors the Tikkun Olam Awards, run by Program Director Erica Aren, formerly of the American Jewish World Service, whose work "examine[s] experiential education through the lens of equity and social justice." The Diller Family Foundation states that it "knows that supporting Jewish teen leadership today means creating and inspiring future generations of strong Jewish leaders in the global community."

"The Diller family's tremendous support will enable us to accelerate the planning process for a hospital at Parnassus Heights that meets the high demand we experience at UCSF for the comprehensive care we provide," said Mark R. Laret, President and CEO of UCSF Health, which includes UCSF Medical Center, UCSF Benioff Children's Hospitals, and other partners and affiliates in the Bay Area.

The Jewish Benjamin N. Breyer is chief of urology at San Francisco General Hospital and is also a professor at UCSF, specializing in transgender surgery. Jewish colleagues Stephen M. Rosenthal and Diane Ehrensaft have worked with hundreds of minors in the UCSF Child and Adolescent Gender Center Clinic. Ehrensaft, a developmental and clinical psychologist, says that out of the hundreds of patients she has seen, only one has ever regretted a medical transition:

> [Her work] helps unlock the door to a gender-expansive world, revealing pathways for positive change in schools, the community, and the world at large. Fueled by over three decades of pioneering work, she explores the interconnected effects of nature, nurture, and culture to explore and explain gender fluidity.

Rosenthal was one of four principal investigators for "The Impact of Early Medical Treatment in Transgender Youth" sponsored by the National Institutes of Health and the Eunice Kennedy Shriver National Institute of Child Health and Human Development. Rosenthal (Columbia University alumnus) was instrumental in the founding of the UCSF Child and Adolescent Gender Center (CAGC), described as:

> A collaboration between UCSF and community organizations, offers comprehensive medical and psychological care, as well as advocacy and legal support, to gender non-conforming/transgender youth and adolescents. A central component of this program is the UCSF CAGC Clinic, housed in the Division of Pediatric Endocrinology.

Rosenthal is the Medical Director of the CAGC and Ehrensaft is the Mental Health Director of the CAGC.

Rosenthal also directs a collaboration with the San Francisco Department of Public Health to "develop community outreach services for gender-diverse youths" and is on the Board of Directors of the Endocrine Society. For Rosenthal, "When I think about why this work touches me deeply, it's because I'm gay and was a bit gender nonconforming in my own right as a young kid." The Clinical Director of the Child and Adolescent Gender Center (CAGC) at UCSF Benioff Children's Hospital Oakland affiliate Rachel Kadakia's fellowship and residency were at Northwestern University/Ann and Robert H. Lurie Children's Hospital.

The UCSF Benioff Children's Hospitals owe a great debt to the Jewish founder, Chairman, and CEO of Salesforce Marc Benioff, who is also on the USC Board of Trustees. To date, Benioff and his wife have given more than $250 million to the University of California-San Francisco for the UCSF Benioff Children's Hospitals. Martin Collier is an Advisory Board member of the UCSF Global Health Group, as well as a member of the Glaser Progress Foundation (established by Rob Glaser), a member of the Global Fund private foundation constituency group, an Advisory Board member of the University of Washington Evans School of Public Affairs, and a member of New Media Mentors, which runs training programs for "progressive" NGOs. New Media Mentors is headed by the Jewish Elana Levin and Liza Pike, formerly with the Natural Resources Defense Council.

Rob Glaser[126] is also a major donor to America Votes, "the coordination hub of the progressive community," which has also received major funding from homosexual "activists"/bankrollers Jon Stryker and Fred Eychaner, and whose national partners include the HRC, EMILY's List, the Sierra Club, Planned Parenthood, the League of Conservation Voters, the American Federation of Teachers, Bend the Arc: Jewish Action, Michael Bloomberg's Everytown for Gun Safety, and the LGBTQ Victory Fund.

In 2008 the Glaser Progress Foundation announced its creation of the Global Health Leadership Institute in partnership with the Yale School of Public Health, "conven[ing] leaders in public health from a group of countries that have demonstrated momentum in strengthening their health care systems, a fundamental goal set out by the World Health Organization and the World Bank."

The Glaser Progress Foundation also provided the initial seed money, with Pfizer and the MAC AIDS Fund as other donors, to the Access Project, primarily-focused in Rwanda and co-founded by Glaser and his foundation along with Columbia University under the auspices of its Earth Institute and the Center for Global Health and Economic Development (which was subsequently moved to the Center for Sustain-

---

[126] Rogers, Ray, "17 Top Music Execs.": "The annual UJA-Federation Music Visionary of the Year Awards luncheon has become the music industry's hot-ticket charity event. With proceeds going to the largest local philanthropic organization in the world (United Jewish Appeal-Federation of Jewish Philanthropies of New York, founded in 1917), top executives are happy to fork it over during the high-profile gathering. 'Our music visionaries are the most important carriers of our message,' says UJA-Federation of New York CEO Eric S. Goldstein, 55 . . . Seventeen of the past UJA-Federation music visionaries photographed on Sept. 24 at The Pierre hotel in New York. In the back row, from left: Julie Greenwald, Daniel Glass, Joel Katz, Neil Portnow, Charlie Feldman, Cary Sherman, Rob Glaser, Fred Davis, Amy Doyle and Jason Flom. In the middle, from left: Avery and Monte Lipman. In the front, from left: Kevin Liles, Craig Kallman, Barry Weiss, Lyor Cohen and Rick Krim."

able Development), and individuals Jeffrey Sachs and Joshua Ruxin in 2002. In December 2013 the Earth Institute's affiliation ended, and in 2014 the infrastructure of Access Project was absorbed by Rwanda Works (founded by Ruxin), which is now Health Builders.

According to *The New York Times* Weddings/Celebrations notice from July 17th, 2005 for the Access Project's co-founder and initial Director Joshua Ruxin and his wife Alissa:

> Alissa Aimée Carlat and Joshua Nalibow Ruxin were married at Clay Head Beach on Block Island on Wednesday by John A.L. Sisto, a town warden of New Shoreham, R.I. Yesterday Daniel J. Carlat, the bride's brother, led a ceremony that drew on Jewish tradition at Sullivan House, a bed-and-breakfast in New Shoreham. Mrs. Ruxin, 30, works as a health-services administrator in New York for CHD Meridian Healthcare, which manages corporate health-care programs and centers. She graduated from Wellesley and received a master's degree in public health from Harvard. She is a daughter of Aurèle and Paul Carlat of San Francisco. Mr. Ruxin, 35, is an assistant clinical professor of public health at the Mailman School of Public Health at Columbia. He is also a project director at the Earth Institute there, working on health systems for the poor in developing nations and leading projects in Nigeria, Kenya, Rwanda and Ethiopia. He is also a chairman of the Task Force on H.I.V./AIDS of the United Nations Millennium Project. The bridegroom, a graduate of Yale, received a master's degree in public health from Columbia and a PhD. in the history of medicine from University College London, where he was a Marshall scholar. In the 1992–93 academic year, he was a Fulbright scholar in La Paz, Bolivia, studying women's reproductive health.

Ruxin was on the faculty at the Mailman School of Public Health at Columbia University. He created Columbia University's first multi-disciplinary course focused on addressing the challenges to achieving the UN's Millennium Development Goals. Ruxin is co-founder and Executive Chairman of GoodLife Pharmacy, a pharmaceuticals chain in Kenya and Uganda. Per the archived Access Project website from February 2012:

> Josh currently oversees an array of initiatives in health, microfinance, agriculture, education, water and sanitation, and is responsible for infrastructure build-out for solar energy, electrification, water points, and transportation. Previously, Josh was co-founder and vice president of ontheFRONTIER, a strategy consulting firm based in Boston, Massachusetts. During his five years there and at Monitor Group, he led projects in a dozen developing countries and was an advisor to government and private sector leaders on business strategy and economic development.

Before we return to the Access Project, another interesting vector here is Blue Haven Initiatives with Liesel Pritzker Simmons as co-founder and principal. Pritzker Simmons is a Columbia University alumnus. Blue Haven's strategic partners include the Omidyar Network, the Shell Foundation, and the US Global Development Lab ("powered by USAID")—we know that USAID and the World Bank have been using microfinance to facilitate mass migration from Central America into the United States.

Blue Haven Senior Advisor Chad Larson was instrumental in pioneering digitized payments in Kenya for solar panels and accessories as co-founder of M-KOPA Solar. As it intersects, for Stephan Faris:

> In 2007 the Kenyan mobile operator Safaricom launched a service called M-Pesa, allowing customers to use a phone to send cash. Originally intended as a way to help microfinance borrowers make and repay loans, M-Pesa was rapidly adopted for everything from salaries to taxi rides, bringing banking to people who were miles from physical bank branches. Today about a third of the Kenyan economy flits across Safaricom's airwaves, and 82 percent of Kenyan adults have a mobile phone. . . . Slogans hand-painted on concrete buildings hawk the power of the Internet in the service of selling smartphones: "Take Google With You" and "You Are Not on Facebook. . . ?" It was [M-KOPA co-founder Nick] Hughes, when he was an executive at Vodafone—which owns 40 percent of Safaricom—who first came up with the idea that would become M-Pesa. M-Kopa's director of operations, Pauline Vaughan, was in charge of the mobile-money service during its early years. . . . In November [2015], M-Kopa received a clear vote of confidence when it completed a $19 million investment round, including $10 million from Generation Investment Management, a fund co-founded by former U.S. Vice President Al Gore that's also invested in SolarCity, the biggest U.S. rooftop solar installer, and digital thermostat maker Nest Labs [acquired by Google in January 2014] . . . . Other investors in the round included Virgin's Richard Branson and AOL co-founder Steve Case.

According to an archived version of the Access Project's website from 2011, "In its first phase, with less than a million dollars, the Access Project successfully leveraged over one billion dollars for AIDS, tuberculosis, and malaria programs from the Global Fund." The site continues:

> The project first helped Rwanda attract Global Fund financing and aided the country in its scale-up of voluntary counseling and testing for HIV. Between 2003 and 2004, in partnership with the Government of Rwanda, the Access Project helped expand the number of testing sites from two to more than 70. . . . Through the Neglected Tropical Disease program, the Access Project is working with the Rwanda Ministry of Health, the Ministry of Education and the World Health Organization to develop a national plan for carrying out necessary interventions at the district level. The plan includes connecting health centers across the country with the research, interventions and training needed to fight these diseases.

The Glaser Progress Foundation expands:

> In 2006 when the Rwandan government decentralized, the Ministry of Health asked Access to provide management technical assistance to health centers at

the local level. Access worked in the Rwandan Ministry of Health office to implement the national decentralization strategy; helped design the TRACnet phone and web-based ART surveillance program [and] helped establish over 200 Voluntary Counseling and Testing Centers nationwide.

Karen Schmidt was the Deputy Director of the Access Project and Millennium Villages Rwanda. According to the archived website, prior to joining the Access Project, Schmidt was:

In Kenya as a Michigan Population Fellow with Program for Appropriate Technology in Health (PATH). With PATH, she worked primarily on the USAID-funded IMPACT project, using behavior change communication for the prevention of HIV and STD's. Focused on adolescent reproductive health, Karen developed a life skills education comic book for girls and young women (partnering with the Kenya Girl Guides Association), and helped develop a program to increase adolescents' access to reproductive health services through private pharmacies. She also managed the development of a behavior change communication strategy and program to improve TB treatment seeking and adherence. Before going to Kenya, Karen worked as the Community Director for Yale University's Center for Interdisciplinary Research on AIDS. Karen also worked as an independent public health consultant for PATH, Family Care International, and Family Health International. Projects included documentation of HIV and AIDS programs in Ethiopia and the Philippines, and research on long-term and permanent contraception in Malawi. Karen earned her M.P.H. at Yale University, where she conducted her master's thesis research on infant feeding decisions in settings with high HIV prevalence. She also holds an M.S. in Journalism from Columbia University, and worked as a newspaper and radio journalist for more than 10 years.

Affiliated project partners listed include Pfizer's Global Health Fellows (GHF) Program, the Elizabeth Glaser Pediatric AIDS Foundation (EGPAF), and IntraHealth in addition to the Global Fund and Columbia's Earth Institute, among others.

IntraHealth is supported by the Gates Foundation, the CDC, USAID, Qualcomm, Pfizer, the Tides Foundation, the David and Lucile Packard Foundation, the NIH, the William and Flora Hewlett Foundation, the UK's DFID, the UN High Commissioner for Refugees, the World Bank, and the World Health Organization. They are committed to "promoting gender equality as an integral part of our work, recognizing that if gender-based disparities and inequalities are not addressed they may undermine the achievement of health care program, service delivery, and development goals."

Columbia's Earth Institute comprises more than thirty research centers and some 850 scientists, postdoctoral fellows, staff, and students. Working across many disciplines, it studies and "create[s] solutions for problems in public health, poverty, energy, ecosystems, climate, natural hazards and urbanization." The Earth Institute's "experts work hand-in-hand with academia, corporations, government agencies, nonprofits and individuals. They advise national governments and the United Nations on issues related to sustainable development." External Advisors have included

Jared Diamond, Harold Varmus (UCSF, WHO, Council on Foreign Relations), Bono, Sean Solomon (MIT), and George Soros.

Adam Pritzker studied under Jeffrey Sachs at Columbia and went on to work for him at the Earth Institute. In October 2017, Pritzker partnered with Sachs and Daniel Squadron, whose father was Chairman of the Conference of Presidents of Major American Jewish Organizations, to form Future Now, which is focused on funding political candidates who are committed to working toward the UN's Sustainable Development Goals/Agenda 2030. Director of Policy and Legal Lauren Popper Ellis is an alum of Harvard and Yale, and her husband Michael Ellis is also a Harvard alum and is the founder of the Lithuania Project, a New York organization that provides financial support for the Jewish community in Lithuania, as well as for its historic sites. COO Seisei Tatebe-Goddu has an MA from Columbia, Jewish author Gayle Forman is a Board member, and Board member Deborah Simon has been involved with the ACLU and Planned Parenthood. Simon is the daughter of deceased Jewish billionaire and Indiana Pacers NBA franchise co-owner Melvin Simon. Planned Parenthood Board of Directors member and the founder and former CEO of transgender recruitment tool Tumblr David Karp is also a Board member and is the Technology Advisor. While with Tumblr, Karp announced an initiative with Planned Parenthood calling on the tech industry to lend more support to Planned Parenthood. Karp's father is Jewish.

Prominent Earth Institute faculty from 2011 include (with excerpted bios reflecting that year):

- Joel E. Cohen, also Head of the Laboratory of Populations at the Rockefeller University: Dr. Cohen's laboratory also studies international migration in collaboration with colleagues at the United Nations Population Division. Newly developed mathematical and statistical models make it possible to account for more than half of the variability in the annual numbers of migrants among 229 countries or regions from 1960 to 2004. These models can be incorporated in deterministic or probabilistic population projections in combination with standard demographic techniques for projecting births and deaths.
- Richard Deckelbaum, Professor of Epidemiology-Mailman School of Public Health, Robert R. Williams Professor of Nutrition in Pediatrics-College of Physicians and Surgeons, Director-Institute for Human Nutrition; He has also led international NIH and USAID programs
- Steven L. Goldstein, Chair and Professor-Department of Earth and Environmental Sciences
- Michael Gerrard, Professor of Professional Practice-Columbia Law School-Director, Center for Climate Change Law (CCCL) at Columbia Law School; Through CCCL, which he launched in January 2009, Gerrard helps train the next generation of leaders in climate change law. With the aim of influencing key decision makers, bringing the latest scientific knowledge into the regulatory system, and developing innovative legal tools to combat climate change and promote sustainable development practices, CCCL is collaborating closely with the Earth Institute and the United Nations.

The Director of Columbia University's Earth Institute from 2002–2016 was the Jewish Harvard graduate Jeffrey Sachs, who had previously helmed the Harvard Institute for International Development (HIID) at the Kennedy School of Government before leaving it just prior to its being shuttered to run Harvard's Center for International Development. The HIID has an extremely interesting history, via Wikipedia:

> The Harvard Institute for International Development originated when Harvard University's Center for International Affairs (CFIA) tried to move away from a controversial role in giving advice on topics such as arms control, foreign aid and development. The CFIA preferred a more academic role of teaching and research. The Ford Foundation and other organizations involved in aid-giving still wanted Harvard to provide hands-on training for their staff. In 1962 the Development Advisory Service was established for this purpose, associated with the CFIA but independent. It was renamed the HIID in 1974. In 1980 the economist Arnold Harberger[127] was selected as head of the institute. . . . He withdrew and Dwight Perkins,[128] an economist and specialist in China, took the job. After the collapse of the Soviet Union, the economist Jeffrey Sachs became head of the institute. . . . In the late 1970s David Korten headed a project funded by the Ford Foundation to assist in organization and management of national family-planning programs. . . . The HIID collaborated with the Women In Development office of USAID in developing the Harvard Analytical Framework, also called the Gender Roles Framework, one of the earliest frameworks for understanding differences between men and women in their participation in the economy. This has great importance in helping policy makers understand the economic case for allocating resources to women as well as men. The framework was described in 1984. . . . In mid-1998 the World Economic Forum [currently the central fixture in formulating and implementing the next globalist evolution in "The Great Reset"] and HIID assembled a team of experts to determine the causes of the Asian financial crisis and the mechanisms of the crisis, to determine methods of reducing the probability of similar crises in the future and to identify policy changes that would help the affected countries resume growth. In the late 1990s, USAID sponsored the Equity and Growth through Economic Research (AGER) project. . . . With the collapse of the Soviet Union, USAID funded a project by the HIID to help rebuild the Russian economy on the basis of western concepts of ethics, democracy and free markets. Jeffrey Sachs was said to have "packaged HIID as an AID consultant." USAID were glad to accept help from Harvard. . . . In 1997, USAID ended a $14 million grant to the Harvard Institute for International Development after [the Jewish] Andrei Shleifer was accused of using the institute to help his wife [the Jewish] Nancy Zimmerman's investments in Russia.

After leaving the Earth Institute, Sachs was appointed to a two-year fellowship at the Arnhold Institute at the Icahn School of Medicine at Mt. Sinai Hospital. Today, Sachs has returned to Columbia to helm the Center for Sustainable Development.

---

[127] University of Chicago, Johns Hopkins, UCLA.
[128] Cornell, Harvard.

Sachs was instrumental in "advising" former Eastern Bloc countries in their rapid transition to capitalism, namely those of Poland, Slovenia, Estonia, and Russia. Sachs was the main architect of Poland's debt reduction plan and teamed up with David Lipton of the IMF on facilitating the rapid conversion of all property and assets from public to private ownership.

Sachs was also as we've seen central in the "transitioning" of Russia to a capitalist economy, serving as an advisor and offering institutional support during the introduction of the shock therapy "reforms" of the early 1990s. We all know what happened to Russia over the rest of the decade. Sachs has also been an advisor to the WHO, the IMF, the World Bank, the UNDP, and the OECD, was Special Advisor to then-United Nations Secretary-General Ban Ki-moon, and from 2002–2006 was Director of the UN Millennium Project and Special Advisor to then-United Nations Secretary-General Kofi Annan on the Millennium Development Goals.

Additionally, Sachs was also involved in the formation of the Global Fund, and as a major proponent of the Sustainable Development Goals has endeavored to incorporate their mission into his various projects such as the Deep Decarbonization Pathways Project. "The arithmetic is really brutal," he says. "We're in such a dreadful situation that every country has to make this transformation, or else this isn't going to work."

Yet another Sachs project was the Millennium Villages Project, a sort of trial run in different African locations for the kinds of initiatives the ruling class is planning on implementing globally; the intent was to display an "integrated approach to rural development" as it aligned with the Millennium Development Goals, which were the precursor to the current Sustainable Development Goals/Agenda 2030. Ruxin was also involved, as his Access Project biography states:

> The MV Project uses a revolutionary and integrated approach to demonstrate that substantive and rapid investments in human development can help poor communities achieve all the Millennium Development Goals in less than five years. In Rwanda, this unique government-led project was designed in cooperation with seven government ministries. It has implemented agricultural interventions that have resulted in a ten-fold increase in maize production between 2005 and 2006. Josh also instituted the first project-wide seed and fertilizer loan program.

As Celia Dugger wrote about the project in 2006:

> Mr. Sachs said he believed that just as donors' spending on global health in recent years had reduced deaths that could be prevented with vaccines, mosquito nets and AIDS drugs, so it could help jump-start economic growth in rural areas through the distribution of fertilizers, higher-yielding seeds and inexpensive small-scale irrigation methods.

Columbia's Earth Institute was a founding partner and George Soros contributed $50 million to the project. Other major partners and/or supporters included: Monsanto, Nestlé, Unilever, the World Bank, Facebook, GlaxoSmithKline, Goldman Sachs, the Glaser Progress Foundation, a number of governments, the William and Flora Hewlett Foundation, the MacArthur Foundation, the Merck Company Foundation, the Nike Foundation, the PepsiCo Foundation, the David and Lucille Packard Foundation, the Albert B. Sabin Vaccine Institute, Sanofi Aventis, Procter & Gamble, the Rockefeller Foundation, the United Nations Foundation, UN World Food Program, UNAIDS, UNFPA, UNOPS, UNICEF, Sony Mobile, the Tides Foundation, Tyson Foods, and Sumitomo Chemical.

Sachs worked with senior officials of the George W. Bush administration to help develop the PEPFAR program, via Wikipedia:

> Housed in the Department of State, the Office of the Global AIDS Coordinator oversees the implementation of PEPFAR and ensures coordination among the various agencies involved in the U.S global response to HIV/AIDS. United States Ambassadors from the State Department provide essential leadership to interagency HIV/AIDS teams and engage in policy discussions with host-country leaders. . . . USAID supports the implementation of PEPFAR programs in nearly 100 countries, through direct in-country presence in 50 countries and through seven other regional programs. . . . Under PEPFAR, the Department of Health and Human Services (HHS) implements PEPFAR-funded prevention, treatment and care programs through the Centers for Disease Control and Prevention (CDC), National Institutes of Health (NIH), Health Resources and Services Administration (HRSA), Food and Drug Administration (FDA), and Substance Abuse and Mental Health Services Administration (SAMHSA). . . . The Centers for Disease Control and Prevention uses PEPFAR funding to implement its Global AIDS Program (GAP). GAP works with highly trained physicians, epidemiologists, public health advisers, behavioral scientists, and laboratory scientists in 29 countries, who are part of USG teams implementing PEPFAR. Through partnerships with host governments, Ministries of Health, NGOs, international organizations, U.S.-based universities, and the private sector, GAP assists with HIV prevention, treatment, and care; laboratory capacity building; surveillance; monitoring and evaluation; and public health evaluation research. . . . The Department of Defense (DoD) implements PEPFAR programs by supporting HIV/AIDS prevention, treatment, care, strategic information, human capacity development and program/policy development in host military and civilian communities. The DoD HIV/AIDS Prevention Program (DHAPP) is the DoD Executive Agent for the technical assistance, management, and administrative support of the global HIV/AIDS prevention, care and treatment for foreign militaries.

Lisa Sachs is the Director of the Columbia Center on Sustainable Investment. According to her biographical description through the Center:

> She teaches a masters seminar at Columbia Law School and Columbia's School of International and Public Affairs on Extractive Industries and Sustainable Development, and lectures at Externado University in Colombia on International Investment Law. She has served on World Economic Forum Global Future Councils on International Governance and on Mining & Metals, and is a co-chair of the UN Sustainable Development Solutions Net-

work's thematic group on the Good Governance of Extractive and Land Resources. She is a 2020–2021 Senior Fellow of NAFSA: Association of International Educators, and sits on several advisory boards, including of the Investor Alliance for Human Rights and SDGAcademy. Before joining CCSI, she worked at the Interfaith Center on Corporate Responsibility and at Amnesty USA, in both cases on shareholder engagement. She received a Bachelor of Arts in Economics from Harvard University, and earned her Juris Doctor and a Masters degree in International Affairs from Columbia University, where she was a James Kent Scholar and recipient of the Parker School Certificate in International and Comparative Law.

Returning to UCSF, six of the nine affiliated members of the UCSF Child and Adolescent Gender Center Clinic are Jewish: Rosenthal, Ehrensaft, Joel Baum, Asaf Orr, J. Jessie Rose Cohen ("a transgender, nonbinary-identified social worker"), and Mere Abrams (another transgender social worker). A seventh, Erica Anderson, psychologist, is a lesbian and is married to a Jewish woman—they have two children who they raised Jewish. Anderson is the USPATH representative on the WPATH Board of Directors.

JoAnne Keatley is Director Emeritus of UCSF's Center of Excellence for Transgender Health and is Co-Chair of IRGT: A Global Network of Transgender Women and HIV which features members from India, South Africa, Guyana, Zambia, the UK, Mexico, and more. Like many of these organizations such as the Global Fund, IRGT also devotes considerable resources to data collection and monitoring. In its Strategic Objectives, IRGT states:

> We are human beings functioning within particular social, political and economic realities. This said, it is important to recognize the intersectionalities that shape our access to health services. The law is often a barrier to accessing comprehensive sexual and reproductive health services for trans women. For this reason, we must ensure that trans women's health promotion initiatives are underpinned by a Human Rights ideology.

The IRGT hosted what they believe to be the first ever transgender networking zone during the International AIDS Conference in Melbourne in 2014, a conference which featured speakers such as Bill Clinton and Richard Branson.

IRGT is part of a consortium of similar organizations such as MPact (receiving additional funding from the Elton John AIDS Foundation, PEPFAR, UNAIDS, the Global Fund, Gilead Sciences, ViiV Healthcare, the Ministry of Foreign Affairs of the Netherlands, the WHO, and USAID; MPact is an organizer of the HIV2020 Conference along with organizations such as the International Network of People who Use Drugs, with financial support from ViiV, Gilead Sciences, UNAIDS, the Open Society Foundations, and more) operating in part on grants from the Robert Carr Fund, which invests in organizations and networks "that address the health and human rights of inadequately served populations (ISPs)," which are considered to be: migrants ("Migrants may have higher HIV risks because of exposure to new sexual partners and networks"), prisoners, women and girls, youth, transgender and intersex people, people living with HIV, sex workers, people who use drugs, and gay and bisexual men "and other men who have sex with men." The Robert

Carr Fund receives funding from the Ministry of Foreign Affairs of the Netherlands, PEPFAR, UKAID, UNAIDS, the Norwegian Agency for Development Cooperation (NORAD), and the Gates Foundation.

Keatley has consulted on transgender health for the World Health Organization, the NIH, CDC, HRSA, SAMHSA, and the White House. In partnership with the Pan American Health Organization (PAHO), Keatley co-authored the PAHO document "Blueprint for the Provision of Comprehensive Care to Transgender and Transsexual persons and their communities in Latin America and the Caribbean."

Like Keatley, Scott Leibowitz is also affiliated with the National LGBTQIA+ Health Education Center, a program of the Fenway Institute; he received a bachelor's degree in human development from Cornell University and his medical degree from the Sackler School of Medicine's American program of Tel Aviv University. He served residencies at the Zucker Hillside Hospital in Queens and the Long Island Jewish Health System at the Albert Einstein College of Medicine. Then, he says, "I heard about a new gender program in endocrinology at Boston Children's Hospital," the Disorders of Sex Development and Gender Management Service, which also is affiliated with Harvard Medical School, the first multidisciplinary clinic of its kind. Along with prescribing HRT, the program also incorporates urology, clinical genetics, social work, and psychology into its practice. "As a gay man who has a sense of what it means to be marginalized and bullied during childhood and adolescence . . . I was interested in LGBT issues," Leibowitz says. He was a co-investigator on a major National Institutes of Health-funded grant for multisite longitudinal research on transgender youth, which involved Boston, Chicago, San Francisco, and Los Angeles sites, and at both Boston Children's Hospital and Lurie Children's Hospital of Chicago, Leibowitz states that he worked with hundreds of children, some as young as four.

Leibowitz is the Co-Chairman of the Sexual Orientation and Gender Identity Issues Committee for the American Academy of Child and Adolescent Psychiatry and is the lead trainer for childhood and adolescence for WPATH's Global Education Initiative. Leibowitz is the Medical Director of Behavioral Health Services for the THRIVE Program—a multidisciplinary gender identity clinic at Nationwide Children's Hospital in Columbus, Ohio—and Associate Professor of Psychiatry at the Ohio State University College of Medicine.

Gender Spectrum in California is another of the many organizations that have been very active in pushing transgenderism, featuring the Jewish Joel Baum, Director of Advocacy with the Child and Adolescent Gender Center Clinic at UCSF and Senior Director of Professional Development at Gender Spectrum. Gender Spectrum claims to have worked with over three million children, and when we look at some of their partnering organizations, we can see this may well be so: the National Association of Elementary School Principals, Teach for America, Massachusetts Department of Elementary and Secondary Education, the California Department of Public Health, Saint Anselm College (NH) Nursing Education, Planned Parenthood, the CDC, Apple, Blue Shield, the Palo Alto Medical Foundation, the US Citizenship and Immigration Service, Mexico City's Council for the Prevention and Elimination of Discrimination (COPRED), the National Association of Independent Schools, the National Alliance for Public Charter Schools, Big Brothers Big Sisters, Lucile Packard Children's Hospital-Stanford, and California State PTA.

The Jewish Community Federation and Endowment Fund of San Francisco, the

Peninsula, Marin, and Sonoma Counties has also donated over $1 million to Gender Spectrum. Then there are the other donations to major players in the institutionalization of transgenderism, such as Boston Children's Hospital, the Children's Hospital of Los Angeles, USC, UCLA, Washington University, and the UCSF Benioff Children's Hospitals Foundation on top of the over $13.5 million they've donated to the UCSF Foundation and the UC Regents General Endowment Pool, not to mention the UCSF Osher Center for Integrative Medicine. They've also donated to Cornell University, which houses the Sackler Institute for Developmental Psychobiology—there's another one at Columbia University—and is part of the Pritzker Neuropsychiatric Disorders Research Consortium with Stanford (which has also received over $5 million from the Jewish Community Federation and Endowment Fund of San Francisco, the Peninsula, Marin and Sonoma Counties), UC Irvine, the University of Michigan, and the HudsonAlpha Institute for Biotechnology.

The Gender Dysphoria Affirmative (GDA) Working Group's membership includes figures such as Johanna Olson-Kennedy, Diane Ehrensaft, and Stephen M. Rosenthal; other prominent Jewish figures pushing and profiting from the transgender agenda such as Randi Kaufman and Rachel Lynn Golden; alums of Boston Children's Hospital and other transgender incubators such as UCSF, Northwestern's Feinberg School of Medicine, the Ann & Robert H. Lurie Children's Hospital; and international representatives from Switzerland, Canada, Norway, the UK, and Australia.

Ehrensaft's most recent book, *The Gender Creative Child*, acts as a "guide for parents who are raising children in a time of progressive change in cultural, medical and legal ideas of gender and identity." Ehrensaft says, "We have lifted the lid culturally." The foreword to *The Gender Creative Child* was written by the Jewish Norman Spack, co-founder of the world's first child-specific "gender clinic" in Boston, Massachusetts in the form of the Gender Management Service in 2007. Since its founding, "we have expanded our program to welcome patients from ages 3 to 25." As Gudrun Schultz reports (emphasis added):

> Led by endocrinologist Dr. Norman Spack, the Gender Management Service Clinic is the first U.S. clinic to initiate medical intervention for healthy children on the basis of a "transgender" identification. A 12-year-old German boy who began receiving puberty-blocking hormone treatments last winter (2006) in preparation for sex-change "transition" surgery was believed to be the youngest child to receive the treatment at the time. The Boston clinic will reportedly offer the treatments to children as young as seven years old. . . . *Dr. Spack's interest in transgender issues has included association with bondage and sadomasochistic groups—he presented a workshop at the Transcending Boundaries conference in Worcester . . . organized by PFLAG and co-sponsored by the New England Leather Alliance.*

These are the people lecturing us on morality and "the good of the children." This is the true face of the LGBTQ agenda. Spack is listed as an authority by TransYouth Family Allies, which is:

> The only National non-profit organization that educates and advocates exclusively for gender variant children and transgender youth. As such, we have

unparalleled expertise and experience to draw on when partnering with educational institutions. We have worked with hundreds of schools and organizations, in every type of political climate, all over the United States.

They offer, among other services, a "Successful Partnering with Schools K-12" program and a "Creating Positive Media Experiences" program. Citing the American Academy of Pediatrics, this 501(c)(3) tax-exempt organization states definitively that "by age 4, children's gender identity is stable, and they know they will always be a boy or a girl." Their website links to the article "How Young is Too Young?" by Reid Vanderburgh who confidently states, "A twelve year old . . . has had eight or nine years of conscious gender identity," and therefore, Vanderburgh concludes without a shred of scientific evidence, "I would unequivocally support this person in beginning hormones just prior to the onset of puberty." We've already gone over the grisly details of what happens to the child when the "medical professionals" decide to go this route, and it is unequivocally evil.

Johanna Olson-Kennedy—WPATH member, Director of the Center for Transyouth Health and Development at the Children's Hospital of Los Angeles, and Assistant Professor of Clinical Pediatrics at the USC Keck School of Medicine—and Ilana Sherer (Perelman School of Medicine at the University of Pennsylvania alumnus) recently released a video describing how they give puberty blockers to children at ages eight or nine. This view is affirmed in an Olson-Kennedy-led paper: "Because pubertal development of people who are assigned female at birth may begin as early as 8 or 9 years of age, completion of puberty is plausible even as young as 12 years," thus "necessitating" early intervention. Olson-Kennedy was part of a research team that received a $5.7 million grant from the National Institutes of Health (NIH) for a five-year study on "trans youth" commencing in the fall of 2015; the study:

Will include youth from two age groups: younger children in early puberty, who will receive hormone blockers, called GnRH agonists, used to suspend the process of puberty – preventing the development of undesired secondary sex characteristics; and older adolescents, who will begin use of masculinizing or feminizing cross-sex hormones that allow them to go through the 'right' puberty – consistent with their gender of identification. . . . The multicenter study will be located at four academic medical centers with dedicated transgender youth clinics. The co-investigators and their institutions include:

- Johanna Olson, MD, Children's Hospital Los Angeles and the Keck School of Medicine of the University of Southern California
- Stephen Rosenthal, MD, UCSF Benioff Children's Hospital San Francisco
- Robert Garofalo, MD, MPH, Ann & Robert H. Lurie Children's Hospital of Chicago and Northwestern University Feinberg School of Medicine
- Norman Spack, MD, Boston Children's Hospital and Harvard Medical School

The Jewish Ilana Sherer, who appeared in the video with Olson-Kennedy and "lives with her wife and two children in Oakland," recalls that, "When I got to UCSF for residency, I was directed to Stephen Rosenthal, who was creating the Child and Adolescent Gender Center"; though she is not listed on the Oakland campus's website as part of the care team, as of July 2019, Gender Spectrum describes her as "car[ing] for patients at the Children's Hospital Oakland site." She has been honored by the American Academy of Pediatrics (AAP) for her work with (on) transgender youth and is a founding member of the AAP's Section on Lesbian, Gay, Bisexual, Transgender Health, and Wellness.

Ilana Sherer admitted in a videotaped 2018 Gender Spectrum symposium response that, "I really struggle . . . there are lots of kids I see that don't have dysphoria" who want to "transition," and so the klezmer-playing pediatrician brings Ehrensaft into her clinic and, as she says in the video while looking at Ehrensaft, "I know you said you don't rubber-stamp, but, you know, basically in my mind that's sort of what it feels like."

Olson-Kennedy's Center for Transyouth Health and Development at the Children's Hospital of Los Angeles offers the following "services":

- Gender-affirming medical treatment and mental health services
- Family support services and linkage to outside resources
- Case management services, including assistance with legal name and gender marker changes
- Peer Support groups
- Sexual health education including groups, one-on-one navigation services and HIV/STD (Sexually Transmitted Disease) screening and treatment.
- Access to PEP (Post Exposure Prophylaxis) and PrEP (Pre Exposure Prophylaxis) for HIV prevention.
- Voluntary participation in ground breaking research

In 2019, the NIH announced it would be providing a $3.4 million research grant to fund "the first study of prepubescent transgender or gender non-conforming children—a highly understudied age group," featuring:

- Marco A. Hidalgo, PhD and Johanna Olson-Kennedy, MD – Children's Hospital Los Angeles and the Keck School of Medicine of USC
- Diane Chen, PhD - Lurie Children's Hospital of Chicago and Northwestern University Feinberg School of Medicine
- Diane Ehrensaft, PhD - UCSF Benioff Children's Hospitals
- Amy Tishelman, PhD - Boston Children's Hospital and Harvard Medical School

Amy Tishelman is also Jewish. Additionally, there is significant overlap in personnel between the USC Keck School of Medicine and the Children's Hospital Los Angeles's Saban Research Institute, named as such following a $40 million donation by Haim and Cheryl Saban and the Saban Family Foundation. Cheryl Saban is an honorary trustee for the Children's Hospital, a member of the American Psychological Association, a former Board member of the Clinton Foundation, and she runs the Saban Family Foundation. Her husband, Haim, is a Jewish billionaire of *Mighty Morphin Power Rangers* fame; he is the founder of Saban Entertainment, the Saban Music Group, and Saban Capital Group, and is a stakeholder in Univision (Saban:

"I'm a one-issue guy, and my issue is Israel."). According to the Saban Research Institute website:

> The Saban Research Institute of Children's Hospital Los Angeles maintains strong scientific and strategic affiliations with the University of Southern California (USC) and the Keck School of Medicine of USC, where CHLA physicians and scientists hold faculty appointments. The Institute's 240 principal investigators are involved in collaborative projects with academic institutions throughout the U.S. and abroad. The Saban Research Institute consistently ranks in the top 10 children's hospitals for funding from the National Institutes of Health. In fiscal year 2019, the hospital reported a total of $129.9 million in research funding across all sources, of which $32.4 million came from the National Institutes of Health.

Now as we head into the home stretch of this book, here's where we put the final pieces of the puzzle together. The top international funders for HIV/AIDS-related "philanthropy" in 2011 included Levi Strauss & Co., the Tides Foundation, the Tides Center, the Open Society Foundations, amfAR, the Conrad N. Hilton Foundation, Gilead Sciences, the American Jewish World Service, Merck, Johnson & Johnson, ViiV Healthcare, the MAC AIDS Fund and MAC Cosmetics, Abbott and the Abbott Fund, the Ford Foundation, the Bill and Melinda Gates Foundation (major funders of the World Health Organization), and Bristol-Myers Squibb.

In May 1989, the Salk Institute filed a patent for Supprelin, a histrelin acetate injectable puberty blocker for children with "central precocious puberty." It was approved in 1991 by the FDA with Johnson & Johnson taking it to market. As Corey Lynn reports:

> Scrip ran a press release about Johnson & Johnson's new Supprelin that has been recommended for approval in precocious puberty by the FDA's Endocrinologic and Metabolic Drugs Advisory Committee at its March 26, 1990 meeting, which wasn't technically licensed by the FDA until December, 1991. In this release, they described how that same committee had narrowly rejected Takeda-Abbott Pharmaceutical's (TAP) Lupron and Lupron Depot. They stated that the data provided by TAP on 62 children injected with Lupron and 20 with Lupron Depot was insufficient to demonstrate either formulation's clinical efficacy in precocious puberty. Just three years later, the FDA did in fact license Lupron Depot-Ped. Takeda had a patent on the Leuprolide acetate compound in 1975, which is the synthetic analogue of GnRH used in the puberty blockers. In 1977, they hooked up with their first US company, which was Abbott Pharmaceuticals (Abbott Laboratories), which was founded in 1888. The patent was then transferred to Abbott in 1977. Abbott obtained FDA licensing in 1993 on Lupron Depot-Ped for central precocious puberty. In 2001, Abbott Laboratories and Takeda Chemicals paid an $875 million settlement to the Department of Justice for aggressively marketing Lupron by giving doctors illegal kickbacks in exchange for prescribing Lupron to patients, and assisted the doctors with billing Medicare or Medicaid hundreds of dollars for each dose. On 2012 FDA documents, it indicates that

Lupron Depot and Lupron Depot-Ped (for children) are manufactured for Abbott Laboratories by Takeda Pharmaceutical Company Ltd. In 2013, AbbVie Inc. was birthed from Abbott as an independent company, which is the current name listed for Lupron products. AbbVie is now the world's sixth largest independent biotech company, with a revenue of $32.75 billion in 2018. They sell Lupron products throughout the US and Canada, while Takeda markets them in Asia, and both sell to Europe. In 2016, Lupron alone generated revenue of $821 million. . . . According to the Saint Louis Zoo and several other websites, Lupron is also being used in captive animals, primarily males, to suppress testosterone and sperm production.

Given what we know about our ruling class, it's probably also in the public water supply as most wastewater-treatment systems aren't designed to remove hormones, antidepressants, and other drugs, and furthermore a docile population is an easy population to control. So is a sick one, which the re-orientation of the medical system to treatment rather than prevention with the embrace of pharmaceutical and surgical interventions concurrent with an intentional marginalization of homeopathic medicine and a neglect of nutrition attests to. The proliferation of harmful chemicals in our environment is also depleting the soil and making us profoundly sick, and the nature of food production has seen the nutritive quality of food decline in conjunction with our health.

Still, they wouldn't intentionally poison us, would they? Ask DuPont, 3M, or any of the other manufacturers of "forever chemicals." The CDC's biomonitoring studies show that the blood of nearly all Americans is contaminated with one of these chemicals called PFAS. High concentrations lead to birth defects, a host of cancers, and other health complications. Consider also Roundup, via *Culture Wars*:

A crucial weapon in the attack is Roundup (glyphosate), a widely used herbicide that's being used for something for which there was never any long-term safety-testing: the forced ripening of crops, called desiccation. This practice all but guarantees that this pesticide will wind up in our food, as well as the animal byproducts that are used in vaccines. It also happens to be a highly questionable agronomic practice. Roundup hinders biosynthesis in plants by poisoning the shikimate pathway. For decades it was only used prior to seeding a crop, and since humans and animals don't rely on the same biology and chemistry as plants do, we were assured we could safely ingest small dosages while applying it. But we were never supposed to actually eat it, much less have it injected into our bloodstream. We now know our bodies rely on trillions of microorganisms integral to our immune systems that do employ on the shikimate pathway, leading to the grave conclusion that, more so than other pesticides, Roundup contributes directly to the suppression of our immune systems. Ignoring this, Bayer execs seek to dominate the fast-growing desiccation market with their recent purchase of Monsanto. . . . Both sides in this battle already agree that farmers will NEVER stop using glyphosate, not here in America, nor over in enviro-conscious Europe. Never. Modern farming is literally addicted to it, and both sides are banking on that fact. Why, it's enough to make you think both sides in this titanic struggle for justice might even be in cahoots.

Randy Roach, author of the incredible *Muscle, Smoke, and Mirrors* series details the role in this by the same foundations we see today continuing the process as well as underwriting mass immigration, the LGBTQ agenda, climate change, and the like as they all originate from the same noxious source—it is all inter-connected:

Vaccinations have been shoved down our throats. The pharmaceutical medical fields now are really upset because . . . the percentage that took flu vaccines dropped dramatically, especially after that garbage scam they pulled off with the H1N1. . . . There's a lot of money being made off that. Then they expose that these doctors in the World Health Organization (WHO) had direct connection to the pharmaceutical companies that are creating the vaccines. . . . Many supplement companies are almost pharmaceutical companies . . . pharmaceutical companies are also profiting out of supplements— even though they would like people to all be on drugs because they can't really patent anything that's natural. . . . We migrated to the notion "we could put back through chemical means" and the subsequent fungicides, pesticides, herbicides; they were all chemicals being put on our land as far back as 100 years ago. . . . It's probably just much worse now with companies like Monsanto totally disrupting the whole farming process all around the world in terms of using GMO crops to make them resilient to their round up. In Iraq and many other places they have come in and totally disrupted century long traditions of fairly sustainable agriculture. . . . It's always more industry, more industry, more industry and everything in our western culture is more and more chemicals and that seems to be the driving force. . . . The world is going in to more and more control in the hands of less and less people. We are being globalized and the food supply is being globalized internationally. . . . They have been doing this for years and there is a lot of money behind these global initiatives, it goes back to the League of Nations . . . and the formation of the Council on Foreign Relations and the Royal Institute of International Affairs [Chatham House]; these are all global initiatives, put out there by not just one particular country. It's like the Federal Reserve thing in the United States, the majority of people think the Federal Reserve is an American institution. . . . The way they name things confuse people who think these initiatives are put out by this country and that country but these are pure global dictates that are driven by dubious characters who I would just call "global architects;" they have no alliance to any country. They want world government and they have been working on it for a long time. . . . These tax shelters, the Carnegie Endowment Fund, Rockefeller, Guggenheim and Ford, they all spawned on to the scene like crazy between 1910 and 1930 because these foundations weren't going to be taxed because they created these shelters. The people who I call the "Global Architects" . . . were highly instrumental in bringing in the Federal Reserve Act of 1913 in the United States which took power from Congress in making money and putting into the private sector which was the Federal Reserve. . . . But in the 1950's there were many people who were concerned in terms of what was going on in the American education system and more and more questions were asked on who was influencing this "education system" and what was going on with these tax shelters—who and what are they and what money has been spent and why were they never audited.

Congressman Eugene Cox in 1951 or 1952 received Congressional approval to investigate them, then he died and Congressman Carroll Reece, a prominent Republican politician, took over the investigation. He hired Norman Dodd as director of research and in turn Norman Dodd hired Katherine Casey, a young lawyer who he assigned to go and research the Carnegie Endowment fund and the Rockefeller Foundation. . . . Katherine Casey went to read the minutes of the meetings of the Carnegie Endowment Fund going back around World War I, and she couldn't believe what she was reading at that time in terms of these elitist leaders talking about taking over the American education system, indoctrinating kids into thinking in a collectivist manner or along the lines of the Social Soviet Union and basically taking apart the United States. She could not deal with what she was reading and she literally lost her mind and had to be institutionalized according to Norman Dodd. She saw in those minutes of the meetings this Carnegie Endowment Fund, these elitists talking about the advantages of World Wars to consolidate power. Hence World War I got the League of Nations, hence World War II, you had the United Nations. . . . It is quite evident that they want international guidelines, international laws and that's why we have NAFTA, GAT over here, the World Trade Organization and the European Union. . . . [Codex Alimentarius is] basically international food guidelines and the matrix of this came out of the World Health Organization (WHO) and other initiatives going quite a ways back. . . . The take-over of the American Medical Association [was] back in 1910 with philanthropic money from the Rockefeller Foundation and the Rockefeller Institute of Medical Research, and the Carnegie Endowment Fund with Doctors Simon and Abraham Flexner[129] who worked for those two organizations and they helped in terms of reformatting in the American Medical Association which was not very impressive at the time. . . . Homeopathy, chiropractic, and naturopathy . . . were prominent as well in terms of choices for medical care. But with the insurgence with this money and reforming along the lines of scientific methods, pharmacology, research labs. . . . [Alternatives] weren't going to receive any funding in their schools. So eventually a lot of those schools shut down and basically the new paradigm of medicine, which was going to be drug-based, took control.

The man-made/destroyed environment of the modern world is weakening our immune systems and both suppressing testosterone and elevating estrogen in men, which in turn also produces a weakened immune system. Perversely, the entire medical establishment claims that *high* testosterone in men causes immunosuppression and dumbs you down, when the opposite, as always, is true.

Furthermore, regarding nutrition, the New York Academy of Sciences, in partnership with The Mortimer D. Sackler Foundation Inc. established The Sackler Institute for Nutrition Science to create "a coordinated effort to support and disseminate nutrition science research." Yes, this is the Jewish Mortimer Sackler who with his brothers built the Purdue Pharma that unleashed OxyContin and spawned the hellish opioid epidemic. The Sackler Institute for Nutrition Science published 2013's

---

[129] Yes, Jewish. Also connected to Johns Hopkins, Columbia, and the University of Pennsylvania.

"A Global Research Agenda for Nutrition Science: Outcome of a Collaborative Process Between Academic and Non-Profit Researchers and the World Health Organization":

> Action must stem from a globalized, collaborative approach to carry out research and disseminate findings relevant to nutrition science. . . . This research topic highlights the need for an analytical toolbox to describe and model an enabling environment for health and nutrition that connects nutritional quality, environmental sustainability, and economic viability. This requires adding the dimensions of household vulnerability and livelihood levels, including in subsistence economies; and policies (using multi-disciplinary approaches including: climate change researchers, scientists working on health system strengthening, economists evaluating the cost of the double burden, environmental and urban engineers). . . . In a real world of very complex and ever-changing interactions, there is a need to better measure economic and sustainability trade-offs in terms of nutrition and health outcomes. . . . How to connect women's economic empowerment with enhanced nutritional status for women and children. . . ? Nutrition-centered approaches in climate changes need to incorporate population trends, various types of food systems (production, processing, trade patterns, and consumption), access to water, sanitation, and overall environmental sustainability, with the capacity to produce various scenarios and projection of nutritional outcomes. Points of convergence also emerged, stressing the following elements in research:

- Thinking and acting holistically (focus on research that can evaluate multiple inputs and address several outcomes together)
- Developing alliances (where is the most convergence of goals and incentives?)
- Building feasible, pragmatic approaches to research
- Building recognition that nutrition both influences, and is influenced by, human, social, and economic development
- Connecting nutrition, economics, and environment
- Capitalizing on the strengths of many disciplines through collaboration and communication
- Placing biology within the social/economic/natural environment
- Paying attention to measurement and delivery issues

The Sackler Institute for Nutrition Science Advisory Group during the development of the research agenda included members of Johns Hopkins, the WHO, Cornell University, the Gates Foundation, and the United Nations Children's Fund. Humanitas Global Development provided additional support; its team members have developed and directed initiatives for the World Bank, the Clinton Foundation, the Mathile Institute for the Advancement of Human Nutrition, UNICEF, the World Health Organization, USAID, the EastWest Institute, the UNDP, Women's Campaign International, the Center for Monitoring Election Violence, Microfinance International Corporation, the International Rescue Committee (IRC), the Global Alliance for Improved Nutrition (GAIN), government health agencies, corporations, and more.

The exclamation mark prior to the agenda's publication was the December 2012 conference in New York of the same name—A Global Research Agenda for Nutrition Science—that featured speakers from the Gates Foundation, DuPont, USDA, Cornell University, CDC China, the OECD, McGill World Platform for Health and Economic Convergence, Aga Khan University, the Ministry of Health of Malaysia, the New York State Department of Health, Columbia University, DFID, the University of Pennsylvania, the World Health Organization, Johns Hopkins University, and the KEMRI Wellcome Trust Research Programme ("The programme was formed in 1989 when the Kenya Medical Research Institute formed a partnership with the Wellcome Trust and the University of Oxford").

The Wellcome Trust is a Core Partner and co-founder of EAT, "a non-profit [also] founded by the Stordalen Foundation [and] Stockholm Resilience Centre . . . to catalyze a food system transformation." On its About page, EAT states:

> Today's global food system is failing both people and planet. . . . How we grow, process, transport, consume and waste food is also driving our global environmental crises. The agricultural sector is the single biggest emitter of greenhouse gases and a major contributor to deforestation, species extinction, and the depletion of both marine systems and fresh water resources. As hunger rises – powered significantly by climate change – greater pressure mounts on an already overstretched, inefficient and unsustainable food system, further accelerating climate change and ecological decline. It is the interlinkages between these great threats that define their urgent potency – but also provide us our greatest opportunities for action. Just as the challenges are intimately intertwined, our actions must be integrated across sectors, disciplines and continents. A core premise of the Sustainable Development Goals (SDGs) is that we will never achieve the future we want by repeating past mistakes, nor by working in silos.

EAT also discusses "scalable action," which is a recurring theme with the proposed overhaul to the "food system transformation." EAT states that it will "work to reform global, national and local governance around food systems [and] influence and align political and business action."

EAT's Action Allies include Chatham House, the Stockholm International Water Institute (privatization of water is an impending threat—John Q. Publius documents this aspect of the system and the grim reality of what it looks like in *The Way Life Should Be?*), and the World Business Council for Sustainable Development. EAT's Strategic Partners include Novo Nordisk, Deloitte, and Aviva ("We understand how important a sustainable future is for our customers, our business and for society and believe the Sustainable Development Goals provide the vision towards the future our planet needs"). EAT's Engagement Allies include Nestlé (mentioned specifically by Publius in great detail in *The Way Life Should Be?*), Google Food Services, and the National Geographic Society. EAT's Knowledge Partners include the Harvard T.H. Chan School of Public Health, the Harvard Global Equality Initiative, MIT, and the Sackler Institute for Nutrition Science.

Gunhild A. Stordalen is the founder and Executive Chair of EAT, a driving force linking climate, health, and sustainability issues across sectors to transform the global food system. Stordalen sits on several boards and advises on councils including the United Nations' Scaling Up Nutrition (SUN) Movement Lead Group, the World Economic Forum (WEF) Stewardship Board on Food Systems, the British Telecom Group's Committee for Sustainable and Responsible Business, the Global Alliance for Improved Nutrition (GAIN) Partnership Council, UNICEF's Advisory Group, and the international advisory board of the Stockholm Resilience Center. GAIN's website states that their:

> Mission is well aligned to the Sustainable Development Goals (SDGs) as nutrition and the SDGs are interlinked. Good nutrition is both a means to and an end result of attaining the SDGs. It is a fundamental cross-cutting investment for countries and the global community. GAIN's work in alleviating the burden of malnutrition in all its forms contributes notably towards at least 11 of 17 SDGs. Of all the global goals, SDG2 best encapsulates GAIN's vision: seeking to end hunger and malnutrition in all its forms.

GAIN's Executive Director Lawrence Haddad was the UK representative on the Steering Committee of the High Level Panel of Experts (HLPE) of the UN Committee on World Food Security (CSF). Sheryl Fofaria, on the Board of Directors, also leads JP Morgan's Philanthropy Center in Europe, the Middle East, and Africa.

Dominic O'Neill is also on GAIN's Board of Directors; he joined the UK Department for International Development (DFID) in 2002 as the Environmental Health policy adviser. In 2003 he was posted to Yemen to establish DFID's first bilateral development program in the country. Over the next ten years he was based in Iraq, Sierra Leone, and Nepal as DFID's Country Director. In 2013, he became the UK's Executive Director on the Board of the African Development Bank. He then returned to DFID and took up the position of Head of United Nations and Commonwealth Department responsible for UK funding to UNICEF, United Nations Population Fund (UNFPA), United Nations Development Program (UNDP), United Nations Human Rights Office of the High Commissioner (OHCHR), Food and Agriculture Organization of the United Nations (FAO), World Food Program (WFP), and International Fund for Agriculture Development (IFAD). O'Neill is the Executive Director of the Water Supply and Sanitation Collaborative Council (WSSCC), a United Nations Office for Project Services-hosted membership organization. O'Neill is the World Wildlife Fund International's Executive Director of Operations.

Stay with me. The World Wildlife Fund Sweden is another Strategic Partner of EAT. You know how cows farting is supposedly boiling the earth so we can't eat meat and need to rely on substandard vegetarian diets? Well Sodexo announced in 2020 it would be "allying" with the World Wildlife Fund (WWF), Impossible Foods and Eat JUST to promote plant-based dining. According to EAT's report "Diets for a Better Future: Rebooting and Reimagining Healthy and Sustainable Food Systems in the G20" from leader author Brent Loken (now with the WWF as Global Food Lead Scientist):

> Food-related per-capita emissions in G20 countries as a whole need to be approximately halved by 2050. Doing so would ensure we can feed 10 billion people healthy diets within planetary boundaries, and enable a more equitable global distribution of food-related GHG emissions.

Loken states:

> The coronavirus pandemic exposes the fragilities and inequalities of the global food system. It is hard to imagine that only 20 countries together use up 75% of carbon emissions that the Paris Agreement allocates to food production. While G20 countries consume at an unsustainable rate, too many countries still have high rates of hunger and malnutrition.

Melissa Ho, Senior Vice President of Freshwater and Food for WWF-US says:

> Achieving healthy diets and a healthy planet will require more ambition on National Dietary Guidelines (NDGs). It will require a shift in many G20 countries in the overconsumption of red meat. . . . At the same time in many other parts of the world, healthy diets may require increased consumption of quality nutrition, including more meat, fruit and vegetables. And always, sustainable diets should reflect the local context, and culture. WWF takes a holistic approach, understanding that while important, dietary shifts alone will not meet the future challenges of sustaining people and planet. WWF is working with a wide range of partners on sustainability solutions including, improved production, food loss and waste reduction, building resilient supply chains that return value to producers and communities, and conservation of critical landscapes. These efforts together with sustainable diets will help transform the global food system for the benefit of people and planet.

Although some of that might sound perfectly reasonable, it's a Trojan horse, designed to facilitate Sustainable Development Goal 10: "Reduce inequality within *and among* countries" (emphasis added). Still think the hollowing-out of industry, the push to marginalize meat, the conditioning of people to live in pods and eat bugs, the experiments on the population, the propaganda, all of it—think any of it was an accident? Jon Miller of the Board of Trustees of Open for Business has created campaigns for WWF in the past, and Melissa Ho (Cornell alum), per the WWF website:

> Came to WWF from the Millennium Challenge Corporation, where she oversaw a $1.5 billion portfolio of infrastructure investments in West Africa. She also served at USAID overseeing the technical team responsible for the strategy development and implementation of Feed the Future. Previously, Dr. Ho developed and implemented the agricultural water management strategy and grant portfolio at the Bill and Melinda Gates Foundation. She has also served in various capacities in the US Congress.

Jared Diamond and Leonardo Di Caprio are on the WWF's Board, Mayari Pritzker is on the National Council, and Adrienne Mars of the Mars Foundation is a Director Emeritus of the WWF.

In November 2015, CNA, a nonprofit research and analysis organization located in Arlington, Virginia, and the Center for American Progress, the World Wildlife Fund, Cargill, and Mars, "developed and executed a policy decision-making game designed to explore issues arising from, and possible responses to, global food system disruptions." From the Abstract of their December 2015 report "Food Chain Reaction—A Global Food Security Game":

The game took place in November 2015 in Washington, D.C., and included senior officials and subject matter experts on teams representing Brazil, Continental Africa, China, the European Union (EU), India, the United States, Multilateral Institutions, and Business and Investors. During four rounds of game play spanning the decade 2020 to 2030, players confronted food system pressure at the intersection of population growth, urbanization, severe weather, and social unrest. In response, players crafted policies, made decisions, and took actions that dynamically influenced the state of the world as the game advanced. As the chain reaction of impacts tied to their choices became apparent, players experienced first-hand how their decisions and actions influenced global food security. At the conclusion of the game, players highlighted significant lessons learned and expressed increased preparedness to collaboratively address food security.

CNA traces its origins to World War II and a small contingent of MIT scientists who worked with the US Navy to study German U-Boat activities. CNA now works with the US Department of Veterans Affairs, the Carnegie Corporation of New York, the MacArthur Foundation (which has granted the WWF roughly $32 million since the 1980s), the Department of Health and Human Services, the White House, the US Navy, the US Marines, the Henry M. Jackson Foundation for the Advancement of Military Medicine, USAID, the US State Department, and more.

Erica Downs is a non-resident senior research scientist at CNA and a Senior Research Scholar at the Center on Global Energy Policy at Columbia University's School of International and Public Affairs, focusing on Chinese energy markets and geopolitics. Downs previously worked as a senior research scientist in the China Studies program of CNA, as a senior analyst in the Asia practice at Eurasia Group, as a fellow in the John L. Thornton China Center at the Brookings Institution, as an energy analyst at the CIA, and as a lecturer at the Foreign Affairs College in Beijing, China. Downs has managed more than fifty publications in the areas of Chinese energy production and development and its geopolitical positioning.

The Jewish Dov Zakheim (Booz Allen Hamilton, fixture in the George W. Bush administration's first term, BA from Columbia, Council on Foreign Relations member, board member of the American Jewish Committee) is a Senior Fellow for CNA. As Steve Clemons wrote in October 2011:

During the very start of George W. Bush's first presidential run in mid-1999, Robert Zoellick—now head of the World Bank—was tasked with organizing a myriad of advisory committees to the Bush Campaign. . . . Mitt Romney [Bain Capital] may be taking a page out of the George W. Bush/Zoellick playbook in the announcement this past Friday of his roster of national security advisers. . . . Some of the more balanced realists in the Romney camp include former Department of Defense Comptroller Dov Zakheim. . . . Among the Advisers are Cofer Black—who used to run some of the key anti-terror black ops before becoming Vice Chairman of Blackwater (which is left off of his official bio tag on Romney's site); former UN Management Official Christopher Burnham who is known to be very close to former US Ambassador to the UN John Bolton; former Department of Homeland Security chief Michael Chertoff and former NSA Director General Michael Hayden—two of the countries leading authorities on cybersecurity and broad homeland security. . . . CFR President Richard Haass' protege Megan O'Sullivan who rise high in the Bush Administration for her counsel on Afghanistan and Iraq is also on the team. . . . Eliot Cohen and Robert Kagan are on the list.

The Jewish Cohen, another Council on Foreign Relations member and Harvard alumnus, is now the Dean of the Johns Hopkins School of Advanced International Studies (SAIS).

Also of great significance, the Center for American Progress receives or has received in recent years financial support from:

- Open Society Foundations
- World Wildlife Fund
- Mars
- Ford Foundation
- Gates Foundation
- Google
- MacArthur Foundation
- Carnegie Corporation of New York
- Pritzker Children's Initiative
- Lisa Stone Pritzker
- Rockefeller Brothers Fund
- Rockefeller Family Fund
- Rockefeller Foundation
- Facebook
- Microsoft
- JP Morgan Charitable Giving Fund
- WK Kellogg Foundation
- Bloomberg Philanthropies
- Joan and Irwin Jacobs Fund of the Jewish Community Foundation
- Walton Family Foundation
- Amazon
- William and Flora Hewlett Foundation
- Silicon Valley Community Foundation
- New York Community Foundation
- New Venture Fund
- Annie E. Casey Foundation
- Bronfman Hauptman Foundation
- David and Lucile Packard Foundation
- Sandler Foundation
- Jonathan and Jeannie Lavine Family Fund
- Unbound Philanthropy
- Henry van Ameringen
- David Bohnett Foundation
- Wells Fargo
- Jewish Communal Fund
- Nathan Cummings Foundation and Jane M. Saks
- Bauman Foundation
- Bank of America
- National Collegiate Athletic Association (NCAA)
- Evelyn and Walter Haas Jr. Fund
- Eli and Edythe Broad Foundation
- American Federation of Teachers (AFT)
- Apple
- AT&T
- BlackRock
- Madeleine K. Albright
- Goldman Sachs Gives
- Comcast NBCUniversal
- Fred P. Hochberg and Thomas P. Healy
- Johnson Family Foundation
- Kohlberg Kravis Roberts
- Lippman Kanfer Foundation for Living Torah
- Barbra Streisand
- Uber
- United Way
- Lawrence H. Summers & Elisa F.

- New Family
- Verizon
- Walmart
- Chan Zuckerberg Initiative
- Arcus Foundation
- National Education Association (NEA)
- Robert E. Rubin
- Visa
- City of London Corporation
- Laura and Gary Lauder
- Blackstone
- Embassy of the Federal Republic of Germany
- Jewish Community Foundation of Los Angeles
- Coca-Cola
- Doctors Council, SEIU
- Everytown for Gun Safety Action Fund
- Heather Podesta + Partners
- James Hormel
- Anglo-American
- Akin Gump Strauss Hauer & Feld LLP
- Citigroup
- America's Health Insurance Plans, or AHIP
- Discovery
- DeVry Education Group
- DRS Technologies / Leonardo DRS (defense contractor)
- Health Care Service Corporation
- Lyft
- Borealis Philanthropy
- Morgan Stanley

- Yale Law School
- S. Donald Sussman
- Embassy of Japan
- CVS Health
- Heinrich-Böll-Stiftung North America
- JUUL Labs Inc.
- Mertz Gilmore Foundation

- Embassy of the United Arab Emirates
- Gill Foundation
- Steven Cohen
- Steven Rattner and Maureen White
- Peter Orszag (a Council on Foreign Relations member)
- Alan Patricof
- National Immigration Law Center
- Northrop Grumman
- Tony Podesta
- Quest Diagnostics
- Tides Foundation and Weston Milliken
- Stephen Silberstein
- American Beverage Association
- Israel Institute
- Eli Lilly and Company
- Fred Eychaner
- BAE Systems North America
- Blanchette Hooker Rockefeller Fund
- Barbaralee Diamonstein-Spielvogel
- DuPont
- Pharmaceutical Research and Manufacturers of America
- Cynthia and George Mitchell Foundation

George Mitchell was a close associate of Jeffrey Epstein and was named by Virginia Roberts Giuffre in a lawsuit against Epstein and Ghislaine Maxwell as one of the men she was forced to have sex with while she was allegedly being trafficked while underage by the Jewish duo.

Circling back to the food supply chain reset—a key component of the impending "Great Reset" helmed by the World Economic Forum—the Global Agriculture and Food Security Program (GAFSP) is a $1.6 billion multilateral financing mechanism that supports resilient and sustainable agriculture systems. GAFSP is a Financial Intermediary Fund (FIF), hosted within the World Bank Group, and was set up to complement and reinforce other existing multilateral and bilateral efforts to tackle food insecurity. The World Bank serves as Trustee as well as hosts a Coordination Unit

(CU) within the Agriculture and Food Global Practice that provides support to GAFSP's Steering Committee. The Steering Committee includes representatives of the UK's DFID, the Gates Foundation, the Norwegian Agency for Development Co-operation (NORAD), Australia's Department of Foreign Affairs and Trade, Global Affairs Canada, and more.

The SecureNutrition Knowledge Platform (SNKP) is another World Bank project, initiated in 2011 by a cross-sectoral team of representatives from three World Bank Group (WBG) sectors: Health, Nutrition, and Population; Agriculture; and Poverty. According to the SNKP:

> Past WBG President Robert Zoellick's 'open knowledge' agenda (open data, open knowledge, open solutions) and new analyses that emerged from the devastating food/fuel/finance crises rejuvenated the Bank's focus on nutrition and the links with food security. This was the genesis of SecureNutrition.

We cannot neglect the Soros vector, either; the Open Society Foundations trains "climate justice activists" and Alexander Soros is a former Board member of and the Alexander Soros Foundation a donor to Global Witness, with "associated charitable entities" in both the UK and the US. Global Witness "protect[s] human rights and the environment by fearlessly confronting corruption and challenging the systems that enable it." Disturbingly, this is how they do it: secret filming, data analysis, satellite imagery, and drone footage. No way this is just a pretense and/or practice for the coming Global Panopticon, right? Global Witness's Advisory Board includes:

- Bennett Freeman, Chair: From 2006–15, he was Senior Vice President-Sustainability Research and Policy at Calvert Investments, the largest family of sustainable and responsible (SRI) mutual funds in the U.S. He led the firm's environmental, social and governance analysis and its shareholder advocacy and public policy initiatives on issues such as Sudan divestment and responsible investment in Burma; extractive revenue transparency and conflict minerals; Internet freedom of expression and privacy. . . . As U.S. Deputy Assistant Secretary of State for Democracy, Human Rights and Labor from 1999–2001, he led the State Department's bilateral human rights diplomacy and the development of the Voluntary Principles on Security and Human Rights, the global human rights standard for the oil and mining industries.
- Honorary Chair is the [previously-discussed] Jewish Aryeh Neier: President of the Open Society Foundations from 1993 to 2012. Before that, he served for 12 years as executive director of Human Rights Watch, of which he was a founder in 1978. He worked 15 years at the American Civil Liberties Union, including eight years as national executive director.
- Anita Ramasastry is the Roland Hijorth Professor of Law and Director of the Sustainable International Development Graduate Program at the University of Washington School of Law. . . . Ramastastry has served as a staff attorney at the Federal Reserve Bank of New York.
- Arlene McCarthy served four terms as a Member of the European Parlia-

ment from 1994 -2014. She was the first UK woman President of the Internal Market and Consumer Affairs committee. In 2009 she was elected Vice-President of the Economic and Monetary Affairs committee and campaigned for greater transparency in financial markets working on the post financial crisis reform agenda. . . . Arlene was named one of the 100 most influential women in European Finance in 2010, 2011 and 2012. . . . Arlene is director of AMC strategy and is a special advisor on financial issues to the chairman of Bloomberg.

- Camille Massey was appointed Founding Executive Director of the Sorensen Center for International Peace and Justice in January 2014. She previously served as Vice President for Global Strategy and Programs at the Council on Foreign Relations, overseeing international initiatives, strategic partnerships, and the corporate program. Prior to the Council, Camille was the Founder and CEO of Cue Global, a consulting business that designs and implements strategic policy, legal, and advocacy plans for global organizations. Other positions held include Senior Advisor at the International AIDS Vaccine Initiative, Director of Communications at Human Rights First, and Human Rights Fellow at The Carter Center.

- Ory Okolloh: Until recently Ory was the Managing Director of Omidyar Network and Luminate Group in Africa, both part of The Omidyar Group. . . . She serves on the Board of Directors of several organisations including the Thomson Reuters Founders Share Company, Stanbic Holdings Plc and Stanbic Bank Kenya.  She is also an Aspen Global Leadership Network (AGLN) Fellow and has in the past served as advisory board member to Twiga Foods, Amnesty International Africa and Endeavor Kenya among other organisations. Prior to this, Ory was Google's policy and strategy manager for Africa. . . . In 2011 Ory was named a Young Global Leader by the World Economic Forum. . . . Ory earned a J.D. from Harvard Law School.

- Mabel Van Oranje: Co-founder and the executive chair of the European Council on Foreign Relations. . . . In 1997, she joined the Open Society Foundations in Brussels as Executive Director, becoming OSF's London-based International Advocacy Director in 2003. . . . She has been actively engaged in the fight against HIV/AIDS. . . . In 2005, the World Economic Forum named her one of its Young Global Leaders.

- Misha Glenny: Former visiting professor at Columbia University.

From the Board of Directors:

- Chinmayi Arun is a resident fellow of the Information Society Project at Yale Law School and an affiliate of the Berkman Klein Center of Internet & Society at Harvard University. . . . She is an alternative board member of the Global Network Initiative, an expert affiliated with the Columbia Global Freedom of Expression project, and a member of the Executive Committee of the Global Network of Center's of Internet and Society. . . . Chinmayi is a member of the United Nations Global Pulse Advisory Group on the Governance of Data and AI, and of UNESCO India's Media

Freedom Advisory Group. She has been consultant to the Law Commission of India and member of the Indian government's multi stakeholder advisory group for the India Internet Governance Forum in the past. Her recent writing has focused on online hate speech and on the impact of AI and algorithms on human rights in the Global South.

- Mark Hannam: Mark spent twelve years working in the City as an investment manager, including stints at the Bank of England and at Citibank. He spent seven years at Barclays Global Investors, where he was a Managing Director, Head of the Investment Solutions team and the European Cash Management Team; in addition, he was the founding Chair of the European Diversity Committee and a member of the Global Index and Markets Group Risk Committee. After leaving mainstream finance, Mark was Chair of Fair Finance, a London based micro-credit lender, for eight years, and Chair of Numbers for Good, a London based social investment consultancy, for three years. He has written and spoken regularly on microfinance and social business.
- Gaby Darbyshire: In 2002, she moved to New York, where she co-founded one of the most pioneering journalism companies of the digital age. During her tenure as Chief Operating Officer, Gawker Media grew to become the largest independent online publisher, with media properties including Jezebel, io9, and Lifehacker.
- Fatima Hassan is a South African human rights lawyer and social justice activist, and the former Executive Director of the Open Society Foundation for South Africa, heading the Foundation for 6 years (mid-2013 to mid-2019). She has dedicated her professional life to defending and promoting human rights in South Africa, especially in the field of HIV/AIDS. She has a BA and LL.B from the University of the Witwatersrand and an LL.M from Duke University. . . . She is the recipient of several fellowships and awards, including the Tom and Andi Bernstein Distinguished Human Rights Fellowship at Yale University's School of Law (2012). She has published on issues related to social justice and HIV/AIDS.

Major donors to Global Witness in addition to the Alexander Soros Foundation include the Open Society Foundations, the Ford Foundation, the Arcus Foundation, the UK's DFID, the Oak Foundation, the Norwegian Agency for Development Cooperation (NORAD), the Department of Foreign Affairs and Trade of Ireland, the Dutch Postcode Lottery, the William and Flora Hewlett Foundation, and the Silicon Valley Community Foundation.

Additionally, because this is all just random and unrelated, "Israel's innovation ecosystem has some 1,900 companies whose solutions fit the UN's Sustainable Development Goals," said Eugene Kandel, the CEO of Start-Up Nation Central.

Now we factor in the specter of COVID-19: in June 2020, EAT and the Rockefeller Foundation co-hosted "a virtual convening to reimagine food systems for a post-COVID world." The press release from EAT's website informs that, "According to the World Food Program [United Nations], the effects of Covid-19 will nearly double the number of people facing acute food insecurity from 135 million in 2019 to 265 million by the end of 2020. The pandemic has also laid bare vulnerabilities and inequities in supply chains, straining grocery stores and food banks while caus-ing farmers to waste millions of pounds of fresh produce," which, by the way, was allowed to rot in the fields on purpose by higher-ups as part of a larger design cen-tered on the specific policies enacted or not enacted where relevant in response to COVID. Stordalen of EAT states:

> EAT's new digital platform, EAT@Home, will bring us together . . . and toward the UN Food Systems Summit 2021. EAT@Home will be a partici-patory series of live broadcasts, workshops, events and maybe even a party. Join us to turn our reimagination into a radical transformation—together.

The Rockefeller Foundation itself published "Reset the Table: Meeting the Moment to Transform the U.S. Food System," which is remarkably similar—what a coinci-dence!—to these other proposals and uses the exact same rationale.

What is also probably coincidental is that with funding from Open Philanthropy (main funders are the Jewish Dustin Moskovitz, a co-founder of Facebook and Asana, and his wife Cari Tuna; also notice how everything is "open" and "inclu-sive"), the Johns Hopkins Center for Health Security in partnership with the World Economic Forum (WEF) and the Bill and Melinda Gates Foundation hosted Event 201, "a high-level pandemic exercise" on October 18th, 2019, in New York City. Following the exercise, the WEF, Johns Hopkins, and the Gates Foundation offered the following recommendations:

> Governments, international organizations, and businesses should plan now for how essential corporate capabilities will be utilized during a large-scale pandemic. . . . Industry, national governments, and international organiza-tions should work together to enhance internationally held stockpiles of med-ical countermeasures (MCMs) to enable rapid and equitable distribution dur-ing a severe pandemic. The World Health Organization (WHO) currently has an influenza vaccine virtual stockpile, with contracts in place with pharma-ceutical companies that have agreed to supply vaccines should WHO request them. As one possible approach, this virtual stockpile model could be ex-panded to augment WHO's ability to distribute vaccines and therapeutics to countries in the greatest need during a severe pandemic. This should also in-clude any available experimental vaccine stockpiles for any WHO R&D Blueprint pathogens to deploy in a clinical trial during outbreaks in collabo-ration with CEPI, GAVI, and WHO.

CEPI is the Coalition for Epidemic Preparedness Innovations, launched at the World Economic Forum's Annual Meeting in Davos in 2017, as their website states:

> By the governments of Norway and India, the Bill & Melinda Gates Founda-tion, the Wellcome Trust, and the World Economic Forum. To date, CEPI has secured financial support from the Bill & Melinda Gates Foundation, Wellcome Trust, the European Commission, and the Governments of Aus-tralia, Belgium, Canada, Denmark, Ethiopia, Finland, Germany, Japan, the Kingdom of Saudi Arabia, the Netherlands, Norway, Switzerland and the UK.

Also according to CEPI:

> Additional investment from sovereign governments, the private sector and philanthropic foundations has also been provided to support our COVID-19 vaccine programmes. In response to call the Governments of Austria, Australia, Belgium, Canada, European Commission, Finland, France, Greece, Germany, Iceland, Italy, Japan, Luxembourg, Kingdom of Saudi Arabia, Norway, the Netherlands, New Zealand, Serbia, Spain, Switzerland, and the United Kingdom, alongside private sector companies and donations through the UN Foundation COVID-19 Solidarity Response Fund, have pledged $1.4 billion in financial contributions.

CEO Richard Hackett is the former Director of the US Biomedical Advanced Research and Development Authority (BARDA), served on the White House Homeland Security Council under President George W. Bush, and was a member of the White House National Security Staff under President Barack Obama. Hackett is a graduate of Vanderbilt University and the Vanderbilt University Medical School, and he completed a residency in internal medicine at the New York Hospital – Cornell Medical Center and a fellowship in medical oncology at Duke University Medical Center.

As of March 2019, CEPI had established eleven partnerships, "reflecting a potential investment of up to $350 million in 12 vaccine candidates (five against Lassa virus, four against MERS-CoV, three against Nipah virus) and three vaccine platforms to develop vaccines against Disease X." CEPI states that:

> "Disease X" represents the knowledge that a serious international epidemic could be caused by a pathogen currently unknown to cause human disease. In February 2018, Disease X was included in the updated WHO R&D Blueprint list of priority diseases. By their very nature, we cannot predict what or where "Disease X" is likely to emerge. What we do know is that new diseases emerge all the time, from locations all around the world. Developing countries, particularly those with high rates of biodiversity, are at heightened risk, because of the increased risk of outbreaks and the limited capacity for surveillance and response in these countries. Coronavirus Disease 2019 (COVID-19) represents a Disease X.

The World Bank and the WHO have non-voting members on CEPI's Board, and voting members include (biographical descriptions provided by CEPI's website):

- Rajeev Venkayya: The President of the Global Vaccine Business Unit of Takeda Pharmaceutical Company Limited. He is responsible for Takeda's commercial vaccine business and a development pipeline that includes vaccine candidates for Dengue, Norovirus, Zika (funded by the U.S. Biomedical Advanced Research and Development Authority [BARDA]), and an affordable inactivated Polio vaccine for developing countries (funded by the Bill & Melinda Gates Foundation). Dr. Venkayya was previously the Director of Vaccine Delivery at the Bill &

Melinda Gates Foundation, where he was responsible for the foundation's top two priorities of polio eradication and new vaccine introduction and an investment portfolio of approximately $500 million/year. He served as the foundation's representative on the Gavi Board. Prior to the Gates Foundation, Dr. Venkayya was Special Assistant to the U.S. President and Senior Director for Biodefense at the White House. He led the development and implementation of the National Strategy for Pandemic Influenza, as well as Presidential directives on medical countermeasures and public health preparedness. . . . Dr. Venkayya received his specialty training and served as an Assistant Professor of Medicine in the Division of Pulmonary and Critical Care Medicine at the University of California, San Francisco (UCSF). He was the principal investigator for a 5-year research grant from the National Institutes of Health to study the immunologic mechanisms leading to asthma. . . . Dr. Venkayya was a Resident and Chief Medical Resident in Internal Medicine at the University of Michigan Medical Center. . . . He is a life member of the Council on Foreign Relations.

- Charlotte Watts: Chief Scientific Adviser to the UK Department for International Development (DFID). . . . She became interested in global health whilst conducting post-doctoral research on the epidemiology of HIV at the University of Oxford. . . . Moving to LSHTM in 1994, after gaining further training in economics and social science, and fieldwork experience in Zimbabwe and other developing countries. She founded the Social and Mathematical Epidemiology Group. The multidisciplinary group uses mathematical, epidemiological and economic research to assess the impact of current and new HIV prevention technologies, and evaluate interventions that tackle the determinants of HIV risk. Professor Watts is a global expert in violence prevention. She was Senior Technical Advisor to the WHO 10 country population surveys on women's health and domestic violence.

- Peter Piot: Director of the London School of Hygiene & Tropical Medicine and Handa Professor of Global Health. . . . He was the founding Executive Director of UNAIDS and Under Secretary-General of the United Nations from 1995 until 2008, and was an Associate Director of the Global Programme on AIDS of WHO. Under his leadership UNAIDS became the chief advocate for worldwide action against AIDS, also spearheading UN reform by bringing together 10 UN system organisations. . . . He is the first Chair to lead Her Majesty's Government's Strategic Coherence of ODA-funded Research (SCOR) Board. He is Vice-Chair of the board of the Global Health Innovative Technology Fund in Tokyo, Chair of the Global Burden of Disease Independent Advisory Committee and Chair of the King Baudouin Foundation US. He is a member of the board for the African Health Research Institute, in Durban, and the Public Health Foundation of India and a member of the Oxford Martin Commission on Future Generations.

- Nadine Gbossa: A development professional with 20 years' experience dedicated to inclusive growth and sustainable development. She initiated her career with the United Nations Conference on Trade and Development in Geneva, and the United Nations Office for Project Services in New York. Since 2004, she has held senior management positions with the United Nations Development Programme (UNDP) and the International Fund for Agricultural Development (IFAD) based in Italy.

The Scientific Advisory Committee includes voting representatives of the FDA, the Gates Foundation, the NIH, the CDC, the Chinese CDC, the Wits Reproductive Health and HIV Institute, and more, and non-voting representatives of the WHO, Johnson & Johnson, Takeda, Pfizer, and Sanofi Pasteur, the vaccines division of the French multinational pharmaceutical company Sanofi. Sanofi Pasteur is the largest company in the world devoted entirely to vaccines.

CEPI also states in its Commitment to Tackling Racism:

A destructive legacy of racism has led to deeply entrenched implicit biases and institutional racism, which have hurt countless people for generations. These inequalities are widespread and, as we have seen in the current COVID-19 pandemic, have led to stark inequities in access to healthcare and poorer health outcomes for affected communities globally. Tackling this inequality is core to CEPI's mission to ensure fair access to all the vaccines we develop. Through our strategic partnerships in countries around the world we also seek to build vaccine Research & Development capacity, strengthen domestic expertise, and nurture scientific talent. In response to COVID-19, we've launched the COVID-19 Vaccine Global Access (COVAX) initiative, in partnership with the World Health Organization (WHO) and Gavi, to ensure equitable access to COVID-19 vaccines for all countries, at all levels of development.

GAVI is the product of founding partners the WHO, UNICEF, the World Bank, and the Gates Foundation. Other significant sources of funding come from a number of national governments such as China, plus the European Commission, Mastercard, Unilever, la Caixa Banking Foundation, Comic Relief, the ELMA Vaccines and Immunization Foundation, and the International Federation of Pharmaceutical Wholesalers, with manufacturer members Bayer Healthcare Pharmaceuticals, Johnson & Johnson, GlaxoSmithKline, Mylan, Merck, Pfizer, and Sanofi. GAVI states that:

Gavi now vaccinates almost half of the world's children, giving it tremendous power to negotiate vaccines at prices that are affordable for the poorest countries and to remove the commercial risks that previously kept manufacturers from serving them. . . . At the same time, the pool of manufacturers producing prequalified Gavi -supported vaccines has grown from five in 2001 (with one in Africa) to 17 in 2017 (with 11 in Africa, Asia and Latin America).

GAVI's 2008 Accelerated Vaccine Introduction initiative (AVI) was a partnership with WHO, UNICEF, and a consortium of technical partners including PATH, Johns Hopkins University, the US CDC, Aga Khan University (Pakistan), the International Vaccine Institute (South Korea), the Norwegian Institute of Public Health, and the University of the Witwatersrand (South Africa).

Returning to the recommendations of the WEF, Johns Hopkins, and the Gates Foundation:

> Countries, international organizations, and global transportation companies should work together to maintain travel and trade during severe pandemics. Travel and trade are essential to the global economy as well as to national and even local economies, and they should be maintained even in the face of a pandemic. . . . Governments should provide more resources and support for the development and surge manufacturing of vaccines, therapeutics, and diagnostics that will be needed during a severe pandemic. . . . In coordination with WHO, CEPI, GAVI, and other relevant multilateral and domestic mechanisms, investments should be made in new technologies and industrial approaches. . . . Global business should recognize the economic burden of pandemics and fight for stronger preparedness. . . . Global business leaders should play a far more dynamic role as advocates with a stake in stronger pandemic preparedness. . . . International organizations should prioritize reducing economic impacts of epidemics and pandemics. . . . The World Bank, the International Monetary Fund, regional development banks, national governments, foundations, and others should explore ways to increase the amount and availability of funds in a pandemic and ensure that they can be flexibly used where needed. . . . Governments and the private sector should assign a greater priority to developing methods to combat mis- and disinformation prior to the next pandemic response. . . . Governments will need to partner with traditional and social media companies to research and develop nimble approaches to countering misinformation. This will require developing the ability to flood media with fast, accurate, and consistent information. . . . National public health agencies should work in close collaboration with WHO to create the capability to rapidly develop and release consistent health messages. For their part, media companies should commit to ensuring that authoritative messages are prioritized and that false messages are suppressed including though the use of technology.

These forces have been acting for some time, but technology has really been the accelerant, the gasoline to the fire.

In the midst of the explosion of coronavirus measures in mid-2020, Columbia University researchers at the Vagelos College of Physicians and Surgeons at Columbia University Irving Medical Center led by David Goldstein with additional support from UCLA and West Los Angeles Veteran Affairs Medical Center proposed that reducing testosterone in male patients with COVID-19 would "lessen its severity" by preventing the new coronavirus from entering lung cells.

And yet, two points: researchers from the University of Turku in 2018 linked estrogen and T cell immune response to autoimmune inflammation; women are more prone to the development of autoimmune diseases because of higher levels of estrogen! Furthermore, HIV increases the risk of lung disease because of ongoing inflammation within the immune system. Whereas COPD for example usually affects HIV-negative men and women in their 50s and 60s, it manifests at much younger ages in people with HIV. There is evidence that COVID-19 damages the male testes and may even cause sterility, and there is also evidence that it may result in long-term diminished lung capacity. "We think eliminating testosterone production is too extreme for patients with mild disease," Goldstein says, but lowering testosterone is fine, with the resultant imbalance a breeding-ground for depression and disease in men, not to mention erectile dysfunction. But there are pills and injections for all of that! Goldstein, by the way, is a founder of and holds equity in Pairnomix and Praxis, serves as a consultant to AstraZeneca, and has received research support from Janssen, Gilead, Biogen, AstraZeneca, and UCB.

Then there's the WHO recommendation that yet another "treatment" for COVID-19 that lowers the strength of the immune system in the form of corticosteroids could be used despite the fact that the CDC states, "People with weakened immune systems are at higher risk of getting severely sick from SARS-CoV-2, the virus that causes COVID-19." Also, and suspiciously, from the CDC: "If you have HIV and a low CD4 cell count or are not on HIV treatment, you might be at higher risk for severe illness from COVID-19." As Jeffrey Kluger writes regarding the WHO's recommendations:

> You'd think a robust immune system would be an awfully good thing to have if you're battling COVID-19—and much of the time it is. But in the most extreme cases—the ones the World Health Organization (WHO) labels as "severe and critical" . . . corticosteroids, a class of drugs that reduce inflammation, could prevent at least some cases of coronavirus-related ARDS and the resulting deaths. . . . WHO also warned against "indiscriminate use" of any anti-COVID-19 therapeutic, including steroids, for fear of creating global shortages.

In case you were wondering, the top key manufacturers in the corticosteroids market according to Industry Research are Pfizer, Novartis, Merck, GlaxoSmithKline, Cipla, Sumitomo, Sanofi, Johnson & Johnson, and AstraZeneca.

In order to promote hormonal contraceptive use, the WHO helps promote World Contraception Day sponsored by Bayer and supported by the UNFPA, USAID, and the International Planned Parenthood Federation, among others. Pfizer manufactures the Depo-Provera Contraceptive Injection the Israelis administer to Ethiopian women they take in to look good for propaganda purposes but who they do not want reproducing. Merck is the manufacturer of the NuvaRing, a combined hormonal contraceptive vaginal ring, and Implanon, a single-rod long-acting hormonal contraceptive birth control subdermal implant that is inserted just under the skin of the upper arm. Johnson & Johnson owns Ortho-McNeil Pharmaceutical, which makes diaphragms, and the oral contraceptive pill brands Ortho Tri-cyclen and Ortho-Evra.

Industry Research lists Abbott Laboratories, Pfizer, Novartis, Bayer, Merck, Eli Lilly, Allergan, and Novo Nordisk as seven of the ten "key players" in the estrogen replacement therapy industry. For testosterone, according to 360 Market Updates:

> AbbVie, Endo International, Eli Lilly, Pfizer, Actavis (Allergan), Bayer . . . are the leaders of the industry. The top five players together held about 80% of the market in the same year and they hold key technologies and patents, with high-end customers [and] have been formed in the monopoly position in the industry.

The Council on Foreign Relations positively point to the work of Merck on developing a COVID-19 vaccine, and according to *Forbes*, among the top nine companies "racing for a COVID-19 vaccine" are included Johnson & Johnson, Pfizer, GlaxoSmithKline in collaboration with Sanofi, AstraZeneca in collaboration with Oxford University, and Moderna in collaboration with Lonza (a Swiss multinational chemical and biotechnology company) and NIAID with Anthony Fauci as Director. Claire Felter, writing for the Council on Foreign Relations, outlines the work being done in this arena:

> Vaccines are frequently collaborative efforts across sectors of society, with private pharmaceutical firms teaming up with public health agencies or university labs. For instance, a recently approved Ebola vaccine was ultimately developed by multinational pharmaceutical company Merck but also involved Canadian and U.S. public health agencies, a tiny Iowa-based biotech firm, U.S. Defense Department researchers, and the WHO.... President Donald J. Trump's administration launched a project known as Operation Warp Speed aimed at developing an effective vaccine and manufacturing enough doses for all three hundred million Americans by early 2021. The effort, which has pledged billions of dollars to companies with promising vaccine candidates, brings together agencies within the Department of Health and Human Services (HHS)—including the Centers for Disease Control and Prevention (CDC), the National Institutes of Health (NIH), and the Food and Drug Administration (FDA)—and the Department of Defense. The European Commission is also funding several candidates; and in a virtual summit hosted by the European Union, world leaders, organizations, and banks pledged $8 billion for vaccine research. In China, the government is closely overseeing efforts on its territory, with state-owned firms making up about two-fifths of the country's vaccine industry. International institutions. The WHO and other multilateral institutions such as the World Bank are focused on financing and manufacturing a COVID-19 vaccine for global use, in particular to ensure fair allocation among all countries. Also at the forefront of multilateral efforts is the Coalition for Epidemic Preparedness Innovations (CEPI), a global alliance that was founded by Norway, India, the Bill & Melinda Gates Foundation, the UK-based Wellcome Trust, and the World Economic Forum. Gavi, the Vaccine Alliance—also founded by the Gates Foundation—is a public-private partnership focused on improving vaccine access for lower-income countries. In June, the WHO, CEPI, and Gavi launched COVAX, a global initiative seeking more than $18 billion in funding to procure two billion doses of a vaccine by the end of 2021.... The pharmaceutical industry is driving much of the push toward a vaccine. Companies ranging from biotech start-ups to giants such as Johnson & Johnson and China-based Sinopharm have rapidly shifted their research and development (R&D) efforts to focus on COVID-19. While early research into a vaccine candidate typically receives government funding, such as NIH grants in the case of the United States, the bulk of financing for clinical development generally comes from private sources.... In July, NIAID Director Anthony Fauci said he felt "good about the projected timetable," and vaccine makers testified before the U.S. Congress that the sped-up process would in no way

compromise the safety or effectiveness of a vaccine. In one deal under Warp Speed, Pfizer signed a $1.95 billion contract to manufacture and distribute one hundred million doses by the end of 2020 at no cost to Americans if phase-three trials of its candidate succeed. . . . Among the most promising treatment candidates is the antiviral drug remdesivir, which was developed by U.S.-based Gilead Sciences and already authorized for emergency use by the FDA. An NIAID trial of remdesivir that involved dozens of sites in the United States, Europe, and Asia showed faster rates of recovery from the virus.

Whether the coronavirus leak was intentional or the subsequent police state actions were the result of not letting a good crisis go to waste, we do know research into the virus probably as a bio-weapon was officially-sanctioned, according to *Newsweek*:

> The National Institute for Allergy and Infectious Diseases, the organization led by Dr. Fauci, funded scientists at the Wuhan Institute of Virology and other institutions for work on gain-of-function research on bat coronaviruses. In 2019, with the backing of NIAID, the National Institutes of Health committed $3.7 million over six years for research that included some gain-of-function work. The program followed another $3.7 million, 5-year project for collecting and studying bat coronaviruses, which ended in 2019, bringing the total to $7.4 million. Many scientists have criticized gain of function research, which involves manipulating viruses in the lab to explore their potential for infecting humans, because it creates a risk of starting a pandemic from accidental release. SARS-CoV-2, the virus now causing a global pandemic, is believed to have originated in bats. U.S. intelligence, after originally asserting that the coronavirus had occurred naturally, conceded last month that the pandemic may have originated in a leak from the Wuhan lab.

How many times during the coronavirus lock-downs did we hear the phrase "the new normal," surely a trial run for the coming top-down One World government that's been building in strength for a century-plus.

With varying degrees of certainty, the origins of HIV (less so) and the coronavirus (more so) can be traced, but the symptoms, treatment, and genesis of coronavirus as they intersect with that of HIV should raise a few eyebrows, not least of which would include Fauci's role. The intentionality of COVID's release as a real-time trial run rather than a simulation—or at the very least the intentional inaction allowing it to spread for the same purposes, including data collection, research, and experimentation—is looking increasingly-likely, however, given what we've discussed and the following, for Whitney Webb:

> The creation of the [University of Pittsburgh Medical Center] UPMC's [Regional Biocontainment Laboratory] RBL was first announced in 2003, when the National Institute of Allergy and Infectious Diseases (NIAID, then and currently led by Anthony Fauci) stated it would fund the laboratory's construction with an $18 million grant. . . . The Center for Vaccine Research was the second such institution to be officially added to the NIAID's "biodefense"

RBL network. . . . In January 2020 . . . UPMC was already at work developing a vaccine to protect against the novel coronavirus that causes Covid-19, known as SARS-CoV-2. That month, before the state of Pennsylvania had a single case of Covid-19, UPMC formed a "coronavirus task force," which was initially focused on lobbying the US Centers for Disease Control and Prevention (CDC) to obtain samples of live SARS-CoV-2 for research purposes. . . . A little over a month after the live SARS-CoV-2 samples were received by UPMC's Center for Vaccine Research, UPMC received a $5 million grant from CEPI. . . . The grant was officially awarded to "an international academic-industry partnership" that the Center for Vaccine Research had recently formed with the Institut Pasteur in France and Austrian vaccine manufacturer Themis [a CEPI partner for Lassa and MERS vaccines— MERS, per the WHO, "is a viral respiratory disease caused by a novel coronavirus (Middle East respiratory syndrome coronavirus, or MERS-CoV) that was first identified in Saudi Arabia in 2012. Coronaviruses are a large family of viruses that can cause diseases ranging from the common cold to Severe Acute Respiratory Syndrome, SARS"]. Soon after, in May, Themis was acquired by vaccine giant Merck. . . . Recently obtained documents reveal that the BSL-3 lab that is part of UPMC's Center for Vaccine Research is conducting eyebrow-raising research involving combining SARS-CoV-2 with *Bacillus anthracis*, the causative agent of anthrax infection. . . . Since 2000, the studies that have examined the use of genetically modified anthrax as a potential vaccine vector have been affiliated with Harvard University. One of these studies was on the use of anthrax as a vector in a potential HIV vaccine and was jointly conducted in 2000 by Harvard researchers and the vaccine company Avant Immunotherapeutics (now part of Celldex). . . . The Harvard researchers involved in that 2000 study, however, continued to investigate the possibility of an anthrax-based HIV vaccine in 2003, 2004, and 2005. . . . The Center for Vaccine Research's director, Paul Duprex . . . is a former chief scientist for Johnson & Johnson whose subsequent foray into academia was largely funded with research grants from the NIH and the Pentagon's Defense Advanced Research Projects Agency (DARPA).

COVID-19 has been colloquially referred-to as "lung AIDS," for a number of reasons including that it may also be sexually-transmitted. Further, as Trenton Straube reported in January 2020:

Health officials in China are including two HIV meds as treatment for pneumonia caused by the new coronavirus (COVID-19). . . . Specifically, the country's National Health Commission in Beijing recommends the HIV drug Kaletra, which is manufactured by AbbVie and is also marketed as Aluvia.

Here's some more fun from Corey Lynn:

In 2013, the AbbVie Foundation, Takeda Pharmaceutical Company Ltd., Microsoft, and several others, as Clinton Global Initiative (CGI) members,[130] partnered to bring a virtual mentoring STEM system to 15 high schools in Illinois. AbbVie went on to donate $40 million to fund the rebuilding of North Chicago's middle school, Neal Math & Science Academy, in 2019, which was part of a $350 million charitable contribution to nonprofit partners. $15 million went to the University of Chicago's Education Lab.[131] In 2014, AbbVie, along with Abbott, Merck, and others, partnered with CGI to deliver emergency equipment to West Africa to fight Ebola. 2014 was a busy year for AbbVie. They also teamed up with Google in a $1.5 billion dollar research partnership. Google Inc.'s secretive biotech company, Calico LLC partnered with AbbVie Inc. to develop anti-aging drugs. By 2018, they were focusing on over two dozen projects with a special interest in neuroscience and targeting cellular stress systems, but have kept very hush hush about it. Each have contributed another $500 million to continue this partnership. Calico went from a staff of 10 to a team of 150-plus, headquartered in San Francisco. [Jewish] Arthur Levinson, the former Chairman of Genentech, is the current Chairman of Apple Inc. and CEO of Google's Calico LLC. In 2015, Abbott Laboratories donated between $50,000 – $100,000 to the Clinton Foundation. In 2016, the Bill & Melinda Gates Foundation granted Takeda Pharmaceutical Company over $40 million "to increase total global capacity to meet potential demand for Inactivated Poliovirus Vaccine (IPV) in 2019/2020, and ensure adequate vaccine supply at an affordable cost." In 2016, AbbVie contributed $44,538 to Hillary Clinton's presidential campaign. In 2017, as a CGI partner, AbbVie stepped up again, along with 43 other companies, to deliver medicine and medical supplies to Puerto Rico. The following year AbbVie donated $50 million each to Direct Relief and Habitat for Humanity International. Direct Relief is who had the "Direct Relief-chartered MD-11 cargo jet" that flew the supplies to Puerto Rico in 2017. Coincidence? Interesting side note: On Adam Schiff's 2016 financial disclosure report, it indicates that he has shares in AbbVie Inc. Sure, a lot of people do. But he also holds shares in Franklin Templeton and BlackRock, and Franklin Templeton Investments was just implicated in the laundering of $7.4 billion in external government loan bonds between 2013 and 2014, allegedly from family members of Ukrainian ex-President Yanukovych. Franklin Templeton Investments has significant ties to the Democratic Party, including former President Obama, as does the managing director of BlackRock who holds the largest share in Franklin Templeton Investments. All of this is related to the $16.5 million that the former Vice President Joe Biden's son Hunter Biden received from Burisma.

BlackRock donates to Chatham House and oversaw the merger of Bayer and Monsanto as a major shareholder in both companies.

---

[130] The reader should recall here the 2015 launch of Open for Business at the Clinton Global Initiative Annual Summit. The ruling class is nothing if not incestuous; it bears repeating that the neo-liberal system's various arms are all inextricably intertwined.

[131] Recall here the Pritzker ties to the University of Chicago.

The UNDP, IRGT: A Global Network of Trans Women and HIV, the United Nations Population Fund, the UCSF Center of Excellence for Transgender Health, the Johns Hopkins Bloomberg School of Public Health, the World Health Organization, the Joint United Nations Programme on HIV/AIDS (UNAIDS), USAID, and the United States President's Emergency Plan for AIDS Relief (PEPFAR) teamed up in 2016 to publish its "Implementing Comprehensive HIV and STI Programmes with Transgender People" based on treatment recommendations from the WHO. This transgender implementation tool is known informally as the TRANSIT and is the third in a series of tools on implementing HIV and STI programs with "key populations" such as the sex worker implementation tool (SWIT) published by the WHO in 2013 and the implementation tool for men who have sex with men (MSMIT) published by the United Nations Population Fund in 2015.

In 2019, UNAIDS called on all countries to "remove discriminatory laws against lesbian, gay, bisexual, transgender and intersex (LGBTI) people" because, in their own words:

> Stigma towards key populations—gay men and other men who have sex with men, sex workers, transgender people, people who inject drugs and prisoners and other incarcerated people—is reinforced by criminal laws. These in turn fuel violence, exploitation and a climate of fear, hindering efforts to make HIV services available to the people who need them.

"We all have a moral and legal obligation to remove discriminatory laws and enact laws that protect people from discrimination," said Gunilla Carlsson, former interim UNAIDS Executive Director and former Swedish Minister for International Development Cooperation, whose resumé also includes Board or Panel membership with the UN Secretary General's High-Level Panel of Eminent Persons on the Post-2015 Development Agenda, the World Bank Group's High Level Advisory Council on Women's Economic Empowerment, the European Council on Foreign Relations, GAVI, the Global Fund, and Annexin Pharmaceuticals. "To end the AIDS epidemic, people need to be protected from harm. We need justice and equality for all." Equality is going to end AIDS?

The Global Fund is a name we've seen come up a lot and it warrants more attention. It is a financing and partnership organization that aims to "attract, leverage and invest additional resources to end the epidemics of HIV/AIDS, tuberculosis, and malaria to support attainment of the Sustainable Development Goals established by the United Nations." It was hosted by the World Health Organization from its inception in 2002 until 2009. It has also collaborated with USAID.

As regards COVID, the Global Fund states:

> Under the World Health Organization's leadership, the Global Fund is using its experience working with partners and governments in more than 100 countries to coordinate our response on a massive global scale. The Global Fund's response to the pandemic makes available more than US$1 billion through our COVID-19 Response Mechanism and grant flexibilities.

Similarly, but more explicitly-intersectional, the Open Society Foundations announced in April 2020 that it would grant more than $16 million in support of "urgent climate crisis priorities related to the COVID-19 pandemic, with a focus on advancing green economic stimulus plans and stopping authoritarian efforts to roll back environmental progress." The package was part of more than a $130 million total "investment."

"The COVID-19 pandemic has made all too real the dangers of ignoring science. Our world is facing two emergencies at once—both the climate crisis and a global pandemic—and it is deepening racial, gender, and economic injustices," said Patrick Gaspard, President of the Open Society Foundations. According to the Open Society Foundations' press release:

> Scientists have long warned that the climate crisis is a 'threat multiplier,' meaning it will unleash and exacerbate existing social inequalities and injustices. The COVID-19 pandemic has made the climate threat even worse, and revealed that urgent, science-based action on both issues is necessary to prevent catastrophic impacts on human health, the environment, and the global economy.

In April 2015, the Open Society Foundations convened a consultation of experts and advocates "concerned about the future" of the Global Fund particularly in the areas of preserving support to "important programs in middle-income countries, realizing the Global Fund's human rights objectives, and the role of the Global Fund in supporting access to essential medicines."

Current Board members of the Global Fund include:

- Chairman Donald Kaberuka (President of the African Development Bank and chairman of its board of directors from 2005–2015. Prior to that he was finance minister of Rwanda from 1997–2005, during which he also served as governor for Rwanda for the International Monetary Fund and the World Bank.)
- Erika Castellanos—alternate (GATE, an HIV positive transgender activists from Belize residing in the Netherlands)
- Joia Mukherjee—alternate (associate professor at Harvard Medical School)
- Birgit Pickel (Deputy Director General for Human Rights, Gender and Social Development at the German Federal Ministry for Economic Cooperation and Development)
- Deborah L. Birx (Coordinator of the United States Government Activities to Combat HIV/AIDS and US Special Representative for Global Health Diplomacy, world-renowned medical expert and leader in the field of HIV/AIDS. Her three-decade-long career has focused on HIV/AIDS immunology, vaccine research, and global health. From her US State Department biography: "The White House has appointed world-renowned global health official and physician Ambassador Deborah Birx to the Office of the Vice President to aid in the whole of government response to COVID-19 as the Coronavirus Response Coordinator. . . . As the U.S. Global AIDS

Coordinator, Ambassador Birx oversees the implementation of the U.S. President's Emergency Plan for AIDS Relief (PEPFAR), the largest commitment by any nation to combat a single disease in history, as well as all U.S. Government engagement with the Global Fund to Fight AIDS, Tuberculosis and Malaria. Serving as the U.S. Special Representative for Global Health Diplomacy, she aligns the U.S. Government's diplomacy with foreign assistance programs. . . . In 1985, Ambassador Birx began her career with the Department of Defense (DoD) as a military-trained clinician in immunology, focusing on HIV/AIDS vaccine research. From 1985–1989, she served as an Assistant Chief of the Hospital Immunology Service at Walter Reed Army Medical Center. Through her professionalism and leadership in the field, she progressed to serve as the Director of the U.S. Military HIV Research Program (USMHRP) at the Walter Reed Army Institute of Research from 1996–2005. Ambassador Birx helped lead one of the most influential HIV vaccine trials in history (known as RV 144 or the Thai trial), which provided the first supporting evidence of any vaccine's potential effectiveness in preventing HIV infection. . . . From 2005–2014, Ambassador Birx served successfully as the Director of CDC's Division of Global HIV/AIDS (DGHA), which is part of the agency's Center for Global Health. As DGHA Director, she utilized her leadership ability, superior technical skills, and infectious passion to achieve tremendous public health impact. She successfully led the implementation of CDC's PEPFAR programs around the world and managed an annual budget of more than $1.5 billion. Ambassador Birx was responsible for all of the agency's global HIV/AIDS activities, including providing oversight to more than 400 staff at headquarters, over 1,500 staff in the field, and more than 45 country and regional offices in Africa, Asia, Caribbean, and Latin America."

- Winnie Byanyima, non-voting (Executive Director of UNAIDS, former Executive Director of Oxfam International and former Director of Gender and Development at the United Nations Development Program)
- Ren Minghui, non-voting (Assistant Director-General at WHO for HIV/AIDS, Tuberculosis, Malaria and Neglected Tropical Diseases)
- Muhammad Ali Pate, non-voting (World Bank Global Director of Health, Nutrition, and Population and the Director of the Global Financing Facility for Women, Children, and Adolescents)
- Kieran Daly (Responsible for HIV, TB, malaria and the Global Fund. With an academic background in development economics, he served as the Chief Executive Officer of the International Council of AIDS Service Organizations (ICASO), and also worked for the International HIV/AIDS Alliance as the Senior Policy Advisor. He has extensive experience with the UN, with particular focus on HIV policy and programming.)
- Marja Esveld (currently leads the Global Health team at the Ministry of Foreign Affairs in the Netherlands. Esveld has over two decades of experience in global and European health, working at the Dutch Ministry of Health, several other governmental health bodies and the World Health Organization)
- Mohsen Asadi-Lari (former member of the Executive Board of the World Health Organization)
- Joshua Tabah (Director General of Health and Nutrition at Global Affairs

Canada. He joined the Canadian International Development Agency in 2003 and has worked in various roles in multilateral affairs and humanitarian assistance. Tabah was previously the Director General of Inclusive Growth, Governance and Innovation.)

- Garrett Grigsby—alternate (From his HHS biography: "Garrett Grigsby has served as Director of the Office of Global Affairs since May 2017. Garrett served on the staff of the U.S. Senate Committee on Foreign Relations (SFRC) throughout the 1990s. As SFRC Deputy Staff Director he was responsible for oversight of all U.S. Government foreign assistance programs, including global health initiatives. Garrett joined the U.S. Agency for International Development (USAID) in 2002 as Deputy Assistant Administrator for the Bureau for Democracy, Conflict, and Humanitarian Assistance where he oversaw global disaster relief and humanitarian programs. In 2005, he was appointed Director of USAID's Center of Faith-Based and Community Initiatives. From 2006–2014, Garrett consulted for U.S. non-profits to support their global health work. From 2014 until joining HHS Garrett served as Executive Director of Christian Connections for International Health, an association of non-profits focused on promoting global health and wholeness.")
- Paul Schaper—alternate (Executive Director, Global Public Policy, Merck & Co., Paul Schaper is responsible for global health policy issues in infectious disease, non-communicable disease, and reproductive health at Merck & Co. His work has involved HIV prevention and treatment issues for over two decades. In previous positions at Merck, he worked in the vaccine division on Merck's HIV and HPV vaccine programs.)

The Global Fund's biggest NGO supporter financially is the Bill and Melinda Gates Foundation, however (RED) is another. (RED)'s partners include Salesforce, Starbucks, Primark, Apple, Bank of America, Beats, and Durex; (RED) also highlights Roche as a featured supporter and Amazon is a product and marketing partner. (RED) is a division of The ONE Campaign, "a global movement campaigning to end extreme poverty and preventable disease by 2030." Its Board of Directors includes Bono (co-founder of (RED) and ONE), Susan Buffett, former UK Prime Minister David Cameron, Joe Cerrell (Gates Foundation), Morton Halperin (Open Society Foundations), Sheryl Sandberg (Facebook), Kevin Sheekey (Bloomberg LP), and Lawrence/Larry Summers. ONE's Global Leadership Circle includes Lynne Benioff and representatives of JP Morgan Chase, Cargill, and the Rockefeller Foundation. Neville Gabriel, CEO of the OTHER Foundation and formerly of the Open Society Foundations, is on the African Policy Advisory Board. Top donors include: the Gates Foundation, SAP, the Rockefeller Foundation, Sheryl Sandberg, Larry Summers, Google, Bank of America, Merck, Johnson & Johnson, the William and Flora Hewlett Foundation, Susan Buffett's Sherwood Foundation, the David Geffen Foundation, Cargill, David Cameron, Lynne and Marc Benioff, and the Open Society Policy Center.

Other donors to the Global Fund include or have included: the Rockefeller Foundation; Takeda Pharmaceutical Company; Comic Relief; Chevron; the United Nations Foundation and its donors; Anglo-American; the MAC AIDS Fund and MAC Cosmetics; and numerous governments and governing bodies.

The United Nations Foundation was created in 1998 with Ted Turner's $1 billion gift to support United Nations causes and activities. Its four current areas of focus are: energy and climate, global health, the United Nations, and women and population. The UN Foundation hosts (and co-founded with the Rockefeller Foundation and the Vodafone Foundation) the mHealth Alliance, which:

> Acts as a convener of the mobile health (mHealth) community and seeks to share the collective lessons learned and best practices developed so that mHealth can continue to advance improved health outcomes, including through the prevention, diagnosis, and treatment of HIV/AIDS.[132]

According to the Global Fund's 2019 Annual Report:

> The Global Fund achieved its goal of securing at least USD 14 billion in donor pledges for the Sixth Replenishment (2020–22) period during the Pledging Conference. This amount is the largest amount ever pledged to a multilateral health organization and represents an increase of 15 percent compared to the amount pledged during the 2017–19 period. The outcome of the Replenishment Pledging Conference demonstrates the international community's willingness to accelerate progress towards ending the epidemics by 2030 in line with SUSTAINABLE DEVELOPMENT GOAL 3: Ensure healthy lives and *promote well-being for all at all ages* (emphasis added). . . . The Global Fund will continue to mobilize funds throughout the Sixth Replenishment period. In Lyon, President Macron committed to support these efforts alongside Mr. Bill Gates and Bono to secure USD 100 million for the Global Fund within the 2020–22 period. . . . In addition, 11 private sector partnerships for innovation and improved implementation were launched, including with new partners such as Google Cloud, Mastercard, Microsoft, Société Générale and the Thomson Reuters Foundation.

In 2011, the Bill and Melinda Gates Foundation was the second-highest funder of HIV vaccine R&D after the US Government (including the National Institutes of Health [NIH], the U.S. Military HIV Research Program [MHRP], and the United States Agency for International Development [USAID]). As Marlee Tichenor and Devi Sridhar write:

---

[132] Dr. Robert Hickson's exquisite article from August 2017 entitled "Hilaire Belloc's 'The Barbarians' (1912) and the Analogy of a Self-Sabotaging Cultural Immune System" offers an apropos analogy, especially in light of the coronavirus, of auto-immune diseases and the Catholic Church's immune system, an analogy which can and should be extended to Western civilization as a whole: "In this context, we might also helpfully recall what the Roman historian, Livy, had earlier (and very trenchantly) written, even back in 19 B.C., and in the general introduction to his own multivolume history of Rome. Livy had then said that Rome had so degenerated and come down in those times even to such a point where 'we can tolerate neither our vices nor their remedies' ('donec ad haec tempora quibus nec vitia nostra nec remedia pati possumus peruentum est').This compact insight about cumulative decadence is certainly 'a terrible thing to think upon' (in the words of Father François Rabelais). Into such a weakened culture — to include a fatigued and weakened culture and immune system of the Catholic Church — there will come various parasites and barbarians. They should be expected (and firmly resisted). For, a certain kind of weakness constitutes a 'provocative weakness' (in the memorable words of Dr. Fritz Kraemer)—'for it is so weak that it is provocative to others.'"

Over the past 20 years, the foundation has grown into one of the leading voices in global health, often sitting at the table with heads of state and heads of multilateral organisations as decisions are made about investment priorities. This has disrupted the nature of global health governance through changing the nature of what it means to be "public." In 2017, the Gates Foundation provided $3.3bn (£2.5bn; €2.9bn) of the world's global health funding, tying the private philanthropic organisation in second with the United Kingdom for development assistance for health. The Gates Foundation's major investment in the World Health Organization, the Global Fund to Fight AIDS, Tuberculosis, and Malaria, and GAVI, the Vaccine Alliance—along with the global health partnerships it helped found, such as the Primary Health Care Performance Initiative and the Global Financing Facility—make clear in budgetary terms how influential the Gates Foundation is in setting the agenda and in managing the world's health. In the process, the Gates Foundation has simultaneously expanded its reach into the production of global health data, the dissemination of these data, and their uptake by global health institutions such as WHO and the World Bank. The expansion of private, albeit philanthropic, interests into domains that are perceived as public and independent raises major questions about the influence of private actors, the effects of the monopolisation of data, and the nature of accountability in global health governance. The present governance system provides no mechanisms to tackle these issues. The Gates Foundation financially backs the Institute for Health Metrics and Evaluation (IHME), part of the University of Washington, through an initial grant of $105m and a follow-up grant of $279m to produce global health data. . . . The Gates Foundation helps increase the influence of these data and shapes how global health problems are discussed, as is evident in the high number of citations of these studies. Furthermore, in May 2018, the IHME and WHO signed a memorandum of understanding, which noted that from 2019 there will be a single global burden of disease study published in the *Lancet*, rather than one produced by WHO and one by IHME. WHO has agreed to use IHME data in their own 2019–23 general programme of work and for their own estimates for burden of disease, and WHO data specialists will be seconded to the IHME.

This is the exact same methodology at play with the globalist institutions' endeavors to re-shape and control the nature of the world's food supply, as witnessed by such proposals in line with the Great Reset! Already the consolidation of production and its nature has occurred to a large degree, but what we are witnessing is the next phase, a kind of globalized feudalism with UBI, nutrient-"reinforced" slop, and mandatory sex changes and "vaccines" containing God-knows-what.

Of further discomfort, projects like the "doomsday seed bank" seem to telegraph the "elites" preparing for something, the details of which we do not know but the nature of which is sure to be terrible, for F. William Engdahl:

The first notable point is who is sponsoring the doomsday seed vault. Here joining the Norwegians are . . . the Bill & Melinda Gates Foundation; the US agribusiness giant DuPont/Pioneer Hi-Bred, one of the world's largest owners of patented genetically-modified (GMO) plant seeds and related agrichemicals; Syngenta, the Swiss-based major GMO seed and agrichemicals company through its Syngenta Foundation; the Rockefeller Foundation, the private group who created the "gene revolution with over $100 million of seed money since the 1970's; CGIAR, the global network created by the Rockefeller Foundation to promote its ideal of genetic purity through agriculture change.

The parallels with the transgender agenda are striking because they are the same actors! Again for F. William Engdahl:

Through the Green Revolution, the Rockefeller Foundation and later Ford Foundation worked hand-in-hand shaping and supporting the foreign policy goals of the United States Agency for International Development (USAID) and of the CIA. One major effect of the Green Revolution was to depopulate the countryside of peasants who were forced to flee into shantytown slums around the cities in desperate search for work. That was no accident; it was part of the plan to create cheap labor pools for forthcoming US multinational manufactures, the 'globalization' of recent years. The Green Revolution was typically accompanied by large irrigation projects which often included World Bank loans to construct huge new dams, and flood previously settled areas and fertile farmland in the process. Also, super-wheat produced greater yields by saturating the soil with huge amounts of fertilizer per acre, the fertilizer being the product of nitrates and petroleum, commodities controlled by the Rockefeller-dominated Seven Sisters major oil companies. Huge quantities of herbicides and pesticides were also used, creating additional markets for the oil and chemical giants. As one analyst put it, in effect, the Green Revolution was merely a chemical revolution. At no point could developing nations pay for the huge amounts of chemical fertilizers and pesticides. They would get the credit courtesy of the World Bank and special loans by Chase Bank and other large New York banks, backed by US Government guarantees.

Speaking of Chase—and speaking *to* Chase—as Bill Gates stated in his January 2018 address at the JP Morgan (Chase) Healthcare Conference in San Francisco, which featured a keynote address by GlaxoSmithKline CEO Emma Walmsley at its 2020 meeting:

We don't have to wait 20 or 30 years. Even in the shorter term, impact and earnings are not mutually exclusive for the private-sector. As you probably know, global health is our primary focus at the Gates Foundation, although we also work in a few other areas that are big levers for impact like agricultural development and public education here in the U.S. Over the last five years, we have invested nearly $12 billion in global health. This includes grants and equity investments in companies with promising technologies that have potential application in global health. . . . The questions driving your research agendas today in biotech and pharma, and the problems we're trying to solve in global health, are starting to converge in exciting ways.

One November 2012 report among various such reports throughout the years authored by Funders Concerned About AIDS (FCAA) and the European HIV/AIDS Funders Group was funded Broadway Cares/Equity Fights AIDS, the New Venture Fund, and UNAIDS to provide a "state of the union" of sorts regarding multilateral and other "philanthropic" funding endeavors by the Establishment. As stated, any number would do, but this one was selected just as a case-in-point. At that time, the FCAA Resource Tracking Advisory Committee consisted of: Anu Gupta, Johnson & Johnson; Alicia Carbaugh and Jen Kates, The Henry J. Kaiser Family Foundation; Erika Arthun, The Bill & Melinda Gates Foundation; Owen Ryan, amfAR; Kevin Fisher, AVAC; and Anja Grujovic, UNAIDS. Its Board featured representatives of amfAR, Johnson & Johnson, the MAC AIDS Fund, the Open Society Foundations, ViiV Healthcare, the Levi Strauss Foundation, and the Bristol-Myers Squibb Foundation, among others.

Funders Concerned About AIDS's 2020 member-supporters included: Gilead Sciences, the Ford Foundation, the American Jewish World Service, ViiV Healthcare, the Open Society Foundations, amfAR, AIDS United, the Conrad N. Hilton Foundation, the Levi Strauss Foundation, the MAC VIVA Glam Fund (the new name of the MAC AIDS Fund), and more. Their Director of Operations Sarah Hamilton:

> Helped to manage collaborations with various peer organizations, such as FRE, Human Rights Funders Network, Funders for LGBTQ Issues, and Planned Parenthood, among others [and] worked for both non-profit and for-private clients including Columbia University and Johnson & Johnson.

Its current Board features people such as:

- Lisa Bohmer: Senior Program Officer of International Programs at the Conrad N. Hilton Foundation. Bohmer leads the Foundation's Children Affected by HIV and AIDS Strategic Initiative. . . . Bohmer is a public health professional with over 25 years of experience with programs, research and grant making in the areas of pediatric HIV/AIDS, OVC, maternal and child health, reproductive rights and the empowerment of women and girls. Prior to joining the Foundation, Bohmer was Director of Program Partnerships with the Elizabeth Glaser Pediatric AIDS Foundation where she led efforts to engage private donors and other NGOs towards the elimination of pediatric HIV. Past positions include HIV/AIDS Director for UNICEF in Ethiopia where she initiated services with partners to prevent mother to child HIV transmission. Bohmer has held other senior positions with Nike Foundation, the Pacific Institute for Women's Health and Ipas (where she was regional representative for East and Southern Africa in the 1990s). Her background includes five years living and working in Ethiopia and consultancies with numerous organizations including UNFPA, International Center for Research on Women and EngenderHealth. Bohmer has a Master's Degree in Public Health from UCLA.
- Kiyomi Fujikawa: A Seattle-based, mixed-race queer trans femme who

has been involved with movements to end gender- and state-based violence since 2001. Her political home is with queer and trans communities of color.

- Julia Greenberg: Director of Governance and Financing in the Open Society Foundations' Public Health Program. In this role she serves as a member of the Board constituency of the Global Fund to Fight AIDS, Tuberculosis and Malaria and as a Board member of Funders Concerned About AIDS. As a founding partner in The Fremont Center (2008–2015), she advised a diverse group of clients, including the Global Fund to Fight AIDS, TB, and Malaria, the Ford Foundation, and the International Treatment Preparedness Coalition, on the development of program, advocacy, and fundraising strategies. As the Director of the Grants Department at American Jewish World Service (AJWS), she developed a program that provided grants and technical assistance to 350 community organizations across Africa, Asia and Latin America working at the intersection of development, public health and human rights. In that role she guided the development of policies that positioned AJWS as a leading grantmaker in the areas of sexual health and rights (with a focus on LGBT and sex worker rights) and natural resource rights. As the Associate Director of AIDS-Free World, she led a successful campaign leading to the establishment of a new international agency for women (UN Women) and spearheaded advocacy and strategic litigation efforts to combat the homophobia and discriminatory laws fueling the epidemic in Jamaica.
- Korab Zuka: Vice President, Public Affairs, Gilead Sciences. Korab also spent 5 years working for the United Nations/OSCE in Kosovo, where he supported several projects focused on promoting education for underserved youth in Kosovo. While at the United Nations/OSCE, Korab also founded and served as Executive Director for the Center for Social Emancipation, a non-profit organization that sought to promote human rights for marginalized communities in Kosovo.
- Amelia Korangy: Senior Manager in External Affairs at ViiV Healthcare, where she leads the company's community giving in the US and Positive Action Programs. . . . She received a Master's degree in Social Enterprise from Columbia University's School of Social Work, where she focused on strategic philanthropy. . . . Prior to joining TCC Group, Korangy worked to design a national grantmaking strategy to end child sexual abuse as part of a partnered initiative between the Ms. Foundation for Women and the NoVo Foundation. She's a trained social worker, and has provided direct services to LGBTQ, HIV+, and homeless young people with organizations including the Hetrick-Martin Institute and Young Ladies of Tomorrow.
- Shari Turitz: Vice President for International Programs at the American Jewish World Service. Before joining AJWS in 2013, Shari served as director of programs for the Open Society Foundation's Public Health Program, co-leading a 55-person global team of international grant makers and advocates. Shari holds an M.A. from the Columbia University School of International and Public Affairs.

Additionally, still more relevant official US "collaborative" efforts are outlined by Jennifer Kates:

USAID, PEFPAR's largest implementing agency, has been addressing the impact of HIV among MSM since it first began carrying out international HIV activities in the 1980s. USAID efforts, funded under PEPFAR, to address the health of key populations have included its AIDSTAR2 and Health Policy Projects, both of which have supported MSM civil society capacity building, as well as its Research to Prevention (R2P) project, which included research to document and measure stigma and discrimination. . . . In December 2013, to support PEPFAR's Blueprint, USAID put out a Request for Application (RFA) for a new five year, $72 million cooperative agreement to address key populations. This RFA, *Linkages Across the Continuum of HIV Services for Key Populations Affected by HIV*, marks the first PEPFAR central procurement dedicated to addressing the needs of key populations. It is intended to strengthen the capacity of governments and civil society in PEPFAR partner countries to "implement high quality, sustainable, evidence-based and comprehensive HIV and AIDS prevention, care and treatment services with key populations at scale," including gay men and other MSM and transgender individuals. . . . Three, smaller-scale PEPFAR initiatives are focused on creating more civil society capacity to help scale up access to PEPFAR's HIV programs among key populations, including LGBT individuals: the "Key Populations Challenge Fund", a $20 million fund launched in June 2012 to support the expansion of interventions and services for key populations, including MSM, at the country level, focusing in 6 countries and two regions; the "Robert Carr Civil Society Network Fund," also launched in June 2012 by the U.S. along with the United Kingdom, Norway, and the Gates Foundation to support civil society organizations in scaling up access for key populations including LBGT individuals. The U.S. is providing $2 million to this effort; and the "Local Capacity Initiative Fund," which provides funding to PEPFAR country and regional teams to support local civil society organizations that advocate for key populations to work to reduce legal and policy structural barriers and stigma and discrimination.

Another representative example from the Global Philanthropy Project's June 2016 paper "The Road to Successful Partnerships: How governments in the Global North can effectively partner with intermediary organizations to support LGBTI communities in the Global South and East" is useful here, in the context of the implementation The LGBTI Global Development Partnership encompassing Albania, Bosnia and Herzegovina, Kosovo, Serbia, Colombia, Ecuador, Honduras, India, Kenya, Peru, South Africa, and the Dominican Republic. "The Partnership aimed to create sustainable replicable models for transformation and so chose countries that were ripe for strategic intervention." Those responsible for intervention are USAID, the Swedish International Development Cooperation Agency (SIDA), the Astraea Lesbian Foundation for Justice, the Swedish Federation for Lesbian, Gay, Bisexual, Transgender and Queer Rights (RFSL), the National LGBT Chamber of Commerce (NGLCC), Olivia Companies, and the Arcus Foundation, with the LGBTQ Victory

Institute and the Williams Institute at UCLA sub-awardees of Astraea under the Partnership.

The William and Flora Hewlett Foundation is yet another granting organization that, in their words, endeavors to "help solve social and environmental problems." In 2011, the Hewlett Foundation supported a Population Action International (PAI) project to monitor national budget expenditures for "reproductive health supplies," typically in the form of contraceptives. It is yet another organization that links climate change, "gender equality," and all the rest of it together: under past president Amy Coen, PAI worked to encourage the use of US power abroad to "fortify the reproductive-health advocacy movement in other countries and the links between population and reproductive health and global issues such as climate change." PAI played a role in the establishment of the Office of Population within USAID, the establishment of the United Nations Population Fund (UNFPA), and the raising of funds for the International Planned Parenthood Federation (IPPF). PAI's "Family Planning: The Smartest Investment We Can Make" brief highlights that, "increased access to contraception for women in developing countries is critical to improving maternal and newborn health, preventing HIV/ AIDS, and reducing unintended pregnancies and the need for abortion." Not all of that is necessarily a bad thing, and the Third World's massive over-population is a major issue especially in light of what we've discussed regarding the food supply, but any good is ultimately ancillary to what is indisputably an insidious agenda.

The Hewlett Foundation provides support to organizations like the International Planned Parenthood Federation, which provides "hormone therapy" and HIV/AIDS-related services in countries around the world as well as the hormonal contraceptives that interfere with natural processes and wreak havoc on women's minds and bodies. As John Q. Publius writes:

> Women who take "the pill" are nearly 10% worse at recognizing subtle expressions of complex emotions like pride or contempt, "blurring social judgement" according to new research. Hormonal contraceptive users, in contrast with non-users, were found to have higher rates of depression, anxiety, fatigue, neurotic symptoms, sexual disturbances, compulsion, anger, and negative menstrual effects, in addition to the physical effects, such as an increase in the risk of breast and cervical cancer, blood clots, and high blood pressure. Current contraceptive use was associated with an increased rate in depression, divorce, tranquilizer use, sexual dysfunction, suicide and other violent and accidental deaths. The definitive link between birth control usage and depression and other harmful side effects cannot be emphasized enough. These, in turn, contribute to and/or are exacerbated by other toxic by-products of modernity. Interestingly enough, however, the depression may not be attributable to the hormones themselves, but rather, "The evidence suggests that most of the side effects of hormonal contraception are a result of a psychological response to the practice of contraception. It is reasonable to hypothesize, given the present data, that contraceptive activity itself is inherently damaging to women." In other words, women become depressed due to a subconscious acknowledgement that they are artificially suppressing the natural instinct toward motherhood. Even more harmful, women then transfer their nurturing impulse toward destructive nonsense. . . . Add to the mix the

dehumanizing and depression-inducing state of modern "living" . . . and it is clear to see why women are so miserable.[133]

Regarding the origin of hormonal contraceptives, Publius continues:

> The deeply harmful mother of hormonal contraceptives the birth control pill owes its origin to two Jewish men. Carl Djerassi, a Jewish chemist, created a version of the birth control pill, but didn't have the funds to produce and distribute it. The Jewish Gregory Pincus was ultimately successful in his endeavor, and in 1957 the FDA approved it for use in regularizing menstrual cycles. Its approval as a contraceptive followed in 1960. The "abortion pill" (RU-486), was invented by the Jewish Etienne-Emile Baulieu (né Blum). Jewish State Senators Anthony Bielenson of California and Albert Blumenthal in New York were at the forefront of pushing for legalized abortion legislation in the US and the Jewish Henekh "Henry" Morgentaler was the leading figure in pushing for legalized abortion in Canada. Oh, and by the way, all four of the founders of the most influential American "abortion activist" group, the National Abortion Rights Action League (NARAL), were Jewish. If the highest moral good is the survival and propagation of each group's genes, then sexuality may—should—be viewed through a moral lens.[134]

As all of this intersects with the International Planned Parenthood Federation (IPPF), major government donors include those of Sweden, Australia, Germany, Norway, Denmark, the Netherlands, the UK, and Canada, among others, plus the European Commission, the EU, USAID, Merck, the William and Flora Hewlett Foundation, the Open Society Foundations, the Bill and Melinda Gates Foundation, GIZ, the Global Fund, UNAIDS, UNFPA, UN Women, and the WHO, among others.

The Executive Director of Planned Parenthood Global, Monica Kerrigan, is described by Planned Parenthood as a "seasoned veteran of the United Nations, the United States Agency for International Development, the Bill and Melinda Gates Foundation, and other leading development and global health organizations."

The Chair of the Planned Parenthood Action Fund is Jennie Rosenthal, a former member of the Global Advisory Council of the Wilson Center. According to the Wilson Center, "Benefits of membership [include] meet-and-greet opportunities and select events with U.S. and global thought-leaders, heads of state, and senior level U.S. and foreign policymakers." Supporters and/or affiliates of the Wilson Center include JP Morgan Chase, AIG, David Simon (Deborah's sister), Johnson & Johnson, Goldman Sachs, the Chevron Corporation, and Bank of America. A Co-Chair of the Global Advisory Council is David Petraeus: Chairman of the private-equity firm KKR's KKR Global Institute; former Commander of the International Security Assistance Force (ISAF), the US-NATO military mission in Afghanistan; former CIA Director.

According to Rosenthal's Planned Parenthood biography:

---

[133] Publius, *The God that Failed*, 247–248.
[134] Publius, *Plastic Empire*, 117–118.

Jennie has led fundraising and grassroots efforts for local, state and, national political campaigns, serving on the national finance committee for President Barack Obama in 2008 and 2012 and Secretary Hillary Clinton in 2016 and as a delegate in 2008 and 2012. . . . For Senator Sherrod Brown, she hosted events with then Senator Barrack Obama, Martin Sheen, Cecile Richards, Cory Booker, and a concert with Carole King attended by 500 donors. . . . Additionally, she held events for the DNC with Debbie Wasserman Schultz and Howard Dean. . . . She hosted Secretary Hillary Clinton in her home in 2015, and President Bill Clinton at several events throughout Cincinnati in 2016.

Would you like to know more? Alright then, let's take a look at some of the International Planned Parenthood Federation's principal figures:

- Director-General Alvaro Bermejo has more than 20 years' experience as a senior executive in global federations, working across HIV and AIDS, humanitarian issues and health policy. He was previously the Executive Director of the *Survive and Thrive* portfolio at the Children's Investment Fund Foundation (CIFF), where he helped build an adolescent sexual and reproductive health portfolio
- Mariama Daramy-Lewis, Director, People, Organization & Culture Division. Mariama is results-oriented with over 20 years of experience in international development, human resources management, performance management, public relations, communications and advocacy and program management. Working with the United Nations system since 1994, Mariama has held senior positions in UNDP, IFAD, UNSSC and UNEP, in Africa, Europe and North America. . . . Her work on gender mainstreaming and parity has be recognized in the UN system.
- Marie-Evelyne Petrus-Barry, Africa Regional Director, joins us from Amnesty International where she has been working as the Regional Director for West and Central Africa based in Dakar, Senegal. . . . Prior to Amnesty International Evelyne has worked for the several UN agencies including as the UN Resident Coordinator in Gabon and representative of UNDP, UNFPA, UN Nations Information Centre, UN Human Rights, Plan International along with other organisations.
- South Asia Regional Director Sonal Mehta joins us from India HIV/AIDS Alliance where she is currently the Chief Executive Officer. . . . Sonal's past career experience includes working for DFID, UNDP, the Government of India, CHETNA (NGO working for women and children) and the Pacific Institute of Women's Health.
- Board of Trustees member Isaac Adewole, Professor of Obstetrics and Gynaecology at the College of Medicine, University of Ibadan, Nigeria since 1997. He was the former Nigerian minister of health from 2015 to 2019 and the 11th Vice-Chancellor of the University of Ibadan from 2010 to 2015 as well as the past President of African Organization for Research and Training in Cancer (AORTIC). His research interest is in the area of human papillomavirus, HIV, and gynaecologic oncology.
- Board of Trustees member Abhina Aher has been Associate Director for

Gender, Sexuality and Rights at the India HIV/AIDS Alliance since 2010. She has been a global activist on LGBTI issues for the last 24 years and has worked with organisations such as The Humsafar Trust (Mumbai), Family Health International (FHI), and the Johns Hopkins University Centre for Communication Programme (CCP).

- Board of Trustees Interim Chair Kate Gilmore has been a Fellow at the Carr Center for Human Rights Policy, Harvard Kennedy School since February 2020. She is researching human rights concerns including: The political economy of sexual and reproductive health and rights; Organizational leadership in a world of 'J curve' change; Acceleration of youth participation in public decision making; and Civil service without fear or favour. Kate was United Nations Deputy High Commissioner for Human Rights from 2014 to 2019 and was Assistant Secretary General and Deputy Executive Director, United Nations Population Fund (UNFPA) from 2012 to 2014. Before this, she was Executive Deputy Secretary General at Amnesty International from 2000 to 2009.

- Board of Trustees member Aurélia Nguyen has been Managing Director, Vaccines and Sustainability at Gavi, the Vaccine Alliance since 2011. She was also Director of Policy and Market Shaping from 2011 to 2018. Previously, she worked as Director, Global Vaccine Policy (Biologicals) at GlaxoSmithKline from 2006 to 2011. She is currently on the Steering Committee for the Global Polio Eradication Initiative; Chair of the Task Force for COVID-19 Vaccine Development at the World Bank; and is Chair of the Procurement and Stockpiling Working Group at the Coalition for Epidemic Preparedness Innovations.

Nothing suspicious there, right?

Speaking of COVID, one of the central themes of the World Economic Forum's (WEF) virtual meeting in June 2020 was that the coronavirus necessitates the acceleration of the process of what the WEF has been referring-to as the Fourth Industrial Revolution and what has been bandied-about in a more rudimentary form in the US as the Green New Deal. What emerged is familiar in its justification—the coronavirus somehow catalyzing a need for systemic overhaul and consolidation due to "climate change"—but new in name: The Great Reset, which builds on the Green New Deal, the Paris Agreement, and the E15 Initiative and represents the most all-encompassing, dystopian, totalitarian globalist system yet conceived, but one that's implementation in some form has been in the works for a very long time now.

The E15 Initiative was launched in 2011 as a project of the WEF and the International Center for Trade and Sustainable Development with sixteen "knowledge partners" to bring together more than 375 international experts in over 80 interactive dialogues between 2012–2015. The recommendations were authored in 2016 as "The E15 Initiative: Strengthening the Global Trade and Investment System in the 21st Century." According to Ricardo Melendez and Richard Samans in the paper's foreword:

An effective global trade and investment system is crucial for reinvigorating economic growth and confronting '21st century global challenges. Yet the system—well performing as it is in many of its functions—is out of date and in need of greater coherence. Recent years have witnessed the emergence of an increasingly complex global trade policy landscape. Hundreds of regional trade agreements—including mega-regionals like the Trans-Pacific Partnership and the Transatlantic Trade and Investment Partnership with potentially systemic implications—have been notified to the WTO, many with investment provisions. In addition, there are over 3,200 bilateral investment treaties and thousands more tax arrangements. At the same time, deadlock in negotiating the WTO Doha Development Agenda has detracted from the trade system's ability to respond to emerging global challenges and priorities such as the UN 2030 Agenda for Sustainable Development, the Addis Ababa Action Agenda on financing for development, and the Paris Agreement on climate change.

The knowledge partners for the E15 Initiative included Chatham House, the Center for International Development at Harvard University, the Graduate Institute of International and Development Studies in Geneva's Center for Trade and Economic Integration, the International Institute for Sustainable Development, the International Food and Agricultural Trade Policy Council, and more. Primary funding was derived from arms of the governments of Switzerland, Canada, the UK, Sweden, the Netherlands, Finland, Denmark, and Norway. These are some of the major recommendations outlined, and provide a glimpse into what the Great Reset will expand upon, as "The Nairobi trade conference (MC10) and the Paris climate conference (COP21) mark important steps, but many more steps must be taken":

- Allow the free flow of data across borders.
- Streamline processes and procedures related to visas and work permits and establish a plurilateral but open "innovation zone" working through GATS within which skilled researchers and technical personnel would be able to migrate freely for up to 10 years.
- Establish a Global Value Chain Partnership, a public-private platform to improve the efficiency and inclusiveness of global supply chains.
- Establish a permanent moratorium on the imposition of customs duties on the electronic transmission of products.
- Establish regional institutions for structured support programs to enhance local capacity to conform to global standards, and provide links to lead firms to increase understanding of international market developments.
- Scale the blended (public-private) financing of infrastructure and industrial investment.
- Develop norms for making regional and plurilateral agreements more inclusive. In addition to more permissive rules of origin, devise methods or principles by which the multilateral system could accommodate newly emerging trade regulatory regimes.
- Establish an Advisory Centre on International Investment Law to level the playing field for developing country governments.
- Expand donor country assistance to support for capacity building to developing countries in the implementation of the new model framework.
- Scale technical assistance from the International Monetary Fund or multilateral development banks to LDC sovereign debt issuers.

- Establish an agricultural subsidy solidarity fund.
- By combining improvements in infrastructure, investment climate institutions and workforce skills with openness to foreign direct investment in key sectors, countries create the possibility for technology and know-how from those foreign firms to be transferred more widely and organically through the bottom-up creation of forward and backward linkages.
- Mandate within the WTO the disclosure and phased prohibition of fossil fuel subsidies, according special and differential treatment to poorer developing countries.
- Promote an integrated Agri-Food Value Chain approach to future negotiations.
- A new dimension of citizen participation modelled on the OECD Guidelines for Multilateral Enterprises.
- Promote the levelling up of social and environmental standards.
- The absence of any agreed definition of what constitutes a "climate measure" in the Paris climate agreement would be a decision de facto to leave the clarification of the meaning of "climate measure" to WTO jurists on a case-by-case basis.
- Mitigation efforts to limit global warming to no more than 2 degrees Celsius or 1.5 degrees Celsius as compared to pre-industrial levels will primarily hinge on a rapid and massive scale-up of clean energy. The December 2015 Paris Agreement on climate change is fundamentally about fostering an urgent and massive transformation to a low carbon or carbon-neutral energy base for the world economy.

Klaus Schwab, Founder and Executive Chairman of the World Economic Forum, declared that:

A Great Reset is necessary to build a new social contract. . . . The global health crisis has laid bare the unsustainability of our old system in terms of social cohesion, the lack of equal opportunities, and inclusiveness. Nor can we turn our backs on the evils of racism and discrimination. We need to build into this new social contract our intergenerational responsibility to ensure that we live up to the expectations of young people. COVID-19 has accelerated our transition into the age of the Fourth Industrial Revolution. We have to make sure that the new technologies in the digital, biological, and physical world remain human-centered.

The most profound arrogance, but pride goeth before destruction, and an haughty spirit before a fall, after all.

The announcement of the Great Reset was made by Prince Charles (who has said that we need a "global Marshall Plan" to save the environment) and Schwab, followed by statements by UN Secretary-General António Guterres and IMF Managing Director Kristalina Georgieva. Their statements were supported by voices from:

All stakeholder groups of global society, including Victoria Alonsoperez, Founder and Chief Executive Officer, Chipsafer, Uruguay, and a Young Global Leader; Caroline Anstey, President and Chief Executive Officer, Pact,

USA; Ajay S. Banga, Chief Executive Officer, Mastercard, USA; Sharan Burrow, General Secretary, International Trade Union Confederation (ITUC), Brussels; Ma Jun, Chairman, Green Finance Committee, China Society for Finance and Banking, and a Member of the Monetary Policy Committee of the People's Bank of China; Bernard Looney, Chief Executive Officer, bp, United Kingdom; Juliana Rotich, Venture Partner, Atlantica Ventures, Kenya; Bradford L. Smith, President, Microsoft, USA; and Nick Stern, Chair, Grantham Research Institute on Climate Change and the Environment, United Kingdom.

For reference, among the unbelievable concentration of NGO, corporate, and financial power partnered with the WEF, of particular relevance to us as names we've either frequently encountered or encountered at critical junctures in this book are numbered: AstraZeneca, the Gates Foundation, Bayer, CVS Health, Gilead Sciences, Johnson & Johnson, Merck, Mylan, Pfizer, Sanofi, Takeda, McKinsey, the Wellcome Trust, Walmart, the Carlyle Group, Salesforce, Goldman Sachs, Google, BlackRock, Barclays, JP Morgan Chase, Soros Fund Management, Cargill, Nestlé, New York Times, Novartis, the Novo Nordisk Foundation, Tyson Foods, Banco Safra Brazil and J. Safra Group, PayPal, Chevron, Apple, Amazon Web Services, Airbus, Anglo-American, Procter & Gamble, Bloomberg, Thomson Reuters, the Blackstone Group, Biogen, and many more, not least of which includes the Mayo Clinic, Hackensack Meridian Health, Hikma Pharmaceuticals, Sun Pharmaceutical Industries, and Ginkgo Bioworks, a biotechnology company founded by five MIT scientists such as Tom Knight, a senior research scientist at the MIT Computer Science and Artificial Intelligence Laboratory.

Ginkgo Bioworks's Concentric offers "COVID-19 testing at scale," and Gingko is part of a joint venture with Leaps by Bayer called Joyn Bio, "engineering plant microbes to solve growers' greatest challenges [and] founded to create sustainable, cost effective, and agronomically meaningful microbial solutions to growers." According to Stuart Anderson:

> Using its platform to program the DNA of living cells allows the company to produce a range of products, including in chemicals and agriculture. For example, Ginkgo Bioworks is working to replace nitrogen-based fertilizers by engineering microbes for crops. In the chemical industry, the company can replace chemical synthesis with engineered cells that make the desired chemical through fermentation. Designing enzymes for food and beverage production is another growth area for the company. Customers include food giants Cargill and ADM.

Ginkgo Bioworks has received funding from the NIH's Rapid Acceleration of Diagnostics (RADx) initiative.

The World Economic Forum's Board of Trustees is comprised of people like:

- Al Gore (daughter Karenna was married to the great-grandson of the Jewish mega-banker and "proto-Soros" Jacob Schiff, Andrew, who is now a Managing Partner at the biotech-focused private equity firm Aisling Capital; Schiff was educated at Cornell, Columbia, and Brown, and has sat on numerous Boards of pharmaceutical, medical technology, and biotechnology companies)

- Christine Lagarde (former Managing Director of the IMF and current President of the European Central Bank)
- Jack Ma (Alibaba, etc.)
- Kristalina Georgieva (Managing Director of the IMF; January 2017 to September 2019, CEO of the World Bank)
- The Jewish David M. Rubenstein (Duke and University of Chicago alumnus; Brookings Institution; numerous Harvard connections; Co-Founder and Co-Executive Chairman of the Carlyle Group; trustee of the University of Chicago and Johns Hopkins Medicine; Chairman of the Board of Directors of the Council on Foreign Relations, preceded by the Jewish Robert E. Rubin: Goldman Sachs, Citigroup during the bailouts, the Board of Trustees of the Carnegie Corporation and Mt. Sinai Hospital, the Board of Directors of the Harvard Corporation, and one of the three Jewish Horsemen along with Larry Summers and Alan Greenspan who spearheaded US-IMF economic interventions across the globe in the late 1990s)
- The Israeli Orit Gadiesh (Hebrew University of Jerusalem; International Advisory Board of the Atlantic Council; Council on Foreign Relations member; Chairman of Bain & Company)
- Mark Carney (Goldman Sachs; former Governor of the Bank of Canada and current Governor of the Bank of England)
- Yo-Yo Ma (cellist; Former Member of the Board of Trustees of the Aspen Institute)
- Peter Brabeck-Letmathe (Chairman Emeritus of Nestlé; former Board member of: Roche, Credit Suisse, L'Oréal, and Exxon Mobil; former Chairman of the 2030 Water Resources Group, a public-private partnership incorporated as part of the World Bank)
- Queen Rania Al Abdullah of the Hashemite Kingdom of Jordan (served on the UN Secretary-General's High Level Panel on the Post-2015 Development Agenda, which contributed to the development of the UN Sustainable Development Goals; co-chaired a panel on the international response to the global "refugee crisis" at the 2016 UN Summit on Refugees and Migrants; member of the Board of Directors of the United Nations Foundation; member of the Board of Advisors of the International Rescue Committee; UNICEF's first Eminent Advocate for Children in 2007— pretty sick when you think about the fate of children under this globalist regime)
- The Jewish Laurence Fink (Chairman and CEO of BlackRock; member of the Council on Foreign Relations)

Lastly, we should not forget another WEF Board of Trustees member in the Jewish founder, Chairman, and CEO of Salesforce Marc Benioff and donor of over $250 million to the UCSF Benioff Children's Hospitals, which as we discussed in great detail are central to the institutionalization of the transgender agenda and its targeting of children.

The aforementioned David M. Rubenstein's Rubenstein Fellowship program at the Brookings Institution's recent fellows offer more insight:

- Madiha Afzal's research lies at the intersection of development, security, and politics, with a focus on Pakistan. . . . She has also taught at Johns Hopkins SAIS, and consulted for international organizations including the World Bank and UK's Department for International Development.
- Matthew Collin is an Anglo-American economist whose research focuses on understanding and addressing spillovers of global institutions and norms as well as helping domestic institutions become more efficient and equitable. . . . Matt has previously worked in the World Bank as an economist in the Global Tax Team and as a Young Professional in the Human Development Chief Economist's office. He has also previously held positions as a Research Fellow at the Center for Global Development and as an ODI Fellow in the Ministry of Finance of Malawi.
- Alex Engler studies the implications of artificial intelligence and emerging data technologies on society and governance. Most recently faculty at the University of Chicago. . . . Alex is also a proud alumnus of Sunlight Foundation's Labs and the Congressional Research Service.
- Annelies Goger applies her knowledge as an economic geographer to develop innovative policy solutions to address rising inequality and improve access to economic opportunity. Her research focuses on workforce development policy, the future of work (processes of industrial transformation), and inclusive economic development.
- Molly Kinder's research explores an equitable future of work and examines the impact of emerging technologies on low wage workers and women. . . . Molly has more than 15 years of experience in innovation, policy, research, and impact investing. Previously, she was co-founder and Vice President of a $200 million social impact fund and served in the Obama administration as director in a new innovation program at USAID.
- Sarah Reber is Associate Professor of Public Policy at the UCLA Luskin School of Public Affairs. Her research focuses on school desegregation, elementary and secondary education finance policy, and college access. She is also a Research Associate at the National Bureau of Economic Research (NBER), a California Center for Population Research (CCPR) affiliate, and a California Policy Lab (CPL) affiliated expert. Previously, she was a Robert Wood Johnson Foundation Scholar in Health Policy Research at UC Berkeley and a Research Assistant and Staff Economist on the Council of Economic Advisers (CEA).
- Mallika Thomas is a professor of economics at Cornell, in the Department of Economics and in the School of Industrial and Labor Relations. She is a labor economist, and her research focuses on examining the causes of persistent wage inequality and the consequences of policy responses. Her most recent work examines the impact of government-mandated family leave policies on the wages and promotion opportunities of young women and the role of employer-based discrimination in the effectiveness of such policies. Thomas' ongoing work focuses on peer effects in education among female MBA students in male-dominated areas of concentration

and the causes of the gender-wage gap upon graduation, the impact of employer-provided benefits on the wages and employment of low-wage workers, and the consequences of rising wage inequality and changing wage structure on the educational investments of men and women. Thomas holds a Ph.D. in economics from the University of Chicago, a B.S. in physics and a B.A. in economics from Yale University. She has received a number of awards during her academic career, including the University of Chicago Presidential Fellowship, the George Stigler dissertation award, and the American Economic Association dissertation fellowship.

Perversely, Rubenstein purchased the only copy of Magna Carta in private hands for $21.32 million (£10.6 million) in December 2007 in "the first auction of the birth certificate of freedom."

Unsurprisingly given everything we've discussed, we also see Jeffrey Epstein played a central role. MIT has launched an investigation into what its president calls the "deeply disturbing" relationship between Epstein and the MIT Media Lab ("an interdisciplinary research lab that encourages the unconventional mixing and matching of seemingly disparate research areas"), whose Director Joi Ito resigned in the aftermath of media reports that Epstein had invested in his private companies as well as donating to the lab. Epstein stated that, "I was very close to Marvin Minsky for quite a long time [and] I funded some of Marvin's projects." Marvin Minsky, whose mother was a "Zionist activist," focused primarily on artificial intelligence and was the co-founder of MIT's AI laboratory.

As part of this approaching "reset," with COVID used as a justification for shelving paper and coin money as a way that the virus can be transported along with the intentional tanking of the US dollar, MIT is at the forefront of researching its fully-digital currency replacement, which is obviously great for the ruling class because every transaction may be tracked and traced. As Vipin Bharathan reports:

Two events took place on August 13 [2020]. One was a speech from Lael Brainard at the Federal Reserve Bank of San Francisco's Innovation Office Hours. The other was the publication of a paper in the FEDS notes series on "Comparing Means of Payment: What Role for a Central Bank Digital Currency?". It is no coincidence that both events happened on the same day. The Federal Reserve Bank (FRB) wants to communicate that it takes CBDCs seriously and is engaged in efforts to research a path toward implementation. . . . Federal Reserve chairman Jerome Powell made it clear that as CBDC is an extremely important part of the national infrastructure and under the purview of the Fed, the Fed would be in charge of the core infrastructure of CBDC. The latest news reveal how the Fed has gone about researching and testing technologies to support a CBDC. . . . A technology lab (TechLab) was established by the Federal Reserve Board (FRB)to build and test distributed ledger based solutions for CBDCs. The TechLab is a multidisciplinary team consisting of technologists from the Federal Reserve Banks of Cleveland, Dallas and New York supporting a policy team studying the monetary policy, financial stability and payments infrastructure through the lens of the

Fed's primary purpose. Dr. Brainard announced a partnership with MIT Digital Currency Initiative (DCI) with the Boston Fed taking the lead as the liaison with DCI. The multi-year partnership is aimed at building and testing a hypothetical CBDC.

You'd better believe a central component of the new digital currency will be a "social credit score," a la China, which in some ways the US already has in your credit score as a marker of your ability to get on the debt hamster wheel and in companies' decisions to decline services to dissidents, a la Chase Bank, Barclays, PayPal, et cetera.

The Ashkenazi Genomics Consortium is a collaborative effort involving more than a dozen investigators from leading institutions (including Columbia University, the Mt. Sinai Icahn School of Medicine, the Albert Einstein College of Medicine, and MIT), using "similar strategies to understand the genetic basis of diseases." In 2012, Jeffrey Epstein created the Southern Trust to develop algorithms to mine DNA databases and sell the resulting data to drug manufacturers.

Recently, 23andMe—founded by the Jewish Anne Wojcicki, ex-wife of Jewish Google co-founder Sergey Brin and sister of Associate Adjunct Professor in Pediatrics at UCSF's School of Medicine Janet Wojcicki and YouTube CEO Susan Wojcicki (UCLA, Harvard), who also played an instrumental role in the founding of Google, actually letting Brin and Larry Page use her garage—signed a massive $300 million deal to sell genetic data to GlaxoSmithKline; Calico, a subsidiary of Alphabet, Inc., teamed up with Ancestry.com LLC at one point.

Calico's CEO is the Jewish Arthur Levinson, who is also the President of Apple and is on the Board of Directors of the Broad Institute, a biomedical and genomic research center based on a partnership between MIT and Harvard (the Boston Children's Hospital is also included in this partnership). The Broad Institute is named for its Jewish benefactor Eli Broad (also known for his "philanthropic commitment to public K–12 education, scientific and medical research and the visual and performing arts") and his wife. In 2015, Broad and Calico announced a partnership to "advance research on age-related diseases and therapeutics." In 2014, Calico announced that in partnership with AbbVie it would be opening up an R&D facility; in December 2017 Hal Barron, its head of R&D, left for GlaxoSmithKline, and in March of the following year Daphne Koller, leading the team's AI projects, left to pursue a venture in applying machine learning techniques to drug design.

Continuing with the Harvard connections, the following is from a 2003 article from *The Harvard Crimson*:

Elusive financier Jeffrey E. Epstein donated $30 million this year to Harvard for the founding of a mathematical biology and evolutionary dynamics program. While the mathematics teacher turned magnate remained unknown to most people until he flew President Clinton, Kevin Spacey and Chris Tucker to Africa to explore the problems of AIDS and economic development facing the region, Epstein has been a familiar face to many at Harvard for years. Networking with the University's leading intellectuals, Epstein has spurred research through both discussions with and dollars contributed to various faculty members. Lindsley Professor of Psychology Stephen M. Kosslyn, former Dean of the Faculty Henry A. Rosovsky and Frankfurter Professor of Law

Alan M. Dershowitz are among Epstein's bevy of eminent friends that includes princes, presidents and Nobel Prize winners. Epstein is also well acquainted with University President Lawrence H. Summers. The two serve together on the Trilateral Commission and the Council on Foreign Relations, two elite international relations organizations. Epstein's collection of high-profile friends also includes newly-recruited professor Martin A. Nowak, who will run Harvard's mathematical biology and evolutionary dynamics program. Like Kosslyn, Rosovsky and Dershowitz, Nowak praises Epstein's numerous relationships within the scientific community. "I am amazed by the connections he has in the scientific world," Nowak says. "He knows an amazing number of scientists. He knows everyone you can imagine."

The $30 million donation figure is contested, but we do know definitively that $6.5 million went to launch Martin Nowak's Program for Evolutionary Dynamics at Harvard in 2003. Nowak thanked Epstein explicitly in at least one of his research papers on the evolution of HIV. Nowak and Jewish physicist Lawrence Krauss (MIT) were apparently point-men in introducing Epstein to many of his contacts in the scientific community. According to *BuzzFeed* of all places:

Nowak also continued to facilitate meetings between Epstein and leading academics at Harvard and MIT. Pictures from one meeting in 2012, on an archived version of one of Epstein's foundation websites, show him at Nowak's office with a group including mathematician and geneticist Eric Lander, director of the Broad Institute of MIT and Harvard, and David Gergen of the Harvard Kennedy School, a CNN political analyst and former adviser to presidents Nixon, Ford, Reagan, and Clinton. Also pictured were [Leon] Black [Jewish co-founder of private equity firm Apollo Global Management, Jewish "junk bond king" Michael Miliken's "right hand man" at Drexel Burnham Lambert and proud owner of a complete set of the Daniel Bomberg Babylonian Talmud acquired at auction for $9.3 million] and [Howard] Gardner [of Harvard], Harvard geneticist George Church; MIT physicist Seth Lloyd; Ted Kaptchuk, a Harvard expert on the placebo effect; and Henry Rosovsky, an economist and former dean of Harvard's Faculty of Arts and Sciences. . . . In September 2013, AI researcher [Ben] Goertzel thanked Epstein in a technical volume for his "visionary funding. . . ." [Joscha] Bach who has worked at Nowak's Harvard Program for Evolutionary Dynamics and the MIT Media Lab, acknowledged support from the Jeffrey Epstein Foundation in a paper presented at meetings on artificial intelligence in 2017 and 2018. Epstein also touted his backing for Bach's work in an October 2013 press release. Bach is now vice president for research with the AI Foundation, a startup in San Francisco. . . . [Ira] Lamster, former dean of the Columbia University College of Dental Medicine, told Reuters in 2015 that he accepted about $100,000 from Epstein. . . . [Doris] Germain, a cancer researcher at the Icahn School of Medicine in New York City, told Reuters in 2015 that she had received a grant from Epstein to study breast cancer. . . . A biotech venture capitalist and former science adviser to Bill Gates, [Boris] Nikolic was named by Epstein as a backup executor for his will, in which he put assets valued at $578 million into a trust just two days before his death. . . . Epstein was also on the advisory board of the Harvard Society of Mind, Brain, and Behavior. . . . The 2016 IRS filing from Epstein's foundation Gratitude America notes a $10,000 donation to the Icahn School of Medicine, part of the Mount Sinai Health System in New York City. . . . Some alleged recipients includ[e] Cornell University [and] Stanford University. . . . In its former guise as the World Transhumanist Association, Humanity+ received $20,000 from Epstein Interests in 2010. . . . In 2009, MIRI, then known as the Singularity Institute for Artificial Intelligence, received $50,000 from Epstein's COUQ Foundation.

The AI research is extremely important because this is going to form the bedrock of the digitalized currency/social credit/monitoring system of the future the transhumanist "elites" are designing. We can clearly see how all of this is connected, with a series of inter-locking networks circulating people, funds, and more.

Continuing in this vein and evidencing yet more connections, we also know that there are ties between Epstein and the Elton John AIDS Foundation. From a January 10th, 2014 press release from the Jeffrey Epstein Foundation:

The New York science philanthropist, Jeffrey Epstein, has put his support behind the celebrated Elton John AIDS Foundation (EJAF) to combat HIV resistance to drugs. . . . .In 2003, Jeffrey Epstein established the Program for Evolutionary Dynamics at Harvard University which, over the past three years, collaborated with Johns Hopkins University to develop a database to predict the effect of drugs on the HIV virus and notably HIV resistance. Using data from thousands of blood tests on more than 20 anti-HIV drugs, the Program's model factors in different drug combinations and dosages, as well as blood type, viral genotype, viral load, HIV stage, treatment history, age, sex and a host of other variables to arrive at the most precisely engineered predictor of results for future patients. . . . Since its inception, EJAF has raised more than $300 million to fund worthy projects across the globe. One of those programs is the outstanding HIV Drug Resistance Database at Stanford University's Clinical Virology Laboratory. . . . The database provides the largest HIV drug resistance surveillance, interpreting HIV drug resistance tests, and new antiretroviral drugs. Obtained from nearly 40,000 patients, the database uses more than 90,000 HIV sequences from approximately 80,000 distinct virus isolations. When presented with an HIV sequence, the genotypic resistance interpretation algorithm considers hundreds of factors including: genotypic data, treatment history, in vitro drug susceptibility and clinical response to a new treatment regimen.

Epstein and Bill Gates met on numerous occasions, and Epstein was also a one-time member of the Board of the Rockefeller University; the following is from an October 17th, 2011 press release from the Rockefeller University:

Rockefeller University President Marc-Tessier Lavigne has been elected to the Institute of Medicine, the health and medicine branch of the National Academy of Sciences. . . . Tessier-Lavigne obtained his Ph.D. from University College London and performed postdoctoral work at the MRC Developmental Neurobiology Unit in London and at Columbia University. He has been on the faculty of the University of California, San Francisco and Stanford University and has been a Howard Hughes Medical Institute investigator. In 2003, Tessier-Lavigne joined Genentech, one of the world's leading biotech companies, where he oversaw 1,400 people in disease research and drug discovery as executive vice president and chief scientific officer. He is the recipient of numerous scientific awards and is an elected member of the U.S. National Academy of Sciences and a fellow of the Royal Societies of the U.K. and Canada. Established in 1970 as the health branch of the National Academy of Sciences, the Institute of Medicine['s] . . . projects during the past year include studies on calculating people's vitamin D and calcium needs; improving the process for clearing medical devices for the market; preventing obesity among infants and toddlers; improving American's access to oral health care; preparing for the future of HIV/AIDS in Africa; ensuring the health of lesbian, gay, bisexual, and transgender people; and enhancing nurses' roles in improving health care. . . . Sixteen Rockefeller University scientists are Institute of Medicine members.

I'm not surprised to see Vitamin D research on there, especially in light of its role in beefing-up the immune system; Vitamin D deficiencies are correlated with increased risks of infection and increased autoimmunity, which may well explain why darker-skinned people living in Northern climes to which they did not evolve have higher rates of many autoimmune disorders beyond genetic predispositions to greater impulsivity and high time preference, as well as higher incidence rates of homosexuality, often reflected in "lifestyle choice."

Vitamin D has been widely-discussed in connection with lowering the risk of contracting coronavirus, which makes perfect sense. An April 2020 study published in *Arthritis and Rheumatology* reveals that the prevalence of antinuclear antibodies (ANA), the most common biomarker of autoimmunity, has been significantly increasing in the United States. "The reasons for the increases in ANA are not clear, but they are concerning and may suggest a possible increase in future autoimmune disease," said corresponding and senior author Frederick Miller, Chief of the Clinical Research Branch at the National Institute of Environmental Health Sciences (NIEHS) at the NIH.

Autoimmune conditions are on the rise in much of the rest of the world as well. The scientific community is generally unsure of what causes many of these diseases, but considering all we've covered in this book, very probably it has to do with nutritive deficiencies and environmental factors like exposure to harmful chemicals. Miller states that:

> Our gene sequences aren't changing fast enough to account for the increases. Yet our environment is—we've got 80,000 chemicals approved for use in commerce, but we know very little about their immune effects. Our lifestyles are also different than they were a few decades ago, and we're eating more processed food.

Returning to Epstein, yet another surprisingly good source for information on the mysterious pedophilic financier proved to be *The Daily Beast*, which is usually busy running pieces like "Bella Thorne's OnlyFans Fiasco Exposes Porn Discrimination":

> [Epstein's] Gratitude America's biggest donations included a $375,000 payout to the International Peace Institute Inc., a New York think tank staffed by former United Nations officials and run by Norwegian diplomat Terje Rød-Larsen, and $225,000 to the Melanoma Research Alliance. . . . Gratitude America Ltd. donated $150,000 each in 2017 to MIT and the Kuhn Foundation, run by writer Robert Lawrence Kuhn. . . . One biography on the Chopra Foundation's site says Kuhn is "an international corporate strategist, investment banker and expert on China" and has "a doctorate in brain research. . . ." Epstein also funded a nonprofit that produces a TV show hosted by the wife of Larry Summers, a Harvard economist and Treasury secretary under former President Clinton. In 2016, Gratitude America Ltd. shelled out $110,000 to Verse Video Education. The Cambridge, Massachusetts-based nonprofit produces the PBS show *Poetry in America*, whose creator and host is Harvard professor Elisa New. New is married to Summers, Harvard University's former president, who hobnobbed with Epstein in elite international relations groups and, like Bill Clinton, flew on Epstein's private jet. . . . The Bruce and Marsha Moskowitz Foundation received $100,000 in 2016 and $50,000 in 2017. . . . [Moskowitz's] name was found in Epstein's "little black book" alongside other doctors [like Eva Andersson-Dubin of Mt. Sinai Hospital, a former girlfriend of Epstein's and wife of the Jewish hedge fund billionaire Glenn Dubin, also allegedly connected to the Epstein child sex ring] under the category "medical" [as well as other figures like the Jewish Victoria's Secret magnate Les Wexner, former Israeli Prime Minister Ehud Barak, and George Soros's nephew Peter Soros]. . . . Gratitude America listed a donation of $50,000 to the Chopra Foundation; $60,000 to a group labeled as "Association Mind Education" in Rome, Italy; and $50,000 to the United Jewish Appeal (UJA) Federation of New York. . . . Gratitude America Ltd. apparently donated to prominent litigator Stephen Susman's[135] fundraising page for Bike MS.

We also know Epstein was a major AIDS activist on the back of a complaint filed by Jennifer Araoz, who alleges Epstein said he was a "big AIDS activist" as he groomed the then-fourteen-year-old whose father had recently died from AIDS complications "before forcibly raping the teenager while not wearing a condom."

One of the most essential aspects of Planned Parenthood's operation is the harvesting of aborted fetal tissue, as according to the Associated Press, "scientists have been using such cells for decades to develop vaccines and seek treatments for a host of ailments, from vision loss and neurological disorders to cancer and AIDS." Though abortions are down in the US, the globalized spread of Planned Parenthoods and the black market have kept the industry humming. Aborted fetuses are essential to powering the medical-industrial complex, via the Associated Press:

---

[135] The reader will be shocked to learn that Susman is Jewish.

From 2011 through 2014 alone, 97 research institutions—mostly universities and hospitals—received a total of $280 million in federal grants for fetal tissue research from the National Institutes of Health. A few institutions have consistently gotten large shares of that money, including Yale, the University of California and Massachusetts General Hospital, which is affiliated with Harvard. . . . Vaccines have been one of the chief public benefits of fetal tissue research. Vaccines for hepatitis A, German measles, chickenpox and rabies, for example, were developed using cell lines grown from tissue from two elective abortions, one in England and one in Sweden, that were performed in the 1960s. German measles, also known as rubella, "caused 5,000 spontaneous abortions a year prior to the vaccine," said Dr. Paul Offit, an infectious-disease specialist at Children's Hospital of Philadelphia. "We wouldn't have saved all those lives had it not been for those cells." Fetal tissue was "absolutely critical" to the development of a potential Ebola vaccine that has shown promise, said Dr. Carrie Wolinetz, an associate director at NIH, which last year handed out $76 million for work involving fetal tissue, or 0.2 percent of the agency's research budget. . . . Scientists are also using fetal tissue to try to identify substances in adults that could be early warning signs of cancer, said Dr. Akhilesh Pandey, a molecular biologist at Johns Hopkins University. Experts at MIT and other research centers use fetal tissue to implant the human immune system into mice. . . . They add tumors to study the immune system's response, then test cancer treatments out on the mice. . . . At Stanford, fetal tissue has been used to study Huntington's disease, "bubble boy disease" and juvenile diabetes. Fetal brain calls are now being used there in research on autism and schizophrenia. [Colorado State University] is pressing ahead with its HIV research with fetal tissue.

In its "Strategic Framework 2016–2022," after listing "values" like "social inclusion" and "diversity," the International Planned Parenthood Federation lists its main priority objectives as including:

- Enable young people to access comprehensive sexuality education and realize their sexual rights
- Engage champions, opinion formers and the media to promote health, choice and rights
- Grow our volunteer and activist supporter base
- Enable services through public and private health providers
- Deliver rights-based services including for safe abortion and HIV

The "human rights" architecture of the UN and its partners is already being used to justify mandating the "educational" and medical aspects of transgenderism on a global scale; with nods to Foucault and "some of the key global documents from the United Nations, Europe and Australia that may influence Western education in this regard," Jenna Gillett-Swan and Lisa van Leent write that:

The right to education encompasses more than the provision or access to education. The right to education is also a means to better assure the realisation of other rights. In this way, access to information (Article 17) is critical to inform rights-based content acquisition as part of an individual's rights in education, through education. Education rights also incorporate guarantees around self-determination, participation and protection. The right to information is, therefore, critical in assuring rights realisation in education. While a human rights framework mandates the indivisibility, interrelatedness, equality and interconnectedness of all rights (United Nations 1948), the interrelationship between (the right to) education and (the right to) information as a means of rights realisation are, therefore, intertwined in the context of a discussion about comprehensive sexuality education.

In July 2010, Vernor Muñoz, United Nations Special Rapporteur on the Right to Education's "Report of the United Nations Special Rapporteur on the right to education" was presented to the UN General Assembly. The report stated that:

> In order to be comprehensive, sexual education must pay special attention to diversity, since everyone has the right to deal with his or her own sexuality without being discriminated against on grounds of sexual orientation or gender identity. Sexual education is a basic tool for ending discrimination against persons of diverse sexual orientations. A very important contribution to thinking in this area was made by the 2006 Yogyakarta Principles on the application of international human rights law in relation to sexual orientation and gender identity. The Special Rapporteur fully endorses the precepts of Principle 16, referring specifically to the Right to Education. . . . The aforementioned Yogyakarta Principles are a fundamental tool for inclusion of the diversity perspective in the public policies that have to be taken into account in education. . . . Sexual education should encourage a rethinking of the stereotypical roles assigned to men and women so that real equality can be achieved. . . . In the Special Rapporteur's view, [abstinence-only education] normalizes, stereotypes and promotes images that are discriminatory because they are based on heteronormativity; by denying the existence of the lesbian, gay, transsexual, transgender and bisexual population, they expose these groups to risky and discriminatory practices. . . . The absence of planned, democratic and pluralist sexual education constitutes, in practice, a model of sexual education (by omission) which has particularly negative consequences for people's lives and which uncritically reproduces patriarchal practices, ideas, values and attitudes that are a source of many forms of discrimination. . . . It should be borne in mind that patriarchy affects everyone by normalizing and stereotyping roles, thereby imposing needs and ways of being and feeling. But, like any social construct, it can be changed.

Sex ed—especially as defined by the Yogyakarta Principles—is a human right/mandated requirement in this ludicrous, insane, and de-humanizing system run by sociopaths who believe that man may defy the rules of nature—may be *above* nature—and that we are all infinitely malleable to be molded into the crude and broken shapes of their choosing. Their vision of progress signals the realization of man's triumph over any and all limitations, a vision that imbues them with the arrogance of believing they can dictate the terms to all life on earth and stay the forces of nature. They truly believe they can live forever through man-made means and bend reality to their will, assured in what is to them the incontrovertible truth that they themselves are not just god-like, but are actual gods. In truth, they actually resemble demons.

More than anything, perhaps, the LGBTQ agenda reveals the metaphysical nature of this struggle. Political solutions alone are not enough—they are tethered to the material and do not account for the evil that finds form behind treacly appeals to human rights and a perversion of man as the center of the universe. As Savitri Devi wrote in *The Lightning and the Sun*:

> People '*in* Time,' consciously self-centered, of the type of those money-mak-ers and power-seekers who would sacrifice anybody and anything—the whole world—to their personal ends . . . hide their cynical self-centeredness under a noisy lip-adherence to the dogma of the 'dignity of all men' . . . while busy causing, directly or indirectly, in view of their goal, the suffering and death of any number of human beings.

Thusly the forces of dissolution and decay marshal their ill-gotten power against the world, treating us as "human resources" to be exploited and sucked dry before dis-carding the husk. In the ultimate irony we are left asking where the humanity is in this system—a system that channels the energies of something much darker, a sys-tem that goes beyond political or even racial or religious quarrels to the heart of something cosmic.

Righteous fury and indignation, the cleansing which must surely take place for us to survive, will have its share of "evil" of a kind, but it is not evil as such. It is the capacity for retribution, for violence, to kill to survive that is harnessed for the good of life itself that is eminently necessary. For Nietzsche, "Despisers of life are they, decaying ones and poisoned ones themselves, of whom the earth is weary: so away with them!" The lover of life is the one who will kill for it, and for his kith and kin, especially his progeny, which is to say that he will have transcended the materialist illusion through his bloodline and his people, using the tools available to him to re-store something that is at once new and eternal, particular and universal, reflecting Truth and Order. Quoting Revilo P. Oliver:

> What do we owe the rest of the world? Nothing, *absolutely nothing*. . . . This is our country. He who would take it from us, by force or by stealth, is our enemy. And it is our purpose—nay, it is our duty to our children and to their children and to our yet unborn posterity—*it is our duty to use all feasible means to destroy him.*

We are now faced with a choice: live—*really live*—in accordance with nature and cosmic principles, or die ignominiously in darkness.

# Appendix A

The list of "activists and leaders from the Lesbian, Gay, Bisexual, and Transgender (LGBT) Jewish community" who signed the endorsement letter for Congressman Jerry Nadler dated April 8th, 2016:

**Liz Abzug**
Feminist / LGBTQ Activist

**Martin Algaze**
Past President & Founding Member, Stonewall Democrats of New York City

**Stuart Appelbaum**
President, Retail, Wholesale Department Store Union (RWDSU)

**Jared Arader, Esq.**

**Steve Ashkinazy**
LGBTQ Advocate

**Andrew Belanfante**
Director of Programs, Mechon Hadar

**Gabriel Blau**
LGBTQ Advocate & Former Executive Director, Family Equality Council

**Jeffrey Campagna**
Attorney

**David Chapman**
Board Member, Congregation Beit Simchat Torah

**Louis Cholden Brown**

**Rose Christ**
Vice President, Stonewall Democrats of New York City

**Alan Cohen**
Board Member, Keshet

**Elizabeth B. Cooper**
Associate Professor, Fordham University School of Law

**Sandi DuBowski**
Filmaker, Director of Trembling Before G-d

**Tony Felzen**

**Rabbi David Dunn Bauer**
Director, Social Justice Programming, Congregation Beit Simchat Torah

**Ari Gershman**
Former Executive Vice President, Lesbian and Gay Democratic Club of Queens

**Emily Giske**
Member, Democratic National Committee

**Deborah J. Glick**
NYS Assembly Member

**Suzanne Goldberg**
Director, Sexuality and Gender Law Clinic Columbia Law School

**Lewis Goldstein**
LGBT Activist

**Dr. Nate Goldstein**
President, Congregation Beit Simchat Torah

**William Hibsher**

**Brad Hoylman**
NYS Senator

**David Sigal**
NYS Senator

**Roberta A. Kaplan**
Partner, Paul Weiss Rifkind Wharton & Garrison & Lead Counsel, *U.S. v. Windsor*

**Ryan Karben, Esq.**

**Amichai Lau-Lavie**
Spiritual Leader, Lab/Shul NYC

**Ryder Kessler**
CEO, DipJar

**Scott Klein**
Co-President of Lambda Independent Democrats of Brooklyn

**Idit Klein**
Executive Director, Keshet

**Rabbi Sharon Kleinbaum**
Congregation Beit Simchat Torah

**Julian Kline**
Former President, Gay & Lesbian Independent Democrats

**Yetta G. Kurland**
Civil Rights Attorney

**Rachel Lavine**
Co-Founder and Chair, NYS Democratic Committee Progressive Caucus & Former Chair, New York LGBT Center

**Aubrey Lees, Esq.**

**Alex Halpern Levy**
Vice President, SKDKnickerbocker & former LGBT Adviser to Senator Charles Schumer

**Chaim Levin**
Plaintiff, *Ferguson v. JONAH*

**Jayson Littman**
Founder, Hebro & LGBT Jewish Community Organizer

**Jonathan Lovitz**
Vice President of External Affairs at National Gay & Lesbian Chamber of Commerce / Director of National Gay & Lesbian Chamber of Commerce NY (NGLCCNY)

**Seth M. Marnin**
Vice-President, Civil Rights, Anti-Defamation League

**Noemi E. Masliah, Esq.**
Co-Founder, Immigration Equality

**Rabbi Jay Michaelson**
Contributing Editor, the Jewish Daily Forward

**Gabe Most**
**Laura Morrison**
Former President, Gay & Lesbian Independent Democrats

**Bruce Patcher**
Co-Chair, Red Ribbon Initiative

**Allen Roskoff**
President, Jim Owles Liberal Democratic Club

**Johanna Sanders**
The Vaid Group

**Melissa Sklarz**
Board Co-Chair, Empire State Pride Agenda

**Rachel B. Tiven**

**Andy Tobias**
Treasurer, Democratic National Committee

**Alan van Capelle**
Former Executive Director, Empire State Pride Agenda

**Andrew Velez**
ACT UP New York

**David Warren**
President, Chelsea Reform Democratic Club

**Janet Weinberg**
Founding Board Member, NYC AIDS Memorial

**Randi Weingarten**
President, American Federation of Teachers

**Edith "Edie" Windsor**
Plaintiff, *U.S. v. Windsor*

**Evan Wolfson**
Former President, Freedom to Marry

**Bob Zuckerman**
Former President, Stonewall Democratic Club of New York City

# Appendix B

After the Orlando attacks in the United States in June 2016, the President Hollande of France announced that the mandate of the Inter-ministerial Delegation to Racism and Antisemitism would be extended to the fight against LGBTphobia and that an action plan would be put in place. The plan is now launched. In order to implement the plan, an annual budget of €1.5 million has been allocated which also comprises support to LGBT organisations. A selection of the most significant items in the plan is as follows:

## At governmental level:
- National campaign against LGBTphobia.
- Network of officials in charge of the fight against LGBTphobia in each ministry.
- Same at local level in each department.
- The public sector as an employer: ministries, public companies, etc. will have to apply for the "diversity label" (which is already inclusive of sexual orientation and gender identity). Interesting examples of existing support groups within ministry of defense (e.g. THEMIS focuses on welcoming trans people in the army) and other ministries. In addition, a report on discrimination within the public sector will be launched (based on 'testing').
- The use of the first name of trans people (both as employees and users) will be facilitated in public services.

## Protect victims of hate crime:
- Communicate on the annual number of victims and on judicial proceedings (already the case for other grounds of discrimination)
- Test a procedure of "pre-complain on line" which aims at facilitating the physical complain (the reception of the victim can be anticipated through that pre-complain).
- In all services in charge of taking care of victims, there should be one person allocated for LGBT issues.
- Putting in place campaigns against LGBTphobia, with a focus on lesbian women (in order to tackle double discrimination).
- Transmit systematically cases of LGBTphobia on the Internet to the Prosecutor.
- Keeping in mind the situation in detention facilities (give access to LGBT detainees to individual wards and also to a helpline).

## Field of education:
- LGBTphobia included in civic education (which has been the case since 2015)
- Education ministry staff will be trained on prevention of LGBTphobia (both pre-service and continuous)
- In December 2015, two campaigns were launched by the ministry of education, they will be renewed.
- A study will be conducted on options for trans students (who are +18 of age only)

who have not legally changed their gender to use their first name (on students cards, exams, etc.).

## Media:
- The body in charge of monitoring media will now also look at incidents of LGBTphobia.
- Journalist students will be trained on LGBT issues.

## Acting against discrimination in daily life:
- Guidance will be developed towards childcare professionals, family associations, social workers, etc. on rainbow families.
- Implementation decrees for the law on Justice (adopted in 2016 and comprising provisions on legal gender recognition) will be published in Feb. 2017. Also a guide for trans people on legal gender recognition will be developed.
- A charter on older LGBT people will be elaborated for long-term care facilities. Staff in those facilities will be trained.
- Raising the awareness of a number of bodies in rural areas (family organisations, farming teaching, etc.) on LGBTphobia.

## Employment:
- Partnerships will be established with companies already doing well on diversity.
- Compulsory training on discrimination for human resources staff in companies with + than 300 employees.

## Health:
- Tissue donations by men who have sex with men: four months ban for plasma donations and 12 months for blood donation following a reform which entered into force in June 2016.
- Special attention to suicidal young LGBT people
- HIV prevention campaigns and focus on STIs among lesbians
- Training of healthcare providers, with a focus on trans people.
- Intersex: France has been condemned three times in 2016 by various bodies of the United Nations: January 2016 by Committee on Children's Rights, May 2016 by Committee Against Torture and July 2016 by Convention on the Elimination of all Forms of Discrimination Against Women (CEDAW). As a result the action plan states that *"when they're not medically necessary, surgeries on intersex kids are mutilations and need to end."*

## Rights of LGBT people abroad:
- Continue to push for decriminalization of homosexuality at UN level
- Support the new independent expert
- Continue to ensure that embassies take initiatives to support LGBT human rights defenders and their participation to international events.

## LGBT refugees:
- Continue to raise awareness of officers in charge of examining asylum cases and supporting LGBT organisations active in the field.
- Moreover the action plan also contains a whole section on culture and sports.

# Appendix C

The Pharmaceutical Research and Manufacturers of America (PhRMA) leadership and Board of Directors with accompanying notable position(s):

- Ramona Sequeira: President of Takeda Pharmaceuticals, Treasurer of the Board of PhRMA, formerly of Eli Lilly, also a member of the Board of Directors for Matter, a Chicago-based healthcare technology incubator, and previously a Board member of the Association of British Pharmaceutical Industry; member of the Board of Trustees for Lake Forest Academy, a college preparatory boarding and day school for grades 9 through 12 located in Lake Forest, Illinois and member of the Chicago Executive Club's Board
- Bill Anderson: CEO of Roche Pharmaceuticals, Genentech Board member, formerly with Biogen
- Peter Anastasiou: President of Lundbeck North America, graduate of the Executive Education Program in Strategic Marketing from the Columbia University Graduate School of Business; formerly of Eli Lilly, Bristol-Myers Squibb, and Neuronetics, Inc.
- Jenny Bryant: Executive Vice President of Policy and Research at PhRMA, Harvard MBA, formerly Vice President the Lewin Group, a national healthcare consulting firm, New York Hospital-Cornell Medical Center, and Blue Cross Blue Shield
- David Ricks: Chairman and CEO of Eli Lilly, President of the International Federation of Pharmaceutical Manufacturers & Associations (IFPMA), and Chairman-Elect of PhRMA
- Giovanni Caforio: Chairman and CEO of Bristol-Myers Squibb, Chairman of the Board of PhRMA
- Wolfgang Maximilian Baiker: President and CEO of Boehringer Ingelheim USA
- Percival Barretto-Ko: Astellas Pharma (Illinois), member of the Board of Chicago United, "an organization committed to achieving parity in economic opportunity for people of color by advancing multiracial leadership in corporate governance, executive level management and business diversity"
- Albert Bourla: Chairman and CEO of Pfizer
- Jean-Jacques Bienaime: Chairman and CEO of BioMarin, formerly of Genentech and Genencor, a biotechnology company focused on industrial bioproducts and targeted cancer biotherapeutics; currently on the Boards of Incyte Corporation, a biotechnology company, and the Biotech Industry Organization
- Robert A. Bradway: Chairman and CEO of Amgen
- Ivan Cheung: Chairman of Eisai Inc.
- James C. Stansel: Executive Vice President, general counsel, and corporate secretary of PhRMA, previously served as acting general counsel of the US Department of Health & Human Services (HHS), where he was the chief legal officer of HHS, including its sub-agencies the Food and Drug Administration, the Centers for Medicare and Medicaid Services, the Centers for Disease Control and

Prevention and the National Institutes of Health; at HHS, he also served as deputy general counsel and as counselor to the secretary, where he coordinated with the White House and advised the secretary on the development of health policy

- Robert Zirkelbach: Executive Vice President of Public Affairs for PhRMA, formerly Vice President of Strategic Communications at America's Health Insurance Plans (AHIP), served as the national spokesman for the health insurance industry and played a lead role in "crafting the association's communications strategy and public policy positioning throughout the health care reform debate and implementation of the Affordable Care Act"
- Lori M. Reilly: COO of PhRMA, named by The Hill as a top lobbyist in 2018; currently oversees PhRMA's advocacy activities, including its federal, state and international government affairs and alliance development work
- Paul Aines: CFO and Executive Vice President of Administration
- Richard Moscicki: Executive Vice President of Science and Regulatory Advocacy and Chief Medical Officer at PhRMA, former Harvard Medical School faculty, formerly of Genzyme Corporation, formerly the deputy center director for science operations for the U.S. Food and Drug Administration's (FDA) Center for Drug Evaluation and Research (CDER)
- Stephen J. Ubl: President and CEO of PhRMA; per their website: "As president and CEO of medical technology association AdvaMed, Ubl helped facilitate landmark reforms related to the U.S. Food and Drug Administration product review process and Medicare's coverage and reimbursement of medical technologies. He led the industry's defense of breakthrough R&D, successfully delaying an innovation-stifling device tax, and, in 2013, was recognized by a leading industry publication as one of 10 people to have a lasting impact on the medical technology industry. Ubl has worked extensively with patient advocacy organizations in health policy, including longstanding service on the board of the National Health Council, a leading umbrella organization for voluntary health care organizations. . . . Prior to AdvaMed, Ubl was vice president of legislation for the Federation of American Hospitals. He began his Washington career on Capitol Hill. . . . He is routinely recognized as one of Washington's most effective advocates, and, in 2019, was named one of B*usiness Insider's* 'DC Healthcare Power Players.' He is consistently named to *Modern Healthcare*'s '100 Most Influential People in Healthcare' list and is identified as a top health influencer by *Medical Marketing & Media* and *PR Week* magazines."
- Emma Walmsley: CEO of GlaxoSmithKline, formerly of L'Oréal
- Michael Vounatsos: CEO of Biogen, formerly of Merck
- Jean-Christophe Tellier: CEO of UCB, "an innovation-driven global biopharmaceutical company focused on the discovery and development of novel medicines and solutions," and President of the Board of the European Federation of Pharmaceutical Associations (EFPIA)
- Jeffrey R. Stewart: President for US Commercial Operations for AbbVie, joined Abbott in 1992 as part of TAP, Abbott's former US joint venture with Takeda
- Pascal Soriot: Executive Director and CEO of AstraZeneca Pharmaceuticals LP, formerly Chief Executive Officer of Genentech where he led its merger with Roche
- Joaquin Duato: Vice Chairman of the Executive Committee of Johnson & Johnson

- Ken Frazier: Chairman and CEO of Merck
- Belen Garijo: Independent Director of the Board of L'Oréal SA, Independent Director of the Board of Banco Bilbao Vizcaya Argentaria SA (BBVA), member of the Executive Board of Merck KGaA, Darmstadt, Germany, and CEO of Healthcare
- Ludwig Hantson: CEO of Alexion
- Brenton Saunders: Chairman, CEO, and President of Allergan, previously served as Chief Executive Officer and President, and as director, of Forest Laboratories, Inc. prior to its acquisition by Allergan, formerly CEO of Bausch + Lomb, formerly of Schering-Plough, and was named head of integration for the company's merger with Merck & Co. and for Schering-Plough's acquisition of Organon BioScience, currently on the Board of Directors of Cisco Systems, Inc.
- Richard F. Pops: Chairman and CEO of Alkermes
- Richard Paulson: Executive Vice President and CEO of Ipsen, formerly of Amgen and Pfizer
- Brendan O'Grady: Executive Vice President, North America Commercial at Teva Pharmaceuticals Industries Ltd.
- Paul Hudson: CEO of Sanofi, previously CEO of Novartis Pharmaceuticals, formerly of AstraZeneca and GlaxoSmithKline UK
- Hervé Hoppenot: Chairman, President, and CEO of Incyte
- Jeff Jonas: CEO of Sage Therapeutics, former Executive Vice President of Forest Laboratories among others positions, MD from Harvard Medical School
- Ken Keller: President and CEO of Daiichi Sankyo, formerly of Amgen, Spectrum Pharmaceutical Inc., and Beecham Laboratories
- Douglas J. Langa: Senior Vice President, Head of North America Operations and President of Novo Nordisk Inc., formerly of Johnson & Johnson and GlaxoSmithKline, and has a professional certificate from Harvard Business School
- Antony Loebel: President and CEO of Sunovion Pharmaceuticals Inc., a Clinical Assistant Professor of Psychiatry at the New York University School of Medicine, a Fellow of the American Psychiatric Association (APA), previously served on the Massachusetts Biotechnology Council (MassBio) Board of Directors
- Vas Narasimhan: CEO of Novartis, has a master's degree in public policy from Harvard's John F. Kennedy School of Government, and a bachelor's degree in biological sciences from the University of Chicago, member of the Board of Fellows of Harvard Medical School, committee member of the Biopharmaceutical CEOs Roundtable at the International Federation of Pharmaceutical Manufacturers & Associations, based in Switzerland
- Kabir K. Nath: President and CEO Otsuka North America Pharmaceutical Business; prior to joining Otsuka, Nath was with Bristol-Myers Squibb, Senior Vice President, Virology, Transplant & Optimized Brands, responsible for the commercialization of a significant portfolio including drugs for HIV
- Stefan Oelrich: Member of the Board of Management and President of the Pharmaceuticals Division of Bayer AG, member of the Supervisory Board of the Berlin Institute of Health, formerly of Sanofi
- Daniel O'Day: Chairman and CEO of Gilead Sciences, formerly CEO of Roche Pharmaceuticals, Columbia University MBA, former Genentech Board member

# Selected Bibliography

*The following selected bibliography contains sources cited as organized by the first chapter in which they appear. Some websites and public annual reports are not included. Please direct any questions about citations to the author.*

**Introduction**

Batty, David. "Mistaken Identity." *The Guardian*, July 30, 2004. https://www.theguardian.com/society/2004/jul/31/health.socialcare.

Batty, David. "Sex changes are not effective, say researchers." *The Guardian*, July 30, 2004. https://www.theguardian.com/society/2004/jul/30/health.mentalhealth.

Costa, Rosalia, Michael Dunsford, Elin Skagerberg, Victoria Holt, Polly Carmichael, and Marco Colizzi. "Psychological support, puberty suppression, and psychosocial functioning in adolescents with gender dysphoria." *The Journal of Sexual Medicine* 12, no. 11 (November 2015): 2206–2214. https://doi.org/10.1111/jsm.13034.

Gliske, Stephen V. "Research Article Theory/New Concepts, Cognition and Behavior A New Theory of Gender Dysphoria Incorporating the Distress, Social Behavioral, and Body-Ownership Networks." *eNeuro* 6, no. 6 (December 2019): 0183–19.2019. https://doi.org/10.1523/ENEURO.0183-19.2019.

Hayes, Peter. "Commentary: Cognitive, Emotional, and Psychosocial Functioning of Girls Treated with Pharmacological Puberty Blockage for Idiopathic Central Precocious Puberty." *Frontiers in Psychology* 8, (January 2017): 44. https://doi.org/10.3389/fpsyg.2017.00044.

Hough, D., M. Bellingham, I. R. H. Haraldsen, M. McLaughlin, M. Rennie, J. E. Robinson, A. K. Solbakk, and N. P. Evans. "A reduction in long-term spatial memory persists after discontinuation of peripubertal GnRH agonist treatment in sheep." *Psychoneuroendocrinology* 77, (March 2017): 1–8. https://doi.org/10.1016/j.psyneuen.2016.11.029.

Hough, D., M. Bellingham, I. R. H. Haraldsen, M. McLaughlin, M. Rennie, J. E. Robinson, A. K. Solbakk, and N. P. Evans. "Spatial memory is impaired by peripubertal GnRH agonist treatment and testosterone replacement in sheep." *Psychoneuroendocrinology* 75, (January 2017): 173–182. https://doi.org/10.1016/j.psyneuen.2016.10.016.

Lombardo, F., L. Toselli, D. Grassetti, D. Paoli, P. Masciandaro, F. Valentini, A. Lenzi, and L. Gandini. "Hormone and genetic study in male to female transsexual patients." *Journal of Endocrinological Investigation* 36, no. 8 (January 2013): 550–7. https://doi.org/10.3275/8813.

Lynn, Corey. "Exploiting Transgenders Part 1: Manufacturing an Industry." *Corey's Digs*, November 15, 2019. https://www.coreysdigs.com/health-science/exploiting-transgenders-part-1-manufacturing-an-industry/.

Mul, D., H. J. Versluis-den Bieman, F. M. Slijper, W. Oostdijk, J. J. Waelkens, and S. L. Drop. "Psychological assessments before and after treatment of early puberty in adopted children." *Acta Paediatrica* 90, no. 9 (September 2001): 965–971. https://doi.org/10.1111/j.1651-2227.2001.tb01349.x.

O'Neil, Tyler. "Medical Expert: Doctors Are Actually Giving Trans Kids a Disease, and It's Child Abuse." *PJ Media*, August 25, 2019. https://pjmedia.com/news-and-politics/tyler-o-neil/2019/08/25/medical-expert-doctors-are-actually-giving-trans-kids-a-disease-its-child-abuse-n68343.

Richardson, Valerie. "Transgender homicide rate 'remarkably low' despite cries of 'national epidemic.'" *The Washington Times*, December 8, 2019. https://www.washingtontimes.com/news/2019/dec/8/transgender-homicide-rate-remarkably-low-despite-h/.

Schneider, Maiko A., Poli M. Spritzer, Bianca Machado Borba Soll, Anna M. V. Fontanari, Marina Carneiro, Fernanda Tovar-Moll, Angelo B. Costa, et al.. "Brain Maturation, Cognition and Voice Pattern in a Gender Dysphoria Case under Pubertal Suppression." *Frontiers in Human Neuroscience* 11, (November 2017): 528. https://doi.org/10.3389/fnhum.2017.00528.

Schuerger, James M., and Anita C. Witt. "The temporal stability of individuality tests intelligence." *Journal of Clinical Psychology* 45, no. 2 (Mark 1989): 294–302. https://doi.org/10.1002/1097-4679(198903)45:2<294::AID-JCLP2270450218>3.0.CO;2-N.

"Sex change hormonal treatments alter brain chemistry." *Elsevier*, October 8, 2015.
https://www.sciencedaily.com/releases/2015/10/151008110522.htm.

Staphorsius, Annemieke S., Baudewijntje P. C. Kreukels, Peggy T. Cohen-Kettenis, Dick J. Veltman, Sarah M. Burke, Sebastian E. E. Schagen, Femke M. Wouters, Henriëtte A. Delemarre-van de Waal, and Julie Bakker. "Puberty suppression and executive functioning: an fMRI-study in adolescents with gender dysphoria." *Psychoneuroendocrinology* 56, (June 2015): 190–9.
https://doi.org/10.1016/j.psyneuen.2015.03.007.

Tannehill, Brynn. "The End of the Desistance Myth." HuffPost, January 1, 2016.
https://www.huffpost.com/entry/the-end-of-the-desistance_b_8903690.

Wolford-Clevenger, Caitlin, Christopher J. Cannon, Leticia Y. Flores, Phillip N. Smith, and Gregory L. Stuart. "Suicide Risk Among Transgender People: A Prevalent Problem in Critical Need of Empirical and Theoretical Research." *Violence and Gender* 4, no. 3 (September 2017): 69–72.
https://doi.org/10.1089/vio.2017.0006.

**Chapter 1: All My Friends Are Going Trans**

Caplan-Bricker, Nora. "Voices of the New Masculinity." *GQ*, October 15, 2019.
https://www.gq.com/story/voices-of-the-new-masculinity.

Christiansen, Jen. "Judge gives grandparents custody of Ohio transgender teen." *CNN*, February 18, 2018. https://www.cnn.com/2018/02/16/health/ohio-transgender-teen-hearing-judge-decision/index.html.

Davidson, Erielle "The Real Crisis Of Masculinity Is Tanking Testosterone Levels." *The Federalist*, January 22, 2019. https://thefederalist.com/2019/01/22/real-crisis-masculinity-tanking-testosterone-levels/.

Doll, Lynda S., Dan Joy, Brad N. Bartholow, Janet S.Harrison, Gail Bolan, John M.Douglas, Linda E.Saltzman, Patricia M. Mossab, and Wanda Delgadoab. "Self-reported childhood and adolescent sexual abuse among adult homosexual and bisexual men." *Child Abuse & Neglect* 16, no. 6 (November–December 1992): 855–864. https://doi.org/10.1016/0145-2134(92)90087-8.

Endrass, Jérôme, Frank Urbaniok, Lea C. Hammermeister, Christian Benz, Thomas Elbert, Arja Laubacher, and Astrid Rossegger. "The Consumption of Internet Child Pornography and Violent and Sex Offending." *BMC Psychiatry* 9, no. 43 (2009). https://doi.org/10.1186/1471-244X-9-43.

Haramis, Nick. "Welcome to the Age of the Twink." *The New York Times*, May 14, 2018.
https://www.nytimes.com/2018/05/14/t-magazine/age-of-the-twink.html.

Kaplan, Michael. "The more porn you watch, the more likely you are to be bisexual." *New York Post*, February 26, 2019, https://nypost.com/2019/02/26/people-who-watch-porn-are-more-likely-to-be-bisexual-study/.

Levy, Dawn. "Two transsexuals reflect on university's pioneering gender dysphoria program." *Stanford Report*, May 3, 2000. https://news.stanford.edu/news/2000/may3/sexchange-53.html.

Littman, Lisa, "Parent reports of adolescents and young adults perceived to show signs of a rapid onset of gender dysphoria," August 16, 2018. *PLOS One* (August 2018).
https://doi.org/10.1371/journal.pone.0202330.

O'Neil, Tyler. "Mother Forcing Transgenderism on 6-Year-Old Son May Suffer From a Mental Disorder, Pediatrician Says." *PJ Media*, December 1, 2018. https://pjmedia.com/parenting/tyler-o-neil/2018/12/01/mother-forcing-transgenderism-on-6-year-old-son-may-suffer-from-a-mental-disorder-pediatrician-says-n114017.

Polletta, Maria. "Why parents are losing custody of trans and gender non-conforming kids." *AZ Central*, April 10, 2018. https://www.azcentral.com/story/news/local/arizona/2018/04/10/why-parents-losing-custody-trans-and-gender-non-conforming-kids/485928002/.

Regnerus, Mark. "Queering Science." *First Things*, December 2018.
https://www.firstthings.com/article/2018/12/queering-science.

Seigfried-Spellar, Kathryn C., and Marcus K. Rogers, "Does Deviant Pornography Use Follow a Guttman-like Progression," 2013. *Computers in Human Behavior* 29, no. 5 (September 2013): 1997–2003. https://doi.org/10.1016/j.chb.2013.04.018.

Voon, Valerie, Thomas B. Mole, Paula Banca, Laura Porter, Laurel Morris, Simon Mitchell, Tatyana R. Lapa, et al. "Neural Correlates of Sexual Cue Reactivity in Individuals with and without Compulsive Sexual Behaviors." *PLOS One* (July 2014).
https://doi.org/10.1371/journal.pone.0102419.

## Chapter 2: The Gaslight Anthem

Allen, James Preston. "Gaslighting America and Congress." *Random Lengths News*, November 21, 2019. https://www.randomlengthsnews.com/archives/2019/11/21/gaslighting-america-and-congress/24680.

Dhejne, Cecilia, Paul Lichtenstein, Marcus Boman, Anna L. V. Johansson, Niklas Långström, and Mikael Landén. "Long-term follow-up of transsexual persons undergoing sex reassignment surgery: cohort study in Sweden." *PLOS One* 6, no. 2 (2011). https://doi.org/10.1371/journal.pone.0016885.

Evans, Patricia. *The Verbally Abusive Relationship: How to Recognize it and How to Respond (2nd ed.)*. Holbrook, MA: Adams Media Corporation, 1996.

King, Michael, Joanna Semlyen, Sharon See Tai, Helen Killaspy, David Osborn, Dmitri Popelyuk, and Irwin Nazareth. "A systematic review of mental disorder, suicide, and deliberate self harm in lesbian, gay and bisexual people." *BMC Psychiatry* 8, no. 70 (2008). https://doi.org/10.1186/1471-244X-8-70.

Open Society Foundations. *License to be Yourself: Responding to National Security and Identity Fraud Argument.* Open Society Foundations, 2016. https://docslib.org/doc/213573/license-to-be-yourself-responding-to-national-security-and-identity-fraud-arguments.

Sansone, Randy A. and Lori A. Sansone. "Sexual Behavior in Borderline Personality: A Review." *Innovations in Clinical Neuroscience* 8, no. 2 (2011): 14–8. https://www.ncbi.nlm.nih.gov/pmc/articles/PMC3071095/.

Semlyen, Joanna, Michael King, Justin Varne, and Gareth Hagger-Johnson. "Sexual orientation and symptoms of common mental disorder or low wellbeing: combined meta-analysis of 12 UK population health surveys." *BMC Psychiatry* 16, no. 67 (2016). https://doi.org/10.1186/s12888-016-0767-z.

Smith, Jenn. "Synanon, the Brainwashing 'Game' and Modern Transgender Activism: The Orwellian Implication of Transgender Politics." *Medium*, August 13, 2017. https://archive.org/details/Synanon00.

Transgender Europe. *Welcome to Stay: Building Trans Communities Inclusive of Trans Asylum Seekers and Refugees in Europe.* Transgender Europe, 2016.

Yong, Ed. "Young Trans Kids Know Who They Are." *The Atlantic*, January 15, 2019. https://www.theatlantic.com/science/archive/2019/01/young-trans-children-know-who-they-are/580366/?fbclid=IwAR0tsy51bUhbDF9jJacLUyISiNz2mQ_vpOZ279lACnWZQ2CDTuRcKvV_-gk.

## Chapter 3: Sex (Education) as a Weapon

Baker, Neal. "LGBT CLASS Primary school kids 'to be taught about gay and trans relationships from age 5 under new curriculum.'" The Sun, February 24, 2019. https://www.thesun.co.uk/news/8497179/primary-school-gay-trans-lessons-curriculum/.

Hope, Allison. "The Right's New Target: LGBTQ Children." *Slate*, March 23rd, 2020. https://slate.com/human-interest/2020/03/lgbtq-kids-anti-trans-legislation.html.

Horn, Erlend. "The Rainbow City of Bergen, Plan for gender and sexual diversity 2017–2021." 2016.

Kan, Lyle Matthew. *The 2018 Diversity Among Philanthropic Professionals Report: A Tale of Two Sectors*. CHANGE Philanthropy, Emerging Practitioners in Philanthropy, and Funders for LGBTQ Issues, 2019. https://lgbtfunders.org/wp-content/uploads/2019/11/2018_DAPP_Report_A_Tale_of_Two_Sectors.pdf.

*LGBTQI Inclusive Education Report 2018.* IGYLO, 2018.

Magić, Jasna, and Bruno Selun. *Safe at school: Education sector responses to violence based on sexual orientation, gender identi-ty/expression or sex characteristics in Europe*. Council of Europe, 2018. https://rm.coe.int/prems-125718-gbr-2575-safe-at-school-a4-web/16809024f5.

Nash, Catherine J. and Kath Browne. "Resisting the mainstreaming of LGBT equalities in Canadian and British Schools: Sex education and trans school friends." *Environment and Planning C: Politics and Space* 39, no. 1 (2019): 74–93. https://doi.org/10.1177/2399654419887970.

*Out in the Open: Education sector responses to violence based on sexual orientation and gender identity/expression.* United Nations Educational, Scientific, and Cultural Organization, 2016. https://unesdoc.unesco.org/ark:/48223/pf0000244832.

Taylor, Catherine. *The Every Teacher Project on LGBTQ-Inclusive Education in Canada's K-12 Schools: Final Report.* Winnipeg, MB: Manitoba Teachers' Society, 2015.

https://healtheducationresources.unesco.org/library/documents/every-teacher-project-lgbtq-inclusive-education-canadas-k-12-schools-final-report.

Zelermyer, Karen. *Forty Years of LGBTQ Philanthropy 1970-2010.* Funders for LGBTQ Issues, 2012. https://lgbtfunders.org/research-item/forty-years-lgbtq-philanthropy/.


**Chapter 4: Drag Me to Hell**

Lewis, Iris. "Updated Medicaid rule may allow youth under 21 to receive gender-affirming surgery." *Vermont Digger*, June 14, 2019. https://vtdigger.org/2019/06/14/updated-medicaid-rule-may-allow-youth-21-receive-gender-affirming-surgery/.

Lothbrook, Kay Elle. "The Money and Masterminds Behind Drag Queen Story Hour." *National Justice*, December 4, 2019. https://archive.ph/yjrqG.

Orr, Asaf and Joel Baum. *Schools in Transition: A Guide for Supporting Transgender Students in K-12 Schools.* National Center for Lesbian Rights, 2015. https://assets2.hrc.org/files/assets/resources/Schools-In-Transition.pdf.

Sales, Ben. "To sway the teachers' union to love Israel, Randi Weingarten criticizes it." *The Times of Israel*, August 14, 2018. https://www.timesofisrael.com/to-sway-the-teachers-union-to-love-israel-randi-weingarten-criticizes-it/.


**Chapter 5: The She-Male Gaze**

Eror, Aleks. "How a Homophobic Country Became a Go-To Spot for Gender Reassignment Surgery." *Vice*, January 5, 2016. https://www.vice.com/en/article/wnwme4/how-a-homophobic-country-became-a-go-to-spot-for-gender-reassignment-surgery.

Gates, Gary J. "How many people are lesbian, gay, bisexual, and transgender?" The Williams Institute, April 2011. https://williamsinstitute.law.ucla.edu/publications/how-many-people-lgbt/.

Hooker, Evelyn. "The Adjustment of the Male Overt Homosexual." *Journal of Projective Techniques* 21, (1957) 18–31. https://doi.org/10.1080/08853126.1957.10380742.

Miller, Yael. "Six Jews Who Changed the Way We Talk About Sex." *Haaretz*, September 3, 2014. https://www.haaretz.com/jewish/2014-09-03/ty-article/.premium/lets-talk-about-sex-jews/0000017f-e8e2-df2c-a1ff-fef3663a0000

Stark, Jill. "Sex-change clinic 'got it wrong.'" *The Sydney Morning Herald*, May 31, 2009. https://www.smh.com.au/national/sexchange-clinic-got-it-wrong-20090530-br3u.html.


**Chapter 6: What's Love Got to Do With It?**

Cassata, Donna. "Gay rights legislation gains bipartisan support." *Associated Press*, November 2, 2013. https://apnews.com/article/12215ffb30754ccb9c1a5fdd2c92a159.

Contrada, Amy and Brian Camenker. "How Elena Kagan helped 'queer' Harvard Law School." *Mass Resistance*, April 20, 2015. https://www.massresistance.org/docs/gen/10b/kagan/index.html.

Cooper, Sean. "Bending the Jews."*Tablet*, May 27, 2020. https://www.tabletmag.com/sections/news/articles/bend-the-arc.

Dean, Amy. "How Jews Brought America to the Tipping Point on Marriage Equality: Lessons for the Next Social Justice Issues." *Tikkun*, March 10, 2014. https://www.tikkun.org/how-jews-brought-america-to-the-tipping-point-on-marriage-equality-lessons-for-the-next-social-justice-issues/.

Ditkoff, Susan Wolf and Abe Grindle. "Audacious Philanthropy." *Harvard Business Review*, September–October 2017. https://hbr.org/2017/09/audacious-philanthropy.

"The Fall of the House of Gilman." *Forbes*, August 11, 2003. https://www.forbes.com/forbes/2003/0811/068.html?sh=2b5457622086.

Foster, William, Gail Perrault, and Bradley Seeman. "Becoming Big Bettable." *Stanford Social Innovation Review*, Spring 2019. https://ssir.org/articles/entry/becoming_big_bettable.

Ghermezian, Shiryn. "Dozens of Jewish Charities Supported by Newly Revealed '$13 Billion Mystery Angels.'" *The Algemeiner*, May 27, 2014. https://www.algemeiner.com/2014/05/27/jewish-charities-heavily-favored-by-newly-revealed-13-billion-mystery-angels/.

Jones, E. Michael. "Revolutionary Jews Promote Porn, Feminism & Homosexual Agenda." Interview, February 17, 2013. https://educate-yourself.org/cn/Revolutionary-Jews-Promote-Porn-Feminism-and-Homosexual-Agenda17feb13.shtml.

Joyce, Andrew. "Vulture Capitalism is Jewish Capitalism." *The Occidental Observer*, December 18, 2019. https://www.theoccidentalobserver.net/2019/12/18/vulture-capitalism-is-jewish-capitalism/.

Kunreuther, Frances, Barbara Masters, and Gigi Barsoum. *At the Crossroads: The Future of the LGBT Movement*. Building Movement Project, 2013. https://buildingmovement.org/wp-content/uploads/2019/08/At-the-Crossroads-The-Future-of-the-LGBT-Movement.pdf.

Nathan-Kazis, Josh. "George Soros Next Generation Steps Up." *Forward*, April 23, 2012. https://forward.com/news/155047/george-soros-next-generation-steps-up/.

PragerU. "I'm Gay...Conservative...So What?" January 22, 2018. Youtube video, 4:46. https://www.youtube.com/watch?v=YTiADvV_PDs.

Sammon, Alexander. "Buttigieg Bundler Is an Executive at Vulture Fund Holding Puerto Rican Debt." *Sludge*, January 5, 2020. https://readsludge.com/2020/01/05/buttigieg-bundler-is-an-executive-at-vulture-fund-holding-puerto-rican-debt/.

Shaw, Donald. "Hedge Fund Billionaires Power New Democratic Super PAC." *Sludge*, January 23, 2020. https://readsludge.com/2020/01/23/hedge-fund-billionaires-power-new-democratic-super-pac/.

Snell, Robert. "Genital mutilation ban ruled unconstitutional; judge drops charges against sect." *The Detroit News*, November 20, 2018. https://www.detroitnews.com/story/news/local/detroit-city/2018/11/20/judge-dismisses-key-count-genital-mutilation-case/2066855002/.

Talusan, Meredith. "Prominent Trans Lawyer Picked To Run National Trans Rights Legal Group." *BuzzFeed*, July 12, 2016. https://www.buzzfeed.com/meredithtalusan/prominent-trans-lawyer-picked-to-run-national-trans-rights-l.

### Chapter 7: Climate of Queer

Andriote, John-Manuel. *Victory Deferred: How AIDS Changed Gay Life in America*. University of Chicago Press, 1999.

Lipshiz, Cnaan. "International LGBT Jews gather in Austria for festive launch of advocacy group." *Jewish Telegraphic Agency*, August 19, 2015. https://www.jta.org/2015/08/19/global/in-austria-jewish-gay-activists-explore-silver-lining-of-a-horrible-year.

"List of Trans Funds and Resources." Google Doc, last modified January 15, 2022. https://archive.ph/pFk82.

Rapp, Linda. "Achtenberg, Roberta (b. 1950)." glbtq, Inc., 2015. http://www.glbtqarchive.com/ssh/achtenberg_r_S.pdf.

Silberman, Charles E. *A Certain People: American Jews and Their Lives Today*. New York: Simon & Schuster, 1985.

### Chapter 8: Transforming Our World

Bilek, Jennifer. "The Billionaires Behind the LGBT Movement." *First Things*, January 21, 2020. https://www.firstthings.com/web-exclusives/2020/01/the-billionaires-behind-the-lgbt-movement.

Borman, Nancy. "Inside the CIA with Gloria Steinem." Reprinted from the *Village Voice*, 1979. https://www.mail-archive.com/ctrl@listserv.aol.com/msg02217.html.

Davies, Caroline. "Sheila Michaels, who brought 'Ms' into mainstream, dies at 78." *The Guardian*, July 7, 2017. https://www.theguardian.com/lifeandstyle/2017/jul/07/sheila-michaels-who-brought-ms-into-mainstream-dies-aged-78.

"Family Planning Summit – London, July 2012: Zero Draft." The London Summit, April 20, 2012. https://pmnch.who.int/docs/librariesprovider9/governance/12th-board-meeting-2may2012-family-planning-summit-en.pdf?Status=Master&sfvrsn=53093522_5.

Labarique, Paul. "Ford Foundation, a philanthropic façade for the CIA." *Voltaire Network*, April 5, 2004. https://www.voltairenet.org/article30039.html.

Morgan, Robert C. Morgan. "Nancy Grossman: Opus Volcanus." *Sculpture Magazine*, July 1, 1998. https://sculpturemagazine.art/nancy-grossman-opus-volcanus/.

Petras, James. "The Ford Foundation and the CIA: A documented case of philanthropic collaboration with the Secret Police," December 15, 2001. https://www.ratical.org/ratville/CAH/FordFandCIA.html.

Publius, John Q. *Plastic Empire*. Ostara Publications, 2020.

Publius, John Q. *The Way Life Should Be?* Ostara Publications, 2020.

"Redstockings' Statement." *Off Our Backs* 5, no. 6 (1975): 8–33. http://www.jstor.org/stable/25772264.

Reichel, Chloe. "What the research says about hormones and surgery for transgender youth." *The Journalist's Resource*, August 7, 2019. https://journalistsresource.org/politics-and-government/gender-confirmation-surgery-transgender-youth-research/.

Saunders, Frances Stonor. "Modern art was CIA 'weapon.'" *The Independent*, October 22, 1995. https://www.independent.co.uk/news/world/modern-art-was-cia-weapon-1578808.html.

Tananbaum, Susan L., "Anna Lederer Rosenberg." Jewish Women's Archive, December 31, 1999. https://jwa.org/encyclopedia/article/rosenberg-anna-marie-lederer.

### Chapter 9: Case Studies: Ireland and South Africa

Baker, Kellan. *Transforming Health: International Rights-Based Advocacy for Trans Health.* Open Society Foundations, 2013. https://www.opensocietyfoundations.org/publications/transforming-health.

Harvey, Brian. *Making a Difference: Catalysing LGBT Equality and Visibility in Ireland.* The Atlantic Philanthropies, 2016. /http://www.atlanticphilanthropies.org/wp-content/uploads/2016/05/Making-a-Difference-Report.pdf.

Riddell, Kelly. "The money behind the transgender movement." *The Washington Times*, August 11, 2016. https://www.washingtontimes.com/news/2016/aug/11/george-soros-the-money-behind-the-transgender-move/.

### Chapter 10: Networks and Frameworks

van den Brink, Marjolein and Peter Dunne. *Trans and Intersex Equality Rights in Europe: A Comparative Analysis.* European Commission, 2018. https://ec.europa.eu/info/sites/default/files/trans_and_intersex_equality_rights.pdf.

Frazer, Somjen and Erin Howe. *Growing Trans\* Funding and Strategy: A report from the field in 2013.* Strength in Numbers Consulting Group for Arcus Foundation and Open Society Foundations, 2015. http://strengthinnumbersconsulting.com/wp-content/uploads/2017/06/Trans-Report-FINAL-May-5-2015.pdf.

ILGA-Europe. *Annual Review of the Human Rights Situation of Lesbian, Gay, Bisexual, Trans and Intersex People in Europe and Central Asia 2020.* Brussels: ILGA-Europe, 2020. https://www.ilga-europe.org/files/uploads/2022/04/annual-review-2020.pdf.

Leszkowicz, Pawel and Tomasz Kitlinski. "The Utopia of Europe's LGBTQ Visibility Campaigns in the Politics of Everyday Life: The Utopic of Social Hope in the Images of Queer Spaces." In *A Critical Inquiry into Queer Utopias*, edited by Angela Jones, page. New York: Palgrave Macmillan, 2013.

Perry, Joanna and Paul Franey. *Policing Hate Crime against LGBTI persons: Training for a Professional Police Response.* The Council of Europe, 2017. https://rm.coe.int/prems-030717-gbr-2575-hate-crimes-against-lgbti-web-a4/1680723b1d.

Tozzi, Piero A. "French UN 'Sexual Orientation' Push Linked to Radical Yogyakarta Principles." The Center for Family and Human Rights, January 1, 2009. https://c-fam.org/friday_fax/french-un-sexual-orientation-push-linked-to-radical-yogyakarta-principles/.

### Chapter 11: Boas Constrictor

Adler, David Adler. "Jews in Britain Are Not Facing an Existential Threat." *Boston Review*, September 5, 2018. https://www.bostonreview.net/articles/david-r-k-adler-no-existential-threat-jewish-life-britain/.

Adler, Rachel. "Feminist Judaism: Past and Future." *Reconsidering Scripture* 51, no. 4 (Winter 2002): 484–488. https://www.jstor.org/stable/24461272.

Bashkow, Ira. "The Boas Circle vs. White Supremacy." *History of Anthropology Review* 44, (2020). https://histanthro.org/reviews/the-boas-circle-vs-white-supremacy/.

Bauer, J. Edgar. "On Behalf of Hermaphrodites and Mongrels: Refocusing the Reception of Magnus Hirschfeld's Critical Thought on Sexuality and Race." *Journal of Homosexuality* 68, no 5. (2019): 777–801. https://doi.org/10.1080/00918369.2019.1661686.

Blumenfeld, Warren J. *Heterosexism and Anti-Jewish Oppression: Making the Links*. Presentation for the World Congress of GLBT Jews: Keshet Ga'avah, July 11, 2015. https://www.slideshare.net/wblumen/making-thelinks.

Blumenfeld, Warren J. "The US needs to teach the Confederacy like Germany teaches Nazism." *LGBTQ Nation*, August 2, 2020. https://www.lgbtqnation.com/2020/08/us-needs-teach-confederacy-like-germany-teaches-nazism/.

Blumenfeld, Warren J. "'Straight pride' makes less and less sense the more you think about it." *LGBTQ Nation*, July 5, 2020. https://www.lgbtqnation.com/2020/07/straight-pride-makes-less-less-sense-think/.

Cooper, Howard. "Book review: A Specter Haunting Europe." *The Jewish Chronicle*, November 26, 2018. https://www.thejc.com/culture/books/book-review-a-specter-haunting-europe-1.473110.

Ehrlich, Claire. "The Lost World of Yiddish Anarchists." *Jewish Currents*, January 15, 2019. https://jewishcurrents.org/the-lost-world-of-yiddish-anarchists.

Falasca, Anina, Miriam Goldmann, and Martina Lüdicke. "'Are there gay Jews?' Date me and find out! – Question of the Month in the Context of the Exhibition 'The Whole Truth'" Jewish Museum Berlin, 2013. https://www.jmberlin.de/en/question-of-the-month-are-there-gay-jews.

Fraenkel, Carlos. "Is Germany's New Anti-Semitism Really New?" *Boston Review*, May 22, 2018. https://www.bostonreview.net/articles/carlos-fraenkel-is-germanys-new-anti-semitism-really-new/.

Gelernter, Josh. "A Conservative Defense of Transgender Rights. " *National Review*, December 17, 2016. https://www.nationalreview.com/2016/12/transgender-bathrooms-conservative-defense-transgender-rights/.

MacDonald, Kevin. *The Culture of Critique: An Evolutionary Analysis of Jewish Involvement in Twentieth-Century Intellectual and Political Movements*, 2nd ed. Authorhouse, 2002.

MacDonald, Kevin. "Foreword to *Battle Lines: Essays on Western Culture, Jewish Influence, and Anti-Semitism* by Brenton Sanderson." *The Occidental Observer,* August 23, 2020. https://www.theoccidentalobserver.net/2020/08/23/foreword-to-battle-lines-essays-on-western-culture-jewish-influence-and-anti-semitism-by-brenton-sanderson/.

Muller, Jerry Z. *Capitalism and the Jews*. Princeton University Press, 2011.

Volkelt, Johannes quoted in Stoddard, Lothrop. *The Revolt Against Civilization: The Menace of the Under Man*. New York: Charles Scribner's Sons, 1924. 139.

## Chapter 12: The Emperor's New Penis

Baskin, April and Idit Klein. "Racial Justice and LGBTQ Equality Are The Same Fight. It's A Jewish Fight." *Keshet*, June 18, 2019. https://www.keshetonline.org/news/racial-justice-and-lgbtq-equality-are-the-same-fight-its-a-jewish-fight/.

Bilefsky, Dan. "The openly gay rabbi who's working to change the face of Judaism." *The Independent*, July 21, 2019. https://www.independent.co.uk/arts-entertainment/lgbt-rabbi-lesbian-women-judaism-religion-lisa-grushcow-a9007231.html.

Borinsky, Alex. "Putting the Pieces Together." *Tablet Magazine*, June 24, 2019. https://www.tabletmag.com/sections/community/articles/putting-the-pieces-together.

Boyarin, Daniel, Daniel Itzkovitz, and Ann Pellegrini (eds.). "Strange Bedfellows: An Introduction." In *Queer Theory and the Jewish Question*. New York: Columbia University Press, 2003.

Branch, Mark Alden. "Back in the Fold." *Yale Alumni Magazine* 66, no. 6 (April 2003). http://archives.yalealumnimagazine.com/issues/03_04/kramer.html.

Branfman, Jonathan, Susan Stiritz, and Eric Anderson. "Relaxing the straight male anus: Decreasing homohysteria around anal eroticism." *Sexualities* 21, no. 1–2 (February 2017). https://doi.org/10.1177/1363460716678560.

Branfman, Jonathan and Susan Stiritz. "Teaching Men's Anal Pleasure: Challenging Gender Norms with 'Prostage' Education." *American Journal of Sexuality Education* 7, no. 4 (October 2012): 404–428. https://doi.org/10.1080/15546128.2012.740951.

Bruenbaum-Fax, Julie. "Transgender Jews: Beyond the Rainbow." *Jewish Journal*, May 7, 2015. https://jewishjournal.com/community/236924/transgender-jews-beyond-rainbow/.

Carrillo, Hector and Amanda Hoffman. "'Straight with a pinch of bi': The construction of heterosexuality as an elastic category among adult US men." *Sexualities* 21, no. 1–2 (February 2017). https://doi.org/10.1177/1363460716678561.

Dolsten, Josefin. "How Judaism inspires the first openly gay politician in Michigan state office." *The Times of Israel*, February 22, 2019. https://www.timesofisrael.com/how-judaism-inspires-the-first-openly-gay-politician-in-michigan-state-office/.

Eisner, Jane. "Forward 50 2015." *The Forward*, 2015. https://forward.com/series/forward-50-2015/.

Fisher, Leda. "Should White Boys Still Be Allowed to Talk?" The Dickinsonian, February 7, 2019. https://thedickinsonian.com/opinion/2019/02/07/should-white-boys-still-be-allowed-to-talk/.

Gilad, Elon. "Judaism and Homosexuality: A Brief History." *Haaretz*, June 2, 2016. https://www.haaretz.com/jewish/2016-06-02/ty-article-magazine/.premium/judaism-and-homosexuality-a-brief-history/0000017f-e6a5-dc7e-adff-f6adec1f0000.

Ilany, Ofri. "Homosexuality Is Part of Jewish Tradition." *Haaretz*, August 5, 2015. https://www.haaretz.com/jewish/2015-08-05/ty-article/.premium/homosexuality-part-of-jewish-tradition/0000017f-f64d-d5bd-a17f-f67f92080000.

Kaplan, Arielle. "King Princess Is the Jewish Queer Pop Icon We've Been Waiting For." *Alma*, February 5, 2019. https://www.heyalma.com/king-princess-is-the-jewish-queer-pop-icon-weve-been-waiting-for/.

Kay, Barbara. "Exploring the phenomenon of the social justice Jewish warrior." *The Post Millenial*, December 16, 2019. https://thepostmillennial.com/exploring-the-phenomenon-of-the-social-justice-jewish-warrior.

Klein, Norma. *Beginner's Love.* Dial Books, 1983.

Marsh, Nina, Dirk Scheele, Justin S. Feinstein, Holger Gerhardt, Sabrina Strang, Wolfgang Maier, and René Hurlemann. "Oxytocin-enforced norm compliance reduces xenophobic outgroup rejection." *PNAS,* 114, no. 35 (August 2017): 9314–9319. https://doi.org/10.1073/pnas.1705853114.

Melloy, Kilian. "First Black Transsexual Delegate Headed to Dems' Convention." *Edge Media Network*, March 31, 2008. https://www.edgemedianetwork.com/story.php?72406.

Meyer, David J. "What the Torah Teaches Us About Gender Fluidity and Transgender Justice." Religious Action Center of Reform Judaism, September 20, 2018. https://rac.org/blog/what-torah-teaches-us-about-gender-fluidity-and-transgender-justice.

Naidoo, Kamban. "The origins of hate crime laws." *Fundamina (Pretoria)* 22, no. 1. (2016). http://dx.doi.org/10.17159/2411-7870/2016/v22n1a4.

Paull, Laura. "Beyond he and she: New expressions of gender arrive in the rabbinate." *The Jewish News of Northern California*, June 7, 2017. https://jweekly.com/2017/06/07/beyond-he-and-she-new-expressions-of-gender-in-the-rabbinate/.

Rothchild, Alice. "On empathy, Yom Kippur, and the NFL." *Mondoweiss*, October 3, 2017. https://mondoweiss.net/2017/10/empathy-yom-kippur/.

Rubin, Edwin L. "Jews, Truth, and Critical Race Theory." *Northwestern University Law Review* 93, no. 2 (Winter 199): 525–45.

Ruttenberg, Danya. "In the Image of God." *Lilith Magazine*, March 19, 2002. https://lilith.org/articles/in-the-image-of-god/.

Sameth, Mark. "Is God Transgender?" *The New York Times*, August 12, 2016. https://www.nytimes.com/2016/08/13/opinion/is-god-transgender.html.

Seigel, Amanda. "Celebrating Transgender Jews." NYPL Blogs: Posts from the Dorot Jewish Division, November 19, 2015. https://dorot1.rssing.com/chan-8213068/article61.html.

Smith, M. "RETRACTED ARTICLE: Going in Through the Back Door: Challenging Straight Male Homohysteria, Transhysteria, and Transphobia Through Receptive Penetrative Sex Toy Use." *Sexuality & Culture* 22, no. 1 (2018): 1542. https://doi.org/10.1007/s12119-018-9536-0.

Teutsch, David. "Understanding Transgender Issues in Jewish Ethics." Reconstructing Judaism, April 18, 2016. https://www.reconstructingjudaism.org/article/understanding-transgender-issues-jewish-ethics/.

Tucker, Karen Iris. "How Harvey Milk's fight for social justice was fueled by Jewish tradition." *Washington Post*, June 22, 2018. https://www.washingtonpost.com/outlook/how-harvey-milks-fight-for-social-justice-was-fueled-by-jewish-tradition/2018/06/22/eb65177a-41b0-11e8-8569-26fda6b404c7_story.html.

## Chapter 13: TERF Wars

Jewish Telegraphic Agency. "Son of Holocaust survivor named president of Harvard." *Jewish Standard*, February 12, 2018. https://jewishstandard.timesofisrael.com/son-of-holocaust-survivor-named-president-of-harvard/.

Joyce, Andrew. "Review of Robin DiAngelo's White Fragility." The Unz Review, August 2, 2020. https://www.unz.com/article/review-of-robin-diangelos-white-fragility/.

Lambert, Josh. *Unclean Lips: Obscenity, Jews, and American Culture*. New York: New York University Press: 2014.

Rothenberg, Paula. *Invisible Privilege: A Memoir about Race, Class, and Gender*. Lawrence, Kansas: University Press of Kansas: 2000.


## Chapter 14: Case Study: Cruel Britannia

Adams, Stephen. "NHS spends as much on patients with HIV as it does on breast cancer care amid fears health tourists with the virus are targeting Britain to access expensive treatment for free." *The Daily Mail*, August 10, 2019. https://www.dailymail.co.uk/news/article-7344937/NHS-spends-patients-HIV-does-breast-cancer-care.html.

Dams, Tim. "UK Channels ITV, 4Music, MTV and Comedy Central Mark 'Blackout Tuesday.'" *Variety*, June 2, 2020. https://variety.com/2020/tv/global/itv-4music-mtv-comedy-central-mark-blackout-tuesday-1234622993/.

Liboni, Luna Lara. "Jewish LGBT Groups Stress Unity Against Antisemitism and Homophobia." *Liberties*, April 6, 2018. https://www.liberties.eu/en/stories/world-congress-of-lgbt-jews/14581.

Manning, Sanchez and Stephen Adams. "NHS to give sex change drugs to nine-year-olds: Clinic accused of 'playing God' with treatment that stops puberty." *The Mail on Sunday*, May 17, 2014. https://www.dailymail.co.uk/news/article-2631472/NHS-sex-change-drugs-nine-year-olds-Clinic-accused-playing-God-treatment-stops-puberty.html.

Stevens, Jenny. "Meet the Doctor Who Runs the Only Clinic for Trans Children in the UK." Vice, November 16, 2016. https://www.vice.com/en/article/exkb4m/meeting-the-doctor-who-runs-the-only-nhs-clinic-for-trans-children.


## Chapter 15: Men Are From Mars, Women Have a Penis

Anderson, Eric. "Generational masculinities." *Journal of Gender Studies* 27, no. 3 (November 2017): 243–7. https://doi.org/10.1080/09589236.2017.1406088.

Kołakowski, Leszek. *Main Currents of Marxism, Vol. II*. Oxford University Press, 1981.

Vogel, Kenneth and Sarah Wheaton. "Major donors consider funding Black Lives Matter." *Politico*, November 13, 2015. https://www.politico.com/story/2015/11/major-donors-consider-funding-black-lives-matter-215814.

Wexelbaum, Rachel S., Katie Herzog, and Lane Rasberry. "Queering Wikipedia." *Library Faculty Publications* 49, (2015). https://repository.stcloudstate.edu/lrs_facpubs/49/.


## Chapter 16: Transgender, Inc.

Gorenfeld, John. "Ambassador de Sade." *AlterNet,* November 8, 2005. https://kipdf.com/alternet-ambassador-de-sade_5aca38e31723dd33c071a597.html.

Green, Jeff. "Goldman to Refuse IPOs If All Directors Are White, Straight Men." *Bloomberg*, January 23, 2020. https://www.bloomberg.com/news/articles/2020-01-24/goldman-rule-adds-to-death-knell-of-the-all-white-male-board.

Ivn1977. "Barbara Lerner Spectre calls for destruction of Christian European ethnic societies." September 9, 2015. YouTube video, 1:17. https://www.youtube.com/watch?v=G45WthPTo24.

Lowbridge, Caroline. "Trans models: From decades of rejection to centre stage." *BBC News*, September 20, 2019. https://www.bbc.com/news/uk-england-49578690.

MacDonald, Kevin. "The AEI, a Major Neocon Thinktank, Implicated in the Sackler Family's Opioid Crisis." *The Occidental Observer*, December 6, 2019. https://www.theoccidentalobserver.net/2019/12/06/the-aei-a-major-neocon-thinktank-implicated-in-the-sackler-familys-opioid-crisis/.

Publius, John Q. *The God that Failed: Liberalism and the Destruction of the West*. london: Black House Publishing Ltd., 2020.

Steinberger, Michael. "George Soros Bet Big on Liber Democracy. Now He Fears He Is Losing." *The New York Times Magazine*, July 17, 2018. https://www.nytimes.com/2018/07/17/magazine/george-soros-democrat-open-society.html.

World Bank. *Inclusion Matters: The Foundation for Shared Prosperity (Advance Edition)*. Washington, DC: World Bank, 2013. https://openknowledge.worldbank.org/handle/10986/16195.


**Chapter 17: Gross Domestic Products**

"Ammon Exits Endo." *Forbes*, April 9, 2007. https://www.forbes.com/2007/04/09/ammon-endo-retirement-face-cx_rs_0409autofacesscan01.html?sh=7f85e2af112b.

Bilek, Jennifer. "Who Are the Rich, White Men Institutionalizing Transgender Ideology?" *The Federalist*, February 20, 2018. https://thefederalist.com/2018/02/20/rich-white-men-institutionalizing-transgender-ideology/.

Bridge, Robert. "Doctors & drugs FOR LIFE: Big Pharma's profit on the transgender craze." *RT*, September 27, 2019. https://www.rt.com/usa/469766-transgender-pharma-drugs-surgery/.

Damonti, John, Patricia Doykos, R. Sebastian Wanless, and Mark Kline. "HIV/AIDS In African Children: The Bristol-Myers Squibb Foundation and Baylor Response." *Health Affairs* 31, no. 7 (July 2012). https://doi.org/10.1377/hlthaff.2012.0425.

Sagonowsky, Eric. "Gilead schemed with J&J, Bristol-Myers to keep their HIV combo monopoly, lawsuit claims." *Fierce Pharma*, May 15, 2019. https://www.fiercepharma.com/pharma/after-decades-activism-patients-hit-gilead-hiv-drug-antitrust-lawsuit.

Shaw, Glenda Fauntleroy. "The Endocrine Society Celebrates A Quarter Century of Diversity." *Endocrine News*, May 2019. https://endocrinenews.endocrine.org/the-endocrine-society-celebrates-a-quarter-century-of-diversity/.


**Chapter 18: Trans America: World Police**

Cotton, Anthony, et al. *Suggested Approaches for Integrating Inclusive Development Across the Program Cycle and Mission Operations*. USAID, July 2018. https://usaidlearninglab.org/sites/default/files/resource/files/additional_help_for_ads_201_inclusive_development_180726_final_r.pdf.

Cronk, Terri Moon. "Pentagon Celebrates Diversity at LGBT Pride Month Observance." US Department of Defense, June 13, 2019. https://www.defense.gov/News/News-Stories/Article/Article/1874601/pentagon-celebrates-diversity-at-lgbt-pride-month-observance/.

DFID Inclusive Societies. "Transgender Inclusive Development." Medium, March 29, 2018. https://medium.com/@DFID_Inclusive/transgender-inclusive-development-5128f899592.

Glassman, Marvin. "Broward Jewish population has declined, but still largest in Florida." *Sun Sentinel*, November 21, 2016. https://www.sun-sentinel.com/florida-jewish-journal/news/broward/fl-jjbs-demography-1123-20161121-story.html.

"Global Equality Fund Annual Report 2015." Bureau of Democracy, Human Rights, and Labor, June 23, 2016. https://2009-2017.state.gov/globalequality/releases/259029.htm.

Gray, Nicole. "Why ViiV Healthcare leads the pharma industry in corporate reputation." BioPharma Dive, March 22, 2016. https://www.biopharmadive.com/news/why-viiv-healthcare-leads-the-pharma-industry-in-corporate-reputation/416103/.

Kates, Jennifer. "The U.S. Government and Global LGBT Health: Opportunities and Challenges in the Current Era." *KFF*, May 28, 2014. https://www.kff.org/global-health-policy/issue-brief/the-u-s-government-and-global-lgbt-health-opportunities-and-challenges-in-the-current-era/.

Laughland, John. "The Chechens' American friends." *The Guardian*, September 8, 2004. https://www.theguardian.com/world/2004/sep/08/usa.russia.

Riley, Charles. "JPMorgan tells staff to boycott Brunei-owned hotels over gay sex death penalty." CNN Business, April 29, 2019. https://www.cnn.com/2019/04/29/business/brunei-hotels-jpmorgan-chase.

Sabbagh, Dan. "BAE Systems sold £15bn worth of arms to Saudis during Yemen assault." *The Guardian*, April 14, 2020. https://www.theguardian.com/business/2020/apr/14/bae-systems-sold-15bn-arms-to-saudis-during-yemen-assault.

**Chapter 19: 50 Shades of Gay, Starring the United Nations**

Associated Press, "Convicted killer gets sex-reassignment surgery on taxpayer's dime." ABC13, January 8, 2017. https://abc13.com/prison-sex-change-operation-prisoner-gender-reassignment-surgery-california/1692155/.

Levinson, Isaiah. "Former South African Victory Institute Trainee Thokozile Nhlumayo to Join Mandela Washington Fellowship." LGBTQ Victory Institute, April 15, 2020. https://victoryinstitute.org/former-south-african-victory-institute-trainee-thokozile-nhlumayo-to-join-mandela-washington-fellowship/.

Lynn, Corey. "Exploiting Transgenders Part 4: Manufacturing a Reality $$." Corey's Digs, November 30, 2019. https://www.coreysdigs.com/health-science/exploiting-transgenders-part-4-manufacturing-a-reality/.

Nasir, Peggy Wilhide. "World Bank Announces New Advisor on Sexual Orientation and Gender Identity Issues." World Bank, October 27, 2016. https://www.worldbank.org/en/news/press-release/2016/10/27/world-bank-announces-new-advisor-on-sexual-orientation-and-gender-identity-issues.

United Nations. *Living Free and Equal: What States Are Doing to Tackle Violence and Discrimination Against Lesbian, Gay, Bisexual, Transgender, and Intersex People.* New York and Geneva: United Nations, 2016. https://www.ohchr.org/sites/default/files/Documents/Publications/LivingFreeAndEqual.pdf.

Zappulla, Antonio. "The simple reason why so many businesses support LGBT rights." World Economic Forum, January 14, 2017. https://www.weforum.org/agenda/2017/01/why-so-many-businesses-support-lgbt-rights/.


**Conclusion**

*2019 Annual Financial Report.* Global Fund, 2019. https://www.theglobalfund.org/media/9603/corporate_2019annualfinancial_report_en.pdf.

Aldhous, Peter. "Jeffrey Epstein's Links to Scientists Are Even More Extensive Than We Thought." *BuzzFeed News*, August 26, 2019. https://www.buzzfeednews.com/article/peteraldhous/jeffrey-epstein-science-donations-apologies-statements.

"Alissa Carlat and Joshua Ruxin." *The New York Times*, July 17, 2005. https://www.nytimes.com/2005/07/17/fashion/weddings/alissa-carlat-and-joshua-ruxin.html.

Anderson, Stuart. "Irish MIT Student Co-Founded Billion-Dollar Gingko Bioworks." *Forbes*, February 5, 2019. https://www.forbes.com/sites/stuartanderson/2019/02/05/irish-mit-student-co-founded-billion-dollar-ginkgo-bioworks/?sh=7218007b3530.

Bharathan, Vipin. "Fed Partners With MIT Based Digital Currency Initiative To Explore Central Bank Digital Currency." *Forbes*, August 30, 2020. https://www.forbes.com/sites/vipinbharathan/2020/08/30/fed-partners-with-mit-based-digital-currency-initiative-to-explore-central-bank-digital-currency/?sh=311872b53fa1.

Binkey, Collin and Carla K. Johnson. "Scientists say fetal tissue remains essential for vaccines and developing treatments." Associated Press, August 11, 2015. https://www.pbs.org/newshour/health/medical-researchers-say-fetal-tissue-remains-essential.

Briquelet, Kate. "REVEALED: We Found Billionaire Pedophile Jeffrey Epstein's Secret Charity." *The Daily Beast*, April 16, 2019. https://www.thedailybeast.com/jeffrey-epstein-has-a-secret-charity-heres-who-it-gave-money-to.

Clemons, Steve. "Romney Foreign Policy Bench Impresses." *The Atlantic*, October 11, 2011. https://www.theatlantic.com/author/steve-clemons/?page=9.

Engdahl, F. William. "'Doomsday Seed Vault' in the Arctic." *Global Research*, December 4, 2007. https://www.globalresearch.ca/doomsday-seed-vault-in-the-arctic-2/23503.

Faris, Stephan. "The Solar Company Making a Profit on Poor Africans." *Bloomberg Businessweek*, December 2, 2015. https://www.bloomberg.com/features/2015-mkopa-solar-in-africa/.

Felter, Claire. "What Is the World Doing to Create a COVID-19 Vaccine?" The Council on Foreign Relations, August 26, 2020. https://web.archive.org/web/20200828214007/https://www.cfr.org/backgrounder/what-world-doing-create-covid-19-vaccine.

*Food Chain Reaction—A Global Food Security Game.* CNA, 2015. https://www.cna.org/reports/2015/IQR-2015-U-012427.pdf.

Gates, Bill. "JP Morgan Healthcare Conference." Speech. *Bill and Melinda Gates Foundation*, January 8, 2018. https://www.gatesfoundation.org/ideas/speeches/2018/01/jp-morgan-healthcare-conference.

Gillett-Swan, Jenna and Lisa van Leent. "Exploring the Intersections of the Convention on the Rights of the Child General Principles and Diverse Sexes, Genders and Sexualities in Education." *Social Sciences* (September 2019). DOI:10.3390/socsci8090260.

Guterl, Fred. "Dr. Fauci Backed Controversial Wuhan Lab with US Dollars for Risky Coronavirus Research." *Newsweek*, April 28, 2020. https://www.newsweek.com/dr-fauci-backed-controversial-wuhan-lab-millions-us-dollars-risky-coronavirus-research-1500741.

Hickson, Robert. "Hilaire Belloc's 'The Barbarians' (1912) and the Analogy of a Self-Sabotaging Cultural Immune System." *Ordo Dei*, August 8, 2017. https://ordodei.net/2020/06/22/hilaire-bellocs-the-barbarians-1912-and-the-analogy-of-a-self-sabotaging-cultural-immune-system/.

Kates, Jennifer. "The U.S. Government and Global LGBT Health: Opportunities and Challenges in the Current Era." *KFF*, May 28, 2014. https://www.kff.org/global-health-policy/issue-brief/the-u-s-government-and-global-lgbt-health-opportunities-and-challenges-in-the-current-era/.

Kluger, Jeffrey. "Affordable Steroids Could Reduce Some COVID-19 Deaths by One-Third, Says World Health Organization." *Time*, September 2, 2020. https://time.com/5885696/corticosteroids-coronavirus-who/.

Lynn, Corey. "Exploiting Transgenders Part 3: The Funders & Profiteers." *Corey's Digs*, November 22, 2019. https://www.coreysdigs.com/health-science/exploiting-transgenders-part-3-the-funders-profiteers/.

Olson-Kennedy, Johanna, Jonathan Warus, Vivian Okonta, Marvin Belzer, and Leslie F. Clark. "Chest Reconstruction and Chest Dysphoria in Transmasculine Minors and Young Adults." *JAMA Pediatrics* 172, no. 5 (May 2018): 431–6. doi:10.1001/jamapediatrics.2017.5440.

Popoff, Mischa. "COVID-19 and Roundup: An Immuno-Compromised Marriage from Hell." *Culture Wars*, June 1, 2020. https://culturewars.com/news/covid-19-and-roundup.

Roach, Randy. "Muscle, Smoke, and Mirrors." Interview by Maximus Mark. *Enterprise Fitness Podcast*, April 2, 2018. https://melbournepersonaltrainers.com/randy-roach/.

Rogers, Ray. "17 Top Music Execs On Giving Back, The Charities They Support and Their Love For UJA." *Billboard*, October 15, 2015. https://www.billboard.com/music/features/music-execs-uja-honorees-philanthropy-lyor-cohen-julie-greenwald-neil-portnow-more-6730150/.

Scharnick, Jaquelyn. "People in the News: Jeffrey E. Epstein." *The Harvard Crimson*, June 5, 2003. https://www.thecrimson.com/article/2003/6/5/people-in-the-news-jeffrey-e/.

Schultz, Gudrun. "Boston Children's Hospital Opens 'Transgender' Children's Clinic." *Life Site News*, April 8, 2013. https://www.lifesitenews.com/news/boston-childrens-hospital-opens-transgender-childrens-clinic/.

Tichenor, Marlee and Devi Sridhar. "Global health disruptors: The Bill and Melinda Gates Foundation." *The BMJ Opinion*, November 28, 2018. https://blogs.bmj.com/bmj/2018/11/28/global-health-disruptors-the-bill-and-melinda-gates-foundation/.

Webb, Whitney. "Engineering Contagion: UPMC, Corona-Thrax And 'The Darkest Winter.'" *The Last American Vagabond*, September 25, 2020. https://www.thelastamericanvagabond.com/engineering-contagion-upmc-corona-thrax-darkest-winter/.

# Index

www.ingramcontent.com/pod-product-compliance
Lightning Source LLC
Chambersburg PA
CBHW021602120626
46545CB00001B/34